AMERICAN FOREIGN
RELATIONS
1976
A DOCUMENTARY RECORD

COUNCIL ON FOREIGN RELATIONS BOOKS

The Council on Foreign Relations, Inc., is a non-profit and non-partisan organization devoted to promoting improved understanding of international affairs through the free exchange of ideas. Its membership of about 1,700 persons throughout the United States is made up of individuals with special interest and experience in international affairs. The Council has no affiliation with, and receives no funding from, the United States government. The Council does not take any position on questions of foreign policy.

The Council publishes the quarterly journal, *Foreign Affairs*. In addition, from time to time, books and monographs written by members of the Council's research staff or visiting fellows, or commissioned by the Council, or written by independent authors with critical review contributed by a Council study group, are published with the designation "Council on Foreign Relations Book" or "Council Paper on International Affairs." Any book or monograph bearing that designation is, in the judgment of the Committee on Studies of the Council's board of directors, a responsible treatment of a significant international topic worthy of presentation to the public. All statements of fact and expressions of opinion contained in Council books, monographs, and *Foreign Affairs* articles are, however, the sole responsibility of their authors.

AMERICAN
FOREIGN RELATIONS
1976
A DOCUMENTARY RECORD

Continuing the Series
DOCUMENTS ON AMERICAN FOREIGN RELATIONS
THE UNITED STATES IN WORLD AFFAIRS

Edited by ELAINE P. ADAM
with an introduction by
RICHARD P. STEBBINS

A Council on Foreign Relations Book
Published by
New York University Press • New York • 1978

PREFACE

This volume offers a condensed historical narrative together with a selection of documents reflecting salient aspects of the foreign relations of the United States in 1976. Continuing the series of foreign policy surveys initiated by the Council on Foreign Relations in 1931 under the title *The United States in World Affairs*, the volume also maintains the service provided annually for more than three decades by the separate *Documents on American Foreign Relations* series, inaugurated by the World Peace Foundation in 1939 and taken over by the Council on Foreign Relations in 1952. The fusion of narrative and documentation, commenced on a trial basis with the inception of the present series in 1971, is designed to provide a single, comprehensive, and nonpartisan record of American foreign policy as it develops during the bicentennial decade and beyond.

The interests of orderly presentation have appeared to be best served by the inclusion of a fairly detailed historical essay that reviews the year's main foreign policy developments and serves as introduction to the accompanying documentary material, which is presented in a parallel sequence to facilitate cross referencing between the two parts of the volume. Some readers will no doubt be satisfied to stop with the introduction; others may wish to go directly to the documents, which are presented in authoritative texts and accompanied by whatever editorial apparatus seemed necessary for independent reference use.

A key to certain abbreviations used in footnotes throughout the volume appears at the end of the Table of Contents, and organizational abbreviations and acronyms are listed and explained in the alphabetical Index. The Appendix presents a selected checklist of historical documents that are referred to in the volume. All dates refer to the year 1976 unless a different year is specifically indicated.

The editorial procedure described above admittedly involves the exercise of a substantial measure of individual judgment and demands all possible objectivity in the handling of controversial events and data. While hopeful that the volume will not be found wanting in this regard, the editors wish to emphasize that the editorial viewpoint is of necessity a personal one and in no way seeks to reflect the outlook of the Council on Foreign Relations or any of its officers and directors, members, or staff.

Among their immediate associates, the editors would note their special indebtedness to Winston Lord, President; John Temple Swing, Vice President and Secretary; Grace Darling Griffin, Publications Manager; and Janet Rigney, Librarian, of the Council

v

on Foreign Relations; and to Despina Papazoglou, Associate Managing Editor, and other friends at NYU Press. They are also indebted to various official agencies which have provided documentary material, and to *The New York Times* for permission to reprint texts or excerpts of documents appearing in its pages. As always, the editors themselves are responsible for the choice and presentation of the documents as well as the form and content of the editorial matter.

Readers in search of additional enlightenment will do well to turn in the first instance to the parallel Department of State volume, *Digest of United States Practice in International Law, 1976*, edited by Eleanor C. McDowell (Department of State Publication 8908; Washington: GPO, 1977). Conceived on wholly different principles and received too late to be of use in editing the present volume, it constitutes a treasure trove of information and documentation on many of the same subjects.

R.P.S.
E.P.A.

February 1, 1978

CONTENTS

KEY TO ABBREVIATED REFERENCES

(The abbreviation GPO refers to
the U.S. Government Printing Office)

"AFR": American Foreign Relations: A Documentary Record (New York: New York University Press, for the Council on Foreign Relations; annual vols., 1971-).

"Bulletin": U.S. Department of State, *The Department of State Bulletin* (Washington: GPO, weekly through 1977, monthly thereafter). Most references are to vols. 74 (Jan.-June 1976), 75 ((July-Dec. 1976), and 76 (Jan.-June 1977).

"Documents": Documents on American Foreign Relations (annual vols., 1939-70). Volumes prior to 1952 published by Princeton University Press for the World Peace Foundation; volumes for 1952-66 published by Harper & Row for the Council on Foreign Relations; volumes for 1967-70 published by Simon and Schuster for the Council on Foreign Relations.

"Keesing's": Keesing's Contemporary Archives (Bristol: Keesing's Publications, Ltd., weekly). Most references are to pp. 27501-28124 (1976).

"Presidential Documents": Weekly Compilation of Presidential Documents (Washington: GPO, weekly). Most references are to vol. 12 (1976).

"Stat.": Statutes at Large of the United States (Washington: GPO, published irregularly).

"TIAS": U.S. Department of State, *United States Treaties and Other International Agreements* (Washington: GPO, published irregularly).

"UST": U.S. Department of State, *United States Treaties and Other International Agreements* (Washington: GPO, published irregularly).

"USUN Press Releases": Press releases of the U.S. Mission to the United Nations, as reprinted in the *Department of State Bulletin.*

PART I: INTRODUCING 1976

INTRODUCING 1976

NINETEEN SEVENTY-SIX will be remembered as the year when 215,000,000 Americans laid aside the cares of world responsibility to join in glad commemoration of their country's birth two centuries earlier. "We were sick at heart for many reasons," Senator Hubert H. Humphrey later recalled, in a typical evocation of the spirit of the mid-decade. "Then all at once we became involved in the Bicentennial celebration, and we changed. We began to look up."[1] The traumas of the 1960s and the earlier 1970s—Vietnam, Watergate, the oil embargo, the shades of crime, inflation, unemployment—were momentarily forgotten as the United States and most of the outside world took time to hail America's first 200 years of membership in the family of nations.

The sense of confidence and national pride that marked the Bicentennial celebrations would also shed its tempering influence upon a second major event of 1976, the presidential election campaign in which incumbent Chief Executive Gerald R. Ford succeeded in wresting the Republican nomination from conservative Ronald Reagan, but failed to avoid a subsequent defeat at the hands of Georgia's former Governor Jimmy Carter, the Democratic nominee who had emerged from relative obscurity to outmaneuver half a dozen better known aspirants. Not without the usual personal and party animosities were the Republican and Democratic nomination contests and the subsequent Ford-Carter race, with its televised debates and hairline finish. Yet underneath the rhetorical excesses was a pervasive sense of balance restored, of renewed respect for oneself and one's fellow citizens, that promised well for the new Democratic administration that would take office January 20, 1977.

In other respects it must be admitted that 1976 was a less than wholly edifying year from either a national or an international standpoint. Recovery from the global economic recession of 1974-75, advancing strongly in the United States in the first half of the

---

[1]Quoted by Laura Foreman in *New York Times*, July 1, 1977.

1

year, subsequently slackened off at a time when many other nations still awaited the breath of economic revival. Détente with the Soviet Union, perhaps the principal American diplomatic achievement of the earlier part of the decade, underwent a similar loss of momentum as mistrust of Soviet intentions and distaste for Soviet conduct combined to banish the very word "détente" from the American vocabulary.

United States relations with the People's Republic of China also failed to advance significantly at a time when the mainland regime was largely absorbed in an internal power struggle over the succession to Prime Minister Chou En-lai and Communist Party Chairman Mao Tse-tung. Progress toward a Middle East peace settlement, moreover, was virtually halted while the world awaited the outcome of a civil war in Lebanon, although American diplomacy could meanwhile be fruitfully applied to some of the complex problems of Southern Africa. Notwithstanding some improvement in the tone of U.S. relations with the "Third World" countries of Asia, Africa, and Latin America, the year brought no real resolution of the deep political, economic, and ideological issues dividing those countries from the "industrial democracies" of North America, Europe, and the Pacific. Among the industrialized countries themselves, an unsatisfactory economic situation represented a noteworthy blot upon an otherwise comparatively harmonious relationship.

Queen Juliana of the Netherlands, who experienced a personal sorrow during 1976 in the official censure of her husband, Prince Bernhard, for imprudent conduct in his financial relations with the Lockheed Aircraft Corporation, offered a particularly gloomy view of the year's experience in her annual Christmas broadcast:

> We see lasting discord, even wars in the world, little reconciliation, little progress and too many people failing. And with all this there is the frightening lack of respect for each other's life and well-being, of all life on earth, that is visible again and again in dozens of terrifying shapes.
>
> However, all of this is no cause for surprise in a world inhabited by 4 billion egoists, all of them inclined to fancy themselves to be the focus points of the world.[2]

Prince Bernhard's misadventure was related to an aspect of the American scene that was distinctly less exemplary, though not less striking, than the euphoria of the Bicentennial observances. Even as it evoked the virtues of the Founding Fathers, the contemporary United States had been doomed to suffer a further impairment of

[2]UPI dispatch, Dec. 25, in *New York Times*, Dec. 26, 1976.

its already tarnished reputation as a global ethical center. In 1975, American and world attention had focused largely on the manifold improprieties being brought to light in the records of the Central Intelligence Agency, the Federal Bureau of Investigation, and other "national security" agencies. In 1976, the spotlight shifted to the giant American corporations whose actions so powerfully influenced the economic, military, and moral patterns of the contemporary world. Disclosures relating to the huge cash disbursements and other favors dispensed by firms like Lockheed in their quest for competitive advantage would literally destroy the careers of prominent public figures, as well as spurring the demand for more effective regulation at national and international levels.

Although the United States itself no longer seemed to ride the wave of political violence that had propelled it through much of the Vietnam period, it still belonged to a world in which violence was seldom far below the surface of public affairs. Admittedly, no formalized international wars were raging at the moment. But the Catholic and Protestant extremists of Northern Ireland continued to prosecute their internecine feuds with a barbarity that largely nullified the healing efforts of those within the two communities who found the courage to raise their voices in behalf of peace. Lebanon's tradition of religious and political tolerance, meanwhile, was ripped to shreds by a civil war that killed an estimated 60,000 people and sputtered ominously even after most of the country had been occupied by a Syrian peacekeeping force. Untold numbers were perishing in the aftermath of the Communist revolution in Cambodia. In the Philippines, a Christmas Eve ceasefire brought only momentary surcease from a four-year-old internal struggle that pitted the Muslims of Mindanao and the Sulu Archipelago against their Christian brethren and the civil government in far-off Manila.

Ethiopia, for years distracted by a national liberation struggle in the northeastern province of Eritrea, experienced mounting turmoil at the center in the wake of the liquidation of its ancient imperial regime. In Angola, one national liberation movement won a doubtful victory over two rivals with the aid of Soviet arms and Cuban troops. Guerrilla warfare was on the increase along the borders of Rhodesia and Namibia, and the troubles that broke out in June in the South African township of Soweto provided masses of fresh evidence of the evils of the *apartheid* system. In Argentina, during this same period, the military rulers who had ousted President Isabel Martínez de Perón would cite a figure of some 1,300 killed in political violence in 1976 alone.[3]

Abridgment or denial of the fundamental rights and freedoms set

[3]*New York Times*, May 15, 1977.

forth in the Universal Declaration of Human Rights of 1948 was so
notoriously prevalent in so many parts of the world of the 1970s as
to have forced itself into the very forefront of international concern. American action, in and out of the United Nations, had long
borne witness to a continuing, if sometimes rather selective, interest
in the protection of human values against the arbitrary action of
governments. This interest was to be further strengthened during
1976, in part by evidence of the widespread trampling on human
rights in other lands and in part by the decision of the Democratic
candidate to make the issue a central element in his campaign for
the presidency. If there is any single, recognizable theme or
unifying principle that is consistently in evidence amid the year's
tumultuous events, it may perhaps be found in this heightened
consciousness of human rights issues and in the related, sometimes
agonizing conflict between the urge to correct abuses and the
crippling limitations of practical diplomacy.

1. A BICENTENNIAL AGENDA

"Operation Sail," the highlight of the Bicentennial observances
in New York harbor, still lay six months in the future as the United
States prepared to face a year whose culminating experience undoubtedly would be the selection of a President and Vice-President
for the 1977-81 quadrennium. The conditions under which this task
would be undertaken were visibly more favorable than would have
been true a mere twelve months earlier, when memories of the
Watergate scandals and the resignation of President Richard M.
Nixon had been fresh in the national mind, and when the beginnings of economic recovery had yet to make themselves felt.
President Ford, addressing the Congress at that time, had acknowledged frankly "that the state of the Union is not good."[4]
This year, he could offer a more temperate judgment to the effect
"that the State of our Union is better—in many ways a lot better—
but still not good enough."

The State of the Union

Recovery from recent travail was the dominant theme of the
President's 1976 address on the State of the Union, delivered to a
joint session of the Congress on January 19 **(Document 1)**.
Reviewing the achievements of the past year—the first full year of
his administration—the President stressed not only the element of
psychic recovery from the war in Indochina but also a virtual
halving of the rate of inflation at a time when reviving economic

[4]*AFR, 1975:* 32.

activity had been providing 1,700,000 more jobs than had been available at the low point of the recession. Admittedly there were many Americans who had yet to feel a beneficent impact on their daily lives. Unemployment, charted the previous month at 7,768,000 or 8.3 percent of the labor force, was obviously much too high. Prices were admittedly rising too fast, despite the fact that the rate of inflation had been cut from 12.2 percent in 1974 to 7 percent in the year just past.

Yet there appeared to be no doubt in the President's mind that he now held the key to what could be "a healthy, noninflationary economy." "The Government," he asserted, must simply "stop spending so much and stop borrowing so much of our money. More money must remain in private hands where it will do the most good. To hold down the cost of living, we must hold down the cost of government." A judicious combination of tax reduction and curtailment in the growth of Federal spending, the President insisted, would make it possible to balance the budget and give the American people incentives to invest in the future.

One major area of expenditure, the President indicated, must nevertheless be exempted from this rule of retrenchment:

> The defense budget I will submit to the Congress for fiscal year 1977 will show an essential increase over the current year. It provides for real growth in purchasing power over this year's defense budget, which includes the cost of the all-volunteer force.
>
> We are continuing to make economies to enhance the efficiency of our military forces. But the budget I will submit represents the necessity of American strength for the real world in which we live.

Doubts About the Russians

Why was it necessary to raise a level of defense expenditure that had already undergone a sharp increase the year before and currently was running at a rate of some $93 billion a year, about a fourth of the entire budget? The United States, the President himself had pointed out, was now at peace; its foreign policy was "sound and strong," its military forces were "capable and ready," and its principal alliances had "never been more solid." Yet it remained a fact that America's relations with at least one foreign power, and that the strongest among contemporary nations, still counseled caution and could, if things went badly, lead to incalculable tragedy for all concerned.

President Ford's address occurred in the midst of a period of widespread disenchantment concerning the relaxation of U.S.-Soviet tensions that had been under way for approximately the last two decades, attaining its climax at the time of President Nixon's visit to the U.S.S.R. in 1972. Since that time, considerable slippage had occurred. U.S.-Soviet economic and political relations had failed to prosper as had been hoped. Plans for a comprehensive limitation of strategic offensive weapons, reaffirmed at Vladivostok in 1974 by President Ford and General Secretary Leonid I. Brezhnev, had encountered unexpected obstacles, as had the Vienna East-West talks on Mutual and Balanced Force Reduction in Central Europe. The lofty humanitarian principles enunciated at the recent 35-nation Conference on Security and Cooperation in Europe were being systematically disregarded in Soviet and Eastern European practice. While pressing a relentless build-up of its armaments and armed forces, the Soviet Union had intermittently displayed a disconcerting readiness to challenge the United States—and perhaps endanger world peace—by unilateral actions in areas remote from its frontiers.

Particularly disillusioning to President Ford and to Secretary of State Henry A. Kissinger had been the Soviet action, initiated in the summer of 1975, in supplying large-scale material and moral support to one of the several factions that were contending for mastery in the former Portuguese African territory of Angola. This intrusion into an area in which the U.S.S.R. had few if any historical interests had been rendered the more flagrant by the participation in the Angola fighting of thousands of Cuban troops, dispatched by Premier Fidel Castro in open collusion with his Soviet patrons. A continuation of such activities, Secretary Kissinger had repeatedly warned, must inevitably damage the whole fabric of U.S.-Soviet relations. In an attempt to counter the Soviet moves, the Ford administration had clandestinely supplied a limited amount of aid to a rival Angolan faction more favored by African moderates. Congress, however, had taken what the President had called a "very short-sighted" view in this matter and was now in the process of barring any further expenditure for such purposes.[5]

In spite of their unwillingness to sanction American involvement in what might, they feared, become a "new Vietnam" in Southern Africa, many members of Congress had been keenly disappointed by Soviet behavior and had become correspondingly doubtful about the real value of U.S.-Soviet "détente." Presidential aspirants in both major parties, like former Republican Governor Ronald Reagan of California and, among Democrats, Senator Henry M. Jackson of Washington and former Governor Jimmy Carter of Georgia, were already disparaging détente in a manner that had begun to enshroud the concept in a haze of domestic

[5]Details in *AFR, 1975:* 604-5.

politics. Even those who lacked a political incentive were bound to acknowledge that the current state of U.S.-Soviet relations left room for justified concern.

Another life-and-death issue for the United States, though it was one to which the President devoted less attention in his State of the Union address, had to do with the global energy crisis and the related financial and monetary dislocations, brought on as they had been by the conjunction of a growing demand for energy with the exaction of ever higher prices by members of the Organization of Petroleum Exporting Countries (OPEC). Without an assured supply of energy, the President pointed out, there could be "neither sustained growth nor more jobs." And yet, he noted, domestic production of oil and gas was still declining; dependence on high-priced foreign oil continued to drain away jobs and dollars "at the rate of $125 per year for every American"; and the legislation thus far enacted by Congress represented at best a late and incomplete start toward implementation of his proposals "to make America invulnerable to the foreign oil cartel." Although the energy question had by this time shed the aura of panic that had surrounded it at the time of the Arab oil embargo of 1973-74, the underlying situation was one that clearly would continue to exert a powerful influence on America's national and world position.

The Budget for FY 1977

More detailed indications of the administration's current planning were included in the Federal budget submitted by the President to Congress on January 21.[6] Unlike previous budgets, this one was geared to a new fiscal calendar whereby the current fiscal year (FY 1976) would end as usual on June 30, 1976 but would be followed by a three-month "transition quarter" before the commencement of the new fiscal year (FY 1977) on October 1, 1976. That year, in turn, would end September 30, 1977. In planning for the period ahead, the President proposed a number of changes in taxes and expenditures in line with the philosophy he had expounded in his State of the Union address. The overall objective, he explained, was to bring the budget into balance within the next three years and, at the same time, improve the prospects for the economy to remain upon a path of sustainable growth. Since, however, the outlays of $394.2 billion projected for the fiscal year would substantially exceed the anticipated receipts of approximately $351.3 billion, the immediate effect would be to pile

[6]Executive Office of the President, Office of Management and Budget, *The Budget of the United States Government, Fiscal Year 1977* (Washington: GPO, 1976); excerpts in Document 2.

a deficit of some $43 billion on top of the earlier deficits of $43.6 billion incurred in FY 1975, the $76 billion projected for FY 1976, and the $16.1 billion anticipated for the transition quarter.

National Defense Needs

Within the record-breaking $394.2 billion outlay projected for fiscal 1977, the largest single category of expenditure bore the label of "human resources" and included Social Security and other forms of social expenditure amounting, in the aggregate, to $205.3 billion or 52.1 percent of the total. Next in magnitude was "national defense," a category that included foreign military assistance as well as the Pentagon budget and was expected to account for $101.1 billion, or 25.6 percent of total outlays. This figure, moreover, was one in what was evidently intended as a series of annual increases in defense outlays. The previous (1976) fiscal year, with estimated defense expenditures of $92.8 billion, had already reversed what President Ford described as "the 7-year decline in real defense resources."[7] In subsequent years, the annual outlays were expected to increase still further, from $101.1 billion in FY 1977 to $112.9 billion in FY 1978, $121.5 billion in FY 1979, $132.4 billion in FY 1980, and $142.8 billion in FY 1981.[8]

Some inkling of why this money was thought needed, and how it would be spent, was provided by those sections of the budget that were specifically devoted to National Defense and to the related category of International Affairs and Finance (**Document 2**). "Despite an increase in Soviet defense spending, military personnel levels, and equipment modernization," this document conceded, "an acceptable military balance exists in the world today." This not unsatisfying state of affairs was attributed in the budget document to the fact that the United States continued to maintain an effective strategic deterrent, had been strengthening and modernizing its own and allied forces, and was improving the combat effectiveness of U.S. forces (including an increase from 13 to 16 Army divisions), all this at a time when much of the Soviet military build-up was being directed toward the Chinese border rather than toward the United States and its allies.

But however favorable the momentary situation, the budget document went on to argue, any hope for a reduction of military expenditures and international tensions must depend upon the forces of the United States and its allies remaining "at least as strong as those of potential adversaries." To ensure the preservation of the existing military balance, it said, the program for the

[7]*Budget*, cited: 61.
[8]Same: 35.

coming fiscal year included plans to "carry forward the increase in Army divisions, continue the modernization of ground, sea, and tactical air equipment, and improve the readiness of the combat forces." Particularly noticeable, in a year when it was hoped to complete a new strategic arms agreement with the U.S.S.R., was a $9.4 billion program for continued modernization of the strategic missile and bomber forces. In military jargon, this would involve the following elements:

- development of the B-1 bomber to strengthen and update strategic bomber forces, and initial procurement of the B-1 if test results are favorable;
- continued development of the Trident missile and submarine to give the seagoing strategic forces greater range and less vulnerability;
- further development of a new intercontinental ballistic missile [later called M-X] for deployment in the mid-1980's;
- full-scale development of long-range strategic cruise missiles for aircraft, submarine, or surface ship deployment;
- increases in the accuracy of ballistic missile warheads;
- improvement of technology for ballistic missile defense systems; and
- further improvements in systems for early warning of attack and for command, control and communications.

A more vigorous justification for the FY 1977 program was offered in the annual "military posture" statement delivered by Secretary of Defense Donald H. Rumsfeld to the House Armed Services Committee on January 27 (Document 3). In one of his first appearances as civilian chief of the Pentagon establishment, the former U.S. Representative to NATO asserted flatly that U.S. interests were being challenged throughout the world, primarily by the Soviet Union—a power which, he noted, had vastly expanded its military capabilities over the past decade and continued to increase them both qualitatively and quantitatively. Though Mr. Rumsfeld professed to find the current U.S. force structure "adequate to perform its missions at the present time," he clearly did not expect this situation to last unless the United States took resolute action to maintain it. ". . . Confidence in the future adequacy of our force structure is gradually declining," he averred. "Because of the trends—reductions on our part and Soviet military expansion—there has been a gradual shift in the power balance over the past fifteen years. And, in light of the momentum of Soviet military programs of all kinds, it will continue to shift unless U.S. defense outlays are increased in real terms, as the President is recommending."

Outlays for Foreign Aid

A minor item in the $101.1 billion the administration planned to spend on maintenance of the military balance over the next fiscal year was the $539 million (elsewhere stated, due to bookkeeping technicalities, as $739 million) to be spent for what was known as "military assistance." This was a catch-all name that covered a variety of defense materials and services provided to selected countries to enable them to strengthen their internal security and self-defense and, in some instances, to participate in regional or collective security arrangements. This, too, was an activity about which Congress had become increasingly dubious in recent years, and President Ford's projections—reduced from an estimated level of more than $2 billion in FY 1976—appeared to take note of this sentiment in citing what he described as "a continued transition from emphasis on grant military assistance to an emphasis on foreign military sales credits." Expatiating on this readjustment in a special message to Congress, the President stated that his 1977 budget reflected "a 28 percent reduction below the 1976 request, the termination of grant materiel assistance to Korea, and elimination of five small grant programs in Latin America."[9]

Although the President suggested that some additional reductions in military grant aid might be feasible in future years, he also warned that "offsetting increases in foreign military sales credits" would be required in most instances "to meet the legitimate military needs of our friends and allies at a time when much of their military equipment is reaching obsolescence and prices of new equipment are increasing drastically." What previously had been given away, in other words, would in future be sold on credit. In line with this policy, the 1977 budget included a request for $840 million in new budget authority to support a military credit sales program amounting to no less than $2.1 billion in direct credits and guaranteed loans.

A substantial portion of the credits in question was already earmarked for Israel, which had been given promises of large-scale military support at the time of the Sinai disengagement agreement negotiated with the aid of Secretary of State Kissinger in September 1975.[10] Nor had Israel and its Middle Eastern neighbors been overlooked in drawing up the 1977 allotments for "International Affairs and Finance." They called for total expenditures of $6.8 billion (and new budget authority of $9.7 billion) for a range of activities that included various forms of foreign economic aid as well as foreign information and exchange programs and diplomatic and consular representation. Prominent in the $5.5 billion of new

[9]Message of Jan. 20, in *Presidential Documents*, 12:53 (*Bulletin*, 74: 158-9).
[10]Cf. *AFR, 1975:* 400 and 497-8.

budget authority requested for "foreign economic and financial assistance" were an item of $1.8 billion for "security supporting assistance" (a kind of security-oriented economic aid), primarily for the Middle East, and an additional $35 million for a "Middle East special requirements fund." Also requested were appropriations of approximately $1.2 billion for multilateral development assistance; $1.1 billion for bilateral development assistance through the U. S. Agency for International Development (AID); and $1.2 billion for the 22-year-old Food for Peace program.

Intelligence and Corporate Payments

In presenting his financial recommendations to the Congress, President Ford had not lost sight of other matters with a foreign policy dimension that had also exercised the nation in recent months. On February 18, he was to announce a partial reorganization of the intelligence services, ostensibly designed to protect the integrity of the intelligence function while at the same time responding to the clamor for far-reaching reforms that would preclude the recurrence of the kind of abuses revealed in recent months—among them, the disclosure that the Central Intelligence Agency (CIA) had at one time taken part in the plotting of assassination attempts against certain foreign chiefs of state. The principal feature of the reorganization was a centralization of the responsibility for policy direction in the National Security Council and in a Committee on Foreign Intelligence that would be headed by the Director of Central Intelligence, George Bush.[11]

Less subject to administrative action were the shady corporate practices, including bribes and other illicit payments, whose disclosure had become a source of mounting international indignation and, in the words of one high State Department official, had occasioned "serious political crises in friendly countries, possible cancellation of major overseas orders for U.S. industries, and the risk of general cooling toward U.S. firms abroad." The administration's initial impulse in this matter was to work toward internationally agreed guidelines and multilateral agreements through such established bodies as the Organization for Economic Cooperation and Development (OECD) and the U.N. Commission on Transnational Corporations.[12] In addition, the President established early in the spring a Cabinet-level Task Force on Questionable Corporate Payments Abroad, chaired by Secretary of

[11]*Presidential Documents*, 12: 227-9 and 234-44 (in part in *Bulletin*, 74: 292-4); for background cf. *AFR, 1975:* 5-7.
[12]Statement of Deputy Secretary of State Robert S. Ingersoll, Mar. 5, in *Bulletin*, 74: 414.

Commerce Elliot L. Richardson, which was directed "to conduct a sweeping policy review"[13] and later recommended a number of legislative initiatives, none of which could be acted upon during the 1976 congressional session.

"No" on Angola

It had been a foregone conclusion that the President's program would be minutely scrutinized by a legislative body that was dominated by the opposition party, as had been true in most of the years since World War II. Much more than partisanship, moreover, had been involved in the reassertion of legislative authority over foreign affairs that had occurred since the beginning of the 1970s. In the course of that period, Congress had successively decreed an end to military involvement in Indochina, imposed harsh limitations on the war powers of the President, rejected the Administration's recommendation of most-favored-nation commercial treatment for the U.S.S.R., and, more recently, insisted on a cutoff of military aid to Turkey (later partially rescinded) because of dissatisfaction with that country's actions in Cyprus.

An equally striking manifestation of independence had been the Senate's action of December 19, 1975, in voting 54 to 22 to bar the use of Defense Department funds to counter Soviet activities in Angola. Vigorously denounced by President Ford and Secretary Kissinger, who insisted that the United States must not sit idly by in face of the Soviet-Cuban intrusion into African affairs, the "hands off Angola" amendment—technically, an amendment to the pending $112.3 billion Department of Defense Appropriation Act for FY 1976[14]—was nevertheless approved in its turn by a 323 to 99 vote of the House of Representatives when that body got around to clearing the bill for the President on January 27, 1976. Unwilling to veto a measure that contained essential funds for other ongoing programs, President Ford contented himself with loosing another volley of criticism at a provision which, he said, not only would "deprive the people of Angola of the assistance needed to resist Soviet and Cuban military intervention in their country" but constituted, in his opinion, "an extremely undesirable precedent that could limit severely our ability to play a positive and effective role in international affairs."[15]

Advice from Dr. Kissinger

The debacle in Angola and the apparent slowdown in the

---

[13]*Presidential Documents*, 12: 519-21 (in part in *Bulletin*, 74: 583-4).
[14]Public Law 94-212, Feb. 9, 1976; for background cf. *AFR, 1975:* 604-5.
[15]Signature statement, Feb. 10, in *Presidential Documents*, 12: 172.

Strategic Arms Limitation Talks (SALT) with the U.S.S.R. did not present the most favorable auguries for U.S. foreign policy at the outset of an election year in which the concept of détente was under heavy attack and even Secretary of State Kissinger, the architect and visible symbol of the U.S.-Soviet relationship, no longer enjoyed his former immunity from criticism. Returning more or less empty-handed from a January visit to Moscow, to be discussed in the next chapter, the Secretary of State seemed fully aware of the threatening currents on the domestic scene. These, indeed, appeared to be his chief preoccupation as he set out at the beginning of February for a brief Western tour that would include a foreign policy address at the University of Wyoming in Laramie as well as a San Francisco speech on U.S.-Soviet relations.

Republished under the title "America's Destiny: The Global Context," Secretary Kissinger's address at Laramie **(Document 4)** was at once a review of American diplomatic history, a warning to the Soviet Union against the temptation to "fish in troubled waters," and a plea to the American people to exhibit the "vision and patience" without which, he warned, the opportunity to shape a new international order would fade and the world would be shaped, amid mounting "conflict and suffering," by "others who do not share our principles."

"The principal danger we face," Dr. Kissinger averred, "is our own domestic divisions." ". . . It is time we recognize that, increasingly, our difficulties abroad are largely of our own making." "We must restore our unity while the essential structure of our foreign policy is still sound and before irreparable damage is done to it." Broadside attacks on the intelligence services, congressional usurpation of executive responsibilities, "acrimonious controversy which thwarts serious discussion of the great issues," were threatening, he said, to nullify the achievements of America's first two centuries and were already imperiling the rich promise of its third.

The weeks that followed were to offer scanty comfort to a senior official who, after being so long hailed as a national hero, was increasingly being attacked by political candidates in all parts of the spectrum and, despite the loyal support of President Ford, increasingly looked upon as an encumbrance in the President's campaign for the Republican nomination. Particularly wounding in a personal sense was the appearance in the press of unauthorized, truncated versions of a report by the House Select Committee on Intelligence, chaired by Democratic Representative Otis Pike of New York, in which the Secretary in effect was charged with betraying the Kurds of Iran, misrepresenting the status of the SALT talks, and committing various other offenses in a blanket indictment that was characterized by Dr. Kissinger himself as "a new version of McCarthyism."[16]

"An orgy of recrimination" was the term the Secretary of State employed a few weeks later to suggest the way in which America seemed "bent on eroding its influence and destroying its achievements in world affairs." "If one group of critics undermines arms control negotiations and cuts off the prospect of more constructive ties with the Soviet Union while another group cuts away at our defense budgets and intelligence services and thwarts American resistance to Soviet adventurism," he asserted, "both combined will—whether they have intended it or not—end by wrecking the nation's ability to conduct a strong, creative, moderate, and prudent foreign policy. The result will be paralysis, no matter who wins in November. And if America cannot act, others will, and we and all the free peoples of the world will pay the price."[17]

As always, however, the Secretary of State seemed confident in the last analysis that the nation's better qualities would ultimately prevail:

In this Bicentennial year [he said in Boston on March 11], we celebrate ideals which began to take shape around the shores of Massachusetts Bay some 350 years ago. We have accomplished great things as a united people. There is much yet to do. This country's work in the world is not a burden but a triumph—and the measure of greatness yet to come.

Americans have always made history rather than let history chart our course. We, the present generation of Americans, will do no less. So let this year mark the end of our divisions. Let it usher in an era of national reconciliation and rededication by all Americans to their common destiny. Let us have a clear vision of what is before us—glory and danger alike—and go forward together to meet it.[18]

2. AVERTING NUCLEAR CATASTROPHE

Implicit in the international programs proposed by President Ford was a conviction that the Soviet Union must continue to hold the central place in American foreign policy calculations that it had occupied since World War II. In spite of all the talk of North-South

[16]News conference, Feb. 12, in *Bulletin*, 74: 289-91. For background on the Pike committee report (partially printed in the *Village Voice* of Feb. 16 and 23, 1976), cf. *AFR, 1975:* 6-7.
[17]Boston speech, Mar. 11, in *Bulletin*, 74: 431-2.
[18]Same: 432.

issues, economic development, and the "New International Economic Order," American authorities still attached preeminent importance to the relationship with the world's other nuclear superpower. "The Soviet Union possesses great industrial prowess and military strength," Winston Lord, Director of the State Department's Policy Planning Staff, reminded a congressional subcommittee early in 1976. "It is directed by leaders dedicated to developing Soviet power and enhancing Soviet influence. Aside from ourselves, only the U.S.S.R. has strategic capabilities and conventional forces with a global reach. It is thus at once our principal rival and an inevitable partner if we are to help shape a more positive globe. There can be no higher imperative than insuring that the vast nuclear arsenals we each hold are never used—for the ensuing holocaust could engulf not only our two countries but civilization itself. Our own security and global stability hinge fundamentally upon the success of our endeavors to manage this relationship."[19]

East-West Disappointments

But though the management of U.S.-Soviet relations had seemed to attain a peak of virtuosity at the time of President Nixon's triumphant visit to the U.S.S.R. in May 1972, it had since run into mounting difficulties that had caused uneasiness to many Americans and, as already noted, had created widespread skepticism about the virtues of East-West "détente." Both powers, it was hoped, continued to share a basic conviction that nuclear war must at all costs be avoided, and that peaceful interchange should be encouraged within the limits of mutual convenience. Yet the two governments had met with unexpected difficulty in translating their aversion to nuclear war into reliable agreements to limit, let alone end, the strategic arms race and the worldwide competition for military advantage; nor could their recent ventures in the area of "peaceful coexistence" by any means be termed an unqualified success. Plans for a vast expansion of mutual trade and economic relations had failed to fructify, in part because of the unwillingness of Congress to grant the U.S.S.R. most-favored-nation tariff treatment in light of its restrictions on the emigration of Soviet citizens, particularly those of Jewish faith. The ceremonial conclusion at Helsinki of the Conference on Security and Cooperation in Europe (CSCE) in the summer of 1975 had done less to promote

[19]Winston Lord, "The Triangular Relationship of the United States, the U.S.S.R., and the People's Republic of China," statement before the Subcommittee on Future Foreign Policy Research and Development of the House Committee on International Relations, Mar. 23 (*Bulletin*, 74:514).

the peaceful exchange of people, ideas, and goods than to focus attention on the denial, by the Soviet and other Communist governments, of many of the rights and freedoms that were regarded in the West as vital to successful "people-to-people" diplomacy or to any long-term accommodation between the two kinds of society.

A Snag in SALT

Not less disquieting to Western observers had been the lack of progress in either of the two main forums of East-West negotiation that were ostensibly concerned with reducing the burdens and dangers of the existing military confrontation. One of these negotiating forums was the Strategic Arms Limitation Talks (SALT) between the United States and the Soviet Union. The other was the Vienna Conference on Mutual Reduction of Forces and Armaments and Associated Measures in Central Europe (MBFR), in which the U.S.S.R. and six of its Warsaw Pact associates confronted the United States and those of its NATO allies (other than France) with forces stationed in the Central European theater.

Of the two negotiations, it was the SALT talks that were most immediately concerned with trying to reduce or exorcise the threat of nuclear warfare. Initiated in 1969 after several years' American efforts, the talks had reached a significant watershed in May 1972 when the two governments had celebrated President Nixon's visit to the Soviet capital by agreeing (1) to limit themselves in future to two launcher sites apiece for antiballistic missiles (ABMs), and (2) to freeze their inventories of ground- and submarine-launched strategic missiles at current levels pending the conclusion of a more complete agreement sometime within the next five years.[20]

Two years later, these arrangements had been further developed through (1) a protocol, signed—subject to ratification—by President Nixon and General Secretary Brezhnev on July 3, 1974, by whose terms the number of ABM launcher sites permitted each side would be reduced from two to one;[21] and (2) an understanding between President Ford and General Secretary Brezhnev, meeting at Vladivostok on November 23-24, 1974, on guidelines for a new strategic arms limitation agreement that would if possible be completed in 1975 and would, in any event, apply to the period from October 1977 through 1985.[22]

Central to the Vladivostok understandings was a principle of "equality and equal security" which—unlike the 1972 agreement, which had involved missiles but not bombers—would impose

[20]*AFR, 1972:* 86-101.
[21]*AFR, 1974:* 226-9.
[22]*AFR, 1974:* 508-17.

identical numerical limits on the strategic delivery vehicles (missiles and bombers) of both sides. Specifically, each side would be permitted an agreed maximum of 2,400 strategic delivery vehicles, and, within that number, could have up to 1,320 intercontinental ballistic missiles (ICBMs) and/or submarine-launched ballistic missiles (SLBMs) equipped with multiple, independently targetable reentry vehicles (MIRVs). Since the Soviets had at the time been well ahead of the United States in numbers of strategic delivery vehicles, their acceptance of equal numbers, as well as their willingness to exclude the NATO forces in Europe from the equation, represented concessions of considerable significance.

Not covered by the Vladivostok understandings, however, had been the status of certain new weapons whose capabilities and availability for inclusion within the agreed ceilings had quickly become a matter of disagreement. On one side was a new Soviet bomber, known in the West as "Backfire," which was classified by Moscow as having an intermediate range but was viewed in the Pentagon as a long-range "strategic" bomber that ought, as such, to be included under the Vladivostok ceiling. On the other side was the American-developed "cruise missile," a subsonic, pilotless drone that could be launched from submarines, surface ships, or aircraft, was credited with a range of some 1,500 miles, and was viewed in Moscow (though not in Washington) as a prime candidate for limitation under the Vladivostok principles. The attempt to reconcile these antithetic positions had gone forward without success through 1975, a year in which the failure to reach definitive agreement had led to the postponement of a transatlantic visit by General Secretary Brezhnev and had contributed to a gradual erosion of American support for the détente concept.

Storm over Angola

On top of these disappointments had come the unexpected Soviet intervention in Angola, where a struggle among contending African nationalist factions had been elevated into an episode of the "cold war" by the sudden appearance of the U.S.S.R. and Cuba as committed supporters of the leftist Popular Movement for the Liberation of Angola (MPLA) led by Agostinho Neto. Such a bid for unilateral advantage, as Secretary Kissinger had repeatedly insisted and again assured the press on January 14, 1976,[23] was viewed by the United States as "incompatible with a genuine relaxation of tensions," "a wholly unnecessary setback to the constructive trends in U.S.-Soviet relations," and a burden on the "general relationship" between the two powers which must, if continued over time, affect the SALT negotiations as well.

[23]*Bulletin*, 74: 125-6.

In spite of these unfavorable auguries, the Secretary of State undertook another visit to the Soviet capital on January 20-23 in what was generally viewed as a last attempt to break the SALT deadlock before the chances of agreement were lost amid the turbulence of the presidential campaign. The precise proposals Dr. Kissinger took with him to Moscow were not officially made public and were, in any case, concerned with issues too abstruse to lend themselves to intelligent public discussion. Although it would later be ascertained that a number of technical points had been resolved in the course of the Secretary's conversations in Moscow, neither then nor later could agreement be reached on such key questions as (1) the number of Backfires to be allowed the Soviet Union above the Vladivostok ceiling, or any lower ceiling that might later be agreed upon; and (2) how many ship- or air-launched cruise missiles with ranges over 375 miles should be allowed the United States, and how these numbers should be related to the over-all ceilings established at Vladivostok.[24]

Moscow's policy concerning Angola also underwent no visible change as a result of the Kissinger visit, and a victory for the Cuban-supported MPLA seemed virtually certain by the time of his return to Washington. Appearing before the Senate Foreign Relations Committee on January 29, the Secretary of State was scathingly critical of the Soviet-Cuban intervention and scarcely less caustic about the congressional resistance which had frustrated the administration's attempts to counter it.[25] This "blatant Soviet and Cuban challenge," Dr. Kissinger repeated in his important address on U.S.-Soviet relations at San Francisco on February 3 (Document 5), imposed a duty on the United States "to make clear to the Soviet Union and Cuba that Angola sets no precedent, that this type of action will not be tolerated again."

Détente in the Doghouse

Scandalized as he appeared to be by Soviet conduct in the Angola affair, the Secretary of State was well aware that the détente he had so labored to bring about was threatened from the American as well as the Soviet side. In his San Francisco address, he tried hard to dispel some prevalent misconceptions on the subject and to focus attention on the realities of the U.S.-Soviet relationship. Even the grave financial consequences of a failure to achieve a SALT agreement, he suggested, underlined the need to persevere in trying to place the relationship between the two superpowers on more secure foundations. "We must strive for an equilibrium of power," Dr. Kissinger insisted, "but we must move beyond it to

[24]Cf. Leslie H. Gelb in *New York Times*, Feb. 17, 1976.
[25]Text in *AFR, 1975:* 605-18.

promote the habits of mutual restraint, coexistence, and ultimately cooperation. We must stabilize a new international order in a vastly dangerous environment, but our ultimate goal must be to transform ideological conflict into constructive participation in building a better world." "This," Secretary Kissinger added, "is what is meant by the process called détente—not the hunger for relaxation of tension, not the striving for agreements at any price, not the mindless search for friendly atmosphere which some critics use as naive and dangerous caricatures."

Yet it was precisely these "naive and dangerous caricatures," rather than the more sophisticated view of détente enunciated by the Secretary of State, that were increasingly gaining ascendancy in the public mind and would soon torpedo the word if not the concept. President Ford himself, his hopes for the Republican nomination increasingly threatened by the upsurge of conservative nationalistic forces identified with former Governor Reagan, would soon begin to avoid the word "détente" even while striving to preserve the substance. ". . . Let me say very specifically that we are going to forget the use of the word détente," the President declared at Peoria on March 5. ". . . The word is inconsequential. What happens in the negotiations between the United States and the Soviet Union, what happens in the negotiations between the People's Republic of China and the United States—those are the things that are of consequence."[26]

Intent on demonstrating the importance of negotiation—rather than confrontation—with the two Communist powers, the President referred particularly to the continuing attempt to "get a SALT Two agreement that will keep a lid on strategic arms in the next 7 or 10 years." "If we had an open thermonuclear arms race," he pointed out, "that's not in the best interest of the United States or the world as a whole. We have an obligation to have rough equivalency that will deter aggression, either by us or by them, and permit us to do some things that are needed and necessary for the world as a whole, as well as for the United States."[27]

But neither the progress of the SALT negotiations nor any other major aspect of the U.S.-Soviet relationship would afford an altogether persuasive substantiation of the Ford-Kissinger thesis. SALT talks during the balance of the year were to produce no resolution of the fundamental issues that clustered around the Backfire and the cruise missile, and hence no letup in the "mad momentum" of the strategic arms race between the two powers. Even the missile "freeze" imposed in 1972 began to look increasingly precarious as the five-year Interim Agreement concluded

[26]*Presidential Documents*, 12: 350.
[27]Same.

in that year approached its formal expiration on October 3, 1977. Not until after Governor Carter's victory in the November election would there be signs of renewed movement, initiated by Brezhnev's assertion that it was "high time to put an end to the freeze imposed on this question by Washington almost a year ago."[28] And still more time would be needed before the next President and his aides could gain an understanding of the substantive difficulties that had prevented progress during the last two years of the Ford administration.

The ABM Protocol

If 1976 thus offered disappointingly little in the way of unambiguous progress toward a comprehensive SALT agreement, it did at least record a number of advances along the peripheries of the U.S.-Soviet arms race.[29] Several of these minor achievements completed initiatives dating from President Nixon's second visit to the U.S.S.R, a few weeks before his resignation in the summer of 1974.

One of the significant accomplishments of the second Nixon visit had been the signature on July 3, 1974, of the ABM Protocol already referred to, a supplement to the 1972 ABM Treaty whereby each of the two powers undertook to limit itself in future to a single ABM site, rather than the two sites agreed upon in 1972.[30] The United States, under this arrangement, proposed at least for the time being to maintain only a single ABM site for the protection of its ICBM launcher site at Grand Forks, North Dakota; the U.S.S.R., similarly, would limit itself to a single ABM site based on its capital at Moscow. Transmitted to the Senate by President Ford in September 1974, the protocol had been approved by a 63 to 15 vote of that body on November 10, 1975, and entered into force with the exchange of ratifications by the two powers on May 24, 1976.

Several months later, agreement was also reached in the U.S.-Soviet Standing Consultative Commission on a pair of technical protocols, one of which established procedures governing replacement, dismantling or destruction, and notification thereof, of the respective ABM systems or their components, while the other established a procedure to facilitate transmissions of immediate notifications in the event of threatened emergencies of the sort

[28]*New York Times*, Dec. 1, 1976.

[29]Additional data on arms control activities in 1976 will be found in U.S. Arms Control and Disarmament Agency (ACDA), *16th Annual Report*, transmitted to Congress Jan. 19, 1977 (House Document 95-58, 95th Cong., 1st sess.; Washington: GPO, 1977).

[30]Text in *AFR, 1974:* 226-8.

foreseen in the 1971 Agreement on Measures to Reduce the Risk of Outbreak of Nuclear War.[31]

TTB and PNE

Another result of Mr. Nixon's second Moscow visit had been the signature, also on July 3, 1974, of a bilateral Threshold Test Ban (TTB) Treaty or Treaty on the Limitation of Underground Nuclear Weapons Tests,[32] the purpose of which was to broaden the prohibitions on nuclear weapon testing contained in the multilateral 1963 Treaty on the Prohibition of Nuclear Weapon Tests in the Atmosphere, in Outer Space, and Under Water. In instituting a prohibition on underground nuclear weapon tests with a yield exceeding 150 kilotons (equivalent to 150,000 tons of TNT), the new treaty did not attempt to outlaw underground testing as such, but undertook to establish a nuclear "threshold" that would at least eliminate the testing of large-scale weapons "going beyond the fractional-megaton range."[33] Even this prohibition, however, would not become effective before March 31, 1976, and would have no binding effect thereafter until the treaty had been formally ratified and entered into force; and it had been mutually understood by the two parties that this would not occur until they had also concluded and ratified a parallel treaty governing underground nuclear explosions for peaceful (as distinct from military) purposes.

Negotiations relating to peaceful nuclear explosions (PNE) were initiated in October 1974 and reached fruition on May 28, 1976 with the signature in Washington and Moscow of a new, bilateral U.S.-Soviet Treaty on Underground Nuclear Explosions for Peaceful Purposes **(Document 6a)**. Its key provision, as paraphrased by the U.S. Arms Control and Disarmament Agency (ACDA), committed the two powers "not to carry out any individual nuclear explosions having a yield exceeding 150 kilotons; not to carry out any group explosion (consisting of a number of individual explosions) having an aggregate yield exceeding 1,500 kilotons; and not to carry out any group explosion having an aggregate yield exceeding 150 kilotons unless the individual explosions in the group could be identified and measured by agreed verification procedures."[34]

---

[31]ACDA, *16th Annual Report:* 8.

[32]Text in *AFR, 1974:* 229-33.

[33]U.S. Arms Control and Disarmament Agency (ACDA), *Arms Control and Disarmament Agreements: Texts and History of Negotiations,* 1977 ed. (ACDA Publication 94; Washington: GPO, 1977): 155.

[34]Same: 166.

These undertakings, which were to remain in effect for a five-year period, were buttressed by unusually stringent provisions for mutual verification, involving not merely the standard reliance on "national technical means of verification" but also an obligation on each party to provide the other party "information and access to sites of explosions." This requirement, spelled out at length in an accompanying protocol,[35] was generally construed as a first victory for the principle of on-site inspection long championed by the United States but always hitherto resisted by the U.S.S.R.

Two months after the conclusion of the PNE Treaty, President Ford in a message sent to the Senate on July 29 **(Document 6b)** requested that body's advice and consent to ratification of both the TTB and the PNE treaties. "Taken together as integrated and complementary components of this important limitation on nuclear explosions," the President suggested, the two treaties represented "one more useful step in our continuing effort to develop comprehensive and balanced limitations on nuclear weapons." Although no action was taken by the Senate during the 1976 session, both the Soviet and the American governments had intimated that they intended to observe the terms of the TTB treaty until its ratification and entry in force.

Banning Environmental Warfare

Even the most comprehensive agreements between the two nuclear superpowers would not in themselves suffice to avert the threat of catastrophe in a world where at least six countries already possessed a military nuclear capability, numerous others appeared capable of acquiring one at comparatively short notice, and still others, including many third world nations, were doing everything possible to acquire the latest in sophisticated conventional weaponry. Difficult if not impossible to justify from an economic point of view, the world's expenditure of some $350 billion a year for military purposes also carried with it a mounting threat to the safety and well-being of every country and every individual on the planet. In such a situation, the professed objective of "general and complete disarmament under effective international control" seemed tragically remote despite the pertinacious efforts carried on from year to year in the Geneva-based Conference of the Committee on Disarmament (CCD) and elsewhere.

The one concrete accomplishment of 1976 in the area of multilateral disarmament negotiation was the completion and preliminary approval of a multilateral "Convention on the Prohibition of Military or Any Other Hostile Use of En-

[35]Same: 168-79 and *Bulletin*, 74: 804-11.

vironmental Modification Techniques." This, too, was a legacy of the Nixon-Brezhnev meeting of 1974, at which both parties had acknowledged the potential dangers of environmental warfare—already widely noted in the U.S. Congress—and had decided to sponsor a meeting of U.S. and Soviet experts on the subject.[36] Subsequent discussion and negotiations, on a bilateral basis and in the CCD, had led by the summer of 1976 to the formulation of an agreed text **(Document 7)** that obligated each of the states subscribing to the convention "not to engage in military or any other hostile use of environmental modification techniques having widespread, long-lasting or severe effects as the means of destruction, damage or injury to any other State Party." Enforcement of this provision was optimistically left to the Security Council of the United Nations. Endorsed by the U.N. General Assembly in a resolution adopted December 10, 1976,[37] the convention was subsequently opened for signature at Geneva on May 18, 1977 and signed immediately by 34 countries, including most members of NATO and all members of the Warsaw Pact.

The Nuclear Proliferation Problem

More immediate dangers were involved in the threatened proliferation of nuclear weapon capabilities as an accompaniment of the growing worldwide shift to nuclear power as an alternative to high-priced petroleum. The dangers of this trend, vividly illustrated by India's acquisition of a military nuclear capability in 1974 and highlighted the following year at the conference to review the 1968 Nuclear Nonproliferation Treaty,[38] continued to preoccupy both the United States and the governments of other technically advanced countries—including the U.S.S.R.—that were currently participating in the London meetings of the so-called Nuclear Suppliers Conference. Especially prominent among the issues agitating the world community throughout the year was the fate of an agreement by West Germany to build a uranium enrichment plant and a nuclear fuel reprocessing facility for Brazil, and of a French agreement to provide a nuclear reprocessing facility to Pakistan. Underlying the controversy provoked by these agreements were the difficult technical and philosophical questions that would be involved in trying to regulate the diffusion of nuclear technology, equipment and fuel in the coming years.

In the absence of effective action on a multilateral basis, the

[36]Statement of July 3, 1974, in *AFR, 1974:* 234.
[37]General Assembly Resolution 31/72, adopted by a vote of 96 (U.S., U.S.S.R.)-8-30.
[38]*AFR, 1975:* 149-56.

demand had grown for the elaboration by the United States of a national nuclear policy commensurate with the increasing scope and complexity of the problem.[39] Following a comprehensive review commissioned in the summer of 1976, President Ford made public on October 28, five days before the election, a detailed statement **(Document 8)** in which he asserted, among other things, that while the United States and other nations "can and should increase their use of nuclear power for peaceful purposes," the avoidance of proliferation must henceforth "take precedence over economic interests"; that success in this endeavor depended on "an extraordinary coordination of the policies of all nations toward the common good"; and that the first priority was to inhibit the accumulation of plutonium, the element most suited to the manufacture of nuclear bombs, either in a separated form suitable for weapons use or in unprocessed spent fuel from nuclear reactors.

As one means to this end, the President announced what amounted to a moratorium on the reprocessing and recycling of used nuclear fuel to produce plutonium until such time as it might appear that the world community could effectively overcome the associated risks of proliferation. Other key points, of a nature scarcely to be welcomed by nations eager to exploit a growing international market, included a proposal "to join us in exercising maximum restraint in the transfer of reprocessing and enrichment technology and facilities by avoiding such sensitive exports or commitments for at least 3 years."

Conventional Arms Transfers

This plan was almost immediately superseded by the outcome of the presidential election, which spelled the opening of still another phase in the battle to put a stop to nuclear proliferation—and, in addition, to stem the ever-increasing dissemination of conventional weaponry to countries which, in many cases, could not readily afford it even if they could be trusted to use it wisely. Conventional arms transfers were even less susceptible to international control than the trade in nuclear materials and processes; and the United States itself, whose arms transfers amounted to approximately half the world total[40] had not as yet attempted to exercise the kind of restraint it was applying in the nuclear field. Security interests, particularly in the case of such major purchasers as Iran and Saudi

[39]For an outline of U.S. "nonproliferation strategy" as of early 1976 see the statement of Secretary Kissinger, Mar. 9, in *Bulletin*, 74: 405-11.
[40]U.S. Arms Control and Disarmament Agency (ACDA), *World Military Expenditures and Arms Transfers, 1966-1975* (ACDA Publication 90; Washington: GPO, 1976): 56 and 74.

Arabia, were felt by the Defense and State Departments to out-weigh any objection to the sales of advanced aircraft, missiles, and other equipment those countries were able to purchase with their increased oil revenues.[41]

But Congress, of late years, had been much less susceptible to this kind of argument. Through a gradual strengthening of its independent influence, it had by now established what amounted to a virtual veto on major governmental sales of military equipment and services. The congressional role was further strengthened with the enactment in June of the International Security Assistance and Arms Export Control Act of 1976,[42] in which it was strongly suggested that, as a matter of policy, the aggregate total of U.S. governmental and commercial arms sales should not be further increased. (An earlier version, vetoed by the President, would have imposed an annual ceiling of $9 billion on total governmental and commercial exports of military equipment and services.) The whole subject remained a source of contention that would gain new layers of complexity with the advent of an administration that tended, like the Congress, to view a country's performance in the human rights area as no less pertinent than traditional security criteria in determining its eligibility to acquire U.S. arms.

3. ATLANTIC ALLIANCE AND DÉTENTE IN EUROPE

Relations with the Soviet Union and its allies were a prime concern not merely for the United States, but for all of the governments that had banded together in the late 1940s and early 1950s for the purpose of deterring Communist aggression or subversion against an allied state in Europe or the North Atlantic area. Though perhaps to a less marked degree than in the United States, the sense of relaxation and relief that had accompanied the détente movement of the early 1970s in Western Europe had lately given way to reviving uneasiness as the European military balance gave evidence of shifting to the detriment of the NATO powers and to the increasing advantage of the Soviet Union and its Warsaw Pact allies.

Ironically, the Warsaw group had been moving toward a position of military preponderance at the very time when the interested governments of East and West, after long years of preparatory maneuvering, had finally begun negotiations at Vienna for the

---

[41]Cf. the statement of Philip C. Habib, Under Secretary of State for Political Affairs, Sept. 21, in *Bulletin*, 75: 447-51.
[42]Public Law 94-329, June 30, 1976.

professed objective of bringing about a mutual reduction of forces and armaments in Central Europe, one that would establish a more stable relationship and strengthen European peace and security even while it ensured that there was no diminution in the security of any individual state.[43]

Eurocommunism and the Helsinki Final Act

While the participating governments exchanged their proposals at the Vienna talks, another novel factor had entered the European scene with the revival, for almost the first time since the late 1940s, of the possibility that national Communist parties might soon take power in one or more of the leading Western countries. The phenomena of what was known as "Eurocommunism"—a somewhat amorphous term that encompassed not only the more moderate, democratic stance adopted by many of the Western Communist parties, but also the ostentatious expressions of independence from Moscow that frequently accompanied it—had occasioned widely varying reactions in the Western world. Such developments as Italy's "opening to the Left," the tactical alliance of France's Communists and Socialists, the political ferment in Portugal following the overthrow of the authoritarian Caetano regime in 1974, the welling up of long suppressed political forces as the Franco dictatorship in Spain approached its end, were viewed by some as a heartening testimony to the political vitality of the old continent and its capacity for democratic renewal.

There were other authorities, however, to whom these same phenomena signified a mortal threat to everything the West had accomplished over the past 30 years. In the view of Secretary of State Kissinger, for instance, a Communist accession to even a limited share of political power in one or more Western countries could defeat the basic purposes of the Western alliance, undermine the foundations of NATO, and subvert the very democratic processes that had successfully resisted external conquest. That Dr. Kissinger's apprehensions might not lack some measure of justification had been demonstrated to the satisfaction of a good many Western observers when the Portuguese Communists—whose leader, Alvaro Cunhal, admittedly was among those least susceptible to the new Eurocommunist influences—had involved themselves in an unsuccessful attempt at a takeover of the Lisbon government in November 1975.

In off-the-record comments to American diplomats in London a few weeks after this occurrence, Dr. Kissinger had maintained not only that "the dominance of Communist parties in the West is

[43]Vienna communiqué, June 28, 1973, in *AFR, 1973:* 290.

unacceptable," but also that "major Communist participation in Western governments" would erode "the foundations of our Atlantic security" and spell the death of the Western alliance in its existing form.[44] "I . . . believe that the United States must not create the impression that it could be indifferent to such development," the Secretary of State repeated on April 13, 1976, after his earlier comments had leaked to the press. ". . . So when I am asked about this issue, I must point out the serious consequences. If it happens, we will then have to deal with it; but it will certainly mark a historic turning point in Atlantic relationships."[45]

Paradoxically, the Soviet Union and the Communist regimes of Eastern Europe had become a prey to apprehensions of a rather similar kind, reflecting, in their case, the congenital failure of the repressive apparatus of Communist rule to quench the thirst for greater personal freedom—and, in the Eastern European countries at least, a fuller affirmation of national identity. Always latent within the Communist world, such trends had been immensely stimulated by the holding of the recent Conference on Security and Cooperation in Europe (CSCE), an exercise originally proposed by the Communist governments themselves and which, as already noted, had culminated at Helsinki in the summer of 1975 with a heads-of-government meeting of leaders from 35 countries, including the United States and Canada as well as every European state except Albania. The high point of the Helsinki ceremonies had been the adoption of a Final Act[46] in which were set forth a wide variety of principles and undertakings relating to peace and security in Europe, the inviolability of existing frontiers, confidence-building measures (such as advance notification of certain military movements), and the determination of the participating governments to promote respect for human rights and foster increased contacts and exchanges among their peoples in the economic, scientific, intellectual and cultural areas.

Particularly mistrusted by the Soviet and associated governments, in spite of their success in watering down the language, were a series of provisions relating to "Cooperation in Humanitarian and Other Fields" (the so-called "Third Basket"),[47] on which the Western governments had insisted as the price of their formal acquiescence in the existing European political and territorial setup. Inspired by an essentially liberal, Western concept of human rights and personal and intellectual freedoms, these prescriptions in many instances ran directly counter to existing Soviet practice in

[44]*AFR, 1975:* 562-4.
[45]*Bulletin*, 74: 568.
[46]Text in *AFR, 1975:* 292-360.
[47]Same: 333-55.

regard to such matters as the reunification of divided families, marriage between citizens of different states, access to information, improvement of working conditions for journalists, and the like. From the standpoint of the Communist authorities in the U.S.S.R. and Eastern Europe, these portions of the Helsinki legacy would seem to have loomed as no less dangerously subversive than current Communist tactics in the West appeared to some Americans. Such reservations, moreover, were coming to seem increasingly well-founded as the Helsinki Final Act began to serve as a rallying point for political dissidence both in the U.S.S.R. and in Poland, Czechoslovakia, and other Eastern European countries.

The Treaty with Spain

The kaleidoscopic political changes of recent years had not impaired the long-established determination of the American government to maintain such military arrangements at home and overseas as it considered essential to the common defense of the West—even, if necessary, at the cost of friction with other allied governments that did not share its views. An example of at least 25 years' standing had to do with the proper role (if any) of Spain in Western defense. Throughout the past quarter-century, there had been chronic differences between the United States, as a devoted partisan of Spain's association with the Western defense system, and those allied countries that had refused to enter on any close relationship with a country governed by the authoritarian regime of General Francisco Franco. Although the old Spanish dictator had died in November 1975, the opening of the new year found his last Prime Minister, Carlos Arias Navarro, still wielding power on behalf of the new King, Juan Carlos I, a relatively inexperienced figure whose political intentions and capabilities had yet to reveal themselves.

Linked with Spain in a bilateral defense cooperation arrangement established as long ago as 1953—and last renewed in 1970 for a five-year period expiring September 26, 1975[48]—the United States had not felt able to await a clarification of the Spanish political picture before taking steps to renew its right to use a number of Spain's key military facilities. Negotiations looking toward a new agreement had in fact begun as early as 1974 and were brought to a culmination on January 24, 1976, when Secretary of State Kissinger, stopping over in the Spanish capital on the way back from Moscow, sat down with Foreign Minister José María de Areilza to sign a complex of documents that included a Treaty of Friendship and Cooperation, seven supplementary agreements, and eight related exchanges of notes.[49]

[48]Partial text and related documents in *Documents, 1970:* 107-14.
[49]Texts in TIAS 8360; summaries in Document 9a.

Examination of these documents, authoritatively summarized in an official report of the Secretary of State **(Document 9a)**, bore witness not only to the importance the United States attached to the Spanish relationship but also to the increased bargaining power of the Spanish government, which had held out for terms substantially more advantageous to Spain than had been true of previous agreements. In a sharp break with precedent, the principal document took the form not of an executive agreement, as hitherto, but of a formal treaty **(Document 9b)**, concluded for a period of five years and subject to a further, five-year extension by mutual agreement. Although it stopped short of directly obligating the two parties to come to one another's aid if attacked, this pact—which, unlike earlier agreements, would require the approval of the U.S. Senate—did call for the development of "the appropriate plans and coordination between their respective armed forces" as well as a common effort "to harmonize their defense relationship with existing security arrangements in the North Atlantic area."

These undertakings were further elaborated in a series of supplementary documents that provided, among other things, for the setting up of a United States-Spanish Council and other coordinating bodies; the promise to Spain of $600 million in military grants and credits, $450 million in Export-Import Bank credits, and other sums to a total of $1,220 million, as well as a maximum effort to provide it with four complete squadrons of F-16 jet fighters and other military items; and continued use by the United States, for a further five-year period, of the military facilities made available to it at Spain's Rota naval base, the Torrejón and Saragossa air bases, and elsewhere. In an important limitation of its rights, the United States agreed to withdraw a strategic wing of tanker aircraft from Spain, to withdraw its nuclear submarine squadron from Rota during the first half of 1979, and not to store nuclear devices or their components on Spanish soil.

These arrangements could hardly fail to inspire a number of misgivings on the part of the Senate, whose advice and consent to ratification were sought in a special presidential message of February 18.[50] Less worrisome than the military and economic details was the question whether it was wise, as a matter of principle, to establish so close a relationship with a country whose political future still appeared decidedly problematical. But the announcement during the spring of plans for far-reaching political reconstruction in Spain was helpful in mitigating these concerns, as was the excellent impression created by the young King and Queen on an official bicentennial visit to the United States at the beginning of June. On June 21, the Senate approved by a vote of 84 to 11 a resolution of ratification **(Document 9c)** in which it signified its

[50]*Presidential Documents*, 12: 233-4 (*Bulletin*, 74: 362).

acquiescence in the treaty's terms and expressed its support for Spain's progress toward free institutions, participation in the regional life of Western Europe, and eventual full cooperation with NATO. Three months later, the treaty entered into force with the formal exchange of ratifications at Madrid on September 21. Prime Minister Arias Navarro had by that time been succeeded by a personal appointee of the King, Adolfo Suárez González, and Spain appeared well started on the road to what it was hoped would turn out to be a progressive democratic regime.

Arrangements with Turkey and Greece

A somewhat comparable situation had developed for the United States at the eastern end of the Mediterranean, where American defense arrangements with Turkey and Greece—both of them members of the NATO alliance—had been gravely impaired by the events that had begun with the Cyprus crisis of 1974 and the Turkish intervention and military occupation of the northern third of that island republic. A congressionally mandated suspension of U.S. military aid to Turkey had led, in July 1975, to a Turkish takeover of American defense installations in that country and a suspension of certain U.S. electronic "intelligence collection" activities, subsequently described as involving "the monitoring of Soviet missile testing," providing "a primary source of vital early-warning information on Soviet missile and satellite launchings," and serving as "an important data link on explosions of Chinese and Soviet nuclear devices."[51]

This situation had persisted, and U.S.-Turkish relations had continued generally unsatisfactory, despite the subsequent enactment by Congress of compromise legislation which had permitted a partial resumption of the aid flow in the autumn of 1975. In a renewed attempt to bring about a restoration of full defense cooperation between the two countries, the United States agreed in March 1976 to Turkey's demand that a completely new, bilateral Defense Cooperation Agreement be drawn up to take the place of the previous agreement concluded in 1969. Negotiated for a four-year period but dependent for validation on an endorsement by Congress, the new agreement paralleled the Spanish treaty in several notable respects. Among other things, it provided for the payment to Turkey of $1 billion in grants, credits and loan guarantees over the four-year period of its prospective life.

But lack of progress toward a settlement in Cyprus, where Turkish forces still remained in occupation of some 36 percent of the national territory, had left the Congress exceedingly lukewarm to any attempt to regain the favor of the Ankara government—the

[51]Habib statement in *Bulletin*, 75: 425.

more so because relations between Turkey and Greece also remained decidedly volatile and subject to periodic flare-ups. The Turkish agreement and accompanying legislation were not even submitted to the Congress until June 16 **(Document 10a)**, and it was not until September 15 that the Senate Foreign Relations Committee got around to holding a one-day hearing on the matter. Nor was any further action taken by the Congress in support of an initiative which, it was suspected, had been undertaken more to placate the Turks than with any expectation of its coming to fruition.

Defense relations between the United States and Greece had also been severely prejudiced by recent developments in the Eastern Mediterranean. In Athens, news of the Turkish-American agreement had raised what were described as "problems" and "serious apprehensions," and Foreign Minister Dimitri S. Bitsios had lost no time in asking Secretary Kissinger to clarify American policy in the area—and, more specifically, to consider the advisability of drawing up new arrangements governing American facilities in Greece as well. In the absence of such arrangements, he seemed to imply, the facilities might cease to be available. After receiving assurances of Washington's fundamental impartiality as between Greece and Turkey, the Minister accepted an invitation to come to the United States with a view to discussing the framework of a new bilateral defense agreement.[52]

The result of these discussions was the drafting of a statement of principles, initialed by Foreign Minister Bitsios and Secretary Kissinger on April 15 **(Document 10b)**, in which it was agreed that the two governments would complete as soon as possible a modernized, four-year defense cooperation agreement, "similar to the United States-Turkish Agreement," that would among other things provide for $700 million in military assistance to Greece, a part of it in the form of grant aid. Unlike the Turks, however, the Greeks preferred to include the detailed technical arrangements governing U.S. facilities in appendixes to the agreement itself, a time-consuming procedure that precluded early completion of the negotiations and would indefinitely delay submission of the eventual agreement for congressional approval.[53] In the meantime, it was understood that American operations conducted from Greek facilities and serving mutual defense interests would be permitted to continue.

Stalemate in Vienna

To most of the NATO countries, these peripheral developments

[52]*Bulletin*, 74: 630.
[53]Habib statement in *Bulletin*, 75: 426-7.

were of less immediate concern than the ongoing Vienna negotiations on Mutual and Balanced Force Reduction (MBFR)—or, to use the official name, the "Conference on Mutual Reduction of Forces and Armaments and Associated Measures in Central Europe." Still another round of talks—the ninth since the opening of the conference on October 30, 1973—had taken place in Vienna in the early months of 1976, but had failed to break the stalemate that had persisted in all essentials since the beginning of the negotiations.

The only significant change over that 26-month period, most experts agreed, had been a further increase in the numerical superiority of the Warsaw Pact forces, particularly in the critical Central European sector. NATO military authorities were by this time showing open concern at the growing disparity between the two groups in ground combat forces, a disparity that was beginning to be described as "the main destabilizing factor in Central Europe."[54] Warsaw Pact ground and air forces in that theater, according to NATO's latest estimates, totaled no less than 1,163,000, of whom 962,000 were ground forces, approximately half that number being Soviet troops organized in 27 ground force divisions and other combat units. (Later in 1976, the Warsaw Pact would admit to a total air and ground strength of 987,300, including 805,000 in ground forces.) NATO's ground combat forces, on the other hand, totaled only 791,000; and the disparity in main battle tanks and tactical aircraft was even greater. Estimates of Warsaw Pact strength in main battle tanks ranged upward from 15,600 to as high as 19,000, more than three times the Western strength of approximately 6,000.[55]

All of the twelve NATO and seven Warsaw Pact countries that were involved in the Vienna negotiations (France being the only notable absentee) professedly subscribed to the overall objective of bringing about a mutual reduction of forces and armaments in such a way that no party's security would be diminished. In practice, however, each side had confined itself to advocating those types of reductions that could be expected to benefit its own position at the expense of its adversaries. The U.S.S.R. and its Warsaw Pact allies had pressed for "across-the-board," "percentagewise" reductions that would apply equally to all national forces in the area—including, notably, those of the Federal Republic of Germany—and would include nuclear weapons and air forces as well as ground forces. The United States and the other NATO powers, in contrast,

---

[54]Statement by Baron De Vos van Steenwijk, Apr. 8, in *NATO Review*, June 1976: 30-31.

[55]Lothar Ruehl, "Die Wiener Verhandlungen über einen Truppenabbau in Mitteleuropa," *Europa-Archiv*, 1977, No. 13: 399-408.

had shied away from a plan that would, among other effects, preserve the Warsaw Pact's existing numerical superiority while weakening NATO in vital areas of nuclear and air strength. Their own plan bypassed air and nuclear forces completely and focused instead on a reduction and equalization of ground forces. Such reductions, under the Western plan, would be carried out in two phases: an initial phase in which the United States would withdraw 29,000 ground troops while the U.S.S.R. withdrew an entire tank army of 68,000; and a second phase in which reductions by other forces would reduce the aggregate numbers on both sides to a common maximum of 700,000.

In an attempt to provide additional inducements in support of their plan, the Western negotiators had also introduced on December 16, 1975, a supplementary offer under which, if the Warsaw Pact countries agreed to the essential features of the Western plan, the United States would also withdraw 1,000 nuclear warheads with their related means of delivery—notably, 54 F-4 Phantom combat aircraft and 36 Pershing short-range missile launchers. To obtain this benefit, however, the Warsaw Pact group would not only have to accept the common ceiling of 700,000 for ground and air personnel, but, as already intimated, would be expected to dispense with a Soviet tank army of 68,000 men together with 1,700 main battle tanks.[56]

The Warsaw Pact response to this proposal took the form of a new three-year plan that was put forward by the Soviet delegation on February 19, 1976. Embodying elements of the Western program yet obviously designed to perpetuate the superiority of the Eastern group, it contemplated a first-stage reduction of 2 to 3 percent in the overall personnel strength of the two alliances during 1976, to be brought about entirely by reductions in the forces of the United States and the U.S.S.R.—each of which would, in addition, withdraw 300 tanks, one army corps headquarters, 54 nuclear-capable combat aircraft or tactical ballistic missile systems, and other conventional and nuclear armaments, including 36 nuclear-capable ground-to-air defense systems. In 1977, both sides would refrain from increasing their forces. In 1978, the European forces in their turn would be reduced by 2 or 3 percent. The ultimate effect, it was calculated by Western experts, would be a reduction of both sides' manpower by 13 to 15 percent, with disproportionately deep cuts in Western air and nuclear strength.[57]

To the NATO group, this "disappointing" offer afforded confirmation that "the East" was still attempting to "contractualize the existing disparities in the area" to its own ad-

[56]*AFR, 1975:* 552.
[57]Ruehl, cited: 402-3.

vantage. Such a plan was clearly unacceptable, the spokesman for the participating Western governments declared as the talks recessed on April 8. Not only would it leave intact the current Eastern superiority in ground forces; it would actually diminish Western security by freezing these inequalities in an international agreement. The Soviet proposal failed, moreover, to take account of the advantages the U.S.S.R. derived from its position contiguous to the reduction area. Under these circumstances, said the Western spokesman, the Western side would continue to press for the acceptance of its own proposals, in the hope that the East would eventually realize that they provided "a practical and equitable basis for agreement."[58]

Political Affirmations

The Western position in the Vienna talks was strongly endorsed by the NATO Foreign Ministers—though France, as a nonparticipant, maintained its customary silence—when the North Atlantic Council held its regular spring meeting at Oslo on May 20-21. A newcomer to this NATO session was Anthony Crosland of the United Kingdom, who had assumed the post of Foreign and Commonwealth Secretary on the designation of his predecessor, James Callaghan, to succeed Harold Wilson as Prime Minister some two months earlier.

A communiqué made public at the conclusion of the NATO meeting (Document 11) rehearsed familiar views on MBFR and other topics of mutual interest. To Secretary Kissinger, just back from an epochal visit to Africa, the Oslo meeting seemed "an extremely harmonious one in which the assessment of the Ministers with respect to East-West relations, with respect to Africa, and with respect to other issues that were discussed were as close to unanimous as I have seen them and in which the conviction existed that NATO is a going concern, that the military equilibrium must be maintained, and that the West has the capabilities and the determination to preserve its security and to maintain its values."[59]

A more formal affirmation of these views was offered by the Secretary of State a few weeks later in a celebrated address in London (Document 12) inaugurating a lecture series in memory of the late Alastair Buchan, sometime Director of the International Institute for Strategic Studies. Asserting that the Western world was passing through a state of crisis, Dr. Kissinger also affirmed that since the crisis was essentially moral and spiritual rather than rooted in material circumstances, it could be transcended by a resolute application of moral and intellectual resources. ". . . Let

[58]De Vos statement, cited.
[59]News conference, Oslo, May 21, in *Bulletin*, 74: 769.

us not paralyze ourselves by a rhetoric of weakness," the Secretary of State exhorted. "Complacency may produce weakness, but exaggeration of danger can lead to a loss of will. . . . We cannot afford either a perilous complacency or an immobilizing pessimism."

Secretary Kissinger seemed at this period to draw particular reassurance from a reviving spirit of cooperation among the Western nations, a spirit symbolized in the economic sphere by the meeting of heads of state and government of leading industrial countries that would soon take place at President Ford's invitation at Dorado Beach, Puerto Rico. The ultimate need, in Dr. Kissinger's eyes, was "the solidarity of the democratic nations in the world . . . both as material support and as a moral symbol." "There could be no greater inspiration of our peoples," he concluded, "than the reaffirmation of their common purpose and the conviction that they can shape their fortune in freedom."

Included in the Kissinger address was another brief, discreetly worded reference to the hotly debated issue of the Communists' eligibility to participate in Western democratic governments. The chances that this issue would be concretely posed in the immediate future appeared, however, to be receding as a consequence of current political developments in a number of European countries. In Italy, a powerful Communist bid for admission to a share of political power had just been turned back in the parliamentary elections of June 20-21, in which the Communists had won a resounding 34.4 percent of the national vote for the Chamber of Deputies but had failed to oust the Christian Democrats from their position as the strongest single party, with 38.7 percent of the vote and the opportunity of forming still another minority government, this one under Giuseppe Andreotti as successor to Aldo Moro. The new government would, however, be dependent on Communist good will in the sense that it could survive for only so long as the Communists refrained from voting against it on major issues.

In Portugal, too, conditions appeared to be stabilizing with the decisive defeat of the extreme leftist and Communist candidates in a presidential election held June 27. Backed by an overwhelming popular mandate, the conservative General Antônio Ramalho Eanes soon afterward redeemed his pre-election pledge to designate the Socialist Mário Soares as Prime Minister. In Spain, as already noted, the outlook for effective political reform was also brightening with the designation of a government headed by Prime Minister Suárez, a trusted collaborator of King Juan Carlos.

Observers of the French scene were not without uneasiness about the outlook for the legislative elections due in 1978, in which a leftist alliance of Communists, Socialists, and Radicals appeared to have at least a chance of supplanting the existing Right-Center majority in the National Assembly. For the moment, however, attention was mainly focused on a contest for the leadership of the nonleftist forces that had pitted President Valéry Giscard d'Estaing against the aggressively conservative Prime Minister Jacques Chirac, who shortly afterward resigned his post in an open challenge to the moderate President. (His successor as Prime Minister was Raymond Barre, while Louis de Guiringaud succeeded Jean Sauvagnargues as Minister of Foreign Affairs.)

West Germany's Social Democratic-Free Democratic coalition government, headed since 1974 by Chancellor Helmut Schmidt and with Hans-Dietrich Genscher as Foreign Minister, was to survive the October 3 elections to the *Bundestag* in good order, though with a considerably reduced majority. As always, too, developments connected with the United States' own presidential election would exert a hypnotic fascination on other NATO countries, and Governor Carter's proclaimed intention of trimming the defense budget, with anything else that could be gleaned about his approach to Atlantic community problems, was endlessly canvassed before and after the November 2 voting. Another North American election with strong if still uncertain implications for NATO was held November 15 in Canada's Province of Quebec, where the decisive victory of the pro-independence Parti Québecois led by René Lévesque portended, at the very least, a period of uneasiness involving not merely Canada's foreign policy but its integrity as a nation.

NATO Looks to the Future

The later months of 1976 brought few significant developments in the relations between East and West, though there were signs of incipient ferment in Poland—where serious food riots occurred in July—and elsewhere in Eastern Europe as the significance of the Helsinki declaration became more widely known and attention began to focus on a follow-up meeting to be held in Belgrade in 1977. In Vienna, a tenth round of MBFR talks concluded in December with nothing more positive than an exasperated comment by the Western spokesman, Baron De Vos van Steenwijk of the Netherlands, to the effect that the West had already rejected the Eastern approach and consequently did not understand why the East continued to adhere to it.[60]

Though obviously unprepared for the kind of troop reductions envisaged by the Western formula, the Warsaw Pact nations were not insensible to the propaganda implications of their position and, as always, displayed a fertile imagination in devising proposals that

[60]Statement of Dec. 16, in *NATO Review*, Feb. 1977: 28.

could embarrass their NATO adversaries. Meeting in Bucharest on November 25-26, General Secretary Brezhnev, Foreign Minister Andrei A. Gromyko, and the Communist leaders and Foreign Ministers of the other Warsaw Pact countries released a lengthy declaration on "international relaxation" in which they suggested, among other things, that both alliance groups refrain from taking in any new members (presumably meaning Spain), and proposed a draft treaty under whose terms governments signatory to the Helsinki Final Act would assume an obligation not to be the first to use nuclear weapons against one another.[61]

Not unexpectedly, these proposals met with a polite rejection at the year-end ministerial session of the North Atlantic Council, which took place at NATO headquarters in Brussels on December 9-10 and was favored with a message from President-elect Carter affirming his determination that "The American commitment to maintaining the NATO alliance shall be sustained and strengthened under my Administration."[62] Referring to the Communist initiative, the NATO Ministers "confirmed that the countries of the Alliance, in the event of an attack on them, cannot renounce the use, as may be required for defense, of any of the means available to them"—an obvious euphemism for the defensive use of nuclear weapons. In addition, said the formal communiqué made public at the conclusion of the session (**Document 13**), "Ministers . . . stated their position that the Alliance will remain a free association open to all European states devoted to the defense of the freedom, common heritage and civilization of their peoples."

The participants in the NATO meeting appeared, as usual, to find a marked discrepancy between the Warsaw group's pacific professions and its warlike preparations. "They viewed with concern the high level of military expenditure in the Soviet Union and the continued disquieting expansion of the military power of the Warsaw Pact on land, air and sea, which are difficult to reconcile with the avowed desire of the Soviet Union to improve East-West relations," said the communiqué. "Faced with this persistent growth in military might, Ministers reiterated their determination to take the measures necessary to maintain and improve their own defensive military forces, in order to ensure credible deterrence and to safeguard their countries from any risk of military aggression or political pressure."

Recognizing "that the basic problems in East-West relations were unlikely to be resolved quickly and that the Alliance must respond with a long-term effort commensurate to the challenges

---

[61] Text in *Soviet News*, Nov. 30, 1976.
[62] *Bulletin*, 76: 9.

confronting it," the Western representatives further observed that
the allied powers "could rely not only on their material resources,
but also on the creative power demonstrated in all fields by their
free and democratic societies. Ministers were confident that, with
the mutual support and solidarity provided by the Alliance, their
governments and peoples would be able to overcome the problems
which faced them."

4. PEACE-SEEKING IN THE MIDDLE EAST

Few parts of the world were unaffected by the relationship
between the United States and the Soviet Union, whose
disagreements and reciprocal distrust had done so much to shape
the global history of the postwar period. The Middle East had been
a leading theater of East-West rivalry since World War II and,
more especially, since the U.S.S.R.'s emergence during the 1950s as
a backer of the Arab states in their perennial quarrel with Israel.
The danger of a military confrontation between East and West—
or, specifically, between the U.S.S.R. and the United States—had
been a prominent ingredient in each of the major international
crises that had accompanied the Arab-Israel wars of 1956, 1967,
and 1973.

Aware of the inherent dangers of such a state of affairs, the
United States and, at least intermittently, the Soviet Union had
sought to restrain their protégés in the area and even to nudge them
by slow degrees along the road to a peace settlement. Provisional
foundations for such a settlement, based among other requirements
on an Israeli military withdrawal from territories occupied in the
1967 war, had been defined in U.N. Security Council Resolution
242 of November 22, 1967,[63] reaffirmed in Resolution 338 of
October 22, 1973,[64] and carried at least one step toward fulfillment
with the two-day meeting of the Geneva Conference on the Middle
East on December 21-22, 1973.[65]

But though the American and Soviet governments still retained
their theoretical status as co-chairmen of the Geneva Conference,
that gathering had never been able to reassemble in view of the
seemingly irreconcilable differences between Israel and its Arab
neighbors, whose basic demand for Israeli withdrawal from *all* the
territories occupied in 1967 was flatly rejected by the Israelis
despite the vigorous condemnation of their stand by the U.S.S.R.
and its less than unequivocal support by the United States. Progress
toward a permanent peace settlement had thus been limited to the

[63]*Documents, 1967:* 169-70.
[64]*AFR, 1973:* 459.
[65]Same: 603-13.

"step-by-step" procedures initiated by Secretary Kissinger in the aftermath of the 1973 war. Dr. Kissinger's protracted exercises in "shuttle diplomacy" had resulted in the signature in 1974 and 1975 of a series of military disengagement agreements whereby the Israeli military forces had been separated from those of Egypt in the south and Syria in the north, with U.N. peacekeeping contingents taking up positions between the hostile armies and a team of U.S. volunteer technicians undertaking to operate an early warning system in the Sinai Peninsula.[66]

Lebanese Background

A novel ingredient had been added to the Mideast confusion with the outbreak in April 1975 of a serious internal conflict in Lebanon, Israel's northern neighbor and an Arab country of mixed Muslim and Christian population and well-established democratic traditions. Although it had thus far avoided major involvement in Arab-Israeli hostilities, Lebanon had long been indirectly involved by reason of the presence in its territory of large numbers of Palestinian refugees and substantial concentrations of Palestinian guerrilla elements, who used the mountainous terrain of southern Lebanon as a base of operations against Israel. Israel had frequently retaliated against objectives within Lebanon, and serious friction had developed between the Palestinians and the Lebanese government, which insisted on its right and duty to maintain law and order throughout the national territory. These antagonisms, in turn, had gradually fused with the internal rivalry between Lebanon's growing Muslim population and the predominantly conservative, Christian establishment that tended to dominate the country's economic and financial life as well as its political institutions.

An escalating series of incidents during the spring of 1975, touched off apparently by mutual animosities between Palestinian groups and Lebanon's right-wing, predominantly Christian Phalangist Party, expanded rapidly into a full-scale civil conflict of extraordinary brutality. Cease-fires were repeatedly concluded only to break down again. While the Palestinians seemed primarily concerned to make good their claim to unrestricted operational rights, their allies in Lebanon's Muslim and Druse communities gave evidence of an increasingly definite intention to "correct" the predominant position accorded the Christians at the time of independence in the 1940s. The more extreme Christians, for their part, seemed bent on fortifying their own position, if necessary even by bringing about a partition of the country into separate Muslim and Christian areas.

[66]*AFR, 1974:* 13-20, 153-64; same, *1975:* 397-416.

Aside from its dismaying human and material toll—casualties, by April 1976, were provisionally estimated at 15,000 killed and 50,000 injured[67]—the conflict was a recognizable source of international danger and one that intensely concerned all parties interested in the Arab-Israeli relationship. While radical Arab governments like those of Libya and Iraq supported the left-wing, Muslim-Palestinian alliance, Syria—Lebanon's next-door neighbor—had pointedly dissociated itself from the left-wing element and endorsed the moderate reform program espoused by Lebanese Prime Minister Rashid Karami, a Muslim supporter of the existing system. Given its presumed unwillingness to tolerate a permanent state of chaos on its own doorstep, the Syrian government of President Hafez al-Assad was widely credited with an intention to occupy Lebanon with its own forces in the event that the Lebanese government was unsuccessful in reestablishing order. Yet such a step would clearly be fraught with extreme danger in view of the likelihood that it would precipitate intervention by Israel and, possibly, by other states opposed to any shift in the existing power balance. In view of these possibilities, the United States had made known from an early date that it was equally opposed to partition and to outside intervention, whether by Syria, by Israel, or by any other country.[68]

Despite these admonitions, the situation had become so grave by late March of 1976 that the U.S. Sixth Fleet was reported standing by for possible emergency evacuation of Americans. In turn, such Palestinian leaders as Yasir Arafat of the Palestine Liberation Organization (PLO) and George Habash of the Popular Front for the Liberation of Palestine (PFLP), neither of whom was counted as a friend to the United States, were quoted as threatening to sink any U.S. warships that entered Lebanese waters. Syrian intervention, limited thus far to inconspicuous movements by units of the Syrian-controlled As-Saiqa guerrilla organization, now began to occur in more direct form as Syrian regular units occupied a number of border positions. Though Secretary Kissinger and President Ford described these Syrian moves as "constructive," an anxious Israel let it be known that it could tolerate no Syrian encroachments south of an undefined "Red Line" that was generally believed to coincide with the course of the Litani River in southern Lebanon.[69]

By early May, hopes for a solution had been renewed with an amendment to the Lebanese constitution and a special meeting of the Lebanese Parliament on May 8 to elect a successor to President

[67]*Le Monde,* Apr. 14, 1976, cited in *Keesing's:* 27765.
[68]*Keesing's:* 27770; also *Bulletin,* 74: 507.
[69]*Keesing's:* 27772-3; cf. map in *AFR, 1974:* 159.

Suleiman Frangié, a Christian and a vigorous conservative who had become anathema to the Muslim-leftist group. Elias Sarkis, the successful presidential candidate, who was governor of the Central Bank and known as a more moderate Christian, promptly appealed for a cessation of fighting and a commencement of national reconstruction. Contrary to expectations, however, President Frangié did not resign in order to permit the induction of his successor, but continued to cling to office—as he was constitutionally entitled to do—while new waves of violence engulfed the country.

Arab-Israeli Repercussions

The developments in Lebanon colored the entire Middle Eastern situation in these early months of 1976. For once, the danger of an explosion seemed not to center in the relationship between Israel and its Arab neighbors, but within the Arab world itself. For once, moreover, the Soviet Union seemed not to be supporting the trouble makers, but to be distinctly embarrassed by the differences that had broken out among its Arab clients, particularly between Syria on the one hand and the Palestinian factions associated with Arafat and the PLO on the other.

In such circumstances, the Arab-Israel relationship as such was at least temporarily relegated to a back burner, the more so because America's "step-by-step" diplomacy appeared to have run its course and no basis for reconvening the Geneva Conference had yet been found. The principal developments of the period thus took place not in the Middle East itself but in the U.N. Security Council, where the United States had occasion to veto two successive resolutions that it considered unduly weighted against Israel.

The first of these negative votes (the thirteenth U.S. veto in the history of the Council) was cast by U.S. Representative Daniel P. Moynihan on January 26 to defeat a resolution that purported to endorse the establishment of an independent Palestinian state and called, in addition, for an Israeli withdrawal from *all* Arab territories occupied since June 1967.[70] Such stipulations lay far outside any language thus far accepted by Israel or the United States. A second U.S. veto (the fourteenth) was cast on March 25 by Moynihan's successor, Ambassador William W. Scranton, to prevent adoption of a resolution deploring Israeli policies in the West Bank and Jerusalem.[71] Supported by the other fourteen members of the Council, this resolution was considered "un-

[70]U.N. Document S/11940, failed of adoption by a vote of 9-1 (U.S.)-3, with 2 states not participating; text and related material in *Bulletin*, 74: 189-97.
[71]U.N. Document S/12022, failed of adoption by a vote of 14-1 (U.S.); text and related material in *Bulletin*, 74: 526-30.

balanced" by the United States. Governor Scranton did, however, remark in the debate that the United States was not entirely satisfied with Israeli actions in the occupied territories and regarded the Israeli settlements established there since 1967 as "an obstacle to the success of the negotiations for a just and final peace between Israel and its neighbors."[72]

In a further Security Council discussion in May, Ambassador Scranton once again dissociated the United States from a majority finding, this one in the form of a "consensus statement," formulated by Louis de Guiringaud of France as President of the Security Council, in which Israeli conduct in the occupied territories was censured with a severity the U.S. Representative again found lacking in balance.[73]

There were other indications during these months that the Ford administration was trying hard to maintain its objectivity, ensure that Israel was given its due, and yet resist the ever-present temptation to embrace Israeli interests without qualification. A number of skirmishes had occurred between the White House and the Congress over the latter's wish to add an extra $500 million in "transition quarter" aid to the $2.2 billion proposed for Israel in the 1976 fiscal year. Entirely characteristic of the administration's attitude was the language used by Secretary Kissinger and the President in addressing American Jewish groups, in which assurances of basic solidarity toward Israel were mingled with intimations that the latter would do well to adopt a more flexible posture in matters pertaining to a negotiated peace.[74]

Meeting of the CENTO Council

Both Lebanon and the Arab-Israeli quarrel were much in the minds of Secretary Kissinger and his colleagues from Iran, Pakistan, Turkey, and the United Kingdom as they gathered in London on May 26-27 for the 23rd meeting of the Council of Ministers of the Central Treaty Organization (CENTO), the regional defense alliance established in the 1950s to protect the "northern tier" of countries adjoining the southern Soviet frontier. Completing a round of visits to Scandinavian and Central European capitals, Dr. Kissinger as head of the U.S. "observer" delegation was listened to with at least as much attention as was accorded the representatives of the four formally allied CENTO governments.

"The United States will stand by its friends," the Secretary of

[72]Statement of March 23, in *Bulletin*, 74: 528.

[73]Texts in same: 797-8.

[74]Kissinger address, May 9, in *Bulletin*, 74: 720-25; Ford remarks, May 13, in *Presidential Documents*, 12: 877-8.

State declared in his formal statement **(Document 14a)**. ". . . It will continue to be a reliable partner to those who defend their freedom against foreign intervention or intimidation." Congratulating Pakistan on recent improvements in relations with its neighbors, particularly India, the Secretary of State expressed a hope that Turkey and Greece would also move to resolve their differences, and that progress toward a Cyprus settlement would contribute to a pacification "essential to the security of the eastern Mediterranean, the Middle East, and Europe as well."

In what was described by the final communiqué **(Document 14b)** as "a wide-ranging and constructive exchange of views on recent international developments," the CENTO Ministers "noted with satisfaction that peace, stability, and economic and social progress were maintained in the Region"; took gratified account of recent progress in regard to economic, military, countersubversive, and cultural cooperation; and "reaffirmed their determination to ensure that the Alliance continues to contribute to the peace, security and stability of the Region, and to promote the social and economic welfare of its people." Unlike the SEATO alliance in Southeast Asia, whose organizational superstructure was now being dismantled, CENTO was still regarded by its members as an organization with an essential role to play.

The Lebanese Denouement

Events in Lebanon were meanwhile hastening toward a gruesome climax. Instead of the hoped-for national pacification, the presidential election on May 8 was followed by a broadening confrontation of hostile forces, an escalation of the Syrian military involvement—notwithstanding vigorous discouragement by the Soviet Union—and intensified fighting in Beirut and elsewhere. On June 16 there occurred the tragic deaths of the U.S. Ambassador, Francis E. Meloy, Jr., the Counselor for Economic Affairs, Robert O. Waring, and the Ambassador's Lebanese chauffeur, Zohair Moghrabi, following their disappearance on a passage through Beirut's "no man's land" en route to a meeting with President-elect Sarkis. "An act of senseless, outrageous brutality," President Ford exclaimed. In similar language, Secretary Kissinger let it be known that the United States would not be "deterred, by brutal and vicious action, from the search for peace" **(Document 15a)**. Investigations undertaken by the Palestine Liberation Organization, which disclaimed responsibility for the murders, were to leave the killers unidentified and presumably unpunished.

Two days later, President Ford announced that in view of the "continuing uncertainty" of the situation in Beirut, the U.S. Embassy would assist those Americans who wished to leave the country in joining convoys of British and other foreign nationals departing overland for Damascus **(Document 15b)**. This plan, in turn, was subsequently modified because of unsafe highway conditions, although approximately 270 Americans and other foreigners were evacuated by sea (with PLO assistance) on June 20 and conveyed to Athens by a U.S. naval vessel. A further 300 persons were evacuated by sea on July 27, among them 20 of the remaining U.S. Embassy staff of 32.

These actions presented a startling contrast to the events of 1958, when the United States had responded to a request from the then Lebanese government by sending in 14,300 Marines and airborne troops "to protect American lives and . . . encourage the Lebanese government in defense of Lebanese sovereignty and integrity."[75] This time it was not the United States but Syria that assumed the responsibility for reestablishing order. Syrian military forces in Lebanon, estimated by August to number as many as 20,000, were rapidly coming to outnumber the warring factions in the country itself. Increasingly, moreover, the Syrian forces were seen to be co-operating directly with Lebanese Christian elements against the PLO, which suffered heavy casualties during the summer in the sieges of Tal Zataar and other refugee camps and appeared to be fast losing its capacity for effective military operations either against Lebanese foes or against Israel.

By mid-September, the Syrian pacification effort had been so far successful that President-elect Sarkis could be formally inducted as constitutional successor to the outgoing President Frangié, although the ceremony was held for security reasons at Chtaura, in Syrian-controlled territory, rather than in the capital. The new executive's appeal for peace and national reconstruction was echoed by a statement from the Department of State in Washington **(Document 15c)** that stressed the importance of restoring Lebanon's national unity and again voiced opposition to any partition into separate Christian and Muslim areas. Although considerable fighting was to continue through the autumn, diplomatic efforts within an Arab League framework were to result in an agreement on a general cease-fire, effective October 21, and the assumption of nominal peacekeeping responsibility by an Arab League "deterrent force"—in which, however, an estimated 25,000 Syrians continued to be the principal element.[76]

For Israel, which had followed these events with anxious attention, it was impossible not to rejoice at the apparent weakening of the Palestinian guerrillas, whose depredations from Lebanese bases had been a source of constant worry and frequent loss of civilian life. To a certain extent, it was rumored, the Israelis had

[75]*Documents, 1958:* 303.
[76]*Keesing's:* 28122-3.

actually been cooperating with the Syrians, as well as the Lebanese Christians, in opposition to their common adversaries. Nor could Israel have been displeased at Syria's involvement in an adventure that engaged the bulk of the Syrian military forces, eased the pressure on Israel's northeastern flank, and had severely strained Syria's relations with the U.S.S.R. as well as Egypt and other Arab governments.

At the same time, however, the Israelis had no reason to favor a permanent installation of Syria, one of its most implacable foes, in a country which had hitherto been a comparatively tractable neighbor. Nor could the Israelis afford to be indifferent about the immediate situation in southern Lebanon, which they regarded as a kind of Israeli security zone and were determined to keep clear of potentially hostile forces, whether Palestinian or Syrian. Israel, accordingly, continued to insist that while willing to accept the presence of units from a reconstituted Lebanese Army in southern Lebanon, it could not tolerate the intrusion of Syrian or pan-Arab forces south of the "Red Line." This stand added to the tension that prevailed throughout the autumn and early winter, even while the situation was gradually stabilizing and the United States continued to make its good offices available in helping the parties to avoid potentially dangerous confrontations.

Israel Under Siege

The world was not permitted, during these months, to forget that there remained a wider range of Arab-Israeli issues that would continue to fester even if conditions in Lebanon should ultimately return to normal. In June there had been the hijacking and flight to Entebbe, Uganda, of an Air France airbus whose captors—two West Germans and two presumed Palestinian Arabs affiliated with the PFLP—demanded the release of 53 terrorist comrades imprisoned in Israel, Europe, and Africa. The sensational rescue operation carried out by Israeli commandos on July 3-4, to be described later, irritated Israel's critics as deeply as it enthralled its friends and admirers.

Even before the Entebbe crisis was resolved, the United States had cast still another veto—its sixteenth—to defeat another "totally" unbalanced Security Council resolution that seemed to preempt the decisions to be taken at a peace conference by endorsing what were described as "the inalienable rights of the Palestinian people to self-determination, including the right to national independence and sovereignty in Palestine."[77] Ten members of the Security Council voted in favor of this text, with

[77]U.N. Document S/12119; text and related material in *Bulletin*, 75: 143-5.

France, Italy, Sweden, and the United Kingdom abstaining and only the United States opposed.

Such incidents forbade complacency about the durability of the "no war, no peace" situation that had generally prevailed since 1973. "If there is anything the history of this conflict should have taught, it is that the Middle East will not stand still," declared the Assistant Secretary of State for Near Eastern and South Asian Affairs, Alfred L. Atherton, in addressing a B'nai B'rith Installation Banquet in Omaha on June 30 **(Document 16a)**. " . . . It is unthinkable that there should be a fifth Arab-Israeli war—and yet that is the grim alternative to negotiation, compromise, and further progress toward peace."

A similar, if somewhat more hopeful, emphasis was heard in Secretary Kissinger's remarks at a September 29 luncheon for heads of Arab delegations to the U.N. General Assembly **(Document 16b)**. Looking back over the series of meetings he had initiated before the war of 1973, the Secretary of State declared: "I feel that despite all the ups and downs very great progress has been made toward peace in the Middle East." Among other hopeful elements, he emphasized what he described as a restoration of "the traditional friendship between the United States and the countries of the Arab world . . . with respect to at least very many of them." "I know that we have not yet traveled except the beginning of the road toward peace," Secretary Kissinger admitted. "But I also believe that we have created conditions from which the rest of the distance can be traveled if we work on it with conviction and with confidence in each other."

However favorable the long-run prospects, however, it was hardly to be expected that the annual session of the General Assembly, that favorite rhetorical battlefield of Arabs and Israelis, should lead to visible movement toward an accepted peace settlement. About the most that could be said concerning the Assembly's 31st Regular Session was that it brought no repetition of the distressing experience of the previous year, when the Arab countries and their friends had flouted American as well as Israeli sensibilities by branding the Zionist movement as "a form of racism and racial discrimination."[78] There was, however, no real change in the embarrassing forensic situation that had developed since 1973 and had left Israel—often with no supporter but the United States—to face the parliamentary assaults of Arab, African, and other third world and Communist states.

Even the alignment of the United States with Israel was not unbreakable. In a renewed discussion in the Security Council on

[78]Resolution 3379 (XXX), Nov. 10, 1975; text in *AFR, 1975:* 507-8.

November 11, a few days after the November election, the United States appeared to modify its earlier position by joining in a new "consensus statement" that was severely critical of Israel's actions in the occupied territories. But Secretary Kissinger promptly explained that this action had been the result of complicated tactical considerations and did not betoken any substantive change in the American attitude.[79] In the General Assembly, meanwhile, the United States supported various resolutions dealing with the Palestine refugee question but strongly opposed a resolution, adopted on November 24, that not only endorsed majority doctrine concerning Palestinian "rights" but indirectly called on Israel to effect a complete withdrawal from the occupied territories by June 1, 1977.[80]

Two further resolutions relating to the Geneva peace conference elicited a decidedly negative reaction on Ambassador Scranton's part when they came before the Assembly for a final vote on December 9. The first resolution, adopted by a vote of 91 to 11 with 29 abstentions, insisted among other things on the need for PLO participation in the Geneva Conference—to which Israel was adamantly opposed—as well as Israeli withdrawal from all Arab territories occupied since June 1967. The second resolution, adopted by 122 votes to 2 (Israel and the United States) with 8 abstentions, called for a reconvening of the Geneva Conference not later than the end of March 1977.[81] Such a deadline, Governor Scranton suggested in his comment on the two drafts **(Document 16c)**, would be peculiarly inappropriate at a time when a new American administration was just preparing to take office.

In spite of these and other disappointments, the outgoing U.S. Representative could cite a widespread belief that a new opportunity for negotiations—"even to the point of a gleam of hope of an *overall* settlement"—was beginning to come into view. Such a prospect should not, he urged, be jeopardized by headline-seeking or irresponsible behavior in any quarter. "Peacekeeping and peacemaking are very difficult; they are very tenuous efforts," Ambassador Scranton pointed out. "No one knows that better than members of the United Nations. In comparison to lasting peace, war comes all too easily. So let us work quietly for negotiation to begin so that peace may come." This was an aim that would surely continue to animate the American government under the new leadership already waiting in the wings.

[79] *Bulletin*, 75: 692-5.
[80] Resolution 31/20, Nov. 24, adopted by 90-16 (U.S.)-30; details in *Bulletin*, 76: 41-2 and *UN Monthly Chronicle*, Dec. 1976: 29-31, 73, and 83.
[81] Resolutions 31/61 and 31/62, Dec. 9; texts in *Bulletin*, 76: 40.

5. THE YEAR OF AFRICA

The involvement of the Secretary of State in the minute details of Middle East peace-seeking was a comparatively recent phenomenon that dated from the advent of Secretary Kissinger and the outbreak, almost immediately afterward, of the "Yom Kippur" War of October 1973. Less than three years later, the commencement of a similar involvement in the problems of Africa, particularly Southern Africa, signaled the emergence of the United States as a leading participant and even a pace-maker in the affairs of a continent where it had hitherto preferred as a rule to leave the initiative to other friendly governments.

Unlike the "shuttle diplomacy" devised to meet the exigencies arising out of military conflict in the Mideast, the line of action adopted by the United States in Southern Africa was aimed essentially at *forestalling* major conflict by defusing critical situations before they could develop explosive force—and, at the same time, promoting an ideal of racial justice more nearly acceptable to the outlook of the contemporary world. Whether this switch to a more active involvement had occurred in time for its purposes to be achieved—if, indeed, they were achievable at all—would be for later years to determine.

Angola Faces East

That the United States had "missed the bus" in regard to Angola came to be admitted even by those American authorities who, like President Ford and Secretary Kissinger, had been most persuaded of the need to resist a seizure of power by the Soviet- and Cuban-supported Popular Movement for the Liberation of Angola (MPLA). American objections, even in this instance, had not been focused on the MPLA "within a purely African context," as William E. Schaufele, Jr., the Assistant Secretary of State for African Affairs, observed in reviewing the situation for the Senate Subcommittee on African Affairs **(Document 17)**. "What we oppose," Mr. Schaufele emphasized, "is the MPLA's effort, as a minority political movement, to impose itself as the government of Angola, with the help of Soviet arms and a Cuban proxy army, on the majority in Angola."

But Washington's attempts to obstruct this process had foundered, as already noted, on the unwillingness of Congress to sanction what might, it was feared, develop into a new Vietnam-type military engagement in Southern Africa. Disappointed in the attitude of Congress and openly concerned for the future of détente with the Soviet Union, administration spokesmen nevertheless were forced to concede the probability of an MPLA victory in Angola even as they warned that the experience must not be viewed as a precedent for U.S. inaction in other situations.

Even without continued U.S. support, however, the Angolan opponents of the MPLA—the National Front for the Liberation of Angola (FNLA), led by Holden Roberto, in the north, and the National Union for the Total Liberation of Angola (UNITA), headed by Jonas Savimbi, in the south—were able to delay an MPLA victory until around the middle of February, when they announced that they were abandoning overt resistance in order to prepare for a long-term guerrilla struggle.

Formal acknowledgment of MPLA predominance by other African countries was similarly delayed. A special summit meeting of the Organization of African Unity (OAU), held in Addis Ababa in mid-January, actually split into two equal factions, one favoring the MPLA and the other demanding a government of national unity that would include the two rival groups. By February, however, a growing number of African countries were joining the MPLA bandwagon, and the MPLA government, headed by President Agostinho Neto, and with its capital at Luanda, was formally admitted to the OAU on February 23 as the organization's 47th member state. Diplomatic recognition was promptly accorded by France, the United Kingdom, and other leading governments in Western Europe and elsewhere, and South African troops, whose presence in southern Angola had been a complicating factor since the previous autumn, were fully withdrawn by the end of March.

But over 10,000 Cuban military personnel still remained in Angola as the principal support of the Luanda regime; and the United States, though it had actively participated in humanitarian relief efforts, displayed no interest in seeking a political accommodation with the new Angolan authorities at a time when guerrilla resistance appeared to be continuing and when Luanda continued to stress its close dependence on the Soviet Union, with which it later concluded a twenty-year treaty of friendship and cooperation. On June 23, the United States employed its fifteenth veto to block a Security Council recommendation looking toward Angolan admission to membership in the United Nations.[82] Washington's negative judgment of the Luanda government was reinforced in July when an American citizen, Daniel Gearhart, was condemned and executed for alleged mercenary activity under circumstances which, in Secretary Kissinger's words, "can only be regarded . . . as a deliberately hostile act toward this country and its people."[83]

---

[82]U.N. Document S/12110; failed of adoption by a vote of 13-1 (U.S.) with China not participating.
[83]*Bulletin*, 75: 163.

Henry Africanus

America's unsuccessful maneuvers with regard to Angola did little to enhance the reputation of the United States as a constructive influence in African affairs. Some well-disposed governments, like those of Zaïre and Zambia, were disappointed and embarrassed by the sudden collapse of American opposition to the MPLA; others, notably the military regime that held power in Nigeria, were incensed by what was seen as the "patronizing" attitude of President Ford in trying to suggest the line of action they might adopt at the OAU summit.[84] Nor, in a wider context, did the U.S. stand on Angola do anything to mitigate the mistrust in which Washington was already held by most African governments because of its refusal to take a stronger stand against the discriminatory, white-dominated regimes that wielded power in the Republic of South Africa, in the former mandated territory of South West Africa (Namibia), and in Southern Rhodesia (Zimbabwe), the self-governing British colony whose white-dominated government had unilaterally declared its independence in 1965.

A more positive effect of the Angola debacle was a quickening of Washington's realization that time was really running out in Southern Africa, that the guerrilla warfare that had developed in frontier areas of Rhodesia and Namibia was tending to increase in scale, and that the search for solutions could no longer be safely postponed, especially now that the U.S.S.R. and Cuba had come upon the African scene. The settlement of the war in Indochina and the current stalemate in the Middle East, which left no immediate opening for further "step-by-step" diplomacy, had opportunely freed the Secretary of State to undertake a more intensive involvement in African matters. A fortnight's trip to Africa in late April and early May marked Dr. Kissinger's debut as one of the determining influences in African affairs.

The "primary objective" of this first African journey, Secretary Kissinger explained before his departure, was "to establish with African leaders a community of concerns with respect to the problem of the political evolution of southern Africa and with respect to the problem of development which affects Africa more than any other region of the world, since all of its countries are really developing countries." For that reason, Dr. Kissinger noted, he would be crisscrossing the continent from east to west and then from west to east, beginning the trip in Nairobi, Kenya, and concluding it by returning to the same city as head of the U.S. delegation to a ministerial conference of the U.N. Conference on Trade and Development (UNCTAD). "I do not consider this trip

[84]*New York Times*, Jan. 8, 1976.

to be the last word in our African policy," the Secretary of State cautioned. "I expect it to be the basis from which an integrated African policy will be developed, and therefore we expect to be in contact with other leaders in both black African countries as well as in white southern African countries, or with southern African regimes, after I return to the United States."[85]

In the course of a journey that began on April 24 and ended May 7, Secretary Kissinger visited no fewer than six African and two European nations, delivering four major addresses as well as innumerable shorter statements at airports, news conferences, and banquets. From England, his itinerary took him to Kenya and Tanzania in East Africa; to Zambia and Zaïre in Central Africa; to Liberia and Senegal in West Africa; then back to Kenya for the UNCTAD meeting, and home to Washington via Paris. An intended visit to Ghana was belatedly canceled by that country's military government, reputedly under pressure from the U.S.S.R. and Nigeria.

The reception accorded the American visitor and his party was generally most cordial. The African leaders he talked with seemed well aware that the United States had turned a new page in African policy, and he himself was "very well impressed" by their "spirit of cooperation." "I've told them frankly what American concerns were," he said; "they have told me frankly what theirs were, and I think we have narrowed the areas where our views do not always coincide and have established many areas of cooperation."[86]

Policy for Southern Africa

Undoubtedly of primary interest to Africans of every race was Dr. Kissinger's vigorous affirmation of the American commitment to "self-determination, majority rule, equal rights, and human dignity for all the peoples of southern Africa—in the name of moral principle, international law, and world peace." The mere enunciation of such goals sufficed to range the United States, far more decisively than in the past, on the side of those black Africans who were working to supplant the existing white-dominated regimes in Southern Africa with new political structures attuned to the aspirations, as well as the numerical preponderance, of the black majority populations.

Passing from generalities to specifics, Secretary Kissinger availed himself of a presidential luncheon in Lusaka, Zambia, on April 27 to deliver a policy address **(Document 18)** in which he detailed

[85]News conference, Apr. 22, in *Bulletin*, 74: 623, 627. For full documentation on the trip see same: 657-710.
[86]Departure statement, Nairobi, May 6, in same: 709-10.

American views on the three key areas of Rhodesia, Namibia, and South Africa.

In Rhodesia, Dr. Kissinger declared, it was "the responsibility of all who seek a negotiated solution to make clear to the Rhodesian minority that the world community is united in its insistence on rapid change." As the vehicle for such change, he strongly endorsed a proposal already put forward by British Foreign Secretary Callaghan on March 22 that had called for early agreement on the principle of majority rule, the holding of elections on that basis within eighteen months to two years, and postponement of formal Rhodesian independence until majority rule had been established. Until a negotiated settlement was achieved, Secretary Kissinger warned, the white minority regime that functioned in Salisbury under Prime Minister Ian D. Smith would "face our unrelenting opposition." On the other hand, he said, the United States would be prepared to contribute to international assistance programs aimed at providing "a secure future and civil rights" for whites as well as blacks in a future independent "Zimbabwe."

Concerning Namibia, the Secretary of State took note of certain limited moves already made by the South African government, presumably with a view to moving the territory toward independence; but he urged the Pretoria authorities to broaden their approach, permit an open expression of opinion by Namibia's inhabitants under U.N. supervision, and establish a definite timetable looking toward "a rapid and acceptable transition to Namibian independence." "We are convinced that the need for progress is urgent," he added.

South Africa's own system of *apartheid* or "institutionalized separation of the races" must also end, Dr. Kissinger went on—and, he added, it must end much sooner than had been generally realized even a few years earlier. "The United States appeals to South Africa to heed the warning signals of the past two years," he said. ". . . Our policy toward South Africa is based upon the premise that within a reasonable time we shall see a clear evolution toward equality of opportunity and basic human rights for all South Africans." In the meantime, he suggested, South Africa could show its good will "by using its influence in Salisbury to promote a rapid negotiated settlement for majority rule in Rhodesia."

Here, in a nutshell, was the concept that was to be simplistically perceived as the key to U.S. strategy in Southern Africa for the remainder of the Ford administration. By helping to expedite independence based on majority rule in Rhodesia and Namibia, it was suggested, the South African government headed by Prime Minister Johannes B. Vorster could reduce the immediate pressure for internal change and thus buy time in which to come to terms with its own domestic problems. Belief in such a "grand design" would persist despite denials by the Secretary of State—who continued to insist that South Africa, too, must move with the times—and despite internal developments which suggested that conditions in South Africa were already nearing the danger level.

Commitment to Africa's Future

Dr. Kissinger also emphasized in his Lusaka speech the United States' concern for African material progress—a concern which would, he stated, be reflected in a trebling of U.S. support for development programs in Southern and Central Africa over the next three years. Additional details of U.S. thinking about African economic problems were offered in subsequent speeches. In Monrovia, Liberia, on April 30, the Secretary of State reviewed American efforts and policies on behalf of developing countries generally, mentioning among other things a proposed initial contribution of $15 million to the African Development Fund.[87] In Dakar, Senegal, on May 1, he addressed himself to the problems of the drought-ridden Sahelian region and called for preliminary discussions of a major regional development program to be sponsored by a new international grouping known as the *Club des Amis du Sahel*.[88] In Nairobi, finally, the Secretary's address at the UNCTAD conference on May 6 **(Document 30)** was to offer a full-dress prescription directed—so far as American authorities thought realistically possible—toward meeting the concerns of developing countries both in Africa and elsewhere.

"We have regained the initiative," the Secretary of State declared as he reviewed his trip before the Senate Foreign Relations Committee on May 13 **(Document 19)**. "We have offered our African friends a welcome alternative for the future, both political and economic. We have told much of the world that America continues to have a positive vision and to stand ready to play an active and responsible role in the world."

Among the important results of his talks with African statesmen, Dr. Kissinger said, was "the agreement by a number of African leaders that outside powers should not in the future deal directly with the liberation movements in southern Africa"—the realization, in other words, that interventions of the Cuban type were neither inevitable nor beyond their power to prevent. Thanks to the new attitude displayed by the United States, the Secretary implied, African leaders now recognized that there existed an alternative, peaceful approach "which moderate and responsible Africans can support and which serves interests we share—for

[87]*Bulletin*, 74: 679-84.
[88]Same: 685-8.

peace, justice, progress, and for an Africa free from outside pressures.''

Soweto and Entebbe

Everything that Dr. Kissinger had said about the quickening pace of African events was startlingly confirmed in the month that followed his trip. On June 16 began the series of clashes in Soweto, a black township outside Johannesburg, South Africa, between police and students protesting the use of Afrikaans in the educational system. Escalating violence, spreading rapidly to other South African areas, caused numerous casualties and quickly developed into a wide-scale protest against the entire *apartheid* system. "The tragic events occurring in South Africa are a sharp reminder that when a system deprives a people of the basic elements of human dignity and expression, only the bitterest results can be expected," declared U.S. Representative Albert W. Sherer, Jr., on June 19 as the Security Council prepared to adopt a resolution "strongly" condemning South Africa's "resort to massive violence against and killing of the African people including school children and students and others opposing racial discrimination.''[89]

New horrors claimed the attention of the civilized world even while the disorders in Soweto and other South African townships continued—resulting, according to one responsible estimate, in the killing of over 1,000 students and young people by South African police in 1976 alone.[90] On June 27 came the hijacking, by self-styled representatives of the "Che Guevara cell, Haifa section" of the Popular Front for the Liberation of Palestine (PFLP), of a Paris-bound Air France airbus en route from Tel Aviv and Athens with 247 passengers and a crew of twelve. After refueling at Benghazi, Libya, the captive aircraft was flown to Entebbe, Uganda, where passengers and crew were granted the ambiguous hospitality of President Idi Amin Dada while the four original hijackers—together with three or more confederates who joined them at Entebbe—threatened to destroy the aircraft and the hostages unless their demands for the release of 53 terrorists imprisoned in Israel and other countries were promptly met.

The most sinister aspect of this affair had to do with the demeanor and uncertain intentions of the Ugandan President, whose hostility toward Israel was already well known and whose behavior toward the hijackers and their victims suggested that he not only sympathized with the former group but had actively

---

[89]Resolution 392 (1976), June 19, adopted by consensus; text and related material in *Bulletin*, 75: 59-60.
[90]Estimate of the National Council of Churches, reported by George Dugan in *New York Times*, Nov. 11, 1977.

cooperated from an early stage of their enterprise. The anti-Israeli focus of the operation emerged with increasing clarity as hostages of other nationalities were gradually released. Of the 110 hostages still being held on July 1, all except the twelve crew members were of Israeli or dual nationality.

On that July 1, the terrorists advanced the final deadline for meeting their demands to 11 A.M. on Sunday, July 4. But by the time Sunday dawned, most of the hostages were already on their way to Israel as a result of a spectacular rescue operation carried out hours earlier by three planeloads of Israeli commandos who had secretly flown to Entebbe. Fatalities resulting from the operation, which was mounted without the knowledge or consent of the Uganda authorities, included seven terrorists, three hostages, 20 Ugandan soldiers, and one Israeli soldier. Another casualty of the hijacking was Mrs. Dora Bloch, a 74-year-old passenger with dual British and Israeli nationality who disappeared, and presumably perished, while hospitalized under Ugandan care. Authorities in nearby Kenya proved most helpful in caring for the survivors but insisted that they had had no advance knowledge of the rescue operation.

"One of the most remarkable rescue missions in history," Governor Scranton remarked to the Security Council a few days later **(Document 20)**: "a combination of guts and brains that has seldom if ever been surpassed. It electrified millions everywhere, and I confess I was one of them." The U.S. Representative was not, however, insensitive to the anger of Uganda and other African states over Israel's admitted, if temporary, breach of Uganda's territorial integrity. Professing nevertheless to find the Israeli action justified under "the unusual circumstances of this specific case," Ambassador Scranton urged the international community to attack the evil at its roots and to delay no longer in taking decisive action to put an end to hijacking and other forms of international terrorism. Yet so divisive had been the effect of the incident that an American-British resolution along the lines of Governor Scranton's speech attracted only six votes as the Security Council ended its debate on July 14; while an alternative draft condemning the Israeli action was not even put to a vote in view of the certainty that it would fail of adoption.[91]

In terms of the international campaign to curb the terrorist evil, the consequences of the Entebbe affair were inconclusive, although West Germany's government was doubtless encouraged in its determination to seek agreement at the forthcoming U.N. Assembly session on an international convention against the taking

[91]U.N. Documents S/12138 and 12139; texts and related matter in *Bulletin*, 75: 181-6.

of hostages.[92] In African terms, the most conspicuous result was Uganda's deepening alienation not only from the West and Israel but also from those among the independent African states, like Kenya, that had generally eschewed fanaticism and terror in the conduct of their national affairs.

Negotiations on Rhodesia

Events like these provided a lurid background for the deployment of American diplomatic skills in what was soon perceived as a full-scale attack on the political problems of Southern Africa, an effort even more vast and intricate than Dr. Kissinger's earlier ventures relating to Indochina and the Middle East. The immediate aim, in line with the strategy announced at Lusaka, was to produce a workable settlement on the basis of majority rule in Rhodesia and in Namibia. The method, as unfolded during the remaining months of 1976, involved the closest possible cooperation not only with the United Kingdom, the nominal sovereign in Rhodesia and an interested party throughout the region, but also with black African leaders and with the Republic of South Africa, whose government still wielded power in Namibia and might also be able to exert a wholesome influence on the policies of Rhodesia's Ian Smith. In three successive meetings with South African Prime Minister Vorster, the first in southern Germany on June 23-24, the second at Zürich on September 4-6, and the third at Pretoria on September 17-19, the Secretary of State was able to obtain South African concurrence in a detailed plan for a settlement in Rhodesia and to reduce somewhat the differences of view regarding Namibia as well.

It was also in Pretoria that there took place on September 19 a crucial face-to-face meeting between the Secretary of State and Rhodesian Prime Minister Smith. At this meeting, according to the Rhodesian leader's later account, he was told on the one hand that the pressure on Rhodesia from the "free world" would continue to mount as long as "present circumstances in Rhodesia prevailed"— but that, on the other hand, both parties shared "a common aim and a common purpose, namely to keep Rhodesia in the free world and to keep it from Communist penetration." Apparently fortified by this assurance, Prime Minister Smith announced on September 24 that Rhodesia was reluctantly accepting what he described as a Kissinger proposal that called, among other things, for agreement on "majority rule within two years," establishment of a biracial interim government, the lifting of sanctions and cessation of all acts of war, and international economic support to provide assurance concerning Rhodesia's economic future.[93]

[92]Cf. note 180 to chapter 9.
[93]Text in *New York Times*, Sept. 25, 1976.

Secretary Kissinger was quick to point out that the proposal attributed to him was not the fruit of any individual initiative but represented an updating of the Callaghan plan of March 22, developed in concert with Foreign Secretary Crosland and with the Presidents of such "front line" African countries as Tanzania and Zambia. Despite the breadth of its authorship, however, it soon became evident that the plan's details as enunciated by Prime Minister Smith were acceptable neither to Rhodesia's African neighbors nor to such Rhodesian black nationalists as Bishop Abel Muzorewa of the African National Council (ANC), the Rev. Ndabaningi Sithole of the Zimbabwe African National Union (ZANU), Joshua Nkomo of the Zimbabwe African People's Union (ZAPU), and the guerrilla leader Robert Mugabe, who soon afterward joined with Nkomo in forming the so-called Patriotic Front. At odds among themselves on many questions of strategy and tactics, these leaders were alike in rejecting crucial details of the Smith formula—especially those relating to the composition of the interim government, the control of the Rhodesian security forces, the suspension of guerrilla warfare during the transitional period, and the date of Zimbabwe's independence.

Differences on these and related issues helped to delay until October 28 the opening of a so-called constitutional conference at Geneva that had been convened on the initiative of Foreign Secretary Crosland and was chaired by Ivor Richard, Britain's Permanent Representative to the United Nations. Nor did recriminations and charges of perfidy abate thereafter. By December 14, when it was announced that the conference would recess until January 17, 1977, not much was left of the optimism engendered by Smith's original announcement. Not to be overlooked, however, were the indications that the Rhodesian government and the white Rhodesian population had crossed a major psychological divide and were beginning to see the transition to majority rule as an inevitable if still unpalatable step.

Outlook for Namibia

A second concern of the Kissinger-Vorster conversations was the situation in Namibia, where South Africa itself had by this time recognized the inevitability of eventual independence and seemed primarily concerned to ensure that South African and white minority interests would continue to remain paramount even after independence took effect. A constitutional conference on the future of South West Africa had been meeting at Windhoek, the territorial capital, since September 1975, and announced on August 18, 1976 a plan for a multiracial government involving a possible independence date of December 31, 1978. For most outside observers, however, the Windhoek exercise had been vitiated from the start by the absence of the South West Africa People's Organization (SWAPO), the spearhead of the independence movement and an organization recognized by the U.N. General Assembly as "the authentic representative of the Namibian people."[94] The apparent intention of excluding SWAPO from a role in the territory's future was sufficient in itself to ensure rejection of the Windhoek plan by the United Nations and the interested African governments.

The United States itself had not been much enamored of SWAPO, whose leader, Sam Nujoma, was on close and friendly terms with the new Angolan government and boasted of substantial Cuban aid in the guerrilla struggle in northern Namibia. At the same time, however, Washington could see no virtue in attempting to bypass both the United Nations and the territory's principal nationalist movement. After discussion with Nujoma himself, Dr. Kissinger reported on his efforts in a major address to the new session of the General Assembly on September 30 **(Document 35a)**:

> In recent months the United States has vigorously sought to help the parties concerned speed up the process toward Namibian independence. The United States favors the following elements: the independence of Namibia within a fixed, short time limit, the calling of a constitutional conference at a neutral location under U.N. aegis, and the participation in that conference of all authentic national forces including, specifically, SWAPO.
>
> Progress had been made in achieving all of these goals. We will exert our efforts to remove the remaining obstacles and bring into being a conference which can then fashion, with good will and wisdom, a design for the new state of Namibia and its relationship with its neighbors. We pledge our continued solicitude for the independence of Namibia so that it may, in the end, be a proud achievement of this organization and a symbol of international cooperation.

"Africa Can Count On Us"

Concentration on the problems of Southern Africa did not diminish the broader, continental interest enunciated by Secretary Kissinger during his first African trip. "The focus of the moment is on the southern part of the continent," the Secretary of State explained at a New York luncheon for African Foreign Ministers and U.N. representatives **(Document 21)**, "but the U.S. commitment applies to all of Africa and to all the great issues I have

---

[94]General Assembly Resolution 3295 (XXIX), Dec. 13, 1974.

mentioned: justice, progress, and independence." There were other problem areas, such as the so-called "Horn of Africa," that also called for vigilant attention in light of such factors as the revolutionary ferment in Ethiopia, the impending accession to independence of the French Territory of the Afars and the Issas, and the irredentist ambitions and Soviet ties of the Somali government headed by President Muhammad Siad Barre.[95]

On the whole, however, the Secretary of State found reason for considerable pride in the accomplishments of a period that had seen dramatic breakthroughs in both the political and economic aspects of African policy. "Last year," he told his African guests,

> I said to the permanent members of the OAU who met with me that strengthening the relationship between the United States and Africa is a major objective of American policy.[96] It was then, it is now, and shall continue to be so in the future. Africa can count on us.
>
> There can no longer be any question that America is committed to Africa's goals and to working with the nations of Africa to solve the continent's problems. In return, we expect to find respect for our concerns and perspectives.
>
> Let us set aside the suspicions of the past and work for our common future. . . .

One manifestation of this new spirit of give and take was the United States' decision, several weeks later, to discontinue its resistance to Angola's admission to the United Nations. "Out of respect for the sentiments of our African friends," Ambassador Scranton explained when the issue again was brought before the Security Council on November 22, the United States would refrain from casting another veto, despite its continuing doubts about the independence of a government that exercised only tenuous control over much of the country and depended for its security on the presence of a "massive contingent" of Cuban troops.[97] U.S. abstention on this occasion paved the way for Angola's admission on December 1 as the United Nations' 146th member state.

There were other matters, however, in which the United States still found great difficulty in accommodating itself to the prevailing African viewpoint. As in 1975, it joined with France and the United Kingdom on October 19 in vetoing another draft Security Council resolution that termed the situation in Namibia a threat to international peace and security and called for a mandatory arms

[95]For details cf. *Bulletin*, 75: 300-303.
[96]*AFR, 1975:* 485.
[97]*Bulletin*, 75: 742.

embargo against South Africa.[98] Such action at such a moment, Ambassador Scranton observed, could hardly "improve the chances to gain a free and independent Namibia. . . . It would be tragic if the delicate fabric of negotiations were to be torn asunder by any precipitate move at this time."

Though Secretary Kissinger's efforts to pave the way for formal talks on Namibia had thus far brought little visible result, Governor Scranton assured the General Assembly on December 20 that "progress has been made and diplomatic consultations continue." Insistence on the virtues of negotiation did not, however, deter the Assembly from adopting a strongly worded resolution which, among other novelties, identified SWAPO as "the sole [sic] and authentic representative of the Namibian people" and expressed support for the "armed struggle," led by SWAPO, "to achieve self-determination, freedom and national independence in a united Namibia."[99]

Concerning South Africa and Rhodesia, there were also differences of emphasis and, at times, of substance between the United States and the African bloc which dictated the form and content of the General Assembly's resolutions. Although the United States was able to join in a consensus resolution expressing support for the Geneva conference on Zimbabwe,[100] the U.S. delegation took particularly strong exception to a related resolution in which the United States was singled out for condemnation on account of its continuing violation of U.N. sanctions through the importation of Rhodesian chrome and nickel pursuant to the "Byrd amendment" of 1971.[101]

Yet even this "petty and unjust" action, as a U.S. delegate termed it, did not unduly discourage American spokesmen as they contrasted the hopeful elements in the present-day African situation with the "downward spiral toward violence" that had seemed to be gaining momentum a year earlier. "As to southern Africa," Ambassador Scranton commented in his valedictory remarks to the Assembly **(Document 35b)**,

determination is strong to bring about majority rule for multiracial nations living in peace. Meaningful talks concerning Rhodesia are in process. Talks on Namibia are within reach—

[98]U.N. Document S/12211, failed of adoption by a vote of 13-3 (U.S.)-2; text and related matter in *Bulletin*, 75: 593-5.
[99]Resolution 31/46, adopted Dec. 20 by a vote of 107-6 (U.S.)-12; text and related matter in *Bulletin*, 76: 43-8.
[100]Resolution 31/154 A, Dec. 20, adopted by consensus; text and related matter on this and the following resolution in *Bulletin*, 77: 53-7.
[101]Resolution 31/154 B, Dec. 20, adopted by 124-0-7 (U.S.). For the Byrd amendment see *AFR, 1971:* 426-7; it was repealed by Public Law 95-12, Mar. 18, 1977.

talks allowing peaceful change, change by negotiations, the only course that will avoid the horror of mass violence.

6. INTER-AMERICAN CROSSCURRENTS

In the midst of his other preoccupations, the Secretary of State found time in 1976 for two extended swings through Latin America, a living witness to the concern of the United States for its southern neighbors even at a period of immersion in the urgencies of the Middle East, Southern Africa, the U.S.-Soviet relationship, and the exigencies of domestic politics.

Although the opening of a new "dialogue" with the Latin American countries had been one of the earliest of Dr. Kissinger's undertakings on becoming Secretary of State in 1973, he would have been the last to pretend that things had always gone smoothly in the intervening years. Among other irritations, Latin American sentiment had been particularly outraged by the action of Congress in excluding Ecuador and Venezuela, as members of OPEC, from the system of generalized trade preferences authorized by the Trade Act of 1974.[102] At the same time, however, there had been progress toward a resolution of at least some of the thornier issues in U.S.-Latin American relations. Examples had to do with the negotiation of new arrangements for the Panama Canal and the Canal Zone, and with accommodating present-day sentiments regarding the status of Castro's Cuba in the hemispheric system.

The year 1976 brought none of these endeavors to final fruition. The recent, promising trend toward better U.S.-Cuban relations was nullified by Cuba's military intervention in Angola and the subsequent continuance of Cuban personnel in Africa in what looked like the beginning of a large-scale revolutionary penetration effort, apparently undertaken in collusion with the Soviet Union. Negotiations for a new treaty or treaties with Panama remained at a standstill after having become embroiled in U.S. presidential politics to a point where any concession to Panamanian national sentiment was sure to be attacked in the United States as betrayal of the national interest. Dissension over trade, raw materials, and other economic matters continued not only in inter-American forums but also in such broader gatherings as the "North-South" Conference on International Economic Cooperation (CIEC) and the Nairobi meeting of the U.N. Conference on Trade and Development (UNCTAD).

Despite this superficially negative record, it was maintained by Secretary Kissinger and others that the current phase of inter-

[102]Public Law 93-618, Jan. 3, 1975; cf. *AFR, 1975:* 24 and 29-30.

American activities displayed a new maturity that had imparted fresh momentum to the pursuit of shared objectives. At least one innovation of more than transitory importance was the increased attention bestowed on the issue of human rights and individual freedoms, a painfully timely topic at a period when repressive military regimes held sway in many Latin American countries and when the use of terror by extremists of both Right and Left appeared to be continually on the increase.

The View from Macuto

The malaise affecting many aspects of U.S.-Latin American relations was frankly acknowledged by Secretary Kissinger in the course of an oft-postponed nine-day trip, conceived as a continuation of the dialogue begun in 1973-74, that commenced in Venezuela in mid-February and took him also to Peru, Brazil, Colombia, Costa Rica, and Guatemala.[103] A highlight of the stay in Venezuela, which featured talks with President Carlos Andrés Pérez and others, was an address at the seaside resort of Macuto to the U.S.-Venezuela Symposium II, the sequel to a bilateral symposium held in Boston the year before.

"The problem we face today," the Secretary declared at the outset of this wide-ranging analysis **(Document 22)**, "is that history, and indeed the very growth and success we have all achieved, have complicated our relationship. What used to be a simple perception of hemispheric uniqueness, and a self-contained exclusive relationship, has become enmeshed in the wider concerns we all now have in the rest of the world." It was precisely "the variety of these intersecting relationships and concerns," in Dr. Kissinger's view, that demanded both a redefinition of the hemispheric condition and a major effort by the United States "to invigorate our hemispheric ties." "It is time that all of us in the hemisphere put aside slogans and turn from rhetoric to resolve. . . . let us focus on our goals and the need for common effort and get down to serious business."

Aside from its pervasive emphasis on the need for mutual understanding, Dr. Kissinger's presentation contained few out-and-out novelties. His principal pledges on behalf of the United States—inspired, he pointed out, by an earlier, common pledge to seek "a new, vigorous spirit of inter-American solidarity"—involved attention to the distinctive economies of Latin America's more industrialized countries, and of the region as a whole, in international economic policy; continued direct assistance to the

---

[103]Full documentation in *Bulletin*, 74: 313-53.

hemisphere's neediest nations; support of Latin American efforts toward regional and subregional cooperation and integration; negotiation of specific differences on the basis of parity and dignity; enforcement of the common commitment to regional security; and continued work to modernize the inter-American system.

Absent from the Macuto speech, save for a passing mention, was the issue of human rights, a topic that would nevertheless engage the Secretary's attention to an increasing extent both during and after his Latin American trip. Not less lightly touched upon was the issue of democratic versus authoritarian government. "Our societies," Dr. Kissinger said at Macuto, "derive their strength from the consent and dedication of our peoples. Can our democratic system cope with the strains of social change and the frustrations of what is inevitably a long historical process?"

It would have been superfluous for Dr. Kissinger to point out that his question had already been given a negative answer, at least provisionally, in those numerous Latin American countries where popular government had in fact been abrogated and replaced by some kind of authoritarian regime. So prevalent had this trend become in recent years that democratically governed countries like Venezuela, Colombia, Costa Rica, and Mexico now seemed quite exceptional. The military dictatorship established in Chile on the overthrow of President Salvador Allende in 1973 was merely the most glaring recent example of a process that had begun at least as far back as 1964, when President João Goulart of Brazil had been ousted by the military chieftains who had since administered the country behind a transparent military façade.

Peru, the second country on Secretary Kissinger's February itinerary, had experienced a military revolution of a rather different sort, one in which the military leaders who had seized power in 1968 had themselves become protagonists of economic and social change with strong populist overtones. But the hostility toward the United States that had characterized the Peruvian revolution in its early stages had waned in recent years, and General Juan Velasco Alvarado, its original leader, had lately been supplanted by a more circumspect colleague, General Francisco Morales Bermúdez. In his talks with Morales Bermúdez and other Peruvian leaders in Lima, Secretary Kissinger went out of his way to express his understanding not only for Peru's nonaligned foreign policy but also for its "struggle to create a social democracy attuned to the needs of all its people."[104]

In Brazil, the giant of South America, the Secretary's con-

[104]*Bulletin*, 75:332.

versations with President Ernesto Geisel and others afforded the opportunity "to learn from various Brazilian officials their ideas about the evolution of this country in the political field and their perception of the role of human rights in this respect"[105]—a tactful allusion to the fact that Brazilian performance in the human rights area had been among the most widely criticized in the Americas. A token of the growing importance of a country that Dr. Kissinger thought predestined "to join the club of the rich"[106] was the signature of a bilateral memorandum of understanding that provided for semiannual consultations between the two governments at Foreign Ministers' level "on the full range of foreign policy matters."[107]

Announcement of the United States' decision to become a party to the newly negotiated International Coffee Agreement was helpful in ensuring Dr. Kissinger's welcome both in Brazil and in Colombia—where, however, his unconcealed preoccupation with Cuba's intervention in Africa elicited no more than a lukewarm response from President Alfonso López Michelsen. In Costa Rica, where the Secretary of State was able to meet both with President Daniel Oduber Quirós and with ministerial colleagues from the other Central American countries, he found the opportunity for a stronger warning against "foreign adventurism," as well as a reaffirmation of the U.S. commitment to hemispheric security, nonintervention, and basic human rights.[108] In Guatemala, his last stop, Dr. Kissinger voiced dismay at the devastation caused by a recent earthquake that had cost over 22,000 lives, injured more than 75,000, and rendered a million persons homeless.

A change was occurring in the nature of the Latin American countries' ties to the United States, Dr. Kissinger told the Senate Foreign Relations Committee in an optimistic report on his trip. "The United States is experiencing a more open relationship with the nations of Latin America, a relationship which now turns not on the memories of an earlier age of tutelage, on pretensions by us to hegemony, or on national inequality, but on mutual respect, common interests, and cooperative problem solving. . . . We can accept and indeed welcome the emergence of the nations of Latin America into global importance. And we must preserve our special hemispheric ties, without slogans, so that our cooperation as equals in this hemisphere can be a model for cooperation in the world arena."[109]

[105]Same: 341.
[106]Same.
[107]Same: 337-8.
[108]Same: 346-9.
[109]Statement of Mar. 4, in same: 357-8.

The View from Santiago

Dr. Kissinger's second Latin American tour of 1976 took place in June on the occasion of the annual session of the General Assembly of the Organization of American States (OAS), which was being held in Chile's capital city in spite of the distaste of several Latin American governments for the right-wing military regime headed by General Augusto Pinochet Ugarte, the leader of the 1973 coup. In the weeks preceding the Santiago meeting, the ranks of South America's military dictatorships had been still further augmented by the action of the Argentine military on March 24 in ousting the incompetent civilian administration of President Isabel Martínez de Perón and substituting a three-man junta in which General Jorge Rafael Videla, the Army commander, had been designated to serve as President. Affirming its commitment to "full observance of the law with respect for order and human dignity," the new regime would prove more adept at repressing leftist violence than at checking the terrorist proclivities of some of its right-wing supporters. Unable to ameliorate a pervasive climate of violence, it would prove equally at a loss to curb an inflation rate extraordinary even by South American standards.

Even without the coup in Argentina, the vicissitudes of human rights and democratic freedoms in Latin America would have been a source of lively concern at the OAS meeting because of the controversial record of the Chilean military junta headed by General Pinochet. Many of the abuses ascribed to his regime by the international press had lately been confirmed in a report from the Inter-American Commission on Human Rights that told of frequent resort to arbitrary imprisonments, persecutions, torture, and the killings of prisoners, as well as a determined withholding of information and the issuance of misleading decrees and statements aimed at "tranquilizing or confusing" world opinion. Estimates of the number of political prisoners still held in Chile, 33 months after the coup against Allende, still ran as high as 10,000. Although some prisoners had been ostentatiously released on the heels of a recent visit by U.S. Secretary of the Treasury William E. Simon, others had been arrested in the weeks before the OAS meeting. Mexico, indeed, had refused to attend a function hosted by "a regime which [it asserted] commits outrages against the lives of thousands of people and restricts the freedom and dignity of a brother people."[110]

Secretary Kissinger, who arrived in Santiago after stopovers in the Dominican Republic and Bolivia,[111] met the human rights issue

---

[110]*Keesing's:* 27899-900.

[111]Full documentation on the Secretary's trip appears in *Bulletin*, 75: 1-36.

head on in a June 8 address to a closed session of the OAS Assembly **(Document 23a)**. ". . . Let us face facts," he said. "Respect for the dignity of man is declining in too many countries of the hemisphere. There are several states where fundamental standards of humane behavior are not observed." Two of these states he went so far as to mention by name, on the basis of the evidence compiled by the Inter-American Commission on Human Rights: Chile, where "The condition of human rights as assessed by the OAS Human Rights Commission has impaired our relationship . . . and will continue to do so," and Cuba, where the Commission's inquiry, conducted in face of a total lack of Cuban cooperation, "confirms our worst fears of Cuban behavior" regarding the "inhuman treatment" of "many Cuban political prisoners." The most suitable immediate response to such a state of affairs, Dr. Kissinger suggested, would be a broadening of the Human Rights Commission's mandate and an enlargement of its budget and staff.

Cooperation for development, Secretary Kissinger's second main concern at Santiago, was the subject of a separate statement **(Document 23b)**, delivered on June 9, in which he undertook to adapt and apply to the special situation of the hemisphere the general principles he had previously expounded at the UNCTAD meeting in Nairobi **(Document 30)**. For the critical areas of commodities, trade, and technology he proposed a variety of procedural and institutional innovations designed to ensure that Latin American countries would gain full benefit from the opportunities that were supposedly being opened up on a global scale. In addition, Dr. Kissinger emphasized the U.S. administration's desire to broaden the recently instituted system of generalized trade preferences, to include Ecuador and Venezuela in its benefits, and to cooperate in plans for regional and subregional integration in Latin America.

Another perennial concern of the inter-American organization was a restructuring of the OAS machinery to make it more responsive to contemporary needs, particularly in the economic and social fields. Secretary Kissinger's views in this area were the subject of still another statement **(Document 23c)** which was made public by the U.S. delegation on June 11. Unceremoniously dismissing the latest redraft of the OAS Charter as "one that our government could neither sign nor recommend that our Senate ratify," the Secretary of State urged a new effort aimed at the threefold objective of a simplified OAS structure, a broadened OAS membership, and a reapportionment of financial burdens "that will, over time, reduce the U.S. share of the assessed costs while insuring that the activities of the OAS in the vital development field are not weakened."

Such fundamental matters were not to be decided at the 1976 Assembly but would be reserved for later special sessions. More routine questions continued to occupy the delegates at Santiago while Secretary Kissinger returned to the United States by way of Mexico City, where he conferred with President Luis Echeverría Alvarez about the transborder drug traffic, the status of American offenders—mostly drug offenders—in Mexican jails, and other matters of mutual concern.

The atmosphere of "mutual respect and perceived common interest" that had prevailed at Santiago, Dr. Kissinger told the House International Relations Committee on June 17, had been "better . . . than at any other inter-American meeting I have ever attended." "The constructive attitude at Santiago and the remarkably good tone to our relationships throughout the hemisphere," he suggested, could be attributed in large measure to the reemergence of the United States since 1974 as an equal partner in inter-American councils, with a coherent policy addressed to the entire catalog of hemispheric issues and animated by "a vision of the future of our relationship."

"We have come to the end of a critical era and are marking the beginning of a new one," Dr. Kissinger summarized. "The United States can now deal with Latin America in a new spirit. We need not hold back on major initiatives for fear of inspiring old notions of paternalism. With consultation and cooperation, our hopes of meeting the challenges of economic and social progress in an age of interdependence and of building a sound and beneficial relationship between developed and developing nations are brightest and most promising here in this hemisphere."[112]

The View from North America

The OAS Assembly in Santiago was the only major inter-American meeting of 1976, and thus the last occasion of the year for comprehensive, high-level examination of topics of hemispheric interest. The year's remaining developments in Latin American policy were somewhat episodic in character and offered few definitive indications of an over-all trend. One positive achievement, completed even before the Santiago meeting, was the passage by the U.S. Congress of legislation designed to help the Inter-American Development Bank (IDB), the hemisphere's chief regional development institution, in spurring the region's economic advance with the aid of a four-year, $6.3 billion capital increase, to which the United States proposed to contribute $2.25 billion. Sanctioned by the same legislation[113] was a proposed enlargement

[112]*Bulletin*, 75: 43-4.
[113]Public Law 94-302, May 31, 1976.

of the IDB membership through the accession of the Bahamas, Guyana, and some dozen "nonregional" countries in Europe and Asia that were expected to increase the institution's resources by some $745 million.

Another source of official satisfaction was the conclusion in September of an agreement with Peru relating to compensation for the assets of the Marcona Mining Company, the iron ore mining complex which had been nationalized in July 1975 shortly before the ouster of former President Velasco Alvarado. A more recent upheaval within the official family of President Morales Bermúdez had shunted the Peruvian revolution onto what seemed a more moderate track and helped pave the way to a settlement that would give the company $37 million in cash as well as a lucrative contract for sales of Peruvian iron ore in the United States. "Because it demonstrates that fair and equitable treatment for foreign capital can be assured within the Peruvian revolutionary process," the State Department exulted, "the settlement constitutes a point of departure for increased private as well as public cooperation and practical progress on a wide variety of fronts."[114]

Decidedly less auspicious from the standpoint of hemisphere relationships were the increasingly heated arguments about the Panama Canal, which had already stymied negotiations for a new treaty and resounded more loudly as America's election campaign approached its climax. Such specific issues as the duration of a new Panama Canal treaty, the division of management and defense responsibilities between the United States and Panama, and the amount of compensation to be paid the latter country were all but lost in a cacophony of high-pitched disputation. Though it was Governor Reagan who appeared most vehemently opposed to surrendering any element of U.S. rights and privileges in the Canal and the adjacent Zone, the type of patriotic sentiment to which he specially appealed could be ignored by none of the candidates.

Relations with Castro's Cuba might also have become a campaign issue had not the Cuban Premier himself elected to embark on new adventures in Africa and thus, in effect, stifled any immediate prospect of better relations with the United States. Late in May, there was a flurry of seemingly trustworthy reports that the Cuban troops in Angola were to be gradually withdrawn; but any withdrawals that might subsequently have taken place were offset by new arrivals as Cuba deepened its involvement not only with Angola's left-wing regime but with other African governments of similar stripe, notably the new regime headed by Lieutenant Colonel Mengistu Haile Mariam in Ethiopia.

In October, U.S.-Cuban relations took a further turn for the

[114]*Bulletin*, 75: 488.

worse after 73 lives had been lost in the crash of a Cuban airliner on October 6, apparently due to a bomb explosion shortly after takeoff from Bridgetown, Barbados. Indications pointed to the complicity of a group of anti-Castro Cuban exiles, working out of Venezuela, who had allegedly been involved in such other terrorist activities as the assassination in Washington on September 21 of Orlando Letelier, Defense Minister of Chile under the late President Allende. Complaining bitterly of acts of anti-Cuban sabotage prepared in neighboring countries—some of them, allegedly, with official U.S. sponsorship—Premier Castro on October 15 accused the United States of direct complicity in the October 6 crash and gave notice that Cuba would abrogate the anti-hijacking agreement the two governments had concluded in 1973. (Concluded for a five-year period but subject to denunciation on six months' notice by either side, this agreement[115] had helped reduce the number of recent hijackings involving the two countries virtually to zero.) With a strong denial of U.S. involvement in the bomb explosion, Secretary Kissinger warned that the United States would "hold Cuba strictly accountable for any encouragement of hijacking or any act of terrorism that may flow from its renunciation of the treaty."[116]

While U.S.-Cuban relations deteriorated, U.S. relations with another close neighbor, Mexico, seemed likely to take a turn for the better with the election of José López Portillo of the Institutional Revolutionary Party to succeed his friend and party colleague, Luis Echeverría, for a presidential term beginning December 1. The U.S.-Mexican frictions inseparable from territorial contiguity had been aggravated to some extent in recent years by Echeverría's posturings as a third world statesman, revolutionary firebrand, and intellectual parent of the 1974 Charter of Economic Rights and Duties of States.[117] What was known about López Portillo suggested a lower-keyed approach that might prove as much a relief to Mexican business interests as it would to official Washington. The rebuilding of U.S.-Mexican amity might also be made easier by the recent signature of a new U.S.-Mexican fishery agreement[118] as well as a novel "Treaty on the Execution of Penal Sentences" which was designed to enable Americans sentenced in Mexico, and Mexicans sentenced in the United States, to serve their sentences in their own countries.[119]

[115]*AFR, 1973:* 122-4.
[116]*New York Times*, Oct. 16, 1976.
[117]*AFR, 1974:* 525-41.
[118]*Bulletin*, 75: 758-9.
[119]Same: 750. Signed at Mexico City on Nov. 25, 1976, the Treaty on the Execution of Penal Sentences (TIAS 8718) entered into force Nov. 30, 1977.

The United States, too, would soon experience a change of leadership, as Secretary Kissinger pointed out when he returned to Mexico City as head of an American inaugural delegation that included both President Ford's son Jack and President-elect Carter's wife Rosalynn. "Nothing," said the Secretary of State, "could express more profoundly [than the makeup of the delegation] the importance that the United States attaches to its relationships in the Western Hemisphere and to its very special relationship to its growing, complicated, difficult, occasionally cantankerous but always close friends in Mexico . . . And just as the transfer of authority is taking place in Mexico with dignity and with continuity and with the assurance that the basic principles of the relationship between our two countries will be maintained, so I am confident that the basic principles of peace, of progress, of interdependence and mutual respect reflect the view of all Americans. . . ."[120]

7. EAST ASIAN TREMORS

In addition to growing disquiet about relations between the two superpowers, 1976 was marked by some uncertainty about the development of the U.S. position in East Asia and the Pacific. This was an area whose place in the American foreign policy design had become as firmly fixed, if not always as clearly defined, as that of Europe, the Middle East, or Latin America. But just as the relationship between East and West was caught in something of a tidal backwash after the years of Nixon-era détente, international relations in the Far East exhibited the effects of a perceived American disinvolvement that had begun with the "Nixon Doctrine" of 1969, continued with the "Vietnamization" policy and the eventual American withdrawal from the war in Indochina, and culminated in the final defeat, in 1975, of the American-supported anti-Communist regimes in South Vietnam, Laos, and Cambodia. It is true that President Ford, in a speech at Honolulu on December 7, 1975, had promulgated a new "Pacific Doctrine" that featured the maintenance by the United States of "a flexible and balanced position of strength throughout the Pacific."[121] But the generalities in which the President had spoken had yet to be translated into concrete, measurable action.

The China Story

Changes of deep though uncertain portent had meanwhile been

[120]*Bulletin*, 75: 749-50.
[121]*AFR, 1975:* 547-52.

occurring on the mainland of China. Prime Minister Chou En-lai, the veteran statesman who had guided his country's recovery from the "Cultural Revolution" and managed its subsequent *rapprochement* with the United States, died on January 8, 1976. To the considerable surprise of the outside world, he was succeeded not by his closest collaborator, First Deputy Premier Teng Hsiao-ping, but by another, relatively unknown Deputy Premier, named Hua Kuo-feng, who was soon afterward elevated to the post of acting Prime Minister. These events were accompanied by a renewed outbreak of the characteristic feuding among Communist factions, with moderates of the Chou En-lai and Teng Hsiao-ping stamp (or "capitalist-roaders," as their adversaries preferred to call them) apparently being thrown on the defensive by a more radical, doctrinaire group which had roots in the Shanghai party organization and whose most prominent single representative was Chiang Ching, the bespectacled wife of the ailing Communist Party Chairman, Mao Tse-tung.

That a major internal crisis was taking place in China became fully evident at the beginning of April when authorities repressed what had appeared to be a series of spontaneous mass demonstrations in honor of the late Chou En-lai—and, presumably, in support of his moderate associates and policies. The immediate sequel, however, was the confirmation of Hua Kuo-feng as Premier and the dismissal of Teng Hsiao-ping from all his posts in what looked at first glance like a sweeping victory for the Shanghai radicals. The ultimate significance of these developments was not, however, immediately evident to American authorities. Their first-hand knowledge of events in China was decidedly limited, although their normal sources of information were supplemented by a report submitted by former President Nixon after a February visit, undertaken at the invitation of Chinese authorities, in the course of which he had talked repeatedly with Hua Kuo-feng and was also received by Chairman Mao.

Late in July, the industrial city of Tangshan near Peking was leveled by one of the worst earthquakes in China's history. Six weeks later, on September 9, occurred the death of the 82-year-old Mao Tse-tung, a long-expected event that brought the political situation in China to a head and ultimately led to a reaffirmation of the moderate trend associated with the Chou En-lai tradition. Clear losers in the overt struggle for power that followed the Chairman's death were the widowed Chiang Ching and her radical associates of the "Gang of Four"—Wang Hung-wen, Chang Chun-chiao, and Yao Wen-yuan. Having failed in an apparent attempt to seize control in the wake of Mao's death, all four were arrested early in October as a smiling Hua Kuo-feng assumed the added posts of Chairman of the Communist Party, Chairman of the Party

Military Affairs Committee, and *ex officio* Commander of the Armed Forces. The public disclosure of these events on October 22 was followed by a campaign to unmask the "Gang of Four," a purge of their supporters, and the beginnings of a move to restore the elderly Teng Hsiao-ping to some semblance of his former position as right-hand man to the titular Prime Minister.

Among the lesser changes involved in this process was the ouster of Foreign Minister Chiao Kuan-hua, whose relations with the "Gang of Four" had apparently been unacceptably close, and his replacement by Huang Hua, a professional diplomat who had previously represented the People's Republic at the United Nations. The substance of China's foreign policy, however, seemed likely to remain essentially unchanged. There would, it appeared, be no mitigation of Peking's hostility toward the Soviet Union, nor would relations with the United States be further "normalized" unless Washington unexpectedly decided to sever its remaining ties with the Republic of China on Taiwan, a move unthinkable in a presidential election year.

Survey at Seattle

The denouement in China had still to occur when Secretary Kissinger appeared in Seattle on July 22 to address a luncheon, sponsored by the Downtown Rotary Club and the Seattle Chamber of Commerce, on the all-inclusive theme of "America and Asia" **(Document 24)**. The region he had come to discuss, the Secretary of State observed, was as dynamic, as diverse, and as complex as any in the world, and one in which American foreign policy had known "both great accomplishment and bitter disappointment." It was also, he implied, an area in which recent American policy had been extraordinarily creative.

"Throughout the first half of this decade," Dr. Kissinger asserted,

we have been fashioning a new policy for Asia. We have been bringing our commitments into balance with our interests. We have helped our allies and friends augment their own strength, while we have gradually reduced our own military presence in Asia by 130,000 men in addition to the 550,000 troops we withdrew from Vietnam. We have strengthened our relations with Japan, begun a new relationship with the People's Republic of China, and searched for political solutions to Asian regional conflicts. We have encouraged Asian nations in their self-reliance and in their efforts at regional cooperation. We have welcomed Asian nations in new multilateral efforts to improve the global economic system.

Fears of a general American retreat from Asia in the wake of the Vietnam collapse had happily subsided, Dr. Kissinger continued;

but Asia nevertheless remained "a region of potential turbulence" that offered "no grounds for complacency":

Soviet activity in Asia is growing. North and South Korea remain locked in bitter confrontation. Hanoi represents a new center of power, and its attitude toward its neighbors remains ambiguous and potentially threatening. Most developing nations remain afflicted by social and political tensions. And the scramble for oil and ocean resources raises the specter of possible future territorial disputes.

". . . All the strands of our global policy meet in Asia," Dr. Kissinger pursued as he entered upon his detailed discussion of the problem of Asian security, the problem of resolving conflicts and easing tensions, and the effort to shape new patterns of international cooperation. In every phase of Asian affairs, the Secretary insisted, much would depend upon American actions and "the confidence of Asian nations in our steadiness." "Our greatest challenge abroad," he summarized,

is to continue to act on the knowledge that neither peace nor prosperity—for ourselves or anyone else on our small planet—is possible without the wisdom and the continuing active involvement of the United States. . . . Our greatest foreign policy need at home is steadiness, cohesion, and a realization that in shaping foreign policy we are engaged in an enterprise beyond party and not bounded by our electoral cycles. . . . We are ready, as Americans have always been ready, to face the future without fear. We shall go where we have to go. We shall do what we have to do.

Adjustments in Southeast Asia

Among the Asian countries, Dr. Kissinger intimated, it was "the friendly nations of Southeast Asia that, in the wake of Indochina, are facing the greatest adjustment to new conditions." "Nations which once looked almost exclusively to us for their security," he added, "have been forced by events into greater self-reliance and broader cooperation with one another." A part of this change of focus, though Dr. Kissinger did not specifically mention it, could be attributed to the post-Vietnam initiative of two of America's Southeast Asian allies, the Philippines and Thailand, in bringing about the abrogation of the U.S.-supported South-East Asia Treaty Organization (SEATO)[122] and throwing in their lot with the Association of Southeast Asian Nations (ASEAN), a nine-year-old

[122]*AFR, 1975:* 487-9.

grouping in which they shared membership with the nonaligned states of Indonesia, Malaysia, and Singapore.

Even after the demise of SEATO, however, important vestiges of the Pacific security system erected after World War II persisted in the United States' bilateral security treaties with the Philippines, Taiwan, and South Korea and in the tripartite ANZUS Pact between the United States, Australia, and New Zealand, Pacific powers whose habit of cooperation had in recent years increasingly extended to the economic as well as the politico-military sphere. The ongoing relationship among the ANZUS allies had in some respects been facilitated of late by the return of conservative governments to power in both Australia and New Zealand, after a period of socialist administration that had begun in both countries in 1972 and had been marked by some tentative flirtation with neutralist ideas. The essential solidarity of the three governments in both world and regional affairs, emphasized in July on the occasion of an official visit to Washington by Australia's Prime Minister J. Malcolm Fraser,[123] was reaffirmed in Canberra a few days later when ministerial representatives of all three powers reviewed the international situation at the 25th meeting of the ANZUS Council, the permanent organ set up under the Tripartite Security Treaty of 1951 **(Document 25).**

More complex conditions faced the United States in the countries of Southeast Asia proper, a point much emphasized by the Assistant Secretary of State for East Asian and Pacific Affairs, Arthur W. Hummel, Jr., in a statement to a House International Affairs subcommittee on September 28 **(Document 26).** Yet despite the apprehensions that had followed the Communist victories in Indochina, this official found reason for optimism in the way the nations of the area had adapted themselves to the changing international environment. The progressive collapse envisaged by the "domino theory" had obviously not occurred. There had been no "major increase in the level of Communist insurgent activity in Southeast Asia," Mr. Hummel reported; nor was any major power at present "aggressively seeking a predominant role in the region."

Admittedly, considerable doubt persisted with regard to the intentions of the Communist regimes that now held sway in the three states of Indochina. Particularly was this true of the recently reunified "Socialist Republic of Vietnam," whose northern and southern portions had been officially reunited on July 2, 1976 under a regime made up of such familiar figures as Premier Pham Van Dong, Communist Party chief Le Duan, and other Communist holdovers from the former, northern-based "Democratic Republic of Vietnam." The former Kingdom of Laos, meanwhile,

[123]*Presidential Documents*, 12: 1211-12 and 1215-20 (in part in *Bulletin*, 75: 291-3).

had become a "People's Democratic Republic," headed since December 1975 by the veteran leftist, Prince Souphanouvong. "Democratic Cambodia," whose postwar regime had emerged as the most fanatically leftist of the three, had severed its last remaining ties with the past in April 1976 when Prince Norodom Sihanouk, the nominal Chief of State, resigned in favor of a new slate of leaders in which the Communist Khieu Samphan was President and one Pol Pot, later identified as head of the Communist Party, was Prime Minister.

An unresolved issue that was of deep and continuing concern to the United States had to do with Vietnam's persistent failure to furnish information and assistance regarding some 795 Americans who were still listed as missing in action in the recent war, together with a larger number who were presumed dead but whose remains had not been recovered. Vietnam's insistence on linking this question with its demands for $3.25 billion in American reconstruction aid, allegedly promised by former President Nixon in 1973,[124] had frustrated any move toward normal relations and was to lead in November to the casting of the United States' eighteenth Security Council veto to block a favorable action on Vietnam's request for U.N. membership. Supported by 14 Security Council members and opposed only by the United States, the Vietnamese application was later endorsed by the General Assembly—with "deep regret and concern" at the American stand—in a nonbinding resolution adopted by the overwhelming vote of 124 to 1 (the United States) with 3 abstentions.[125]

Assistant Secretary Hummel's statement, though not of great consequence in itself, stands out as one of the few reviews of Southeast Asian affairs from an official standpoint to be made public during 1976. Surveying U.S. relations with the non-Communist countries of the region, Mr. Hummel laid special emphasis on Thailand and the Philippines, both still nominally aligned with the United States, and on Indonesia, whose nonaligned position had not prevented the development of a close relationship in which, among other things, it was currently supplying the United States some 8 percent of its imported oil supplies.

The American military presence in Thailand, though continued even after the conclusion of the war in Indochina, had recently been terminated in consequence of a failure to agree on the conditions under which the United States might still retain residual facilities in the country. Despite this disappointment, Assistant Secretary Hummel expressed good hopes for the success of Thailand's three-year-old civilian government, currently headed by

[124]Cf. *AFR, 1975:* 40.
[125]Resolution 31/21, Nov. 26; details in *UN Monthly Chronicle,* Dec. 1976: 16-23.

Prime Minister Seni Pramoj. In point of fact, however, that government had already been undermined by disputes about the treatment of banished military leaders. On October 6, approximately one week after the Hummel statement, it was overthrown in another military coup whose most conspicuous leader was Admiral Sa-ngad Chaloryu, a quondam Supreme Commander of the Armed Forces.

The U.S. military bases in the Philippines were described by Mr. Hummel as retaining their importance both for the mutual defense of the two countries and for the security of the Pacific region. President Ferdinand E. Marcos' post-Vietnam insistence on a "reassessment" of the American military presence had consequently led to the initiation of new negotiations, based on "the clear recognition of Philippine sovereignty," looking toward a revision of existing arrangements. In spite of numerous difficulties, Mr. Hummel expressed confidence that the negotiations would "eventually prove successful." Noting that discussions looking toward a new economic and commercial agreement were also going forward, the Assistant Secretary refrained from entering upon such Philippine internal problems as the Muslim revolt in the south or the abridgement of political and personal freedoms under the martial law regime maintained by President Marcos since 1972.

These matters had not, however, been overlooked by a vocal segment of American opinion. A sense of strain already pervaded the atmosphere of U.S.-Philippine relations, and matters were not improved by the misunderstandings that arose late in the year in connection with a proposal by Secretary Kissinger that the United States be given a five-year extension on its use of the Philippine bases and pay to the Philippines the sum of $1 billion, to be equally divided between military and economic aid. Supposedly suggested to Philippine Foreign Secretary Carlos P. Romulo at the December 1 inauguration ceremonies in Mexico City, the offer is said to have been turned down by the Manila government with an intimation that the Philippines would require $1 billion in military aid alone, economic aid being a separate matter requiring a separate agreement. Any further discussion would obviously have to be left to the incoming Carter administration.[126]

Korean Difficulties

Problems arising from the practice of authoritarian government loomed even more prominently in the United States' relations with the Republic of Korea (ROK), where President Park Chung Hee had responded to the Nixon Doctrine and the U.S.-China thaw of

[126]*New York Times*, Dec. 5 and 7, 1976.

the early 1970s by setting up a thinly veiled dictatorship in which the former army leader exercised virtually unlimited powers while critics and opponents were ruthlessly silenced. Not widely known, as yet, was the fact that President Park's regime had also been engaged since early in the decade on a deliberate, large-scale campaign to cultivate American support by means of favors, gifts, and outright bribes to congressmen and other influential Americans. Such efforts, however, had clearly not succeeded in tempering the bad impression created by the Seoul government's domestic policies, which had been harshly criticized in Congress and elsewhere and had resulted in increasing resistance to the military aid allotments the Ford administration considered necessary to maintain a friendly South Korea with an adequate defense capability.

Despite admitted disapproval of some aspects of South Korean official conduct, Dr. Kissinger and other administration spokesmen had tempered their reproofs in recognition of the fact that South Korea did, after all, occupy an exposed position in which it was under constant threat of attack from the northern, Communist-ruled Democratic People's Republic of Korea (DPRK) headed by Marshal Kim Il Sung. ". . . We will continue to remind the South Korean Government," Secretary Kissinger said in Seattle **(Document 24)**, "that responsiveness to the popular will and social justice are essential if subversion and external challenge are to be resisted. But we shall not forget that our alliance with South Korea is designed to meet an external threat which affects our own security and that of Japan as well."

The meeting of this external threat had in fact been the key to U.S. policy in the Korean peninsula ever since the war of 1950 and the armistice agreement concluded in 1953 and still remaining in force. "North Korea," as one U.S. official observed, "remains intransigently committed to unification on its own terms and has embarked on a major campaign to isolate the Republic of Korea internationally";[127] and it was to block the accomplishment of such designs that the United States had felt it necessary to bolster the ROK with a security relationship that comprised not only a mutual defense treaty but also an American military presence of some 40,000, plus a substantial military assistance program that was expected to continue on a credit basis even after grant assistance was phased out.

Existing conditions and commitments in the area, administration authorities believed, would not allow for any further significant reduction of American forces beyond those already carried out at the beginning of the 1970s, when authorized U.S. strength in South

---

[127] Habib statement, Apr. 8, in *Bulletin*, 74: 558.

Korea had been reduced from 63,000 to 43,000.[128] This, however, was a view that would be sharply challenged by Governor Carter, whose successful campaign for the office of Chief Executive would prominently feature a plan for phased withdrawal of U.S. ground forces from South Korea.

Not less reflective of its overriding concern for South Korean security were Washington's recurrent efforts to promote political arrangements that would ease tensions on the Korean peninsula and make renewed hostilities less likely. Unwilling to accede to North Korea's agitation for a unilateral withdrawal of U.S. forces and dissolution of the U.N. Command, which still remained in being as a relic of the 1950-53 conflict, Secretary Kissinger had proposed in 1975 a conference, to include North and South Korea, the United States, and the People's Republic of China, to discuss ways of preserving the armistice agreement and explore other possible tension-reducing measures, including a larger conference to negotiate a more fundamental arrangement.[129] This offer the Secretary of State reiterated, at President Ford's direction, in his Seattle address of July 22, in which he proposed specifically that the parties meet in New York or elsewhere during the coming U.N. Assembly session. In repeating the American offer, Dr. Kissinger specifically rejected a series of alternative proposals from North Korea, whose true object, he asserted, was "not to promote peace but to isolate our ally, to precipitate unilateral American withdrawal, and to dissolve the existing legal arrangements into amorphous general negotiations."

That Kim Il Sung's regime was more concerned with creating tension than with reducing it seemed all the more evident in light of a series of events which took place a few weeks later and found the North Koreans engaging in a calculated display of anti-U.S. violence, perhaps designed in part to impress participants in the Fifth Conference of Heads of State or Government of Nonaligned Countries, then meeting in Colombo, Sri Lanka. As dispassionately recounted by Assistant Secretary Hummel in a later statement to congressional subcommittees **(Document 27)**, these North Korean actions were marked by a brutality more frequently met with in the conduct of private terrorist groups than in that of organized governments in the 1970s.

This truculent North Korean demonstration occurred on the morning of August 18 within the Joint Security Area of the Demilitarized Zone at Panmunjon, the headquarters of the Military Armistice Commission set up under the armistice agreement. A small work party of the U.N. Command, engaged in

[128]Same: 559.
[129]U.N. address, Sept. 22, 1975, in *AFR, 1975:* 471.

"routinely trimming branches" with a view to improving visibility and security, was ordered to desist by North Koreans on the scene and, on its failure to comply, was set upon by some 30 North Korean guards. Responding to an alleged incitement "to kill" the offending U.N. personnel, the assailants attacked with "axes, metal pikes and axe handles," taking the lives of two American officers—the first such deaths in the Joint Security Area since the 1953 armistice—and injuring four other Americans as well as five ROK military personnel.[130]

President Ford's response to this "vicious and unprovoked murder" recalled his vigorous actions in the *Mayagüez* incident the year before. The 40,000 U.S. troops in South Korea were promptly placed on alert status, the carrier *Midway* and two squadrons of fighter-bombers were dispatched to the area, and flights of B-52 bombers from Guam were added to the overwhelming show of force that was brought to bear within the Joint Security Zone on August 21, when the disputed tree was cut down—rather than trimmed—in the presence of several hundred U.S. and South Korean troops. Marshal Kim himself seemed disconcerted by the vigor of the U.S. reaction, and moved to defuse the situation with a message to the American chief of the U.N. Command in which he termed the August 18 incident "regretful" and called for mutual efforts to prevent a recurrence.[131] Responding to a further North Korean initiative, the interested parties soon afterward negotiated a modification of the relevant agreement that would reduce the occasions for contact between military personnel of the opposing sides.[132]

A further indication that Pyongyang's homicidal move had backfired was the subsequent withdrawal, at North Korea's own request, of the usual draft resolution in which the U.N. General Assembly was asked to call for the dissolution of the U.N. Command, withdrawal of foreign troops from South Korea, and replacement of the armistice agreement by a peace treaty. Likewise withdrawn by prearrangement was a U.S.-supported, pro-South Korea resolution calling for resumption of the dialogue between the two Korean governments and for negotiations to permit a dissolution of the U.N. Command through adaptation of the armistice agreement or its replacement by more permanent arrangements.

As a result of these actions, it became evident early in the General Assembly session that the Korean question would be bypassed for the first time since 1947. Secretary Kissinger, in

---

[130]State Department statement, Aug. 18, in *Bulletin*, 75: 392-3.

[131]*New York Times*, Aug. 23, 1976.

[132]*Bulletin*, 75: 393-4.

addressing the Assembly on September 30 **(Document 35a)**, put forward still another reformulation of his proposal for a four-party conference—which could, he now suggested, be brought into being by stages if some of the parties were unwilling to take the full plunge immediately. There would, however, be no further action on the Korean question until there had been an opportunity to assess the implications of Governor Carter's election victory, his reiterated intention to remove at least the U.S. ground troops from South Korea, and the mounting indications that the Seoul regime, in addition to its disregard for human rights at home, had overstepped all ordinary bounds in its attempts to manipulate the foreign policy of the United States.

Japan: No Problems

"No relationship," Secretary Kissinger had said in Seattle, "is more important to the United States than our alliance with Japan. Mutual security remains fundamental to our collaboration; but in a new era we have extended our partnership to a broad range of common interests: easing tensions in Asia, solving regional and global problems, and combining our vast economic strength to spur stable and noninflationary world economic growth."

Although the United States and Japan had traversed a period of difficult adjustment in the early 1970s, the Secretary of State continued,

Today our relations with Japan are better than they have ever been. There are no significant bilateral disputes. We have developed a clearer common perception of our security requirements. . . . We have injected greater balance and reciprocity into our economic relations. We have learned to identify and deal with potential difficulties before they become politically explosive. We have consulted with greater frequency and frankness and in greater depth than in any previous period. Both nations are displaying sensitivity to the intangibles of our relationship and have built a wide base of public support for closer cooperation.

An equal measure of satisfaction pervaded a subsequent address on U.S.-Japanese relations that was delivered by Assistant Secretary Hummel before the Japan-America Society in Washington on October 19 **(Document 28)**. "Many of those cliches about Japan and the United States are true," Mr. Hummel rejoiced. "We do think that the essential foundation of the U.S.-Japan relationship, constructed of common interests and shared values, will endure." Bilateral economic ties, the Assistant

Secretary continued, were now "remarkably trouble-free"; and the Japanese were showing increased awareness of "the essentiality of a Japanese defense role, albeit limited, and of Japan's security relationship with the United States." Both countries, moreover, shared "a fundamental goal . . . of preserving and strengthening democratic institutions and values in a world increasingly hostile to them."

Even the upheaval known as the "Lockheed affair," according to Mr. Hummel, had "not significantly damaged U.S.-Japan relations," thanks mainly to the wise decision of the two governments to treat the matter as a legal issue removed from the political arena. Yet this undoubtedly salutary arrangement had failed to spare Japan a shattering political experience, as devastating in its own way as Watergate had been for the United States.

One blow to Japanese complacency had occurred as early as 1974, when the revelation of certain financial irregularities unrelated to Lockheed had led to the resignation of Premier Kakuei Tanaka and his replacement by Takeo Miki as Liberal Democratic Party leader and Prime Minister. New shocks had begun to occur in February 1976 as the U.S. Senate Subcommittee on Multinational Corporations heard evidence of multimillion dollar payments allegedly made by the Lockheed Aircraft Corporation in the early 1970s—among them a payment of $7,000,000 to a single individual, Yoshio Kodama—to promote the purchase of its TriStar aircraft by All Nippon Airways, Japan's principal domestic airline. It was in response to urgent demands from Prime Minister Miki, who professed to fear a "fatal blow" to democracy in Japan, that the United States agreed in March to an exchange of relevant information, on the understanding that it would be kept confidential except in legal proceedings.[133]

But powerful elements in the ruling Liberal Democratic Party had not been slow to take alarm at Prime Minister Miki's insistence on full investigation of the Lockheed and related scandals; and the danger of a split in the ruling party had been dramatized in July when former Premier Tanaka himself was arrested on charges (which he consistently denied) relating to his alleged receipt of the equivalent of $1,700,000 as a return for using his influence in behalf of TriStar.[134] Pressure from other party chieftains for Miki's resignation, staved off by a cabinet reorganization in September, continued to intensify even as Assistant Secretary Hummel extolled the measures taken to ensure "that cooperative efforts to investigate the scandal and punish the guilty should insofar as

[133]*Keesing's:* 27840-4.
[134]Same: 28005.

possible be removed from the political arena and placed in a legal framework.''

The climactic moment for Japan occurred on December 5 with the holding of the regular quadrennial elections to the 511-member lower house of the national Diet. For the first time since its formation in 1955, the scandal-ridden Liberal Democratic Party lost its over-all majority in the lower chamber, winning only 41.78 percent of the vote and only 249 seats, to 262 for the combined opposition. (Promises of support from eleven independents subsequently gave the LDP a narrow majority of 260 to 251). ''A major defeat'' and ''the worst political crisis in our postwar history,'' said the 69-year-old Prime Minister Miki, whose tenure of office was clearly at an end and who was succeeded soon afterward by the 71-year-old Takeo Fukuda, a veteran of earlier cabinets who had spearheaded the anti-Miki campaign.

He, too, intended to pursue the thorough ''unraveling'' of the Lockheed affair, Fukuda told a Christmas news conference. In addition, he said, he planned to give priority to revitalizing the Japanese economy and, with this in mind, was hoping for an early meeting with President-elect Carter—to be followed, perhaps, by another economic ''summit'' of the kind that had been held at Rambouillet in 1975 and at Dorado Beach, Puerto Rico, in June 1976.[135] The new Prime Minister thus bore independent testimony to the predominant influence that international economic affairs were coming to exert not only on Japanese-American relations but on the life of the whole non-Communist world. It was this economic dimension, far more than the transient phenomena associated with the Lockheed scandal, that would condition the relationship of the two powers and of their friends and allies in the coming years.

8. THE ECONOMIC DIMENSION

''The world economy has come a long way from the gloom and uncertainty of two years ago,'' President Ford reported shortly before leaving office in January 1977. ''Despite many divisive economic pressures, international cooperation has not broken down but has, in fact, improved. U.S. initiatives to strengthen international economic cooperation have led to real progress. Our major allies and trading partners have cooperated with us and have reciprocated our desire for strengthened economic ties.'' ''The United States can be proud of its leadership in these areas,'' Mr.

[135]Same: 28157-9.

Ford added. "International economic cooperation is stronger today than at any time since the Second World War."[136]

In the background of these optimistic comments lay a record of continued economic recovery in the United States and, to a lesser extent, abroad as the world emerged from its deep recession of 1974-75. Paced by accelerating economic expansion in the United States, West Germany, and Japan, the economies of the industrial world had advanced strongly through the spring of 1976, continuing thereafter at a somewhat slackened pace that reflected, among other things, the wariness of governmental authorities in face of a threatened revival of excessive inflationary pressures. As industrial production picked up, the OPEC nations reaped the benefit of reviving demand for their high-priced oil exports, while even the poorer developing countries that had to buy their oil experienced some increase in the demand for their particular exports.

Within the United States itself, the gross national product increased in 1976 by 6 percent in real terms and, in terms of current dollars, by 11.6 percent, from $1,528.8 billion in 1975 to $1,706.5 billion in 1976. The rate of increase in consumer prices, in contrast, declined from 7 percent in 1975 to 4.8 percent in 1976. Unemployment, which had averaged 8.5 percent through 1975, decreased to a 1976 average of 7.7 percent, or 7,288,000, while average employment grew from 84,783,000 to 87,485,000. The stock market, too, continued its upward course of the previous year, the Dow Jones Industrial Average gaining 152.24 points and closing at 1004.65, the highest year-end closing in history. No one seemed much alarmed by the appearance of a $5.9 billion trade deficit in place of the unusual $11.1 billion surplus recorded in 1975. If imports had increased more rapidly than exports, this was attributed simply to the comfortable fact that the United States had been recovering faster than its major trading partners. Related to these same circumstances was a shift in the overall balance of payments on current account from a 1975 surplus of $11.6 billion to a 1976 deficit of $1.3 billion.

Halting and precarious though it still appeared at times, the broad-scale economic revival both at home and abroad provided a favorable climate for the various institutional reforms through which the industrial nations had for several years been endeavoring

---

[136]Message on the International Economic Report, Jan. 18, 1977, in *Presidential Documents*, 13: 58-9 (*Bulletin*, 76: 129-30). This discussion draws heavily on the accompanying *International Economic Report of the President* [including the Annual Report of the Council on International Economic Policy], *Transmitted to the Congress January 1977* (Washington: GPO, 1977).

to effect a general streamlining and reshaping of the world economy—or, at any rate, of the economy of the non-Communist world. This was an endeavor in which the industrialized countries considered that they were acting not only in their own direct interest but also in the interest of the more than 100 developing nations that made up the so-called Group of 77, the principal pressure group for the promotion of developing country interests. To whatever degree this may have been true, some progress was undoubtedly achieved in 1976 on each of the major enterprises that made up the international economic agenda of the 1970s: reform of the international monetary system, revision of international trade rules, and a general overhaul of economic development policies.

Reforming the Monetary System

Undoubtedly the most definitive achievement of the year was the completion of the first general revision of the Articles of Agreement of the International Monetary Fund (IMF), the U.N. specialized agency that served as arbiter of international monetary affairs. In recent years, the IMF had been severely weakened by the progressive abandonment of the system of currency exchange rates based on gold and the increasing resort to "floating" rates determined basically by market conditions. Protracted bargaining between the United States and France, as chief upholder of the old system, had paved the way for a critical meeting of the so-called Interim Committee of the IMF, held in Kingston, Jamaica, on January 7-8, 1976, at which the United States was represented by Secretary of the Treasury William E. Simon. At this meeting, a comprehensive agreement was reached on both the long-term structural reform of the monetary system and measures to meet immediate balance-of-payments needs.

Prominent among the detailed principles accepted at Jamaica, and set forth in the Interim Committee's official communiqué **(Document 29)**, were a legalization of floating and other current exchange rate practices; a further reduction of the role of gold in the monetary system, including its replacement by the so-called Special Drawing Right (SDR) as the official IMF unit of account; disposal of one-third of the IMF's existing gold holdings, in part through sales for the benefit of developing countries and in part through direct return to the member states; a liberalization of special credit facilities developed to meet the oil crisis; and the establishment of a special Trust Fund to provide balance-of-payments aid on concessional terms to the poorest IMF member states. In endorsing the pending revision of the IMF Articles of Agreement, the Jamaica conferees also agreed to recommend a 32.5 percent increase in total IMF quotas that would expand the

Fund's resources from about SDR 29.2 billion to SDR 39 billion (roughly, from $35 billion to $46 billion) and, among other things, substantially increase the participation of the oil-rich OPEC countries.

These arrangements would not, in some cases, become fully operative until they had been implemented by the IMF Executive Directors, approved by the organization's Board of Governors, and, in the case of the most important changes, accepted by a specified proportion of the 128 IMF member countries. Initial progress was fairly rapid. A proposed Second Amendment to the IMF Articles of Agreement, already many months in preparation, was duly completed by the Executive Directors in March,[137] was approved by the Board of Governors in April, and was submitted to the U.S. Congress in May, together with a proposed $2 billion increase in the U.S. quota that would raise the U.S. monetary stake in the institution to approximately $9.8 billion. Congress, in turn, signified its concurrence by passing the Bretton Woods Agreement Act Amendments, which were duly signed by the President on October 19.[138] Although the way was thus cleared for full U.S. participation in the new system, its entry into force would still have to wait for parallel action by other countries over the next few months.

Negotiations on International Trade

No such decisive results were to be looked for in the parallel negotiations aimed at a revision of international trade rules, which were being conducted under the auspices of another UN-related agency, the General Agreement on Tariffs and Trade (GATT). Getting off to a promising start at Tokyo in 1973, these negotiations had since run into mounting difficulties and delays that had already led to a postponement of their targeted completion date from 1975 to 1977. Instead of the intended far-reaching liberalization of existing trade practices, the immediate problem had turned out to be one of staving off a piecemeal return to protectionist policies in response to current economic difficulties. President Ford was less than ebullient in his description of developments in this area. "Although the recession and large balance of payments deficits of the oil consuming countries led several of them to move in the direction of new restrictive trade

[137]*Proposed Second Amendment to the Articles of Agreement of the International Monetary Fund: A Report by the Executive Directors to the Board of Governors* (Washington: IMF, March 1976); text in *International Legal Materials*, 15: 499-590 (May 1976).

[138]Public Law 94-564, Oct.19, 1976; signature statement in *Presidential Documents*, 12: 1542 (*Bulletin*, 75: 626).

policies," he reported, "on the whole, considerable success has been achieved in maintaining an open world trading system."[139]

Modest progress in several areas was recorded by the more than 90 nations participating in the negotiations at GATT Headquarters in Geneva, a highly complex enterprise that involved both industrial and agricultural products and focused on both tariffs and nontariff barriers (NTBs) as they affected both industrial and developing countries. Among the year's highlights was the submission of alternative tariff-cutting formulas by the United States and the European Community, with the United States stressing percentage cuts "across the board" while the Europeans favored a concept of "harmonization" that singled out the highest tariffs for the sharpest cuts. The search for a reconciliation of these alternative approaches, each aimed at maximizing the benefit to its own proponents, would constitute one aspect of a lengthy negotiating process that was expected to continue well into the next U.S. administration.

Encounter at Nairobi

Promotion of the economic development of less developed countries (LDCs) was another leading concern of U.S. policy, as well as a recognized goal of international endeavor within the framework of the U.N. Second Development Decade and other multinational programs. Increasingly in recent years, the problems of economic development had also become a subject of tenacious and sometimes heated argument between the LDCs themselves and the industrial countries whose help remained essential to their further progress. The various forms of help provided or envisaged by the advanced countries—including, in the case of the United States, bilateral aid programs, Food for Peace, the Peace Corps, support of multilateral development programs under the United Nations and the World Bank, and, most recently, a newly instituted system of Generalized Trade Preferences (GTP) available only to developing countries—were regarded, by and large, by the LDCs as both inadequate in scale and poorly adapted to the needs they were supposedly designed to meet.

Sharpened by the world financial crisis that had accompanied the energy emergency of 1973-74, the differing philosophies that animated developing and industrial countries had already been ventilated at a series of major international meetings, notably the Sixth Special Session of the U.N. General Assembly in 1974;[140] the Seventh Special Session of the same body in 1975;[141] and, again in

[139] *Presidential Documents*, 13: 60 (*Bulletin*, 76: 130).
[140] *AFR, 1974:* 91-112.
[141] Same, *1975:* 417-46.

1975, the meeting in Paris of the Conference on International Economic Cooperation (CIEC), the celebrated "North-South" dialogue involving 19 developing and 8 industrialized countries that had originally been proposed by President Giscard d'Estaing of France.[142] Four commissions set up by the CIEC were currently at work on the problems of energy, raw materials, development, and related financial issues, in preparation for another meeting of the conference to be held at ministerial level during the first half of 1977. In the meantime, still another full-dress encounter between industrial and developing countries had been scheduled to take place at the Fourth Ministerial Session of the U.N. Conference on Trade and Development (UNCTAD-IV), to be held in Nairobi, Kenya, beginning May 3, 1976.

The main desiderata with which the developing nations intended to approach the Nairobi conference were placed on record at a preparatory meeting of the so-called Group of 77 that took place at Manila in February. Addressed primarily to the areas of commodities, debt, and transfer of technology, the so-called Manila Declaration and Program of Action included, in addition to noncontroversial items, a number of features that were opposed by the United States on both theoretical and practical grounds. With regard to commodities, for instance, the United States took particular exception to (1) the concept of "indexation," or the attempt to establish a fixed relationship between the prices of raw materials and industrial goods, and (2) the concept of a Common Fund to promote higher commodity prices by financing the formation of buffer stocks. The American approach, reflected in adherence to the recently completed international agreements on tin and coffee, was based on a case-by-case examination of the problems of particular commodities, rather than an "across-the-board" procedure. With regard to the debt burden of the LDCs, the United States opposed demands for "generalized" relief and favored a more discriminating approach tailored to the needs of individual countries.[143]

Secretary Kissinger's much-publicized address at Nairobi on May 6 (**Document 30**) provided a detailed exposé of American thinking in these matters and offered a significant alternative to the Common Fund in the form of a proposed $1 billion International Resources Bank that would be designed, among other functions, to promote "more rational, systematic, and equitable development of resources in developing nations" by mobilizing and encouraging the flow of foreign private capital, management and technology. Other novel proposals included the formation of an International

[142]Same: 571-92.
[143]For background cf. especially *Bulletin*, 74: 631-5.

Industrialization Institute to encourage research and development of industrial technology appropriate to developing countries, and an International Energy Institute to facilitate energy research and the application of energy-related technologies to the special needs of such countries.

To the disappointment of Secretary Kissinger and Secretary of the Treasury Simon, who worked closely with him in formulating the American proposals, a resolution calling for further study of the International Resources Bank was rejected on May 31, the final day of the Nairobi conference, by a vote of 33 to 31 (with 44 abstentions and 46 absences) as the result of a parliamentary maneuver that had little to do with its intrinsic merits. American disappointment was all the keener because the U.S. delegation at Nairobi had tried hard to show a conciliatory spirit and had even joined with other delegations in a consensus statement that contemplated, among other things, a negotiating conference on the establishment of a common commodity fund.[144] Without committing itself to actual participation in such a conference, the United States made clear its readiness to join in UNCTAD-sponsored discussions of individual commodities and to proceed with the implementation of other commitments it had undertaken at Nairobi or earlier.

Meeting of the OECD Council

A leading theme of the developing countries at Nairobi had been the need for a code of conduct to regulate the behavior of transnational or multinational corporations in such a way as to maximize the benefits and minimize the possible harmfulness of foreign private investment in their economies. Without denying that past experience with multinational corporations, including instances of corporate wrongdoing, made this a legitimate concern, the United States had emphasized its own view that the "host countries" also had important obligations in this area, particularly in providing a favorable legal, political, and economic climate for foreign private investment. In addition, the United States had maintained that the problem of corporate behavior could be best addressed through the formulation of voluntary guidelines rather than by trying to draw up a rigid, enforceable code of conduct.

The elaboration of such a set of guidelines, applying to both corporations and host countries, had already been undertaken by a special committee of the Organization for Economic Cooperation and Development (OECD), and its adoption by the 23 governments composing that organization was the highlight of the annual

[144]Kissinger-Simon statement, June 1, in *Bulletin*, 75: 133-4; additional material in same: 134-8.

ministerial-level meeting of the OECD Council that was held in Paris on June 21-22. Once again it fell to Secretary Kissinger, as co-chairman with Secretary Simon of the U.S. delegation, to establish a general perspective in an opening statement **(Document 31a)** that ranged widely over the field of current international economics. Citing the recent accomplishments of the OECD group—among them an agreement on a long-term energy program within the framework of the International Energy Agency (IEA),[145] and an agreement to establish the $25 billion Financial Support Fund or "safety net" originally proposed by Dr. Kissinger as a safeguard against balance-of-payments emergencies[146]—the Secretary of State as usual emphasized the need for continuing and still closer cooperation among industrialized countries in facing the challenges of the contemporary world.

The stress on interdependence and enhanced cooperation was echoed in a formal communiqué that listed the main decisions reached by the OECD Council **(Document 31b)**. Conspicuous among them was the acceptance of a "go-slow" economic strategy, aimed at a combination of sustained expansion and reduced inflation, that would involve the setting of a collective OECD growth target of not much over 5 percent a year for the five years 1976-80. In addition, the ministers renewed for a further year their 1974 declaration renouncing certain types of trade and related restrictions,[147] and, as already noted, adopted a new Declaration on International Investment and Multinational Enterprises with guidelines on the principles of good corporate behavior.[148] The basic aim of the meeting, said Dr. Kissinger at its conclusion, had been to highlight the capacity of the industrial democracies, given proper coordination, to help themselves and the rest of the world in constructing an international order "—for the first time in history on a global basis—in which all or at least most nations have a sense of participation."[149]

The Puerto Rico Summit

The themes of coordination and cooperation were even more emphatically sounded the following weekend at a meeting of the leaders of seven of the principal industrial democracies (Canada, France, West Germany, Italy, Japan, the United Kingdom, and the United States) that had been convoked by President Ford and took place at Dorado Beach, Puerto Rico, on June 27-28. A sequel to the

---

[145]Details in *Bulletin*, 74: 261-2.
[146]*AFR, 1974:* 460-61; further details in *Bulletin*, 74: 818-20.
[147]*AFR, 1974:* 150-51.
[148]Text in *Bulletin*, 75: 83-7.
[149]News conference, Paris, June 22, in same: 89.

five-power "economic summit" held at Rambouillet in November 1975,[150] the Puerto Rico summit could build upon the substantial measure of economic recovery accomplished in the intervening months. Future economic policy, according to the Joint Declaration issued at the conclusion of the meeting **(Document 32)**, would be dominated by the need "to manage effectively a transition to expansion which will be sustainable, which will reduce the high level of unemployment which persists in many countries and will not jeopardize our common aim of avoiding a new wave of inflation."

To an extent unprecedented in previous experience, the conferees in Puerto Rico faced the problem of differential rates of growth, inflation, employment, and trade and payment flows within a group of countries whose economies had become so closely intertwined that events in one inevitably affected all the others. Countries with high inflation and persistent external deficits, like Britain and Italy, inevitably took a different view from those, like Japan and West Germany, with lower inflation rates and surpluses in their external payments. Such difficulties could at least be discussed with mutual benefit in the "very free and relaxed atmosphere" which, according to Secretary Kissinger, characterized both formal and informal discussions at the Dorado Beach meeting. "What no communiqué can reflect," the Secretary of State suggested, "is the many conversations that took place at the side, the attitude of the participants that reflected the conviction that they represented parallel values and the realization that their destinies were linked together."[151]

Stocktaking at Manila

Economic recovery in the industrialized world still lagged behind expectations as Finance Ministers from all parts of the globe converged on Manila early in the autumn for the annual meetings of the Boards of Governors of the International Monetary Fund and the International Bank for Reconstruction and Development (IBRD), twin pillars of the international economic order established late in World War II. The "healthy and balanced" economic expansion that had been taking place in the United States, Secretary Simon reported in his major address to this gathering on October 5,[152] was proceeding at a satisfactory pace and was expected to continue into 1977, although at gradually moderating rates of growth. Already perceptible, however, were

[150] *AFR, 1975:* 515-26.
[151] News conference, June 28, in *Presidential Documents*, 12: 1094.
[152] Text in *Vital Speeches*, 43: 34-42 (Nov. 1, 1976).

the beginnings of a reverse movement in several industrial countries as the surging expansion of the first half year was curbed, in part by a moderation of consumer spending and inventory buildups and in part by policies deliberately designed to restrain external deficits and domestic inflation rates.

Economic policy, monetary reform, development problems, and the freeing of international trade and investment all came within the purview of the Bank and Fund; and no one was surprised that Secretary Simon in his address should adopt a relatively conservative approach to all these issues, consistent with his view that it was the duty of Finance Ministers "to call for prudence in an age of fiscal adventure." International cooperation, Mr. Simon pointed out, provided "a framework of opportunity"; but "what really counts for each of our countries and for the world economy is how efficiently we all manage our own domestic affairs."

A matter of particular interest at the Manila meeting was the need for an expansion of the resources of the various international development institutions that made up the "World Bank Group" and served as a major instrumentality for the transfer of capital resources from developed to developing countries. Addressing the Manila conferees on October 4, World Bank President Robert S. McNamara had strongly supported a proposed $8.4 billion expansion in the resources of IBRD, as well as a $9 billion replenishment of the affiliated International Development Association (IDA), which provided needed development financing on concessional terms in cases where other sources of financing were not available. Without contesting the overall target figures, Secretary Simon weighed in strongly against any relaxation of the IBRD's lending policies that could undermine its ability to meet the challenges of the coming years. Displaying somewhat greater solicitude for the IDA (whose fifth replenishment was later cut from $9 billion to $7.6 billion, of which the United States proposed to furnish $2.4 billion), Mr. Simon also welcomed an agreement to increase the capital resources of the small but efficacious International Finance Corporation (IFC), which specialized in channeling private funds into economic development.

"In my stay at the Treasury, I have seen the world economy pass through some extremely rough weather," the U.S. spokesman observed.

Our management, though imperfect, has enabled us to survive— and a bit more.

We survived in the sense that our economies did not collapse, markets continued to function, and we avoided a wave of restrictions on flows of goods and capital among nations. This achievement in itself was considerable. But beyond that, the foundation we have laid can lead to a great deal more—if we do the right things from here on.

We all know that the present situation has both risk and opportunity. We should not fear the risk and we must not fail to grasp the opportunity. Much has been accomplished—much remains to be accomplished. With determination, we can now strengthen the foundation of individual economic stability. With courage, we can eliminate restrictions on trade and investment, in recognition of our interdependence. With patience, we can work together and find the proper balance of opportunity and responsibility for rich and poor alike that is essential in today's world. . . .

Food and Energy

Accorded only a passing mention in Secretary Simon's review were two global economic problems that had occasioned acute anxieties within the recent past and, if current indications could be believed, might do so again before many years had passed.

For the moment, interest in the world food problem had markedly subsided as the sporadic famines of the early 1970s, and the World Food Conference held in Rome in 1974,[153] receded into history. World agricultural output gained over a broad front in 1976, as an 8.2 percent increase in world grain production made possible an anticipated 40-million-ton addition to world grain stocks in the 1976-77 marketing year—at the same time adding to farmers' woes by bringing about a sharp decline in prices of wheat and coarse grains. Discussion of a U.S. proposal for an international system of nationally held grain reserves continued in the International Wheat Council, but in a desultory atmosphere that only too obviously reflected the abatement of any general sense of urgency. One positive occurrence was the opening for signature in late December of the agreement establishing the U.N. International Fund for Agricultural Development (IFAD), to which the United States had promised to contribute $200 million out of total pledges exceeding $1 billion.[154] Its primary purpose would be the encouragement of increased food output in developing countries.

In energy matters, too, the sense of urgency had waned in most of the industrialized consumer nations in a year when consumption increased, conservation lagged, and OPEC imposed still another increase in the export price of crude petroleum. Although the decreasing oil consumption patterns of 1974-75 were reversed throughout the non-Communist world in 1976, it was the United

[153]*AFR, 1974:* 427-42.
[154]*UN Monthly Chronicle*, Jan. 1977: 44.

States that most spectacularly disregarded its own advice by importing no less than 21 percent more oil in the first half of 1976 than in the corresponding period of 1975. Inevitably, such a performance cast some doubt on the potentialities of the new, 19-nation International Energy Agency (IEA), a U.S. brain child which, as noted earlier, had developed elaborate plans for oil stockpiling and emergency allocation, cooperation to reduce dependence on imported oil, and strategy for the North-South dialogue. A further disappointment for the Ford administration was the failure of Congress to act upon the $25 billion OECD "safety net" or Financial Support Fund, which, as already observed, had been proposed by Secretary Kissinger and had since been accepted by numerous OECD members.[155]

The frailty of existing energy arrangements was further dramatized by the action of the OPEC states in decreeing yet another increase in world oil prices at a meeting held in Doha, Qatar, in December 1976. The fact that this action was less than unanimous may have given comfort to those in the United States who had considered "breaking up the oil cartel" to be one of the supreme aims of U.S. policy. But there was no blinking the fact that the United States and the other consuming countries would be paying more for their oil in the future. Eleven of OPEC's thirteen members, accounting for two-thirds of the group's production, decided to raise the "participation" or "buyback" price by 10 percent—from $11.51 to $12.70 per barrel—on January 1, 1977 and by another 5 percent—to $13.30—on July 1, 1977. (These prices compared with $2.33 per barrel in January 1973.) Saudi Arabia, the largest single producer, and the United Arab Emirates decided, however, to limit themselves to a single 5 percent increase which would bring their price to $12.085 per barrel as from January 1.

"A course which can only be termed irresponsible," was President Ford's judgment of the action of the OPEC majority—an action that signally failed, in his opinion, to meet the elementary requirement "that nations avoid actions which harm one another." This latest price increase, said the President, "can only serve as a sharp reminder for all Americans of the need to take urgent action to strengthen our conservation efforts and develop new sources of energy in order to reduce our dependence. And it must serve as a reminder to all oil-consuming nations of the need to work closely together to reduce our reliance on imported oil and our vulnerability to arbitrary OPEC decisions."[156] These were strong words that would soon be echoed by Mr. Ford's successor.

---

[155] Cf. notes 145-6.
[156] *Presidential Documents*, 12: 1720-21 (*Bulletin*, 76: 67).

9. CALMER WEATHER AT THE UNITED NATIONS

That the concerns of U.S. foreign policy were constantly expanding and diversifying was no longer news in 1976. Recent experience with matters as heterogeneous as the environment, hijacking and terrorism, the drug problem, outer space, multinational corporations, food and energy, human rights, and population growth bore witness to the comprehensive scope of what President Nixon, earlier in the decade, had called the "New Dimensions of Diplomacy."[157] In the meantime, a proliferation of new states endowed with at least the formal attributes of national sovereignty had complicated the day-to-day management of world affairs; while the political and ideological obsessions affecting many members of the world community had accentuated the polemical side of international life in a way that sometimes interfered with the handling of even the most technical and supposedly noncontroversial issues.

These tendencies had naturally found their fullest expression in the United Nations organization and in some of its specialized and related agencies. With a membership that stood at 144 at the beginning of 1976 and had increased to 147 by its end, the United Nations by this time encompassed all but a handful of the world's sovereign governments. Apart from Switzerland, which had never sought U.N. membership, the principal remaining absentees in 1976 were the two Koreas, the Republic of China on Taiwan (ousted in 1971 to make room for the Communist People's Republic of China), and the newly reunified Socialist Republic of Vietnam, whose application for membership, as already noted, was blocked by a U.S. veto in the Security Council on November 15. (As noted earlier, the United States also vetoed Angola's membership bid in June, but subsequently relented and enabled that country to become a U.N. member during the autumn session of the General Assembly.)

A "Time of Turbulence"

As it approached its longstanding goal of universality, the United Nations had not become more hospitable toward differences of political and social outlook among its members. On the contrary, the increasing preponderance of newly emancipated and incompletely developed states in Asia, Africa, and, in many instances, Latin America, had swelled the chorus of "third world" voices to a Niagara-like roar which, though reasonably consonant with the aims of the Communist countries, threatened to obliterate

[157]Cf. *AFR, 1971:* 532-43.

entirely the voices of the United States and other representatives of the Western democratic tradition. In the Security Council, the United States was still protected by the veto against the possibility of intemperate actions sparked by third world emotions; and the records of the Security Council testified to a growing American willingness to invoke a procedure that had formerly been thought of as one that should be utilized only in cases of extreme necessity. But in the General Assembly and other U.N. bodies governed by majority rule, the U.S. delegation was by now accustomed to being outvoted by a crushing majority of third world and Communist states.

One of the more contentious issues between the United States and the Communist-third world majority had been resolved in 1971 with the decision of the General Assembly to seat the representatives of Communist China and oust the delegation from the Republic of China on Taiwan.[158] But the handling of other questions had continued to highlight the difficult forensic plight of the United States and its friends. The year 1974 had been made especially memorable by such developments as the adoption of the "Declaration and Programme of Action on the Establishment of a New International Economic Order" and the "Charter of Economic Rights and Duties of States,"[159] the exclusion of South Africa from participation in the General Assembly,[160] and the admission of the Palestine Liberation Organization (PLO) to observer status in the Assembly and in international conferences convened under its auspices.[161] All of these actions had been taken against most vigorous American opposition.

There had, of course, been more harmonious developments, among them the narrowing of the gap on "third world" economic issues that had taken place at the Seventh Special Session of the General Assembly in September 1975.[162] But that felicitous interlude had been immediately followed by the "high contention" of the 30th Regular Session, at which, in the words of Samuel W. Lewis, Assistant Secretary of State for International Organization Affairs, "the United States and some of its friends, particularly Israel, seemed to take it on the chin."[163] For many Americans, the ultimate obscenity had been the General Assembly's action of November 10, 1975 in declaring, by a vote of 72 to 35 with 32

[158]Same: 500-514.
[159]Same, *1974:* 103-7 and 528-41.
[160]Same: 391-406.
[161]Same: 415-22.
[162]Same, *1975:* 417-46.
[163]Document 33.

abstentions, that Zionism—the movement for the return of Jews to Palestine—was "a form of racism and racial discrimination."[164]

It was indeed a "time of turbulence" in the relationship between the United States and the United Nations, as Assistant Secretary Lewis later observed in a review of U.N. developments before the Senate Foreign Relations Committee (Document 33). American opinion, moreover, had been still further scandalized by the trend in some of the U.N. specialized agencies. Particularly resented had been the anti-Israeli actions voted by the Eighteenth General Conference of UNESCO, the U.N. Educational, Scientific and Cultural Organization, in Paris in the fall of 1974. Their consequence had been a congressional ban on further U.S. financial support for UNESCO until such time as that organization should return to its assigned objectives and "correct its recent actions of a primarily political character."[165]

American dissatisfaction with the International Labour Organisation (ILO) was of a more fundamental kind, the natural consequence of an organizational setup that equated the state-dominated labor organizations of the Communist countries with the free labor unions of the West. But a grant of observer status to the PLO in 1975 had deepened U.S. discontent, and Secretary Kissinger had given formal notice on November 5, 1975 that in view of the organization's increasing "politicization" and deviation from basic principles, the United States intended to withdraw from membership at the end of the prescribed two-year waiting period.[166]

Closely related to the rift between the United States and the third world-Communist majority were the controversies that had boiled up around the person of Ambassador Daniel Patrick Moynihan, U.S. Representative to the United Nations from mid-1975 until his resignation on January 31, 1976. In an official cablegram obtained by the New York Times and published a few days before his departure from office,[167] Ambassador Moynihan bewailed what he described as the failure of the State Department to support more fully his efforts "toward a basic foreign policy goal, that of breaking up the massive blocs of nations, mostly new nations, which for so long have been arrayed against us in international forums and in diplomatic encounters generally."

Acting on the direct instructions of the President and the Secretary of State, Ambassador Moynihan asserted, his mission had initiated a new tactic at the United Nations by undertaking "to

[164]Resolution 3379 (XXX), in AFR, 1975: 507-8. For official use of the term "obscene act" cf. same: 8.
[165]AFR, 1974: 422-3 and 575.
[166]Same, 1975: 418.
[167]Text in New York Times, Jan. 28, 1976.

respond to attack by counterattack"—a procedure which, he claimed, had presented such a contrast to established custom "that our counterattacks made it look like all hell was breaking loose up here." Nevertheless, the Ambassador contended, there was evidence that other governments were "beginning to think that anti-American postures at the U.N. and elsewhere are not without cost and that the cost has to be calculated." Such successes, he implied, would be more readily appreciated but for the existence within the Department of State of what he described as "a large faction which has an interest in our performance being judged to have failed."

Although such statements were naturally given no direct endorsement by President Ford or Secretary Kissinger, both of the latter professed to expect that Mr. Moynihan's successor, former Pennsylvania Governor William W. Scranton, would operate along essentially similar lines. "Bill Scranton has a big job to do," the President remarked in announcing his appointment on February 25. In an obvious effort to spare the feelings of the outgoing U.S. Representative, Mr. Ford continued:

We have great responsibilities in the United Nations. We are stronger there today. Starting with the Secretary's speech to the Seventh Special Session of the United Nations last fall,[168] where we, I think, made great progress with the underdeveloped countries and, of course, the policy of standing up for the United States against some of these unfair attacks—the actions of Ambassador Moynihan—I think, have been good from the point of view of the United States.[169]

Ambassador Scranton, who would later be remembered as one of the more conciliatory holders of the U.N. post, readily concurred. "It will be a very difficult job," he agreed.

I think everybody is aware that the United States is being attacked in the UN a great deal. I am a Pat Moynihan fan, and I was delighted with the way he handled it. And I had a long talk with him yesterday in New York. I think we are on the upbend in the United Nations, primarily due to the policy of the President and the Secretary and the activity of Ambassador Moynihan. And I am proud and happy to be his successor and be the delegate from the President of the United States.[170]

[168]*AFR, 1975:* 419-46.
[169]*Presidential Documents*, 12: 280.
[170]Same.

A U.N. Panorama

Such polemical notes were absent from the review of U.N. affairs which Assistant Secretary Lewis presented to the Senate Foreign Relations Committee in the course of its hearings on the Scranton nomination **(Document 33)**. Mr. Lewis' more immediate concern was to combat the negative impressions of the United Nations that had arisen from recent experience, and to encourage a more balanced view in which the usefulness—indeed, the indispensability—of the world organization would be as fully recognized as its shortcomings. Admittedly, "serious questions" had been raised "in the minds of many Americans about the United Nations itself and about the utility of U.S. participation in its work"; but many Americans, Mr. Lewis asserted, also understood "that global cooperation is more than ever essential to meet inescapable global problems," and that in assessing the role of the United States in the United Nations it was necessary to "take into account not merely the issues of the moment but our fundamental interests and the basic ideals of the American people."

Judged from this angle, the Assistant Secretary implied, the United Nations still offered essential advantages to the United States as well as to other member countries. In the area of international peace and security, it had made and was still making vital contributions to the maintenance of peace in the Middle East and elsewhere; while there were any number of outstanding achievements to illustrate its importance in the field of international economic and social cooperation. Even the General Assembly, the scene of most of the "parliamentary abuses" and "irresponsible actions" of recent times, had—he pointed out—played a necessary supporting role not only in the financing of peacekeeping operations but in the conduct of U.N. efforts relating to international drug control, the law of the sea, population activities, the environment, international food problems, disaster relief, and the promotion of disarmament agreements.

"We have recently experienced a serious low point," Mr. Lewis admitted. "But we have also experienced some points that are very high indeed." Though some had advocated outright withdrawal from the United Nations—or, at least, a cessation of U.S. participation in the General Assembly or a punitive reduction in U.S. financial contributions—Assistant Secretary Lewis insisted that success was achieved "not by withdrawing but by participating—by staying and fighting for what we know to be right."

That, Mr. Lewis emphasized, was what the administration intended to do: "to continue to support in an effective, vigorous, and tough-minded way all of those programs in the United Nations which offer benefits to the American people," while continuing "selectively to refuse to participate in U.N. activities which we believe are fundamentally unsound or grossly irresponsible." This latter category, the Assistant Secretary confirmed, included the 1973-83 "Decade for Action to Combat Racism and Racial Discrimination," the program which had given rise to the Assembly's anti-Zionist resolution.

Tempest over "Habitat"

Assistant Secretary Lewis spoke too early in the year to catalog the major U.N. developments of 1976, which would later be surveyed in an official book-length report released by President Carter on November 1, 1977.[171] "In sum," Mr. Carter was to state in a covering message to the Congress, "the report portrays an active year during which our country worked hard with others in the UN to advance the causes of peace, economic progress, and justice."[172]

Many of the more dramatic episodes of the period took place in the Security Council, especially in its deliberations on the Middle East and Southern Africa, and have been mentioned earlier in this introductory survey. There were also a number of specialized international meetings which—like the earlier U.N. conferences on the environment, population, food, and the International Women's Year—would be remembered as milestones in the evolving relationship between industrial and developing nations. One such conclave, the Fourth Ministerial Session of the U.N. Conference on Trade and Development (UNCTAD-IV) in Nairobi, has already been mentioned as the scene of an important U.S. overture in the area of international economic policy. More specialized in focus, and even more "ideological" in temper, was "Habitat," otherwise known as the U.N. Conference on Human Settlements, which was held at Vancouver on May 31-June 11 with the participation of 134 countries and numerous specialized organizations and national liberation movements.

Nominally convened with the objective of promoting a broad exchange of information about solutions to problems of human settlements, "Habitat" was promptly seized upon by representatives of less developed countries as one more opportunity to vent their grievances against the more advanced nations—and, in addition, to renew their attacks upon such favorite political targets as Israel. These manifestations were visibly disconcerting to the U.S. delegation, which was headed by Carla A. Hills, the Secretary of

---

[171]*U.S. Participation in the UN: Report by the President to the Congress for the Year 1976* (Department of State Publication 8916; Washington: GPO, 1977). The report was distributed too late for use in preparing the present text.

[172]Transmittal message, Nov. 1, 1977, in *Presidential Documents,* 13: 1704.

Housing and Urban Development, with Russell W. Peterson, Chairman of the Council on Environmental Quality, as her alternate.

Particularly painful to the United States and some other countries in the Western tradition was the inclusion in the conference's final document, the "Vancouver Declaration on Human Settlements, 1976,"[173] of an indirect but unmistakable endorsement of the General Assembly's anti-Zionist resolution. This harping on political issues essentially extraneous to the substantive work of the conference, Mr. Peterson warned in a concluding statement, "does not bode well for my country's support and participation in future U.N. conferences concerned with substantive global problems demanding international attention." Only several months later would the Department of State make public a broader evaluation that stressed the positive as well as the negative aspects of the Vancouver experience.[174]

The Law of the Sea Negotiations

Of much more critical concern to the American government was the lagging progress of the Third United Nations Conference on the Law of the Sea, at which some 150 nations had been attempting since 1973 to establish a legal regime for the ocean spaces that cover 70 percent of the earth's surface and contribute in manifold ways to the life of every individual on the planet. No nation could be more interested than the United States in the integrity of an element so vital from the standpoint of communications, trade, resources, strategy, and ecology. Nor could any nation be more intensely aware that failing some form of regulation by international agreement, individual nations would attempt to protect their interests by unilateral actions which would, in many cases, predictably traduce the interests of the international community as a whole.

The United States itself, by 1976, was beginning to respond to what had already come to be recognized as a growing trend toward unilateral preemption of various forms of oceanic rights. Ignoring administration pleas to await the actions of the U.N. conference, Congress determined in the Fishery Conservation and Management Act of 1976[175] that the United States should hold exclusive fishing

[173]Text, adopted by a vote of 89-15 (U.S.)-10, in *Report of Habitat: United Nations Conference on Human Settlements* (U.N. Document A/CONF. 70/15; U.N. Sales No. E.76/IV.7; New York: United Nations, 1976): 2-9.

[174]Stanley D. Schiff, "The U.N. Conference on Human Settlements (Habitat), May-June 1976," *Bulletin*, 75: 461-6.

[175]Public Law 94-265, Apr. 13, 1976; presidential signature statement in *Presidential Documents*, 12: 644.

rights beginning March 1, 1977 in a 200-mile-wide fishery conservation zone extending outward from all its coasts and encompassing approximately one-tenth of the world's traditional fish resources. Likewise in prospect was the early commencement by American mining interests of operations directed toward exploiting the manganese and other mineral resources of the deep seabed. "Our country cannot delay in its efforts to develop an assured supply of critical resources through our deep seabed mining projects," Secretary Kissinger pointed out on April 8 in a New York address devoted to the issues confronting the Law of the Sea Conference:[176]

> We strongly prefer an international agreement to provide a stable legal environment before such development begins, one that insures that all resources are managed for the good of the global community and that all can participate. But if agreement is not reached this year, it will be increasingly difficult to resist pressure to proceed unilaterally.

That the Conference on the Law of the Sea had by 1976 arrived at a critical stage was generally recognized by participants in its fourth session, held in New York on March 15-May 17, with H.S. Amerasinghe of Sri Lanka continuing as its President and with Ambassador at Large T. Vincent Learson heading the U.S. delegation.[177] On some important points, the previous negotiating sessions at Caracas in 1974 and at Geneva in 1975 had resulted in at least a broad, general consensus, if not yet in definite agreement. Among them were the delimitation of a twelve-mile-wide territorial sea, with free transit through and over straits used for international navigation, and of a 200-mile-wide economic zone in which coastal states would have special though not exclusive rights; likewise, a definition of rights and responsibilities in exploiting the resources of the continental margin at distances over 200 miles from the coast; and measures to protect the marine environment. Major issues still awaiting resolution had to do mainly with the regulation of marine scientific research, the settlement of disputes, and, most difficult of all, the exploitation of the mineral resources of the deep seabed.

Even more than the other issues before the conference, the question of seabed resources and their exploitation had given rise to a typical confrontation between developed and developing countries, one in which the former (especially the United States) possessed the capital and technology for seabed exploitation, while

[176]*Bulletin*, 74: 533-42.
[177]For background cf. *AFR, 1973:* 581-2; same, *1974:* 315-26; same, *1975:* 141-8 and 373-80.

the latter group brought to the issue an ideological fervor and a demand for special consideration that had thus far precluded any agreement. For the developing countries, the resources of the deep seabed were literally the "common heritage of mankind," and, as such, should be exploited for the benefit of those in need rather than for private profit. The United States, on the other hand, pointed out with equal insistence that if private profit were eliminated, there would be no one to do the job at all. Continued failure to reach agreement on this and other pending matters, Dr. Kissinger warned in his April 8 speech, would throw away the conference's opportunity "to devise the first truly global solution to a global problem," and could inaugurate "an era of unrestrained commercial rivalry, mounting political turmoil, and eventually military conflict."

In an attempt to avoid such consequences—and, if possible, promote agreement on a treaty before the end of 1976—Secretary Kissinger took the opportunity of his April 8 speech to present a bulky "package" of new proposals, encompassing the totality of the unagreed issues and openly directed toward accommodating the wishes of the less advanced countries in so far as these were found compatible with the basic interests of the United States. Especially noted was his proposal that the seabeds be opened to a system of "dual access" or parallel exploitation whereby certain locations would be reserved for private exploitation while others would be earmarked for exploitation in the interest of the developing countries, either directly or through an international enterprise.

Secretary Kissinger's initiative did not, however, suffice to bring about the hoped-for general agreement at the spring session of the conference, where the main achievement was a revision—unsatisfactory to the United States in many particulars—of the "informal single negotiating text" that had previously been prepared by Ambassador Amerasinghe and the chairmen of the conference's three main committees.[178] Nor did any full agreement emerge from a further (fifth) session that took place in New York from August 2 to September 17 and resulted in a decision to schedule still another seven- to eight-week session beginning May 23, 1977.

Secretary Kissinger was personally much in evidence at the summer session of the conference, at which he lobbied actively for agreement while there was still time and put forward a number of refinements of earlier proposals in an attempt to make them more widely palatable. Concerning the deep seabeds, for example, he advanced a number of new ideas for financial and technological

[178]U.N. Document A/CONF/WP.8/Rev.1/Parts I-III and WP.9/Rev.1. For details cf. *UN Monthly Chronicle*, June 1976: 23-4 and *Bulletin*, 74: 764-7.

assistance to the proposed international enterprise, as well as periodic reviews of the system's efficacy.[179] But while a number of delegations expressed interest in this approach, the Secretary later reported, "some delegations chose tactics of confrontation"—tactics which, he warned, "cannot work and will inevitably lead to deadlock and unilateral action."

"I continue to believe that a law of the sea convention can be achieved," the Secretary of State affirmed in an official review made public as the summer session concluded on September 17 **(Document 34)**. "The United States will seek to build on the progress made to date and will continue its intensive efforts to achieve a treaty." At the same time, Dr. Kissinger warned, "we will continue vigorously to safeguard essential American interests. We will work cooperatively with other nations, but we expect a reciprocal attitude of good will and reasonableness. There are limits beyond which the United States will not go, and we are close to such limits now."

The 31st General Assembly

Secretary Kissinger returned to this theme in his major address of September 30 to the General Assembly, whose 31st Regular Session had convened a few days earlier and elected Ambassador Amerasinghe as its President. "The United States," the Secretary of State declared **(Document 35a)**, "believes that this 31st General Assembly must free itself of the ideological and confrontational tactics that marked some of its predecessors and dedicate itself to a program of common action. . . . Today there is no single crisis to conquer. There is instead a persisting challenge of staggering complexity—the need to create a universal community based on cooperation, peace, and justice."

Twelve weeks later, when the Assembly suspended its 31st Session after having admitted three new members to the United Nations (Seychelles, Angola, and Western Samoa), adopted 245 resolutions, and appointed Austria's Kurt Waldheim to a second five-year term as Secretary-General, it could be generally agreed that Dr. Kissinger's hopes for a diminution of the "confrontational" emphasis had been largely realized. "In contrast with the last General Assembly," Ambassador Scranton observed as he addressed the closing plenary session **(Document 35b)**, "this session has had a lessening of confrontation. Some significant changes in the world situation combined with a more mature tone

---

[179]Remarks of Sept. 1, in *Bulletin*, 75: 395-9; additional details in same, 327-8 and 333-6; and *UN Monthly Chronicle*, Oct. 1976: 22-5.

here to alter the atmosphere for the better. A small but perceptible change of mood took place. The U.N.'s cup, last year half empty, this year became half full.''

Ambassador Scranton's caution that there was ''no reason for euphoria'' was thoroughly borne out by the detailed records of the session, which—apart from a few positive actions like the approval of the Environmental Warfare Convention—consisted for the most part of the reiteration of familiar positions and the repetition of familiar voting patterns. Especially disappointing to the United States was the lack of more effective action for the protection of human rights and for the combating of international terrorism, a field in which the Assembly's only concrete action was a decision, pursuant to a West German initiative, to establish a 35-nation Ad Hoc Committee on the Drafting of an International Convention against the Taking of Hostages.[180] As regards other prime U.N. responsibilities, however—and notably those relating to peacekeeping and to economic development—Ambassador Scranton found reason to be encouraged ''not only by the demands on the United Nations but by its response, even though it is limited.''

Additional grounds for encouragement might be discovered in the record of UNESCO's Nineteenth General Conference, which had been meeting in Nairobi from October 26 to November 30 while the General Assembly was being held in New York. Here, too, there had been evidence of a trend toward ''conciliation and consensus'' that was all the more noteworthy after the ''bitter confrontation on political subjects, particularly on issues relating to Israel,'' that had marked the previous session in 1974. Fears that the United States might continue its financial nonsupport of UNESCO, or even withdraw from the organization, had abated after the Conference approved a recommendation that would enable Israel to participate in the European program group, a right denied it in 1974. Although the Nairobi conference once again adopted resolutions condemning Israeli educational and archaeological policies in the occupied Arab territories, the outcome of the session could nevertheless be judged ''generally favorable'' from a Western point of view. Credit for this result could be attributed in large measure to ''the desire of most delegations to avoid open confrontation and work towards consensus,'' and to ''the moderating influence of the Director-General, Mr. Amadou-Mahtar M'Bow and other Africans who sought to make a success of the first UNESCO General Conference held on African soil.''[181]

[180]Resolution 31/103, adopted Dec. 15, 1976 by consensus.
[181]*Australian Foreign Affairs Record* (Canberra), 48: 73-5 (Feb. 1977).

10. FOREIGN POLICY AND PRESIDENTIAL POLITICS

There is perhaps more truism than truth in the assertion that American foreign policy is doomed to stagnate whenever the rhythm of government requires the choice of a President and Vice-President. Foreign nations, it is claimed, are too much in doubt about America's future course to take important decisions on their own responsibility. The United States, in turn, is supposedly too obsessed with its electoral campaign to burden its mind with overseas matters.

The experience of 1976 affords a measure of disproof of these assertions, at least as they apply to the conduct of American foreign policy under President Ford and Secretary of State Kissinger. The fact that the former Harvard professor was himself subjected to political attack from various directions during the 1976 campaign appeared to prejudice neither his intellectual leadership of the official foreign policy community nor his penchant for initiating novel diplomatic ventures reminiscent of the breakthrough to China, the Vietnam peace negotiations, and the Sinai and Golan disengagement agreements. If little follow-up to those particular endeavors was possible under the conditions obtaining in 1976, Southern Africa, in contrast, presented American foreign policy with a challenge as urgent as it was novel. The principal American initiatives in this area, moreover, occurred precisely during the tense and climactic months when President Ford and Ronald Reagan were battling for the Republican nomination and when Democrat Jimmy Carter, in a series of remarkable primary victories, was eliminating such better-known rivals as Henry M. Jackson, George Wallace, Frank Church, Edmund G. Brown, and Morris K. Udall.

Carter vs. Kissinger

Apart from President Ford and Senator Jackson, none of the leading candidates had been particularly identified with foreign affairs before the beginning of 1976. It was only natural, therefore, that an aspirant who desired to establish credentials in this area should try to define his position by contrasting it with that of Secretary Kissinger, the fountainhead and incarnation of recent American foreign policy. Senator Jackson's differences with the Secretary of State, over SALT and over Soviet trade and emigration policy, were already well known and had been echoed in varying degrees by candidates as unlike as Governors Reagan, Wallace, and Carter. Attacked on one hand for naïve credulity and excessive leniency toward the Russians, the Secretary of State was denigrated at one and the same time as a Metternichean patron of global reaction, the Bismarckian practitioner of a ruthless *Realpolitik*, and, in Governor Carter's celebrated phrase, the exponent of a secretive, "Lone Ranger" system of diplomatic spectaculars which the former Georgia Governor appeared to find as Machiavellian in inspiration as it was deficient in substance.[182]

Described by one campaign observer as sounding "more anti-Kissinger than pro-anything,"[183] Governor Carter from an early stage evinced his disagreement with the Secretary of State on matters of content as well as style. In language that frequently recalled the unsuccessful presidential campaign of Senator George McGovern in 1972,[184] the Georgian candidate inveighed against the balance-of-power concept, denounced America's alleged neglect of its allies and indifference toward developing nations, and castigated what he characterized as an excessive preoccupation with military strength to the neglect of other values. By early May, Governor Carter was telling Dean E. Fischer of *Time* magazine that if he was elected he would withdraw American troops from South Korea in five to seven years, would reduce the American military presence in Western Europe and elsewhere, and believed the defense budget could be reduced by $7 billion by cutting waste and eliminating costly weapon systems like the B-1 bomber—proceeding at the same time, however, with the construction of Trident missile-carrying submarines and other naval vessels.[185]

Further refined and elaborated in a June 23 address to the Foreign Policy Association in New York,[186] Governor Carter's views were clearly reflected in the foreign policy plank that was being drafted by former Ambassador Moynihan and others in the knowledge that the Georgian was already assured of the nomination when the Democratic National Convention met in New York in mid-July. Moderate if partisan in tone, the platform's foreign policy sections **(Document 36)** reaffirmed the high-minded objectives of U.S. foreign policy while promising its liberation from the deplorable imperfections that had allegedly marred its conduct by Republican administrations. Again, a $5 to $7 billion reduction in defense spending and a phased withdrawal of U.S. ground forces from South Korea were prominent among the

[182]E.g., address to the Foreign Policy Association, New York, June 23, in *New York Times*, June 24, 1976. This discussion owes much to B.K. Shrivastava, "Foreign Policy Issues in the 1976 US Presidential Election," *Foreign Affairs Reports* (New Delhi: Indian Council of World Affairs), 26: 62-83 (Mar. 1977).

[183]Same: 67.

[184]*AFR, 1972:* 26-8, 34-7 and 264-71.

[185]*Time*, May 10, 1976, quoted in Shrivastava, *loc. cit.:* 68-9.

[186]*New York Times*, June 24, 1976.

specific objectives mentioned. Noticeable both here and in the Carter address of June 23 was a strengthened emphasis on the need for a restoration of morality and moral purpose in American foreign policy, the promotion of human rights, and the denial of economic and military aid to dictatorial regimes.

Ford vs. Reagan

Apart from the call for reduced defense spending and the occasionally savage disparagement of the Republican foreign policy performance, the Democratic platform represented less of a departure from established policy than might have been expected. What it put forward, in most respects, was a restatement of precisely those bipartisan principles and policies for which administrations of both parties had labored in alternation through most of the postwar period. Although it unquestionably tended to minimize the importance of military strength and to accord unusual prominence to humanitarian and ethical values, the platform's qualified and balanced language seemed to recognize that both factors—the ethical and the military—were rooted in the heart of American foreign policy.

President Ford's political achievement of 1976 lay not so much in any refutation of Democratic foreign policy doctrine as in his successful defense of this essentially bipartisan heritage against a determined challenge from within his own party. Long celebrated as one of the perennial aspirants to the Republican nomination, Governor Reagan had emerged by the fall of 1975 as the recognized favorite of most of those right-wing elements who sought to limit the role of government at home while insisting on an uncompromising, maximalist posture in relations with the outside world. To a nation still experiencing the aftereffects of Watergate and Vietnam, and patently disinclined to continue the heavy international involvement of the preceding period, Reagan offered a simplified world picture in which American military strength and self-assertiveness were made to appear as the only effective formula for national salvation, whether the point at issue had to do with "standing up to" the Russians or holding on to the Canal Zone.

Though there were elements of this approach in President Ford's own thinking, the Reagan philosophy in its essentials (like the somewhat similar position espoused by Governor Wallace on the Democratic side) was almost as antithetic to the Nixon-Ford-Kissinger world outlook as it was to the position being developed by Governor Carter—who also seemed in his own way to be offering an attractive alternative to the experience of recent years.

In resisting such isolationist and/or hypernationalist trends, President Ford displayed increasing readiness to sacrifice at least the trappings of established policy in order to preserve as much as possible of the substance. A salient instance was his abandonment of the term "détente" even as he continued to defend the policy's aims and methods. It is true that the President did not abandon Secretary Kissinger in even a symbolic sense, at one time going so fas as to declare him "one of the greatest Secretaries of State in the history of the United States." But the President also made an obvious effort to convey the impression that the leadership in foreign policy was his and no one else's.

Despite the President's efforts, the possibility of a Reagan nomination remained very much alive as late as August 16, when the Republican National Convention was called to order in Kansas City. The influence of the former California Governor had already been strongly felt in the committee charged with drafting the Republican campaign platform, whose foreign policy sections **(Document 37a)** abounded with such Reaganisms as "Military strength is the path to peace," and "A sound foreign policy must be rooted in a superior defense capability, and both must be perceived as a deterrent to aggression and supportive of our national interests."

But even these vigorous affirmations had not sufficed to satisfy the Reagan forces. Failing to impose the totality of their views upon the platform committee, Governor Reagan's supporters had adopted the tactic of submitting to the full convention a specially drafted platform amendment whose title, "Morality in Foreign Policy," implied without much subtlety that morality had been a neglected value under the Ford-Kissinger regime—the very charge the Democrats had been making from their own quite different perspective. Invoking the anti-Soviet message of Aleksandr Solzhenitsyn (whom President Ford had neglected to invite to the White House the year before), this draft amendment **(Document 37b)** lashed out at détente, at the Helsinki Final Act of 1975, and at "secret agreements, hidden from our people," such as Secretary Kissinger was supposed to specialize in. Reluctant to precipitate a floor fight, President Ford chose not to oppose this statement, which was adopted by voice vote of the convention early on August 18.

The President none the less retained sufficient delegate strength to scrape a narrow victory over the man in whose interest the amendment had been formulated. The final vote on the first ballot, decided early on August 19, was 1,187 for Ford to 1,070 for Reagan. In thus eliminating the Reagan candidacy, the convention automatically eliminated the possibility of a fundamental foreign policy challenge and ensured that the presidential contenders on both sides would remain faithful to the essentials of the bipartisan tradition. So far as international affairs were concerned, the campaign seemed likely to hinge rather less on matters of principle than on the contrast between President Ford, portrayed as the experienced national and world leader, and the self-proclaimed "outsider" from the Deep South who might initially be presumed to know no more of foreign policy than his advisers chose to tell him.

Ford vs. Congress

The months of President Ford's tenacious battle to win the Republican nomination had also been a time of unremitting struggle with the Congress in whose ranks the Chief Executive had passed the greater part of his own political life. Mr. Ford, in this election year, had been compelled to operate with much less than 100 percent congressional support for his endeavors both at home and abroad. "Few Congresses," he declared four weeks before the November election, "have been presented with such a clear challenge to deal forthrightly with the Nation's problems than the Congress that has just adjourned—and few Congresses have fallen so short of meeting the challenge."[187] Although the President referred primarily to the performance of the Democratic-controlled Congress in dealing with fiscal, energy, and social welfare matters, the same complaint could easily have been documented by reference to Congressional actions and omissions in the field of foreign, defense, and international economic policy.

Examples of congressional refusal to submit to administration guidance in the international area are almost too numerous for separate mention.[188] Some, like the refusal of funds for Angola early in the year, were clothed by the administration in hues of deepest tragedy; others were described merely as regrettably perverse. An example of the latter kind was the enactment of the Fishery Conservation and Management Act, establishing a 200-mile fishing zone without waiting for action at the Law of the Sea Conference.[189] In May, Congress in a somewhat similar action gave evidence of its mistrust of Soviet policies in the field of détente and human rights—and also, perhaps, its doubts about the administration's readiness to hold the U.S.S.R. to its commitments—by insisting, despite official coolness, on the establishment of a joint congressional-executive Commission on Security and

---

[187]Statement of October 5, in *Presidential Documents*, 12: 1443.

[188]For details see especially U.S. Senate, 94th Cong., 1st sess., Committee on Foreign Relations, *Legislative Activities Report of the Committee on Foreign Relations, United States Senate; Ninety-fourth Congress, January 14, 1975-October 1, 1976* (Senate Report 95-21; Washington: GPO, 1977).

[189]Public Law 94-265, Apr. 13; signature statement in *Presidential Documents*, 12: 644.

Cooperation in Europe to monitor the actions of governments signatory to the Final Act of the Helsinki Conference.[190]

The 1976 congressional session witnessed the usual legislative-executive clashes on foreign aid and military policy. In May, the President went so far as to veto an authorization bill for "security assistance" for the ongoing fiscal period because of what he termed "fundamental constitutional problems" and "unwise restrictions that would seriously inhibit my ability to implement a coherent foreign policy."[191] A substitute measure, authorizing $6.96 billion in military and security assistance to Israel and other countries over the 27-month period ending September 30, 1977, was signed June 30, not without sharp presidential criticism of its remaining restrictions and limitations.[192]

Many of these restrictions reflected the persistent congressional misgivings about the whole subject of foreign military aid and overseas arms sales, particularly to countries whose observance of human rights was open to criticism. Such controversies played a somewhat less prominent role in the consideration of the Foreign Assistance and Related Programs Appropriations Act, 1976, which was also signed June 30 and appropriated $5.94 billion in economic and military assistance—much of it for the Middle East—for the fifteen-month period ending September 30, 1976.[193] Three months later, Congress passed and the President signed a second foreign aid appropriation bill providing a total of $5.13 billion for the fiscal year 1977, over half of this amount being allocated to Israel and other Middle Eastern countries.[194]

On military policy, too, Congress of late years had developed a habit of challenging administration judgments and, in many cases, scaling down administration programs, occasionally substituting alternative projects for which the administration had little use. President Ford's expressed determination to bring about "a significant increase in military spending for 1977" was nevertheless respected in its essentials in the $32.5 billion military procurement bill that Congress passed at the beginning of July;[195] and tenacious

[190]Public Law 94-304, June 3, 1976.

[191]Veto message on S. 2662, 94th Cong., May 7, in *Presidential Documents*, 12: 828-30.

[192]International Security Assistance and Arms Export Control Act of 1976 (Public Law 94-329, June 30, 1976); signature statement in *Presidential Documents*, 12: 1104-5 (*Bulletin*, 75: 198-200).

[193]Public Law 94-330, June 30, 1976; signature statement in *Presidential Documents*, 12: 1104 (*Bulletin*, 75: 199-200).

[194]Foreign Assistance and Related Programs Appropriation Act, 1977 (Public Law 94-441, Oct. 1, 1976).

[195]Department of Defense Appropriation Authorization Act, 1977 (Public Law 94-361, July 14, 1976); signature statement in *Presidential Documents*, 12: 1162-3.

efforts from within the Senate to delay the B-1 bomber program until a new administration took office were defeated in advance of final passage.

But though he commended Congress for its unusual promptness in passing this annual measure, President Ford in signing the legislation nevertheless complained of a failure to approve a number of essential programs, the addition of funds for unneeded programs, and the lack of congressional action on proposals for management economies. Similar complaints were to be heard in September when the President signed a $104.43 billion defense appropriation bill[196] that would help reverse the decline in real defense spending but, among other shortcomings cited by the President, would bypass an administration-supported shipbuilding program and would temporarily restrict B-1 expenditures to a mere $87 million a month. Thus a final decision on this controversial weapon system would after all be left to the next administration.

Not every piece of foreign affairs legislation considered during these months occasioned legislative-executive conflict. No serious controversies developed, for instance, around the request for congressional approval of the 1975 Covenant to Establish a Commonwealth of the Northern Mariana Islands, designed to provide the United States a permanent foothold in the Western Pacific;[197] of increased U.S. participation in the Inter-American Development Bank, and participation in the African Development Fund;[198] of the recently negotiated changes in the Articles of Agreement of the International Monetary Fund;[199] of the Act for the Prevention and Punishment of Crimes Against Internationally Protected Persons,[200] designed to give effect to the anti-terrorism conventions concluded in recent years' under the auspices of the Organization of American States and the United Nations; or of the Immigration and Nationality Act Amendments of 1976, which redistributed the annual immigration quota of 120,000 assigned to Western Hemisphere countries.[201]

In discharging its responsibilities in the treaty area, the Senate made no particular difficulty about approving the newly negotiated Treaty of Friendship and Cooperation with Spain, or the most

---

[196]Department of Defense Appropriation Act, 1977 (Public Law 94-419, Sept. 22, 1976); signature statement in same: 1365-6.

[197]Public Law 94-241, Mar. 24, 1976; signature statement in same: 482-3.

[198]Inter-American Bank Act (Public Law 94-302, May 31, 1976).

[199]Bretton Woods Agreements Act Amendments (Public Law 94-564, Oct. 19, 1976); signature statement in *Presidential Documents*, 12: 1547.

[200]Public Law 94-467, Oct. 8, 1976; signature statement in same: 1485-6.

[201]Public Law 94-571, Oct. 20, 1976; signature statement in same: 1548 (*Bulletin*, 75: 639).

recent International Coffee, Wheat, and Tin Agreements. It took no action, however, on the 28-year-old Convention on Genocide, the 1975 amendments to the Inter-American Treaty of Reciprocal Assistance, or the pending U.S.-Soviet treaties on the Limitation of Underground Nuclear Weapon Tests and on Underground Nuclear Explosions for Peaceful Purposes (which were not submitted for its consideration until July 29, 1976).[202]

More disappointing to the administration was the failure of Congress to authorize U.S. membership in the $25 billion OECD Financial Support Fund or "Safety Net," which seemed less necessary than when it had been proposed by Secretary Kissinger in 1974. Other matters remaining unresolved as the 94th Congress concluded its labors on October 1 had to do with compliance by U.S. firms with the Arab boycott of Israel, the problem of illegal corporate payments, and the pending authorization of a $50 million U.S. contribution to the Asian Development Fund.

Carter vs. Ford

Complaints about the Democratic-controlled Congress would obviously be repeated many times as President Ford plunged into the final battle with his Democratic opponent. It was to be a campaign devoid of oratorical triumphs for either contestant, with few if any of the inspiring, thought-provoking speeches that might have merited preservation in a collection such as this. What did distinguish the 1976 campaign was the series of televised, face-to-face "debates," originally suggested by President Ford, which brought the two candidates together on three occasions (with a fourth debate between the vice-presidential candidates, Republican Senator Robert J. Dole of Kansas and Democratic Senator Walter F. Mondale of Minnesota) to answer questions put to them by selected newspaper and radio-television correspondents.

It was the second of these debates, held in San Francisco on October 6, that offered the closest approximation to a comparative survey of the presidential candidates' foreign policy views. The verbatim transcript of the debate, as subsequently made public by the White House **(Document 38)**, affords an insight into the weaknesses as well as the strengths of the two contenders. In a discussion ranging over many areas and honeycombed with factual pitfalls, Governor Carter talked much about the need for leadership, principle, and truth to national character; President Ford, who saw these qualities as eminently characteristic of his own administration, preferred to stress the importance of experience

---

[202]Details in Senate Report 95-21 (cited in note 188): 20-31.

and the folly, as he saw it, of reducing defense expenditures as the Democrats proposed to do.

Most morning-after pundits agreed that Governor Carter had held a slight advantage in the foreign policy debate, thus redeeming a somewhat ineffective performance in an earlier debate on the national economy. In part, however, the advantage in the second debate was handed to him by the President's unaccountable slip in insisting, in indignant tones and with embarrassing reiteration, that "There is no Soviet domination of Eastern Europe, and there never will be under a Ford administration." This patently unfactual assertion, which outraged masses of American voters with ties to Eastern Europe, was later understood to have cost the President a good many votes in spite of a series of clarifying statments in which Mr. Ford explained that what he had meant to say was merely that the United States did not *acquiesce* in the Soviet domination of Eastern Europe.[203]

Governor Carter committed an infelicity of his own with reference to Eastern Europe when he was asked a few days later what action he would take in the event that an Eastern European country were to revolt against Soviet domination. "I don't know what I would do, but I wouldn't send American troops in," the Democratic candidate replied,[204] perhaps remembering the similar stand adopted by the Eisenhower administration in 1956 and the Johnson administration in 1968.

According to one version, a further question to Governor Carter about a possible Soviet attempt to reassert control over a post-Tito Yugoslavia elicited the response: "I would not go to war in Yugoslavia even if the Soviet Union sent in troops." Questioned about this statement in the course of the third Ford-Carter debate on October 22, the Governor insisted that his stand was the correct one and that such action by the U.S.S.R. was highly unlikely in any event. President Ford, for his part, limited himself to a moderate-sounding comment to the effect "that it's unwise for a President to signal in advance what options he might exercise if any international problem arose."[205] Secretary Kissinger, who thought it "important that the other side understand that pressure on Yugoslavia would have grave consequences for the relationship with the United States," reacted more strongly. If Governor Carter were elected, said the Secretary of State, he would presumably reconsider a statement that was "inconsistent with the entire postwar policy of every Democratic and Republican Ad-

[203]E.g., statement of Oct. 12, in *Presidential Documents*, 12: 1488-9.

[204]AP dispatch, Oct. 16, in *New York Times*, Oct. 17, 1977.

[205]*Presidential Documents*, 12: 1567-8.

ministration, incompatible with the views of our West European allies, and would be dangerous if it became American policy."[206]

Appearing on the "Face the Nation" television and radio program on October 24, Secretary Kissinger also produced what may well have been the best concise list of specific foreign policy differences between the Ford and Carter camps:

> We would have a difference in attitude toward Communist participation in the governments of Europe [he said]. We would have a difference with respect to arms sales to many countries, because our view would be that if we cannot be the world's policeman and if we cannot sell arms to threatened countries, then there is bound to be a vacuum that somebody is going to fill. There is a difference in the attitudes toward countries, for example, like Kenya and Zaïre. There is a difference in the degree of explicitness with which we should state what we will or will not do in the case of certain contingencies, such as came up with respect to Yugoslavia. And there is a difference about the level of the defense expenditures.[207]

Significant as such differences undoubtedly were, however, they still lay within the bipartisan parameters of a traditional foreign policy which, in its essentials, both Democratic and Republican candidates appeared to respect. In the end, as Dr. George Gallup was to write in a post-election analysis, "foreign policy, for the first time since 1936, was not a major issue in the campaign."[208] More pertinent factors, in Dr. Gallup's opinion, were the state of the economy, the overriding public concern with the cost of living and unemployment, and the pride of Southern voters at having the chance to vote for a candidate from their own region. The Democratic candidate, in addition, would seem to have been more successful than his opponent in conveying a sense of active concern for the plight of disadvantaged Americans—insisting at the same time that the Federal budget could be brought into balance by the end of his first term.

"A beautiful new spirit in this country" was Governor Carter's dominant perception as returns rolled in from the November 2 voting, assuring the election of Carter and Mondale with 40,249,963 votes (50.4 percent of the national total) and 297 electoral votes in 23 States and the District of Columbia. Their opponents, Ford and Dole, were credited with 38,498,496 votes (48.3 percent), with 241 electoral votes in 27 States, among them all

[206] Interview, Oct. 24, in *Bulletin*, 75: 606-7.
[207] Same: 606.
[208] Quoted by Shrivastava, *loc. cit.*: 79.

of the Western States as well as several Midwest and Atlantic States. Former Senator Eugene McCarthy of Minnesota, running as an independent candidate in 29 States, led the minor contenders with 657,340 votes or 0.8 percent of the total. The outcome of the congressional races would leave the Senate with a Democratic majority of 61 to 38, with 1 independent; in the House, Democrats would outnumber Republicans by 292 to 143.

"A City Upon a Hill"

The exemplary demeanor of both candidates, and their respective associates, did much to assure the success of the process of transition that began on November 3 and was to continue until Governor Carter's inauguration as the nation's 39th President on January 20, 1977. The Democratic victor, who had made something of a point of his independence of the Eastern foreign policy "establishment," occasioned some surprise by his choice of such familiar figures as Cyrus R. Vance as Secretary of State, W. Michael Blumenthal as Secretary of the Treasury, Dr. Harold Brown as Secretary of Defense, Professor Zbigniew Brzezinski, his principal foreign affairs mentor, as Assistant for National Security Affairs, Theodore E. Sorensen as Director of Central Intelligence, and former Defense Secretary James R. Schlesinger as Adviser on Energy. The rather conventional character of some of these appointments was balanced, however, by the choice of two fellow Georgians, Thomas Bertram Lance and Congressman Andrew J. Young, to serve respectively as Director of the Office of Management and Budget and as U.S. Permanent Representative to the United Nations.

Not forgotten in the excitement of the presidential transition was the fact that the United States was still observing its bicentennial year, a circumstance that gave a special accent to the nonpartisan philosophising traditional at such times. Winston Lord of the State Department went all the way back to John Winthrop's vision of "a City upon a Hill" to characterize the sense of unique American destiny that, he said, had animated Winthrop's countrymen from 1630 down into the 1970s.[209]

America has traversed many frontiers [the Policy Planning Director recalled]—independence, continental expansion, global involvement. The next frontier is within ourselves.

During the past decade and a half Americans felt the sting of discord between races and generations, the turmoil of great social and cultural change, and the cynicism and division

---

[209]Washington address, Nov. 11, in *Bulletin*, 75: 677.

aroused by a foreign war. Serious abuses of power occurred in government, business, and other institutions. We lost three successive Presidents—through assassination, Vietnam, and scandal. We have had to recover our balance under a President who had not been elected. And perhaps most crucial for our role abroad, there has been struggle between two branches of government. . . .

And yet, the speaker insisted, in language that may fittingly close the present survey, the nation had emerged triumphant over these vicissitudes:

Our institutions have shown a remarkable resiliency through domestic turbulence and constitutional crisis.

And the American people are beginning to heal the wounds of recent years and recover a sense of pride and purpose.

. . . Americans have learned that if we are not innocent in our relations with the world, neither are we corrupt; if we are not young, neither are we old; if we are not paramount, neither are we pawns of destiny.

America remains "a City upon a Hill": unique, endowed, an example to others. Now we are also part of a wider human community, engaged in creating a better world—a peaceful commonwealth for all peoples.[210]

---

[210]Same: 685-6.

PART II: DOCUMENTS

1. A BICENTENNIAL AGENDA

(1)   The State of the Union: Address by President Gerald R. Ford before a Joint Session of the Congress, January 19, 1976. [1]

(Excerpts)

Mr. Speaker, Mr. Vice President, [2] *Members of the 94th Congress, and distinguished guests:*

As we begin our Bicentennial, America is still one of the youngest nations in recorded history. Long before our forefathers came to these shores, men and women had been struggling on this planet to forge a better life for themselves and their families.

In man's long upward march from savagery and slavery— throughout the nearly 2,000 years of the Christian calendar, the nearly 6,000 years of Jewish reckoning—there have been many deep, terrifying valleys but also many bright and towering peaks.

One peak stands highest in the ranges of human history. One example shines forth of a people uniting to produce abundance and to share the good life fairly and with freedom. One union holds out the promise of justice and opportunity for every citizen: That union is the United States of America.

We have not remade paradise on Earth. We know perfection will not be found here. But think for a minute how far we have come in 200 years.

We came from many roots, and we have many branches. Yet all Americans across the eight generations that separate us from the stirring deeds of 1776, those who know no other homeland and those who just found refuge among our shores, say in unison:

I am proud of America, and I am proud to be an American. Life will be a little better here for my children than for me. I believe this

[1] Text from *Presidential Documents*, 12: 43-52.
[2] Speaker of the House Carl Albert and President of the Senate Nelson A. Rockefeller.

not because I am told to believe it, but because life has been better for me than it was for my father and my mother. I know it will be better for my children because my hands, my brains, my voice, and my vote can help make it happen.

It has happened here in America. It has happened to you and to me.

Government exists to create and preserve conditions in which people can translate their ideas into practical reality. In the best of times, much is lost in translation. But we try. Sometimes we have tried and failed. Always we have had the best of intentions.

But in the recent past, we sometimes forgot the sound principles that guided us through most of our history. We wanted to accomplish great things and solve age-old problems. And we became overconfident of our abilities. We tried to be a policeman abroad and the indulgent parent here at home.

We thought we could transform the country through massive national programs, but often the programs did not work. Too often they only made things worse. In our rush to accomplish great deeds quickly, we trampled on sound principles of restraint and endangered the rights of individuals. We unbalanced our economic system by the huge and unprecedented growth of Federal expenditures and borrowing. And we were not totally honest with ourselves about how much these programs would cost and how we would pay for them. Finally, we shifted our emphasis from defense to domestic problems while our adversaries continued a massive buildup of arms.

The time has now come for a fundamentally different approach—for a new realism that is true to the great principles upon which this Nation was founded.

We must introduce a new balance to our economy—a balance that favors not only sound, active government but also a much more vigorous, healthy economy that can create new jobs and hold down prices.

We must introduce a new balance in the relationship between the individual and the government—a balance that favors greater individual freedom and self-reliance.

We must strike a new balance in our system of federalism—a balance that favors greater responsibility and freedom for the leaders of our State and local governments.

We must introduce a new balance between the spending on domestic programs and spending on defense—a balance that ensures we will fully meet our obligation to the needy while also protecting our security in a world that is still hostile to freedom.

And in all that we do, we must be more honest with the American people, promising them no more than we can deliver and delivering all that we promise.

The genius of America has been its incredible ability to improve the lives of its citizens through a unique combination of governmental and free citizen activity.

History and experience tells us that moral progress cannot come in comfortable and in complacent times, but out of trial and out of confusion. Tom Paine aroused the troubled Americans of 1776 to stand up to the times that try men's souls because the harder the conflict, the more glorious the triumph.

Just a year ago I reported that the State of the Union was not good. Tonight, I report that the State of our Union is better—in many ways a lot better—but still not good enough.

To paraphrase Tom Paine, 1975 was not a year for "summer soldiers and sunshine patriots." It was a year of fears and alarms and of dire forecasts—most of which never happened and won't happen.

As you recall, the year 1975 opened with rancor and with bitterness. Political misdeeds of the past had neither been forgotten nor forgiven. The longest, most divisive war in our history was winding toward an unhappy conclusion. Many feared that the end of that foreign war of men and machines meant the beginning of a domestic war of recrimination and reprisal. Friends and adversaries abroad were asking whether America had lost its nerve. Finally, our economy was ravaged by inflation—inflation that was plunging us into the worst recession in four decades. At the same time, Americans became increasingly alienated from big institutions. They were steadily losing confidence not just in big government, but in big business, big labor, and big education, among others. Ours was a troubled land.

And so, 1975 was a year of hard decisions, difficult compromises, and a new realism that taught us something important about America. It brought back a needed measure of common sense, steadfastness, and self-discipline.

Americans did not panic or demand instant but useless cures. In all sectors, people met their difficult problems with the restraint and with responsibility worthy of their great heritage.

Add up the separate pieces of progress in 1975, subtract the setbacks, and the sum total shows that we are not only headed in a new direction, a direction which I proposed 12 months ago, but it turned out to be the right direction.

It is the right direction because it follows the truly revolutionary American concept of 1776, which holds that, in a free society, the making of public policy and successful problem-solving involves much more than government. It involves a full partnership among all branches and all levels of government, private institutions, and individual citizens.

Common sense tells me to stick to that steady course.

Take the state of our economy. Last January, most things were rapidly getting worse. This January, most things are slowly but surely getting better.

The worst recession since World War II turned around in April. The best cost-of-living news of the past year is that double-digit inflation of 12 percent or higher was cut almost in half. The worst—unemployment remains far too high.

Today, nearly 1,700,000 more Americans are working than at the bottom of the recession. At year's end, people were again being hired much faster than they were being laid off.

Yet, let's be honest. Many Americans have not yet felt these changes in their daily lives. They still see prices going up far too fast, and they still know the fear of unemployment.

We are also a growing nation. We need more and more jobs every year. Today's economy has produced over 85 million jobs for Americans, but we need a lot more jobs, especially for the young.

My first objective is to have sound economic growth without inflation.

We all know from recent experience what runaway inflation does to ruin every other worthy purpose. We are slowing it. We must stop it cold.

For many Americans, the way to a healthy, noninflationary economy has become increasingly apparent. The Government must stop spending so much and stop borrowing so much of our money. More money must remain in private hands where it will do the most good. To hold down the cost of living, we must hold down the cost of government.

In the past decade, the Federal budget has been growing at an average rate of over 10 percent a year. The budget I am submitting Wednesday cuts this rate of growth in half. I have kept my promise to submit a budget for the next fiscal year of $395 billion. In fact, it is $394.2 billion.

By holding down the growth of Federal spending, we can afford additional tax cuts and return to the people who pay taxes more decision making power over their own lives.

Last month I signed legislation to extend the 1975 tax reductions for the first 6 months of this year. I now propose that effective July 1, 1976, we give our taxpayers a tax cut of approximately $10 billion more than Congress agreed to in December.

My broader tax reduction would mean that for a family of four making $15,000 a year, there will be $227 more in take-home pay annually. Hard-working Americans caught in the middle can really use that kind of extra cash.

My recommendations for a firm restraint on the growth of Federal spending and for greater tax reduction are simple and straightforward. For every dollar saved in cutting the growth in the

Federal budget, we can have an added dollar of Federal tax reduction.

We can achieve a balanced budget by 1979 if we have the courage and the wisdom to continue to reduce the growth of Federal spending.

One test of a healthy economy is a job for every American who wants to work. Government—our kind of government—cannot create that many jobs. But the Federal Government can create conditions and incentives for private business and industry to make more and more jobs.

* * *

Taking a longer look at America's future, there can be neither sustained growth nor more jobs unless we continue to have an assured supply of energy to run our economy. Domestic production of oil and gas is still declining. Our dependence on foreign oil at high prices is still too great, draining jobs and dollars away from our own economy at the rate of $125 per year for every American.

Last month, I signed a compromise national energy bill[3] which enacts a part of my comprehensive energy independence program. This legislation was late, not the complete answer to energy independence, but still a start in the right direction.

I again urge the Congress to move ahead immediately on the remainder of my energy proposals to make America invulnerable to the foreign oil cartel.

My proposals, as all of you know, would:

— reduce domestic natural gas shortages;
— allow production from Federal petroleum reserves;
— stimulate effective conservation, including revitalization of our railroads and the expansion of our urban transportation systems;
— develop more and cleaner energy from our vast coal resources;
— expedite clean and safe nuclear power production;
— create a new national Energy Independence Authority to stimulate vital energy investment; and
— accelerate development of technology to capture energy from the Sun and the Earth for this and future generations.

* * *

The protection of the lives and property of Americans from foreign enemies is one of my primary responsibilities as President.

---

[3]Energy Policy and Conservation Act (Public Law 94-163, Dec. 22, 1975). Background in *AFR, 1975:* 20.

In a world of instant communications and intercontinental ballistic missiles, in a world economy that is global and interdependent, our relations with other nations become more, not less, important to the lives of Americans.

America has had a unique role in the world since the day of our independence 200 years ago. And ever since the end of World War II, we have borne—successfully—a heavy responsibility for ensuring a stable world order and hope for human progress.

Today, the state of our foreign policy is sound and strong. We are at peace, and I will do all in my power to keep it that way.

Our military forces are capable and ready. Our military power is without equal, and I intend to keep it that way.

Our principal alliances with the industrial democracies of the Atlantic Community and Japan have never been more solid.

A further agreement to limit the strategic arms race may be achieved.

We have an improving relationship with China, the world's most populous nation.

The key elements for peace among the nations of the Middle East now exist.

Our traditional friendships in Latin America, Africa, and Asia continue.

We have taken the role of leadership in launching a serious and hopeful dialog between the industrial world and the developing world.

We have helped to achieve significant reform of the international monetary system.

We should be proud of what America, what our country, has accomplished in these areas, and I believe the American people are.

The American people have heard too much about how terrible our mistakes, how evil our deeds, and how misguided our purposes. The American people know better.

The truth is we are the world's greatest democracy. We remain the symbol of man's aspiration for liberty and well-being. We are the embodiment of hope for progress.

I say it is time we quit downgrading ourselves as a nation. Of course, it is our responsibility to learn the right lesson from past mistakes. It is our duty to see that they never happen again. But our greater duty is to look to the future. The world's troubles will not go away.

The American people want strong and effective international and defense policies. In our constitutional system, these policies should reflect consultation and accommodation between the President and the Congress. But in the final analysis, as the framers of our Constitution knew from hard experience, the foreign relations of the United States can be conducted effectively only if there is strong central direction that allows flexibility of action. That responsibility clearly rests with the President.

I pledge to the American people policies which seek a secure, just, and peaceful world. I pledge to the Congress to work with you to that end.

We must not face a future in which we can no longer help our friends, such as Angola, even in limited and carefully controlled ways. We must not lose all capacity to respond short of military intervention.

Some hasty actions of the Congress during the past year—most recently in respect to Angola—were, in my view, very shortsighted. Unfortunately, they are still very much on the minds of our allies and our adversaries.

A strong defense posture gives weight to our values and our views in international negotiations. It assures the vigor of our alliances. And it sustains our efforts to promote settlements of international conflicts. Only from a position of strength can we negotiate a balanced agreement to limit the growth of nuclear arms. Only a balanced agreement will serve our interests and minimize the threat of nuclear confrontation.

The defense budget I will submit to the Congress for fiscal year 1977 will show an essential increase over the current year. It provides for real growth in purchasing power over this year's defense budget, which includes the cost of the all-volunteer force.

We are continuing to make economies to enhance the efficiency of our military forces. But the budget I wlll submit represents the necessity of American strength for the real world in which we live.

As conflict and rivalry persist in the world, our United States intelligence capabilities must be the best in the world.

The crippling of our foreign intelligence services increases the danger of American involvement in direct armed conflict. Our adversaries are encouraged to attempt new adventures while our own ability to monitor events and to influence events short of military action is undermined. Without effective intelligence capability, the United States stands blindfolded and hobbled.

In the near future, I will take actions to reform and strengthen our intelligence community. I ask for your positive cooperation. It is time to go beyond sensationalism and ensure an effective, responsible, and responsive intelligence capability.

Tonight I have spoken about our problems at home and abroad. I have recommended policies that will meet the challenge of our third century. I have no doubt that our Union will endure, better, stronger, and with more individual freedom. We can see forward only dimly—one year, five years, a generation perhaps. Like our forefathers, we know that if we meet the challenges of our own time with a common sense of purpose and conviction, if we remain true to our Constitution and to our ideals, then we can know that the future will be better than the past.

I see America today crossing a threshold, not just because it is our Bicentennial but because we have been tested in adversity. We have taken a new look at what we want to be and what we want our Nation to become.

I see America resurgent, certain once again that life will be better for our children than it is for us, seeking strength that cannot be counted in megatons and riches that cannot be eroded by inflation.

I see these United States of America moving forward as before toward a more perfect Union where the Government serves and the people rule.

We will not make this happen simply by making speeches, good or bad, yours or mine, but by hard work and hard decisions made with courage and with commonsense.

I have heard many inspiring Presidential speeches, but the words I remember best were spoken by Dwight D. Eisenhower. "America is not good because it is great," the President said. "America is great because it is good."

President Eisenhower was raised in a poor but religious home in the heart of America. His simple words echoed President Lincoln's eloquent testament that "right makes might." And Lincoln in turn evoked the silent image of George Washington kneeling in prayer at Valley Forge.

So, all these magic memories which link eight generations of Americans are summed up in the inscription just above me. How many times have we seen it? "In God We Trust."

Let us engrave it now in each of our hearts as we begin our Bicentennial.

(2)   The Budget for Fiscal Year 1977, January 21, 1976: Defense and International Affairs.[4]

NATIONAL DEFENSE

The national defense function includes the funds to develop, maintain, and equip the military forces of the United States and to provide military assistance to foreign governments.

The fundamental goal of the defense establishment is to ensure the freedom and security of the United States and to protect the vital interests of the United States throughout the world.

[4]Text from Executive Office of the President, Office of Management and Budget, *The Budget of the United States Government, Fiscal Year 1977* (Washington: GPO, 1976): 61-79. Tables and charts omitted.

To ensure that American defense forces remain adequate to meet these goals, an increase in funding—beyond what is necessary to offset inflation—is essential. This increase will permit the development and procurement of up-to-date military equipment needed to improve the effectiveness of our combat forces. Proposed outlays for national defense programs rise from $92.8 billion in 1976 to $101.1 billion in 1977, and to $112.9 billion in 1978.

To achieve the improvements needed, while staying within the proposed budget, requires further increases in the efficiency of the defense establishment. Toward this objective reductions are proposed in personnel levels, benefits, and support activities that make only marginal contributions to combat effectiveness. Many of these reductions will require legislation. Without such legislation additional funds would be required.

Department of Defense.—The national security goals of the Department of Defense are to:

- maintain a worldwide military balance, in conjunction with our allies, and thus reduce the threat of war;
- deter any attack against the United States, its allies, and other nations vital to United States security; and, if deterrence fails, ensure an outcome favorable to the United States; and
- assure the flow of ocean-going trade and supplies by protecting the sea lanes that are vital to the national security and economic well-being of the United States, its allies, and its trading partners.

United States forces as proposed in this budget, together with allied forces, are sufficient to meet these goals. Despite an increase in Soviet defense spending, military personnel levels, and equipment modernization, an acceptable military balance exists in the world today, primarily due to four factors:

- An effective strategic deterrent has been maintained through selected force improvements.
- United States and allied forces have been strengthened by the introduction of modern tactical aircraft, the continuing modernization of the surface fleet, and increased purchases of tanks, antitank weapons, and other ground force equipment and munitions.
- The fighting capability of the defense establishment has been improved—without an increase in overall personnel levels—by the conversion of support resources into combat

resources. The number of Army divisions has been expanded from 13 in 1974 to 16 in 1976, while the total number of military personnel has remained at 2.1 million. The combat effectiveness of the tactical air forces and naval forces has also been improved.

- Much of the Soviet military increase has been directed toward the Chinese border.

The United States seeks to reduce military expenditures and international tensions through negotiations. These include the strategic arms limitation talks with the Soviet Union and discussions on mutual and balanced force reductions in central Europe between NATO and Warsaw Pact members. Effective agreements can be reached, however, only if United States and allied forces remain at least as strong as those of potential adversaries.

To maintain the military balance in the interim, the 1977 budget contains proposals to carry forward the increase in Army divisions, continue the modernization of ground, sea, and tactical air equipment, and improve the readiness of the combat forces. These measures will require continuing budget increases, over and above amounts needed to offset inflation.

To moderate the increases in resources that are required to maintain U.S. military strength, the 1977 budget contains the following proposals to increase the efficiency of the defense establishment:

- restrain the growth in compensation levels;
- reduce civilian personnel positions by consolidating headquarters and other base facilities;
- phase out subsidies for the operating costs of military commissaries over a 3-year period;
- eliminate dual compensation of Federal employees on active duty for training with the National Guard or Reserve;
- reduce temporary duty and permanent change-of-station travel;
- reduce petroleum consumption for proficiency flying programs through greater use of smaller aircraft and ground training aids;
- reduce the scope of the civil defense program, while continuing to support nuclear attack preparedness activities at the State and local level;
- hold new construction below 1976 levels; and
- reduce the paid drill strength of the Naval Reserve by 40,000.

Most of these actions require the approval of Congress. If these actions are not approved, additional defense appropriations of up to $2.8 billion would be required in 1977. These amounts cannot be offset by reductions in resources needed for basic defense preparedness.

As shown in the accompanying chart, increases in the total current dollar military budget were insufficient to offset inflation during the 1968-75 period. This resulted in a 7-year decline in Department of Defense military functions and military assistance budget resources when measured in dollars of constant 1977 purchasing power. This decline was reversed in 1976, and further increases proposed for 1977 would continue to improve purchasing power. This chart is in terms of total obligational authority— current budget authority enacted each year by Congress, plus previously enacted authority that is transferred to subsequent years.

The following table summarizes the total obligational authority for Department of Defense military functions and military assistance on the basis of major missions.

Strategic forces.—The principal objective of strategic forces is to deter nuclear attack, or the threat of attack, against the United States or its allies by maintaining:

- overall balance with Soviet strategic forces;
- no perceived advantage to the Soviet Union of a first use of strategic weapons; and
- the ability to counter rapidly any adverse change in the strategic balance.

Arms control negotiations are being pursued to stabilize the strategic balance and eventually to reduce the level of forces. Both as an aid to these negotiations and as a safeguard if they are not successful, research and development efforts will continue to improve weapon systems.

The 1977 strategic program of $9.4 billion in total obligational authority continues the planned modernization of strategic forces and provides options for more extensive future modernization. Major efforts, including those funded under research and development, are:

- development of the B-1 bomber to strengthen and update strategic bomber forces, and initial procurement of the B-1 if test results are favorable;
- continued development and procurement of the Trident

missile and submarine to give the seagoing strategic forces greater range and less vulnerability;

- further development of a new intercontinental ballistic missile for deployment in the mid-1980's;
- full-scale development of long-range strategic cruise missiles for aircraft, submarine, or surface ship deployment;
- increases in the accuracy of ballistic missile warheads;
- improvement of technology for ballistic missile defense systems; and
- further improvements in systems for early warning of attack and for command, control and communications.

General purpose forces.—Land, sea, and air forces in this category are intended to deter or counter threats short of strategic nuclear conflict. These threats range from isolated incidents to major sustained conventional warfare and tactical nuclear conflict. The objective of general purpose forces is to deter such conflicts wherever possible and, where deterrence is not possible, to ensure an outcome favorable to the United States. Recommended total obligational authority for general purpose forces is $40.2 billion in 1977.

For the last 2 years a major effort has been underway to increase combat readiness and effectiveness so that U.S. forces are better prepared for short, intense conflicts. New combat units have been established by making offsetting reductions in headquarters and general support activities. A major initiative in the 1976 budget was to increase the number of active Army divisions from 13 to 16. All 16 divisions have now been established and further actions in 1977 will bring the new divisions up to combat strength. The Administration's efforts in this direction will continue in 1977 with a program that adds the equivalent of four wings to the Air Force with no overall increase in total military personnel.

Both qualitative and quantitative improvements in *land forces* are provided for in the 1977 budget. The production of helicopters and antitank guided missiles will continue, and tank production will be increased in order to permit the eventual conversion of two light infantry divisions into mechanized divisions and to rebuild inventory levels by replacing tanks provided to Israel. Major new systems under development for support of land forces include the advanced XM-1 tank, a mechanized infantry combat vehicle, and an attack helicopter.

The combat effectiveness of the *tactical air forces* will be increased as more F-14 and F-15 fighters are purchased. Air Force air-to-ground capabilities will be improved with the introduction of the A-10 aircraft, specifically developed to support ground combat units. Air combat fighters are under development for both the Air

Force and Navy, with initial production of the Air Force F-16 air combat fighter scheduled in 1977. This aircraft will meet the varied defense requirements of the United States and a number of NATO nations. Significant savings will be realized through shared production and a high rate of procurement. Inventory requirements for the Navy A-6 attack aircraft have been met and production of this aircraft will be discontinued.

Procurement of 15 new ships in 1977 will support continued efforts to modernize general purpose *naval forces* and rebuild the size and capability of the fleet. In 1965 the United States had 936 warships with an average age of 16 years. In 1976 the fleet will have 480 active warships with an average age of 14 years. Fleet readiness will be improved through increasing overhauls and intermediate maintenance. Three nuclear-powered attack submarines, designed to hunt down and destroy enemy submarines, will be procured in 1977. Procurement of eight guided-missile frigates will provide increased protection of amphibious force ships, replenishment ships, and merchant convoys from air, surface, and subsurface attacks.

The 1977 shipbuilding program includes a nonnuclear destroyer and long-lead funding for a nuclear-powered strike cruiser. Both ships will carry the Aegis weapon system that will increase the ability of the fleet to counter the air and cruise missile threat in the 1980's and beyond. Maintenance capability will be increased through the purchase of several fleet support vessels. These vessels will replace aging units and provide the additional facilities needed to repair, maintain, and supply the new combat ships now entering the fleet.

Airlift and sealift forces.—Effective transportation is required to enable U.S. forces to respond on short notice to threats against U.S. interests throughout the world, to assist nations whose security is important to the welfare of the United States, and to sustain American forces abroad. Strategic transport capabilities will be increased to enable adequate U.S. forces to be deployed and sustained in the critical early days of an intense conflict overseas. To achieve these objectives, total obligational authority of $1.6 billion is being requested for 1977.

Proposed modifications will improve and extend the service life of the C-5 and C-141 aircraft. In addition, there will be an evaluation in 1977 among existing large transport aircraft to select a new tanker/cargo aircraft to be procured in 1978. Portions of the Civil Reserve Air Fleet will be modified to permit the air transport of oversized cargo. This will enable commercial aircraft to support active forces more effectively in either a mobilization or a combat situation.

The sealift program provides transportation for heavy armored equipment and munitions, as well as petroleum products and dry cargo. Special ships are also necessary for oceanography, cable maintenance, and the tracking of missiles and space vehicles.

Guard and Reserve forces.—The effectiveness of Reserve forces will be increased by modernizing equipment and associating designated National Guard and Reserve units more closely with specific active force units. Emphasis will be placed on better management of Reserve personnel. Naval Reserve paid drill strength will be reduced by 40,000 through the transfer of these positions to the Individual Ready Reserve in those cases where readiness still can be maintained through summer training.

Research and development.—Technological superiority of U.S. forces depends upon adequate investment in research and development. To maintain this superiority, recommended total obligational authority will increase to $10.5 billion in 1977, $1.8 billion above the 1976 level.

Strategic weapon systems development will continue on the B-1 aircraft, the Trident submarine and missile system, a new intercontinental ballistic missile system, strategic cruise missiles and warhead improvements, as will research on ballistic missile defense technology.

Research and development activities will also continue the major modernization of general purpose forces started in previous years. The Army development program includes a new tank, infantry combat vehicle, attack and transport helicopters, and air defense system. The Navy will develop the F-18 air combat fighter to complement the sophisticated F-14 fleet defense aircraft. The Navy will also continue development of improved fleet air defense and antisubmarine systems. Full-scale development of a tactical cruise missile will lead to a more effective attack capability for ships.

The Air Force will continue development of the F-16 air combat fighter. In addition, work will proceed on systems capable of neutralizing enemy air defenses and on exploration of the combat potential of high-energy lasers and vehicles piloted by remote control. Funding for a major new aeropropulsion systems test facility will be provided in 1977. This facility will be required for the development and testing of advanced military aircraft engines and will result in substantial future savings in the development costs of such engines.

Training, medical, and other general personnel support activities.—The increased wages and other pay and benefit improvements associated with pay comparability and the decision to shift to an all-volunteer military force have significantly raised the cost of personnel. As shown in the accompanying table, total personnel-related costs increased from 43% of the Department of Defense budget in 1964 to over 54% beginning in 1974.

Several actions are proposed to moderate the increase in pay-related costs.

- Civilian personnel employment levels will be reduced.
- The housing system of the Department of Defense will be reformed gradually to eliminate inequities between the value of housing directly received and the allowances provided in lieu of housing. As a first step, future military pay raises will be allocated differently among the various pay components.
- Enlistment bonuses are being reduced, and the need to extend legislation authorizing annual bonuses for physicians as a recruitment and retention device will be reexamined.
- Legislation to replace the basic pay of future cadets at the Service academies with a method of compensation more appropriate for students—the payment of expenses plus a monthly allowance—will be requested.
- Congress will be requested to enact the Defense Officer Personnel Management Act. This act is designed to match better the military work force with job requirements, in terms of rank and length of service.
- New personnel policies will reduce both the costs of military travel and the adverse effects of frequent transfers on the morale of military personnel and their dependents.
- Training times will be reduced, personnel will be assigned to permanent duty stations as soon as possible after training, and training sites will be consolidated where feasible.
- Legislation has been proposed to reform gradually the career incentives in the military retirement system. Legislation is also proposed to revise the formula for the cost-of-living adjustment for civilian and military retired pay. This will eliminate provisions that increase annuities by one percentage point more than the Consumer Price Index increase.
- Legislation will be proposed to reform aspects of the law governing wage-board pay rates that result in Government civilian blue-collar workers earning more than their non-Government counterparts. The budgetary effect of this legislation on outlays of the Department of Defense is included in the defense function.

Further savings will result as the recommendations of a recently completed comprehensive review of the military health care system are implemented. Developed by the Department of Defense, the Department of Health, Education, and Welfare, and the Office of Management and Budget, these recommendations would result in more efficient operations and reduced outlays for the military health care system in the future.

Military assistance.—Military assistance grants, credit sales, and training of foreign military personnel furnish other countries the support necessary to strengthen their own defense efforts. These programs are discussed in the section on international affairs.

Atomic energy defense activities.—Nuclear weapons research, development, underground testing, and production activities are expected to remain at about 1976 levels. Additional funds are requested for safety, environmental, and waste storage improvements as well as cost increases. The physical security of nuclear weapons and nuclear materials at Government sites will continue to be improved.

Defense-related activities.—To end the annual registration for the draft during peacetime, the Selective Service System will be reformed. This reform will yield an annual outlay savings of $33 million beginning in 1977.

Realization of an estimated $870 million in stockpile receipts is dependent upon market conditions and the passage by Congress of $746 million in disposal authority for certain commodities that are in excess of current needs. Receipts from the sale of excess strategic stockpile commodities under existing disposal authority are estimated at $124 million in 1976.

INTERNATIONAL AFFAIRS

The international affairs function includes programs to achieve a range of United States economic and security objectives. It is composed of foreign economic and financial assistance, the conduct of foreign affairs, foreign information and exchange activities, and international financial programs.

The achievement of peace throughout the world is this Nation's foremost international goal. The most immediate threat to that peace has been in the Middle East, an area of great importance to the United States. This country has made a major effort to bring peace to the region, and the recent agreement between Israel and Egypt is an encouraging sign of progress. The United States, in concert with the nations of the area, will continue its efforts to promote a durable settlement.

America's prosperity and the health of the world economy are closely linked. The United States must, therefore, promote a world economic system that ensures stability and progress for both developed and developing nations alike. The United States is committed to work with the other industrial nations to assure the rapid recovery of their economies, to accelerate completion of trade negotiations, to achieve monetary reform, and to foster economic growth in the developing nations. Outlays for international affairs are expected to total $6.8 billion in 1977 and $7.8 billion in 1978.

FOREIGN AID

The United States undertakes a variety of programs designed to further U.S. objectives by directly assisting developing countries. Foreign aid programs consist of two major components: military assistance (included in the national defense function) and foreign economic and financial assistance.

Military assistance.—Defense materiel and services are provided by the United States to selected countries for their internal security and self-defense, and to permit the recipient country to participate in regional or collective security arrangements. Military assistance, administered by the Department of Defense and included in the national defense function, is an integral part of the overall American foreign aid effort.

Budget authority of $840 million is requested to support a military credit sales program of $2.1 billion, a substantial portion of which will be for Israel. About $704 million will be in direct credits requiring budget authority of the same amount. The remainder of the program will be guaranteed loans for which the funds will be provided by the Federal Financing Bank. These loans require a guaranty reserve of 10% and thus budget authority of $136 million.

The Administration's budget proposals are based upon a continued transition from an emphasis on grant military assistance to an emphasis on foreign military sales credits. In 1977, budget authority for grant military assistance will decline from the 1976 level of $394 million to $279 million, and the number of recipient countries will also be reduced. Total outlays for military assistance are estimated to be $739 million in 1977. This estimate is $200 million higher than that shown in the section on national defense because of the exclusion here of net trust fund outlays related to military cash sales.

Foreign economic and financial assistance.—Provided bilaterally and multilaterally, this assistance is designed to: contribute to U.S. security objectives; facilitate the economic growth of the developing countries; and respond to the needs of the poorest people of the world for food, shelter and other necessities of life.

Security supporting assistance provides economic assistance to selected countries and encourages progress toward a lasting negotiated settlement in the Middle East. Budget authority of $1.8 billion is being requested in 1977, primarily for aid to the Middle East.

A *Middle East special requirements fund* of $35 million is also being requested to defray the costs of the Sinai Support Mission and to allow an additional measure of flexibility in responding to unforeseen events.

Multilateral development assistance.—This assistance is provided through contributions to the international financial institutions (the World Bank Group and the regional development banks) and for development programs of international organizations (principally within the United Nations system). It has become an increasingly important component of foreign economic development assistance. Multilateral assistance encourages increased contributions from other donors and mobilizes private resources for the development effort. For 1977, $1.2 billion in budget authority is requested for this assistance, with estimated outlays of $1.1 billion.

The international financial institutions extend long-term loans to developing countries to finance development projects. It is proposed that in 1977 the United States contribute $375 million to the International Development Association, $171 million to the Asian Development Bank, and $440 million toward a new capital replenishment of the Inter-American Development Bank. In addition, a United States contribution of up to $42 million is proposed for the International Finance Corporation to stimulate private sector activities in the developing nations.

Voluntary contributions of $178 million are proposed for 10 international organizations and programs primarily oriented toward economic assistance and humanitarian relief. The largest of these is the United Nations Development Program.

Authorization has been granted to allow the United States to contribute one-fifth, but no more than $200 million, of the total amount mobilized in a new International Fund for Agricultural Development to help finance agricultural production projects in developing countries. Contributions from all sources are expected to total $1 billion.

Two other major initiatives to hasten the economic growth of the developing nations are being pursued through the International Monetary Fund (IMF). Neither of these affects the budget totals. The United States has proposed a special trust fund within the IMF to extend concessional aid to the poorer developing nations, financed in part with funds received by the sale of gold now held by the IMF. The United States also supports changes in the operations of the IMF's compensatory financing facility that will make increased IMF resources available to developing nations that suffer sudden shortfalls in their export earnings.

Bilateral development assistance, provided primarily by the Agency for International Development (AID), concentrates aid on the neediest people in the poorer countries. This program emphasizes expanding agricultural development, checking rapid population growth, and improving basic health and education services.

Because the economies of some developing countries have progressed, they no longer need highly concessional assistance from AID. This, combined with the availability to many developing nations of other public and private sector sources of capital and technical assistance, has permitted the Administration to reduce its budget request somewhat below the amount originally sought in authorizing legislation for 1977.

Food for Peace helps alleviate hunger and malnutrition in developing countries by providing concessional loans and grants to finance agricultural imports from the United States. Most of the food goes to the poorer countries, with grants focused on the poorest-fed groups in those countries.

Migration and refugee assistance is conducted through American voluntary agencies, the United Nations, and the Intergovernmental Committee on European Migration. A 1976 appropriation of $25 million is requested to establish a new emergency refugee and migration assistance fund. No additional budget authority is requested for the fund in 1977.

International narcotics control assistance is provided to foreign governments and international organizations to control the production, processing, and illegal trafficking in dangerous drugs in an effort to curtail their flow into the United States.

The *Peace Corps*, which will have approximately 5,700 volunteers in 67 countries during 1977, will concentrate its efforts on agriculture, health and nutrition, education, and conservation.

OTHER INTERNATIONAL ACTIVITIES

Conduct of foreign affairs.—Outlays for the administration of worldwide U.S. diplomatic and consular responsibilities will increase by $73 million in 1977. About $45 million of this increase results from the State Department financing certain administrative services provided to, and previously funded by, other agencies. It does not represent a net increase in budget totals. Most of the remaining increase is due to sharply rising wages and prices abroad. Budget authority is also requested to begin construction of a new embassy complex in Moscow.

Outlays for international organizations and conferences increase by $21 million, primarily reflecting increased assessments for membership in international organizations. Outlays for the Arms Control and Disarmament Agency and the International Trade Commission increase slightly in 1977, while those for the Foreign Claims Settlement Commission decrease due to the completion of two claims programs.

Foreign information and exchange activities.—Proposed outlays will decrease $13 million in 1977. The decrease in foreign information activities largely reflects savings to the Board for International Broadcasting resulting from the consolidation of the management and operation of Radio Free Europe and Radio Liberty. The activities of the U.S. Information Agency and the educational exchanges of the Department of State will also decline in 1977.

International financial programs.—The Export-Import Bank promotes United States exports by extending direct loans to overseas buyers, discount loans and guarantees to American banks, and insurance to American exporters. Direct loans in 1977 are estimated to increase from $3.0 billion to $4.0 billion; discount loans will be reduced to $1.0 billion as a step toward eventual termination of the program; and insurance and guarantees are projected at $8.8 billion. The Bank's budget authority and outlays, excluded by law from the budget totals since 1971, is included again beginning in 1977. Outlays to finance these activities are estimated at $1.3 billion in 1977.

Pending legislation would enable the United States to provide loan guarantees to the Financial Support Fund for the industrial countries. The fund will be available to member countries with major balance of payments difficulties. No budget authority is required in 1977.

Tax expenditures.—The international affairs function contains a number of tax expenditures that promote international trade and investment. The largest—the deferral of taxes on profits of domestic international sales corporations—is expected to reduce U.S. Treasury receipts by $1.6 billion in 1977.

Credit programs.—The international affairs loan and loan guarantee programs are summarized in the table below.

(3) *Military Posture of the United States: Statement by Secretary of Defense Donald H. Rumsfeld to the Committee on Armed Services, House of Representatives, January 27, 1976.*[5]

Mr. Chairman and Members of the Committee:

I am pleased to present the proposed defense budget for FY 1977 and its implications for the defense authorization request for FY 1978, and a preliminary five-year defense projection for FY 1977-1981.

In FY 1977, the Department proposes a defense budget of $112.7 billion in total obligational authority and $100.1 billion in estimated outlays.[6] The details of this request as well as its justification are set forth in the annual Defense Department Report. I will touch on some of the points of particular interest.

I. The Defense Budget

We estimate that because of a declining rate of inflation, the defense budget for FY 1976 could permit some small real growth in defense funding for the first time since FY 1968. The budget request for FY 1977 and the preliminary five-year defense projection reflect our conviction that there must be a real program growth in the years immediately ahead.

The Defense establishment is engaged in a crucial function of

[5]Text from *Annual Defense Department Report: Report of Secretary of Defense, Donald H. Rumsfeld to the Congress on the FY 1977 Budget and Its Implications for the FY 1978 Authorization Request and the FY 1977-1981 Defense Programs, Jan. 27, 1976:* 1-13.

[6]These figures are for Department of Defense programs only. Because they exclude atomic energy defense activities and certain other items, they are smaller than the over-all "National Defense" figures cited in the budget statement (Document 2) and in the Introduction.

government—providing for the common defense—contributing to peace, stability, and the preservation of freedom. I know it will receive your most serious consideration.

Within roughly three months, as prescribed by the new budget reform guidelines, you and your colleagues in the House and Senate will determine the total federal spending level, and the portion of that total which will be devoted to defense and deterrence.

These two decisions are of enormous importance to the nation and the world. They will be of major significance today and in the years to come, and they will be among the most important decisions which will be made by the Congress this year.

After careful deliberation, the President and the Defense Department have made their judgments. We recognize the importance of your decision. Representatives of the Defense Department will be explicit and candid about the requirements of national security as they appear before you concerning this budget.

II. The International Context

It is useful to consider defense strategy, force structure, and budget requests within a broad international context, as is required by law. That context has five major implications for defense planning:

—First, military power and the international appreciation of it remain basic arbiters of international disputes and major determinants of our capabilities to achieve the objectives of our foreign policy.

—Second, the United States has political, economic, and strategic interests in the world which must be fostered through foreign policies which are supported by our military posture.

—Third, U.S. interests remain under challenge, primarily by the USSR, which continues to add to its military capabilities qualitatively and quantitatively. These challenges can be seen in Europe, along the Mediterranean littoral, in the Middle East and Africa, in the Persian Gulf and, indirectly, in Northeast Asia.

—Fourth, the United States cannot escape the principal role in defending interdependent interests and maintaining world stability: If we falter or fail, there is no other power to take our place.

—Finally, the United States must maintain a military establishment which permits it—in conjunction with allies—to safeguard its interests in the face of a growth in adversary capabilities. The U.S. establishment must be both nuclear and non-nuclear. Much of it must be ready at all times. Security is not available at bargain-basement rates, and the instruments of security cannot expand and contract on short notice.

Today, there are a number of misunderstandings about the relationship between defense and the international environment. I want to address two in particular. The first misunderstanding is that there is an inconsistency between detente and a strong national defense. The second is that there is a contradiction between increases in the U.S. defense budget and the maintenance of international stability.

To deal with the first misunderstanding, it is important to be precise about the meaning of *detente*, this word borrowed from the French. Literally, in French, detente is applied to a number of things having to do with weapons. For example, the entire trigger mechanism of a pistol is called "detente"—the part you pull to fire it, the hammer, the firing pin, and the spring mechanism. Detente is the word, also, for uncocking a cocked pistol—that is, releasing the tension on the spring which moves the hammer. In similar ways, detente is used to describe relaxing the tension on a taut bowstring, or reducing the pressure of a gas in a closed container.

In none of these meanings is there any hint that detente means friendship, trust, affection, or assured peace. In all uses, detente means relaxation of tension that exists—for real, not imaginary, reasons.

On our side, detente is also a hope and an experiment. In this age of nuclear weaponry, it makes sense to seek a reasonable accommodation of our differences with the USSR. But, keeping the basic meaning of detente in mind, we should be under no illusion as to when and how accommodations might be reached. Strength is a prerequisite to acceptable agreements. That is why there is no inherent contradiction among the three main objectives of U.S. policy: defense, deterrence, and the effort to see if it is possible to achieve some relaxation of tension—detente. That is why successive Presidents, including President Ford, have emphasized the connection between strength and peace, between weakness and war.

A wise Frenchman recently noted, "that the Soviet Union today is one of the two main military powers in the world, and this power is ruled according to methods which are substantially and essentially different from . . . Western methods. Why therefore should it not be tempted to extend its influence, if not its rule, if it does not come up against any form of resistance on the part of a power comparable to its own?" That is why I have stressed that weakness, too, can be provocative.

To address the second misunderstanding, it is well to consider some conspicuous trends in Soviet military capabilities—trends that are facts, not projections—before making any judgments about the desirability of increasing U.S. strength:

—Over the past decade, Soviet defense spending has been increasing steadily in real terms.

—In that same period, the Soviet military establishment (not counting border guards and internal security forces) has expanded by a million men from 3.4 to 4.4 million men.

—Between 1965 and 1975, Soviet strategic offensive forces have also increased:

—Intercontinental Ballistic Missiles (ICBMs) from 224 to 1,600 (an increase of nearly 1,400);

—Sea launched Ballistic Missiles (SLBMs) from 29 to 730 (an increase of about 700);

—Strategic warheads and bombs, from 450 to 2,500 (an increase of about 2,000).

—The momentum of this buildup shows no sign of slackening. Qualitative improvements continue, such as:

—The development of four new ICBMs, two of which are currently being deployed with multiple independently targetable reentry vehicles (MIRVs);

—The production of a new generation of Ballistic Missile Submarines (SSBNs), one version of which has been deployed with a new 4,200 mile range SLBM;

—Accuracy improvements which could give their ICBMs a significantly reduced circular error probable (CEP);

—Large MIRVs with high-yield warheads;

—Development of a mobile IRBM (in the form of the SS-X-20).

—Since the early 1960's, Soviet general purpose forces have also expanded substantially. Some of the significant developments have been:

—An expansion in the number of divisions from 141 to 168, with added tanks, artillery, and armored personnel carriers;

—An addition of nearly 2,000 tactical aircraft, combined with the introduction of more sophisticated fighter/attack aircraft;

—A similar growth in the sophistication of Soviet naval forces, with greater missile firepower, more nuclear-powered attack submarines, greater fleet range, more underway replenishment support, and the construction of three small aircraft carriers.

—While much of the increase in ground and tactical air forces has gone to the Far East, Soviet forces oriented toward NATO have improved both quantitatively and qualitatively as well, and the Soviet Navy has become increasingly a worldwide force.

It must be emphasized that while these developments have been occurring in the Soviet Union, U.S. force levels and defense expenditures (in real terms) have been going down. The U.S. force structure is substantially smaller today than it was a decade ago, although it is qualitatively improved in some respects. The crucial issue, however, is not so much why these trends have occurred, or who has led whom into the competition. It is whether the United States is still able to meet its international responsibilities. The nation must also ask itself whether the United States will have a sufficient military capability for defense, deterrence, and detente in the future if these adverse trends continue. This budget says it will not, and sets out to change the trends.

III. Defense Objectives

The primary U.S. objective is, of course, deterrence and international stability. We do not try to do everything, everywhere ourselves. We are not the world's policeman and we do not pretend to be. We do bear the principal burden of nuclear deterrence—both for ourselves and our allies—and hence have the responsibility, along with the USSR, for restraining nuclear competition and maintaining a stable balance of power.

The basic objectives for the strategic nuclear forces are four in number:

—To have a well-protected, second-strike force to deter attacks on our cities and people, at all times;
—To provide a capability for more controlled and measured responses, to deter less than all-out attacks;
—To ensure essential equivalence with the USSR, both now and in the future, so that there can be no misunderstandings or lack of appreciation of the strategic nuclear balance; and
—To maintain stability in the strategic nuclear competition, forsaking the option of a disarming first-strike capability and seeking to achieve equitable arms control agreements where possible.

Obviously, the United States is not responsible for the deterrence of all international disorders. Nor can U.S. nuclear forces credibly deter all contingencies of concern to the nation. For many purposes, non-nuclear forces must carry the main burden of deterrence. In order to plan the conventional forces with restraint and realism, we seek to maintain—in conjunction with our allies—two principal areas of strength and stability—in Western Europe and in Northeast Asia. Insuring stability in these two vital regions requires forward deployed forces as well as strategic reserves.

If we and our allies have the forces to perform those tasks—particularly in response to a major conventional assault on NATO—the United States will also have the necessary capabilities (both active and reserve) to deal with other contingencies which might arise separately, as could be the case in the Middle East. A conventional force structure with this capability and flexibility will strengthen deterrence, enhance stability, and lower the probability of nuclear war.

IV. The Adequacy of Our Forces

An assessment of opposing forces is difficult and tentative in the best of circumstances. I will not presume to speak conclusively on this subject, nor with the certainty that flows from long study and thorough probing and analysis. Nevertheless, there are two judgments about U.S. capabilities that I want to convey. The first is that the current force structure is adequate to perform its missions at the present time. The second is that confidence in the future adequacy of our force structure is gradually declining. Because of the trends—reductions on our part and Soviet military expansion—there has been a gradual shift in the power balance over the past fifteen years. And, in light of the momentum of Soviet military programs of all kinds, it will continue to shift unless U.S. defense outlays are increased in real terms, as the President is recommending.

1. The Strategic Nuclear Situation

As of today, the U.S. strategic nuclear forces retain a substantial, credible capability to deter an all-out nuclear attack. Their ability to execute controlled and limited responses is being enhanced as a result of improvements in plans, command and control, and the increasing flexibility being introduced into the Minuteman force. However, there remains a basis for concern in three areas, and that concern will deepen in succeeding years.

—First, the submarine and bomber forces are aging; at the same time the Soviets are improving their antisubmarine warfare capabilities and their defense against bombers.

—Second, there is an increasing possibility that major asymmetries will develop between U.S. and Soviet strategic offensive forces because of the momentum in Soviet offensive and defensive programs, and that the Soviet strategic capability will come to be seen as superior to that of the United States.

—Third, a continuation of current Soviet strategic programs—even within the constraints of SALT—could threaten the survivability of the Minuteman force within a decade. If that should be allowed to happen, our ability to respond to less-than-full-scale attacks in a controlled and deliberate fashion would be severely curtailed, and strategic stability could be endangered.

2. The Situation in Europe

The defense of Western Europe continues to be one of our fundamental interests. We are naturally concerned, therefore, about certain vulnerabilities that have developed along the southern flank of NATO. In the crucial center region, we and our allies have the basic capabilities necessary to respond to a Warsaw Pact attack. Even here, however, there are two vulnerabilities which will grow in seriousness if we fail to take remedial action.

First, we do not have sufficient long-range airlift capability to deploy our reinforcements to Europe in a timely fashion.

Second, we are concerned that, unless we counterbalance them, increasing Soviet firepower and mobility will begin to give the Pact an unacceptable advantage in the two contingencies against which we design our forces: an attack coming with little or no warning, and one coming after a large-scale mobilization and deployment of Pact forces.

3. The Situation in Northeast Asia

The situation in Northeast Asia is directly influenced by the status of Sino-Soviet relations. At present, we do not anticipate that either power is likely to encourage or support North Korea in an attack on South Korea. If there is no outside aid to North Korea, South Korea should be able to repulse a North Korean attack with relatively modest U.S. assistance.

U.S. ground forces continue to have a deterrent and stabilizing effect on this balance. It would be unwise, therefore, to withdraw U.S. ground forces from the Peninsula and jeopardize the stability we have had in Northeast Asia during the last 20 years.

4. The Situation at Sea

A major non-nuclear conflict in Europe or in Northeast Asia would make it essential for the United States to keep open sea lines of communication to both regions, as well as to other continents and areas. A war in Europe might well become worldwide in character, but even if it were to remain contained, we would have to be concerned about Soviet land and naval deployments in the Far East. We require the major elements of a two-ocean Navy.

Maintenance of a fleet of the proper size and composition to fulfill that role is a problem which requires the most thorough consideration. The present assessment is that the current fleet can control the North Atlantic sea lanes to Europe, but only after serious losses to U.S. and allied shipping, and that our ability to operate in the Eastern Mediterranean would be, at best, uncertain. The fleet in the Pacific could hold open the sea lanes to Hawaii and Alaska but, because of a shortage of surface combatants, would have difficulty in protecting our lines of communication into the Western Pacific. This situation will presumably grow more precarious as the capabilities of Soviet nuclear attack submarines increase.

V. Proposed Programs

This general assessment of the planning contingencies which have been important to the shaping and testing of U.S. forces suggests where—if not corrected—our current and future vulnerabilities lie. It also suggests the direction that the FY 1977 budget should take. Accordingly, assessing the FY 1977 request requires examination of the larger picture which has been set forth. Judgments in the next few months which fail to weigh adequately the need to check present adverse trends will inexorably lead to a conclusion in the world that the United States has decided to allow the trends to continue to the point of imbalance, insufficiency and, possibly, ultimately, instability. We should not be surprised if the discounting of U.S. power and will, which would follow from such a conclusion, would bring unpleasant consequences.

Expert witnesses will be appearing before you to discuss the specific details of the FY 1977 request. In light of the objectives set forth, the expanding capabilities of the Soviet Union, and the trends described, my chief purpose today is to underline the importance of five major program areas I consider essential.

1. Strategic Nuclear Forces

U.S. strategic nuclear deterrence continues to be based on a Triad of strategic forces. These forces are designed to be able to ride out a surprise attack and retaliate in a controlled second-strike at Presidential direction. A combination of ballistic missiles—land- and sea-based—and heavy bombers is necessary to diversify the strategic forces sufficiently, so that neither system failures nor enemy ingenuity could prevent retaliation. Responsive command and control of these forces is essential to deal with the possibility of less than all-out attacks and to terminate a nuclear exchange at the earliest moment possible if, despite best efforts, deterrence should fail.

At the present time, one component of the Triad—the Minuteman force—is essential to both diversity and control. And, it is the Minuteman force that the increasingly sophisticated Soviet ICBM capability threatens to neutralize eventually. Accordingly, we must move steadily, but with deliberation, to retain the option to move toward a more secure basing mode for the ICBM force.

—The Trident program is necessary in any event to replace the aging SLBM forces in the mid-1980s. We are also concerned with possible Soviet advances in anti-submarine warfare capabilities, and the quieter Trident boat with its longer range missiles hedges against any significant Soviet ASW gains.

—The B–1 bomber represents a suitable successor to the B–52. Its ability to penetrate at low altitude and high speed will allow us to offset any Soviet air defense improvements. Most important, the B–1's advances in structural design, hardening against nuclear effects, and the ability to fly out from under nuclear attack, with minimum warning time, would represent a valuable improvement in survivability.

—The M–X missile, either in fixed silos or in a multiple-aim-point mode, with a combination of larger throw-weight and increased accuracy, should improve on the desirable features of the Minuteman, without Minuteman's potential vulnerabilities. We should develop M–X at a rate that would allow us to supplement part or all of the Minuteman force in the 1980s, should that prove necessary.

In order to keep open the option to diversify further the nuclear forces, exploiting new technology in which we lead the Soviets, we are developing two cruise missiles—sea-launched (SLCM) and air-launched (ALCM).

With these major programs, we should be able to ensure a modern strategic deterrent force through the next decade, and remove, as necessary, the vulnerabilities that could increasingly degrade elements of our present posture. As our deterrent improves, so will our contribution to strategic stability.

2. General Purpose Forces

The primary U.S. contribution to the non-nuclear defense of Western Europe continues to be a combination of ground forces and tactical airpower. Because a war in Europe could break out suddenly, we keep the initial defense capability largely in the active force structure rather than in the guard and reserve. The added weight in men, armor, and guns that the Soviets have been providing to a potential assault force in Central Europe is a fundamental reason why the active Army is being expanded from 13 to 16 divisions (within a constant level of manpower). We are adding two combat brigades to the European deployments (also within the manpower constraints established by Congress). Two more steps need to be taken:

—First, we should "heavy up" the additional Army divisions now programmed, to give them the increased firepower and mobility necessary for combat in the European theater.
—Second, we should consider adding aircraft to fill out the Air Force's twenty-six fighter/attack wings, both to complement planned Army divisions and to increase firepower and mobility across the European front.

The present assessment of the situation at sea leads to the requirement for additional surface combatants and submarines in a two-ocean capability for simultaneous protection of Atlantic and Pacific sea lanes. The difficult remaining issue is one of determining how many vessels of what kind and mix will be needed to perform the mission. The basis for additional nuclear attack submarines and relatively inexpensive surface combatants, as well as the arguments for more mines and improved undersea surveillance equipment, are well-founded.

Questions concerning additional large-deck carriers, strike cruisers, and the broad adoption of nuclear propulsion merit close attention in the weeks ahead. You will find a tentative five-year shipbuilding forecast outlined in the Annual Report, as requested by Congress. It may prove to be the right program. However, we are examining some options within the Department now and it will be a few weeks before I am in a position to make specific recommendations to the President and the Congress.

3. Strategic Mobility Forces

Long-range mobility forces are critical to our capability, in conjunction with allies, to offset a major Warsaw Pact mobilization and deployment in Central Europe. There remains considerable difference of opinion as to how long it would take the Soviets to fill out and move the tank and mechanized divisions they retain in the western military districts of the USSR. For planning purposes, the United States should be able to reinforce NATO rapidly by moving a substantial number of divisions from the continental United States to the European theater within a few weeks. Current strategic lift forces cannot today fully meet that requirement for these reasons:

—C-5A wing fatigue problems and flying hour limits reduce our capacity to move outsize cargo;

—Strategic airlift squadrons are not manned or supported with spare parts sufficient for the requisite number of sorties; and

—We have yet to achieve essential reductions in preparation and marry-up time (at CONUS and overseas terminals) to exploit the potential of the airlift and sealift resources we own.

The Department is moving to correct some of these defects. We continue to recommend modifications in the civil reserve air fleet (CRAF) so as to improve our capacity to move outsize cargo in the requisite amounts during the early days of a reinforcement effort.

In short, the faster we can move to reinforce, the better NATO's chances will be and the lower the probability that the Warsaw Pact will be tempted to undertake any kind of an attack. This is also why we need to continue large-scale mobility exercises which demonstrate reinforcement capabilities.

4. Readiness

Logistics capabilities undergird the readiness of forces and their ability to sustain combat. The logistics base is of particular concern at a time when competing demands on the defense budget require increasing combat productivity from both men and machines. Despite the resources previously allocated to logistics, the United States has not maintained the levels of equipment readiness and stocks of war reserves required for a fully credible posture of deterrence.

The precise impact of deficiencies in readiness on combat effectiveness is difficult to measure. However, it is widely agreed that:

—Too many U.S. ships are overdue for overhaul, and the number is still growing;

—Too many tactical aircraft are grounded awaiting repair, which in too many instances is delayed because spare parts are lacking;

—The materiel readiness of U.S. land forces is improving, but remains substandard in some important respects;

—Finally, we are running unnecessary risks because of

shortfalls in war reserve stocks, especially of modern and more efficient munitions.

I will not belabor the reasons for the present level of readiness. I am persuaded that we must make a significant and sustained effort to correct the four major weaknesses just outlined. U.S. combat capabilities are already strained when judged against their tasks; we should not further reduce their effectiveness and ability to sustain themselves in combat because of weaknesses in logistics support.

5. Research and Development

A vigorous program of research, development, test, and evaluation is critical to the achievement of long-term U.S. national security objectives. The effectiveness of our strategic and general purpose forces in relation to the modernized Soviet forces depends on the quality of our R&D. We try continuously to hedge against the uncertainties of a rapidly changing future. We also attempt to reduce costs and improve effectiveness.

Overall U.S. technological leadership is as directly challenged by the Soviet Union as is our military capability. During the past decade, Soviet investment in military and space R&D appears to have at least equalled our own; now it is growing at a more rapid rate. The Soviets have been producing and deploying large quantities of advanced weapons, seizing the technological lead or closing the gap in almost every class of weapon.

Reversing these trends in R&D is vital, and FY 1976 appropriations appear to have halted the downward trend in the U.S. RDT&E program. Nearly $11 billion is requested in FY 1977, an amount essential to correct the divergent U.S./USSR trends and provide real growth needed to:

—Strengthen the U.S. technology base to create options for future development;
—Demonstrate selected alternatives chosen from among new options;
—Select the best system or systems and manage the resulting development and production program efficiently and effectively;
—Concentrate on completing current U.S. development programs to achieve improved deployed capabilities.

VI. Restraints on Defense Planning

The improvements being made in the U.S. force structure, and the efforts to maintain a superior technological base through research and development, are essential if we are to have continued deterrence, stability, and detente in this period ahead—a period which will almost certainly include increases in Soviet military capabilities. Without improvements, the vulnerabilities which can be anticipated from the momentum of present trends will become a reality—with all that could mean. To reduce the danger, we must begin to act now.

I recognize that national defense accounts for about 25 percent of the President's proposed outlays for FY 1977, and that roughly half of the total increase in Federal spending from FY 1976 to FY 1977 is proposed for the Department of Defense. All of us wish that it could be otherwise. But the Constitution requires that we "provide for the common Defence," and war, as Alexis de Tocqueville pointed out, is "an occurrence to which all nations are subject, democratic nations as well as others. Whatever taste they may have for peace, they must hold themselves in readiness to repel aggression . . ."

This much we must continue to do, but we must do it with continuing attention to economy and efficiency. In order to improve our "readiness to repel aggression," and restrain our requests, we are recommending nine key measures to reduce Defense costs. We propose to:

—Restrain the growth in compensation levels for military and civilian personnel;

—Eliminate 26,000 civilian positions by consolidating headquarters and other facilities;

—Phase out subsidies for the operating costs of military commissaries over a three-year period;

—Eliminate dual compensation of Federal employees on active duty for training with the National Guard or Reserve;

—Reduce temporary duty and permanent change-of-station travel;

—Decrease petroleum consumption for proficiency flying programs through greater use of smaller aircraft and ground training aids;

—Narrow the scope of the civil defense program so that it concentrates on the support of measures at the state and local level to reduce losses from a nuclear attack;

—Hold new military construction below the levels of FY 1976;

—Reduce the paid drill strength of the Navy Reserve by 40,000.

These nine steps enabled us to reduce our request for budget authority by approximately $2.8 billion in FY 1977. Most of the proposed actions require the approval of the Congress. These decisions will not be easy to make. It should be recognized, however, that if these actions are not approved, additional defense appropriations of up to $2.8 billion, and total obligational authority of as much as $116 billion will be required. Within the budget of $112.7 billion that the President has presented, an amount of $2.8 billion cannot be absorbed without a reduction in combat effectiveness.

VII. Conclusion

We live in an age of paradoxes, at a time when hope and peril run side by side. To be just and compassionate, we must be strong. As you consider this budget, you will inevitably consider the military environment, the state of our defenses, and the facts of the world situation, as I have done. The arithmetic is not encouraging; the facts are not kind, but the task is fundamental. I urge your support of this request.

(4) "America's Destiny: The Global Context": Address by Secretary of State Henry A. Kissinger at the University of Wyoming, Laramie, February 4, 1976.[7]

It is good to be here in the West. The people of this land remind me once again that America is not the cynical, confused, and tired nation so many in Washington would have us believe it is. Instead, as I have so often seen in my trips, the American people continue to have pride in their country. They know that America has done more for the world, and for peace, over the past 30 years than any nation in history. They know we have given more of our resources, fed more of the starving, taken in more immigrants, and educated more people from other lands than any other nation before us.

The American people are tired of hearing how evil we are, how terrible are our mistakes, and how misguided our purposes. They know better. And they want better.

It is true that we have passed through a decade and more of tragedy—we have been witness to assassination; we have suffered through a tragic war that shattered our domestic unity; and we have endured our greatest constitutional crisis since the Civil War.

But we have come through these difficult times with our institutions as strong as ever. We remain the world's greatest democracy; we continue to be the bastion to which other nations look for their protection; and we remain the symbol of hope to the

[7]Department of State Press Release 47; text from Bulletin, 74: 249-56.

millions around the world who live in tyranny and poverty but yearn for freedom and prosperity.

America, from its birth, has meant much to the world. The Founding Fathers were animated by a sense of obligation, and of mission, to other peoples and to posterity. Our Revolution, our independence, and our democracy set examples which excited and encouraged imitation around the globe. America represented an inspiration and the most important political experiment of modern history—the spectacle of successful self-government, economic opportunity, social equality, civil and religious liberty, and the tremendous capacities of a free people to shape their own destiny.

Later in our history these values affected the world in a new way—as a powerful magnet drawing great tides of immigration. It was a movement of ideas as well as people, which not only shaped this nation but vastly altered the assumptions and social structures of the Old World.

In recent decades, America's impact on the world has been more immediate. For much of this century, global peace and prosperity have depended upon our contribution. When World War II ended, we took the lead in helping a shattered globe rebuild from devastation. We shaped the commercial and financial system that spread prosperity and economic opportunity to far corners of the world. We built peacetime alliances to maintain global stability and defend the values we share with the great industrial democracies. We resisted aggression. We mediated conflicts. We helped ease the process of decolonization. And we led the fight against disease, hunger, ignorance, and the forces of oppression and terror that have scarred this century.

No other nation has made such a contribution. No other nation can make such a contribution now. The best hope for a planet still beset by war, poverty, and tyranny is a strong, committed, vigilant America.

We must never forget that in serving peace and progress we both serve ourselves and live up to our best traditions.

We declared our independence in "decent respect to the opinions of mankind." Our Founding Fathers were sophisticated statesmen who understood the European balance of power and knew how our country could profit from it. Our independence was not won by American arms alone. The shrewd diplomacy of Franklin and Jefferson led to the involvement of Britain's enemies—France, Spain, and Russia—and eventually engineered the only defeat Britain suffered in the modern era. We then cut loose from our temporary allies when John Jay won the British Crown's recognition and liquidated the residual problems of our war with England.

For more than three decades after we gained our independence, we lived in an age of international turmoil that saw us go to the brink of war with France and suffer the capture of our capital by Britain. Again, alert to new opportunities provided by changes on the international scene, we moved astutely to take advantage of them. The effective elimination of France and Spain from the hemisphere, the expansion of Russia in the Pacific Northwest, and the growing disaffection of Great Britain from the European powers led us in 1823 to concert the Monroe Doctrine with Great Britain.

Thereafter, for the hundred years between Waterloo and 1914, America benefited from the existence of a world balance of power, presided over by Britain, which maintained global stability and prevented international war. In the words of Prime Minister Canning, the doctrine "called the New World into existence to redress the balance of the Old."

Thus, the balance of power in Europe and our skill in using it protected the young United States; it enabled us, in reliance upon the British Navy, to turn our back on the Atlantic and open the continent before us.

Theodore Roosevelt noted that long before Jefferson negotiated an end to the French claim to Louisiana, foreign claims had been effectively undermined by the great western movement of Americans and the free communities they quickly founded. But the consolidation of their pioneering achievement was made possible by those negotiations and by the subsequent series of remarkable diplomatic successes. The annexation of Florida, the Oregon boundary settlement with Great Britain, the Treaty of Guadalupe Hidalgo, the Gadsden Purchase, Secretary of State Seward's purchase of Alaska from Russia—all were triumphs of diplomacy during decades when most citizens believed America did not have, or need, a foreign policy.

Indeed, our very achievements in dealing with the world brought Americans under the sway of a shared mythology. As a society made up of men and women who had fled the persecutions and power politics of the Old World, Americans—whether Mayflower descendants or refugees from the failed revolutions of 1848—came to assume that we were beyond the reach of the imperatives of traditional foreign policy.

While our security continued to be assured by our place in the international structure of the time, we became bemused by the popular belief that President Monroe's obligation to defend the Western Hemisphere and, indeed, almost any obligation we might choose to assume, depended on unilateral American decisions to be entered into or ended entirely at our discretion. Shielded by two oceans and enriched by a bountiful nature, we proclaimed our special situation as universally valid even while other nations with a narrower margin of survival knew that their range of choice was far more limited.

The preoccupation of other nations with security only reinforced our sense of uniqueness. We came increasingly to regard diplomacy with suspicion. Arms and alliances were seen as immoral and reactionary. Negotiations were considered less a means of reconciling our ideals with our interests than a device to entangle us in the endless quarrels of a morally questionable world. Our native inclination for straightforwardness brought increasing impatience with diplomacy, whose essential attribute is ambiguity and compromise.

In this atmosphere even the purchase of Alaska—which excluded Russia from our continent—was regarded in its day as a towering folly explainable only in terms of American gullibility in the face of Old World diplomatic guile. Congress was prevailed upon only with the greatest difficulty to provide the $7 million to complete the deal. The mythology of American ineptitude in its diplomatic pursuits has carried into the 20th century. Will Rogers was always assured of a laugh when he cracked, "America never lost a war and never won a conference." With the humility for which I am famous, I of course reject this attitude.

Forgetful of the wisdom and skilled statecraft by which the Founding Fathers won our independence and secured our safety, and disdainful of the techniques by which all nations—even the United States—must preserve their interests, America entered the 20th century—the most complex and turbulent time in history—largely unprepared for the part we would be called upon to play.

As Lord Bryce said in his "American Commonwealth," America had been sailing "on a summer sea," but a cloud bank was "on the horizon and now no longer distant, a time of mists and shadows, wherein dangers may be concealed whose form and magnitude she can scarcely conjecture."

U.S. Ascendancy: Maintaining Global Stability

In the early years of this century, America seemed to face a choice between continued detachment and active involvement in world affairs. But this was more apparent than real, for the Pax Britannica on which we had relied for so long was coming to an end. We had become—almost without noticing it—the world's major economic power. Increasingly, we were the only democratic nation with sufficient power to maintain a precarious world balance. But nothing in our experience had equipped us to recognize our new responsibility. We continued to reject the demands of the politics of security and abhorred alliances as contrary to American principles. In the place of foreign policy we fell back on our tradition of law, in repeated and unsuccessful attempts to legislate solutions to international conflicts. Many thought that power and principle were forever incompatible.

Our entry into World War I was produced by real geopolitical interests, such as freedom of the sea and the threat of the domination of Europe by a hostile power; but we chose to interpret our participation in legal and idealistic terms—we fought the war "to end war." The inevitable disillusion with an imperfect outcome led to a tide of isolationism. We responded again with moral and legal gestures—humanitarian relief, new disarmament schemes, the Kellogg-Briand Pact to ban war—at a time when the very nature of the international order was being brought into question by the convulsions of the new century. We sought security in aloofness, just as we looked for scapegoats—rooting out the so-called "munitions makers"—to explain why we had ever engaged in such an undertaking as the First World War. The Great Depression drew our energies further inward to deal with the problems of our own society, even while economic upheaval simultaneously generated overwhelming perils abroad.

Our refusal to admit that foreign policy should be related to interests led us, in the years between the wars, to treat allies as rivals, whose armaments had to be limited because they contributed to international tensions. On the brink of World War II, isolationism had been transformed from a comfortable assumption to a deeply felt conviction. Just as the world was about to impinge upon us as never before, we had virtually abandoned the basic precautions needed to preserve our national security. Only with the greatest difficulty could President Franklin D. Roosevelt begin to assert international leadership openly and take steps against the mounting global threat by preparing America for war.

World War II was well underway before we were shocked out of isolation by external attack. Total victory, and the refusal to consider the security of the postwar world in terms of any notion of equilibrium, ill prepared us for the war's aftermath—when the destruction of Europe's traditional power centers suddenly drew Soviet power into the heart of the European Continent.

Yet in the first postwar years America found within itself extraordinary capacities of statesmanship and creativity. Leaders of both parties and many backgrounds—Truman and Eisenhower, Vandenberg and Marshall, Acheson and Dulles—built a national consensus for responsible American world leadership, for a foreign policy based on both principle and pragmatism.

Albert Einstein said at the outset of the nuclear age that "everything has changed, except our mode of thinking." To cope with a world whose basic conditions were so radically altered was a task comparable in magnitude to that which faced the Founding Fathers. When Dean Acheson said he was "present at the creation," he referred not only to the creation of our postwar policy but to a new era in the history of mankind.

American foreign policy had come full circle. With sophistication, the Founding Fathers had manipulated the balance of power to gain our independence and then drew on the international system to assure our survival. A century and a quarter of almost total security had tempted us into isolationism. And now, after two World Wars in this century, we have learned that the responsibilities—and the burdens—of world leadership are inescapable.

Americans can be enormously proud of what their country has accomplished in the postwar decades to build a more stable, secure. and prosperous world. The recovery of Western Europe and Japan, the creation and revitalization of peacetime alliances, the shaping of the global trade and monetary system, the economic advance of newer and poorer nations, the measures to control the nuclear arms race—these comprise an enduring achievement of American statesmanship.

America has been thrust into the role of global leadership with a dual responsibility; we must maintain our security and global peace by the traditional methods of balance of power and diplomacy. But we know that nuclear war could destroy civilization, and therefore we must go beyond traditional foreign policy to shape a more cooperative world reflecting the imperatives of interdependence and justice.

The Traditional Agenda of War and Peace

Our well-being begins with strength at home. To keep America strong and secure, we will maintain the military power needed to meet any challenge. But security cannot be achieved in isolation. Our close ties with the industrial democracies of Western Europe, Canada, and Japan have been the cornerstone of world stability and peace for a generation. We share a common conception of human dignity, a common interest in peace and prosperity, and a common conviction of linked destiny. Today we and our allies look beyond military issues to joint endeavors across a broad range of human activity: we have coordinated our diplomacy to ease global tensions, our policies for economic growth, and our efforts in new fields such as energy.

A secure and stable world requires as well that we seek a

reconciliation of interests with potential adversaries. We shall never lose sight of the fact that in an age threatened by thermonuclear extinction, the search for peace is a moral imperative; without it nothing else we do will be of enduring value.

Peace, to be stable and durable, must place on a more reliable basis the relations between nations that possess the power to destroy our planet. The suspicion and rivalry of two generations will not soon be swept away, and we have no illusions about the continuing moral and ideological conflict. But we will spare no effort to seek reliable reciprocal measures for containing the strategic arms race; we will continue to pursue cooperative arrangements across a wide range of technical, cultural, and commercial fields to deepen the mutual stake in peace.

Progress toward relaxation of tensions, and our overall attitude toward those who would oppose us, have always depended upon restrained and responsible conduct on their part—on issues where America's interests are affected directly, as in Europe, as well as in peripheral conflicts, such as Angola. Let no nation misconstrue America's commitment to an easing of tensions as a license to fish in troubled waters. Let no country believe that Americans will long remain indifferent to the dispatch of expeditionary forces and vast amounts of materiel to impose minority governments—especially when that expeditionary force comes from a nation of the Western Hemisphere. Americans may be slow to rouse, but they will do their duty implacably once a threat is clear.

If the world is to remain at peace and advance in progress, an active American role in the world is essential. The Middle East is perhaps the most critical example. We must be involved there because of our historical and moral commitment to Israel, because of our important interests and friendships in the Arab world, because continued instability in the Middle East strains our relations with allies and risks severe global economic dislocation, and because continuing crisis risks direct U.S.-Soviet confrontation.

The broad implications and imminent dangers of regional conflicts such as those in Angola and the Middle East have compelled us to play an active part. But it would be wrong to conclude from this that the United States seeks to operate as the world's policeman. There are innumerable local conflicts around the globe in which we neither have nor seek any role. We do not seek to police the world—but neither will we accept it if the Soviet Union attempts to do so.

The Soviet and Cuban pattern of conduct in Africa, if continued in other areas, could unravel global security. The tensions of the Middle East, if not overcome, could threaten global peace. With prudence and wisdom, we can prevent dangers to our wider interests by engaging ourselves now at far less cost than we will inevitably have to pay later if we abdicate responsibility. We cannot escape the fundamental reality that it is the United States, alone among the free nations of the world, that is capable of—and therefore responsible for—maintaining the global balance against those who would seek hegemony and shaping a new world of hope and progress.

The New Agenda

True progress requires more than security. We must seek to break past patterns of confrontation and response. It is no longer possible for America or any other nation to achieve its purposes by physical power alone; in today's world, influence derives not only from military strength but also from economic, social, and political factors, from the ability to inspire other nations with the conviction that they have a stake in a shared future.

On a shrinking planet of diffused power and linked destinies, we are called upon to demonstrate vision and patience. Our generation has the opportunity to shape a new international order. If we succeed, the prospects for America and the world are bright. If we fail, the world will be shaped by others who do not share our principles; our period will witness mounting conflict and suffering.

We can approach these new challenges with confidence. Our technological advance, our managerial genius, our achievements in science and medicine, the productivity of our farms and industries, our physical resources, our commitment to the rule of law, insure for us a role of leadership. And we have been demonstrating the resiliency of our economy by emerging from a global recession faster and more steadily than any other nation.

Fundamental to our well-being is international economic cooperation. In the past few years, Americans have seen clearly just how much international economic relations determine the progress of all nations, including our own. The oil embargo of 1973 and the subsequent price increases with their devastating global consequences have reminded us to what extent far-off events affect our prosperity and how important international economic cooperation is for our own well-being and for the prosperity of the rest of the world.

The United States has taken far-reaching steps to lay the foundations for international economic cooperation:

—We have worked closely with the other great industrial democracies on trade, energy, and monetary reform.

—We have organized a comprehensive international program to expand food production in developing countries and to channel resources, including the new wealth of the oil producers, into improving the financing, production, storage, and. distribution of food.

—We have developed and implemented a strategy to end our domestic and international energy vulnerability. We have joined with the other industrial consuming countries in solidarity programs to protect us against further oil embargoes and against destabilizing movements of assets held by oil-producing countries. Only last week the International Energy Agency, a group of industrial consuming countries brought together at our initiative, adopted a sweeping program of cooperative action. We consider this one of the most significant cooperative efforts of the past decade. The industrial democracies will now begin to coordinate their research and development effort to develop alternative supplies of energy, both nuclear power and the more exotic sources such as synthetic and solar energy.

—And the United States has presented to the U.N. General Assembly special session a comprehensive and practical program for a multilateral effort to promote economic development.

Thus we have not only tackled the traditional issues of peace and war but made a good beginning in helping to fashion more cooperative relationships in new dimensions of world concern.

The structure of our foreign policy is sound and ready to encounter the future.

But America cannot hope to shape the future of the world unless we are a confident and united people.

America's Imperative: Domestic Unity

For more than three decades America has, despite setbacks and mistakes, conducted a remarkably effective foreign policy. We have done so because we recognized, even when we disagreed, that what we did beyond our borders was done in the name of the nation as a whole. Partisan interests were channeled into positive accomplishments. We acted as a confident people. We did not doubt ourselves; we did not consume ourselves in self-hatred.

That was the ultimate underpinning for the role of world leadership that was thrust upon us; it was the true measure of our greatness. It is a strength we must not lose.

History has made America the repository and guardian of the best values of mankind, for no other free nation is strong enough to replace us. Without our commitment there can be no progress. We must have the steadiness to oppose military pressures and the vision to work for a more peaceful international order. Moderation has meaning only when practiced by the strong, and strength has purpose only when tempered by conciliation.

These twin strands of firmness and conciliation reflect the permanent interests of our nation. Yet our ability to pursue either course has been, in recent months, increasingly threatened. A strong, coherent, and effective international role is jeopardized by acrimonious controversy which thwarts serious discussion of the great issues and by the growing tendency of too many in the Congress not only to supervise but to legislate the day-to-day conduct of foreign policy.

The slogans of a past we thought we had transcended are suddenly reappearing. We now hear again that suffering is prolonged by American involvement, that injustice is perpetuated by American commitments, that defense spending is wasteful at best and produces conflict at worst, that American intelligence activities are immoral, that the necessary confidentiality of diplomacy is a plot to deceive the public, that flexibility is cynical, and that tranquillity is somehow to be brought about by an abstract purity of motive for which history offers no example.

If these attitudes shape our policies, we will deprive our diplomacy of its essential tools; conciliatory policies and firm measures alike will be undermined by growing doubt about the steadiness of our national will. An atmosphere of suspicion and a lack of even the most elementary confidentiality will make impossible the management of the government and the conduct of negotiation. If a national consensus does not exist, our policy will be driven by narrow interest groups and short-term political considerations.

In an era when the danger of war has been reduced but the rivalry of communism and freedom continues, the gray area between foreign policy and overt conflict continues to be important and, indeed, takes on increasing significance. Yet leaks, sensational investigations, and the demoralization of our intelligence services— at a time when our adversaries are stepping up their own efforts— are systematically depriving our government of the ability to respond.

An effective foreign policy requires a strong national government which can act with assurance and speak with confidence on behalf of all Americans. But when the executive is disavowed repeatedly and publicly, other governments wonder who speaks for America and what an American commitment means. Our government is in danger of progressively losing the ability to shape events, and a great nation that does not shape history eventually becomes its victim.

Too much depends upon a strong and confident America to

allow this state of affairs to continue. When America abdicates from shaping the future, when its policy falls prey to the passions of the moment and the play of pressure groups, it disheartens friends, emboldens adversaries, and gives pause to the wavering and thus undermines international order.

We must restore our unity while the essential structure of our foreign policy is still sound and before irreparable damage is done to it. We retain the capacity, if we have the will, to prevent military expansion by our adversaries. Our alliances with the industrialized nations have never been more solid. A further agreement to limit the strategic arms race is within reach. We are well launched on a durable and improving relationship with the world's most populous nation. The elements for peace in the Middle East exist. A dialogue with the developing world has begun on a hopeful note. The threat of war around the globe has been reduced. The principal danger we face is our domestic divisions.

The American people have a right to demand of their leaders in and out of government an end to the destructive debate that has in recent months come to mark our political process. They know, as the world knows, that the United States is still a great country. And they know how much damage these continuing attacks on their country's institutions have done and will do to undermine America's ability to keep the peace.

We have every obligation to draw the right lessons from our past mistakes and to see that they never happen again. But we have an equally compelling duty to remember that a faltering of will on the part of a country that has for decades been the principal guarantor of peace and progress can have disastrous consequences for the prospects of a better and safer world.

America now finds itself in a world of proliferating, often competitive, and sometimes threatening power. We must often make choices that will not solve but only manage problems; we must occasionally make compromises that by definition will not produce ideal results. We need confidence in ourselves to master a complicated period in which the United States can no longer overwhelm problems with resources—when it needs purpose, firmness, coherence, flexibility, imagination, and above all, unity.

The formulation and conduct of our foreign policy must of course be the product of consultation and accommodation between the Congress and the President. Neither branch can, alone, determine the course we will pursue abroad. The Congress, entitled by the letter and spirit of the Constitution and by the practices of 200 years, must be an equal partner in the process.

But if that partnership is to flourish, each branch must respect the role of the other, and each must recognize the limitations—constitutional and practical—on its authority. The Congress can set broad guidelines and decide basic policies. But the Congress does not have the organization, the information, or the responsibility for deciding the tactical questions that arise daily in the conduct of our foreign relations or for executing a coherent, consistent, comprehensive policy. The President has this responsibility and must be permitted to exercise it on behalf of the entire nation. For in the last analysis, the United States, when it deals with other nations, must speak with one voice.

It is time we recognize that, increasingly, our difficulties abroad are largely of our own making. If America is to be safe, we must cease dismantling and demoralizing our intelligence services. If America is to preserve its values and maintain the global balance of stability, we must have a strong defense. And if America is to help build a world environment in which our citizens can thrive and be free, we cannot deny ourselves the essential tools of policy. Without these our only option is to retreat, to become an isolated fortress island in a hostile and turbulent global sea, awaiting the ultimate confrontation with the only response we will not have denied ourselves—massive retaliation. Our branches of government, special interests, and ordinary citizens must pursue their legitimate concerns with an understanding that there are basic overriding national interests which, if neglected, will render pointless all else we do.

In our age, whose challenges are without precedent, we need once again the wisdom of our Founding Fathers. Our pragmatic tradition must help us understand reality and shape it, rather than be diverted by an obsession with technical detail or method without purpose. Our love of our country must inspire us to persevere with dedication and unity and not to consume our substance in civil strife. Our idealism should remind us that we remain the beacon of hope for all those who love liberty and that this imposes a heavy responsibility upon us.

Our international role is not a burden; it protects the lives and well-being of our people. It has been a historical success. In our first two centuries we have done great things as a united people. We can accomplish even more in our third century. America remains the strongest nation in the world; our government continues to be the noblest experiment undertaken by man; we still are an inspiration to all the world's millions who are much less fortunate than we. Our past achievements should be but prologue to the exciting future that crowds in upon us. It is, in the final analysis, up to us.

2. AVERTING NUCLEAR DISASTER

(5)   *"The Permanent Challenge of Peace: U.S. Policy toward the Soviet Union": Address by Secretary of State Kissinger at a luncheon sponsored by the Commonwealth Club of San Francisco and the World Affairs Council of Northern California, San Francisco, February 3, 1976.*[1]

America enters its third century and its 48th Presidential election with unmatched physical strength, a sound foreign policy design—yet scarred by self-doubt. In the past decade and a half, we have seen one President assassinated, another driven from office, and a third resign. We have lived through the agony of Viet-Nam and Watergate. We are still struggling to overcome the bitterness and division that have followed in their wake. We face no more urgent task than to restore our national unity and our national resolve.

For we, the strongest free nation, cannot afford the luxury of withdrawing into ourselves to heal our wounds. Too much depends upon us—peace or war, prosperity or depression, freedom or tyranny. Too much is at stake for America to paralyze itself tearing up the past, seeking sensational headlines in the present, or offering panaceas for the future. For our own well-being—American lives and American jobs—will be affected if we permit our domestic disunity and turmoil to cause us to falter in meeting our international responsibilities.

And so it is imperative that the national debate in this election year—the greatest demonstration of how free people govern themselves—strengthen, not undermine, our confidence and our capacity to carry out an effective national policy. It is essential that we quickly rebuild our national unity, the sense that we are all part of a shared enterprise.

It is in this spirit that I intend today to discuss America's relations with the world's other superpower, the Soviet Union. In

[1]Department of State Press Release 44; text from *Bulletin*, 74: 201-12.

recent months that relationship has become, as it should be, an important part of our national debate. I want to explain the Administration's view of the conditions that gave rise to the policy known as détente, the goals we seek, and the relationship of our Soviet policy to the overall design of American diplomacy.

The United States is today confronted by one challenge unprecedented in its own history and another challenge without precedent in the history of the world. America finds itself for the first time permanently and irrevocably involved in international affairs. At the same time, the catastrophic nature of nuclear war imposes upon us a necessity that transcends traditional concepts of diplomacy and balance of power: to shape a world order that finds stability in self-restraint and, ultimately, cooperation.

For the first century and a half of our history, our peace and security were provided for us by two oceans, the shield of the British Navy, and equilibrium among the European powers. The success of our democracy at home, and the absence of direct threat from abroad, nourished our sense of uniqueness and fostered the illusion that it was up to America to choose whether and when we would participate in the world.

Since De Tocqueville it has been a cliche that Americans, as a people, are slow to arouse but that, once aroused, we are a tremendous and implacable force. Thus, even when we ventured forth in foreign affairs, we identified our exertion as a temporary disruption of our tranquillity. Our history, except for the Civil War, was without the tragedies and the sense of practical external limits that so colored the experience of almost every other people.

Our successes seemed to teach us that any problem could be solved once and for all by determined effort. We considered peace natural, stability normal, and foreign involvement appropriate only so long as needed to remove some temporary threat or disorder. We entered World War I as "the war to end war" and to "make the world safe for democracy." We fought World War II until "unconditional surrender."

Even in the first 25 years after World War II, an era of great creativity and unprecedented American engagement in foreign affairs, we acted as if the world's security and economic development could be conclusively insured by the commitment of American resources, know-how, and effort. We were encouraged, even impelled, to act as we did by our unprecedented predominance in a world shattered by war and the collapse of the great colonial empires. We considered our deployment of troops in Europe and elsewhere to be temporary. We thought that the policy of containment would transform the Soviet Union and that a changed Soviet society would then evolve inexorably into a compatible member of a harmonious international community.

At the same time, the central character of moral values in American life always made us acutely sensitive to the purity of means—and when we disposed of overwhelming power we had a great luxury of choice. Our moral certainty made compromise difficult; our preponderance often made it seem unnecessary.

Today, while we still have massive strength, we no longer enjoy meaningful nuclear supremacy. We remain the world's most productive and innovative economy—but we must now share leadership with Western Europe, Canada, and Japan; we must deal with the newly wealthy and developing nations; and we must make new choices regarding our economic relations with the Communist countries. Our democratic principles are still far more valued by the world's millions than we realize, but we must also compete with new ideologies which assert progressive goals but pursue them by oppressive methods.

Today, for the first time in our history, we face the stark reality that the challenge is unending, that there is no easy and surely no final answer, that there are no automatic solutions. We must learn to conduct foreign policy as other nations have had to conduct it for so many centuries—without escape and without respite, knowing that what is attainable falls short of the ideal, mindful of the necessities of self-preservation, conscious that the reach of our national purpose has its limits. This is a new experience for Americans. It prompts nostalgia for a simpler past. As before in our history, it generates the search for scapegoats, holding specific policies responsible for objective conditions.

It is precisely because we no longer predominate but must pursue a long-term course that there is a premium today on our constancy and purposefulness. We cannot afford to swing recklessly between confrontation and abdication. We must not equate tough rhetoric with strong action, nor can we wish away tough realities with nostalgic hopes. We can no longer act as if we engage ourselves in foreign affairs only when we choose, or only to overcome specific problems, so that we can then shift our priorities back to our natural concern with ourselves. The reality is that there can be no security without our vigilance and no progress without our dedication.

It is in this context that U.S.-Soviet relations must be seen.

The Contemporary Challenge of Relations

The issue of how to deal with the Soviet Union has been a central feature of American policy for three decades. What is new today is the culmination of 30 years of postwar growth of Soviet industrial, technological, and military power. No American policy caused this; no American policy could have prevented it. But American policy can keep this power from being used to expand Soviet influence to our detriment; we have the capacity to enable allies and friends to live with a sense of security; we possess the assets to advance the process of building an international order of cooperation and progress.

We must do so, however, in unprecedented conditions. In previous periods, rivalry between major powers has almost invariably led to war. In our time, when thermonuclear weapons threaten casualties in the hundreds of millions, such an outcome is unthinkable. We must manage a fundamental clash of ideologies and harness the rivalry of the nuclear superpowers, first into coexistence, and then mold coexistence into a more positive and cooperative future. For as President Kennedy once said:[2]

> . . . in the final analysis our most basic common link is that we all inhabit this small planet. We all breathe the same air. We all cherish our children's future. And we are all mortal.

In the period after World War II, our nightmare was that the Soviet Union, after consolidating its occupation of Eastern Europe, might seek to spread its control to other contiguous areas in Europe and Asia. Our policies therefore sought to build alliances and positions of military strength from which we could contain and isolate the Soviet Union. In this manner the Soviet Union might be forced to settle for peace; transformations might occur within Soviet society that would curb expansionist tendencies and make the U.S.S.R. over time into a more cooperative participant in the international system.

These policies served us and our allies well. Soviet expansion was checked. Behind our shield of security and with our assistance, our friends and allies in Western Europe restored their economies and rebuilt their democratic institutions.

Yet the hope that these policies would produce permanent stability, positive evolution of the Soviet system, and greater normality was only partially realized. In the immediate postwar period, the aggressiveness of Soviet ideology in the Stalinist era obscured some of the real weaknesses of the Soviet state. Indeed, as late as 1962 during the Cuban missile crisis, the United States enjoyed a five-to-one superiority in strategic missiles, a three-to-one superiority in strategic bombers, total naval superiority everywhere, and rough equality on the ground in Europe.

Gradually, with the acquisition of nuclear technology and the

[2]Address of June 10, 1963, American University, Washington, in *Documents, 1963:* 119-20.

transformation of the international system through decolonization, the Soviet Union began to emerge as a first-class military power.

In strategic military terms the U.S.S.R. has achieved a broad equality with the United States, as was inevitable for a large nation whose rulers were prepared to impose great sacrifices on their people and to give military strength the absolute top priority in resources. With only half of our gross national product, Soviet military expenditures exceed those of the United States.

For the first time in history, the Soviet Union can threaten distant places beyond the Eurasian landmass—including the United States. With no part of the world outside the range of its military forces, the U.S.S.R. has begun to define its interests and objectives in global terms. Soviet diplomacy has thrust into the Middle East, Africa, and Asia. This evolution is now rooted in real power, rather than a rhetorical manifestation of a universalist doctrine which in fact has very little validity or appeal.

Coping with the implications of this emerging superpower has been our central security problem for the last several years. This condition will not go away. And it will perhaps never be conclusively "solved." It will have to be faced by every Administration for the foreseeable future.

Our policy must deal with the consequences. The emergence of ambitious new powers into an existing international structure is a recurrent phenomenon. Historically, the adjustment of an existing order to the arrival of one or more new actors almost invariably was accompanied by war—to impede the upstart, to remove or diminish some of the previously established actors, to test the balance of forces in a revised system. But in the nuclear era, when casualties in a general nuclear war will involve hundreds of millions in a matter of days, the use of force threatens utter catastrophe. It is our responsibility to contain Soviet power without global war, to avoid abdication as well as unnecessary confrontation.

This can be done, but it requires a delicate and complex policy. We must strive for an equilibrium of power, but we must move beyond it to promote the habits of mutual restraint, coexistence, and ultimately cooperation. We must stabilize a new international order in a vastly dangerous environment, but our ultimate goal must be to transform ideological conflict into constructive participation in building a better world.

This is what is meant by the process called détente—not the hunger for relaxation of tension, not the striving for agreements at any price, not the mindless search for friendly atmosphere which some critics use as naive and dangerous caricatures.

The policies pursued by this Administration have been designed to prevent Soviet expansion but also to build a pattern of relations in which the Soviet Union will always confront penalties for aggression and also acquire growing incentives for restraint. These goals are well within our capacities. Soviet power is evolving with considerable unevenness. Soviet society is no longer totally cut off from contact with or the influences of the world around it, nor is it without its own needs for outside relationships. It is the great industrial democracies, not the Soviet Union, that are the engine of the world economy and the most promising partners for the poorer nations.

The industrial democracies, if they face their challenges with confidence, if they do not mesmerize themselves with the illusion of simple solutions, possess vast strengths to contain Soviet power and to channel that power in constructive directions.

Our essential task is to recognize the need for a dual policy that simultaneously and with equal vigor resists expansionist drives and seeks to shape a more constructive relationship. We must prevent the Soviet Union from translating its growing strength into global or regional preponderance. But we must do so without escalating every crisis into a massive confrontation. In recent years, the United States has firmly resisted attempts by the Soviet Union to establish a naval base in Cuba, to impede the access routes to Berlin, to exploit the explosive situation in the Middle East. Recently we have sought to halt blatant intervention in Angola—until prevented from doing so by congressional action.

At the same time, we have a historic obligation to mankind to engage the Soviet Union in settlements of concrete problems and to push back the shadow of nuclear catastrophe. At the very least we owe it to our people to demonstrate that their government has missed no opportunity to achieve constructive solutions and that crises which have occurred were unavoidable. For whatever the rhetoric, Americans will not support confrontations they consider contrived.

This is why the United States has set forth principles of responsible relations in the nuclear age: Respect for the interests of all, restraint in the uses of power, and abstention from efforts to exploit instability or local conflicts for unilateral advantage. The United States has sought to give life to these principles in major negotiations on arms control, the prevention of accidental war, and in the settlement of political issues such as Berlin. And we have begun to construct a network of cooperative agreements in a variety of functional areas—economic, scientific, medical, environmental, and others—which promise concrete benefits if political conditions permit their full implementation and further development.

It has been our belief that, with patience, a pattern of restraints and a network of vested interests can develop which will give coexistence a more hopeful dimension and make both sides conscious of what they would stand to lose by reverting to the politics of pressure, confrontation, and crisis.

This policy reflects the deepest aspirations of the American people.

In the early 1970's when current U.S.-Soviet relations were shaped, our nation had already passed through traumatic events and was engaged in an anguishing war. There were riots in the streets and on the campuses demanding rapid progress toward peace. Every new defense program was challenged—including the ABM, which was approved by only one vote, the development of multiple warheads, the Trident submarine, and the B-1 bomber. Successive Congresses passed resolutions urging the Administration to reorder our national priorities away from defense. We were continually attacked for not making concessions in the SALT talks. The Congress and many interest groups pressed continually for the opening up of East-West trade and agitated against the Administration's approach of linking progress in economic relations with prior progress in political relations. Throughout the course of 1970 and 1971, we were involved in a series of crises with the Soviet Union and were often accused of provocation or bellicosity in the process.

Thus, only a few short years ago, the pressures in this country and from our allies were overwhelmingly to move rapidly toward better relations with Moscow. We resisted these pressures then, just as we now refuse to let ourselves be stampeded in the opposite direction. In the Administration's view the country needs a balanced policy, combining firmness and conciliation, strong defense and arms control, political principles and economic incentives. And it must be a policy for the long term that the American people can sustain, offering promise of a constructive future.

It is therefore ironic that our national debate seems now in many respects to have come full circle. The conditions in which détente originated are largely forgotten. Those who pressed for concessions and unilateral restraint toward Moscow now accuse the government of being too conciliatory. Those who complain about our failure to respond with sufficient vigor to Soviet moves are often the very ones who incessantly seek to remove this country's leverage for influence or action—through restrictions on trade and credit, through weakening our intelligence capabilities, through preventing aid to friends who seek to resist Soviet aggression.

The restrictions on trade and credit are a case in point. The human rights issue is a matter of deep and legitimate concern to all Americans. But the congressional attempt to link it openly with economic relations, without subtlety or understanding of Soviet politics, both deprived us of economic levers and sharply reduced Soviet emigration. Other industrial countries have stepped in to provide credits and technology, with less concern for the objective of inducing political restraint which we had envisaged.

So let us understand the scope and limits of a realistic policy:

—We cannot prevent the growth of Soviet power, but we can prevent its use for unilateral advantage and political expansion.

—We cannot prevent a buildup of Soviet forces, but we have the capacity, together with our allies, to maintain an equilibrium. We cannot neglect this task and then blame the Soviet Union if the military balance shifts against us.

—We have the diplomatic, economic, and military capacity to resist expansionism, but we cannot engage in a rhetoric of confrontation while depriving ourselves of the means to confront.

—We must accept that sovereign states, especially of roughly equal power, cannot impose unacceptable conditions on each other and must proceed by compromise.

—We must live with the reality of the nuclear threat, but we have it in our power to build a new relationship that transcends the nuclear peril.

So let us end the defeatist rhetoric that implies that Soviet policy is masterful, purposeful, and overwhelming while American policy is bumbling, uncertain, and weak. Let us stop pretending that somehow tough rhetoric and contrived confrontations show confidence in America. The opposite is true. Those who are prepared to base their policy on reality, those who assert that the American people will support a complex policy of firmness and conciliation and that this policy will succeed, show a real faith in our capacities and our future. We have a design and the material assets to deal with the Soviet Union. We will succeed if we move forward as a united people.

Against this background let me discuss two current issues that illustrate the two strands of policy that we are concurrently pursuing:

—The Strategic Arms Limitation Talks, in which we are seeking to shape a more positive future.

—The Angolan situation, where we are attempting to curb Soviet expansionism.

Strategic Arms Limitation

There is one central fact that distinguishes our era from all previous historical periods: the existence of enormously destructive weapons that can span unlimited distances almost instantaneously. No part of the globe is beyond reach. No part of the globe would be •spared the effects of a general nuclear exchange.

For centuries it was axiomatic that increases in military power could be translated into almost immediate political advantage. It is now clear that new increments of strategic weaponry do not automatically lead to either political or military gains. Yet, in the nature of things, if one side expands its strategic arsenal, the other side will inevitably match it. The race is maintained partly because a perceived inequality is considered by each side as politically unacceptable even though it has become difficult to define precisely what purely military purpose is served.

We thus face a paradox: At current and foreseeable levels of nuclear arms, it becomes increasingly dangerous to invoke them. In no crisis since 1962 have the strategic weapons of the two sides determined the outcome. Today these arsenals increasingly find their purpose primarily in matching and deterring the forces of the opponent. For under virtually no foreseeable circumstance could the United States—or the Soviet Union—avoid 100 million dead in a nuclear exchange. Yet the race goes on because of the difficulty of finding a way to get off the treadmill.[3]

This condition imposes a unique and heavy responsibility on the leaders of the two nuclear superpowers. Sustaining the nuclear competition requires endless invocations of theoretical scenarios of imminent or eventual nuclear attack. The attempt to hedge against all conceivable contingencies, no matter how fanciful, fuels political tensions and could well lead to a self-fulfilling prophecy. The fixation on potential strategic arms imbalances that is inherent in an unrestrained arms race diverts resources into strategically unproductive areas—particularly away from forces for local defense, where shortfalls and imbalances could indeed be turned rapidly to our disadvantage. If no restraint is developed, the competition in strategic arms can have profound consequences for the future of international relations and indeed of civilization.

[3]To be sure, there exist scenarios in planning papers which seek to demonstrate how one side could use its strategic forces and how in some presumed circumstance it would prevail. But these confuse what a technician can calculate with what a responsible statesman can decide. They are invariably based on assumptions such as that one side would permit its missile silos to be destroyed without launching its missiles before they are actually hit—on which no aggressor would rely where forces such as those possessed by either the United States or the U.S.S.R. now and in the years ahead are involved. [Footnote in original.]

The United States therefore has sought and achieved since 1963 a series of arms control agreements which build some restraint into nuclear rivalry. There was a significant breakthrough to limit strategic weapons in 1972. If the 1974 Vladivostok accord leads to a new agreement, an even more important advance will have been made.

Yet, at this critical juncture, the American people are subjected to an avalanche of charges that SALT is a surrender of American interests. There are assertions that the United States is falling behind in the strategic competition and that SALT has contributed to it. There are unsupportable charges that the Soviets have systematically violated the SALT agreements.

None of this is accurate. What are the facts?

First of all, American policy decisions in the 1960's set the level of our strategic forces for the 1970's. We then had the choice between continuing the deployment of large, heavy-throwweight missiles like the Titan or Atlas or undertaking development and deployment of large numbers of smaller, more flexible ICBM's or combinations of both types. The Administration then in office chose to rely on an arsenal of 1,000 small, sophisticated, and highly accurate ICBM's and 656 submarine-launched missiles on 41 boats, along with heavy bombers; we deployed them rapidly and then stopped our buildup of launchers unilaterally in the 1960's when the programs were complete. Only 54 of the heavy Titans were retained and still remain in the force.

The Soviets made the opposite decision; they chose larger, heavier missiles; they continued to build up their forces through the 1960's and 1970's; they passed our numerical levels by 1969-70 and continued to add an average of 200 missiles a year until stopped by the first SALT agreement.

Thus, as a consequence of decisions made a decade ago by both sides, Soviet missiles are superior in throwweight while ours are superior in reliability, accuracy, diversity, and sophistication and we possess larger numbers of warheads. In 1972 when the SALT agreement was signed, the Soviet Union was still building at the rate of 90 land-based and 120 sea-based launchers a year—while we were building none, as a result of our own repeatedly reaffirmed unilateral decisions of a decade previously. Since new American programs to redress the balance had only recently been ordered, there was no way to reduce the numerical gap before the late seventies when more modern sea-based missiles and bombers were scheduled to become operational.

The interim SALT agreement of 1972 froze overall numbers of launchers on both sides for five years, thereby limiting the momentum of Soviet programs without affecting any of ours. It stopped the Soviet buildup of heavy missile launchers. It forced the

Soviets to agree to dismantle 210 older land-based missiles to reach permitted ceilings on missile-carrying submarines. The agreed-upon silo limitations permitted us to increase the throwweight of our own missiles, if we decided on this avenue of improving our strategic forces. We have so far chosen not to do so, although, through research and development, we retain the option. By any measure, the SALT agreements prevented the then-evolving gap in numbers from widening while enabling us to retain our advantage in other categories and easing the problem of redressing the balance when new programs became operational. What no negotiation could do is reverse by diplomacy the results of our own longstanding decisions with respect to weapons design and deployment.

Moreover, the SALT agreements ended for an indefinite period the prospect of a dangerous and uncertain competition in antiballistic missile defense—a competition that promised no strategic advantage, but potentially serious instabilities and the expenditure of vast sums of money.

The first SALT agreements were therefore without question in the American national interest. In the five-year respite gained by the 1972 interim agreement, it was our intention to negotiate a long-term pact on offensive weapons that would firmly fix both sides at an equal level once our new programs became operational. This is precisely what President Ford achieved at Vladivostok in November 1974.

In this accord in principle, both sides agreed on a ceiling of 2,400 strategic weapons covering strategic systems and heavy bombers—but not counting any of our forward-based aircraft in Europe, or our allies' strategic weapons, many of which can reach Soviet soil. The ceiling of 2,400 is lower than the level the Soviet Union already has reached; it would require the dismantling of many Soviet weapons, while the planned levels and composition of our forces would not need to be reduced or changed. An equal ceiling of 1,320 was placed on numbers of strategic weapons with multiple warheads. Soviet heavy missile launchers will remain frozen. These limits would cap the strategic competition in numbers for a 10-year period, yet preserve all the programs we need to assure deterrence and strategic sufficiency.

Obviously no single agreement can solve every problem. This is not a question of loopholes, but of evolving technology, with respect to which we intend to remain vigilant. We will negotiate carefully to make certain that the national interest and national security are protected. But if we succeed in turning the Vladivostok accord into a 10-year agreement, we will have crossed the threshold between total unrestrained competition and the difficult but promising beginning of long-term strategic equilibrium at lower levels of forces. The United States and the Soviet Union have already agreed to turn to reductions in strategic forces in the next phase of the negotiations, starting in 1977.

One would have thought that these accomplishments would speak for themselves. Instead, they have triggered a flood of charges which mislead the American people and our friends, give a wrong impression of irresoluteness to our adversaries, and complicate the prospects for a new agreement that is in the overriding national interest.

No charge is more irresponsible and potentially more dangerous than the allegation that the United States has knowingly tolerated violations of the first SALT agreements.

What are the facts? A Standing Consultative Commission[4] was created by the agreements of 1972 precisely to consider disputes or ambiguities in implementation. Such incidents were almost certain to arise in a first, quite limited agreement between longstanding adversaries possessing weapons systems of great complexity whose growth is verified not by some neutral policing mechanism but by each side's own intelligence systems. Every questionable activity that has arisen has been systematically analyzed by this government and considered by the President and his advisers. Whenever any question remained, it was then promptly raised with the Soviets. All instructions to the American representative on the Consultative Commission reflected the unanimous views of all U.S. agencies concerned and the data and assessment produced jointly by them. No one had a bias in favor of absolving the Soviets—an inherently malicious charge. No one prevented all questionable or suspicious activities from being raised with the Soviets. And not all the questioned activities were on the Soviet side.

All of these issues have been and will continue to be seriously handled and dealt with through a process that has proved effective. Yet irresponsible charges continue to lump together incidents that have been explained or are still being considered with wild allegations that have no foundation. They sometimes put forward inaccurate figures and data which often can be refuted only by divulging sensitive intelligence information. Yet with all the recent flurry of allegations, no recommendations are made of what countermeasures we should take or how to assess the significance of any given alleged violation.

In what way do the alleged violations affect the strategic equation? In what manner, if any, have we been foreclosed from protecting ourselves? Would those who inaccurately allege violations simply throw over all the agreements regardless of the benefits they provide the United States? Would they halt the negotiation of further agreements? What purpose is served by leading our public and the Soviet Union to believe—totally incorrectly—that the United States is blind to violations or that its government deliberately deceives its people? Can anyone seriously believe that this Administration which has strenuously resisted Communist advances in every part of the world—and is often strongly criticized for it—would ignore Soviet violations of a formal agreement?

I can assure you that this Administration will not tolerate violations. It will continue to monitor Soviet compliance meticulously. It will pursue energetically all ambiguities or signs of noncompliance. But it will not be driven by demagoguery to make false or hasty judgments. No department or agency charged with responsibility for this problem holds the view that any violations have occurred.

As we assess SALT we must face squarely one question: What is the alternative to the agreement we have and seek? If the SALT process falters, we must consider what new or additional strategic programs we would undertake, their likely cost, and above all, their strategic purpose.

An accelerated strategic buildup over the next five years could cost as much as an additional $20 billion. Failing a satisfactory agreement, this will surely be the path we must travel. It would be a tragically missed opportunity. For in the process of such a buildup, and the atmosphere it would engender, it would be difficult to return to serious negotiations for some time. Tensions are likely to increase; a new, higher baseline will emerge from which future negotiations would eventually have to begin. And in the end, neither side will have gained a strategic advantage. At the least, they will have wasted resources. At worst, they will have increased the risks of nuclear war.

Of course the Soviet Union must ponder these alternatives as well. Their sense of responsibility must equal ours if there is to be an equitable and durable agreement based on strict reciprocity. We consider a SALT agreement important, but we will take no chances with our national security.

Let me sum up:

—We will never stand for the violation of a solemn treaty or agreement, and we will remain alert.

—We will never tolerate a shift in the strategic balance against us—by violations of agreements, by unsatisfactory agreements, or by neglect of our own programs. We will spend what is necessary to maintain strategic sufficiency.

—The President is determined to pursue the effort to negotiate a saner strategic balance on equitable terms—because it is in our interest and because we have an obligation to our own people and to world peace.

The Soviet Union and Angola

As the United States strives to shape a more hopeful world, it can never forget that global stability and security rest upon an equilibrium between the great powers. If the Soviet Union is permitted to exploit opportunities arising out of local conflicts by military means, the hopes we have for progress toward a more peaceful international order will ultimately be undermined.

This is why the Soviet Union's massive and unprecedented intervention in the internal affairs of Africa with nearly 200 million dollars' worth of military equipment, its advisers, and its transport of the large expeditionary force of 11,000 Cuban combat troops must be a matter of urgent concern.

Angola represents the first time that the Soviets have moved militarily at long distance to impose a regime of their choice. It is the first time that the United States has failed to respond to Soviet military moves outside the immediate Soviet orbit. And it is the first time that Congress has halted national action in the middle of a crisis.

When one great power tips the balance of forces decisively in a local conflict through its military intervention—and meets no resistance—an ominous precedent is set, of grave consequence even if the intervention occurs in a seemingly remote area. Such a precedent cannot be tolerated if a lasting easing of tensions is to be achieved. And if the pattern is not broken now, we will face harder choices and higher costs in the future.

The United States seeks no unilateral goals in Angola. We have proposed a cease-fire; withdrawal of all outside forces, Soviet, Cuban, and South African; cessation of foreign military involvement, including the supply of equipment; and negotiations among all three Angolan factions. This approach has the support of half the nations of Africa.

Last summer and fall, to halt a dangerously escalating situation, the United States provided financial support through African friends to those in Angola—the large majority—who sought to resist Soviet and Cuban domination. Using this as leverage, we undertook an active diplomacy to promote an African solution to an African problem. We acted quietly, to avoid provoking a major crisis and raising issues of prestige.

At first it was feared that the Soviet-backed faction, because of massive Soviet aid and Cuban mercenaries, would dominate totally by Independence Day, November 11. Our assistance prevented that. African determination to oppose Soviet and Cuban intervention became more and more evident. On December 9 the President warned Moscow of the consequences of continued meddling and offered to cooperate in encouraging a peaceful outcome that removed foreign influence. The Soviet Union appeared to have second thoughts. It halted its airlift from December 9 until December 24.

At that point, the impact of our domestic debate overwhelmed the possibilities of diplomacy. It was demanded that we explain publicly why our effort was important—and then our effort was cut off. After the Senate vote to block further aid to Angola, Cuba more than doubled its forces and Soviet military aid was resumed on a large scale. The cooperativeness of Soviet diplomacy declined. Since then the situation has continued to deteriorate.

As our public discussion continues, certain facts must be understood. The analogy with Viet-Nam is totally false; this nation must have the maturity to make elementary distinctions. The President has pledged that no American troops or advisers would be sent to Angola, and we were prepared to accept legislative restrictions to that effect, in addition to the War Powers Act which already exists. What was involved was modest assistance to stabilize the local balance of forces and make possible a rapid political settlement in cooperation with African countries.

It is charged that the Administration acted covertly, without public acknowledgment. That is correct; for our purpose was to avoid an escalated confrontation that would make it more difficult for the Soviets to back down, as well as to give the greatest possible scope for an African solution. Angola was a case where diplomacy without leverage was likely to be impotent, yet direct military confrontation would involve needless risks. This is precisely one of those gray areas where unpublicized methods would enable us to influence events short of direct conflict.

And we complied totally with Congress' new standard of executive-legislative consultation on secret activities. Beginning in July, and through December, we discussed the Angolan situation and what we were doing about it with more than two dozen Senators, 150 Congressmen, and over 100 staff members of both Houses. Eight congressional committees were briefed on 24 separate occasions. We sought in these briefings to determine the wishes of Congress, and there was little sign of active opposition to our carefully limited operations.

It is said that the Russians will inevitably be eased out by the Africans themselves over a period of time. This may or may not prove true. But such an argument, when carried to its logical conclusion, implies that we can abandon the world to interventionist forces and hope for the best. And reliance on history is of little solace to those under attack, whose future is being decided now. The degree of Soviet and Cuban intervention is unprecedented; they will have effectively determined the outcome. There is no evidence to support the claim that they will be quickly removed or that other nations may not draw damaging conclusions dangerous to our long-term interests.

It is maintained that we should meet the Soviet threat in Angola through escalated methods of pressure such as altering our position on SALT or grain sales. But these arrangements benefit us as well as the Soviet Union and are part of the long-term strategy for dealing with the Soviet Union. History has proved time and again that expansion can be checked only when there is a local balance of forces; indirect means can succeed only if rapid local victories are foreclosed. As the President has pointed out, the Soviet Union has survived for nearly 60 years without American grain; it could do so now. Cutting off grain would still lose Angola. We would duplicate the experience of the Trade Act, which interrupted the trade relationship with the U.S.S.R. to insure emigration—and ended up with neither.

Let us not bemuse ourselves with facile slogans about not becoming the world's policeman. We have no desire to play such a role. But it can never be in our interest to let the Soviet Union act as the world's policeman. There are many crises in the world where the United States cannot and should not intervene. But here we face a blatant Soviet and Cuban challenge, which could have been overcome if we had been allowed to act prudently with limited means at the early stage. By forcing this out onto center stage, our divisions simultaneously escalated the significance of the crisis and guaranteed our impotence.

To claim that Angola is not an important country, or that the United States has no important interests there, begs the principal question. If the United States is seen to waver in the face of massive Soviet and Cuban intervention, what will be the perception of leaders around the world as they make decisions concerning their future security? And what conclusions will an unoppposed superpower draw when the next opportunity for intervention beckons?

Where are we now? The government has a duty to make clear to the Soviet Union and Cuba that Angola sets no precedent, that this type of action will not be tolerated again. It must reassure adjacent countries they will not be left exposed to attack or pressure from the new Soviet-Cuban foothold. Congress and the executive must come together on this proposition—in the national interest and in the interest of world peace.

The Administration will continue to make its case, however

unpopular it may be temporarily. Let no nation believe that Americans will long remain indifferent to the dispatch of expeditionary forces and vast supplies of arms to impose minority governments—especially when that expeditionary force comes from a nation in the Western Hemisphere.

National Strength and the Debate at Home

We live in a world without simple answers. We hold our values too dear to relinquish defending them; we hold human life too dear to cease the quest for a secure peace. The first requirement of stability is to maintain our defenses and the balance of power. But the highest aim of policy in the nuclear age must be to create out of the sterile equilibrium of force a more positive relationship of peace.

America has the material assets to do the job. Our military might is unmatched. Our economic and technological strength dwarfs any other. Our democratic heritage is envied by hundreds of millions around the world.

Our problems therefore are of our own making—self-doubt, division, irresolution. We must once again become a confident, united, and determined people.

Foreign countries must be able to deal with America as an entity, not as a complex of divided institutions. If our divisions paralyze our international efforts, it is America as a whole that will suffer. We have no more urgent task than restoring the partnership between the American people, the Congress, and the executive. A new partnership can enable the President of the United States, in his constitutionally determined role, to address the world with the central authority of the spokesman of a united and purposeful America.

Debate is the essence of democracy. But restraint is the cement of national cohesion. It is time to end the self-torment and obsession with our guilt which has threatened to paralyze us for too many years. It is time to stop dismantling our national institutions and undermining our national confidence.

Let us learn—even in an election year—the self-discipline to shape our domestic debates into a positive, not a destructive, process.

One of the forgotten truths of our history is that our Founding Fathers were men of great sophistication in foreign affairs. They understood the balance of power; they made use of the divisions of Europe for the advantage of our own Revolution. They understood the need for a strong executive to conduct the nation's diplomacy. They grasped that America required economic, political, and moral links with other nations. They saw that our ideals were universal, and they understood and welcomed the impact of the American experiment on the destinies of all mankind.

In our age, whose challenges are without precedent, we need once again the wisdom of our Founding Fathers. Our ideals must give us strength—rather than serve as an excuse for abdication. The American people want an effective foreign policy. They want America to continue to help shape the international order of the coming generation according to our ideals. We have done great things as a united people. We have it in our power to make our third century a time of vibrancy and hope and greatness.

(6)   The Threshold Test Ban (TTB) and Peaceful Nuclear Explosion (PNE) Treaties.

(a)   Treaty between the United States of America and the Union of Soviet Socialist Republics on Underground Nuclear Explosions for Peaceful Purposes, signed in Washington and Moscow on May 28, 1976.[5]

(Not in force as of the close of 1977)

The United States of America and the Union of Soviet Socialist Republics, hereinafter referred to as the Parties,

Proceeding from a desire to implement Article III of the Treaty between the United States of America and the Union of Soviet Socialist Republics on the Limitation of Underground Nuclear Weapon Tests, which calls for the earliest possible conclusion of an agreement on underground nuclear explosions for peaceful purposes,

Reaffirming their adherence to the objectives and principles of the Treaty Banning Nuclear Weapon Tests in the Atmosphere, in Outer Space and Under Water, the Treaty on Non-Proliferation of Nuclear Weapons, and the Treaty on the Limitation of Underground Nuclear Weapon Tests, and their determination to observe strictly the provisions of these international agreements,

Desiring to assure that underground nuclear explosions for peaceful purposes shall not be used for purposes related to nuclear weapons,

[5]Text from *Bulletin*, 74: 802-4.

Desiring that utilization of nuclear energy be directed only toward peaceful purposes,

Desiring to develop appropriately cooperation in the field of underground nuclear explosions for peaceful purposes,

Have agreed as follows:

Article I

1. The Parties enter into this Treaty to satisfy the obligations in Article III of the Treaty on the Limitation of Underground Nuclear Weapon Tests, and assume additional obligations in accordance with the provisions of this Treaty.

2. This Treaty shall govern all underground nuclear explosions for peaceful purposes conducted by the Parties after March 31, 1976.

Article II

For the purposes of this Treaty:

(a) "explosion" means any individual or group underground nuclear explosion for peaceful purposes;

(b) "explosive" means any device, mechanism or system for producing an individual explosion;

(c) "group explosion" means two or more individual explosions for which the time interval between successive individual explosions does not exceed five seconds and for which the emplacement points of all explosives can be interconnected by straight line segments, each of which joins two emplacement points and each of which does not exceed 40 kilometers.

Article III

1. Each Party, subject to the obligations assumed under this Treaty and other international agreements, reserves the right to:

(a) carry out explosions at any place under its jurisdiction or control outside the geographical boundaries of test sites specified under the provisions of the Treaty on the Limitation of Underground Nuclear Weapon Tests; and

(b) carry out, participate or assist in carrying out explosions in the territory of another State at the request of such other State.

2. Each Party undertakes to prohibit, to prevent and not to carry out at any place under its jurisdiction or control, and further

undertakes not to carry out, participate or assist in carrying out anywhere:

(a) any individual explosion having a yield exceeding 150 kilotons;

(b) any group explosion:

(1) having an aggregate yield exceeding 150 kilotons except in ways that will permit identification of each individual explosion and determination of the yield of each individual explosion in the group in accordance with the provisions of Article IV of the Protocol to this Treaty;

(2) having an aggregate yield exceeding one and one-half megatons;

(c) any explosion which does not carry out a peaceful application;

(d) any explosion except in compliance with the provisions of the Treaty Banning Nuclear Weapon Tests in the Atmosphere, in Outer Space and Under Water, the Treaty on the Non-Proliferation of Nuclear Weapons, and other international agreements entered into by that Party.

3. The question of carrying out any individual explosion having a yield exceeding the yield specified in paragraph 2(a) of this article will be considered by the Parties at an appropriate time to be agreed.

Article IV

1. For the purpose of providing assurance of compliance with the provisions of this Treaty, each Party shall:

(a) use national technical means of verification at its disposal in a manner consistent with generally recognized principles of international law; and

(b) provide to the other Party information and access to sites of explosions and furnish assistance in accordance with the provisions set forth in the Protocol to this Treaty.

2. Each Party undertakes not to interfere with the national technical means of verification of the other Party operating in accordance with paragraph 1(a) of this article, or with the implementation of the provisions of paragraph 1(b) of this article.

Article V

1. To promote the objectives and implementation of the

provisions of this Treaty, the Parties shall establish promptly a Joint Consultative Commission within the framework of which they will:

   (a) consult with each other, make inquiries and furnish information in response to such inquiries, to assure confidence in compliance with the obligations assumed;
   (b) consider questions concerning compliance with the obligations assumed and related situations which may be considered ambiguous;
   (c) consider questions involving unintended interference with the means for assuring compliance with the provisions of this Treaty;
   (d) consider changes in technology or other new circumstances which have a bearing on the provisions of this Treaty; and
   (e) consider possible amendments to provisions governing underground nuclear explosions for peaceful purposes.

   2. The Parties through consultation shall establish, and may amend as appropriate, Regulations for the Joint Consultative Commission governing procedures, composition and other relevant matters.

Article VI

   1. The Parties will develop cooperation on the basis of mutual benefit, equality, and reciprocity in various areas related to carrying out underground nuclear explosions for peaceful purposes.
   2. The Joint Consultative Commission will facilitate this cooperation by considering specific areas and forms of cooperation which shall be determined by agreement between the Parties in accordance with their constitutional procedures.
   3. The Parties will appropriately inform the International Atomic Energy Agency of results of their cooperation in the field of underground nuclear explosions for peaceful purposes.

Article VII

   1. Each Party shall continue to promote the development of the international agreement or agreements and procedures provided for in Article V of the Treaty on the Non-Proliferation of Nuclear Weapons, and shall provide appropriate assistance to the International Atomic Energy Agency in this regard.

2. Each Party undertakes not to carry out, participate or assist in the carrying out of any explosion in the territory of another State unless that State agrees to the implementation in its territory of the international observation and procedures contemplated by Article V of the Treaty on the Non-Proliferation of Nuclear Weapons and the provisions of Article IV of and the Protocol to this Treaty, including the provision by that State of the assistance necessary for such implementation and of the privileges and immunities specified in the Protocol.

Article VIII

1. This Treaty shall remain in force for a period of five years, and it shall be extended for successive five-year periods unless either Party notifies the other of its termination no later than six months prior to its expiration. Before the expiration of this period the Parties may, as necessary, hold consultations to consider the situation relevant to the substance of this Treaty. However, under no circumstances shall either Party be entitled to terminate this Treaty while the Treaty on the Limitation of Underground Nuclear Weapon Tests remains in force.

2. Termination of the Treaty on the Limitation of Underground Nuclear Weapon Tests shall entitle either Party to withdraw from this Treaty at any time.

3. Each Party may propose amendments to this Treaty. Amendments shall enter into force on the day of the exchange of instruments of ratification of such amendments.

Article IX

1. This Treaty including the Protocol which forms an integral part hereof, shall be subject to ratification in accordance with the constitutional procedures of each Party. This Treaty shall enter into force on the day of the exchange of instruments of ratification which exchange shall take place simultaneously with the exchange of instruments of ratification of the Treaty on the Limitation of Underground Nuclear Weapon Tests.

2. This Treaty shall be registered pursuant to Article 102 of the Charter of the United Nations.

Done at Washington and Moscow, on May 28, 1976, in duplicate, in the English and Russian languages, both texts being equally authentic.

For the United States of America:

GERALD R. FORD
The President of the United States of America

For the Union of Soviet Socialist Republics:

L. I. BREZHNEV
*General Secretary of the Central Committee of
the CPSU*

(b) Request for Advice and Consent to Ratification: Message from President Ford to the Senate, July 29, 1976.[6]

To the Senate of the United States:

With a view to receiving the advice and consent of the Senate to ratification, I transmit herewith the Treaty between the United States of America and the Union of Soviet Socialist Republics on the Limitation of Underground Nuclear Weapon Tests, and the Protocol thereto, referred to as the Threshold Test Ban Treaty (TTB Treaty), and the Treaty between the United States of America and the Union of Soviet Socialist Republics on Underground Nuclear Explosions for Peaceful Purposes, and the Protocol thereto (PNE Treaty). The TTBT was signed in Moscow on July 3, 1974 and the PNE Treaty was signed in Washington and Moscow on May 28, 1976. For the information of the Senate, I transmit also the detailed report of the Department of State on these Treaties.[7]

These Treaties together establish procedures for the conduct of all underground nuclear explosions by the United States and the Soviet Union. All nuclear explosions other than underground nuclear explosions are prohibited by the Treaty Banning Nuclear Weapon Tests in the Atmosphere, in Outer Space and Under Water (the Limited Test Ban Treaty) of 1963. The TTB Treaty and PNE Treaty are the first agreements since the Limited Test Ban Treaty to impose direct restraints on nuclear explosions by the Parties and, as such, contribute to limiting nuclear arms competition.

These two Treaties represent approximately two years of intensive effort. Negotiation of the TTB Treaty began in the Spring of 1974 and was completed in July of that year. However, the

[6]Text from *Presidential Documents*, 12: 1222-3.
[7]Ex. N, 94th Cong., 2d sess.

question of the relationship of underground nuclear explosions for peaceful purposes to limitations on nuclear weapon testing was not then resolved. As a result, Article III of the TTB Treaty provided that the Parties would negotiate and conclude an agreement governing underground nuclear explosions for peaceful purposes. Work on the PNE Treaty began in the Fall of 1974 and after six lengthy negotiating sessions was completed in April of 1976.

The TTB Treaty and the PNE Treaty are closely interrelated and complement one another. The TTB Treaty places a limitation of 150 kilotons on all underground nuclear weapon tests carried out by the Parties. The PNE Treaty similarly provides for a limitation of 150 kilotons on all individual underground nuclear explosions for peaceful purposes.

During the negotiation of the PNE Treaty, the Parties investigated whether individual explosions with yields above 150 kilotons could be accommodated consistent with the agreed aim of not providing weapon-related benefits otherwise precluded by the TTB Treaty. The Parties did not develop a basis for such an accommodation, largely because it has not been possible to distinguish between nuclear explosive device technology as applied for weapon-related purposes and as applied for peaceful purposes. The Parties therefore agreed that the yield limitations on individual explosions in the two Treaties would be the same.

The TTB Treaty and the PNE Treaty contain numerous provisions to ensure adequate verification, including some concepts, more far-reaching than those found in previous arms control agreements, which are not only important in themselves but which will have significant precedential value as well. For example, the Limited Test Ban Treaty is verified only by national technical means. The TTB and PNE Treaties add requirements for exchange of specific information in advance to assist verification by national technical means, and the PNE Treaty establishes procedures for on-site observation under certain conditions on the territory of the Party conducting the explosion.

The TTB Treaty provides for an exchange of data on the geography and geology of nuclear weapon test sites as well as the yields of some actual weapons tests conducted at each site. The PNE Treaty requires that the Party conducting any underground nuclear explosion for peaceful purposes provide the other Party in advance with data on the geography and geology of the place where the explosion is to be carried out, its purpose, and specific information on each explosion itself. These requirements are related to the yield of the explosion and become more detailed as the magnitude of the explosions increase.

In addition to the limitation on individual nuclear explosions of 150 kilotons, the PNE Treaty provides for an aggregate yield limitation of 1.5 megatons on group underground nuclear explosions for peaceful purposes. A group explosion consists of substantially simultaneous individual explosions located within a specific geometrical relationship to one another. The Treaty provides for mandatory on-site observer rights for group explosions with an aggregate yield in excess of 150 kilotons in order to determine that the yield of each individual explosion in the group does not exceed 150 kilotons and that the explosions serve the stated peaceful purposes. The Treaty also provides for on-site observers for explosions with an aggregate yield between 100 and 150 kilotons if both Parties agree, on the basis of information provided, that such observers would be appropriate for the confirmation of the yield of the explosion.

The TTB Treaty and the PNE Treaty, taken together as integrated and complementary components of this important limitation on nuclear explosions, provide that very large yield nuclear explosions will no longer be carried out by the Parties. This is one more useful step in our continuing efforts to develop comprehensive and balanced limitations on nuclear weapons. We will continue our efforts to reach an adequately verifiable agreement banning all nuclear weapon testing, but in so doing we must ensure that controls on peaceful nuclear explosions are consistent with such a ban. These treaties are in the national interest, and I respectfully recommend that the Senate give its advice and consent to ratification.

GERALD R. FORD

The White House,
   July 29, 1976.

(7)   Convention on the Prohibition of Hostile Uses of Environmental Modification Techniques, approved by the General Assembly of the United Nations December 10, 1976 and signed at Geneva May 18, 1977.[8]

(Not in force as of the close of 1977)

The States Parties to this Convention,
   Guided by the interest of consolidating peace, and wishing to contribute to the cause of halting the arms race, and of bringing

[8]Text from U.S. Arms Control and Disarmament Agency (ACDA), *Arms Control and Disarmament Agreements: Texts and History of Negotiations,* 1977 ed. (ACDA Publication 94; Washington: GPO, 1977): 183-6.

about general and complete disarmament under strict and effective international control, and of saving mankind from the danger of new means of warfare,

Determined to continue negotiations with a view to achieving effective progress towards further measures in the field of disarmament,

Recognizing that scientific and technical advances may open new possibilities with respect to modification of the environment,

Recalling the Declaration of the United Nations Conference on the Human Environment adopted in Stockholm on 16 June 1972,

Realizing that the use of environmental modification techniques for peaceful purposes could improve the interrelationship of man and nature and contribute to the preservation and improvement of the environment for the benefit of present and future generations,

Recognizing, however, that military or any other hostile use of such techniques could have effects extremely harmful to human welfare,

Desiring to prohibit effectively military or any other hostile use of environmental modification techniques in order to eliminate the dangers to mankind from such use, and affirming their willingness to work towards the achievement of this objective,

Desiring also to contribute to the strengthening of trust among nations and to the further improvement of the international situation in accordance with the purposes and principles of the Charter of the United Nations,

Have agreed as follows:

Article I

1. Each State Party to this Convention undertakes not to engage in military or any other hostile use of environmental modification techniques having widespread, long-lasting or severe effects as the means of destruction, damage or injury to any other State Party.

2. Each State Party to this Convention undertakes not to assist, encourage or induce any State, group of States or international organization to engage in activities contrary to the provisions of paragraph 1 of this article.

Article II

As used in article I, the term "environmental modification techniques" refers to any technique for changing—through the deliberate manipulation of natural processes—the dynamics, composition or structure of the earth, including its biota, lithosphere, hydrosphere, and atmosphere, or of outer space.

Article III

1. The provisions of this Convention shall not hinder the use of environmental modification techniques for peaceful purposes and shall be without prejudice to generally recognized principles and applicable rules of international law concerning such use.

2. The States Parties to this Convention undertake to facilitate, and have the right to participate in, the fullest possible exchange of scientific and technological information on the use of environmental modification techniques for peaceful purposes. States Parties in a position to do so shall contribute, alone or together with other States or international organizations, to international economic and scientific cooperation in the preservation, improvement, and peaceful utilization of the environment, with due consideration for the needs of the developing areas of the world.

Article IV

Each State Party to this Convention undertakes to take any measures it considers necessary in accordance with its constitutional processes to prohibit and prevent any activity in violation of the provisions of the Convention anywhere under its jurisdiction or control.

Article V

1. The States Parties to this Convention undertake to consult one another and to co-operate in solving any problems which may arise in relation to the objectives of, or in the application of the provisions of, the Convention. Consultation and co-operation pursuant to this article may also be undertaken through appropriate international procedures within the framework of the United Nations and in accordance with its Charter. These international procedures may include the services of appropriate international organizations, as well as of a consultative committee of experts as provided for in paragraph 2 of this article.

2. For the purposes set forth in paragraph 1 of this article, the Depositary shall, within one month of the receipt of a request from any State Party, convene a consultative committee of experts. Any State Party may appoint an expert to this committee whose functions and rules of procedure are set out in the annex, which constitutes an integral part of this Convention. The committee shall transmit to the Depositary a summary of its findings of fact, incorporating all views and information presented to the committee during its proceedings. The Depositary shall distribute the summary to all States Parties.

3. Any State Party to this Convention which has reason to believe that any other State Party is acting in breach of obligations deriving from the provisions of the Convention may lodge a complaint with the Security Council of the United Nations. Such a complaint should include all relevant information as well as all possible evidence supporting its validity.

4. Each State Party to this Convention undertakes to co-operate in carrying out any investigation which the Security Council may initiate, in accordance with the provisions of the Charter of the United Nations, on the basis of the complaint received by the Council. The Security Council shall inform the States Parties to the Convention of the results of the investigation.

5. Each State Party to this Convention undertakes to provide or support assistance, in accordance with the provisions of the Charter of the United Nations, to any Party to the Convention which so requests, if the Security Council decides that such Party has been harmed or is likely to be harmed as a result of violation of the Convention.

Article VI

1. Any State Party may propose amendments to this Convention. The text of any proposed amendment shall be submitted to the Depositary who shall promptly circulate it to all States Parties.

2. An amendment shall enter into force for all States Parties which have accepted it, upon the deposit with the Depositary of instruments of acceptance by a majority of States Parties. Thereafter it shall enter into force for any remaining State Party on the date of deposit of its instrument of acceptance.

Article VII

This Convention shall be of unlimited duration.

Article VIII

1. Five years after the entry into force of this Convention, a conference of the States Parties to the Convention shall be convened by the Depositary in Geneva. The conference shall review the operation of the Convention with a view to ensuring that its purposes and provisions are being realized, and shall in particular examine the effectiveness of the provisions of article I, paragraph 1, in eliminating the dangers of military or any other hostile use of environmental modification techniques.

2. At intervals of not less than five years thereafter a majority of the States Parties to this Convention may obtain, by submitting a proposal to this effect to the Depositary, the convening of a conference with the same objectives.

3. If no review conference has been convened pursuant to paragraph 2 of this article within 10 years following the conclusion of a previous review conference, the Depositary shall solicit the views of all States Parties to this Convention on the holding of such a conference. If one third or 10 of the States Parties, whichever number is less, respond affirmatively, the Depositary shall take immediate steps to convene the conference.

Article IX

1. This Convention shall be open to all States for signature. Any State which does not sign the Convention before its entry into force in accordance with paragraph 3 of this article may accede to it at any time.

2. This Convention shall be subject to ratification by signatory States. Instruments of ratification and instruments of accession shall be deposited with the Secretary-General of the United Nations.

3. This Convention shall enter into force upon the deposit with the Depositary of instruments of ratification by 20 Governments in accordance with paragraph 2 of this article.

4. For those States whose instruments of ratification or accession are deposited after the entry into force of this Convention, it shall enter into force on the date of the deposit of their instruments of ratification or accession.

5. The Depositary shall promptly inform all signatory and acceding States of the date of each signature, the date of deposit of each instrument of ratification or of accession and the date of the entry into force of this Convention and of any amendments thereto, as well as of the receipt of other notices.

6. This Convention shall be registered by the Depositary in accordance with Article 102 of the Charter of the United Nations.

Article X

This Convention, of which the Arabic, Chinese, English, French, Russian, and Spanish texts are equally authentic, shall be deposited with the Secretary-General of the United Nations who shall send certified copies thereof to the Governments of the signatory and acceding States.

IN WITNESS WHEREOF, the undersigned, duly authorized thereto, have signed this Convention.

DONE at Geneva
On May 18, 1977

(8)   Controlling Nuclear Proliferation: Statement by President Ford, October 28, 1976.[9]

We have known since the age of nuclear energy began more than 30 years ago that this source of energy had the potential for tremendous benefits for mankind and the potential for unparalleled destruction.

On the one hand, there is no doubt that nuclear energy represents one of the best hopes for satisfying the rising world demand for energy with minimum environmental impact and with the potential for reducing dependence on uncertain and diminishing world supplies of oil.

On the other hand, nuclear fuel, as it produces power also produces plutonium, which can be chemically separated from the spent fuel. The plutonium can be recycled and used to generate additional nuclear power, thereby partially offsetting the need for additional energy resources. Unfortunately—and this is the root of the problem—the same plutonium produced in nuclear power-plants can, when chemically separated, also be used to make nuclear explosives.

The world community cannot afford to let potential nuclear weapons material or the technology to produce it proliferate uncontrolled over the globe. The world community must ensure that production and utilization of such material by any nation is carried out under the most stringent security conditions and arrangements.

Developing the enormous benefits of nuclear energy while simultaneously developing the means to prevent proliferation is one of the major challenges facing all nations of the world today.

The standards we apply in judging most domestic and international activities are not sufficiently rigorous to deal with this extraordinarily complex problem. Our answers cannot be partially successful. They will either work, in which case we shall stop proliferation, or they will fail and nuclear proliferation will accelerate as nations initially having no intention of acquiring nuclear weapons conclude that they are forced to do so by the actions of

[9]Text from *Presidential Documents*, 12: 1624-31.

others. Should this happen, we would face a world in which the security of all is critically imperiled. Maintaining international stability in such an environment would be incalculably difficult and dangerous. In times of regional or global crisis, risks of nuclear devastation would be immeasurably increased—if not through direct attack, then through a process of ever expanding escalation. The problem can be handled as long as we understand it clearly and act wisely in concert with other nations. But we are faced with a threat of tragedy if we fail to comprehend it or to take effective measures.

Thus, the seriousness and complexity of the problem place a special burden on those who propose ways to control proliferation. They must avoid the temptation for rhetorical gestures, empty threats, or righteous posturing. They must offer policies and programs which deal with the world as it is, not as we might wish it to be. The goal is to prevent proliferation, not simply to deplore it.

The first task in dealing with the problem of proliferation is to understand the world nuclear situation.

More than 30 nations have or plan to build nuclear powerplants to reap the benefits of nuclear energy. The 1973 energy crisis dramatically demonstrated to all nations not only the dangers of excessive reliance on oil imports, but also the reality that the world's supply of fossil fuels is running out. As a result, nuclear energy is now properly seen by many nations as an indispensable way to satisfy rising energy demand without prematurely depleting finite fossil fuel resources. We must understand the motives which are leading these nations, developed and developing, to place even greater emphasis than we do on nuclear power development. For unless we comprehend their real needs, we cannot expect to find ways of working with them to ensure satisfaction of both our and their legitimate concerns. Moreover, several nations besides the United States have the technology needed to produce both the benefits and the destructive potential of nuclear energy. Nations with such capabilities are able to export their technology and facilities.

Thus, no single nation, not even the United States, can realistically hope—by itself—to control effectively the spread of reprocessing technology and the resulting availability of plutonium.

The United States once was the dominant world supplier of nuclear material equipment and technology. While we remain a leader in this field, other suppliers have come to share the international market—with the U.S. now supplying less than half of nuclear reactor exports. In short, for nearly a decade the U.S. has not had a monopoly on nuclear technology. Although our role is large, we are not able to control worldwide nuclear development.

For these reasons, action to control proliferation must be an international cooperative effort involving many nations, including both nuclear suppliers and customers. Common standards must be developed and accepted by all parties. If this is not done, unrestrained trade in sensitive nuclear technology and materials will develop—with no one in a position to stop it.

We in the United States must recognize that interests in nuclear energy vary widely among nations. We must recognize that some nations look to nuclear energy because they have no acceptable energy alternative. We must be sure that our efforts to control proliferation are not viewed by such nations as an act to prevent them from enjoying the benefits of nuclear energy. We must be sure that all nations recognize that the U.S. believes that nonproliferation objectives must take precedence over economic and energy benefits if a choice must be made.

Previous Action

During the past 30 years, the U.S. has been the unquestioned leader in worldwide efforts to assure that the benefits of nuclear energy are made available widely while its destructive uses are prevented. I have given special attention to these objectives during the past 2 years, and we have made important new progress, particularly in efforts to control the proliferation of nuclear weapons capability among the nations of the world.

In 1974, soon after I assumed office, I became concerned that some nuclear supplier countries, in order to achieve competitive advantage, were prepared to offer nuclear exports under conditions less rigorous than we believed prudent. In the fall of that year, at the United Nations General Assembly, the United States proposed that nonproliferation measures be strengthened materially.[10] I also expressed my concern directly to my counterparts in key supplier and recipient nations. I directed the Secretary of State to emphasize multilateral action to limit this dangerous form of competition.

At U.S. initiative, the first meeting of major nuclear suppliers was convened in London in April 1975. A series of meetings and intensive bilateral consultations followed. As a result of these meetings, we have significantly raised international standards through progressive new guidelines to govern nuclear exports. These involve both improved safeguards and controls to prevent diversion of nuclear materials and to guard against the misuse of nuclear technology and physical protection against theft and sabotage. The United States has adopted these guidelines as policy for nuclear exports.

[10]Cf. Kissinger address to U.N. General Assembly, Sept. 23, 1974, in *AFR, 1974:* 350-52.

In addition, we have acted to deal with the special dangers associated with plutonium.

—We have prohibited export of reprocessing and other nuclear technologies that could contribute to proliferation.

—We have firmly opposed reprocessing in Korea and Taiwan. We welcome the decisions of those nations to forego such activities. We will continue to discourage national reprocessing in other locations of particular concern.

—We negotiated agreements for cooperation with Egypt and Israel which contain the strictest reprocessing provisions and other nuclear controls ever included in the 20-year history of our nuclear cooperation program.

—In addition, the United States recently completed negotiations to place its civil nuclear facilities under the safeguards of the International Atomic Energy Agency—and the IAEA has approved a proposed agreement for this purpose.

New Initiatives

Last summer, I directed that a thorough review be undertaken of all our nuclear policies and options to determine what further steps were needed. I have considered carefully the results of that review, held discussions with congressional leaders, and benefited from consultations with leaders of other nations. I have decided that new steps are needed, building upon the progress of the past 2 years. Today, I am announcing a number of actions and proposals aimed at:

—strengthening the commitment of the nations of the world to the goal of nonproliferation and building an effective system of international controls to prevent proliferation;

—changing and strengthening U.S. domestic nuclear policies and programs to support our nonproliferation goals; and

—establishing, by these actions, a sound foundation for the continued and increased use of nuclear energy in the U.S. and in the world in a safe and economic manner.

The task we face calls for an international cooperative venture of unprecedented dimensions. The U.S. is prepared to work with all other nations.

Principal Policy Decisions

I have concluded that the reprocessing and recycling of

plutonium should not proceed unless there is sound reason to conclude that the world community can effectively overcome the associated risks of proliferation. I believe that avoidance of proliferation must take precedence over economic interests. I have also concluded that the United States and other nations can and should increase their use of nuclear power for peaceful purposes even if reprocessing and recycling of plutonium are found to be unacceptable.

Vigorous action is required domestically and internationally to make these judgments effective.

—I have decided that the United States should greatly accelerate its diplomatic initiatives, in conjunction with nuclear supplier and consumer nations, to control the spread of plutonium and technologies for separating plutonium.

Effective nonproliferation measures will require the participation and support of nuclear suppliers and consumers. There must be coordination in restraints so that an effective nonproliferation system is achieved, and there must be cooperation in assuring reliable fuel supplies so that peaceful energy needs are met.

—I have decided that the United States should no longer regard reprocessing of used nuclear fuel to produce plutonium as a necessary and inevitable step in the nuclear fuel cycle, and that we should pursue reprocessing and recycling in the future only if they are found to be consistent with our international objectives.

We must ensure that our domestic policies and programs are compatible with our international position on reprocessing and that we work closely with other nations in evaluating nuclear fuel reprocessing.

—The steps I am announcing today will assure that the necessary increase in our use of nuclear energy will be carried on with safety and without aggravating the danger of proliferation.

Even with strong efforts to conserve, we will have increasing demands for energy for a growing American economy. To satisfy these needs, we must rely on increased use of both nuclear energy and coal until more acceptable alternatives are developed. We will continue pushing ahead with work on all promising alternatives such as solar energy but now we must count on the technology that works. We cannot expect a major contribution to our energy supply from alternative technologies until late in this century.

To implement my overall policy decisions, I have decided on a number of policies that are necessary and appropriate to meet our nonproliferation and energy objectives.

—First, our domestic policies must be changed to conform to my decision on deferral of the commercialization of chemical reprocessing of nuclear fuel which results in the separation of plutonium.

—Second, I call upon all nations to join us in exercising maximum restraint in the transfer of reprocessing and enrichment technology and facilities by avoiding such sensitive exports or commitments for a period of at least 3 years.

—Third, new cooperative steps are needed to help assure that all nations have an adequate and reliable supply of energy for their needs. I believe, most importantly, that nuclear supplier nations have a special obligation to assure that customer nations have an adequate supply of fuel for their nuclear powerplants, if those customer nations forego the acquisition of reprocessing and uranium enrichment capabilities and accept effective proliferation controls.

—Fourth, the U.S. must maintain its role as a major and reliable world supplier of nuclear reactors and fuel for peaceful purposes. Our strong position as a supplier has provided the principal basis for our influence and leadership in worldwide nonproliferation efforts. A strong position will be equally important in the future. While reaffirming this Nation's intent to be a reliable supplier, the U.S. seeks no competitive advantage by virtue of the worldwide system of effective nonproliferation controls that I am calling for today.

—Fifth, new efforts must be made to urge all nations to join in a full-scale international cooperative effort—which I shall outline in detail—to develop a system of effective controls to prevent proliferation.

—Sixth, the U.S. must take new steps with respect to its own exports to control proliferation, while seeking to improve multilateral guidelines.

—Seventh, the U.S. must undertake a program to evaluate reprocessing in support of the international policies I have adopted.

—Finally, I have concluded that new steps are needed to assure that we have in place when needed, both in the U.S. and around the world, the facilities for the long-term storage or disposal of nuclear wastes.

Actions to Implement Our Nuclear Policies

In order to implement the nuclear policies that I have outlined, major efforts will be required within the United States and by the many nations around the world with an interest in nuclear energy. To move forward with these efforts, I am today taking a number of actions and making a number of proposals to other nations.

I. Change in U.S. Policy on Nuclear Fuel Reprocessing

With respect to nuclear fuel reprocessing, I am directing agencies of the executive branch to implement my decision to delay commercialization of reprocessing activities in the U.S. until uncertainties are resolved. Specifically, I am:

—Directing the Administrator of the Energy Research and Development Administration (ERDA)[11] to:

• change ERDA policies and programs which heretofore have been based on the assumption that reprocessing would proceed;

• encourage prompt action to expand spent fuel storage facilities, thus assuring utilities that they need not be concerned about shutdown of nuclear reactors because of delays; and

• identify the research and development efforts needed to investigate the feasibility of recovering the energy value from used nuclear fuel without separating plutonium.

II. Restraint in the Transfer of Sensitive Nuclear Technology and Facilities

Despite the gains in controlling proliferation that have been made, the dangers posed by reprocessing and the prospect of uncontrolled availability of plutonium require further, decisive international action. Effective control of the parallel risk of spreading uranium enrichment technology is also necessary. To meet these dangers:

—I call upon all nations to join with us in exercising maximum restraint in the transfer of reprocessing and enrichment technology and facilities by avoiding such sensitive exports or commitments for a period of at least 3 years.

This will allow suppliers and consumers to work together to establish reliable means for meeting nuclear needs with minimum risk, as we assess carefully the wisdom of plutonium use. As we proceed in these efforts, we must not be influenced by pressures to approve the export of these sensitive facilities.

[11]Dr. Robert Seamans.

III. Assuring an Adequate Energy Supply
for Customer Nations

—I urge nuclear suppliers to provide nuclear consumers with fuel services, instead of sensitive technology or facilities.

Nations accepting effective nonproliferation restraints have a right to expect reliable and economic supply of nuclear reactors and associated, nonsensitive fuel. All such nations would share in the benefits of an assured supply of nuclear fuel, even though the number and location of sensitive facilities to generate this fuel is limited to meet nonproliferation goals. The availability of fuel-cycle services in several different nations can provide ample assurance to consumers of a continuing and stable source of supply.

It is also desirable to continue studying the idea of a few suitably-sited multinational fuel-cycle centers to serve regional needs, when effectively safeguarded and economically warranted. Through these and related means, we can minimize incentives for the spread of dangerous fuel-cycle capabilities.

The United States stands ready to take action, in cooperation with other concerned nations, to assure reliable supplies of nuclear fuel at equitable prices to any country accepting responsible restraints on its nuclear power program with regard to reprocessing, plutonium disposition, and enrichment technology.

—I am directing the Secretary of State to initiate consultations to explore with other nations arrangements for coordinating fuel services and for developing other means of ensuring that suppliers will be able to offer, and consumers will be able to receive, an uninterrupted and economical supply of low-enriched uranium fuel and fuel services.

These discussions will address ways to ensure against economic disadvantage to cooperating nations and to remove any sources of competition which could undermine our common nonproliferation efforts.

To contribute to this initiative, the U.S. will offer binding letters of intent for the supply of nuclear fuel to current and prospective customers willing to accept such responsible restraints.

—In addition, I am directing the Secretary of State to enter into negotiations or arrangements for mutual agreement on disposition of spent fuel with consumer nations that adopt responsible restraints.

Where appropriate, the United States will provide consumer nations with either fresh, low-enriched uranium fuel or make other equitable arrangements in return for mutual agreement on the disposition of spent fuel where such disposition demonstrably fosters our common and cooperative nonproliferation objectives. The United States seeks no commercial advantage in pursuing options for fuel disposition and assured fuel supplies.

Finally, the U.S. will continue to expand cooperative efforts with other countries in developing their indigenous nonnuclear energy resources.

The U.S. has proposed and continues to advocate the establishment of an International Energy Institute, specifically designed to help developing countries match the most economic and readily available sources of energy to their power needs. Through this Institute and other appropriate means, we will offer technological assistance in the development of indigenous energy resources.

IV. Strengthening the U.S. Role as a Reliable Supplier

If the U.S. is to continue its leadership role in world-wide nonproliferation efforts, it must be a reliable supplier of nuclear reactors and fuel for peaceful purposes. There are two principal actions we can take to contribute to this objective.

—I will submit to the new Congress proposed legislation that will permit the expansion of capacity in the United States to produce enriched uranium, including the authority needed for expansion of the Government-owned plant at Portsmouth, Ohio. I will also work with Congress to establish a framework for a private, competitive industry to finance, build, own, and operate enrichment plants.

U.S. capacity has been fully committed since mid-1974 with the result that no new orders could be signed. The Congress did not act on my full proposal and provided only limited and temporary authority for proceeding with the Portsmouth plant. We must have additional authority to proceed with the expansion of capacity without further delay.

—I will work closely with the Congress to ensure that legislation for improving our export controls results in a system that provides maximum assurance that the U.S. will be a reliable supplier to other nations for the full period of agreements.

One of the principal concerns with export legislation proposed in the last Congress was the fear that foreign customers could be subjected to arbitrary new controls imposed well after a long-term agreement and specific contracts for nuclear powerplants and fuel had been signed. In the case of nuclear plants and fuels, reliable longterm agreements are essential, and we must adopt export controls that provide reliability while meeting nonproliferation objectives.

V. International Controls Against Proliferation

To reinforce the foregoing policies, we must develop means to establish international restraints over the accumulation of plutonium itself, whether in separated form or in unprocessed spent fuel. The accumulation of plutonium under national control, especially in a separated form, is a primary proliferation risk.

—I am directing the Secretary of State to pursue, vigorously, discussions aimed at the establishment of a new international regime to provide for storage of civil plutonium and spent reactor fuel.

The United States made this proposal to the International Atomic Energy Agency and other interested nations last spring.

Creation of such a regime will greatly strengthen world confidence that the growing accumulation of excess plutonium and spent fuel can be stored safely, pending reentry into the nuclear fuel cycle or other safe disposition. I urge the IAEA, which is empowered to establish plutonium depositories, to give prompt implementation to this concept.

Once a broadly representative IAEA storage regime is in operation, we are prepared to place our own excess civil plutonium and spent fuel under its control. Moreover, we are prepared to consider providing a site for international storage under IAEA auspices.

The inspection system of the IAEA remains a key element in our entire nonproliferation strategy. The world community must make sure that the Agency has the technical and human resources needed to keep pace with its expanding responsibilities. At my direction, we have recently committed substantial additional resources to help upgrade the IAEA's technical safeguards capabilities, and I believe we must strengthen further the safeguard functions of the IAEA.

—I am directing the Secretary of State and Administrator of ERDA to undertake a major international effort to ensure that adequate resources for this purpose are made available, and that we mobilize our best scientific talent to support that Agency. Our principal national laboratories with expertise in this area have been directed to provide assistance, on a continuing basis, to the IAEA Secretariat.

VI. U.S. Nuclear Export Policies

During the past 2 years, the United States has strengthened its own national nuclear export policies. Our interests, however, are not limited to controls alone. The United States has a special responsibility to share the benefits of peaceful nuclear energy with other countries. We have sought to serve other nations as a reliable supplier of nuclear fuel and equipment. Given the choice between economic benefits and progress toward our nonproliferation goals, we have given, and will continue to give, priority to nonproliferation. But there should be no incompatibility between nonproliferation and assisting other nations in enjoying the benefits of peaceful nuclear power, if all supplier countries pursue common nuclear export policies. There is need, however, for even more rigorous controls than those now commonly employed, and for policies that favor nations accepting responsible nonproliferation limitations.

—I have decided that we will henceforth apply new criteria in judging whether to enter into new or expanded nuclear cooperation:

• Adherence to the nonproliferation treaty will be a strong positive factor favoring cooperation with a nonnuclear weapon state.

• Nonnuclear weapons states that have not yet adhered to the nonproliferation treaty will receive positive recognition if they are prepared to submit to full fuel cycle safeguards, pending adherence.

• We will favor recipient nations that are prepared to forego, or postpone for a substantial period the establishment of national reprocessing or enrichment activities or, in certain cases, prepared to shape and schedule their reprocessing and enriching facilities to foster nonproliferation needs.

• Positive recognition will also be given to nations prepared to participate in an international storage regime, under which spent fuel and any separated plutonium would be placed pending use.

Exceptional cases may occur in which nonproliferation will be served best by cooperating with nations not yet meeting these tests. However, I pledge that the Congress will not be asked to approve any new or amended agreement not meeting these new criteria unless I personally determine that the agreement is fully supportive of our nonproliferation goals. In case of such a determination, my reasons will be fully presented to the Congress.

—With respect to countries that are current recipients of U.S. nuclear supply, I am directing the Secretary of State to enter into negotiations with the objective of conforming these agreements to established international guidelines, and to seek through diplomatic initiatives and fuel supply incentives to obtain their acceptance of our new criteria.

We must recognize the need for effective multilateral approaches to nonproliferation and prevent nuclear export controls from becoming an element of commercial competition.

—I am directing the Secretary of State to intensify discussions with other nuclear suppliers aimed at expanding common guidelines for peaceful cooperative agreements so that they conform with these criteria.

In this regard, the United States would discuss ways of developing incentives that can lead to acceptance of these criteria, such as assuring reliable fuel supplies for nations accepting new restraints.

The reliability of American assurances to other nations is an asset that few, if any, nations of the world can match. It must not be eroded. Indeed, nothing could more prejudice our efforts to strengthen our existing nonproliferation understandings than arbitrary suspension or unwarranted delays in meeting supply commitments to countries which are dealing with us in good faith regarding effective safeguards and restraints.

Despite my personal efforts, the 94th Congress adjourned without passing nuclear export legislation which would have strengthened our effectiveness in dealing with other nations on nuclear matters.

—In the absence of such legislation, I am directing the Secretary of State to work closely with the Nuclear Regulatory Commission to ensure proper emphasis on nonproliferation concerns in the nuclear export licensing process.

I will continue to work to develop bipartisan support in Congress for improvements in our nuclear export laws.

The terrible increase in violence and terrorism throughout the world has sharpened our awareness of the need to assure rigorous protection for sensitive nuclear materials and equipment. Fortunately, the need to cope with this problem is now broadly recognized. Many nations have responded to the initiatives which I have taken in this area by materially strengthening their physical security and by cooperating in the development of international guidelines by the IAEA. As a result of consultations among the major suppliers, provision for adequate physical security is becoming a normal condition of supply.

We have an effective physical security system in the United States. But steps are needed to upgrade physical security systems and to assure timely international collaboration in the recovery of lost or stolen materials.

—I have directed the Secretary of State to address vigorously the problem of physical security at both bilateral and multilateral levels, including exploration of a possible international convention.

The United States is committed to the development of the system of international controls that I have here outlined. Even when complete, however, no system of controls is likely to be effective if a potential violator judges that his acquisition of a nuclear explosive will be received with indifference by the international community.

Any material violation of a nuclear safeguards agreement—especially the diversion of nuclear material for use in making explosives—must be universally judged to be an extremely serious affront to the world community, calling for the immediate imposition of drastic sanctions.

—I serve notice today that the United States will, at a minimum, respond to violation by any nation of any safeguards agreement to which we are a party with an immediate cutoff of our supply of nuclear fuel and cooperation to that nation.

We would consider further steps, not necessarily confined to the area of nuclear cooperation, against the violator nation. Nor will our actions be limited to violations of agreements in which we are directly involved. In the event of material violation of any safeguards agreement, particularly agreements with the IAEA, we will initiate immediate consultations with all interested nations to determine appropriate action.

Universal recognition of the total unacceptability of the abrogation or violation of any nonproliferation agreements is one of the most important steps which can be taken to prevent further proliferation. We invite all concerned governments to affirm publicly that they will regard nuclear wrongdoing as an intolerable violation of acceptable norms of international behavior, which would set in motion strong and immediate countermeasures.

VII. Reprocessing Evaluation Program

The world community requires an aggressive program to build the international controls and cooperative regimes I have just outlined. I am prepared to mount such a program in the United States.

—I am directing the Administrator of ERDA to:

• Begin immediately to define a reprocessing and recycle evaluation program consistent with meeting our international objectives outlined earlier in this statement. This program should complement the Nuclear Regulatory Commission's (NRC) ongoing considerations of safety safeguards and environmental requirements for reprocessing and recycling activities, particularly its Generic Environmental Statement on Mixed Oxide Fuels.

• Investigate the feasibility of recovering the energy value from used nuclear fuel without separating our [*sic*: out?[plutonium.

—I am directing the Secretary of State to invite other nations to participate in designing and carrying out ERDA's reprocessing and recycle evaluation program, consistent with our international energy cooperation and nonproliferation objectives. I will direct that activities carried out in the U.S. in connection with this program be subjected to full IAEA safeguards and inspections.

VIII. Nuclear Waste Management

The area of our domestic nuclear program dealing with long-term management of nuclear wastes from our commercial nuclear powerplants has not in the past received sufficient attention. In my 1977 Budget, I proposed a four-fold increase in funding for this program, which involves the activities of several Federal agencies. We recently completed a review to determine what additional actions are needed to assure availability in the mid-1980's of a federally-owned and managed repository for long-term nuclear wastes, well before significant quantities of wastes begin to accumulate.

I have been assured that the technology for long-term management or disposal of nuclear wastes is available but demonstrations are needed.

—I have directed the Administrator of ERDA to take the necessary action to speed up this program so as to demonstrate all components of waste management technology by 1978 and to demonstrate a complete repository for such wastes by 1985.

—I have further directed that the first demonstration depository for high-level wastes which will be owned by the Government be submitted for licensing by the independent NRC to assure its safety and acceptability to the public.

In view of the decisions announced today, I have also directed the Administrator of ERDA to assure that the waste repository will be able to handle spent fuel elements as well as the separated and solidified waste that would result if we proceed with nuclear fuel reprocessing.

The United States continues to provide world leadership in nuclear waste management. I am inviting other nations to participate in and learn from our programs.

—I am directing the Secretary of State to discuss with other nations and the IAEA the possibility of establishing centrally located, multinationally controlled nuclear waste repositories so that the number of sites that are needed can be limited.

Increased Use of Nuclear Energy in the United States

Even with strong conservation efforts, energy demands in the United States will continue to increase in response to the needs of a growing economy. The only alternative over the next 15 to 20 years to increased use of both nuclear energy and coal is greater reliance on imported oil which will jeopardize our Nation's strength and welfare.

We now have in the United States 62 licensed nuclear plants, providing about 9 percent of our electrical energy. By 1985, we will have from 145 to 160 plants, supplying 20 percent or more of the Nation's electricity.

In many cases, electricity from nuclear plants is markedly cheaper than that produced from either oil or coal-fired plants. Nuclear energy is environmentally preferable in a number of respects to other principal ways of generating electricity.

Commercial nuclear power has an excellent safety record, with nearly 200 plant-years of experience (compiled over 18 chronological years) without a single death from a nuclear accident. I have acted to assure that this record is maintained in the years ahead. For example, I have increased funds for the independent Nuclear Regulatory Commission and for the Energy Research and Development Administration for reactor safety research and development.

The decisions and actions I am announcing today will help overcome the uncertainties that have served to delay the expanded use of nuclear energy in the United States. While the decision to delay reprocessing is significant, it will not prevent us from increasing our use of nuclear energy. We are on the right course with our nuclear power program in America. The changes I am announcing today will ensure that we continue.

My decisions today do not affect the U.S. program of research and development on the breeder reactor. That program assumes that no decision on the commercial operations of breeder reactors, which require plutonium fuel, will be made before 1986.

Conclusion

I do not underestimate the challenge represented in the creation of a world-wide program that will permit capturing the benefits of nuclear energy while maintaining needed protection against nuclear proliferation. The challenge is one that can be managed only partially and temporarily by technical measures.

It can be managed fully if the task is faced realistically by nations prepared to forego perceived short-term advantages in favor of fundamental long-term gains. We call upon all nations to recognize that their individual and collective interests are best served by internationally assured and safeguarded nuclear fuel supply, services, and storage. We ask them to turn aside from pursuing nuclear capabilities which are of doubtful economic value and have ominous implications for nuclear proliferation and instability in the world.

The growing international consensus against the proliferation of nuclear weapons is a source of encouragement. But it is certainly not a basis for complacency.

Success in meeting the challenge now before us depends on an extraordinary coordination of the policies of all nations toward the common good. The U.S. is prepared to lead, but we cannot succeed alone. If nations can work together constructively and cooperatively to manage our common nuclear problems, we will enhance our collective security. And we will be better able to concentrate our energies and our resources on the great tasks of construction rather than consume them in increasingly dangerous rivalry.

3. ATLANTIC ALLIANCE AND DÉTENTE IN EUROPE

(9) . The Treaty with Spain, January 24, 1976.

   (a) Report of the Department of State on the. Treaty and Related Agreements, February 6, 1976.[1]

DEPARTMENT OF STATE,
Washington, February 6, 1976.

The PRESIDENT,
The White House.

I have the honor to submit to you, with a view to its transmission to the Senate for advice and consent to ratification, the Treaty of Friendship and Cooperation between the United States of America and Spain, signed at Madrid on January 24, 1976, together with its seven Supplementary Agreements and its eight related exchanges of notes.[2] This agreement would supersede the 1970 Agreement between the United States and Spain on Friendship and Cooperation, which expired on September 26, 1975, at which time a one-year transitional period began.

The new agreement is in the form of a Treaty. This solemn form was deemed appropriate not only because of the wide scope and importance of the subject matter covered but also because both Spanish and United States authorities wanted to assure the soundest political basis for the new stage in United States-Spanish relations symbolized by the agreement.

The Treaty covers a broad spectrum of areas of mutual concern in United States-Spanish relations, with specific articles and supplementary agreements treating cooperation in the areas of economic affairs, education and culture, science and technology,

[1] Text from *Bulletin*, 74: 362-4.
[2] Texts of the supplementary agreements (signed Jan. 24) and exchanges of notes (signed Feb. 3) appear in TIAS 8360: 10-39 and 68-9 respectively.

and defense matters. It also provides an institutional framework to enhance the effectiveness of cooperation in all these areas. The principal new elements of substance are in this institutional area, and include the creation of a high-level United States-Spanish Council, to oversee the implementation of the entire agreement, and a set of subordinate bodies, including joint committees for the various areas of cooperation and a Combined Military Coordination and Planning Staff. The agreement specifies the military and nonmilitary assistance to be given Spain over the five-year initial term of the agreement, and grants to the United States essentially the same rights to use military facilities in Spain which it enjoyed under the 1970 arrangements. The principal changes in military facilities are a reduction and relocation of United States tanker aircraft within Spain and establishment of a date for withdrawal of the nuclear submarine squadron from the Rota Naval Base.

Article I of the Treaty, together with Supplementary Agreement Number One, and a related exchange of notes, establishes the United States-Spanish Council, under the joint chairmanship of the Secretary of State of the United States and the Foreign Minister of Spain. The Council, which is to meet at least semi-annually, will have headquarters in Madrid, a permanent secretariat, and permanent representatives serving as deputies to the Chairmen to assure its ability to function in their absence. An important aspect of the new arrangement is the integration of the military cooperation into the Council structure.

Article II, together with Supplementary Agreement Number Two, calls for the development of closer economic ties between the United States and Spain, placing emphasis on cooperation in those fields which facilitate development. In this connection, the agreement takes into account the current readiness of the Export-Import Bank to commit credits and guarantees of approximately $450 million to Spanish companies. The agreement also specifies general principles to guide United States-Spanish relations in the economic field.

Article III, together with Supplementary Agreement Number Three and a related exchange of notes, provides for a broad program of scientific and technical cooperation for peaceful purposes with principal emphasis on areas having significance to the social and economic welfare of the peoples of Spain and the United States as well as to developmental progress. A total of $23 million would be provided by the United States in the form of grant to support this five-year program. One of the first matters of concern in scientific and technological cooperation will be studies relating to a solar energy institute which Spain wishes to establish, with some seed money for the studies being drawn from the U.S. grant.

Article IV of the Treaty, together with Supplementary Agreement Number Four and a related exchange of notes, provides for a continuation and expansion of educational and cultural cooperation. The agreement contemplates a grant from the United States in the amount of $12 million to support this five-year program, which is considered to be of particular importance in strengthening the relationship between the United States and Spain.

Articles V and VI of the Treaty, together with Supplementary Agreements Five, Six and Seven, and related exchanges of notes, deal with cooperation in the area of defense. The defense relationship which these provisions represent is one woven firmly into the fabric of existing United States philosophy and planning for the defense of the North Atlantic area. It represents a decision to assist Spain in developing a role which will contribute actively to that defense, and provides transitional institutions to prepare the way for an appropriate Spanish role in NATO. These provisions do not constitute a security guarantee or commitment to defend Spain. They do, however, constitute a recognition of Spain's importance as a part of the Western World.

To this end, a Combined Planning and Coordination Staff, with no command functions, is provided for by Supplementary Agreement Number Five, which sets forth a carefully drawn mandate and geographic area of common concern. All activities of the staff focus on the contingency of a general attack on the West. There is no commitment, express or implied, in the drawing up of the contingency plans.

To further the purposes of the Treaty, Spain grants the United States the right to use and maintain for military purposes those facilities in or connected with Spanish military installations which the United States has heretofore enjoyed, with the exception that the number of KC–135 tankers in Spain will be reduced to a maximum of five and the remaining tankers relocated; and that the nuclear submarines will be withdrawn from Spain by July 1, 1979, a date which corresponds with our changing requirements. In addition, the United States undertakes not to store nuclear devices or their components on Spanish soil. Details concerning the facilities granted are set forth in Supplementary Agreement Number Six, a related exchange of notes which includes U.S. military strength levels authorized in Spain, and an exchange of notes confirming United States military overflight rights and rights to use facilities in Spain for military aircraft transiting to third countries.

The details of the military assistance to be provided Spain are set forth in Supplementary Agreement Number Seven and a related exchange of notes. Under these arrangements, the United States would provide to Spain, over the five-year initial term of the Treaty, repayment guarantees under the Foreign Military Sales program for loans of $600 million, $75 million in defense articles on a grant basis, $10 million in military training on a grant basis, and a U.S. Air Force contribution, on a cost-sharing basis, of up to $50 million for the aircraft control and warning network used by the U.S. Air Force in Spain. In addition, provision is made to transfer to Spain five naval vessels and 42 F4E aircraft on terms which benefit that country.

The notes exchanged include United States assurances to Spain on settlement of damage claims which might result from nuclear incidents involving a United States nuclear powered warship reactor. These assurances are based on Public Law 93-513.[3] Finally, there is an exchange of notes relating to the possible transfer of petroleum storage and pipeline facilities presently used by United States forces in Spain.

Associated with the Treaty and its supplementary agreements and exchanges of notes are an Agreement on Implementation and procedural annexes thereto[4] which regulate such matters as the status of United States forces in Spain and the use of the facilities there. These documents are being provided to the Congress for its information.

Respectfully submitted,

HENRY A. KISSINGER.

(b) . Treaty of Friendship and Cooperation between the United States of America and Spain, signed at Madrid January 24, 1976 and entered into force September 21, 1976.[5]

TREATY OF FRIENDSHIP AND COOPERATION BETWEEN SPAIN AND THE UNITED STATES OF AMERICA

The Governments of Spain and of the United States of America;

Impelled by their shared concern for the maintenance of world peace and security;

Affirming that their cooperation is beneficial for the security of both countries; strengthens the defense of the West; plays an

---

[3]Signed Dec. 6, 1974.
[4]TIAS 8361, signed at Madrid Jan. 31, 1976 and entered into force Sept. 21, 1976.
[5]Text from TIAS 8360: 5-9.

important part in the security arrangements for the North Atlantic and Mediterranean areas; and contributes to the achievement of their shared goals;

Desiring to reaffirm and strengthen the friendship between their peoples and to continue and enrich the cooperative relationship which exists between the two countries, in the spirit of the Declaration of Principles between Spain and the United States of America, of July 19, 1974;[6]

Agree as follows:

Article I

The close cooperation between the two countries on all matters of common concern or interest will be maintained and developed on a basis of sovereign equality. This cooperation shall encompass economic, educational, cultural, scientific, technical, agricultural, and defense matters, as well as other matters upon which they may mutually agree.

The Governments of Spain and the United States of America will keep their cooperation in all these areas under continuous review and seek to identify and adopt all appropriate measures for carrying out this cooperation in the most effective manner possible with a view to maintaining a balance of benefits, equal and effective participation of both parties, and coordination and harmonization of their efforts with those which may be being made in other bilateral and multilateral contexts.

For these purposes, a Spanish-United States Council is established under the chairmanship of the Foreign Minister of Spain and the Secretary of State of the United States of America. The functions and organization of the Council are set forth in Supplementary Agreement Number One. The Council will meet at least semi-annually.[7]

Article II

Given the increasing international importance of economic affairs, the two parties will seek to develop their economic relations so as to ensure mutual benefit under conditions of equitable reciprocity and to promote, in particular, cooperation in those fields which facilitate development. That cooperation shall also take into account the impact which the state of the economy of

[6]Text in *Bulletin*, 71: 231; cf. *AFR, 1974:* 201 n. 22.

[7]The U.S.-Spanish Council was formally constituted Oct. 1, 1976; text of joint communiqué of the inaugural session in *Bulletin*, 75: 563-4.

each country has on its defense efforts. Their economic relationship will be carried out in accordance with Supplementary Agreement Number Two.

Article III

Given the relations of friendship which exist between the peoples of Spain and the United States of America, and recognizing that science and technology are essential factors in meeting the growing needs and in furthering the general economic development of both countries, the two Governments will carry out a broad program of scientific and technical cooperation for peaceful purposes. In the framework of that cooperation, they will direct their efforts principally to areas having the most significance to the social and economic welfare of their peoples, and to developmental progress. Their relations in these areas will be carried out in accordance with Supplementary Agreement Number Three.

Article IV

In order to continue to expand their cooperation in the educational and cultural fields with a view to furthering the familiarity of their peoples with the important cultural achievements of the other and to strengthen the friendship and understanding between their peoples which provide the necessary foundation for the overall cooperative relationship between the two countries, their relations in these areas will be carried out in accordance with Supplementary Agreement Number Four.

Article V

Having recognized that their cooperation has strengthened the security of the Western World, and contributed to the maintenance of world peace, there is established a defense relationship between Spain and the United States of America. Consistent with the Declaration of Principles of July 19, 1974, they will, through this defense relationship, seek to enhance further their own security and that of the Western World. To such end, they will seek to develop the appropriate plans and coordination between their respective armed forces. This coordination will be carried out by a coordinating body as set forth in Supplementary Agreement Number Five.

To further the purposes of this Treaty, the United States of America may use specific military facilities on Spanish territory, in accordance with the provisions set forth in Supplementary

Agreement Number Six. The two parties will also, for these ends, cooperate in the acquisition as well as the production of appropriate materiel for their armed forces, in accordance with the provisions of Supplementary Agreement Number Seven.

Article VI

In view of the contribution the use of the facilities mentioned in Article V makes to the defense of the West, the parties, through mutually agreed steps, will seek on the basis of reciprocity and equality to harmonize their defense relationship with existing security arrangements in the North Atlantic area. To this end, they will, periodically, review all aspects of the matter, including the benefits flowing to those arrangements from the facilities and make such adjustments as may be mutually agreed upon.

Article VII

This Treaty and its Supplementary Agreements shall enter into force upon the exchange of instruments of ratification between the two Governments and will remain in force for five years, whereupon they may be extended for an additional five year period if the parties so agree.

Article VIII

In order to facilitate the withdrawal of the personnel, property, equipment and materiel of the Government of the United States of America located in Spain pursuant to Article V of this Treaty and its Supplementary Agreements, a period of one year from the termination of the Treaty is provided for the completion of withdrawal which will begin immediately after such termination. During that one year period, all the rights, privileges and obligations deriving from Article V and its Supplementary Agreements shall remain in force while United States forces remain in Spain.

DONE in Madrid, this 24th day of January, 1976, in duplicate, in the English and Spanish languages, both texts being equally authentic.

FOR THE UNITED STATES OF AMERICA:
(*Signed*) Henry A. Kissinger

FOR SPAIN:
(*Signed*) J. Areilza

(c) Resolution of Ratification adopted by the United States Senate, June 21, 1976.[8]

SENATE OF THE UNITED STATES
IN EXECUTIVE SESSION

JUNE 21, 1976

RESOLVED, (two-thirds of the Senators present concurring therein), That the Senate advise and consent to the ratification of the Treaty of Friendship and Cooperation between the United States of America and Spain, signed at Madrid on January 24, 1976, together with its seven Supplementary Agreements and its eight related exchanges of notes (Executive E, Ninety-fourth Congress, second session) subject to the declaration that:

(1) the United States, recognizing the aspiration of Spain to achieve full participation in the political and economic institutions of Western Europe, and recognizing further that the development of free institutions in Spain is a necessary aspect of Spain's full integration into European life, hopes and intends that this Treaty will serve to support and foster Spain's progress toward free institutions and toward Spain's participation in the institutions of Western European political and economic cooperation;

(2) the United States, while recognizing that this Treaty does not expand the existing United States defense commitment in the North Atlantic Treaty area or create a mutual defense commitment between the United States and Spain, looks forward to the development of such an expanded relationship between Western Europe and a democratic Spain as would be conducive to Spain's full cooperation with the North Atlantic Treaty Organization, its activities and mutual defense obligations;

(3) the United States, recognizing that this Treaty provides a framework for continued nuclear cooperation for peaceful purposes with Spain, looks forward to a continued relationship in this field commensurate with steps taken by Spain toward becoming a party to the Treaty on the Non-Proliferation of Nuclear Weapons or placing all of its nuclear facilities under safeguards administered by the International Atomic Energy Agency;

(4) Senate advice and consent to ratification shall be understood to apply only to the initial five-year period of the Treaty, so that

any United States agreement to an extension of the Treaty shall require the further advice and consent of the Senate; and

(5) the sums referred to in the Supplementary Agreement on Cooperation Regarding Materiel for the Armed Forces and Notes of January 24, 1976, appended to the Treaty, shall be made available for obligation through the normal procedures of the Congress, including the process of prior authorization and annual appropriations, and shall be provided to Spain in accordance with the provisions of foreign assistance and related legislation.

Attest: FRANCIS R. VALEO

Secretary

(10) Defense Arrangements with Turkey and Greece.

> *(a) Defense Cooperation Agreement of March 26, 1976 between the United States and Turkey: Message from President Ford to the Congress, June 16, 1976.*[9]

To the Congress of the United States:

I am hereby requesting that Congress approve and authorize appropriations to implement the Agreement Between the Governments of the United States of America and of the Republic of Turkey Relative to Defense Cooperation Pursuant to Article III of the North Atlantic Treaty in Order to Resist Armed Attack in the North Atlantic Treaty Area, signed in Washington, March 26, 1976, and a related exchange of notes. Accordingly, I am transmitting herewith draft legislation in the form of a Joint Resolution of the Congress for this purpose.[10]

The United States and Turkey have long enjoyed a close mutual security relationship under the North Atlantic Treaty, as well as bilateral cooperation in accordance with Article III of that Treaty. The new Agreement, like its predecessor, the Defense Cooperation Agreement of 1969 which this Agreement would supersede, implements the Treaty. It has been signed as an executive agreement. The Agreement was negotiated with the understanding that it would be subject to Congressional approval and expressly provides that it shall not enter into force until the parties exchange notes in-

---

[9]Text from *Presidential Documents*, 12: 1061-2.
[10]Texts of draft legislation, the agreement and related exchange of notes were printed as H. Doc. 94-531.

dicating approval of the Agreement in accordance with their respective legal procedures. Full Congressional endorsement of this Agreement will give new strength and stability to continuing U.S.-Turkish security cooperation which has served as a vital buttress on NATO's southeast flank for more than two decades.

The new Agreement is consistent with, but not identical to, the preceding Defense Cooperation Agreement of 1969. Founded on mutual respect for the sovereignty of the parties, the Agreement (Articles II and III) authorizes U.S. participation in defense measures related to the parties' obligations arising out of the North Atlantic Treaty. It is understood that when the Agreement enters into force pursuant to Article XXI, activities will resume which were suspended by the Government of Turkey in July 1975, when the Turkish Government requested negotiation of a new defense cooperation agreement.

The Agreement provides a mutually acceptable framework for this important security cooperation. The installations authorized by the Agreement will be Turkish Armed Forces installations under Turkish command (Articles IV and V). Article V clearly provides for U.S. command and control authority over all U.S. armed forces personnel, other members of the U.S. national element at each installation, and U.S. equipment and support facilities.

The installations shall be operated jointly. In order to facilitate this objective, the United States is committed to a program of technical training of Turkish personnel.

Other provisions of the Agreement deal with traditional operational and administrative matters, including: operation and maintenance of the installations; ceilings on levels of U.S. personnel and equipment; import, export and in-country supply procedures; status of forces and property questions.

Article XIX specifies the amounts of defense support which the United States plans to provide Turkey during the first four years the Agreement remains in force. We have provided such support to this important NATO ally for many years to help Turkey meet its heavy NATO obligations. The Article provides that during the first four years the Agreement remains in force, the United States will furnish $1,000,000,000 in grants, credits and loan guaranties, to be distributed equally over these four years in accordance with annual plans to be developed by the Governments. It further provides that during the first year of the defense support program, $75 million in grants will be made available, with a total of not less than $200 million in grants to be provided over the four-year life of the program. The Article also sets forth our preparedness to make cash sales to Turkey of defense articles and services over the life of the Agreement.

The related exchange of notes details defense articles we are prepared to sell to the Republic of Turkey at prices consistent with U.S. law. It further provides for Turkish access to the U.S. Defense Communications Satellite System, and for bilateral consultations regarding cooperation in modernizing Turkish defense communications.

The defense support specified in Article XIX and in the related exchange of notes will be provided in accordance with contractual obligations existing and to be entered into by the Governments, and with the general practices applicable to all other recipient countries. The accompanying draft legislation accordingly provides that the generally applicable provisions of our foreign assistance and military sales Acts will govern this defense support, and that it will be exempted from the provisions of section 620(x) of the Foreign Assistance Act as amended. The draft legislation further provides that it fulfills the requirements of section 36(b) of the Foreign Military Sales Act as amended and section 7307 of Title 10 of the United States Code with respect to the transfer of materiel pursuant to the related exchange of notes.

The Agreement will have a duration of four years, and will be extended for subsequent four-year periods in the absence of notice of termination by one of the parties. As the four-year defense support program comes to an end, the Agreement provides for consultation on the development of a future program as required in accordance with the respective legal procedures of the two Governments. Article XXI stipulates the procedures under which the Agreement can be terminated by either party, and provides for a one-year period following termination during which the Agreement will be considered to remain in force for the purposes of an orderly withdrawal.

This Agreement restores a bilateral relationship that has been important to Western security for more than two decades. I believe it will promote U.S. interests and objectives on the vital southeastern flank of NATO and provide a framework for bilateral cooperation designed solely to reinforce NATO and our common security concerns. To the extent that the Agreement restores trust and confidence between the United States and Turkey, it also enhances the prospects for a constructive dialogue on other regional problems of mutual concern.

I therefore request that the Congress give this Agreement and the accompanying draft legislation prompt and favorable consideration, and approve its entry into force and authorize the appropriation of the funds necessary for its execution.

GERALD R. FORD

The White House,
    June 16, 1976.

(b) Principles for Future Defense Cooperation between the United States and Greece, initialed in Washington April 15, 1976.[11]

PRINCIPLES TO GUIDE FUTURE
UNITED STATES-GREEK DEFENSE
COOPERATION

1. The Governments of the United States of America and Greece will complete as soon as possible a new defense cooperation agreement to replace the 1953 United States-Greek military facilities agreement and other related agreements. The United States Government will submit this Agreement to Congress for approval.

2. The new Agreement will be designed to modernize the United States-Greek defense relationship reflecting the traditionally close association between the United States and Greece and the mutuality of their defense interests in the North Atlantic Alliance.

3. This new Agreement will define the status and set forth the terms for operations of military installations in Greece where United States personnel are present. It will be similar to the United States-Turkish Agreement and will embody, *inter alia*, the following principles:

(A) Each installation will be a Greek military installation under a Greek commander.

(B) The installations shall serve only purposes authorized by the Government of Greece. Their activities shall be carried out on the basis of mutually agreed programs.

(C) There shall be participation of Greek personnel up to 50% of the total strength required for agreed joint technical operations and related maintenance activities and services of the facilities and there shall be provisions for the training of such personnel for this purpose.

(D) All intelligence information including raw data produced by the installations shall be shared fully by the two Governments according to mutually agreed procedures. A joint use plan for the United States forces communications system in Greece shall be agreed upon.

(E) The Agreement shall remain in effect for four years and there shall be provisions for the termination thereof before its expiration, as well as for its renewal.

[11]Text from *Bulletin*, 74: 794-7.

(F) Within this framework there shall be annexes to this Agreement covering each major installation (Nea Makri, Souda Bay, Iraklion), the United States element at the Hellenikon Greek Air Force Base, as well as annexes dealing with status of forces (SOFA), and command and control.

(G) The annex covering Souda Bay will be a revision of the 1959 Souda Bay Agreement. Meanwhile it is understood that United States operations at this airfield will be in accordance with the 1959 Agreement.

(H) It is understood that, pending the conclusion of the new Agreement within a reasonable time, United States operations now being conducted from facilities in Greece, which serve mutual defense interests, will be allowed to continue.

4. As an integral part of the new defense cooperation agreement, provision will be made for a four-year commitment to Greece of military assistance totaling 700 million dollars, a part of which will be grant aid. This commitment will be designed to further develop the defense preparedness of Greece and meet its defense needs in pursuit of North Atlantic Alliance goals.

WASHINGTON, *April 15, 1976.*

(11) Ministerial Session of the North Atlantic Council, Oslo, May 20-21, 1976: Final communiqué.[12]

The North Atlantic Council met in Ministerial Session in Oslo on 20th and 21st May, 1976. Ministers reaffirmed their adherence to the central purposes of the Alliance and their determination to maintain and, where necessary, enhance the cooperation and solidarity of the Allies, as well as their deterrent and defensive strength. Only if the security of the peoples of the Alliance is guaranteed in this way can East-West relations continue to improve.

2. After reviewing recent trends in East-West relations, Ministers agreed that, while there were certain encouraging aspects, others gave cause for concern. They remained convinced that Allied Governments, intent on building a more constructive and stable relationship with the East, must continue to strive for a relaxation of tensions and to try to devise further practical measures of cooperation in areas of common interest, while preserving the cohesion and strength of the Alliance. They stated that such a

[12]Department of State Press Release 259, May 21; text from *Bulletin*, 74: 774-5.

policy, entailing a dialogue attuned to current realities, has the full support of the member countries.

However, the pursuit of a genuine and durable détente is possible only if all states concerned exercise restraint both in their relations with each other and in their actions in other parts of the world. The necessary confidence could not be established between East and West if crises and tensions were to be avoided in Europe only to appear elsewhere. In this regard, Ministers underlined that all signatories of the CSCE Final Act have recognized the close link between peace and security in Europe and in the world as a whole.

Accordingly, Ministers felt that they must once again voice their concern at the sustained growth in the Warsaw Pact countries' military power, on land, at sea and in the air beyond levels apparently justified for defensive purposes. Should this trend continue, it could lead to an arms race of dangerous dimensions. Ministers again stressed the determination of their governments to take the measures necessary to maintain and improve the efficiency of their forces, as an essential safeguard for the security of member countries, whether against military aggression or political pressure.

3. Ministers examined the progress made in implementing the provisions of the Final Act of the CSCE. They emphasized the importance they attach to full implementation of all parts of the Helsinki Final Act by all signatories, so that its benefits may be felt not only in relations between states, but also in the lives of individuals. Ministers recognized that some steps have been taken affecting human contacts and working conditions for journalists. However, in view of the importance of what still remains to be done, they expressed the hope that progress in this field would gather momentum during the coming months and that progress would also be recorded in cooperation in economic relations and in other spheres, as well as in the observance of the principles guiding relations between participating states.

In the field of confidence-building measures, they noted that a number of military maneuvers in Europe had been notified and observers had been invited to some of them. They stated their intention to continue fully to comply with the relevant provisions of the Final Act and expressed the expectation that all signatories would do the same.

Ministers expressed the view that the meeting to be held in Belgrade in 1977 would provide an opportunity not only to exchange views on the implementation of the Final Act of the CSCE, but also to consider the further progress that could be made toward the objectives agreed in Helsinki.

4. Ministers heard a report from the United States Secretary of State on the continuing United States efforts toward the further

limitation of strategic offensive arms and toward embodiment of the Vladivostok understanding in a SALT Agreement. The Ministers discussed how the negotiations affect common security interests. They expressed the hope that further efforts would lead to the resolution of outstanding issues and to the conclusion of a satisfactory SALT Agreement. The Ministers also underlined the value of continuing consultations within the Alliance with respect to SALT.

5. The Ministers of those countries which participate in the Vienna negotiations on Mutual and Balanced Force Reductions (MBFR) reviewed the state of these negotiations. They again stressed that MBFR must result in eliminating the ground force manpower disparity in Central Europe and in mitigating the disparity in main battle tanks if the agreed aim of contributing to a more stable relationship and to the strengthening of peace and security in Europe is to be achieved. They reiterated, therefore, the importance which they attach to the Western proposal to establish, in the area of reductions, approximate parity in ground forces in the form of a common collective ceiling for ground force manpower on each side and to reduce the disparity in tanks. As proposed by the participating Allies, agreement to the goal of a common collective ceiling and reductions of American and Soviet ground forces in the first phase would be an important and practical first step leading to a common collective ceiling in the second phase.

The Ministers expressed their continuing resolve to press for achievement of the objectives of the Western participants. They recalled their important specific additional offer of December 1975 which was made conditional upon agreement to the objectives as set out in the Western proposals. They expressed the hope that these would be given the most serious consideration.

These Ministers reaffirmed their conviction that their proposals provide a reasonable foundation for a just and equitable agreement which would in its turn constitute an indispensable contribution to a further relaxation of tensions. These Ministers are convinced that the realization of the aims pursued by the West in the negotiations would lead to a more stable military situation which would ensure undiminished security for all countries concerned and would thus be to the advantage of both sides.

The Ministers noted with satisfaction that solidarity is fully maintained and that their public opinion supports the Western position as logical and fair. They reaffirmed the principle that NATO forces should not be reduced except in the context of Mutual and Balanced Force Reductions Agreements.

6. The Ministers reviewed the developments relating to Berlin

and Germany as a whole which have occurred since their last meeting in December 1975.

They took note of the agreements concluded on 19th December 1975, by the two German States, agreements which will bring, in the interest of the German people, further improvements to the traffic to and from Berlin.

As regards Berlin, the Ministers discussed the further experience gained in the implementation of the Quadripartite Agreement of 3rd September, 1971, and especially of those provisions of the Agreement which concern the Western sectors of Berlin. They noted, in particular, that the provisions of this Agreement which concern the traffic to and from Berlin were being implemented in a satisfactory way.

Noting that Berlin's participation in international activities is an important element of the viability of the city, the Ministers viewed with concern attempts of certain countries to impose limitations on the right of the Federal Republic of Germany, as confirmed in the Quadripartite Agreement, to represent the interests of the Western sectors of Berlin abroad. They expressed the hope that, in the interest of the Berliners and of progress in cooperation in Europe, all provisions of the Quadripartite Agreement and, especially, the provisions which relate to the representation abroad of the interests of the Western sectors of Berlin by the Federal Republic of Germany, will be fully implemented and strictly observed.

7. Ministers took note of the report on the situation in the Mediterranean prepared on their instructions. They emphasized the importance they attach to maintaining the Balance of Forces throughout the Mediterranean area. They requested the Council to continue its consultations on this subject and to report to them at their next meeting.

Ministers noted with satisfaction the progress made regarding new defense cooperation agreements that will open the way to enhancing Allied defenses in the South-Eastern region.

They expressed concern at the serious situation arising from the continuing instability in the Middle East and reaffirmed that rapid progress must be made toward a just and lasting settlement of the conflict.

8. The Fisheries Dispute between Iceland and the United Kingdom was again raised and discussed.

9. As part of their continuing efforts to improve the military capability of the Alliance and to make more effective use of available resources, Ministers addressed the general subject of standardization and discussed an interim report on equipment interoperability. This report, which had been prepared by an Ad Hoc Committee set up after the December Ministerial Meeting, concentrated on certain priority areas. The need for full im-

plementation of existing standardization agreements was stressed. The Ministers noted that there were encouraging prospects for improving operational flexibility of Allied forces. They asked for a full report in December, 1976.

10. The Ministers reaffirmed the commitment of their countries to the principles of democracy, respect for human rights, justice and social progress which inspire the Alliance and on which their political institutions and way of life are founded. They expressed the confidence that, on the basis of the security provided by the Alliance, their governments would overcome the problems confronting them now and in the future.

11. The next Ministerial session of the North Atlantic Council will be held in Brussels on 9th and 10th December, 1976.

(12)   "The Western Alliance: Peace and Moral Purpose": Address by Secretary of State Kissinger before the International Institute for Strategic Studies, London, June 25, 1976.[13]

On my arrival in Washington seven years ago, one of my first acts was to gather a group of senior scholars of European affairs to have them give their advice to a new President on relations with our allies. The chairman of that group was Alastair Buchan.

He should not be held responsible for the results. But it was only natural to seek his counsel. For Alastair was more than a distinguished expert; he was a consummate man of the West. A Scot by birth, he considered himself, and referred to himself, as a European. He lived many years in the United States and visited us often, applying his incisive mind to the study of America and its role in the world. He was a champion of the importance, indeed, the inevitability, of the transatlantic tie between North America and Europe.

Beneath the skeptical air was a passionate commitment to the values and traditions we cherish as Western civilization. Sir Peter Ramsbotham [U.K. Ambassador to the United States] said in his eulogy of Alastair in Washington that no other countryman of his had contributed more to the understanding of international affairs and the strategic implications of nuclear power in the latter half of the 20th century. But Alastair's focus was not simply the structure of global politics and the roots of war; it was the central role of the West in preserving peace and giving it moral purpose.

This institute is a monument to his quest.

Alastair had that combination of intellect and compassion

[13]Department of State Press Release 329; text from *Bulletin*, 75: 105-15.

known as wisdom. It motivated the great contribution he made to scholarship and to a generation's understanding of the transformation of international relationships. He has left his mark on every person in this hall. During the last seven years he never hesitated to scold me, in all friendship, when he thought that American policy did not do justice to the great cause of European-American cooperation.

I would like to think that had he lived he would feel that after many starts we have made great strides in strengthening the unity of the West. And if that were his conviction, I for one would be very proud.

Alastair wrote:

Structural changes are occurring in the relative power and influence of the major states; there has been a quantitative change of colossal proportions in the interdependence of Western societies and in the demands we make on natural resources; and there are qualitative changes in the preoccupations of our societies.

He then posed the question:

Can the highly industrialized states sustain or recover a quality in their national life which not only satisfies the new generation, but can act as an example or attractive force to other societies?

All of us who wish to honor Alastair's memory must do so in the way he would want most of all—by proving that the answer to his question is "Yes." A world that cries out for economic advance, for social justice, for political liberty, and for a stable peace needs our collective commitment and contribution. I firmly believe that the industrial democracies working together have the means, if they have the will, to shape creatively a new era of international affairs. Indeed, we are doing so on many fronts today, thanks no little to the clarity Alastair brought to our purposes and directions.

A generation ago, Western statesmen fashioned new institutions of collaboration to stave off a common threat. Our progress after 30 years has been striking. Global war has been deterred, and all of the industrial democracies live with an enhanced sense of security. Our economies are the most prosperous on earth; our technology and productive genius have proven indispensable for all countries seeking to better the welfare of their peoples, be they Socialist or developing. Our societies represent, more than ever, a beacon of hope to those who yearn for liberty and justice and progress. In no part of the world and under no other system do men live so well and in so much freedom. If performance is any criterion, the contest between freedom and communism, of which so much was made three decades ago, has been won by the industrial democracies.

And yet at this precise moment, we hear in our countries premonitions of decline, anxieties about the travail of the West and the advance of authoritarianism. Can it be that our deeper problems are not of resources but of will, not of power but of conception?

We who overcame great dangers 30 years ago must not now paralyze ourselves with illusions of impotence. We have already initiated the construction of a new system of international relations, this time on a global scale; we must summon the determination to work toward it in unity and mutual confidence.

For America, cooperation among the free nations is a moral, and not merely a practical, necessity. Americans have never been comfortable with calculations of interest and power alone. America, to be itself, needs a sense of identity and collaboration with other nations who share its values.

Our association with Western Europe, Canada, and Japan thus goes to the heart of our national purpose. Common endeavors with our sister democracies raise the goals of our foreign policy beyond physical survival toward a peace of human progress and dignity. The ties of intellectual civilization, democratic tradition, historical association, and more than a generation of common endeavor bind us together more firmly than could any pragmatic conception of national interest alone. The unity of the industrial democracies has been the cornerstone of American foreign policy for 30 years, and it will remain so for as far ahead as we can see.

So I would like to pay tribute to Alastair this evening by addressing the issues he raised: Can America, Europe, and the industrial democracies meet the challenge of the world's future? What is the state of our relationship?

The United States and a United Europe

In 1973, with Viet-Nam at last behind us, and fresh from new initiatives with China and the Soviet Union, the United States proposed that the collaboration of the industrial democracies be given new impetus. Military security, while still crucial, was no longer sufficient to give content or political cohesion to our broader relationship or to retain support for it from a new generation. We faced important East-West negotiations on European security and force reductions, a fresh agenda of international economic problems, the challenge of shaping anew our relationship with the developing world, and the need to redefine relations between America and a strengthened and enlarged European community.

It is academic to debate now whether the United States acted too theoretically in proposing to approach these challenges through the elaboration of a new Atlantic Declaration, or whether our European friends acted wisely in treating this proposal as a test case of European identity. The doctrinal arguments of 1973 over the procedure for Atlantic consultations, or whether Europe was exercising its proper global role, or whether economic and security issues should be linked, have in fact been settled by the practice of consultations and cooperation unprecedented in intensity and scope. The reality and success of our common endeavors have provided the best definition and revitalization of our relationship.

There is no longer any question that Europe and the United States must cooperate closely under whatever label and that the unity of Europe is essential to that process.

In its early days, the European Community was the focus of much American idealism, and perhaps of some paternalism, as we urged models of federal unity and transatlantic burden sharing on our European friends. By now, leaders on both sides of the Atlantic have come to understand that European unity cannot be built by Americans or to an American prescription; it must result from European initiatives.

The evolution of European initiatives—both its successes and its setbacks—inevitably gives rise to new questions about whether the United States still welcomes European unification. Let me take this occasion to emphasize our conviction that European unity is crucial for Europe, for the West, and for the world. We strongly support and encourage it.

We have perhaps become a little more sophisticated about our contribution to the process. We no longer expect that it will grow from the desire to ease American burdens. If Europe is to carry a part of the West's responsibilities in the world, it must do so according to its own conceptions and in its own interest.

Alastair Buchan wrote:

It is impossible to inspire Western Europe to political unity or to encourage Japanese self-reliance unless they have the freedom and confidence to define their interests in every sphere, interests which must be reconciled with those of the United States but not subordinated to them.

The United States endorses this principle wholeheartedly. It is not healthy for the United States to be the only center of initiative and leadership in the democratic world. It is not healthy for Europe to be only a passive participant, however close the friendship and however intimate the consultation.

We therefore welcome the fact that Europe's role in global affairs is gaining in vigor and effectiveness. A vital and cohesive Western Europe is an irreplaceable weight on the scales of global diplomacy; American policy can only gain by having a strong partner of parallel moral purposes.

Of course we do not want Europe to find its identity in opposition to the United States. But neither does any sensible European. Of course there will be disagreements between us of tactics and sometimes of perspectives, if not of ends. But I do not believe that we Americans have so lost confidence in ourselves that we must inhibit the role of others with whom we may have occasional differences but who share our highest values. The wisest statesmen on the two sides of the ocean have always known that European unity and Atlantic partnership are both essential and mutually reinforcing.

So let us finally put behind us the debates over whether Europe's unity has American support. We consider the issue settled. Let us, rather, address ourselves to the urgent challenges of mutual concern which a uniting Europe, the United States, and all industrial democracies must face together—common defense, East-West relations, and the international economy.

Security and the Democracies

Security is the bedrock of all that we do. A quarter century ago, the American defense commitment to Europe provided the shield behind which Western Europe recovered its economic health and political vitality. Today, our collective defense alliance—and the U.S.-Japanese relationship—continue to be essential for global stability. But the nature of security and strategy has fundamentally changed since the time when our alliances were founded:

—The Soviet Union has recovered from the devastation of World War II and pressed vigorously ahead on the path of industrial growth. Possessing resources on a continental scale and imposing on its people enormous sacrifices in the name of its ideology, the U.S.S.R. has developed its economic strength and technology to a point where it can match the West in many sectors of industrial and military power. It shows no signs of changing its priorities.

—For centuries, it was axiomatic that increases in military power could be translated into almost immediate political advantage. It is now clear that in strategic weaponry, new increments of weapons or destructiveness do not automatically lead to either military or political gains. The destructiveness of strategic weapons has contributed to the emergence of nuclear stalemate. Neither side, if it acts with minimum prudence, will let the balance tip against it, either in an arms race or in an agreement to limit arms.

—Beneath the nuclear umbrella, the temptation to probe with regional forces or proxy wars increases. The steady growth of Soviet conventional military and naval power and its expanding global reach cannot be ignored. Conventional forces and military assistance to allies assume pivotal importance. We must insure that the strength and flexibility of all forces capable of local defense are enhanced. And we must conduct a prudent and forceful foreign policy that is prepared to use our strength to block expansionism.

These new realities demand from us steadiness, above all. Democratic societies have always fluctuated in their attitude toward defense—between complacency and alarmist concern. The long leadtimes of modern weapons and their complexity make both these aberrations dangerous. We cannot afford alternation between neglect and bursts of frenzy if we are to have a coherent defense program and public support for the necessary exertions. We need an allied defense posture that is relevant to our dangers, credible to both friends and adversaries, and justifiable to our peoples. And we must be prepared to sustain it over the long term.

It is imperative that we maintain the programs that insure that the balance is preserved. But we owe it to ourselves to see the military balance in proper perspective. Complacency may produce weakness, but exaggeration of danger can lead to a loss of will. To be sure, there has been a steady buildup of Soviet military power. But we have also seen to the steady growth and improvement of our own forces over the same period.

—We have always had to face Soviet ground forces larger than our own, partly because of the Soviet Union's definition of its needs as a power in the heart of the Eurasian landmass, with perceived threats on both flanks. Its naval power, while a growing and serious problem, is far weaker than combined allied naval strength in terms of tonnage, firepower, range, access to the sea, experience, and seamanship.

—The United States, for its part, is expanding its Army from 13 to 16 divisions through new measures of streamlining forces; we are increasing our combat forces in Europe; we plan to station a new Army brigade on the critical sector of the north German plain; we are augmenting our naval forces. Our

European allies have completed major programs to build common infrastructure. We have undertaken new joint efforts of standardization and interoperability of allied forces.

—U.S. strategic forces are superior in accuracy, diversity, reliability, survivability, and numbers of separately targetable nuclear warheads. We have a commanding lead in strategic bombers. In addition, there are American deployments overseas and the nuclear forces of two Atlantic allies.

—Even with our different priorities, the economic and technological base which underlies Western military strength remains overwhelmingly superior in size and capacity for innovation. The Soviet Union suffers endemic weakness in its industry and agriculture; recent studies indicate that this chronic inefficiency extends even into their military sector to a much greater extent than realized before.

These strengths of ours demonstrate that our present security posture is adequate and that it is well within our capacities to continue to balance the various elements of Soviet power. To maintain the necessary defense is a question of leadership more than of power. Our security responsibility is both manageable and unending. We must undertake significant additional efforts for the indefinite future. For as far ahead as we can see, we will live in a twilight area between tranquillity and open confrontation.

This is a task for both sides of the Atlantic. Our defense effort within the alliance will be importantly affected by the degree to which the American public is convinced that our allies share similar perceptions of the military challenge and a comparable determination to meet it. The greatest threat to the alliance would occur if, for whatever reason—through misreading the threat, or inattention to conventional forces or reductions of the defense efforts of allies, or domestic developments within NATO members—U.S. public support for NATO were weakened.

The challenge of building sufficient hardware is easier than those of geopolitical understanding, political coordination, and above all, resolve. In the nuclear age, once a change in the geopolitical balance has become unambiguous, it is too late to do anything about it. However great our strength, it will prove empty if we do not resist seemingly marginal changes whose cumulative impact can undermine our security. Power serves little purpose without the doctrines and concepts which define where our interests require its application.

Therefore let us not paralyze ourselves by a rhetoric of weakness. Let us concentrate on building the understanding of our strategic interests which must underlie any policy. The fact is that nowhere has the West been defeated for lack of strength. Our setbacks have been self-inflicted, either because leaders chose objectives that were beyond our psychological capabilities or because our legislatures refused to support what the executive branch believed was essential. This—and not the various "gaps" that appear in the American debate in years divisible by four—is the deepest security problem we face.

East-West Relations

As long ago as the Harmel report of December 1967,[14] the Atlantic alliance has treated as its "two main functions" the assurance of military security and realistic measures to reduce tensions between East and West. We never considered confrontation—even when imposed on us by the other side—or containment an end in itself. Nor did we believe that disagreements with the Soviet Union would automatically disappear. On the contrary, the very concept of "détente" has always been applicable only to an adversary relationship. It was designed to prevent competition from sliding into military hostilities and to create the conditions for the relationship to be gradually and prudently improved.

Thus, alliance policy toward the East has two necessary dimensions. We seek to prevent the Soviet Union from transforming its military power into political expansion. At the same time, we seek to resolve conflicts and disputes through negotiation and to strengthen the incentives for moderation by expanding the area of constructive relations.

These two dimensions are mutually reinforcing. A strong defense and resistance to adventurism are prerequisites for efforts of conciliation. By the same token, only a demonstrated commitment to peace can sustain domestic support for an adequate defense and a vigilant foreign policy. Our public and Congress will not back policies which appear to invite crises, nor will they support firmness in a crisis unless they are convinced that peaceful and honorable alternatives have been exhausted. Above all, we owe it to ourselves and to future generations to seek a world based on something more stable and hopeful than a balance of terror constantly contested.

However we label such a policy, it is imposed by the unprecedented conditions of the nuclear age. No statesman can lightly risk the lives of tens of millions. Every American President, after entering office and seeing the facts, has come to President Eisenhower's view that there is no alternative to peace.

Our generation has been traumatized by World War II, because we remember that war broke out as a result of an imbalance of

[14]On Future Tasks of the Alliance; text in *Documents, 1967:* 110-14.

power. This is a lesson we must not forget. But neither must we forget the lesson of World War I, when war broke out despite an equilibrium of power. An international structure held together only by a balance of forces will sooner or later collapse in catastrophe. In our time this could spell the end of civilized life. We must therefore conduct a diplomacy that deters challenges if possible and that contains them at tolerable levels if they prove unavoidable—a diplomacy that resolves issues, nurtures restraint, and builds cooperation based on mutual interest.

This policy has critics in all our countries. Some take for granted the relative absence of serious crises in recent years, which the policy has helped to bring about, and then fault it for not producing the millennium, which it never claimed. Some caricature its objectives, portraying its goals in more exalted terms than any of its advocates, and then express dismay at the failure of reality to conform to this impossible standard. They describe détente as if it meant the end of all rivalry; when rivalry persists, they conclude that détente has failed and charge its advocates with deception or naivete. They measure the success of policy toward adversaries by criteria that should be reserved for traditional friendships. They use the reality of competition to attack the goal of coexistence, rather than to illustrate its necessity.

In fact, this policy has never been based on such hope or gullibility. It has always been designed to create conditions in which a cool calculus of interests would dictate restraint rather than opportunism, settlement of conflicts rather than their exacerbation. Western policies can at best manage and shape, not assume away, East-West competition.

A pivot of the East-West relationship is the U.S.-Soviet negotiation on limitation of strategic arms. Increasingly, strategic forces find their function only in deterring and matching each other. A continuing buildup of strategic arms therefore only leads to fresh balances, but at higher levels of expenditures and uncertainties. In an era of expanding technological possibilities, it is impossible to make rational choices of force planning without some elements of predictability in the strategic environment. Moreover, a continuing race diverts resources from other needed areas such as forces for regional defense, where imbalances can have serious geopolitical consequences. All these factors have made arms limitation a practical interest of both sides, as well as a factor for stability in the world.

We have made considerable progress toward curbing the strategic arms race in recent years. We will continue vigorously to pursue this objective in ways which protect Western interests and reflect the counsel of our allies.

In defining and pursuing policies of relaxing tensions with the East, the unity of the industrial democracies is essential. Our consultations have been intensive and frequent, and the record of Western cohesion in recent years has been encouraging—in the negotiations leading to the Four Power Agreement on Berlin, in the mutual and balanced force reduction talks, in the SALT negotiations, and in the preparation for the European Security Conference.

Allied cooperation and the habits of consultation and coordination which we have formed will be even more important in the future. For as the policy of relaxing tensions proceeds, it will involve issues at the heart of all our interests.

No one should doubt the depth of our commitment to this process. But we also need to be clear about its limits and about our conception of reciprocity:

—We should require consistent patterns of behavior in different parts of the world. The West must make it clear that coexistence requires mutual restraint, not only in Europe and in the central strategic relationship but also in the Middle East, in Africa, in Asia—in fact, globally. The NATO Foreign Ministers, at their Oslo meeting last month, stressed the close link between stability and security in Europe and in the world as a whole. We must endorse this not only by our rhetoric but above all by our actions.

—We should make clear the tolerable definition of global ideological rivalry. We do not shrink from ideological competition. We have every reason for confidence in the indestructible power of man's yearning for freedom. But we cannot agree that ideology alone is involved when Soviet power is extended into areas such as southern Africa in the name of "national liberation" or when regional or local instabilities are generated or exploited in the name of "proletarian internationalism."

—We should not allow the Soviet Union to apply détente selectively within the alliance. Competition among us in our diplomatic or economic policies toward the East risks dissipating Western advantages and opening up Soviet opportunities. We must resist division and maintain the closest coordination.

The process of improving East-West relations in Europe must not be confined to relations with the Soviet Union. The benefits of relaxation of tensions must extend to Eastern as well as Western Europe. There should be no room for misconceptions about U.S. policy:

—We are determined to deal with Eastern Europe on the basis of the sovereignty and independence of each of its countries. We recognize no spheres of influence and no pretensions to hegemony. Two American Presidents and several Cabinet officials have visited Romania and Poland as well as nonaligned Yugoslavia, to demonstrate our stake in the flourishing and independence of those nations.

—For the same reason, we will persist in our efforts to improve our contacts and develop our concrete bilateral relations in economic and other fields with the countries of Eastern Europe.

—The United States supports the efforts of West European nations to strengthen their bilateral and regional ties with the countries of Eastern Europe. We hope that this process will help heal the divisions of Europe which have persisted since World War II.

—And we will continue to pursue measures to improve the lives of the people in Eastern Europe in basic human terms— such as freer emigration, the unification of families, greater flow of information, increased economic interchange, and more opportunities for travel.

The United States, in parallel with its allies, will continue to expand relationships with Eastern Europe as far and as fast as is possible. This is a long-term process; it is absurd to imagine that one conference by itself can transform the internal structure of Communist governments. Rhetoric is no substitute for patient and realistic actions. We will raise no expectations that we cannot fulfill. But we will never cease to assert our traditional principles of human liberty and national self-determination.

The course of East-West relations will inevitably have its obstacles and setbacks. We will guard against erosion of the gains that we have made in a series of difficult negotiations; we will insure that agreements already negotiated are properly implemented. We must avoid both sentimentality that would substitute good will for strength and mock toughness that would substitute posturing for a clear conception of our purposes.

We in the West have the means to pursue this policy successfully. Indeed, we have no realistic alternative. We have nothing to fear from competition: If there is a military competition, we have the strength to defend our interests; if there is an economic competition, we won it long ago; if there is an ideological competition, the power of our ideas depends only on our will to uphold them.

We need only to stay together and stay the course. If we do so, the process of East-West relations can, over time, strengthen the fabric of peace and genuinely improve the lives of all the peoples around the world.

Our Economic Strength

One of the greatest strengths of the industrial democracies is their unquestioned economic preeminence. Partly because we are committed to the free market system which has given us this preeminence, we have not yet fully realized the possibilities—indeed, the necessity—of applying our economic strength constructively to shaping a better international environment.

The industrial democracies together account for 65 percent of the world's production and 70 percent of its commerce. Our economic performance drives international trade and finance. Our investment, technology, managerial expertise, and agricultural productivity are the spur to development and well-being around the world. Our enormous capacities are multiplied if we coordinate our policies and efforts.

The core of our strength is the vitality and growth of our own economies. At the Rambouillet economic summit last November, at the Puerto Rico summit next week, in the OECD, and in many other forums, the major democratic nations have shown their ability to work together.

But an extensive agenda still summons us. We will require further efforts to continue our recovery and promote noninflationary growth. We will need to facilitate adequate investment and supplies of raw materials. We must continue to avoid protectionist measures, and we must use the opportunity of the multilateral trade negotiations to strengthen and expand the international trading system. We need to reduce our vulnerability and dependence on imported oil through conservation, new sources of energy, and collective preparations for possible emergencies. And we must build on the progress made at Rambouillet and at Jamaica last January to improve the international monetary system.

Our central challenge is to pool our strengths, to increase our coordination, and to tailor our policies to the long term. On the basis of solid cooperation among ourselves, we must deal more effectively with the challenges of the global economy—such as our economic relations with the centrally planned Communist economies and with the scores of new nations concerned with development.

East-West economic interchange, while small in relative scale, is becoming an important economic and political factor. This growth reflects our fundamental strength. It carries risks and complications, both political and economic. But it also presents opportunities for stabilizing relations and involving the Communist countries in responsible international conduct. If the democracies pursue parallel policies—not allowing the Communist states to stimulate debilitating competition among us or to manipulate the process for their own unilateral advantage—East-West economic relations can be a factor for peace and well-being.

We must insure that benefits are reciprocal. We must avoid large trade imbalances which could open opportunities for political pressure. We should structure economic relations so that the Communist states will be drawn into the international economic system and accept its disciplines.

When dealing with centrally controlled state economies, we have to realize that economic relations have a high degree of political content and cannot be conducted solely on the normal commercial basis. Obviously, profitability must be one standard, but we need a broader strategy, consistent with our free enterprise system, so that economic relations will contribute to political objectives.

The industrial democracies should coordinate their policies to insure the orderly and beneficial evolution of East-West relations. To these ends, the United States has proposed to the OECD that we intensify our analyses of the problems and opportunities inherent in East-West trade with a view to charting common objectives and approaches.

If the economic strength of the industrial democracies is important to the Socialist countries, it is vital for the developing world. These nations seek to overcome pervasive poverty and to lift the horizons of their peoples. They ask for an equitable share of global economic benefits and a greater role in international decisions that affect them.

The process of development is crucial not only for the poorer nations but for the industrial nations as well. Our own prosperity is closely linked to the raw materials, the markets, and the aspirations of the developing countries. An international order can be stable only if all nations perceive it as fundamentally just and are convinced that they have a stake in it. Over the long term, cooperative North-South relations are thus clearly in the interest of all, and the objectives of industrial and developing countries *should* be complementary.

However, the North-South dialogue has been far from smooth. Tactics of pressure and an emphasis on rhetorical victories at conferences have too often created an atmosphere of confrontation. Such attitudes obscure the fundamental reality that development is an arduous long-term enterprise. It will go forward only if both sides face facts without illusions, shunning both confrontation and sentimentality.

Far more is involved than the mechanical application of technology and capital to poverty. There must be within the developing country a sense of purpose and direction, determined leadership, and perhaps most important, an impulse for change among the people. Development requires national administration, a complex infrastructure, a revised system of education, and many other social reforms. It is a profoundly unsettling process that takes decades.

For many new countries it is in fact even more difficult than similar efforts by the Western countries a century ago, for their social and geographic conditions reflect the arbitrary subdivisions of colonial rule. Some face obstacles which could not be surmounted even with the greatest exertions on their own. Their progress depends on how well the international community responds to the imperatives of economic interdependence.

It is senseless, therefore, to pretend that development can proceed by quick fixes or one-shot solutions. Artificial majorities at international conferences confuse the issue. Confrontational tactics will in time destroy the domestic support in the industrial countries for the forward-looking policy which the developing countries so desperately need.

The industrial democracies have special responsibilities as well. Development requires their sustained and collective cooperation. They represent the largest markets and most of the world's technology and capital. They have an obligation to show understanding for the plight of the poorest and the striving for progress of all developing nations. But they do the developing countries no favor if they contribute to escapism. If they compete to curry favor over essentially propagandistic issues, contributions will be diluted, resources will go unallocated, and unworkable projects will be encouraged.

The developing countries need from us not a sense of guilt but intelligent and realistic proposals that merge the interests of both sides in an expanding world economy:

—First, we must develop further the mechanisms of our own cooperation. To this end the United States has made a number of concrete proposals at the recently concluded OECD meeting.

—Second, the industrial democracies should coordinate their national aid programs better so that we use our respective areas of experience and technical skill to best advantage. President Giscard d'Estaing's proposal for an integrated Western fund for Africa is an imaginative approach to regional development.

—Third, we should regularly consult and work in close parallel in major international negotiations and conferences. The Conference on International Economic Cooperation; the multilateral trade negotiations; U.N. General Assembly special sessions; world conferences on food, population, environment, or housing; and UNCTAD all can achieve much more if the industrial democracies approach them with a clear and coherent purpose.

—Fourth, we should stop conducting all negotiations on an agenda not our own. We should not hesitate to put forward our own solutions to common problems.

—And finally, we need a clear longer term strategy for development. The diverse elements of the process, including various forms of assistance, technology transfer, and trade and financial policy, must be better integrated.

Cooperation among developed countries is not confrontation between North and South, as is often alleged. The fact is that a responsible development policy is possible only if the industrial democracies pursue realistic goals with conviction, compassion, and coordination. They must not delude themselves or their interlocutors by easy panaceas, or mistake slogans for progress. We make the greatest contribution to development if we insist that the North-South dialogue emphasize substance rather than ideology and concentrate on practical programs instead of empty theological debates.

The Future of Democratic Societies

In every dimension of our activities, then, the industrial democracies enter the new era with substantial capacities and opportunities. At the same time, it would be idle to deny that in recent years the moral stamina of the West has been seriously challenged.

Since its beginnings, Western civilization has clearly defined the individual's relationship to society and the state. In southern Europe, the humanism of the Renaissance made man the measure of all things. In northern Europe, the Reformation, in proclaiming the priesthood of all believers and offering rewards for individual effort, put the emphasis on the individual. In England, the sense of justice and human rights and responsibilities evolved in the elaboration of the common law. Two hundred years ago the authors of our Declaration of Independence drew upon this heritage; to them every human being had inalienable rights to life, liberty, and the pursuit of happiness. The state existed to protect the individual and permit full scope for the enjoyment of these rights.

Today in the West, 30 years after the Marshall plan, our deepest challenge is that a new generation must explore again the issues of liberty and social responsibility, in an era when societies have grown vastly in size, complexity, and dynamism.

The modern industrial society, though founded in freedom and offering prosperity, risks losing the individual in the mass and fostering his alienation. The technical complexity of public issues challenges the functioning of democracy. Mass media and the weakening of party and group structures further the isolation of the individual; they transform democratic politics, adding new elements of volatility and unpredictability. The bureaucratic state poses a fundamental challenge to political leadership and responsiveness to public will.

Basic moral questions are raised: How do we inspire a questioning new generation in a relativistic age and in a society of impersonal institutions? Will skepticism and cynicism sap the spiritual energies of our civilization at the moment of its greatest technical and material success? Having debunked authority, will our societies now seek refuge in false simplifications, demagogic certitudes, or extremist panaceas?

These questions are not a prediction but a test—a test of the creativity and moral fortitude of our peoples and leaders.

Western civilization has met such tests before. In the late 15th century, Europe was in a period of gloomy introspection, preoccupied with a sense of despair and mortality. The cities which had sparked its revival following the Islamic conquests were in decline. Its territory was being diminished by the depredations of a powerful invader from the East. Its spiritual, economic, and cultural center—Italy—was a prey to anarchy and dismemberment.

And yet Europe at that very moment was already well launched on one of the world's periods of greatest political and intellectual advance. The Renaissance and Reformation, the great discoveries, the revival of humanistic values, the industrial and democratic revolutions—these were all to create the character and the dynamism of the Western civilization of which we, on both sides of the Atlantic, are the heirs.

Similarly today, the West has assets to meet its challenges and to draw from them the material for new acts of creation. It is our nations that have been the vanguard of the modern age. Intellectually and morally, it is our societies that have proven themselves the vast laboratory of the experiment of modernization. Above all, it is the Western democracies that originated—and keep alive today—the vision of political freedom, social justice, and economic well-being for all peoples. None of us lives up to this vision ideally or all the time. But the rigorous standard by which we judge ourselves is what makes us different from totalitarian societies, of the left or the right.

This, then, is our moral task:

—First, as democratic governments we must redeem, over and

over again, the trust of our peoples. As a nation which has accepted the burden of leadership, the United States has a special responsibility: we must overcome the traumas of the recent period, eradicate their causes, and preserve the qualities which world leadership demands. In Europe, wherever there has been a slackening in governmental responsiveness to the needs of citizens, there should be reform and revival.

—Second, we must confront the complexities of a pluralistic world. This calls for more than specific technical solutions. It requires of leaders a willingness to explain the real alternatives, no matter how complicated or difficult. And it requires of electorates an understanding that we must make choices amidst uncertainty, where the outcome may be neither immediate nor reducible to simple slogans.

—Third, we must clarify our attitudes toward political forces within Western societies which appeal to electorates on the ground that they may bring greater efficiency to government. But we cannot avoid the question of the commitment of these forces to democratic values nor a concern about the trends that a decision based on temporary convenience would set in motion. At the same time, opposition to these forces is clearly not enough. There must be a response to legitimate social and economic aspirations and to the need for reforms of inadequacies from which these forces derive much of their appeal.

—Finally, the solidarity of the democratic nations in the world is essential both as material support and as a moral symbol. There could be no greater inspiration of our peoples than the reaffirmation of their common purpose and the conviction that they can shape their fortune in freedom.

We cannot afford either a perilous complacency or an immobilizing pessimism. Alastair Buchan posed his questions not to induce paralysis, but as a spur to wiser action and fresh achievement.

We know what we must do. We also know what we can do. It only remains to do it.

(13) Ministerial Session of the North Atlantic Council, Brussels, December 9-10, 1976: Final communiqué.[15]

The North Atlantic Council met in Ministerial session in Brussels

[15]Department of State Press Release 602, Dec. 13; text from *Bulletin*, 76: 9-12.

on 9th and 10th December. Ministers recognized the indispensable role of a strong alliance in ensuring the security of member countries, and in providing the foundation for their efforts to establish a more constructive and stable relationship with the Warsaw Pact countries. They expressed their determination to maintain and enhance the cohesion and strength of the Alliance.

2. Ministers stressed the need for East-West relations to develop at a more satisfactory pace. They recognized nonetheless that progressive improvement of these relations may be slow and sometimes difficult, and that it calls for perseverance and steadiness over the years. They emphasized that their governments would continue to seek realistic opportunities to resolve points of difference with the East and to build on mutual interest, and look for corresponding efforts by the Warsaw Pact countries.

Ministers stressed, however, that if détente is to progress, with the necessary public support, and not to falter, there must be real improvements across the entire range of international relations. It should not be assumed that heightened tensions in one area of relations would not have repercussions on other areas. In all parts of the world, confrontation can and should be avoided by respect for the accepted principles of international behavior.

Ministers also emphasized the cardinal importance they attached to reducing the risks of confrontation in the military sphere. They viewed with concern the high level of military expenditure in the Soviet Union and the continued disquieting expansion of the military power of the Warsaw Pact on land, air and sea, which are difficult to reconcile with the avowed desire of the Soviet Union to improve East-West relations. Faced with this persistent growth in military might, Ministers reiterated their determination to take the measures necessary to maintain and improve their own defensive military forces, in order to ensure credible deterrence and to safeguard their countries from any risk of military aggression or political pressure.

3. At the same time, Ministers expressed their concern that the continued expansion of armaments would increasingly endanger not only world security but also the economic well-being of all nations. They stressed that these dangers could only be averted if all countries concerned joined in realistic efforts to achieve genuine and controlled measures of disarmament and arms control.

Ministers confirmed that the countries of the Alliance, in the event of an attack on them, cannot renounce the use, as may be required for defense, of any of the means available to them. Ministers also stated their view that all States which participated in the CSCE should respect strictly the renunciation of the threat or use of force as laid down in the Charter of the United Nations and reaffirmed in the Final Act of Helsinki. This renunciation must apply to all types of weapons. It is essential for the strengthening of peace that there should be no build-up of armaments of any type beyond the needs of defense, a policy which has always been followed by the Alliance. Ministers also stated their position that the Alliance will remain a free association open to all European states devoted to the defense of the freedom, common heritage and civilization of their peoples. Furthermore, Ministers recalled that the right of states to belong or not to belong to treaties of alliance was confirmed in the Final Act of Helsinki. It is in light of these considerations that they have concluded that the recently published Warsaw Pact proposals could not be accepted.

4. Ministers stated again the determination of their governments to continue to comply with all the principles and provisions of the Final Act of the CSCE and expected that all other signatories would take steps to fully implement them. They noted that some progress had been made in implementation. However, much remains to be done before the benefits of the Final Act become significantly apparent in tangible improvements, not only in relations between states, but also in the lives of peoples and individuals. Ministers recalled that the Final Act acknowledges that wider human contacts and dissemination of information would contribute to the strengthening of peace and expressed the hope that the Warsaw Pact countries would take measures leading to significant progress in the pace of implementation of the Final Act in the months to come.

Ministers also noted that Allied governments had fully and scrupulously implemented the provisions of the Final Act dealing with confidence-building measures. They noted that the practice of notifying major maneuvers was beginning to be established; however, unlike Allied countries, Warsaw Pact countries had still not notified maneuvers involving less than 25,000 men. They regretted that the Warsaw Pact countries had failed up to now to accept invitations to send observers to Western maneuvers.

Ministers looked forward with interest to the follow-up meeting to be held in Belgrade during 1977. The meeting provides an opportunity for a thorough and objective review of the situation prevailing in all the signatory countries as regards all the areas covered by the Final Act, and also for considering the further progress that could be made towards the objective agreed in Helsinki. Allied governments intend to play their full part in seeking positive results, with the aim of furthering the cause of peace and cooperation in Europe.

5. Ministers heard a report from the United States Secretary of State on the progress and prospects of the United States-USSR Strategic Arms Limitation Talks and discussed the relationship between the SALT negotiations and Allied security interests.

Ministers found the report on SALT both useful and informative and welcomed continued United States efforts towards achievement of a satisfactory SALT agreement which takes into account Allied interests and concerns.

6. Ministers of the participating countries reviewed the state of negotiations in Vienna on Mutual and Balanced Force Reductions (MBFR). They expressed their conviction that these negotiations would achieve their agreed aim of contributing to a more stable relationship and to the strengthening of peace and security in Europe only if they were to result in eliminating the existing ground force manpower disparity in Central Europe and in mitigating the disparity in main battle tanks.

These Ministers reaffirmed their position that these objectives would be achieved by their proposal to establish, in the area of reductions, approximate parity in ground forces in the form of a common collective ceiling for ground force manpower on each side and to reduce the disparity in main battle tanks. These Ministers stressed that agreement to the goal of a common collective ceiling and reductions of United States and Soviet ground forces in the first phase would be an important and practical first step leading to the common collective ceiling which would be reached through additional reductions in the second phase.

These Ministers noted with regret that the important specific additional offer they made one year ago had thus far not met with an adequate response. They reaffirmed their conviction that the Western proposals provided a reasonable foundation for a just and equitable MBFR agreement. They reemphasized their continuing resolve to press for the achievement of the objectives of the Western participants which would ensure undiminished security for all countries concerned. They expressed satisfaction with their governments' continuing solidarity, and reaffirmed the principle that NATO forces should not be reduced except in the context of Mutual and Balanced Force Reduction agreements.

7. In connection with Germany and Berlin, Ministers reviewed the developments which had occurred since their last meeting in May 1976.

Ministers expressed themselves satisfied with the progress which has been possible in matters relating to Berlin on the basis of the Quadripartite Agreement during the five years since its signature. In particular, the agreement had significantly alleviated the lives of many Germans.

Ministers confirmed the continued commitment of their countries to the security and viability of Berlin. These remain essential elements of Western policy, and of détente between East and West. They noted the need for Berlin fully to benefit from any improvement in East-West relations, in particular through its ties to the Federal Republic of Germany as they are confirmed in the Quadripartite Agreement.

Ministers emphasized that the Quadripartite Agreement was part of a greater balance of interests which had, to a very great degree, made possible and contributed to the development of better relations between East and West in Europe. They noted that this process would be placed in serious jeopardy if any of the signatories failed fully to observe the commitments which it undertook in the Quadripartite Agreement.

8. Ministers reviewed developments in the Mediterranean area since their last meeting. They welcomed the end of hostilities in the Lebanon and expressed the hope that there would be continued progress towards stability and reconstruction in that country. They considered, nonetheless, that the continuing instability in the Middle East still gave cause for serious concern and could have dangerous consequences. They underlined the urgency of continuing efforts designed to achieve an overall settlement resulting in a just and durable peace in the Middle East.

Ministers took note of the report on the situation in the Mediterranean prepared on their instructions. They emphasized the need to preserve the balance of forces throughout the Mediterranean area. They requested the Council in Permanent Session to continue its consultations on these questions and report to them again at their next meeting.

In this context, Ministers reaffirmed their view that the coming into operation of defense cooperation agreements between Allied countries will strengthen the Allied defenses in the Mediterranean.

The Ministers voiced their satisfaction on the agreement between Greece and Turkey on the procedure to be followed for the delimitation of the continental shelf and expressed their hope for the successful solution of this issue and the Aegean air space matters.

9. In the context of improving the military capability of the Alliance and making more effective use of available resources, Ministers discussed various aspects of standardization and interoperability of equipment and procedures. They approved the second report by the *ad hoc* Committee on Equipment Interoperability and agreed to take a number of actions, particularly in respect to tactical area communications, rearming of tactical aircraft and the implementation of NATO standardization agreements. They authorized the Committee to continue its efforts for the time being, both in specific areas and in the elaboration of procedures for ensuring the interoperability of future equipment. They also noted the progress in standardization achieved by the Conference of National Armaments Directors in promoting cooperation among member nations in selected equipment areas.

10. Ministers took note of the progress achieved by the Committee on the Challenges of Modern Society (CCMS), and its contribution to effective international cooperation in dealing with environmental problems confronting our societies. They took note of the completion of the pilot studies on advanced health care and urban transportation, and of the Committee's continuing emphasis on implementation by member countries of action resolutions. Ministers noted and endorsed the initiation of two new pilot studies, one to assist in world-wide efforts to clean the marine environment and the other to permit environmentally acceptable utilization of high-sulfur coal and oil. Ministers noted too that the Committee's discussions focused attention on global issues such as the effect of fluorocarbons on the stratosphere and long-range transport of air pollutants.

11. Ministers recognized that the basic problems in East-West relations were unlikely to be resolved quickly and that the Alliance must respond with a long-term effort commensurate to the challenges confronting it. The Allies could rely not only on their material resources, but also on the creative power demonstrated in all fields by their free and democratic societies. Ministers were confident that, with the mutual support and solidarity provided by the Alliance, their governments and peoples would be able to overcome the problems which faced them.

12. The next Ministerial session of the North Atlantic Council will be held in London on 10th and 11th May, 1977.[16]

[16]Held in London May 10-11, 1977; text of communiqué in *Bulletin*, 76: 601-2.

4. PEACE-SEEKING IN THE MIDDLE EAST

(14) *Meeting of the Council of Ministers of the Central. Treaty Organization (CENTO), London, May 26-27, 1976.*

(a) *Statement by Secretary of State Kissinger to the Council, May 26, 1976.*[1]

Mr. Secretary General, Ministers, Excellencies, distinguished delegates, ladies and gentlemen: It is a pleasure for me to meet again with my colleagues, the Ministers of the nations joined in this organization and dedicated to common action for peace.

History shows that changing conditions are a test of the solidarity of alliances. This association has met this test. It has proven its durability; the range of issues on our common agenda has expanded, not diminished, over the decades. Our experience demonstrates that traditional friendships can become more significant and more valued amid change and challenge. President Ford has asked me to convey to you the continuing commitment of the United States to work with you for our common security and well-being and for the security and well-being of mankind.

My country, Mr. Secretary General, celebrates this year the Bicentennial of its independence. And we are engaged as well in the great democratic enterprise of our Presidential election.

Our electoral process affords full play to competition and debate. It gives no rewards for reticence; it therefore seems to emphasize divisions. But our Bicentennial reminds us of the deeper reality. It is, in its essence, a celebration of the remarkable continuity of the American nation. The fundamental principles of U.S. foreign policy have been constant for the past 30 years, through all Administrations, and they will remain constant.

The American people have learned the lessons of history. They

[1]Department of State Press Release 272, May 25; text from *Bulletin*, 74: 794-7. The Secretary-General of CENTO during 1976 was Ümit Halûk Bayülken.

247

are committed to a permanent, active, and responsible American role in the world. They are dedicated to standing by our friends and allies; they are determined to resist aggression; they deeply believe in the moral necessity of building a more stable peace; they are prepared to cooperate in the dialogue between industrial and developing countries for promoting human progress. These basic objectives are permanent interests of the United States. They will not be diminished; they will not change; they will be reaffirmed.

The main lines of U.S. policy are clear.

First is our commitment to solidarity with our allies and friends. America's partners in the world comprise many nations of different stages of development, cultures, and political structures. But we have in common a determination to collaborate to insure against external domination and to cooperate in many positive ways for the greater well-being of our peoples. The American people regard these friendships and alliances as our most valuable assets in our foreign relations.

Three NATO members are represented here. The United States is gratified at the close collaboration that exists today among all the major industrial nations of the Atlantic community and Japan, which is so crucial to the maintenance of the balance of power and the world's hopes for economic advance. I have just come from a ministerial meeting of the Atlantic alliance in Oslo, where our solidarity on all the basic issues facing us was strongly reaffirmed. Our sense of common purpose has never been stronger. Our peoples have shown a continuing appreciation of the need to enhance our common defense. Our efforts to reduce tensions are reflected in coordinated policies. And our collective economic recovery is well underway, reminding us all of how global interdependence can be an engine of common prosperity if we manage our affairs with wisdom and dedication.

This organization, CENTO, embodies similar principles. The countries assembled here are interested in the stability and economic progress of a pivotal region of the world. The strategic importance of this area has never been greater. The United States reaffirms its continuing interest in the security and progress of this region.

Peace rests fundamentally on an equilibrium of strength. The United States will stand by its friends. It accepts no spheres of influence. It will not yield to pressure. It will continue to be a reliable partner to those who defend their freedom against foreign intervention or intimidation.

The second enduring principle of U.S. foreign policy is a commitment to use our strength to promote a secure peace and the reduction of tensions.

We shall never forget that in a world of intercontinental missiles and thermonuclear weapons, building a firmer foundation for peace must be the inescapable imperative of all our action. In this age the very survival of mankind depends upon nurturing among nations fragile habits of restraint, negotiation, peaceful resolution of differences, and striving to transform present conflicts in time into a structure of cooperation. We owe our children a future based on something more secure than a balance of terror constantly contested. The nuclear powers, above all, have a responsibility for self-restraint; they owe it not only to their own people but to mankind. This is why the United States, while striving for an easing of tensions, cannot accept selective relaxation of tensions. Peace is indivisible; claims to coexistence in one part of the world cannot be coupled with disruptive conduct in another.

History is replete with the tragedies of the breakdown of world order. In the nuclear age, the scale of potential catastrophe staggers the imagination. But the potentiality of statesmanship, of creative diplomacy and peacemaking, is equally great. If we act confidently—with a courage worthy of the ideals we defend and represent—we have it within our means to shape the world's peace, and our own.

So we will not succumb to a sentimentality that seeks to found peace on good intentions alone. Nor will we confuse policy with a posturing which leaves man's tremendous capacities for destruction in the service of no positive conception. We will pursue a steady course, guided by our ideals and our interests striving for a more peaceful and secure world, always mindful of the security and concerns of our allies and others who rely on us.

In the CENTO region, a hopeful evolution has taken place in the last year toward more peaceful relations. We applaud these efforts.

Pakistan has moved imaginatively and effectively to improve relations with her neighbors. We welcome this. The United States has a continuing interest in the security and territorial integrity of Pakistan. We will continue to strengthen our cooperation with Pakistan bilaterally as well as within the CENTO framework. At the same time, we support all efforts to reduce tensions, restore normalcy, and advance the prospects for secure and peaceful economic development in the region.

We are impressed as well by Iran's initiatives to expand ties of friendship and cooperation with her neighbors. Iran plays a key role in regional stability and has acted with statesmanship. It has made major efforts to provide for its security and at the same time to promote rapid economic development, on which its security and the well-being of its people must rest in the long run. Iran has also been generous in sharing its resources with others, especially on a regional basis. The United States values its traditional friendship with Iran.

Thirdly, the United States and Turkey signed in March a defense cooperation agreement underlining the importance we attach to this longstanding friendship and to overcoming the difficulties of the recent past. For the solidarity of NATO, we will continue to urge our two allies Turkey and Greece to resolve the differences between them. We hope to see early progress on the constitutional and territorial issues on Cyprus in ways that meet the economic and security requirements of the two communities and respect their dignity. We hope to see the disputes over the Aegean peacefully resolved. These steps are essential to the security of the eastern Mediterranean, the Middle East, and Europe as well.

The Middle East, an area of special concern to CENTO, has also seen hopeful developments. We should not let the present ferment and turmoil in the area or the temporary interruption of the negotiating process obscure either what has been accomplished or the opportunities for further progress. Step-by-step diplomacy brought significant results, including the Sinai agreement last September. The time is approaching when new impetus must be given to movement toward an overall peace.

The United States remains dedicated to helping achieve a just and lasting peace in accordance with Resolutions 242 and 338. We look to all parties to show dedication and willingness to take risks for peace. We are actively exploring the most fruitful possibilities for renewing the negotiating process.

Unfortunately the tragedy of Lebanon has preoccupied the attention of many of the parties in the Middle East. We hope the election of a new Lebanese President will begin the necessary process of reconciliation within Lebanon and among those in the area who wish Lebanon well. The continuing toll of death and destruction in Lebanon must end, for the sake of Lebanon and her suffering people and also for the sake of peace and stability in the entire region. The United States supports the sovereignty, territorial integrity, and national unity of Lebanon and continues to urge outside powers to practice the utmost restraint in an already difficult situation.

The third permanent principle of U.S. policy is a commitment to build international economic cooperation to promote prosperity, development, economic justice, and social progress for all nations. The world's economic concerns have come to the forefront of international diplomacy. In their scale and complexity, these issues mock the efforts of any single nation or group of nations to solve them in isolation. In the last quarter of the 20th century the world community has the technical capacity to work a massive transformation of the quality of life in every region of the globe. Hunger, disease, illiteracy, degradation—decisive steps can be taken in mankind's age-old struggle against these scourges. They wait only on our collective political will and determined decision.

The United States has pledged itself to major efforts for reform and assistance if we are met in a spirit of mutual respect. Last September at the seventh special session of the U.N. General Assembly, we worked for multilateral consensus on a comprehensive program of action on trade, investment, technology, and the special plight of the poorest nations. We have carried these efforts further in the Paris Conference on International Economic Cooperation last December, and three weeks ago at the U.N. Conference on Trade and Development in Nairobi. Many of our proposals have already been implemented. We shall continue in all these fields of endeavor.

This organization includes both consumers and producers of energy, both industrial nations and developing nations severely affected by the recent crisis in energy. This continues to be an important issue on the international agenda. It affects all of us. The United States is convinced that the interdependence of the global economy compels, from all of us, an unprecedented commitment to multilateral cooperation. The world is beginning to understand that amid all the diversity and multiplicity of states, we are dependent on a single global economic system which makes us prosper or suffer together. The rhetoric of conflict, the doctrines of struggle, have nothing to offer save a contest without issue. Reality makes our economic problems common problems, and our moral convictions compel us to engage ourselves in their practical solution.

The last decade has shown conclusively that only the industrial democracies have the resources or the managerial skill to promote sustained development. They must cooperate with each other and with the developing countries to shape a better future. Extraordinary cooperative steps have been taken in a few short months in a series of international forums. The United States will make every effort to maintain this momentum and accelerate it.

Mr. Secretary General, the nations participating in the Central Treaty Organization have an important responsibility in all of these areas: maintaining our solidarity, promoting peace and reduction of tension, and fostering international economic cooperation.

I want to pay special tribute to the energy and imagination you have brought to CENTO as our Secretary General. Our alliance is unique in the diversity of its members and in the enduring partnership we have enjoyed through many changing conditions. CENTO has been a forum for intimate discussions, an instrument of common action, and a symbol of independent nations' determination to remain free.

At last year's meeting in Ankara, I stated the continuing commitment of the United States: "We will remain fully engaged because of our own self-interest, because of the responsibility our wealth and power confer upon us, and because only by standing by our friends can we be true to the values of freedom that have brought progress and hope to our people."[2] These are the values my country celebrates in its Bicentennial year, and they will be the principles of our policy in the decades to come.

(b) Final press communiqué, May 28, 1976.[3]

ANKARA, May 28, 1976—The Council of Ministers of the Central Treaty Organization held its 23rd Session in London on May 26-27, 1976.

The delegations were led by:

IRAN	—H.E. Dr. Abbas Ali Khalatbary Minister of Foreign Affairs;
PAKISTAN	—H.E. Mr. Rafi Raza Minister for Production;
TURKEY	—H.E. Mr. Ihsan Sabri Çaglayangil Minister of Foreign Affairs;
UNITED KINGDOM	—The Rt. Hon. Anthony Crosland Secretary of State for Foreign and Commonwealth Affairs;
UNITED STATES	—The Hon. Dr. Henry A. Kissinger Secretary of State.

H.E. Mr. Ümit Halûk Bayülken, the Secretary General of the Central Treaty Organization presided at the opening meeting of the session. A message of welcome from Her Majesty The Queen was delivered by the Rt. Hon. Anthony Crosland, Secretary of State for Foreign and Commonwealth Affairs of the United Kingdom. This was followed by opening statements by the Secretary General of CENTO and by the leaders of the visiting delegations expressing their appreciation for Her Majesty's gracious message and the warm hospitality of the host government, and by the Rt. Hon. Anthony Crosland, Secretary of State for Foreign and Commonwealth Affairs who presided at subsequent Council meetings.

[2]*AFR, 1975:* 190.
[3]Text from CENTO Press Release No. 33, May 28, 1976 (Central Treaty Organization, Public Relations Bureau, Ankara).

The Ministers had a wide-ranging and constructive exchange of views on recent international developments, giving special attention to matters of interest in the CENTO Region and noted with satisfaction that peace, stability, and economic and social progress were maintained in the Region.

The Ministers also reviewed progress towards further promoting co-operation within the Alliance in the economic and cultural fields. They pledged continuing support for the Central Treaty Organization. The Ministers reaffirmed the vital importance they attached to the preservation of the independence and territorial integrity of each of the Member States in the Region.

Members of the Council explained their position and views regarding problems and developments for peace and security which are of special interest and importance for their respective countries.

The Ministers reviewed developments in the Middle East since their last meeting.[4] They agreed that the prolonged conflict in the Area continued to constitute a grave threat to world peace, and they reaffirmed the importance they attached to the continuation of efforts designed to achieve an overall settlement resulting in a just, honourable and durable peace in the Middle East in accordance with the principles and provisions of the United Nations Security Council Resolutions 242 of November 22, 1967 and 338 of October 22, 1973. The Ministers noted with concern the tragic situation in the Lebanon, and expressed the hope that the Lebanese people as a whole might find a satisfactory solution to their problems in preserving their national independence and territorial integrity.

The Council of Ministers exchanged views on developments in Europe and expressed their satisfaction over the conclusion of the Conference on Security and Co-operation in Europe (CSCE). In this context, the Ministers stressed that security in the CENTO Region constituted an important element in European security.

Ministers noted with deep satisfaction the recent agreement between India and Pakistan as a result of the initiative taken by Pakistan towards normalization of the situation in the South Asian Sub-Continent. They expressed the hope that other outstanding issues in the Sub-Continent would be resolved, thus paving the way for a durable peace and security in the Area.

The Council reaffirmed its agreement that the Economic Programme constitutes an important element of the CENTO partnership.

The Ministers, bearing in mind the important contributions made by CENTO to the strengthening of the economic link between the Regional Countries, endorsed the recommendations of

[4]May 22-23, 1975; communiqué in *AFR, 1975:* 190-93.

the Economic Committee to consider several new projects to expand research in agriculture, aimed at increasing productivity and improving marketing of food production in the Regional Countries, and also expressed their pleasure at the continuing progress in the improvement of transportation and communication facilities in the Region. They welcomed the plans for further upgrading the microwave system linking Iran, Pakistan and Turkey. The Ministers also welcomed the offer from the United Kingdom to increase its programme for the provision of scientific equipment, and that of the Iranian Government to establish a book programme for the supply of Persian language books to Pakistan and Turkey. They also agreed on expanding the Programme of Scientific Research Collaboration and will increase their contributions to the CENTO Multilateral Scientific Fund for this purpose.

The Ministers noted the report of the Military Committee and expressed satisfaction with the progress made during the past year in the improvement of co-operation among the partners in the military field.

The Ministers noted the progress made in countering the threat of subversion directed towards the Region and reaffirmed their resolve to continue to take the necessary measures to eliminate this threat.

The Ministers also endorsed a recommendation for strengthening the Public Affairs Programme and cultural co-operation among the members of the Alliance.

Concluding their review, the Ministers noted with appreciation the Annual Report of the Secretary General. They reaffirmed their determination to ensure that the Alliance continues to contribute to the peace, security and stability of the Region, and to promote the social and economic welfare of its people.

The Council accepted the invitation of the Government of Iran to hold the next session in the second half of April, 1977 in Iran.[5]

(15) *Civil Conflict in Lebanon.*

(a) *Kidnapping and Murder of American Diplomatic Personnel: Statements by President Ford and Secretary of State Kissinger, June 16, 1976.*

Statement by President Ford.[6]

The assassination of our Ambassador in Beirut, Francis E.

---

[5]The CENTO Council held its 24th session in Tehran, May 14-15, 1977; text of communiqué in *Bulletin*, 76: 618.

[6]Text from *Presidential Documents*, 12: 1062-3.

Meloy, Jr., and of our Counselor for Economic Affairs, Robert O. Waring, and of their driver is an act of senseless, outrageous brutality. I extend to their families my own deep sense of sorrow and that of all the American people.

These men were on their way to meet with President-elect Sarkis. They were on a mission of peace, seeking to do what they could in the service of their country to help restore order, stability, and reason to Lebanon. Their deaths add another tragedy to the suffering which the Lebanese people have endured beyond measure.

These men had lived with danger for many weeks and did so with dedication and disregard of personal safety as we have come to expect of the Foreign Service.

The goals of our policy must remain unchanged. The United States will not be deterred in its search for peace by these murders. I have instructed Secretary Kissinger to continue our intensive efforts in this direction. I will name a new Ambassador to Lebanon[7] within the very near future to resume the mission of Ambassador Meloy, which he performed so brilliantly. I have also instructed the Secretary to get in touch with all of the governments in the area and with the Lebanese leaders to help identify the murderers and to see that they are brought to justice. I have also ordered that all appropriate resources of the United States undertake immediately to identify the persons or group responsible for this vicious act.

Those responsible for these brutal assassinations must be brought to justice. At the same time, we must continue our policy of seeking a peaceful solution in Lebanon. That is the way we can best honor the brave men who gave their lives for this country and for the cause of peace.

Statement by Secretary Kissinger.[8]

I learned this morning with profound sorrow of the kidnaping and brutal murder of our Ambassador to Lebanon, Francis E. Meloy, Jr., the Economic Counselor of our Embassy in Beirut, Robert O. Waring, and the Ambassador's Lebanese chauffeur, Zohair Moghrabi. Ambassador Meloy and Mr. Waring were—as part of our intensive effort to bring peace to Lebanon—on their way to a meeting with President-elect Sarkis. They disappeared en route; the three bodies were later found and their identities confirmed.

The President's statement expressed the shock and revulsion that

[7]On June 22, President Ford named Talcott Seelye as Special Representative in temporary charge of the U.S. Embassy. Richard B. Parker was nominated to succeed Ambassador Meloy on Feb. 4, 1977.
[8]Department of State Press Release 316; text from *Bulletin*, 75: 98-9.

all of us feel at this tragic, cowardly, and senseless act. It also expresses our determination not to be deterred, by brutal and vicious action, from the search for peace. But equally, no nation or group should believe that the United States will not find ways to protect its diplomatic personnel.

I have commented before on the particularly monstrous injustice in violent death coming to those engaged in the work of peace. The vicious cycle of violence and counterviolence which has engulfed Lebanon for months has now cost the American people two of their ablest public servants.

The two American diplomats had served their country long and faithfully at many posts throughout the world. Ambassador Meloy, at the President's request, had gone to Beirut only a few weeks ago from his previous post in Guatemala on very short notice, fully realizing the dangers and challenges of this important assignment. Mr. Waring had performed brilliantly in Beirut over the past year under the most difficult and hazardous circumstances. Mr. Moghrabi has worked for our Embassy for over 20 years with distinction and courage.

These men had faced the necessity of living with constant mortal danger in order to carry out their mission. They served the cause of peace and died for their cause. They did so with the dedication and disregard of personal safety which we have come to expect of our distinguished Foreign Service.

The men, sadly, are gone, But duty remains. These senseless murders remind us of the urgency of that duty, and of the need for a world free of terror and living with a consciousness of peace. We shall not forget that, and we shall be inspired by the courage and sacrifice of our colleagues.

(b) Evacuation of United States Citizens: Statements by President Ford, June 18 and 20, 1976.[9]

Statement of June 18.

Due to the continuing uncertainty of the situation in Beirut, I have directed the United States Embassy there to assist in the departure by overland convoy to Damascus of U.S. citizens who wish to depart Lebanon at this time.

The convoy is expected to leave Beirut Saturday,[10] and American citizens are being alerted both by the Embassy and by broadcast on the Voice of America to be prepared for departure at that time, if they so wish.

The remains of Ambassador Francis Meloy and Mr. Robert

---

[9] Texts from *Presidential Documents*, 12: 1067 and 1072 respectively.
[10] June 19.

Waring have been brought to Damascus overland. They will be picked up by a U.S. plane and returned to the United States, arriving on Saturday.

Only those Embassy officials not essential to our continuing operations will be leaving Lebanon. The American Embassy in Beirut is to remain open to continue our efforts to help bring an end to the strife which has brought this tragedy to Lebanon.

Statement of June 20.

The evacuation operation in Beirut today was completed successfully without incident. The success of this operation was made possible through the combined efforts of our Armed Forces and State Department personnel both here and in the field.

I want to express my deep appreciation and pride in the outstanding performance of all the men and women who contributed to this effort. We are grateful, as well, for the assistance of other governments and individuals that facilitated the evacuation. The United States will continue to play a positive role in seeking to restore stability and bring peace to Lebanon.

I would like to express to all those who played a part in the success of this operation my heartfelt thanks.

(c) Reaffirmation of United States Policy: Department of State Statement, September 23, 1976.[11]

The United States is convinced that the occasion of the installation of a new President of Lebanon offers an opportunity which must not be lost to bring an end to the fighting and to begin rebuilding national institutions. It will be essential for all parties in Lebanon to support and strengthen the authority of Lebanon's new President elected by legitimate processes so that all Lebanese may promptly begin their return to productive life.

The violence and destruction in Lebanon have gone on far too long. The costs in human suffering have been far too high. It is clear that no one can gain from continued fighting: countless more men, women, and children will lose lives, property, and hope for the future. It is a time for magnanimity, restraint, and compromise.

The United States believes that a solution can be found that will preserve the country's independence, territorial integrity, and national unity. Solutions based on the partition of Lebanon are

[11]Department of State Press Release 464; text from Bulletin, 75: 459-60. The statement was read to news correspondents by Frederick Z. Brown, Director, Office of Press Relations.

invitations to further strife and instability. The states so created would not be viable and would invite external intervention.

We continue to believe that the principles for a political accommodation among the Lebanese parties enunciated last January and February provide a basis for institutions that will meet the needs of the Lebanese people and nation. We hope that President Sarkis will be able to bring his countrymen to the roundtable talks he has proposed as soon as possible so that the process of reconciliation and rebuilding can begin.

The major objective in negotiating a solution will be to preserve a united country, led by a central government which will assure security and opportunity for all individuals and communities in the country. The principles proposed in January and February were designed to give practical political expression to the concept that there should be a partnership of equals in a reunited Lebanon. In our view, this calls for political, economic, and social adjustments that all Lebanese will perceive as fair and equitable. It presupposes that the government will have at its disposal security forces loyal to it which can restore confidence in the authority and ability of the government to maintain domestic order. And it will require that the Palestinians in Lebanon live in peace with their Lebanese hosts and neighbors without challenging the authority of a central Lebanese administration.

The governments of the area and the Arab League are in a position, each in its own way, to make constructive contributions to a political solution of the conflict. Continuation of the fighting cannot serve their interests. Peace in the Middle East and international stability will be in jeopardy as long as the fighting continues. An end to the fighting in turn would create conditions more conducive to a resumption of the search for a negotiated settlement of the broader Middle East question which would take into account the concerns of the states of the area for their security and territorial integrity, as well as the legitimate interests of the Palestinian people.

We are prepared to help to bring an end to the fighting in Lebanon and to achieve a political solution. The interests of the United States lie in alleviation of human suffering, in the restoration of unity and stability based on justice in Lebanon, and in the reduction of tension and the establishment of peace among the nations of the Middle East. We will be prepared to support or undertake any diplomatic initiative requested by the parties.

We will continue our humanitarian programs, which already amount to more than $10 million in hospital and other medical equipment and supplies and foodstuffs distributed as fairly as possible on both sides of the lines. We will do this and more as necessary. We are considering ways of shipping substantial quantities of wheat under Public Law 480.

We will also play our part, after a settlement is achieved, in helping President Sarkis and his government rebuild Lebanese institutions and the Lebanese economy. We have invited him to send a personal envoy to Washington as soon as he considers it appropriate in order to discuss specific ways in which we can be helpful. We have sought from the Congress an appropriation of $20 million to begin the process.

This is a time of opportunity and hope for a suffering people in an area already too long devastated by war. The United States shares the conviction that this opportunity must not be lost.

(16) The Arab-Israeli Conflict.

(a) "The United States and the Middle East": Address by Alfred L. Atherton, Jr., Assistant Secretary of State for Near Eastern and South Asian Affairs, before the 108th Annual Convention Installation Banquet of B'nai B'rith, District 6, Omaha, June 30, 1976.[12]

It is particularly appropriate, just four days before the Bicentennial of our Declaration of Independence, to be meeting with members of an organization whose history goes well back into the first century of America's independence. For 133 of America's 200 years, B'nai B'rith has been a guardian of the principles of freedom, justice, tolerance, and individual dignity which are the essence of this nation.

I do not feel a stranger among you. For as long as I can remember, and long before I knew what the words "B'nai B'rith" meant, that name has been synonymous to me with the highest ideals of service and brotherhood.

In more recent years, I have had a fruitful dialogue with your representatives in Washington on the subject I want to speak about tonight: U.S. policy in the Middle East. This dialogue has helped me understand the special feeling of American Jews for Israel. It has also, I believe, helped your representatives understand the complex considerations which those of us who deal daily with the problems of the Middle East must weigh in conducting our relations with this area of such vital importance to our national interests.

[12]Text from *Bulletin*, 75: 174-9.

This gathering this evening is an extension of that dialogue. I welcome it, and I am glad to be here. This kind of interchange is indispensable to the formulation of foreign policy in a democracy. Foreign policies must be based on an informed public opinion, and they must have public support, if they are to be sustained. I hope my words this evening will find a response among you that will contribute to the national consensus we must strive for in the search for peace in the Middle East.

All of us here tonight would agree that the security and survival of Israel must be a nonnegotiable premise of American Middle East policy. No significant body of opinion in this country would disagree with that premise.

Our national commitment to Israel's security and survival is not at issue. The issue, precisely stated, is to define and pursue a national policy that puts us in the strongest possible position to continue to meet that commitment. A responsible Middle East policy for America must assure that we retain the capacity to influence the course of events in the Middle East commensurate with our bilateral and global responsibilities as a major power.

The United States, with the good will which it uniquely has among all the parties in the Middle East, is in a position to help shape events, to help prevent wars, and to help the parties to find their way along the hard road to a negotiated peace. To continue to play this role, we must pursue policies which take into account the broad range of American concerns and interests in the Middle East.

It is therefore important, as a starting point, to identify what those concerns and interests are:

—I have already mentioned our strong commitment to the security and survival of Israel. It is a commitment rooted deeply in history. It has been reaffirmed by every Administration in this country since the modern State of Israel came into existence almost 30 years ago. As recently as last May 13, President Ford told the annual meeting of the American Jewish Committee in Washington:[13]

A strong Israel is essential to a stable peace in the Middle East. Our commitment to Israel will meet the test of American steadfastness and resolve. My Administration will not be found wanting. The United States will continue to help Israel provide for her security.

[13]*Presidential Documents*, 12: 877-8.

A concrete manifestation of President Ford's policy toward Israel can be seen in the fact that for the fiscal years 1976 and 1977 he has requested over $4 billion in economic and military assistance, compared to a total of only $6 billion in U.S. assistance since the founding of the State of Israel.

—We also have good and mutually beneficial relations with most of the nations of the Arab world. This is important to them. They seek American technology and managerial know-how for their development programs. Moderate Arab leaders also look to military assistance from the United States as a buttress to their moderation and as a means of protecting themselves against more radical forces in the area. These good relations are also important to us. They are important economically, for example, in jobs created in this country by the growing volume of exports to, and investment in, Arab countries. They are important in helping meet our energy requirements for the years ahead. They are also important politically, in a world where the interdependence of developed and developing nations is a condition for the well-being of all.

Our relations with the Arab world, wisely nurtured, can enhance our ability to strengthen the forces of moderation in the Middle East and advance the cause of peace. A return to the estrangement that so long marred our relations with many Arab nations would, in today's interdependent world, have negative effects on our interests extending far beyond the Middle East.

—A third interest of the United States is the preservation and strengthening of our alliances. Each crisis in the Middle East places severe strains on the fabric of those alliances.

—Finally, we have an interest, dictated by our global responsibilities in this nuclear age, to prevent conflict in the Middle East from again becoming a flashpoint of superpower confrontation.

Fundamental Issues in Peace Process

We cannot pursue our interests in the Middle East selectively. Yet so long as the Arab-Israeli conflict persists, there are potential contradictions among them.

Simple logic therefore requires us—indeed, impels us—to persevere in the search for a comprehensive settlement of the Arab-Israeli conflict. In no other way can we guard against an evolution of events that could bring our multiple interests and concerns into conflict, benefiting only those, both within and outside the region, who seek to inflame or polarize or exploit the conflict. An Arab-Israeli peace settlement which had the strong backing of the United

States and of the world community generally would constitute in the long run the best guarantee of Israel's security and survival.

The question we must therefore ask ourselves is whether or not conditions exist which make a settlement of the Arab-Israeli conflict attainable. What are the fundamental issues which must be dealt with if there is to be tangible progress toward peace? Briefly stated, the issues are these:

—Israel seeks from the Arabs recognition of its legitimacy and right to exist, with all this implies: an end to belligerency, an end to threats of force, and commitments to live together in peace and security.

—The Arab states seek the restoration of occupied territories and, in their words, justice for the Palestinian people.

The suspicions between Arabs and Israelis are so deep, the absence of meaningful communication between them so absolute, that each tends to put the worst interpretation on the stated objectives of the other. When Israel says it seeks security, the Arabs take this to mean that Israel seeks to retain major parts, if not all, of the territories occupied in the 1967 war. When the Arabs speak of the national rights of the Palestinians, Israelis hear a call for the destruction of Israel as a Jewish state.

Undoubtedly some on both sides do harbor such extreme feelings. But there are also those who do not. Public opinion is not monolithic in either Israel or the Arab world; it is in flux, and there is a great yearning on both sides for an end to the killing and conflict. The present generation of Arab and Israeli leaders has an opportunity to lead their peoples to a genuine peace between them—an opportunity that has not existed before and that may not come again soon if the present opportunity is missed.

Achievements and Beginnings

Support for a peaceful settlement can only be consolidated, the true intentions of both sides can only be tested, in the give-and-take of a process of negotiations between the parties that holds out hope for peace. The precise form of negotiations—whether face-to-face, indirect through a third party, or some combination of the two—is less important than the dynamics of the process itself.

To generate such a process has been the central purpose of American diplomacy for years, and in particular throughout the active and creative period since the Arab-Israeli war of October 1973. Through all the drama of shuttle diplomacy, Geneva Conference, and debates in the United Nations, our efforts have been directed toward this objective—to engage Arabs and Israelis in a process of negotiations that they themselves will come to recognize as in their own best interests.

Because there is so far yet to go, it is easy to forget how much has already been achieved. Between 1949 and 1974, there were no Arab-Israeli negotiations on the fundamental issues and no agreements to which they were direct parties. In two short years, 1974 and 1975, there were four negotiations and three agreements—two between Egypt and Israel, one between Syria and Israel.

Measured against the absolutes of final peace, the territorial and political distance covered by these agreements is modest. In psychological terms, it represents a quantum leap forward. For the first time in a quarter of a century, the rigid mindsets and sterile rhetoric that for so many years made progress toward peace impossible have given way to the beginnings of a new pragmatism and of a new vision of what the Middle East could be.

Like all changes that touch the deepest emotions, fears, and hopes of nations, that demand a break with past patterns of thought and behavior and a step into the unknowable future, these fragile beginnings have created new tensions and awakened old traumas. The internal debate in Israel, the dissensions within the Arab world, the travail of Lebanon, have in the first instance their own internal causes. But it is equally clear that these developments, which prolong and increase the ferment in the Middle East, are infinitely more intense and less amenable to solution precisely because they are caught in the crosscurrents of the Arab-Israeli conflict.

Risks of Prolonged Stalemate

The resumption of negotiations looking toward a solution of that conflict must remain a high priority on the agenda of unfinished business in the foreign relations of the United States. We cannot change the imperatives of history. If our government does not retain the initiative in dealing with these issues, we will be forced to respond to the initiatives of others, and to events themselves. The same is true of our friends in the Middle East, who are much more directly concerned.

They recognize, as we do, that time is needed to prepare for the difficult decisions which lie ahead. We are not today at the moment of decision between war and peace.

But neither can that moment be postponed indefinitely. Sometime in the months and years ahead the Middle East will come to the crossroad where all concerned—both within and outside the region—must make the hard decision whether they will this time take the road toward peace or the road toward yet another Arab-

Israeli war. That decision will confront all concerned with difficult and agonizing choices, as they come to grips with the basic issues between them—the issue of how to live together for the first time in peace after so many decades of belligerency and war, the issue of territorial withdrawals and final borders, and the issue of the future of the Palestinian people.

All these questions are the proper subject for negotiations. It would be tragic if the world community despaired of the hope that Arabs and Israelis could find the answers to their own destiny and concluded that peace should be imposed on the nations of that troubled region. This is not our way. We prefer to work instead for a peace through negotiations among the parties themselves—with whatever assistance we and others can provide, in whatever forums prove the most practical and acceptable.

But in the absence of a negotiating process, and of the compromises that will be necessary to make such a process possible, pressures will grow to seek an alternative way. If there is anything the history of this conflict should have taught, it is that the Middle East will not stand still. It has experienced four wars in 25 years. The intervals between wars have grown shorter and have been marked by sporadic tension and violence, including acts of terrorism which feed on the unresolved hatred and frustration of the basic conflict. The cost of each successive war, in blood and money, has increased appallingly; and each war has had increasingly dangerous global economic and political repercussions. It is unthinkable that there should be a fifth Arab-Israeli war—and yet that is the grim alternative to negotiation, compromise, and further progress toward peace.

The risks of moving toward peace are great for the leaders on both sides; witness, for example, the storm of criticism unleashed against Egypt for President Sadat's statesmanlike decision, in concluding the most recent Sinai agreement, to commit Egypt to seek a final settlement through peaceful and not military means. For Israel, the risks it perceives are agonizing. Israelis feel they are being asked to exchange something tangible—territory occupied in 1967—for something intangible—commitments by their neighbors to recognize Israel's right to exist and to live in peace. Seen through Arab eyes, however, these commitments are also tangible, representing as they do an abandonment of the claim to recover all of former Palestine—a claim which was the unanimous Arab position for many years.

Whatever the risks of moving toward peace, the risks in not doing so are infinitely greater. I do not need to dwell on the costs and risks, should there be another war. But consider the costs even in the absence of war, not least of all the risk that prolonged stalemate will set in motion forces which will undermine moderate leaders in the region, seek to isolate the United States and Israel in the world, and erode our ability to influence the course of events.

The Balance Sheet for Further Progress

If there were no alternative to this scenario of despair, the prospects for the Middle East and for the world would be grim indeed. I believe, however, that an alternative does exist. Let us look at the balance sheet.

On the one hand, the factors which make progress difficult are clear:

—The Lebanese crisis, which is in a sense an Arab crisis, makes more difficult the achievement of agreement by the Arab governments on how to move toward a settlement with Israel.

—Second, the leadership of the Palestinian movement has not accepted the framework for peace hammered out in U.N. debates and embodied in Security Council Resolutions 242 and 338 following the 1967 and 1973 wars. That framework calls for withdrawal from occupied territory and clear recognition of Israel's right to exist in the context of a peace settlement. While the legitimate interests of the Palestinian people must be taken into account in a final settlement, it is not reasonable to ask Israel to negotiate with them so long as they do not agree that part of a final settlement must be an agreement to live in peace with a sovereign, Jewish State of Israel.

—A third factor is the continuing debate in Israel about peace goals; for example, how to deal with the Palestinian issue and what should be given up in return for peace. Meanwhile, policies such as the continued establishment of settlements in occupied territories raise questions in Arab minds about Israel's ultimate intentions.

—Similarly, voices of extremism in the Arab world and anti-Israel actions in international forums—usually supported for opportunistic reasons by many governments not directly involved in the Arab-Israeli conflict—raise questions in Israeli minds about ultimate Arab intentions.

Let us look now at the plus side of the ledger:

—An internationally sanctioned framework for a negotiated peace exists in Security Council Resolutions 242 and 338. Israel, the principal Arab governments concerned, and the overwhelming majority of the world community—including the

United States and the Soviet Union—are formally committed to and have accepted that framework. This framework was explicitly reaffirmed in the agreements between Israel, Egypt, and Syria.

—Second, while active negotiations are not presently going on, we have been exploring with the Arab governments concerned, and are prepared to continue to do so, an Israeli proposal for negotiations based on the concept of a termination of the state of war and further territorial withdrawals on one or more fronts. In our view, this would offer a practical way—though not necessarily the only way—of continuing the negotiating process.

—Third, for the first time in the history of the Arab-Israeli conflict, and despite continued outbursts of shrill rhetoric from some quarters, there is today in much of the Arab world a moderate leadership which has accepted the principle of making peace with Israel and no longer espouses the goal of Arab sovereignty over all of what was Palestine.

—Fourth, the Soviet Union no longer has the same position of major influence it once enjoyed in certain Arab countries. Arab leaders perceive increasingly that while Soviet support may help them make war, only the United States—of the major powers—can produce progress toward peace, and the Soviet Union is well aware of the risks to it of continuing conflict, including setbacks to U.S.-Soviet relations.

—Fifth, there has been a constructive evolution in public understanding in this country of the complexities of the Middle East conflict, of its shades of gray as well as its blacks and whites, and of the importance of continued progress toward peace. This strengthens the ability of your government to speak with authority in its peacemaking efforts.

—Finally, the United States today enjoys the kind of relationship with both sides to the conflict which permits us to play a unique and positive role to the benefit of all who seek a reasonable, just, and lasting peace settlement.

If all the parties concerned act with the vision that distinguishes true statesmanship, I believe these factors on the plus side of the ledger can prevail. This will require difficult decisions by Arab and Israeli leaders; it will require putting aside dreams of absolute objectives for the sake of achieving realistic compromises; it will require each side to understand the fears and legitimate national aspirations of the other; it will require a determined and prolonged test of intentions in the crucible of negotiations; and it will require that the United States persist in its efforts to keep the peace process alive, to avoid stagnation, to help the parties find solutions which are in their best interests—and ours. The United States will work *with* Israel throughout this process. I want to read you a brief quotation:

> I note with satisfaction that during the past two years, relations between the United States and Israel have become closer.
>
> Our governments have arrived at a common approach regarding the desirable political direction on the road to peace and in the development of the processes of peace . . . . There has been no erosion in the position and attitude vis-a-vis Israel of the Administration, the Congress or the American public.
>
> Relations between the United States and Israel remain firm.

This was a statement by Prime Minister Rabin in the Knesset on June 15, two weeks ago.

Yet the challenge remains, with all its dangers and opportunities. The issues are clear, and they will neither change nor disappear. The imperatives for the nations of the Middle East, and for the interests of the United States, will be the same tomorrow as they are today. Our responsibilities to Israel, to ourselves, and to world peace and stability therefore leave us no realistic alternative but to continue on course, sustained by the hope that someday our children will look back on this period of history as the time when the Middle East—after a quarter century of strife—chose the road to peace.

(b) Reaffirmation of United States Peace Principles:. Toast by Secretary of State Kissinger at a luncheon in honor of Arab Heads of Delegations and Permanent Representatives to the United Nations, New York, September 29, 1976.[14]

This is the fourth time I have met with you since I've become Secretary of State. I have just returned from Africa, and I don't want to say anything insulting to my Arab friends; but I must tell you that compared to the passions that exist in Africa the Middle East has almost Anglo-Saxon restraint. [Laughter.]

I have visited many of your countries, and I know we cannot compete in hospitality. With respect to hospitality, we are the

[14]Department of State Press Release 482, Sept. 29; text from *Bulletin*, 75: 562-3. A toast by Tunisian Foreign Minister Habib Chatty and the opening paragraph of Secretary Kissinger's toast, which are included in the press release, are not printed here.

underdeveloped region compared to our experiences in the Middle East.

But as I look back over the four meetings we have had, the first time we assembled here everyone wanted to know with great suspicion what we were going to do. And I said all the conventional things about Security Council Resolution 242.

You saw to it that, soon after, another Security Council resolution became necessary. But as I look back, I feel that despite all the ups and downs very great progress has been made toward peace in the Middle East. First of all, the traditional friendship between the United States and the countries of the Arab world has been restored with respect to at least very many of them. And we have had an opportunity to make a contribution to three agreements that have begun the difficult and complicated process toward peace.

When I met with you last year,[15] I pointed out four principles which I would like to repeat today:

—The first was that the only durable solution is a just and comprehensive peace and that the United States remains committed to that objective.

—Second, we recognize that peace in the Middle East is not divisible. Each nation and people which is party to the Arab-Israeli problem must find a fair satisfaction of its legitimate interests.

—Third, it is in the nature of movement toward peace that all the key problems must be dealt with in a balanced way. The questions of territory, borders, military deployments, cannot be dealt with unless at the same time political and economic settlement are given equal attention.

—And fourth, any step taken must be judged in the light of the alternatives that are available.

We have proceeded on a step-by-step basis, but we believe that now conditions exist that make comprehensive solutions the most useful approach. And we believe also that conditions are coming about in which the search for peace can be resumed with energy and with conviction. And I want to assure you that the United States remains committed to this objective and that we hope that significant progress can be made in the months ahead.

Since we last met, also there has been the tragedy of the civil war in Lebanon. As we stated on the occasion of the inauguration of the new Lebanese President, the United States is committed to an independent, sovereign, and united Lebanon. We do not favor

[15]Remarks of Sept. 29, 1975, in *Bulletin*, 73: 582.

partition. We favor an opportunity for the people of Lebanon to live their own lives and to determine their own destinies. And we will be available to give any advice and assistance that the parties may request of us.

We can only express the hope now that this tragic conflict will soon come to an end, because it is the unity of the Arab nations that is an essential precondition to an effective policy of peace in the Middle East. And if we are to achieve the objectives of a just and lasting peace about which we have spoken so long, which we must strive to implement, then unity among the Arab nations is of the greatest importance.

Our countries are also concerned with many economic problems and the relations between the developed and developing nations. The countries of the Middle East are playing an increasingly important role. The oil-producing countries, because of their wealth and because of their influence on the global economy, have an unparalleled responsibility which must be exercised for the benefit of all. We are discussing it with them and other countries of the Middle East in the United Nations, in the Conference on International Economic Cooperation; and we are doing so with the attitude that the dialogue between the industrial and the developing world is perhaps the deepest challenge of our time.

We must solve it cooperatively. We cannot create a world community in which one party is condemned to permanent poverty. We cannot create a world community either through tactics of confrontation. So the United States is prepared to work cooperatively and constructively with the nations assembled in this room for the common benefit of all mankind.

Now, distinguished friends, let me conclude by saying that I know that we have not yet traveled except the beginning of the road toward peace. But I also believe that we have created conditions from which the rest of the distance can be traveled if we work on it with conviction and with confidence in each other.

I have personally valued the associations that have been formed with so many of you over the years. And I am grateful that you have done me the honor of joining me again for this meeting. So I would like to propose a toast to peace in the Middle East and to the lasting friendship between the peoples of the Middle East and the American people.

(c) *The Middle East Question before the United Nations General Assembly: Statement by William W. Scranton, United States Representative, in plenary session, December 9, 1976.*[16]

[16]USUN Press Release 184, Dec. 9; text from *Bulletin*, 76: 37-9.

As we move through the final debates of this General Assembly session, we are also approaching the end of a very difficult period in the history of the Middle East—the year of the tragedy of Lebanon. I want to express my government's profound gratification that the long travail of the people of Lebanon is drawing to an end. We will give every feasible support to President Sarkis as he faces the task of the reconstruction of his country; and we look forward to the day when Lebanon—its territorial integrity, its political independence, and its national unity preserved—will resume its proud and rightful place among the nations of the Middle East.

In the calmer atmosphere in the area created by the healing process now going on in Lebanon, it is natural that attention is turning again to the overriding issue in the Middle East—the need for progress toward a peaceful settlement of the conflict that has so long burdened that region, and without which no period of calm can endure. There is today—and we welcome it—fresh insistence that the negotiating process recommence and a sense of impatience with the status quo, which we share with the parties to the conflict. For our part, we believe conditions are now conducive to the resumption of efforts to solve the underlying problems both of Lebanon and of the region as a whole.

We welcome the recent encouraging statements of President Sadat of Egypt and Prime Minister Rabin of Israel. And here in the United Nations, I for one was encouraged by some of the comments made in the most recent Middle East debate, particularly those of the Jordanian and the Israeli Representatives. And now in this debate we have witnessed a unique experience—the introduction of resolutions advocating a peace conference by both Egypt and Israel.[17]

In the past, events in the Middle East have often seemed to run ahead of diplomatic efforts to shape them into a peaceful course. This need not and must not be the pattern for the future. Out of this conviction were born the U.S. initiatives in the aftermath of the 1973 war, taken at the request of the parties. These efforts have yielded the first tangible, practical steps toward an agreed settlement in nearly three decades of fighting and uneasy truces. The three agreements reached in 1974 and 1975 are partial and interim accords, but they have helped give substance to the framework for negotiation established in December 1973 in Geneva. They have

[17]The Israeli draft resolution, A/31/L.24, was introduced Dec. 6, but was withdrawn after amendments calling for PLO participation in the peace conference (A/31/L.25) were introduced by Sri Lanka on behalf of a group of nonaligned states. Other resolutions dealing with the issue are discussed in the text. Details in *UN Monthly Chronicle*, Jan. 1977: 17-19.

begun to build patterns of cooperation, of interaction, of negotiation which are necessary prerequisites to successful negotiations for an overall settlement.

Mr. President, a new Administration will take office in Washington on January 20. Obviously I do not speak with authority on the details of its policies. There is, however, consistency in the approach of the United States to the problems of the Middle East, which reflects principles and policies enjoying overwhelming public support in our country. With full conviction and confidence, I therefore say to those parties with whom we have worked in the Middle East to advance the cause of peace that they can rest assured we will continue to work with them in this vital effort in the months and the years ahead. Much has been accomplished already. Mutual commitments have been made to pursue the negotiating process; and there is a balanced and comprehensive framework in the form of Resolutions 242 and 338, which contain the fundamental elements for those negotiations. The United States will not now abandon its determined and urgent search for peace. We will persevere, and we are convinced that a settlement will be achieved. The alternative is unthinkable.

I turn now to the resolutions under consideration in connection with our discussion of the situation. The omnibus resolution [A/31/L.26] is similar in many respects to a resolution we opposed last year. We shall do so again.

We do not believe that the blanket condemnations of one side contained in this resolution are warranted or will have any positive effect. Nor do we see any logic in a call on all states to desist from supplying military and other aid to one side but not to the other. The United States cannot support and will not be guided by this proposal if it is endorsed.

This resolution also lacks balance in its reference to the potential elements of a peace. One side cannot be expected to give everything and gain nothing.

There is no reference (1) to the end of the state of war; (2) to an agreement which provides not only for the legitimate interests of the Palestinians but for the security of Israel as well; and (3) to the right of a free and independent Israel to exist in the Middle East.

This resolution contains a request to the Security Council that carries at least the implication that somehow it ought to impose a settlement on the parties and that this should be done within an "appropriate time-table," as it says. The parties to this dispute have accepted the framework for a negotiating position which is aimed at producing an agreed solution. This is the essence of what has been accomplished—a mutual commitment to negotiate rather than to rely on timetables or imposed solutions. The Security Council has in the past and can in the future make important contributions to peace in the Middle East. However, we do not believe it is either appropriate or practical to look to the Council to impose its will on the parties to the negotiations.

The temptation to write prescriptions in advance is a natural one, but it is also dangerous. Such prescriptions, hastily formed, can close the door to peace rather than opening it—because there are still differences among us, and especially among the parties directly involved in the dispute, and those differences can only be resolved by negotiation between those parties. We cannot write a peace agreement here, not among 146 nations, nor can we bring about a detailed prescription for the procedure for reconvening the Geneva Conference without raising the possibility of alienation of one or more of the parties, which would doom the conference before it began.

This brings me to the second draft before us, resolution A/31/L.27. The motivation and a good deal of the resolution itself is consistent with our view of the urgency of resuming the negotiating process. We are compelled, however, to vote "No" because of serious problems in two areas. First, this resolution sets an artificial deadline for reconvening of the Geneva Conference. This is not a matter for the General Assembly but, rather, for the parties themselves to decide. It also sets out a time frame for a meeting of the Security Council, a decision which we believe should be subject to consultations among Council members in light of the situation at that time and not prejudged by this Assembly. Secondly, the request to the Secretary General to resume his contacts with the parties to the conflict is phrased in such a way as to imply that the Palestine Liberation Organization should be one of the parties consulted in preparation for reconvening the Geneva Conference. We believe that the question of additional participants at the Geneva Conference is one which can only be addressed by the original participants themselves.

And now the United States is in a special position which we recognize concerning this particular resolution and, indeed, with regard to the reconvening of the Middle East Peace Conference—a position with which all of you are intimately familiar. A new U.S. Administration will take office in Washington on January 20, and we therefore do not consider it appropriate to join now in a definition of detailed options or time limits governing the evolution of this crucial negotiating process. The procedures and timing of a resumed Geneva Conference are matters which rightly must be determined by the participants themselves and by the cochairmen. This is obviously a question which will be addressed by the new American Administration. Accordingly, we will vote "No" on this resolution. However, in so doing we join with all the rest of the nations here represented who sincerely desire that negotiations toward an overall settlement resume promptly and that peace be the result therefrom for all the peoples of the Middle East.

In this connection, Mr. President, I would like to recall the words of Secretary of State Kissinger in speaking to this Assembly on September 22, 1975:[18]

> In the Middle East today there is a yearning for peace surpassing any known for three decades. Let us not doom the region to another generation of futile struggle. Instead, let the world community seize the historic opportunity before it. The suffering and bravery of all the peoples of the Middle East cry out for it; the hopes and interests of all the world's peoples demand it. The United States promises its full dedication to further progress toward peace.

Those words have gained in urgency in the months since they were spoken, but the opportunity for peace still remains with us.

And now, Mr. President, I ask for the indulgence of this body for a few moments more to recount a personal experience. Some of you may remember that in 1968 there was also a change of Administration in the United States, that I was sent by the then President-elect on a short mission to the Middle East. Upon returning from consultations with leaders there, I reported that many believed there was then an opportunity for negotiations toward a peaceful settlement. Some experts and some of us nonexperts agreed.

Such negotiations did not materialize. Historians may argue forever as to whether or not an opportunity was missed. But that experience of disappointment runs deep in my memory and lingers on and on.

Right now there appears to be another opportunity. Many experts and many of us who are nonexperts believe that negotiations are possible now and should be undertaken. Apparently more are of this opinion now than in 1968. The possibility is exciting—it's enticing—even to the point of a gleam of hope of an *overall* settlement. And with this excitement comes a new responsibility, a deep and abiding responsibility, to us all in this body. Rhetoric for home consumption, polemics for home headlines, should be avoided. In advance of negotiations, beguiling prescriptions for results that will be "your way," or "my way," or "our way" can block that opportunity for negotiation. The slightest error, a misstatement, a mismeaning here can ruin that chance.

[18]*AFR, 1975:* 469.

I know it is no time for lectures either, especially from an American who is in comparative safety thousands of miles away—no lecture to an Egyptian or a Syrian or a Jordanian or an Israeli or a Palestinian who has lived on the brink of war or experienced war itself over decades and who even today wonders, "Will it come again next year, or next month, or next week, or tomorrow?" This is no lecture. I simply request with all my heart that we all think before we speak now, that we all think before we act, so that like those of us who had some hopes in 1968 we will not witness and feel our hopes dashed.

Peacekeeping and peacemaking are very difficult; they are very tenuous efforts. No one knows that better than members of the United Nations. In comparison to lasting peace, war comes all too easily. So let us work quietly for negotiation to begin so that peace may come.

5. THE YEAR OF AFRICA

*(17) "The African Dimension of the Angolan Conflict": State-
ment by William E. Schaufele, Jr., Assistant Secretary of
State for African Affairs, before the Subcommittee on
African Affairs of the Committee on Foreign Relations,
United States Senate, February 6, 1976.*[1]

Mr. Chairman:[2] When Secretary Kissinger met with you and
your distinguished colleagues on January 29, he asked you to look
at what is happening in Angola in its larger global context. He
discussed the implications of Moscow's effort to obtain a position
of special influence in central Africa through military intervention
by Cuban proxy. There is little that I can say either to add to or
detract from this global analysis of what Angola means in the
context of our future relations with the U.S.S.R.

What I would like therefore to do today is to examine the
African dimension of this conflict in greater detail. At the risk of
boring you with some history, I would like to convey our perception of how the Angolan conflict developed from being an
African to being an international problem.

As you know, a part of our basic policy for many years in Africa
has been to do what we could to insulate that continent from great-
power conflicts. We have sought to avoid confrontation except
when it was forced upon us. In the case of the Soviet and Cuban
thrust into Angola, we feel that the confrontation was forced upon
us.

Within a purely African context, we are not opposed to the
Popular Movement for the Liberation of Angola (MPLA). In fact,

[1]Text from *Bulletin*, 74: 278-83. Secretary Kissinger's statement of Jan. 29, referred
to in the first paragraph, is printed in *AFR, 1975:* 605-18.
[2]Senator Richard (Dick) C. Clark, Democrat of Iowa.

before our consulate officers left Luanda last November, they had more contact with representatives of the MPLA than with the other two political movements, the National Front for the Liberation of Angola (FNLA) and the Union for the Total Independence of Angola (UNITA). What we oppose is the MPLA's effort, as a minority political movement, to impose itself as the government of Angola, with the help of Soviet arms and a Cuban proxy army, on the majority in Angola.

A few words will perhaps help us understand why the U.S.S.R and Cuba should be prepared to underwrite a minority political movement thousands of miles from home. According to a Soviet handbook, "Africa Today," published in 1962, the MPLA was founded in 1956 "on the initiative of the Communist Party and the allied Party of Joint Struggle of the Africans of Angola," a clandestine anti-Portuguese organization. This was a period of growing Soviet interest in Africa, where the process of decolonization was unfolding and Moscow evidently saw opportunities to implant its influence in place of the departing metropole powers.

There are obvious parallels between Soviet efforts to move in on the Congo after independence in 1960 and Moscow's behavior in Angola today. In that case, the Soviets worked through the Belgian Communist Party and their own Central Committee apparatus concerned with relations with foreign Communists. This time Moscow worked through the Portuguese Communist Party, following the overthrow of the Caetano regime and the temporary ascendancy in Portugal of a radical military leadership with close ties to the Communists.

In 1964 the MPLA began to receive financial and military assistance through Portuguese Communist Party leaders. Moscow had previously financed an MPLA leader, [Daniel] Chipenda, who now is allied with the FNLA. Moscow slackened its aid in the early 1970's when the MPLA was in the middle of one of its periodic power struggles but at a time when the "national liberation" struggle against Portugal was still in full swing. When the Soviets decided to renew full-scale assistance to the MPLA in 1974, this was no contribution to "national liberation" with independence around the corner; it was a cynical move for political power after Portugal had already agreed to Angolan independence.

Based on my 17 years of work with Africa, I am convinced that the Africans could have worked out some consensus agreement bringing the factions together in Angola if they had been left to themselves. It was the Soviet decision, in my judgment, to step up arms aid to what it apparently regarded as an organization in which it had influence which destroyed Portugal's effort through the

Alvor accord of January 1975[3] to establish a provisional coalition government embracing the three factions. With the prospect of being a minority partner in a post-independence government and the promise of Soviet arms, the MPLA had no incentive to compromise.

It was precisely this sort of lack of restraint in pursuit of unilateral advantage in a situation of opportunity which the U.S.S.R. and this country solemnly agreed to avoid in the declaration of principles which they signed in May 1972 in Moscow.[4]

To argue that the Soviet and Cuban intervention represented a response to action taken by this government, by Zaïre, or by South Africa ignores the facts and the chronology. I would suggest this line of argument begs the question of our unwillingness to face our responsibilities as the only power in the world able—if willing—to protect weaker nations against Soviet intervention in their domestic political quarrels.

Chronology of Events

A succinct chronology of events in Angola that led up to our decision to provide assistance to the FNLA and UNITA forces and subsequent developments should make perfectly clear—and I want to emphasize these points—that our actions were *reactive* to those of the Soviet Union and Cuba, *independent* of those of South Africa, and designed to achieve a military situation which would promote a government of national unity composed of all three factions.

The Soviet Union began extensive rearming of the MPLA, then based in Congo (Brazzaville), in October 1974. Previous to this, we had *rejected* requests to provide military support to the FNLA. The Soviet arms shipments continued up through the January 1975 independence talks among the Portuguese and the three liberation movements which culminated in the Alvor accord.

In January 1975 we provided funds to the FNLA for political purposes, reflecting our judgment that the FNLA was at a disadvantage operating in Luanda, an MPLA-dominated city. This sum was to be doled out over many months and was insignificant compared to Moscow's military aid.

During the skirmishes between the FNLA and MPLA in February and the major battles of March and April, we noticed an increasing tendency on the part of the MPLA forces to *ignore* the cease-fires called for by the leaders of all three movements and to

[3]Cf. *AFR, 1975:* 609-10.
[4]Text in *AFR, 1972:* 75-8.

act independently to achieve their maximum military goals. From March through May, not only did the quantity of the Soviet and Communist-bloc arms flow increase, reflecting delivery decisions taken several months earlier, but the nature of the weaponry escalated as well, with quantities of large mortars and several armored vehicles showing up inside Angola by May.

MPLA intransigence increased along with the Soviet aid in June and July, and on July 9 the MPLA drove the FNLA and UNITA completely out of Luanda, thereby destroying even the pretext of a coalition government. After separate pleas from Zambia and Zaïre, each of which saw their security threatened by the specter of a Soviet-supported MPLA, we reversed our earlier decision not to provide military support to any faction, and on July 18 we authorized the use of covert funds for the FNLA and UNITA forces. Our goal was to strengthen the two movements sufficiently to *preserve* a military balance and thereby encourage the establishment of a compromise coalition government. We hoped, at the same time, to signal the seriousness of our concern by this decision to the Soviets and allow them to scale down their intervention without open confrontation.

After our decision was made but before any U.S. assistance could become apparent, the first Cuban forces arrived in Angola in August as part of an arrangement among the Soviet Union, the MPLA, and Cuba to enable the MPLA to extend its military control over all of the nation.

It was at about this same time that South African forces occupied several damsites inside Angola that are connected with a joint Portuguese-South African hydroelectric project in Angola and Namibia. Later, probably in late September, the South Africans apparently decided to intervene militarily in the conflict. We had nothing to do with their decision, were not consulted, and were not aware of their involvement in the fighting until *after* their entry. Large numbers of Cuban forces, including combat units, arrived in Angola almost *simultaneously* with the South Africans. This coincidence, plus reports from Cuban prisoners taken in Angola, indicates that the Cuban decision to intervene with combat forces was made, and forces dispatched, before the South Africans undertook their own intervention.

Commencing in late October, there was again a marked increase in the quantity and sophistication of the Soviet weapons, with tanks, rockets, and a large number of armored vehicles pouring in to be manned by the Cuban forces. This escalation has continued until now, except for a halt of some two weeks from December 9 to 25 when the Soviet Government may have been reevaluating its position in the light of ever firmer U.S. military and diplomatic signals which the Secretary has already outlined to you. However, the vote of this body on December 19 provided a general indication to everyone that U.S. ability and willingness to provide assistance was highly questionable.

At this point the FNLA has been driven back to the northern corner of its previously held territory and UNITA forces are still strongly resisting the MPLA advance in the south even with reduced resources and against over 11,000 well trained and equipped Cuban troops. Savimbi has said that he will carry on the battle against the MPLA again from the bush if he cannot get any outside assistance.

Reactions in Africa

Our African friends—and even some countries which are not so friendly—are acutely aware of the implications for their security of Soviet and Cuban intervention including a massive expeditionary force in Africa. After all, there are few developing countries which do not have to deal with radical internal factions which would be quite capable of calling upon the U.S.S.R. to assist them in the name of "proletarian internationalism."

Even some of our critics are visibly disturbed by the turn of events in Angola. The weekly magazine *Jeune Afrique* [Paris], which is usually quite critical of the United States, sharply attacked the MPLA in its January 30 edition for allowing itself to become a pawn on the Soviet international chessboard, stating that it did "not believe that the MPLA, very much a minority movement, politically and ethnically, was able to govern all of Angola alone or to preserve the independence of the country." In its issue a week earlier the *Jeune Afrique* editorial, which also criticized U.S. policy, stated:

> The strategy of the MPLA that we cannot support is: The monopolization of power on the very day of independence, at the predictable, therefore accepted, price of a civil war by a minority and Communist political party, with massive military and human assistance from far-off foreign places (except ideologically), against all the neighboring countries.
>
> It is absolutely without precedent and one cannot see how it can succeed or, in addition, how it can be defended.

The Nigerian Herald complained on January 30 of the uncritical view then taken of Soviet activity in Africa. It argued that if Angola were to go Socialist, it should not be by force of arms. There are many other examples I could cite of public support for our position, not the least of which was the article in the New Republic, reprinted in the Washington Star last Sunday, by Colin

Legum, a highly respected authority on Africa often critical of our African policy.

I can tell you frankly from my meetings with five chiefs of state during my visit to Africa in December, and from numerous reports from our Ambassadors, that the 22 countries which followed existing OAU policy to recognize no faction during the summit of the Organization of African Unity meeting in Addis Ababa this past January are watching closely to see whether the United States will be prepared to support its friends in Africa—or whether they should now adjust their policies to what they conceive of as new realities.

No one questions our power; but certainly many leaders around the world—friends, critics, and adversaries—question whether we still have the will to use our power in defense of what appear to them as obvious American, not merely African, interests. As one distinguished African leader expressed it to our Ambassador, it is ironic that when half of Africa is for once actively looking to the United States for support and leadership, the U.S. Government has its hands tied and cannot respond. Pleas to "do something" can be heard from all corners of Africa.

In the first place, of course, it is the countries neighboring the Communist military buildup in Angola and Congo (Brazzaville)—namely, Zaïre, Zambia, and Gabon—which are particularly concerned for their security. In supporting the FNLA and UNITA, and the idea of a coalition government, Zambia and Zaïre wish to insure that Angola, which controls an important outlet for their economies, the Benguela Railroad, is run by a sovereign African government which is not dependent on foreign powers who pursue their own special interests in central and southern Africa.

Extension of Soviet Influence

We are told that we are overreacting—that the Africans will never be Communists and we should not worry about what the Soviets are doing. This argument misses the whole point of Moscow's strategy in less developed areas like Africa. When the Soviets speak about changing the "correlation of forces" in the world, they are talking about extending their influence in countries where it has not been strong before and, conversely, neutralizing Western influence in countries where it was previously dominant. It is true that Moscow claims to see this as a long, slow process growing out of internal social and other conflicts. It also believes, however, that Communist countries have a certain role to play as "midwives of progress" assisting leftist forces in each country.

We know well from other Soviet press articles this year that the FNLA and UNITA forces are what the upside-down Soviet lexicon calls "reactionaries" and "splitters." The same sort of language was used to describe the vast majority of the Czech people when they also resisted Soviet efforts to impose a minority Soviet-style democracy.

Angola is an illustration of how the U.S.S.R. now feels it can behave in one of these conflict situations in Africa. The issue here is not merely one of principle: real democracy versus totalitarianism, something which used to concern American liberals. But it is also a basic question of how social change is to come about in the developing world. We and the Soviets can both agree that many changes are needed, and we also thought we had agreed to use mutual restraint and avoid trying to take unilateral advantage of each other in future conflict situations; but certainly the sending of a 12,000-man Cuban army to Angola to promote "progressive" social change is a curious form of restraint.

Now we are hearing from various MPLA leaders, reputedly the more moderate ones, that they have no intention of selling out to the Russians, that they will respect our economic interests, that they want to have close relations with us, et cetera. I would simply note that these statements come at a time of divisive internal debate in the United States and when the MPLA feels sure it will win the conflict but is aware of other African concern about the foreign presence. No one knows exactly what will happen in Angola. But it is reasonable to assume that countries with an expeditionary force in place are in the best position to call the shots.

Some say that African nationalism will take care of the Russians and the Cubans and cite countries where excessive Soviet influence has been eliminated.

But there is no precedent in Africa for a government of a newly independent African state which owes its very existence to the Soviet Union. Certainly the fact that the Soviet Union was permitted to mount such a massive intervention from neighboring Congo (Brazzaville) would not indicate that its influence has seriously diminished in the 10 years it has had a privileged position there.

Certainly the fact that there are some 3,300 Soviet military and civilian advisers in certain African states would not indicate that this influence is diminishing. Certainly the fact that Soviet military assistance deliveries have been three times their delivery of economic assistance is a clear indication of what they really seek in Africa.

I will not pretend to predict in what category an MPLA government might fall, except to note that with the obligations it will have incurred it may become one of the most dependent African governments on the continent. This dependence and Soviet-Cuban ambitions in Africa lead me to question whether we will be seeing any early departure of this foreign army. I hope I am wrong.

Only now are many Americans and Africans beginning to see the implications of the presence of 12,000 Cubans in Angola. When the Cuban Deputy Prime Minister announced during the OAU summit meeting that Cuba would continue to send its troops to Angola as long as Neto wanted them, the Daily Mail of Lusaka exploded at this arrogant insistence that Cuba "would continue to send troops to Angola to kill Africans whether the OAU liked it or not."

Risks in U.S. Failure To Respond

I tell you very frankly, as one who has spent many years in Africa and with Africans and who has also spent the equivalent of many days talking to African leaders of different viewpoints about the Angolan problem, I am very concerned. I believe that we had a good chance in the fall to persuade the Soviets that they would have to choose between the priorities of détente and their self-assumed role as champion of "national liberation" in central and southern Africa. But we never had the opportunity to find out.

On the ground in Angola, the lack of sophisticated military equipment in quantities sufficient to handle Soviet rockets, tanks, and now planes has placed the FNLA and UNITA forces in an increasingly desperate situation. Further recognitions of the MPLA flow directly from this deteriorating military situation and the belief that the United States will not provide the response to balance Soviet-Cuban intervention.

The results are too easily predictable:

—Two groups representing a majority of Angolans are prevented from their rightful participation in the government of an independent nation because of outside intervention and the inability of the United States adequately to respond.

—Moscow and Havana may see themselves shortly in a position to pursue their ambitions elsewhere under the dangerously mistaken notion that in succeeding once they can succeed again.

—In the post-Angolan atmosphere of insecurity and disillusionment with the lack of U.S. support, the states neighboring Angola—Zaïre and Zambia—would be under great pressure to seek an accommodation disadvantageous to them or see their vital exit to the ocean threatened.

—Other African states would adjust to the realities of power so vividly demonstrated in Angola by the Soviet airlift and the Cuban expeditionary force.

—Those Soviet officials who pushed this "national liberation" struggle on the heels of Viet-Nam will have been proven right. Indeed, the sweeping returns in Africa from involvement in a single internal power struggle can only encourage similar adventures elsewhere.

—And in the last analysis we risk bringing on other confrontations in the future under conditions less advantageous to us and more dangerous to us all.

I share what I think is your wish, Mr. Chairman, that such problems could be resolved without the use of arms, that Africans be allowed to solve their own problems, that the United States not get involved in internal politics in Africa or elsewhere, that our attention be devoted to peaceful and successful evolution in Africa. But it takes two to tango—and while we are gyrating on the floor, the Soviet Union has taken somebody down the garden path. The African attitude, based on its perception of Soviet power, will make it even more difficult for Africans to realize their own legitimate aspirations without outside interference.

At this juncture, if the Congress is determined not to provide the wherewithal successfully to resist this Soviet-Cuban effort to establish their influence by force in this part of Africa, I believe it is imperative that members of this Congress express their deep concern about the possibility that either of these two countries might engage in similar adventures elsewhere. To my knowledge that concern, which I know exists, has not surfaced in any public hearings in which I have participated. In fact the debate has largely been directed at U.S. involvement. Secondly, I urge you seriously to consider what the United States can and should do to counter the effects of our unwillingness to meet our responsibilities in Angola on our relationships in Africa and on the security of our friends there.

(18) "United States policy on Southern Africa": Address by Secretary of State Kissinger at a luncheon hosted by President Kenneth D. Kaunda, Lusaka, Zambia, April 27, 1976.[5]

President Ford has sent me here with a message of commitment and cooperation.

I have come to Africa because in so many ways the challenges of Africa are the challenges of the modern era. Morally and politically, the drama of national independence in Africa over the last generation has transformed international affairs. More than

[5] Department of State Press Release 205: text from *Bulletin*, 74: 672-9.

any other region of the world, Africa symbolizes that the previous era of world affairs, the colonial era, is a thing of the past. The great tasks you face—in nation building, in keeping the peace and integrity of this continent, in economic development, in gaining an equitable role in world councils, in achieving racial justice—these reflect the challenges of building a humane and progressive world order.

I have come to Africa with an open mind and an open heart to demonstrate my country's desire to work with you on these great tasks. My journey is intended to give fresh impetus to our cooperation and to usher in a new era in American policy.

The United States was one of the prime movers of the process of decolonization. The American people welcomed the new nations into the world community and for two decades have given aid and encouragement to economic and social progress in Africa. And America's responsibilities as a global power give us a strong interest today in the independence, peace, and well-being of this vast continent comprising a fifth of the world's land surface. For without peace, racial justice, and growing prosperity in Africa, we cannot speak of a just international order.

There is nothing to be gained in a debate about whether in the past America has neglected Africa or been insufficiently committed to African goals. The United States has many responsibilities in the world. Given the burden it has carried in the postwar period, it could not do everything simultaneously. African nations, too, have their own priorities and concerns, which have not always accorded with our own. No good can come of mutual recrimination. Our differing perspectives converge in a common purpose to build a secure and just future for Africa. In active collaboration there is much we can do; in contention or apart we will miss great opportunities. President Ford and the American Government and people are prepared to work with you with energy and good will if met in the same spirit.

So it is time to put aside slogans and to seek practical solutions. It is time to find our common ground and act boldly for common ends.

Africa is a continent of hope, a modern frontier. The United States from the beginning has been a country of the frontier, built by men and women of hope. The American people know from their history the meaning of the struggle for independence, for racial equality, for economic progress, for human dignity.

I am not here to give American prescriptions for Africa's problems. Your program must be African. The basic decisions and goals must be African. But we are prepared to help.

Nor am I here to set African against African, either among your governments or among factions of liberation movements. African problems cannot be solved, and your destiny cannot be fulfilled, except by a united Africa.

America supports African unity. We urge all other countries to do the same.

Here in Africa the range of mankind's challenges and potential can be seen in all its complexity and enormous promise.

The massive power and grandeur of nature is before us in all its aspects—as the harsh master and as a bountiful servant of mankind.

Here we can feel the rich and living cultures which have changed and invigorated art, music, and thought around the world.

And here on this continent we are tested, all of us, to see whether our future will be determined for us or by us, whether humanity will be the victim or the architect of its destiny.

The Issues of Southern Africa

Of all the challenges before us, of all the purposes we have in common, racial justice is one of the most basic. This is a dominant issue of our age, within nations and among nations.

We know from our own experience that the goal of racial justice is both compelling and achievable. Our support for this principle in southern Africa is not simply a matter of foreign policy but an imperative of our own moral heritage.

The people of Zambia do not need to be reminded of the importance of realizing this goal. By geography and economic necessity, Zambia is affected directly and grievously by strife in southern Africa. Political stability in this region means more to Zambia than to many others. Yet Zambia has chosen to stand by her principles by closing her border with Rhodesia and enduring the economic consequences. This is a testimony to the determination of the people of this country and to the statesmanship of its great leader, President Kaunda.

And it was in this city seven years ago that leaders of east and central African states proclaimed their Manifesto on Southern Africa.

One is struck by the similarity of philosophy in the American Declaration of Independence and in the Lusaka Manifesto.[6] Two hundred years ago Thomas Jefferson wrote:

> We hold these truths to be self-evident, that all men are created equal, that they are endowed by their Creator with certain unalienable Rights, that among these are Life, Liberty,

[6] Apr. 16, 1969; cf. *Documents, 1968-69:* 375; same, *1970:* 297 n. 14.

and the Pursuit of Happiness. That to secure these rights, Governments are instituted among Men, deriving their just powers from the consent of the governed.

And seven years ago the leaders of east and central Africa declared here in Lusaka that:

> By this Manifesto we wish to make clear, beyond all shadow of doubt, our acceptance of the belief that all men are equal, and have equal rights to human dignity and respect, regardless of colour, race, religion or sex. We believe that all men have the right and the duty to participate, as equal members of the society, in their own Government.

There can be no doubt that the United States remains committed to the principles of its own Declaration of Independence. It follows that we also adhere to the convictions of the Lusaka Manifesto.

Therefore, here in Lusaka, I reaffirm the unequivocal commitment of the United States to human rights, as expressed in the principles of the U.N. Charter and the Universal Declaration of Human Rights. We support self-determination, majority rule, equal rights, and human dignity for all the peoples of southern Africa—in the name of moral principle, international law, and world peace.

On this occasion I would like to set forth more fully American policy on some of the immediate issues we face—in Rhodesia, Namibia, and South Africa—and then to sketch our vision of southern Africa's hopeful future.

The U.S. Position on Rhodesia

The U.S. position on Rhodesia is clear and unmistakable. As President Ford has said, "The United States is totally dedicated to seeing to it that the majority becomes the ruling power in Rhodesia."[7] We do not recognize the Rhodesian minority regime. The United States voted for, and is committed to, the U.N. Security Council resolutions of 1966 and 1968 that imposed mandatory economic sanctions against the illegal Rhodesian regime.[8] Earlier this year we cosponsored a Security Council resolution, which was passed unanimously, expanding mandatory sanctions.[9] And in March of this year we joined others to commend

---

[7] Interview for the *Chicago Sun-Times*, Mar. 13, quoted in *Bulletin*, 74: 496.
[8] *Documents, 1966:* 320-22 and same, *1968-69:* 370-72 respectively.
[9] Security Council Resolution 388 (1976), adopted Apr. 6, 1976.

Mozambique for its decision to enforce these sanctions even at great economic cost to itself.[10]

It is the responsibility of all who seek a negotiated solution to make clear to the Rhodesian minority that the world community is united in its insistence on rapid change. It is the responsibility of those in Rhodesia who believe in peace to take the steps necessary to avert a great tragedy.

U.S. policy for a just and durable Rhodesian solution will therefore rest on 10 elements:

—First, the United States declares its support in the strongest terms for the proposals made by British Prime Minister Callaghan, then Foreign Secretary, on March 22 of this year: that independence must be preceded by majority rule, which in turn must be achieved no later than two years following the expeditious conclusion of negotiations. We consider these proposals a basis for a settlement fair to all the people of Rhodesia. We urge that they be accepted.

—Second, the Salisbury regime must understand that it cannot expect U.S. support either in diplomacy or in material help at any stage in its conflict with African states or African liberation movements. On the contrary, it will face our unrelenting opposition until a negotiated settlement is achieved.

—Third, the United States will take steps to fulfill completely its obligation under international law to mandatory economic sanctions against Rhodesia. We will urge the Congress this year to repeal the Byrd amendment, which authorizes Rhodesian chrome imports to the United States, an act inconsistent with U.N. sanctions. In parallel with this effort, we will approach other industrial nations to insure the strictest and broadest international compliance with sanctions.

—Fourth, to insure that there are no misperceptions on the part of the leaders of the minority in Rhodesia, the United States, on the conclusion of my consultations in black Africa, will communicate clearly and directly to the Salisbury regime our view of the urgency of a rapid negotiated settlement leading to majority rule.

—Fifth, the U.S. Government will carry out its responsibility to inform American citizens that we have no official representation in Rhodesia nor any means of providing them with assistance or protection. American travelers will be advised against entering Rhodesia; Americans resident there will be urged to leave.

[10]Security Council Resolution 386 (1976), adopted Mar. 17, 1976; text and related material in *Bulletin*, 74: 496-7.

—Sixth, as in the case of Zambia a few years ago, steps should be taken—in accordance with the recent U.N. Security Council resolution—to assist Mozambique, whose closing of its borders with Rhodesia to enforce sanctions has imposed upon it a great additional economic hardship. In accordance with this U.N. resolution, the United States is willing to provide $12.5 million of assistance.

—Seventh, the United States, together with other members of the United Nations, is ready to help alleviate economic hardship for any countries neighboring Rhodesia which decide to enforce sanctions by closing their frontiers.

—Eighth, humanitarian provision must be made for the thousands of refugees who have fled in distress from Rhodesia into neighboring countries. The United States will consider sympathetically requests for assistance for these refugees by the U.N. High Commissioner for Refugees or other appropriate international organizations.

—Ninth, the world community should give its support to the people of Rhodesia as they make the peaceful transition to majority rule and independence and should aid a newly independent Zimbabwe. To this end, we are ready to join with other interested nations in a program of economic, technical, and educational assistance to enable an independent Zimbabwe to achieve the progress and the place in the community of nations to which its resources and the talents of all its people entitle it.

—Finally, we state our conviction that whites as well as blacks should have a secure future and civil rights in a Zimbabwe that has achieved racial justice. A constitutional structure should protect minority rights together with establishing majority rule. We are prepared to devote some of our assistance programs to this objective.

In carrying out this program we shall consult closely with the Presidents of Botswana, Mozambique, Tanzania,[11] and Zambia.

We believe these are important measures. We are openminded with respect to additional actions that can help speed a resolution. The United States will consult closely with African leaders, especially the four Presidents, and with other friends on the Rhodesian problem. For the central fact that I have come here to stress is this: The United States is wholly committed to help bring about a rapid, just, and African solution to the issue of Rhodesia.

Namibia

Rhodesia is the most urgent but by no means the only critical

[11]Sir Seretse Khama, Samora Machel, and Julius K. Nyerere.

problem in southern Africa. The status of Namibia has been a source of contention between the world community and South Africa for over three decades.

The Territory of South West Africa turned into a source of serious international discord following World War II. When the United Nations refused to accede to South Africa's proposal for annexation of the territory, South Africa declined to enter into a trusteeship agreement and since then has refused to recognize the United Nations as the legal sovereign. In 1966 the General Assembly terminated South Africa's mandate over the territory.[12] In 1971 the International Court of Justice concluded that South Africa's occupation of Namibia was illegal and that it should withdraw.[13]

The United States voted for the 1966 General Assembly resolution. We were the only major power to argue before the International Court that South African occupation was illegal. And in January 1976 the United States voted in favor of the U.N. resolution condemning the occupation of Namibia and calling for South Africa to take specific steps toward Namibia's self-determination and independence.[14]

We are encouraged by the South African Government's evident decision to move Namibia toward independence. We are convinced that a solution can be found which will embody equal rights for the entire population and at the same time protect the interests of all who live and work there. But we are concerned that South Africa has failed to announce a definite timetable for the achievement of self-determination, that all the people and all political groupings of Namibia have not been allowed to take part in determining the form of government they shall one day have, and that South Africa continues to deny the United Nations its proper role in establishing a free and independent Namibia.

Therefore the U.S. position is as follows:

—We reiterate our call upon the South African Government to permit all the people and groups of Namibia to express their views freely, under U.N. supervision, on the political future and constitutional structure of their country.

—We urge the South African Government to announce a definite timetable, acceptable to the world community, for the achievement of self-determination.

---

[12]General Assembly Resolution 2145 (XXI), Oct. 27, 1966 in *Documents, 1966:* 309-11.

[13]Excerpts from ICJ opinion in *AFR, 1971:* 403-5.

[14]Security Council Resolution 386 (1976), Jan. 30; adopted unanimously. For text of statement by Ambassador Moynihan see *Bulletin,* 74: 246.

—The United States is prepared to work with the international community, and especially with African leaders, to determine what further steps would improve prospects for a rapid and acceptable transition to Namibian independence. We are convinced that the need for progress is urgent.

—Once concrete movement toward self-determination is underway, the United States will ease its restrictions on trade and investment in Namibia. We stand ready to provide economic and technical assistance to help Namibia take its rightful place among the independent nations of the world.

South Africa

Apartheid in South Africa remains an issue of great concern to those committed to racial justice and human dignity.

No country, no people, can claim perfection in the realm of human rights. We in America are aware of our own imperfections. But because we are a free society, our problems and our shortcomings are fully aired and made known to the world. And we have reason to take pride in our progress in the quest for justice for all in our country.

The world community's concern with South Africa is not merely that racial discrimination exists there. What is unique is the extent to which racial discrimination has been institutionalized, enshrined in law, and made all-pervasive.

No one, including the leaders of black Africa, challenges the right of white South Africans to live in their country. They are not colonialists; historically, they are an African people. But white South Africans must recognize as well that the world will continue to insist that the institutionalized separation of the races must end. The United States appeals to South Africa to heed the warning signals of the past two years. There is still time to bring about a reconciliation of South Africa's peoples for the benefit of all. But there is a limit to that time—a limit of far shorter duration than was generally perceived even a few years ago.

A peaceful end to institutionalized inequality is in the interest of all South Africans. The United States will continue to encourage and work for peaceful change. Our policy toward South Africa is based upon the premise that within a reasonable time we shall see a clear evolution toward equality of opportunity and basic human rights for all South Africans. The United States will exercise all its efforts in that direction. We urge the Government of South Africa to make that premise a reality.

In the immediate future, the Republic of South Africa can show its dedication to Africa—and its potential contribution to Africa—by using its influence in Salisbury to promote a rapid negotiated settlement for majority rule in Rhodesia. This, we are sure, would be viewed positively by the community of nations as well as by the rest of Africa.

A Vision of the Future

Southern Africa has all the prerequisites for an exciting future. Richly endowed with minerals, agricultural and hydroelectric potential, a favorable climate, and most important, great human resources, it needs only to overcome the human failure of racial strife to achieve bright prospects for all its peoples. Let us all strive to speed the day when this vision becomes a reality.

The United States stands ready to work with the nations of southern Africa to help them achieve the economic progress which will give meaning to their political independence and dignity to their struggle for equality.

As you know, Deputy Secretary Robinson,[15] an expert in economic development, is accompanying me on this visit. This is the first time that an American Secretary of State and Deputy Secretary together have come on such a mission, reflecting the importance we attach to the economic development of southern Africa. Mr. Robinson and I are discussing development needs with African officials in the various capitals, and we shall continue these consultations at the UNCTAD meeting in Nairobi next week. After my return to Washington, based on what we have learned, we will urgently study a new aid program for this continent.

Africa and its friends face a dual challenge: immediate and long-term growth. In the short term, economic emergencies can arise from natural disasters or sharp swings in global economic conditions over which developing nations have little control. These economic shocks must be dealt with if the nations of the region are to maintain their hard-won progress toward development. For example, the sharp drop in world copper prices has had a devastating impact on the economies of Zambia and Zaïre. The United States will deal with this problem in its bilateral assistance programs for these countries and in our programs for multilateral action—to be proposed at UNCTAD next week—for resource development, buffer stocks, and earnings stabilization.

But our basic concern must go beyond responding to emergencies. We need to develop urgently programs to lay the foundations for sustained growth to enable the developing nations of southern Africa to deal effectively with global economic shocks and trends.

Let me mention four that are especially relevant to southern Africa: trained local manpower, rural development, advanced technology, and modern transportation.

[15]Deputy Secretary of State Charles W. Robinson.

—For Namibia and Zimbabwe, training programs should be intensified now so that needed manpower will be ready when majority rule is attained. Existing programs to train Namibian and Zimbabwean refugees as administrators and technicians should be expanded as rapidly as possible. We have requested additional funds from Congress for this purpose. We urge other donors and international organizations to do more.

—Development for all of southern Africa involves a process of transforming rural life. We are prepared to assist in agricultural development, in health programs, in manpower training, in improving rural transportation, through both bilateral and multilateral programs.

—A revolution in development planning could be achieved by the use of satellites to collect vital information on crops, weather, water resources, land use, and mineral exploration. The United States has already shared with developing nations information from our earliest earth resources survey satellites. We are now prepared to undertake much larger programs to apply this technology to Africa, including training programs and the development of training facilities and satellite-receiving stations in Africa itself.

—Perhaps the most critical long-term economic need of southern Africa is a modern system of regional transportation. The magnitude of the effort extends beyond the capacity of any one nation or group of nations. For this reason the United States proposes that the World Bank undertake as a priority matter the organization of a multilateral consultative group of donors to develop a modern regional transportation system for southern Africa. For our part we promise our full cooperation in working out a long-term program and in financing appropriate portions of it.

And finally, I can announce today that we expect to triple our support for development programs in southern and central Africa over the next three years.

In addition, the United States has offered leadership in many international forums to promote development through multilateral cooperation. The industrial nations, the newly wealthy oil producers, and the developing countries themselves must collaborate for the goal of development. Africa is a principal beneficiary of the many U.S. initiatives in multilateral institutions and programs—to enhance economic security through supporting export earnings in the face of sharp economic swings, to promote growth through better access to capital markets and technology transfers, to accelerate agricultural production, to improve the conditions of trade and investment in key commodities, and to address the special needs of the poorest nations.

Many of the proposals we have made are already being implemented. Next week in Nairobi, I will put forward new proposals to further advance progress in relations between developed and developing nations.

Today I have outlined the principles of American policy on the compelling challenges of southern Africa.

Our proposals are not a program made in America to be passively accepted by Africans. They are an expression of common aspirations and an agenda of cooperation. Underlying the proposals is our fundamental conviction that Africa's destiny must remain in African hands.

No one who wishes this continent well can want to see Africans divided either between nations or between liberation movements. Africans cannot want outsiders seeking to impose solutions or choosing among countries or movements. The United States, for its part, does not seek any pro-American African bloc confronting a bloc supporting any other power. Nor do we wish to support one faction of a liberation movement against another. But neither should any other country pursue hegemonial aspirations or bloc policies. An attempt by one will inevitably be countered by the other. The United States therefore supports African unity and integrity categorically as basic principles of our policy.

There is no better guarantee against outside pressure from any quarter than the determination of African nations in defense of their own independence and unity. You did not build African institutions to see outside forces fragment them into competing blocs. The United States supports Africa's genuine nonalignment and unity. We are ready for collaboration on the basis of mutual respect. We do so guided by our convictions and our values. Your cause is too compatible with our principles for you to need to pursue it by tactics of confrontation with the United States; our self-respect is too strong to let ourselves be pressured either directly or by outside powers.

What Africa needs now from the United States is not exuberant promises or emotional expressions of good will. What it needs is a concrete program, which I have sought to offer today. So let us get down to business. Let us direct our eyes toward our great goals—national independence, economic development, racial justice, goals that can be achieved by common action.

Africa in this decade is a testing ground of the world's conscience and vision. That blacks and whites live together in harmony and equality is a moral imperative of our time. Let us prove that these goals can be realized by human choice, that justice can command by the force of its rightness instead of by force of arms.

These are ideals that bind all the races of mankind. They are the mandate of decency and progress and peace.

This drama will be played out in our own lifetime. Our children will inherit either our success or our failure. The world watches with hope, and we approach it with confidence.

So let it be said that black people and white people working together achieved on this continent, which has suffered so much and seen so much injustice, a new era of peace, well-being, and human dignity.

(19) "The United States and Africa": Statement by Secretary of State Kissinger before the Committee on Foreign Relations, United States Senate, May 13, 1976.[16]

I am pleased to have this opportunity to report to you on my visit to Africa and on the state of our relations with this increasingly important continent.

A sound relationship between America and Africa is crucial to an international structure of relations that promotes peace, widening prosperity, and human dignity. When I began my African trip, war had already begun in the south of the continent, risking possible great-power conflict. Africa's hopes for steady economic development were being distorted by increasingly radical forces, and the course of peaceful social change threatened to degenerate into widespread bloodshed. For this reason President Ford directed me to go to Africa to present proposals aimed at bringing about moderate, negotiated solutions to the urgent political problems of southern Africa; the long-term economic development of the continent; and strengthening our ties with Africa in the service of interests we share—peace, independence, prosperity, respect for human dignity, and justice.

I believe that we have laid a sound foundation for progress in these areas. It is this progress which I want to discuss with you today.

Africa is of immense size, strategically located, with governments of substantial significance in numbers and growing influence in the councils of the world. The interdependence of America and our allies with Africa is increasingly obvious. Africa is a continent of vast resources. We depend on Africa for many key products:

[16]Department of State Press Release 246; text from Bulletin, 74: 713-19.

cobalt, chrome, oil, cocoa, manganese, platinum, diamonds, aluminum, and others. In many of these commodities, Africa supplies from 30 to 60 percent of our total imports.

In the last two decades, American investments in black Africa have more than quadrupled, to over $1½ billion. Trade has grown at an even faster rate; Africa's importance to us as a commercial partner—as a producer of energy and commodities and as a market for our own products—is substantial and bound to grow in the future.

The reliance of Europe and Japan on Africa for key raw materials is even greater than our own. For example, three-quarters of the manganese imported by the European Community, and over half that imported by Japan, comes from Africa. The continent provides a growing area of investment for our allies and is an important trading partner as well. Western Europe's and Japan's combined trade with Africa now exceeds $30 billion a year.

Thus, an independent and prospering Africa is of considerable consequence to the security, political, and economic interests of all the great industrial democracies.

For her part, Africa recognizes full well the crucial importance of our markets and investments to her own prosperity. And politically, the emphasis which African leaders placed in conversations with me on the need and importance of American action and support is proof that our assets and our moral influence are recognized and valued on the continent.

We are, in addition, bound by a moral dimension—the cultural heritage of 23 million Americans and the moral sympathy of over 200 million Americans who understand the motivations of peoples who would establish their freedom and prosperity against great odds.

Thus, the formulation of a sound relationship between America and Africa is of considerable importance to our country. It is, as well, a complex and difficult task:

—Never before in history has so revolutionary a change occurred with such rapidity as Africa's transition from colonialism to independence. Many African states are but a decade or so old.

—Moreover, a continent of nearly 50 nations cannot easily, if at all, be encompassed by a single, coherent policy. Africa's drive for unity is a reality; yet Africa's great diversity makes clear-cut general formulations difficult to achieve and apply.

—If Africa is not to become a grave source of great-power conflict and of international tensions, Africa's problems must be for Africans to solve. They must not be permitted to become the subject of great-power rivalry and confrontation. Their ultimate resolution lies in the processes of Africa's own internal political and social evolution.

Significant developments in recent years make it clear that Africa occupies an important place in the course and the conduct of international affairs. The spread of national independence in Africa has done much to transform the numerical and the political makeup of world institutions and the nature of international affairs. Political and social pressures, especially in southern Africa, have raised the threat that the continent might once again become an arena for big-power competition, with profound implications for global stability. And major changes have taken place in the international economy, leading the developing nations of Africa to claim more control over their economic destiny and a greater share in global prosperity.

To take account of such changes on the international scene, and with the aim of strengthening the relationship between the United States and Africa, President Ford in 1974 ordered a review of our African policy. As part of this effort, I announced one year ago that I would visit Africa in the spring of 1976. Last September, I set forth the fundamental elements of our policy toward Africa to members of the Organization of African Unity assembled in New York for the United Nations.

I said then that America had three major concerns:[17]

—That the African Continent be free of great-power rivalry or conflict;
—That all of the continent should have the right of self-determination; and
.—That Africa attain prosperity for its people and become a strong participant in the global economic order—an economic partner with a growing stake in the international system.

Late last year the situation in Africa took on a new and serious dimension. For the first time since the colonial era in Africa was largely brought to an end in the early 1960's, external interventions had begun to control and direct an essentially African problem.

In the hope of halting a dangerously escalating situation in Angola, we undertook a wide range of diplomatic and other activity pointing toward a cessation of foreign intervention and a negotiated African solution.

But the impact of our domestic debate overwhelmed the possibilities of diplomacy. In January, on behalf of the Ad-

[17]Remarks of Sept. 23, 1975; *AFR, 1975:* 480.

ministration I put before the Senate our views on the consequences of our inaction on Angola. I shall not review those arguments again today.

Soviet-Cuban intervention had contributed to an increasingly dangerous situation turning the political evolution away from African aspirations and toward great-power confrontation:

—The Soviets and Cubans had imposed their solution on Angola. Their forces were entrenched there, and fresh opportunities lay before them.

—With the end of the Portuguese era in Africa, pressure was building on Rhodesia, regarded by Africans as the last major vestige of colonialism. Events in Angola encouraged radicals to press for a military solution in Rhodesia.

—With radical influence on the rise, and with immense outside military strength apparently behind the radicals, even moderate and responsible African leaders—firm proponents of peaceful change—began to conclude there was no alternative but to embrace the cause of violence. By March of this year, guerrilla actions had begun to break out against Rhodesia.

—On a broader scale, our friends in Africa were increasingly dismayed by our irresolution in countering external pressures and embarrassed by what they interpreted as passivity or worse on the most central issue of African politics, the future of southern Africa. The possibility grew of an emerging pattern of accommodation to the reality of the Soviet presence and American inaction. We saw ahead the prospect of war—which indeed had already begun—fed by outside forces; we were concerned about a continent politically embittered and economically estranged from the West; and we saw ahead a process of radicalization which would place severe strains on our allies in Europe and Japan.

—There was no prospect of successfully shaping events in the absence of a positive political, moral, and economic program of our own for Africa.

It was for these reasons that President Ford and I determined that the African trip which had long been planned as part of an unfolding process of policy development now had a compelling focus and urgency. Indeed, it had become an imperative. We had these aims:

—To provide our African friends once again with a moderate and enlightened alternative to the grim prospects so rapidly taking shape before them—prospects which threatened African unity and independence and indicated growing violence and widened economic distress;

—To strengthen U.S.-African relations by applying our policy to the critical problems of the moment—the issues of self-determination and economic development;

—To stress the positive elements in our policy around which our friends could rally, to make it possible for responsible African leaders to identify with the United States and to work with us; and

—To give friendly and moderate African governments the perception that their aspirations for justice can be achieved without resort to massive violence or bloodshed and that their hopes for prosperity and opportunity can best be achieved through the open economy of the West rather than by sub-mission to the determinist economic dogma of the Communist world.

In short, we sought to show that there was a moderate and peaceful road open to fulfill African aspirations and that America could be counted on to cooperate constructively in the attainment of these objectives.

My trip addressed the three major issues facing Africa:

—Whether the urgent problems of southern Africa will be solved by negotiation or by conflict;

—Whether Africa's economic development will take place on the basis of self-respect and open opportunity or through perpetual relief or the radical regimentation of societies; and

—Whether the course of African unity and self-determination will once again be distorted by massive extracontinental in-terference.

It is clear that these issues are interrelated. A just, negotiated, and peaceful resolution of the problems of majority rule, minority rights, and economic progress can only take place in a continent which remains free from great-power intervention. But American calls for an end to outside intervention would receive scant if any attention from African leaders who did not also perceive that we shared their aspirations that justice, self-determination, and prosperity spread throughout the continent.

The Political Dimension: Southern Africa

The issue of overriding concern to Africans is the question of southern Africa—most urgently, the question of Rhodesia.

When my trip began, armed struggle had already been declared from the nations bordering Rhodesia. At the same time, it was clear that if the United States put forward a package of proposals on Rhodesia which moderate governments could support, they would be prepared to concentrate on an African solution, stressing a peaceful evolution to majority rule, around which the nations of Africa could rally. I believe we have achieved this; the possibilities of a negotiated solution have been greatly enhanced.

In Lusaka, on behalf of the President, I set forth a 10-point program aimed at helping achieve an outcome that would end bloodshed, permit a negotiated solution, block external encroachment, and make possible the eventual achievement of an independent and multiracial society under majority rule and with guarantees of minority rights.

The cumulative substantive thrust of these points and the fact that the speech was made on African soil signaled a new departure for American policy. We made, I believe, an immense and welcome impact in Africa on those—of all political persuasions—who truly care for peace, independence, and justice. These themes were also the basis of my subsequent private talks and public statements in Africa. The reactions were universally positive.

An important development is the agreement by a number of African leaders that outside powers should not in the future deal directly with liberation movements in southern Africa. We agreed to this and urge all other countries to do the same. This represents a significant step in the direction of African solutions to African problems—and toward direct negotiations between the African groups involved, whether black or white.

Unfortunately, the violence in southern Africa has already begun. But the United States has lent its weight to the only route that can stop the fighting and achieve objectives which I believe all Americans can support—the goals of independence, self-determination, majority rule, minority rights, and peaceful change. It is clear from my conversations with the African leaders that they recognize and welcome this strong endorsement of a policy which offers a peaceful and principled resolution of the major problems facing Africa.

There was always considerable suspicion in other African countries of the Cuban presence in Angola and considerable apprehension as to where they might direct their energies next. But instead of seeing such intervention as inevitable—or, worse, beyond their power to prevent—I believe many African leaders now see that there is an alternative and that they can coalesce around a peaceful approach. I believe that it is becoming more unlikely that other African countries will invite Cuban troops and the opportunities for other external intervention are being reduced.

In sum, I believe we have achieved a platform which moderate and responsible Africans can support and which serves interests we share—for peace, justice, progress, and for an Africa free from outside pressures.

—The possibility of a negotiated settlement now exists; our active concern has increased the possibility that the moderate African leaders can take the lead away from "the men with the guns" and that the burning questions of southern Africa can be solved without the great loss of life which seemed inevitable only a short while ago.

—By offering a realistic alternative to violent change the possibilities have been enhanced for black and white to work out themselves the mode of their future coexistence and cooperation. The Republic of South Africa is offered the opportunity to turn away from its increasingly isolated position and positively engage in a moderate and hopeful process of peaceful change.

—African leaders recognize that our support and their best chance for continued independence depends on the absence of external military intervention. This is, above all, in the interest of Africa. Big-power intervention can only undermine unity, set African against African, and involve the risk of conflict. I can state categorically that the United States has no such designs on the continent and that therefore further Soviet or Cuban military intervention would raise the gravest questions.

The Economic Dimension

Beyond the immediate crisis of southern Africa lies the long-term problem of the continent's economic future. Africa has emerged as a continent of 48 states whose boundaries, based on the former colonial frontiers, have brought not only political and social consequences but economic fragmentation, as naturally complementary regions are often divided among two or more states. Consequently there has been a lack of coherence in economic development programs.

In addition, many of the poorest nations of the world are in Africa. Their plight has required massive relief efforts from the United States and other major donor countries of the industrialized world.

It is for these reasons that during my African trip we put forth proposals aimed at providing moderate African states with positive programs through which they can work together toward common objectives. And we proposed measures aimed at ultimately ending Africa's heavy reliance on international relief efforts and setting them on the road toward greater self-reliance. The idea that the

United States, along with other industrial nations, can hope to solve or even basically alleviate the economic problems of others simply by massive applications of emergency relief is no longer tenable. Today what is most needed is not relief but assistance programs designed to solve ultimately fundamental development problems by enhancing the possibilities for developing nations either individually or in regional cooperation to attain self-sustaining economic growth.

In this regard, at Dakar, and at the U.N. Conference on Trade and Development (UNCTAD) in Nairobi, I presented the Administration's views on how best to overcome two major causes of persistent economic distress: the recurrent natural disasters which nullify development progress and the problems which many developing nations experience in adjusting to the dynamics of the global market economy—problems of trade, technology, and investment which often interrupt their progress toward sustained economic advance.

Until long-term goals are reached, foreign assistance will continue to be an important element of our efforts to strengthen the global economic system. Aid will continue to be a crucial response of the international community to natural disasters, other national economic emergencies, and the need to come to grips with basic economic problems which have prevented the achievement of self-sustaining growth.

In this regard, I strongly welcome and support the action of the Senate Foreign Relations Committee this week in taking the initiative to provide assistance for Zambia, Zaïre, and for other countries affected by the problems of change in southern Africa. This is a critically important initiative to meet immediate needs of the area, and we will be working closely with you during the legislative process.

The responsibility to assist cannot be a purely American effort, requiring large new outlays. We need a reorientation of programs and a new sense of direction coupled with strategic new initiatives. These should overcome the fragmented national approaches of current programs and involve all key industrial and recipient nations.

We welcome the proposals of French President Giscard D'Estaing as a most valuable initiative. President Giscard has proposed an exceptional fund for the advancement of Africa which will incorporate two basic institutions: a council of donors and a council of recipients. Its primary objectives will be to improve transportation, agriculture, and mineral development in Africa and to control drought in the Sahel.

In addition, President Giscard has proposed a European-African

Institute to facilitate the transfer of technology to enable African countries to process their own raw materials.

These are the kinds of major and coordinated efforts with participation by all concerned which are required if the root causes of development problems are to be addressed. We welcome President Giscard's proposals and will be discussing them further with him next week. It is especially important to recognize that these are not proposals for further handouts, but efforts to rationalize and coordinate existing programs with the aim of turning relief programs into self-sustaining development.

In recent years, the drought-stricken area of the Sahel has been a major recipient of relief assistance. The time now has come, as we pointed out in Dakar, to strike at the heart of the problem.

At Dakar we pointed out that the United States strongly supports the efforts of the international group of donor countries called the *Club des Amis du Sahel.* The Club is working on mobilizing foreign and local investment on a major scale over the next decade with the aim of reversing the current economic and ecological decline of the area. I know the Congress shares this view and had already requested the Administration to prepare a long-term comprehensive development proposal for the area. This report, sent to the Congress on April 30, outlines the basic strategy which we and all nations concerned believe will lay the foundations for future growth in the Sahel.

At the UNCTAD Conference in Nairobi I sought on behalf of President Ford to advance the positive trend in the North-South dialogue which has been evident since the United States set forth our comprehensive proposals at the U.N. seventh special session last September. Our aim, then and now, has been to address the issues most troubling the developing nations, commodities, trade, technology, investment, balance of payments, and the needs of the poorest countries, not only in their interest but in ours.

We hope that by the end of the conference a consensus will emerge on the broad outlines of our comprehensive and constructive approach. We would then look to smaller international groups to deal with the individual proposals we have made.

With the critical political issues of southern Africa—including Namibia and South Africa as well as Rhodesia—dominating the scene, the economic dimension of our policy could not in itself be decisive. But it is essential. With the platform established by the Lusaka speech our economic policy strongly reinforces our position. Over time, as the problems of southern Africa are resolved, the relative importance of development issues will increase. At Nairobi we have laid a firm foundation for constructive, mutually beneficial cooperation on those issues.

Mr. Chairman,[18] I found in África a great concern with three cardinal objectives:

—That aspirations for self-determination be achieved;
—That Africa must take its place as a responsible and healthy participant in the global economic system; and
—That Africa should be free from external intervention.

And I found a warm welcome for the concrete proposals by which we applied this policy to the issues of most immediate concern to Africa.

I believe that our policy is moderate and reasonable. More than that, it is right.

—We have advanced the possibilities for peaceful change by giving African nations an alternative to the path of bloodshed that had already started and was certain to escalate.

—We have fostered an economic process aimed at giving all nations a stake in a fair and mutually beneficial global economic system and aimed at the ultimate termination of handouts from rich to poor nations by enabling developing countries to move toward more basic economic self-reliance.

—We have laid the foundation for a strengthened relationship between the United States and Africa, a continent with vast potential for the future.

—We have taken important steps to resist Communist encroachment and preserve the balance of global stability—not by truculently throwing our weight around, but by identifying ourselves with principles which America has always stood for and which the world still looks to us to foster and defend.

Thus our African policy is an important element in our overall international effort to help build a structure of relations which fosters peace, widening prosperity, and fundamental human dignity.

We have regained the initiative. We have offered our African friends a welcome alternative for the future, both political and economic. We have told much of the world that America continues to have a positive vision and to stand ready to play an active and responsible role in the world.

But we should have no illusions. A two-week trip cannot solve all our problems. Africa will be watching us closely to see that we match our speeches with concrete action.

[18] John Sparkman, Democrat of Alabama.

Over the long term the crucial factor in Africa—as in our dealing with all parts of the world—will be the restoring of our domestic fabric and projecting ourselves with coherence and steadiness in the world.

The African Continent today presents us with a major challenge. We are on the way to meeting that challenge successfully. Our actions will have to continue to be comprehensive and well integrated. We have a solid base from which to work. And we have the essential assets to carry out a successful policy. Much will depend on our performance—Congress and the executive together—over the next few months.

And if we carry out these policies together, America will vindicate what it has always stood for: conciliation rather than violence; human dignity rather than oppression; self-determination and not colonialism, new or old; progress and hope.

(20) The Entebbe Rescue: Statement by Ambassador Scranton to the Security Council of the United Nations, July 12, 1976.[19]

This Council has been convened to discuss the military operation of Israel to rescue the hostages that were held by air hijackers at Entebbe Airport in Uganda. The Government of Uganda has condemned Israel for what is termed "aggression against Uganda." Israel has been accused of violating the territorial sovereignty and integrity of Uganda, of wantonly destroying sections of Entebbe Airport, and of killing a number of Ugandan soldiers. These are very grave charges, and it is clearly the duty of this Council to consider them in light of the facts and international law.

As members of this Council know, I have spoken several times earlier this year in this Council defending the principle of territorial sovereignty in Africa. I reaffirm that today. In addition to that principle, there are other basic principles and issues at stake in the question that is before us. We must be deeply concerned with the problem of air piracy and the callous and pernicious use of innocent people as hostages to promote political ends. This Council cannot forget that the Israeli operation in Uganda would never have come about had the hijacking of the Air France flight from Athens not taken place.

Let us review the circumstances surrounding the Israeli action at Entebbe Airport. On July 4, in order to rescue the remaining 100 hostages that had been hijacked in the Air France airbus and taken

[19]USUN Press Release 81, July 12; text from *Bulletin*, 75: 181-5.

to Uganda, Israel sent a small military force to Entebbe Airport. This force succeeded in rescuing the hostages and returning to Israel. Three of the hostages, one Israeli soldier, seven of the terrorists, and a number of Ugandan soldiers were apparently killed, and several Ugandan aircraft were destroyed. The Israeli force was on the ground for an hour and a half and departed for Israel as soon as it was possible to do so in safety.

Israel's action in rescuing the hostages necessarily involved a temporary breach of the territorial integrity of Uganda. Normally such a breach would be impermissible under the Charter of the United Nations. However, there is a well-established right to use limited force for the protection of one's own nationals from an imminent threat of injury or death in a situation where the state in whose territory they are located either is unwilling or unable to protect them. The right, flowing from the right of self-defense, is limited to such use of force as is necessary and appropriate to protect threatened nationals from injury.

The requirements of this right to protect nationals were clearly met in the Entebbe case. Israel had good reason to believe that at the time it acted Israeli nationals were in imminent danger of execution by the hijackers. Moreover, the actions necessary to release the Israeli nationals or to prevent substantial loss of Israeli lives had not been taken by the Government of Uganda, nor was there a reasonable expectation such actions would be taken. In fact, there is substantial evidence that the Government of Uganda cooperated with and aided the hijackers.

A number of the released hostages have publicly related how the Ugandan authorities allowed several additional terrorists to reinforce the original group after the plane landed, permitted them to receive additional arms and additional explosives, participated in guarding the hostages, and according to some accounts, even took over sole custody of some or all of the passengers to allow the hijackers to rest. The ease and success of the Israeli effort to free the hostages further suggests that the Ugandan authorities could have overpowered the hijackers and released the hostages if they had really had the desire to do so.

The apparent support given to the hijackers by the Ugandan authorities causes us to question whether Uganda lived up to its international legal obligations under the Hague Convention. The rights of a state carry with them important responsibilities which were not met by Uganda in this case. The Israeli military action was limited to the sole objective of extricating the passengers and crew and terminated when that objective was accomplished. The force employed was limited to what was necessary for that rescue of the passengers and crew.

That Israel might have secured the release of its nationals by complying with the terrorists' demands does not alter these conclusions. No state is required to yield control over persons in lawful custody in its territory under criminal charges. Moreover, it would be a self-defeating and dangerous policy to release prisoners, convicted in some cases of earlier acts of terrorism, in order to accede to the demands of the terrorists.

It should be emphasized that this assessment of the legality of Israeli actions depends heavily on the unusual circumstances of this specific case. In particular, the evidence is strong that, given the attitude of the Ugandan authorities, cooperation with or reliance on them in rescuing the passengers and crew was impracticable. It is to be hoped that these unique circumstances will not arise in the future. We, of course, strongly defend the concept of national sovereignty and territorial integrity. Moreover, the United States deplores the loss of life and property at Entebbe and extends its sympathy to those families who were bereaved by events originating in acts of terrorism that they neither supported nor condoned.

But the U.S. delegation believes very strongly that this Council should address itself to the causes of incidents such as that which occurred last week in Uganda. We believe that this Council should once again take positive action to put an end to such senseless violence. We believe the United Nations should do everything within its power to insure against a recurrence of this brutal, callous, and senseless international crime of hijacking—the crime which gave rise to the Israeli action.

At the very least, it seems to us, this Council should immediately record its collective view that international terrorism—and specifically hijacking—must be stopped. There is ample precedent for taking such action. The United Nations has spoken out strongly against hijacking and interference with international civil aviation a number of times.

On September 9, 1970, the Security Council adopted by consensus Resolution 286 appealing "for the immediate release of all passengers and crew without exception, held as a result of hijackings . . . ." It called on states "to take all possible legal steps to prevent further hijackings or any other interference with international civil air travel."

Later in the autumn of 1970 the General Assembly adopted its detailed Resolution 2645 (XXV) condemning "without exception whatsoever, all acts of aerial hijacking . . . ."[20] The resolution, which the Assembly adopted by an overwhelming vote of 105 in favor and none against, with eight abstentions, further declared

[20]Nov. 25, 1970; text in *Documents, 1970:* 348-9.

that "the exploitation of unlawful seizure of aircraft for the purpose of taking hostages is to be condemned," and it called for every effort to make a success out of the then forthcoming Hague Conference negotiations for an antihijacking treaty.

Again acting by consensus, the Security Council on June 20, 1972, stated its grave concern "at the threat to the lives of passengers and crew arising from the hijacking of aircraft . . . ."[21] The Council called upon states "to deter and prevent such acts and to take effective measures to deal with those who commit such acts."

In addition, there already exists an international legal obligation for all states to prevent terrorist acts. The U.N. Declaration on Friendly Relations and Cooperation Among States, contained in General Assembly Resolution 2625 (XXV), declares:

Every State has the duty to refrain from organizing, instigating, assisting or participating in acts of civil strife or terrorist acts in another State or acquiescing in organized activities within its territory directed toward the commission of such acts, when the acts referred to in the present paragraph involve a threat or use of force.

Concerning air hijacking in particular, 12 members of this Council have ratified the Convention for the Suppression of Unlawful Seizure of Aircraft, signed at The Hague on December 16, 1970. Over half the members of the international community have accepted this convention, including Uganda and Israel. The purpose of the Hague Convention is to promote the safety of international civil aviation. It seeks to discourage hijacking by creating the realistic prospect of severe treatment by states against persons hijacking aircraft.

To achieve this objective the convention requires every contracting state to make hijacking an offense punishable by severe penalties. Each contracting state is also bound to take such measures as may be necessary to establish its jurisdiction over the offense of hijacking and any other act of violence against passengers or crew of a hijacked aircraft which comes within its territory.

According to the convention, a contracting state shall take all appropriate measures to restore control of the aircraft to its lawful commander. It must also facilitate the continuation of the journey of the passengers and crew as soon as practicable and shall without delay return the aircraft and its cargo to persons lawfully entitled to

---

[21]Text of decision in *Resolutions and Decisions of the Security Council, 1972,* Security Council, Official Records, 27th Year: 18.

its possession. Finally, it must take the hijackers into custody and either prosecute or extradite them.

These are high standards—nobody denies that—but they are reasonable standards. My government does not believe that the Government of Uganda has lived up to its legal obligations under the Hague Convention, to which it is a party.

The United States believes that the United Nations should go much further in addressing itself to the evils of international terrorism. In 1972, we proposed a draft convention to the General Assembly,[22] which provided, inter alia, that a signatory state either prosecute persons in its jurisdiction who commit any acts of international terrorism or extradite them to the state in which the crime was committed. Unfortunately, nothing has yet come of our initiative, because of disagreement over the definition of terrorism.

With regard to air hijacking in particular, the United States has repeatedly pressed in the International Civil Aviation Organization for the adoption of an independent convention enabling states parties to act in concert against a state, even if not a party, that harbors hijackers or saboteurs or that fails to return an aircraft, passengers, or crew. We will continue to urge the adoption of such a convention, because we believe that it could provide for worldwide enforcement of the fundamental legal principles that are reflected in the Hague Convention.

Mr. President,[23] this Council can and should reaffirm its own stand in opposition to air hijacking which was expressed in the Council's consensus decision on hijacking adopted on June 20, 1972. Let us condemn the taking of innocent people as hostages. Let us deplore the threat to innocent human life at the hands of terrorists. Let us also reaffirm our dedication to the preservation of the national sovereignty and territorial integrity of every member state. Most important, let us take a firm stand against terrorist hijacking—one of the most dangerous threats to peace and security in the world today.

Mr. President, these are the measured and considered views of my government concerning this episode, views with which I totally concur. But I ask you and my colleagues here to bear with me a few minutes longer, for I wish to make some personal comments about this episode in the context of the image of the United Nations itself and particularly the Security Council.

My tenure here, as you all well know, has been of very short duration—approximately four months. In that period of time the Security Council has been in session almost continuously. With

---

[22]U.N. Document A/C.6/L.850, Sept. 25, 1972; text in *AFR, 1972:* 501-7.
[23]Piero Vinci (Italy).

rare exceptions the issues before it have been exclusively those of the Middle East, outstandingly, and southern Africa.

To my Arab friends here and elsewhere: the U.S. delegation has made it clear on several occasions that problems in the Middle East are by no means totally one-sided. Each of us, I am sure, has individual pictures and vivid images that dwell in our minds whenever matters—as they have over the last four months many times—concerning the Middle East confront us.

In my own personal experience, there is outstandingly a visit to a refugee camp southwest of Amman, where decent people were living under very trying conditions only with the help of UNRWA, having been expelled from their homes in some cases not once but twice, in 1948 and 1967. And another picture which will never leave my mind ever—the condition of Karameh after the raid on that village.

On the other hand there is an equally vivid picture of Jews with access now to pray at the Wailing Wall. Or, even more vivid—and you must all remember these—those horrors of Buchenwald, Dachau, and Auschwitz.

To my African friends here and elsewhere: on the issue of the liberation of southern Africa, my government has put itself squarely on the side of those who seek majority rule with the determination that it be achieved by peaceful means. I am very happy that policy has been adopted while I am here.

But to my Arab and African friends I say here and now, loud and strong, there may have been mixed pictures concerning some of the questions that have confronted the Security Council in the immediate past, but to my mind there is no doubt on this one, not one iota.

Why do I say that so strongly and so deeply? Yes, there was a temporary breach of the territorial sovereignty of Uganda, and let us hope that that never happens again. But there is another value, another judgment which surpasses that one in importance.

Like most of you I have never been the head of a nation nor had the responsibilities thereof, but I have been accountable for the safety and protection of 12 million people in the Commonwealth of Pennsylvania. During that period of time, even though hardly under the same circumstances, I know, there were several occasions in which incidents concerning the safety, the protection, and the lives of Pennsylvanians came to my office. Action thereon had to be decided by me, the ultimate executive authority in the Commonwealth. That was my first and foremost responsibility. It is the first and foremost responsibility of all governments.

In this episode, that responsiblity lay with the Government of Israel to protect her citizens, hostages threatened with their very lives, in mortal danger in a faraway place. Those innocent people were subjected to the terrorist hijacking of the airplane on which they were rightfully flying and further subjected to a six-day terrorizing experience in a foreign country—seeing other persons freed while the Jews were forced to remain—subjected at gunpoint to seven hijacker terrorists who know no law—aware that the only possibility of freedom came from a government whose head had previously rejoiced at the slaying of Israeli athletes at Munich,[24] called for the extinction of Israel, and praised that madman Hitler, who had on his evil conscience, if he had a conscience at all, the murder of 6 million Jews.

Under such circumstances, it seems to me, the Government of Israel invoked one of the most remarkable rescue missions in history, a combination of guts and brains that has seldom if ever been surpassed. It electrified millions everywhere, and I confess I was one of them.

Justified, truly justified, because innocent, decent people have a right to live and be rescued from terrorists who recognize no law and are ready to kill if their demands are not met.

Who has a conscience about this? We should. Every single one of us.

I assume that every one of us wants to do all in our power to avoid such episodes in the future. This is one episode in a series of cases of hijackings by terrorists—about which we can do a great deal. I believe that if we really want to, the Security Council and the United Nations can wipe such episodes off the face of this earth.

As my government has stated in this message I have just finished delivering, we can do this; I pointed out how. We must do this, and then and only then will our consciences be clear for the future. They will never be clear for the past.

(21) *"Strengthening the Relationship between the United States and Africa": Toast by Secretary of State Kissinger at a luncheon in honor of African Foreign Ministers and Permanent Representatives to the United Nations, New York, October 8, 1976.*[25]

I've been so much in Africa in the past year that I am filing an application to be an honorary member of the OAU. Then you will have to sit through even more of my speeches.

[24]On the Munich tragedy and its aftermath, cf. *AFR, 1972:* 206-14.
[25]Department of State Press Release 501; text from *Bulletin*, 75: 559-62.

When we met here a year ago, I said that America's policy toward Africa was founded upon three principles:[26]

—That self-determination, racial justice, and human rights spread to all of Africa;
—That Africa attain prosperity for its people and become a strong participant in the international economic order; and
—That the continent be free of great-power rivalry or conflict.

I think none of us could then have foretold the dramatic events which have taken place this past year in pursuit of each of these goals.

A year ago, events in Rhodesia seemed to be moving inexorably and swiftly toward war, a war that would have had devastating consequences for that country and its neighbors. There was every prospect of conflict that would leave a legacy of bitterness, division, and confrontation that could well set back the progress of southern Africa for generations.

Today, as a result of the resolute determination of the African people and the responsible and far-seeing decisions of their leaders, the situation has changed dramatically. A breakthrough has been achieved. A negotiation is about to begin; the framework of a settlement exists. An opportunity is now before us for a peaceful transition to a majority-ruled multiracial society in Zimbabwe.

A year ago the prospects were dim that the Namibian problem could be rapidly or satisfactorily resolved.

Today, the inevitability of Namibian independence is accepted by all parties concerned. More important, a way toward agreement among Namibia, South Africa, and the United Nations now appears open. Determined efforts are now underway to bring about a constitutional conference at a neutral location under U.N. aegis in which all authentic national forces, specifically including SWAPO, will be able to fashion a design for the new state of Namibia.

And in the course of the year past, the forces of change have asserted themselves dramatically in South Africa. It is manifest that the internal political, economic, and social structure of that country must change. A system based on institutionalized injustice, and that brings periodic violence and upheaval, cannot last. The leaders of South Africa have taken responsible steps to help facilitate a process of change in Rhodesia. The world now looks to them to exercise the same wisdom to bring racial justice to South Africa.

[26]*AFR, 1975:* 479-85.

The past year also has brought the beginnings of what could be a new economic era for Africa. And it is clear that ultimately it is economic development which will determine whether the aspirations of the African people for progress and human dignity will be fulfilled.

Africa's great natural wealth and considerable potential for agricultural and industrial development have long been impeded by an array of problems:

—Recurrent drought and natural disaster;
—Heavy reliance by many nations on the production of a single commodity and, as a result, extraordinary dependence on the vagaries of the world economy; and
—A crushing historical burden of poverty.

In the past year the international community has laid the groundwork for an attack on all these problems. It is increasingly recognized that in place of sporadic relief efforts to ease the aftereffects of natural disasters, what is needed is comprehensive international programs to address fundamental conditions. Last May in Dakar I outlined one such program, a program for international cooperation to help the nations of the Sahel develop additional water resources, increase crop acreage through modern agricultural techniques, and improve food storage—all aimed at making the Sahel less vulnerable to crisis in the future.

Broad-based multinational cooperation has been accelerated to reform the global economic system for the benefit of the developing nations. In the past year—since the seventh special session—major steps proposed at that session have been implemented and promising new measures discussed. Steps have not only been proposed but carried out—to expand agricultural production worldwide, to improve the earnings potential and market stability of key raw materials, to reduce trade barriers to tropical product exports into the United States, to help those hard hit by increasing energy costs, and to stimulate the flow of modern technology so as to promote growth and diversify economies now excessively dependent on a single commodity. Africa is a principal beneficiary of these reforms in the international economy.

Africa's trade with and investment from the United States and the industrial nations of the West are crucial and expanding. Africa wants to earn its way. But for some, particularly the poorest and least developed, trade and investment are not enough to overcome the legacy of pervasive poverty. U.S. bilateral assistance programs will therefore concentrate increasingly on these countries, and in sectors where the need is greatest.

The United States also believes that closer cooperation among the industrial democracies of North America, Western Europe, and Japan can mean a much greater contribution to the economic development of Africa. Therefore we welcome the proposal of President Giscard d'Estaing of France for a fund to organize and coordinate Western assistance efforts to Africa. We hope to move ahead on this proposal. And we are seeking to further strengthen coordination through the OECD to insure that the collective efforts of the industrial nations are efficiently organized to bring the maximum benefit to Africa.

Economic development is a painful and long-term process which depends most of all on the sustained and substantial efforts of the developing countries themselves. But this has been a historic year in the effort of the community of nations to narrow the gulf between North and South both economically and politically. All those who seek either order or progress are beginning to recognize that we can have neither unless the last quarter of this century is an era of international cooperation.

The advances made toward racial justice and economic progress, if they are maintained and built upon, can strengthen the basis of African unity and self-determination and thereby serve as a bulwark against unwanted outside intervention in the affairs of the African people.

The United States is firmly committed to the concept of Africa for Africans. That is why, for example, we have agreed with the Presidents of Botswana, Mozambique, Tanzania, and Zambia that non-African nations should not deal directly with the liberation movements of southern Africa. The United States seeks no bloc and plays no favorites among groups or leaders; we will not oppose any African faction or group, regardless of its ideology, if it is truly independent and African. We will continue our firm opposition to the extension of great-power rivalry or conflict to the African Continent.

Thus, in the course of the past year, Africa's drive for justice, for progress, for true independence, has been severely tested in every dimension. Africa has survived those tests and finds itself at a possible turning point in its history.

The statesmanship of Africa's leaders has won widespread recognition. The resilience of Africa's economies and the determination of its peoples to achieve racial justice have been amply demonstrated to the world.

But progress achieved will not continue automatically. Difficult decisions must be made, additional statesmanship must be shown, if just solutions are to be achieved.

Yet continued progress is crucial. For we are all aware that the important steps toward peace and justice in Rhodesia, steps to avert bloodshed and widening war, can easily be undone. And there are those who, for their own purposes, do not want to see a peaceful settlement in either Rhodesia or Namibia.

Together, African states, the United Kingdom, and the United States have fashioned an opportunity for peace and foundation for progress in southern Africa. Essential elements of a negotiated settlement have been achieved:

—The authorities in Rhodesia have accepted the principle of majority rule within two years.

—The parties have agreed that an interim government will be established immediately.

—Agreement has been reached on the time and place for a conference.

—A number of Western governments have agreed to participate in a fund to facilitate the transition to majority rule and to enhance the economic future of an independent Zimbabwe.

For the first time in 11 years, a rapid, satisfactory, and peaceful end to the Rhodesian crisis is within reach. To lose this opportunity would be monumental tragedy. To seize it can mean a new day of hope to southern Africa. History will not forgive a failure to seize the moment. Whether by neglect or design, such a failure will be tantamount to a decision to choose violence, chaos, and widening destruction over a rapid and peaceful solution. No country in southern Africa will be spared either the pain of warfare or the judgment of history.

Continued movement toward an accord for Namibia is also crucial. My talks with leaders of black African states, the South African Prime Minister, and Mr. Sam Nujoma of the South West Africa People's Organization lead me to believe that those involved want a peaceful solution and are willing to modify their positions in order to achieve it. As in Rhodesia, success is not assured. Nevertheless, with determination and a readiness to compromise, the parties are now in a position to end the dispute that has been a source of serious international discord for almost three decades.

The focus of the moment is on the southern part of the continent, but the U.S. commitment applies to all of Africa and to all the great issues I have mentioned: justice, progress, and independence.

Last year I said to the permanent members of the OAU who met with me that strengthening the relationship between the United States and Africa is a major objective of American policy. It was then, it is now, and shall continue to be so in the future. Africa can count on us.

There can no longer be any question that America is committed to Africa's goals and to working with the nations of Africa to solve the continent's problems. In return, we expect to find respect for our concerns and perspectives.

Let us set aside the suspicions of the past and work for our common future. Together we can reconstitute the community of man on the basis of mutual benefit and shared endeavor. We can show that races can live together, that there is an alternative to hatred.

If Africa succeeds, it will have much to teach the world, and so much to contribute to it.

I therefore ask you to join me in a toast:

—To the well-being of the peoples of Africa;

—To friendship and cooperation between the United States and Africa; and

—To peace, prosperity, and justice for peoples everywhere.

6. INTER-AMERICAN CROSSCURRENTS

(22) *"The Americas in a Changing World": Address by Secretary of State Kissinger before the U.S.-Venezuelan Symposium II at Macuto, Venezuela, February 17, 1976.*[1]

I am most pleased to be here today, at the invitation of President Pérez. This symposium is symbolic of the effort of our two nations to strengthen our ties and to consult on issues of deep concern to our two peoples. I come here not merely to demonstrate my country's interest in its relationships with you but to address with you the global challenges to our common future.

The Western Hemisphere has for centuries symbolized man's readiness to grasp his own destiny. When I placed a wreath at the tomb of Simón Bolívar yesterday, I recalled the depth of his faith and wonder at the future of the Americas. Today, more than a century later, the promise of our hemisphere is more alive than ever—and more important to each of our countries and to the world.

Today I want to discuss with you the challenges that history has posed to our hemispheric friendship, the efforts we have made in the recent period to address these challenges, and the compelling responsibility we face today and tomorrow.

I have come to this continent because the United States believes that Latin America has a special place in our foreign policy.

This belief is the product of history. We won our national independence together in the same era. We confronted the similar challenges of pioneer peoples developing the resources of bountiful unexplored continents. We shaped democratic institutions and spurred economic growth, conscious that we benefited greatly from our relationship with each other. We have long shared a common interest in shielding our hemisphere from the intrusion of others.

[1] Text from *Bulletin*, 74: 313-21.

We led the world in building international organizations to serve our cooperative endeavors for both collective security and economic progress.

The United States has always felt with Latin America a special intimacy, a special bond of collaboration, even in the periods of our isolation from world affairs. Even now, when our countries are major participants in world affairs, when our perceptions of contemporary issues are not always identical, there remains a particular warmth in the personal relationships among our leaders and a special readiness to consider the views of our neighbors. On many issues of U.S. policy—economic, political, or security—the American people and Congress give special consideration to our hemispheric ties.

The problem we face today is that history, and indeed the very growth and success we have all achieved, have complicated our relationship. What used to be a simple perception of hemispheric uniqueness, and a self-contained exclusive relationship, has become enmeshed in the wider concerns we all now have in the rest of the world.

—The United States is conscious of a global responsibility to maintain the world balance of power, to help resolve the age-old political conflicts that undermine peace, and to help shape a new international order encompassing the interests and aspirations of the 150 nations that now comprise our planet. And so our vision now reaches beyond the Western Hemisphere. We have major alliances with the Atlantic community and Japan, as well as this hemisphere; we have growing ties of friendship with many nations. In a nuclear age, we have an inescapable responsibility to manage and stabilize our relations with the major Communist powers and to try to build a safe and more constructive future. The problem of peace in this generation means for us, the United States, a permanent involvement in world affairs in all their dimensions—maintaining security, promoting a healthy trade and monetary system and economic development, and creating a stable and just and universal system of political relations.

—At the same time, Latin American nations have grown in power and influence and become major forces in their own right on the world scene. This is one of the most striking events of this era. Your economies are among the most advanced of the developing world. But your role is not a product of economic strength alone; its roots are deeper: your traditions of personal and national dignity, concern for legal principle, and your history of peace. Your sense of regional identity has become more important—to you—and to the world. We accept and respect these developments, and the new organizations, like SELA,[2] which now speak to your own collective interests. We trust that they will not be used for confrontation; for that could complicate our relations and hinder solutions to problems. We are confident that the increased sense of Latin American identity, and the institutions which serve it, can be a constructive and vital force for cooperation on a wider basis. This will be our attitude toward these institutions.

—The countries of Latin America have done more than grow internally and strengthen their regional associations. They have established new ties outside the hemisphere—trade relations with the European Community and Japan and a growing sense of solidarity with developing nations in Africa and Asia. Such global involvement is inevitable; inevitably also, it creates new and conflicting pressures on more traditional friendships.

—The challenge of economic development has become a worldwide concern and is being addressed on a global, and not simply hemispheric, basis. Venezuela is now cochairman of the Conference on International Economic Cooperation (CIEC)[3] and has discharged this responsibility with great wisdom. Similarly, the energies of the United States are increasingly focused on international organizations and issues of global scope. We have made major and comprehensive proposals to the U.N. General Assembly special session, the World Food Conference, and the Conference on International Economic Cooperation. Recent events have taught us all that global prosperity is indivisible; no nation can prosper alone.

—Finally, the United States continues in this era to feel a special concern for its hemispheric relations. Our profound conviction is that if we cannot help to solve the burning issues of peace and progress with those with whom we have such long-standing ties of sentiment and experience of collaboration, we have little hope of helping to solve them elsewhere. To put it positively, we feel strongly that our cooperation as equals in this hemisphere can be a model for cooperation in the world arena.

The challenge we face is that we must reconcile these distinct but intersecting dimensions of concern. We must define anew the nature and purposes of our hemispheric condition. We must understand its meaning and its promise. We must adapt it to our new global condition. We must summon it, develop it, and use it for our common objectives.

[2] Latin American Economic System.
[3] With Canada.

The United States values its bilateral ties with your countries, without any intention of pursuing them in order to break up your regional solidarity. We want to preserve our hemispheric ties and adapt them to the moral imperatives of this era—without hegemony, free of complexes, aimed at a better future.

All the nations of the hemisphere are mature countries. The variety of intersecting relationships and concerns reflects the vitality of our nations and the increasingly important roles we play in the world. We in the Americas are granted by history a unique opportunity to help fashion what your Foreign Minister[4] has called a "new equilibrium" among all nations.

Dialogue and Progress

The experience of our recent past has much to teach us.

During the early 1960's, the Alliance for Progress stimulated great expectations of rapid development. The enthusiasm with which our countries embraced the Alliance Charter clearly exceeded our collective perseverance and understated the magnitude of the challenge. But great human and financial resources were mobilized; new institutions were created that remain basic instruments for cooperation. And ultimately the Alliance left an even greater moral imprint. By the end of the 1960's, internal development and social change had become an imperative for all governments in Latin America, regardless of political coloration. The United States is proud of its contribution.

In this decade, this hemisphere has been swept up in the tides of the global economy that now have an increasing significance to our national plans and expectations.

At Viña del Mar in 1969,[5] the nations of Latin America staked out a new agenda of issues reflecting what we have since come to call interdependence—the conditions of world trade, multinational corporations, and technology transfer—as well as more traditional issues such as economic assistance. In the spirit of inter-American cooperation, the United States attempted to respond. My government endorsed, and worked for, measures to improve Latin America's access to our markets and those of other industrial countries, to improve the flow of private capital, to reform the inter-American system, and to insure consideration for Latin American concerns in international forums.

Less than a month after becoming Secretary of State in 1973, I called for a new dialogue between Latin America and the United States[6] to reinvigorate our relations by addressing together the new

[4]Ramón Escovar Salom.
[5]Cf. *Documents, 1968-69:* 431 n. 75.
[6]Cf. Secretary Kissinger's remarks, Oct. 5, 1973, in *AFR, 1973:* 415-17.

challenges of an interdependent world. I believed that in the past the United States had too often sought to decide unilaterally what should be done about inter-American relations. I felt that Latin America must have a stake in our policies if those policies were to be successful. I said that we were ready to listen to all Latin American concerns in any forum.

Latin America chose to conduct the dialogue on a strictly multilateral basis, presenting common positions to the United States. First in Bogotá,[7] then in Mexico City,[8] the agenda of issues that had been set out in Viña del Mar was updated to account for changed circumstances and new concerns. At Tlatelolco, and again in Washington, I joined my fellow Foreign Ministers in informal meetings, supplementing our regular encounters in the OAS and United Nations. A thorough and heartening dialogue took place. For the next 12 months, U.S. and Latin American representatives met in a continuous series of political and technical discussions. These meetings were interrupted almost precisely a year ago in reaction to certain provisions of the U.S. Trade Act of 1974, the very act that implemented the system of generalized preferences first proposed in Viña del Mar.

All of us have something to learn from this experience.

First, we can now see that the new dialogue, as it was conducted, only partially met the psychological requirements of our modern relationship.

The United States was prepared to work with the other nations of the hemisphere to improve and perfect the undeniable community that has existed under the name of the inter-American system for almost a century. Yet the explicitness of our approach to the concept of community led many in Latin America to think that the United States wanted to maintain or create a relationship of hegemony. This misunderstanding obscured the reality that the hemisphere was in transition, between dependence and interdependence, between consolidation and political growth, and that the old community based on exclusivity was being transformed into a more open community based on mutual interests and problem solving.

The Latin American nations still seemed to think that the United States, with its great strengths and responsibilities, could act unilaterally to resolve all issues, that any compromise was surrender, that Latin America should propose and the United States should respond. The United States, on the other hand,

[7]Conference of Foreign Ministers of Latin America for Continental Cooperation, Nov. 14-16, 1973; cf. *AFR, 1974:* 66.
[8]Conference of Tlatelolco, Feb. 18-23, 1974; *AFR, 1974:* 57-71.

looked upon dialogue as a prolonged process of give-and-take in which progress would come incrementally as our representatives analyzed the problems and negotiated solutions.

Latin America demanded quick results: each meeting became a deadline by which time the United States had to show "results" or be judged lacking. But as economic difficulties beset us all in a period of world recession, it became obvious that if Latin American aspirations were expressed to the people of the United States in terms of categorical and propagandistic demands, they could not elicit a sufficiently positive response.

Both sides oversimplified the nature of the problem: the Latin American nations did not always perceive that the issues were among the most difficult that the international community has faced because they go to the heart of the structure and interaction of entire societies. The United States did not sufficiently take into account that Latin America had experienced years of frustration in which lofty promises by the United States had been undone by the gradualism of the American political system, which responds less to abstract commitments than to concrete problems. Hence the charge of neglect on one side and the occasional feeling on the other side of being besieged with demands.

But if the new dialogue has not yet yielded results, it nevertheless expresses a constructive mode of dealing with our problems and realizing the aspirations of the hemisphere. The United States is prepared to make a major effort to invigorate our hemispheric ties. My trip here underlines that purpose.

We have learned something basic about the hemisphere itself. In the past, both the United States and Latin America have acted as if the problems of the hemisphere could be solved exclusively within the hemisphere. Today, the Americas—North and South— recognize that they require a global as well as a regional vision if they are to resolve their problems. For the United States a homogeneous policy toward an entity called "Latin America" presents new problems, in terms both of global concerns and of the real diversity of Latin America. Nor can the burden of adjustment to a new hemispheric equilibrium be borne wholly by the United States. We are prepared to make a major contribution, and we are willing to cooperate fully with Latin American regional institutions that come into being to this end.

Both sides need a new approach. The United States is prepared to give more systematic consideration to Latin America's quest for regional identity. On the other hand, Latin America must overcome its own apprehensions about our policies. In the past, whenever we emphasized the regional aspects of our relationships, we have been accused of forcing problems into an inter-American system which we dominated; when we emphasized the bilateral mode, we were accused of a policy of divide and rule. Each side must understand the problems and purposes of the other.

We thus all know our challenge. We must now turn it into our opportunity. As far as the United States is concerned, we are prepared to make a major effort to build upon our historic ties a cooperative effort to construct a better future.

Interdependence and Our Common Future

Where do we go from here? What is the answer? Wherein lies the purpose of our relationship in the modern era?

Our starting point must be to recognize that an era of interdependence makes collaborative endeavor more, not less, important to any country that wishes to preserve control over its own national destiny.

We in this hemisphere won our glory in fighting for national independence and defending it in the face of foreign threats; we have built societies embodying the tradition of democracy; we have dedicated our human energies to the development of our natural resources, with impressive results.

Yet even as we celebrate our birth as nations and our centuries of achievement, we encounter a new challenge to our independence. It comes not from foreign armies, but from gaps and strains revealed within the very international economic system that each of our nations, in its own way, has done much to create.

Since the Enlightenment, which produced the faith in reason and progress that inspired our revolutions, we have all believed that the growth of a global economy would nurture a world community bringing universal advancement. Yet now we find that the international system of production—which still has the potential to provide material progress for all—has become subject to uncertainties and inefficiencies and international conflicts.

Nowhere is this challenge more vivid than in Latin America. With the higher stage of development that your economies have reached has come the awareness of greater vulnerability to fluctuations in export earnings, to increases in the costs of imports, and to the ebb and flow of private capital. Yet your more complex and more open economies can also respond more vigorously to, and profit more readily from, positive trends in the world economic system.

Interdependence for the Americas is therefore a positive force and an opportunity. We must manage it, harness it, and develop it for our common benefit.

Our economic dilemmas give rise, in our times, to political imperatives. Rapidly changing external events affect all our peoples profoundly—their livelihoods, their material standards, their hopes for the future, and most fundamentally, their confidence that our systems of government can successfully encounter the challenges before us. And the requirement for action is political will.

Our societies derive their strength from the consent and dedication of our peoples. Can our democratic system cope with the strains of social change and the frustrations of what is inevitably a long historical process? Can nations find the wisest path in an era when our problems are too vast to be solved by any nation acting alone? Will we succumb to the temptation of unilateral actions advantageous in their appearance but not their reality? Can we reconcile our diversity and the imperative of our collaboration?

I believe we have every cause for optimism. The requirements of interdependence make patent the genius of our special hemispheric traditions, our values, and our institutions. Pluralism and respect for the rights of others are indispensable to the harmony of the international order. For to seek to impose radical changes without the consent of all those who would be affected is to ignore political reality. Equally, to deny a voice to any who are members of the international community is to insure that even positive achievement will ultimately be rejected.

Therefore the traditions of this hemisphere—democracy, justice, human and national dignity, and free cooperation—are precisely the qualities needed in the era of global interdependence. National unity without freedom is sterile; technological progress without social justice is corrupt; nationalism without a consciousness of the human community is a negative force.

Therefore our permanent quest for progress in this hemisphere must take into account global as well as regional realities. It must reflect the differing interests of each country. And our global efforts respectively must draw on the vitality of our own relationships as a source of dynamism, strength, and inspiration.

The United States has attempted to make a constructive contribution in this context.

Last September in New York, addressing the Latin American Foreign Ministers attending the U.N. General Assembly,[9] I pointed out that several of our initiatives before the seventh special session had been designed to be particularly relevant to Latin American concerns. And I pledged that in the necessary negotiations in other forums, and in all aspects of our relations, we would remember that each Latin American country was different and we would be responsive to the distinctive national interests of our friends in the hemisphere.

[9]Sept. 30, 1975; text in *Bulletin*, 73: 584-7.

My New York comments raised contradictory speculations. The explicit introduction of global considerations into our Latin American policy was variously interpreted as implying either that the United States denied the existence of a special relationship with Latin America or that it sought to build on that relationship to constitute a new bloc in world affairs. The recognition of the uniqueness of each country, and particularly my statement that no "single formula" could encompass our desire for warm and productive relations with each nation in the hemisphere, were interpreted by some to imply that the United States was about to embark on a new crusade to maintain its power through a policy of special bilateral deals designed to divide the countries of Latin America against one another and preclude their ties with countries outside the hemisphere.

These speculations reflect the suspicions and uncertainties of a fluid global environment. They reflect problems we must jointly overcome. They do *not* reflect U.S. policy.

The fundamental interests of the United States require an active and constructive role of leadership in the task of building peace and promoting economic advance. In this hemisphere the legacy of our history is a tradition of civilized cooperation, a habit of interdependence, that is a sturdy foundation on which to seek to build a more just international order. And it is absurd to attempt to create a broader world community by tearing down close cooperative relations that have already existed in our part of the globe.

Therefore the United States remains committed to our *common* pledge at Tlatelolco to seek "a new, vigorous spirit of inter-American solidarity."[10] This must mean today not an artificial unanimity or unrealistic pleas for unilateral action. As we agreed at Tlatelolco, interdependence has become a physical and moral imperative: it is a reality of mutual dependence and a necessity of cooperation on common problems. To face real problems, we must now deal effectively among ourselves; we must identify our real needs and priorities—given the hemisphere's diversity, that can often be achieved bilaterally and subregionally better than regionally.

In this spirit of working solidarity, the United States pledges itself:

—*To take special cognizance of the distinctive requirements of the more industrialized economies of Latin America, and of the region as a whole*, in our efforts to build a more equitable international order. We believe the major Latin American countries

[10]*AFR, 1974:* 67.

need concessional foreign assistance less than they need support for their drive to participate in the international economy on a more equal footing with the industrialized nations. To help overcome fluctuations in export earnings and continued import and debt-servicing needs, we have secured a development security facility in the IMF and a substantial increase in access to IMF resources. To facilitate access to long-term development capital on commercial terms, we have proposed a new international investment trust and have begun a program of technical assistance to countries entering established capital markets.

In a similar vein, we support expanded capitalization of international financial institutions such as the International Finance Corporation and the Inter-American Development Bank. A U.S. contribution of $2.25 billion to a new multi-year replenishment of the Inter-American Development Bank is now before the U.S. Congress. President Ford has given his full support.

To promote the growth and market stability of commodities of importance to Latin America, we favor producer-consumer cooperation in specific commodities and a reduction in the barriers to increased processing of raw materials in exporting countries.

We are prepared to undertake other practical steps:

The nations of Latin America have shown considerable interest in the transfer of modern technology. We support this, in principle and in practice. The challenge here, as elsewhere, is to develop mechanisms to achieve practical results. It may be that SELA can turn to this question and suggest the means by which we could cooperate. We are prepared to respond positively.

In addition we must recognize that the private sector, private initiative, and private capital can play important roles in the development and application of new scientific and technological advances to local needs and conditions. The degree to which private capital is prepared to devote its considerable resources of talent and knowledge to this task will depend on the climate for its participation. It is for this reason that we state again our willingness to discuss codes of conduct which can provide guidelines for the behavior of transnational enterprises. No subject is more sensitive or more vital—for the private sector has played the critical role in bringing about growth; its resources exceed by far those now available for governmental aid. Yet for it to be effective the proper environment must be created. This is a major test for our cooperative efforts.

To increase trading opportunities we now permit many industrial products of developing countries to enter the United States without duty. And we favor special and differentiated treatment in the multilateral trade negotiations through concentration on products of interest to Latin America. This is already apparent in the talks we have had on tropical products. On all such multilateral issues we are prepared to have prior consultation with the nations of Latin America.

—*To maintain direct assistance to the neediest nations in this hemisphere* still oppressed by poverty and natural disaster. The great bulk of our bilateral concessional assistance to Latin America—nearly $300 million annually—is now allocated to the region's poorest nations to meet basic needs in health, education, and agriculture. At this moment, the United States has joined other countries in a massive response to the devastating earthquake in Guatemala. In addition we continue to support expansion of multilateral concessional assistance through the Fund for Special Operations of the Inter-American Development Bank and the soft-loan windows of other international financial institutions active in Latin America. These activities, supplemented by new programs in agricultural development and to assist balance-of-payments shortfalls, make an important contribution to our common responsibility toward the neediest.

In this regard let me mention the critical problem of food—which is especially important to Latin America, where food production over recent years has barely kept pace with population.

Following my proposal of a year ago, the Inter-American Development Bank established the International Group for Agricultural Development in Latin America. This hemispheric agricultural consultative group will consist of major donors and all Latin American nations and focus on overcoming constraints to agricultural growth and rural development in the hemisphere. The first meeting is scheduled for May in Mexico, and preparatory work will begin next week.

The United States attaches great importance to this effort. It is crucial if Latin America is to fulfill its potential as a food-surplus region. It can be another powerful example of how inter-American cooperation can show the way toward solving mankind's most urgent problems.

—*To support Latin American regional and subregional efforts to organize for cooperation and integration.* The United States has provided technical and financial assistance to the movement of regional and subregional integration, including the development banks of the Andean Pact, the Central American Common Market, and the Caribbean Common Market. We are eager to assist these integration movements and others that may arise in the future. In addition, we see in SELA a new possibility for cooperation among the nations of Latin America on common regional problems and projects. We welcome SELA and will support its efforts at mutual cooperation as its members may deem appropriate.

—*To negotiate on the basis of parity and dignity our specific differences with each and every state, both bilaterally and, where appropriate, multilaterally.* We intend to solve problems before they become conflicts. We stand ready to consult with other governments over investment disputes when those disputes threaten relations between our governments. As you all know, the United States and Panama are continuing to move forward in their historic negotiations on a Panama Canal treaty to establish a reliable long-term relationship between our two nations. In the interim between now and the final Law of the Sea Conference, we will continue to attempt to find solutions to issues relating to fisheries and the seas which have complicated our relations in the past. It is the earnest hope of my country that within a year a Treaty of Caracas will be signed on the law of the sea.

—*To enforce our commitment to mutual security* and the Bolivarian ideal of regional integrity against those who would seek to undermine solidarity, threaten independence, or export violence. Last July at San José the nations of the Americas agreed upon revisions to the Inter-American Treaty of Reciprocal Assistance,[11] the Rio Treaty. In so doing, they reaffirmed their commitment to take collective action against aggression—whether it comes from without or within the hemisphere. The United States regards this treaty as a solemn international obligation. We are resolved to carry out the commitment it places upon us.

—*To work to modernize the inter-American system* to respond to the needs of our times, to give direction to our common actions. The member states have already taken a major step forward in revising and reaffirming the Rio Treaty. In the months ahead, the OAS will be considering the report of its special committee on reform. More is at stake than the text of the charter; the member states are also beginning to focus on the structure and processes of the organization itself. The United States believes that the OAS has an important future of service to the hemisphere. We stand ready to work with others to modernize and strengthen it, to make it a more effective instrument for regional cooperation.

The application of these principles is a matter of common

---

[11] Summary of the Protocol of Amendment to the Rio Treaty in *AFR, 1975:* 270-75.

concern. We have had a special relationship for 150 years and more; the very intimacy of our ties imposes upon us the duty of rigorous and responsive self-assessment. We should set ourselves concrete deadlines—to complete the process before the end of this year.

We should use the months ahead constructively and productively. It is time that all of us in the hemisphere put aside slogans and turn from rhetoric to resolve. Let us go beyond the debate whether the United States is patronizing or neglecting or seeking to dominate its neighbors. Let us not dispute whether the Latin American nations are being unreasonable or peremptory or seeking to line up against their northern partner.

Instead, let us focus on our goals and the need for common effort and get down to serious business. Many forums and forms are available. I propose that we identify the most fruitful areas for our common effort and set ourselves the goal of major accomplishment this year. At the OAS meeting in June, we can review where we stand and discuss what further needs to be done. At the last General Assembly we adopted the informal style of the new dialogue, successfully, to facilitate open and frank discussions of major issues. I propose that we do so again and that we concentrate, at this next ministerial meeting, on the nature of our fundamental relationship.

Our common problems are real enough; a common response will give living reality to the heritage and promise of the hemisphere and the enduring truth that the nations of this hemisphere do indeed have—and will continue to have—a special relationship.

The United States and Venezuela

The ties between the United States and Venezuela illustrate the sound foundation upon which we can build. Our democracies, our economic strength, our tradition of trust and working together, give us hope; it is our duty to go forward together. This is the strong desire of my country.

We have set an example together. Our collaboration is traditional, extensive, intensive, and—patently—mutually beneficial.

Venezuela is a country at peace in a continent at peace. Its considerable energies can happily be directed toward the highest aspirations of human well-being in the spirit of its democratic ideals. Now those ideals have been given new strength by the acquisition of new prosperity and power.

Last December in Paris, 27 nations gathered in the Conference on International Economic Cooperation, a milestone in the world's struggle to manage the challenges of interdependence.

Decisions in CIEC are to be taken by consensus rather than by majority vote. The structure of the conference reflects the diversity of nations. It is not a club of the powerful: the developing countries as well as the industrialized participate on a fully equal basis. It is representative, but not so unwieldy as to frustrate all practical action. It is a tribute to common sense and to the strength of our collective commitment to achieve real solutions and real progress for our peoples and for the world.

Appropriately, Venezuela—whose leaders have long projected a vision of greater democracy among nations as well as within their own country—is now cochairman of CIEC.

Since the early days of our nation when Francisco de Miranda befriended George Washington, Venezuela's and the United States' struggle for liberty, national dignity, and progress have been intertwined. Only a few miles up this coast at Puerto Cabello, there is a monument to 10 North Americans who lost their lives in the first attempt by Miranda to win Venezuelan independence. And Henry Clay, whose statue stands in Caracas, expressed the enduring wish of my nation when he wrote to Simón Bolívar in 1828:

> . . . the interest which was inspired in this country by the arduous struggles of South America, arose principally from the hope, that, along with its independence, would be established free institutions, insuring all the blessings of civil liberty.

We have a right to be proud, for these hopes are a living reality. Few societies have transformed themselves so profoundly and so rapidly as our two countries. And those transformations have been neither aimless nor ideological, but the dynamic product of institutions created by free peoples.

Venezuela and the United States have built an economic relationship that is sturdy and valuable to both sides—and is increasingly so. Venezuela has for decades been an important and reliable supplier of energy to the United States—through World War II and the recent oil embargo. The U.S. private sector has participated actively in the dynamic growth of the Venezuelan economy.

We recognize that we often have differing perspectives and differing interests. At times the fervor of our respective convictions has led us to disagree even when our interests basically coincided. Venezuela and the United States can debate without confrontation. We can discuss without rancor, as friends. And most importantly, we can pursue our respective goals with a dignity born of mutual respect.

Like a masterpiece by Soto or Otero, our relationship is therefore a shimmering and changing pattern of reality. My discussions with your distinguished President Carlos Andrés Pérez and Foreign Minister Escovar have convinced me that the farsighted prophecy of the Liberator speaks for both our countries. Bolívar envisioned a world "imbibing the American principles and seeing the effects of liberty on the prosperity of the American peoples. . . ."

We have it in our power to transform such a world from a dream into a practical reality. All great achievements began as dreams. With realism, reason, and the will to work together, we can insure that the dreams of Bolívar and Jefferson, of Miranda and Washington, will endure—for our two countries, for the hemisphere, and for all mankind.

The challenge for both our nations now is to draw new inspiration from the long tradition that unites us, to bring into harmony the diverse roles we are destined to play in world affairs. There is little we can accomplish apart; there are tremendous things we can achieve together.

(23) Sixth Regular Session of the General Assembly of the Organization of American States (OAS), Santiago, Chile, June 4-18, 1976.

(a) Human Rights: Statement by Secretary of State Kissinger to the Assembly, June 8, 1976.[12]

One of the most compelling issues of our time, and one which calls for the concerted action of all responsible peoples and nations, is the necessity to protect and extend the fundamental rights of humanity.

The precious common heritage of our Western Hemisphere is the conviction that human beings are the subjects, not the objects, of public policy, that citizens must not become mere instruments of the state.

This is the conviction that brought millions to the Americas. It inspired our peoples to fight for their independence. It is the commitment that has made political freedom and individual dignity the constant and cherished ideal of the Americas and the envy of nations elsewhere. It is the ultimate proof that our countries are linked by more than geography and the impersonal forces of history.

Respect for the rights of man is written into the founding documents of every nation of our hemisphere. It has long been part of the common speech and daily lives of our citizens. And today, more than ever, the successful advance of our societies requires the

[12]Department of State Press Release 293; text from *Bulletin*, 75: 1-5.

full and free dedication of the talent, energy, and creative thought of men and women who are free from fear of repression.

The modern age has brought undreamed-of benefits to mankind—in medicine, in technological advance, and in human communication. But it has spawned plagues as well, in the form of new tools of oppression, as well as of civil strife. In an era characterized by terrorism, by bitter ideological contention, by weakened bonds of social cohesion, and by the yearning for order even at the expense of liberty, the result all too often has been the violation of fundamental standards of humane conduct.

The obscene and atrocious acts systematically employed to devalue, debase, and destroy human life during World War II vividly and ineradicably impressed the responsible peoples of the world with the enormity of the challenge to human rights. It was precisely to end such abuses and to provide moral authority in international affairs that a new system was forged after that war— globally in the United Nations and regionally in a strengthened inter-American system.

The shortcomings of our efforts in an age which continues to be scarred by forces of intimidation, terror, and brutality—fostered sometimes from outside national territories and sometimes from inside—have made it dramatically clear that basic human rights must be preserved, cherished, and defended if peace and prosperity are to be more than hollow technical achievements. For technological progress without social justice mocks humanity; national unity without freedom is sterile; nationalism without a consciousness of human community—which means a shared concern for human rights—refines instruments of oppression.

We in the Americas must increase our international support for the principles of justice, freedom, and human dignity; for the organized concern of the community of nations remains one of the most potent weapons in the struggle against the degradation of human values.

The Human Rights Challenge in the Americas

The ultimate vitality and virtue of our societies spring from the instinctive sense of human dignity and respect for the rights of others that have long distinguished the immensely varied peoples and lands of this hemisphere. The genius of our inter-American heritage is based on the fundamental democratic principles of human and national dignity, justice, popular participation, and free cooperation among different peoples and social systems.

The observance of these essential principles of civility cannot be taken for granted even in the most tranquil of times. In periods of stress and uncertainty, when pressures on established authority grow and nations feel their very existence is tenuous, the practice of human rights becomes far more difficult.

The central problem of government has always been to strike a just and effective balance between freedom and authority. When freedom degenerates into anarchy, the human personality becomes subject to arbitrary, brutal, and capricious forces. When the demand for order overrides all other considerations, man becomes a means and not an end, a tool of impersonal machinery. Clearly, some forms of human suffering are intolerable no matter what pressures nations may face or feel. Beyond that, all societies have an obligation to enable their people to fulfill their potentialities and live a life of dignity and self-respect.

As we address this challenge in practice, we must recognize that our efforts must engage the serious commitment of our societies. As a source of dynamism, strength, and inspiration, verbal posturings and self-righteous rhetoric are not enough. Human rights are the very essence of a meaningful life, and human dignity is the ultimate purpose of government. No government can ignore terrorism and survive, but it is equally true that a government that tramples on the rights of its citizens denies the purpose of its existence.

In recent years and even days, our newspapers have carried stories of kidnapings, ambushes, bombings, and assassinations. Terrorism and the denial of civility have become so widespread, political subversions so intertwined with official and unofficial abuse and so confused with oppression and base criminality, that the protection of individual rights and the preservation of human dignity have become sources of deep concern and—worse— sometimes of demoralization and indifference.

No country, no people—for that matter no political system—can claim a perfect record in the field of human rights. But precisely because our societies in the Americas have been dedicated to freedom since they emerged from the colonial era, our short- comings are more apparent and more significant. And let us face facts. Respect for the dignity of man is declining in too many countries of the hemisphere. There are several states where fun- damental standards of humane behavior are not observed. All of us have a responsibility in this regard, for the Americas cannot be true to themselves unless they rededicate themselves to belief in the worth of the individual and to the defense of those individual rights which that concept entails. Our nations must sustain both a common commitment to the human rights of individuals and practical support for the institutions and procedures necessary to insure those rights.

The rights of man have been authoritatively identified both in the U.N.'s Universal Declaration of Human Rights and in the OAS's American Declaration of the Rights and Duties of Man. There will, of course, always be differences of view as to the precise extent of the obligations of government. But there are standards below which no government can fall without offending fundamental values, such as genocide, officially tolerated torture, mass imprisonment or murder, or the comprehensive denial of basic rights to racial, religious, political, or ethnic groups. Any government engaging in such practices must face adverse international judgment.

The international community has created important institutions to deal with the challenge of human rights. We here are all participants in some of them: the United Nations, the International Court of Justice, the OAS, and the two Human Rights Commissions of the United Nations and the OAS. In Europe, an even more developed international institutional structure provides other useful precedents for our effort.

Procedures alone cannot solve the problem; but they can keep it at the forefront of our consciousness, and they can provide certain minimum protection for the human personality. International law and experience have enabled the development of specific procedures to distinguish reasonable from arbitrary government action on, for example, the question of detention. These involve access to courts, counsel, and families; prompt release or charge; and if the latter, fair and public trial. Where such procedures are followed, the risk and incidence of unintentional government error, of officially sanctioned torture, of prolonged arbitrary deprivation of liberty, are drastically reduced. Other important procedures are habeas corpus or amparo, judicial appeal, and impartial review of administrative actions. And there are the procedures available at the international level: appeal to, and investigations and recommendations by, established independent bodies such as the Inter-American Commission on Human Rights, an integral part of the OAS and a symbol of our dedication to the dignity of man.

The Inter-American Commission has built an impressive record of sustained, independent, and highly professional work since its establishment in 1960. Its importance as a primary procedural alternative in dealing with the recurrent human rights problems of this hemisphere is considerable.

The United States believes this Commission is one of the most important bodies of the Organization of American States. At the same time, it has a role which touches upon the most sensitive aspects of the national policies of each of the member governments. We must insure that the Commission functions so that it cannot be manipulated for international politics in the name of human rights. We must also see to it that the Commission becomes an increasingly vital instrument of hemispheric cooperation in defense of human rights. The Commission deserves the support of the Assembly in strengthening further its independence, evenhandedness, and constructive potential.

Reports of the Human Rights Commission

We have all read the two reports submitted to this General Assembly by the Commission. They are sobering documents, for they provide serious evidence of violations of elemental international standards of human rights.

In its annual report on human rights in the hemisphere, the Commission cites the rise of violence and speaks of the need to maintain order and protect citizens against armed attack. But it also upholds the defense of individual rights as a primordial function of the law and describes case after case of serious governmental actions in derogation of such rights.

A second report is devoted exclusively to the situation in Chile. We note the Commission's statement that the Government of Chile has cooperated with the Commission, and the Commission's conclusion that the infringement of certain fundamental rights in Chile has undergone a quantitative reduction since the last report. We must also point out that Chile has filed a comprehensive and responsive answer that sets forth a number of hopeful prospects which we hope will soon be fully implemented.

Nevertheless the Commission has asserted that violations continue to occur; and this is a matter of bilateral as well as international attention. In the United States, concern is widespread in the executive branch, in the press, and in the Congress, which has taken the extraordinary step of enacting specific statutory limits on U.S. military and economic aid to Chile.

The condition of human rights as assessed by the OAS Human Rights Commission has impaired our relationship with Chile and will continue to do so. We wish this relationship to be close, and all friends of Chile hope that obstacles raised by conditions alleged in the report will soon be removed.

At the same time, the Commission should not focus on some problem areas to the neglect of others. The cause of human dignity is not served by those who hypocritically manipulate concerns with human rights to further their political preferences nor by those who single out for human rights condemnation only those countries with whose political views they disagree.

We are persuaded that the OAS Commission, however, has avoided such temptations.

The Commission has worked and reported widely. Its survey of human rights in Cuba is ample evidence of that. Though the report was completed too late for formal consideration at this General Assembly, an initial review confirms our worst fears of Cuban behavior. We should commend the Commission for its efforts—in spite of the total lack of cooperation of the Cuban authorities—to unearth the truth that many Cuban political prisoners have been victims of inhuman treatment. We urge the Commission to continue its efforts to determine the truth about the state of human rights in Cuba.

In our view, the record of the Commission this year in all these respects demonstrates that it deserves the support of the Assembly in strengthening further its independence, evenhandedness, and constructive potential.

We can use the occasion of this General Assembly to emphasize that the protection of human rights is an obligation not simply of particular countries whose practices have come to public attention. Rather, it is an obligation assumed by all the nations of the Americas as part of their participation in the hemispheric system.

To this end, the United States proposes that the Assembly broaden the Commission's mandate so that instead of waiting for complaints it can report regularly on the status of human rights throughout the hemisphere.

Through adopting this proposal, the nations of the Americas would make plain our common commitment to human rights, increase the reliable information available to us, and offer more effective recommendations to governments about how best to improve human rights. In support of such a broadened effort, we propose that the budget and staff of the Commission be enlarged. By strengthening the contribution of this body, we can deepen our dedication to the special qualities of rich promise that make our hemisphere a standard-bearer for freedom-loving people in every quarter of the globe.

At the same time, we should also consider ways to strengthen the inter-American system in terms of protection against terrorism, kidnaping, and other forms of violent threats to the human personality, especially those inspired from the outside.

Necessity for Concern and Concrete Action

It is a tragedy that the forces of change in our century—a time of unparalleled human achievement—have also visited upon many individuals around the world a new dimension of intimidation and suffering.

The standard of individual liberty of conscience and expression is the proudest heritage of our civilization. It summons all nations.

But this hemisphere, which for centuries has been the hope of all mankind, has a special requirement for dedicated commitment.

Let us then turn to the great task before us. All we do in the world—in our search for peace, for greater political cooperation, for a fair and flourishing economic system—is meaningful only if linked to the defense of the fundamental freedoms which permit the fullest expression of mankind's creativity. No nations of the globe have a greater responsibility. No nations can make a greater contribution to the future. Let us look deeply within ourselves to find the essence of our human condition. And let us carry forward the great enterprise of liberty for which this hemisphere has been— and will again be—the honored symbol everywhere.

(b) Cooperation for Development: Statement by Secretary of State Kissinger to the Assembly, June 9, 1976.[13]

For two centuries, the peoples of this hemisphere have been forging a record of cooperation and accomplishment of which we can be proud. It is a record which gives good cause for the confidence we bring to the tasks we face today. But of greater importance is the truly special relationship we have achieved. The ties of friendship, mutual regard, and high respect that we have forged here set this hemisphere apart. The bond between the American republics is unmatched in the world today in both depth and potential.

First, we have maintained the awareness that our destinies are linked—a recognition of the reality that we are bound by more than geography and common historical experience. We are as diverse as any association of nations, yet this special relationship is known to us all, almost instinctively.

Second, ours is a hemisphere of peace. In no other region of the world has international conflict been so rare, or peaceful and effective cooperation so natural to the fabric of our relationships.

Third, we work together with a unique spirit of mutual respect. I personally am immensely grateful for the warm and serious relationships I have enjoyed with my colleagues and other Western Hemisphere leaders. I am convinced that this sense of personal *amistad* can play a decisive role in the affairs of mankind, and nowhere more so than in our hemisphere.

Fourth, we share the conviction that there is much to do and that working together for concrete progress is the surest way to get it done. Even our criticism presumes the feasibility of cooperation.

Fifth, we respect each other's independence. We accept the

[13]Department of State Press Release 296; text from *Bulletin*, 75: 5-10.

principle that each nation is—and must be—in charge of its own future; each chooses its mode of development; each determines its own policies. But we know that our capacity to achieve our national goals increases as we work together.

Sixth, despite the differences among our political systems, our peoples share a common aspiration for the fulfillment of individual human dignity. This is the heritage of our hemisphere and the ideal toward which all our governments have an obligation to strive.

Finally, and of immediate importance, we are achieving a new and productive balance, based on real interests, in our relations within the Americas, within other groupings, and with the rest of the world. All of us have ties outside the hemisphere. But our interests elsewhere do not impede our hemispheric efforts. Our traditions of independence and diversity have served us well.

This is both a strength and a challenge to us now, as this Assembly takes up the issue of development.

The United States is dedicated to cooperate in development throughout the world. But as we seek to make progress in all our global development efforts, we recognize close and special ties to the nations of the Americas. We regard the concerns of this hemisphere as our first priority.

It is for this reason that we support the suggestions which have been made for a Special Assembly of the OAS to be devoted to hemispheric cooperation for development. Such an Assembly should deal with concrete problems capable of practical solutions. To this end, the United States proposes that a preparatory meeting of experts be held in advance of the Special Assembly.

But we do not intend to delay our efforts while we await the processes of international institutions and conferences. The U.S. Administration will begin now:

—First, to give special attention to the economic concerns of Latin America in every area in which our executive branch possesses the power of discretionary decision.

—Second, to undertake detailed consultations with Latin American nations to coordinate our positions on all economic issues of concern to the hemisphere prior to the consideration of those issues in major international forums.

—Third, to consider special arrangements in the hemisphere in economic areas of particular concern to Latin America, such as the transfer and development of technology.

—In addition, we will put forth every effort to bring about the amendment of the U.S. Trade Act to eliminate the automatic exclusion of Ecuador and Venezuela from the generalized system of preferences.

The United States is prepared to proceed in these four areas whatever may occur in other development forums. But this Assembly offers an excellent opportunity to advance our joint progress. The United States believes that there are three major issues that this Assembly should address: commodities, trade, and technology. These involve:

—More stable and beneficial conditions for the production and marketing of primary commodities upon which the economic aspirations of so many countries in Latin America rely;
—Expansion of the trade opportunities and capabilities that are an essential part of the development strategies of all countries in the hemisphere; and
—Improved arrangements for the development, acquisition, and utilization of higher technology to speed the modernization of the hemisphere.

Let me address each of these issues in turn.

Commodities

Most of our members depend heavily on the production and export of primary commodities for essential earnings. Yet production and export of these resources are vulnerable to the cycles of scarcity and glut, underinvestment and overcapacity, that disrupt economic conditions in both the developing and the industrial world.

At the U.N. Conference on Trade and Development (UNCTAD) last month, we joined in the common commitment to search for concrete, practical solutions in the interests of both producers and consumers.

Despite reservations about some aspects of the final resolution at Nairobi, the United States believes that the final commodities resolution of the conference represented a major advance in the dialogue between North and South; we will participate in the major preparatory conferences on individual commodities and in the preparatory conference on financing.

One key element, however, is missing from the final catalogue of Nairobi's proposals: machinery to spur the flow of new investment for resource production in the developing countries. The United States made a proposal aimed at that problem—an International Resources Bank. A resolution to study the IRB was rejected by a vote that can best be described as accidental. Ninety nations abstained or were absent. Those nations of Latin America that reject such self-defeating tactics can make a special contribution to insure that the progress of all is not defeated by the sterile and outmoded confrontational tactics of a few.

As a contribution to the commitment we undertook at Nairobi to deal comprehensively with commodities problems, the United States proposes that the nations of the hemisphere undertake a three-part program to secure the contribution of commodities to development in this hemisphere.

First, I propose that we establish a regional consultative mechanism on commodities. This mechanism could well be under the aegis of the OAS. It should bring together experts with operational responsibilities and experience. The inter-American commodities mechanism could precede, or at least supplement, those established with a global mandate, where we are prepared to exchange views regularly and in depth on the state of commodities markets of most interest to us—including coffee, grains, meat, and the minerals produced in this hemisphere. Our objective will be to concert our information on production and demand in order to make the best possible use of our investment resources. These consultations will provide us with an early-warning system to identify problems in advance and enable us to take appropriate corrective action nationally, regionally, or through worldwide organizations.

Second, I propose we give particular attention to global solutions for commodities important to one or more countries of the hemisphere. The United States has signed the Coffee and Tin Agreements; it is crucial to the coffee- and tin-producing countries of this hemisphere that those agreements be implemented in a fashion that will most appropriately contribute to their development.

In Nairobi and at other forums the United States proposed that we examine on a global basis other commodities of particular importance to Latin America—bauxite, iron ore, and copper. I suggest that we in the hemisphere have a special role to play in considering how these steps might be taken and in identifying other high-priority subjects for global commodity discussions.

Third, I propose that the consultative group take a new look at the problem of insuring adequate investment in commodities in this hemisphere under circumstances that respect the sovereignty of producers and provide incentive for investment. We should examine all reasonable proposals, especially those which would help to assure effective resource-development financing. If global solutions are not possible, we are willing to consider regional mechanisms.

Trade

Trade has been an engine of growth for all countries; and for many developing countries—above all, those in Latin America—it is an essential vehicle of development. Recognizing the importance of trade to sustained growth, the United States has taken, within our global trade policy, a number of initiatives of particular significance to Latin America. We have reduced trade barriers, especially those affecting processed goods; provided preferential access to our market for many exports of developing countries; worked in the multilateral trade negotiations in Geneva for reduction of barriers, giving priority to tropical products; and recognized in our general trade policy the special needs of developing countries.

Today, at this Assembly, we can begin to consider ways in which our commitment to trade cooperation can contribute to economic progress in our hemisphere. The United States sees three key areas which this organization could usefully address:

—The need to provide opportunities for developing countries to expand and diversify exports of manufactured and semiprocessed goods;
—The need to promote the hemisphere's trade position through the multilateral trade negotiations at Geneva; and
—The need for effective regional and subregional economic integration.

Let me turn to each of these three points.

No single element is more important to Latin America's trade opportunities than the health of the U.S. economy. I can confirm to you today that our economy is in full recovery, with prospects brighter than they have been for years.

The preferences system contained in the U.S. Trade Act has been in effect since January. It gives Latin American countries duty-free entry on more than 1 billion dollars' worth of their exports to the United States. Even more important, it provides vast opportunities for Latin America to diversify into new product areas in its exports to the United States.

In addition to the effort we will undertake to end the exclusion of Ecuador and Venezuela from the benefits of the U.S. Trade Act, President Ford has asked me to state today that:

—He will make every effort to add to the preferences system products that are of direct interest to Latin America.
—The executive branch will bend every effort to ac-

commodate the export interests of Latin America in all matters in which we have statutory discretion. President Ford's recent choice of adjustment assistance rather than import restrictions in response to the petition of the U.S. footwear industry clearly demonstrates the commitment of the U.S. Government to a liberal trade policy and the use of the Trade Act to expand trade in the hemisphere.

—The President will direct the U.S. Department of Commerce to respond positively to requests from your governments for assistance in the development of export promotion programs. The Department of Commerce will make available technical advice on promotion techniques and personnel training to help develop new markets for Latin American exports worldwide.

The United States believes that the multilateral trade negotiations in Geneva warrant the special attention of Latin America. Our view is that the international codes on subsidies and countervailing duties and on safeguards actions now being negotiated should recognize the special conditions facing developing countries. To this end:

—The United States will seek agreement at Geneva that the code on countervailing duties and subsidies now being negotiated should contain special rules to permit developing countries to assist their exports under agreed criteria for an appropriate time linked to specific development objectives.

—The United States next month will propose that the safeguards code under negotiation in Geneva grant special treatment to developing countries that are minor suppliers or new entrants in a developed-country market during the period that safeguards are in effect.

—The United States will send a trade policy team to Latin America shortly to identify ways to promote increased hemisphere trade through the Geneva negotiations; we are prepared to intensify consultations in Geneva and Washington with Latin American delegations to explore both general issues and positions for specific meetings.

Finally, the United States supports the concept and practice of regional and subregional economic integration as a means of magnifying the positive impact of trade on development. Expanded trade, based on the development of industries that will be able to compete successfully within and outside the integration area, will strengthen the growth process of participating countries. We seek means to support the far-reaching integration plans that have been drawn up in the hemisphere—for the Andean Group, the Caribbean Community, the Central American Common Market, and the Latin American Free Trade Area.

We are ready to support responsible efforts to further integration. The administration of U.S. trade laws and the improvement of our preferences system on matters such as rules of origin are two possible incentives to greater Latin American integration. We welcome your views as to a further U.S. role toward enhancing the momentum of economic integration in Latin America.

We are not persuaded, however, that we have fully exploited all the possibilities of how best to provide expanded trade opportunities to Latin America. We know that the issue is complex and that it involves not only expanded access to the markets of the United States but also measures to enhance opportunities for Latin American products in Europe and Japan and throughout Latin America itself.

Some permanent expert forum is necessary. We therefore propose that within the OAS there be established a special inter-American commission for trade cooperation. If the suggestion for a Special Assembly on cooperation for development prospers, we think that Assembly should set guidelines for the functioning of the commission. We see the commission as an opportunity, in major part through the multilateral trade negotiations in Geneva, to bring together those policy-level officials most familiar with the actual trade problems and opportunities for trade creation under a firm mandate to seek innovative means of cooperating to expand exports—expanding, in short, on a regular and long-term basis the catalogue of trade-expansion proposals I have elaborated above.

Technology

Technology is basic to economic development. It is technology that enables us to master the raw gifts of nature and transform them into the products needed for the well-being of our peoples.

But technology is not evenly distributed. There are impediments to its development, to its transfer, and most importantly, to its effective utilization. The United States believes that technology should become a prime subject of hemispheric cooperation. The countries in this region have reached stages of development that enable them to adapt and create modern technologies. Our potential thus matches the urgency of practical needs.

At this point, what are the new directions we should take together? We have three proposals. The United States believes we in the hemisphere should:

—Take immediate advantage of promising global initiatives. To seek maximum benefit from the U.N. Conference on Science and Development set for 1979, we propose that the nations here today undertake preparatory consultations on that subject in the Economic Commission for Latin America, whose meeting has been prescribed as a regional forum within the conference program. We will enlist the experience and resources of leading U.S. technology institutions in this hemispheric preparatory effort.

—Increase public and private contacts on research, development, and the application of technology. To this end, the United States will:

Open a technology exchange service for Latin America to provide information on U.S. laws and regulations relating to technology flows and to sources of public and private technology;

Explore cooperative ventures in which small and medium-sized U.S. firms would provide practical technologies to individual Latin American firms, along with the management expertise needed to select, adapt, and exploit those technologies; and

Expand and strengthen Latin America's access to the National Technical Information Service and other facilities of the technology information network of the U.S. Government, which covers 90 percent of the technical information that flows from the $20 billion worth of research that the U.S. Government sponsors annually.

—Develop new regional and subregional structures of consultation and cooperation on problems of technology. To this end, the United States proposes:

First, that we establish a consultative group under the OAS to address and provide recommendations on information problems that Latin America faces in acquiring technology.

Second, that the OAS, in line with the UNCTAD IV consensus, establish a regional center on technology. The center would facilitate cooperative research and development activities, drawing on both public and private sources. It could stimulate exchanges of qualified technical personnel. And it could begin to attack the problem of incentives to the thousands of technologically trained Latin Americans now living abroad to return to and serve with their own countries. In the view of the United States, such a center should be a cooperative enterprise requiring commitment and contributions in funds, technological resources, and personnel from all of the countries that take part. To get us underway, I propose that we convene a group of experts to examine the need, feasibility, characteristics, and role of an inter-American technology center and report to us before the next OAS General Assembly.

The Importance of Cooperative Development

Economic development is a central concern of all nations today. The community of nations has become, irrevocably, a single global economy. We know that peace and progress will rest fundamentally on our ability to forge patterns of economic cooperation that are fair, productive, and open to all.

We in this hemisphere have a special opportunity and responsibility to advance the recent favorable mood and the practical achievements in cooperation between the developed and developing nations. We start from a firmer foundation today; our prospects for working together are brighter than ever before—more so in this hemisphere than in any other region of the world. We should have reason for confidence in our ability to advance our own people's well-being, while simultaneously contributing to a more prosperous world. It is in this sense that I have sought today to advance our practical progress in important areas.

The United States stands ready to give its sister republics in the hemisphere special attention in the great task of cooperation for development. We shall make a major effort to prepare for the Special Assembly on development. We shall listen to your proposals, work with you in a serious and cooperative spirit of friendship, and commit ourselves to carry on the great heritage of the Americas as we go forward together.

(c) Reform of the OAS: Statement by Secretary of State Kissinger, circulated by the United States delegation and released June 11, 1976.[14]

The Organization of American States is the cornerstone of the inter-American system, the oldest institution of regional cooperation in the world. Its member states have exceptional ties of respect and a common heritage, and a considerable stake in maintaining those ties for the future.

[14]Department of State Press Release 302; text from *Bulletin,* 75: 10-12.

The inter-American system pioneered the principles of nonintervention and collective security among cooperating sovereign states. Because the Americas also have enormous vitality and achievement, we have a major opportunity and obligation to continue to provide an example and impetus to the global search for better ways to mediate the common destiny of mankind.

Many ask, why think of OAS reform? Why, some wonder, does our Secretary General[15] refer to an "identity crisis" in his latest annual report?

The answer lies in the fact that the pace and complexity of the international and domestic changes of the recent past have made the organization as it is presently constituted less effective as an instrument of our respective foreign policies and less significant to the real issues of the new inter-American agenda than our minimum efforts deserve.

This hemisphere is unique; there is no other grouping like it in the world. We have indeed a special relationship. The fundamental purpose of the OAS must be to continue to nurture and strengthen our fundamental, shared values. We must have an organization that reflects our permanent and irrevocable engagement to work together and maintain our continent as a hemisphere of peace, cooperation, and development.

The United States is committed to the OAS. We have pledged to make it a continually more effective instrument for action in pursuit of the common goals of prosperity and human dignity.

It was to that end that the member states agreed three years ago to an effort to reform, restructure, and modernize the OAS.[16] The results of that effort are disappointing. A proposed new draft of the Charter of the OAS has emerged from the Permanent Council. I regret to say that it is one that our government could neither sign nor recommend that our Senate ratify. It includes prescriptive and hortatory statements of general principle which are as poorly defined as they are ominous. No effort is made in the new charter draft to come to grips with the need to modernize or improve the structure of the organization. We believe the real shortcomings of the OAS have yet to be adequately addressed.

We propose a new effort to reform, modernize, and restructure the organization. We think that effort should concentrate not on words, but on three major substantive issues: structure, membership, and finance.

A.   As to structure,

---

[15]Alejandro Orfila (Argentina).
[16]Background in *AFR, 1973:* 407-8.

The United States would like to advance four points as possible guidelines for the future effort, in the interest of modernization of the organization.

1. The purposes of the organization should be stated simply and clearly in the new charter.
Those purposes should be:

—The promotion of cooperation for development;
—The maintenance of the peace and security of our region; and
—The preservation of our common tradition of respect for human dignity and the rights of the individual.

2. The structure of the organization serving these goals should be flexible.
We should write a constitutive document for the organization which will serve us well into the future. That an organization finds it necessary to rewrite its charter every 5 to 10 years does not speak well for that organization's sense of its role or function. We are now in an age of great change. Our efforts in the coming years to achieve the three basic goals of the organization will take place under rapidly changing circumstances. Thus, flexibility and adaptability must be the key consideration guiding the reform effort. We should not hamstring ourselves with a charter brimfull of the details of the day, with procedural minutiae, or with regulatory prescriptions hindering our ability to meet contingencies.

3. The governance of the organization should be in the hands of the Ministers.
Over the years, the proliferation of functions assigned haphazardly to the OAS has produced an overelaborated organization that is ponderous and unresponsive. Instead of closer and more frequent contact between Foreign Ministers in ways that truly reflect our foreign policies as we are attempting to manage them from our respective capitals, we find ourselves insulated from each other by a plethora of councils and committees with conflicting mandates and a cumbersome permanent bureaucracy.
To strengthen communication, we must cut through the existing organizational underbrush and replace it with a structure capable of responding to the authentic foreign policies of our governments as expressed directly by Foreign Ministers and of relating concretely to our institutions and the needs of our peoples. Par-

ticularly, the three-council system has not fulfilled the hopes which led to its adoption in 1967.

The General Assembly, as the central pillar of the inter-American system, might well be convened more frequently, perhaps twice a year, with special additional sessions to consider our common concerns, particularly the great challenges of cooperation for development. As contacts at the ministerial level intensify, the need for an elaborate structure of councils will disappear. Our encounters at the General Assembly will offer sufficient opportunities to set organizational policy.

This is all of the organizational superstructure we really need. A leaner, more responsive organization would be serviced by a smaller expert Secretariat responsive to the guidelines established by the General Assembly and the functional committees the General Assembly may create.

4. We should improve the OAS mechanisms for promoting respect for human rights in the Americas.   .

B.   As to membership,

To insure that the OAS represents all of the peoples in our region, we should open up the organization to the newly in-dependent states and those which may become independent, both on the continent and in the Caribbean. Although these questions of membership require further study, we believe article 8 of the present charter, which automatically excludes certain states, is an anachronism and should be removed.

C.   As to financing,

A serious effort to reform the Organization of American States should include a review of present provisions for its financing.   .

You are all aware of the critical attention the Congress of the United States has focused on the proportion of the organization's cost the United States is now bearing. Obviously, this has been a factor in recent U.S. budget cuts affecting the OAS. We do not claim that the United States is paying too much or more than its fair share of the cost in terms of our relative ability to pay. It is only that it is wrong and damaging for an organization of two dozen—soon to be 25—sovereign states, whose purpose is to advance the interests of each, to be so heavily dependent on the contributions of a single member. It places the organization in a vulnerable position and projects a false image of the OAS.

It is important to find some basis for OAS financing that will, over time, reduce the U.S. share of the assessed costs while insuring that the activities of the OAS in the vital development assistance field are not weakened.

The United States is committed to the Organization of American States. We know that it provides an institutional base which will continue to be vital to our common progress. In these years of great change, the nations of the world have seen fresh proof of an old truth—that the most durable and responsive institutions are those which bear a lighter burden of bureaucratic machinery and whose procedures permit the flexibility required for swift and imaginative action.

We believe our proposals can help bring the drawn-out reform debate to a successful conclusion over the course of the next year. And we believe this is the kind of organization we can and must have if we in the Americas are to fulfill our promise and our responsibility to advance international cooperation in an era of interdependence.

7. EAST ASIAN TREMORS

(24) *"America and Asia": Address by Secretary of State Kissinger at a luncheon sponsored by the Downtown Rotary Club and the Seattle Chamber of Commerce, Seattle, July 22, 1976.* [1]

A little more than two weeks ago this nation celebrated its 200th birthday. In the process of that celebration, Americans learned that despite the agony, the turmoil, and the constitutional crisis of the last decade, we are still proud to be Americans and still proud of what America means to the world. We felt once again that our country is free and vibrant with life and change. We saw that tolerance and hope and dedication are far more a part of the American national character today than hatred, division, and despair.

To the generation that came to maturity in the late sixties or early seventies, these truths may have been apparent for the first time. For my generation, it was, rather, a reminder of basic verities about America which had been in danger of being obscured by the turmoil of a decade. But for all of us, of whatever generation, it was an uplifting experience.

Certainly the events of one celebration, however inspiring, cannot by themselves solve the long-term problems that our nation will face in its third century. But they illuminate the road before us as we enter our electoral campaign. They tell us that it is time to move away from the counsels of timidity, fear, and resentment which have done so much to corrupt our public dialogue.

Ours is not a nation bent on domination, as we were told four years ago. Ours is not a nation in retreat, as we have been told too often this year. Ours is a nation which understands that America cannot be at peace if the world is at war, that America cannot be prosperous if the world is mired in poverty, that America cannot be

[1] Department of State Press Release 351, July 22; text from *Bulletin*, 75: 217-26.

true to its heritage unless it stands with those who strive for freedom and human dignity. In short, we know that our lives, liberty, and pursuit of happiness depend on the world in which we live and that America's leadership is crucial to shaping what kind of world that will be.

We face today, as we have for several years, international conditions quite unlike those known by earlier generations of Americans. We have designed a foreign policy capable of mastering those new challenges, a foreign policy for the last quarter of the 20th century, based on four propositions:

—First, American strength is essential to the peace of the world and to the success of our diplomacy. We should not bemuse ourselves with false choices between defense or domestic needs, between security or social justice. Unless we pursue all these objectives we are likely to achieve none of them. Security cannot be the sole goal of our policy, but no other achievements can endure without it.

—Second, our alliances with the great democracies of North America, Western Europe, and Asia are the bedrock and the top priority of our foreign policy.

—Third, in an age of thermonuclear weapons and strategic balance, we have a moral as well as a political obligation to strive mightily toward the overriding goal of peace. We are ready to use our strength to resist blackmail or pressure; we must also be prepared to negotiate longstanding disputes, foster habits of moderation, and develop more constructive ties with potential adversaries. The American people and the people of the world ask for a peace more secure than a balance of terror constantly being contested.

—Fourth, security and peace are the foundations for addressing the positive aspirations of peoples. Prosperity, human rights, protecting the environment, economic development, scientific and technical advance, and cultural exchange have become major concerns of international diplomacy. In these spheres, the destinies of nations are interdependent and a world of order and progress requires new forms of cooperation among all nations, rich and poor, industrialized and developing.

We want our children to live in a world of greater peace and justice. We want them to have the opportunity to apply their own genius, in their own time, to the betterment of mankind. To enable them to do so we, in our time, must help shape an international order that welcomes the participation of all nations and responds to the deepest concerns of all peoples.

We have come a long way already. We are at peace for the first time in more than 15 years. Our collaboration with the great industrial democracies is steadily expanding into new fields, while its fundamental basis is stronger than it has been in years. We have made progress toward peace in the Middle East, and partly because of our unique role there, the elements for major new advances exist. In Asia, we have—as I will discuss in greater detail—solidified our ties with both our friends and our potential adversaries. Here in the Western Hemisphere we are building a new relationship based on equality and mutual respect. We have inaugurated a hopeful new policy in Africa. And with respect to the Soviet Union, we have combined a determination to resist expansion with a readiness to build relations on a more stable and lasting basis—we are, and will be, conciliatory but vigilant.

The people of the Pacific Northwest hardly need to be told of the strength or role of America. Yours is a region but recently carved from a wilderness by men and women of courage and vision. Here the pioneer spirit that is so much a part of our history lives on, and from here America looks out across the Pacific toward the nations—new and old—of Asia.

And it is America's relations with Asia that I would like to discuss with you today.

The Asian Dimension

No region in the world is more dynamic, more diverse, or more complex than Asia:

—In the past generation, Americans have fought three major wars in Asia. We have learned the hard way that our own safety and well-being depend upon peace in the Pacific and that peace cannot be maintained unless we play an active part.

—Our prosperity is inextricably linked to the economy of the Pacific Basin. Last year our trade with Asian nations exceeded our trade with Europe. Asian raw materials fuel our factories; Asian manufactures serve our consumers; Asian markets offer outlets for our exports and investment opportunities for our business community.

—Our ties with Asia have a unique human dimension. For generations Americans have supplied an impulse for change in Asian societies; Asian culture and ideas in turn have touched our own intellectual, artistic, and social life deeply.

American foreign policy has known both great accomplishment and bitter disappointment in Asia. After World War II we sought

above all to contain Communist expansion. We essentially succeeded. We forged a close alliance with a democratic Japan. We
and our allies assisted South Korea in defeating aggression. We
provided for the orderly transition of the Philippines to full independence. We strengthened the ties with Australia and New
Zealand that had been forged as allies in two wars. We spurred the
development of the Pacific Basin into a zone of remarkable
economic vitality and growth.

By the late 1960's, however, old policies confronted new
realities: American disenchantment with a war we would not win
and could not end, acute rivalry between the major Communist
powers, and above all, Japan's burgeoning power and prosperity.
It was becoming apparent that our commitments in Asia too often
dictated our interests, that we sometimes acted as though our stake
in our allies' security was greater than their own, that estrangement
with China no longer served either nation's interests or the cause of
global stability, that our economic dealings not infrequently
resembled patron-client relationships.

Throughout the first half of this decade, therefore, we have been
fashioning a new policy for Asia. We have been bringing our
commitments into balance with our interests. We have helped our
allies and friends augment their own strength, while we have
gradually reduced our own military presence in Asia by 130,000
men in addition to the 550,000 troops we withdrew from Viet-Nam.
We have strengthened our relations with Japan, begun a new
relationship with the People's Republic of China, and searched for
political solutions to Asian regional conflicts. We have encouraged
Asian nations in their self-reliance and in their efforts at regional
cooperation. We have welcomed Asian nations in new multilateral
efforts to improve the global economic system.

While a great deal has been accomplished, Asia remains a region
of potential turbulence. The collapse of Viet-Nam last year
produced concern about a more general American retreat from
Asia. Happily, such fears have subsided, largely because American
policy has buttressed the inherent strength and resilience of the
nations of Asia.

But there are no grounds for complacency. Soviet activity in Asia
is growing. North and South Korea remain locked in bitter confrontation. Hanoi represents a new center of power, and its attitude
toward its neighbors remains ambiguous and potentially
threatening. Most developing nations remain afflicted by social and
political tensions. And the scramble for oil and ocean resources
raises the specter of possible future territorial disputes.

Much will depend on our actions and on the confidence of Asian
nations in our steadiness. Indeed, all the strands of our global
policy meet in Asia:

—Peace in Asia is crucial for global peace.

—The need to resolve conflicts and to ease tensions is nowhere more acute than in Asia.

—The effort to shape new patterns of international cooperation holds great promise in Asia, where the developing nations are among the world's most dynamic and self-reliant.

Let me now discuss each of these challenges in turn.

Asian Security

First, the problem of security in Asia.

All the world's major powers—the United States, Japan, China, the Soviet Union, Western Europe—have significant interests in Asia. All would be directly affected by conflict there. Yet the security of none of these powers is determined exclusively—and in some cases not even primarily—by events in Asia. Therefore no nation should believe that it can enhance its security by deflecting conflicts from one continent to another. If the European balance is upset, our security and the security of Asian countries will be affected. If the Asian balance is jeopardized, serious repercussions will be felt in Europe. Neither in Europe nor in Asia can we permit others to dictate our destiny or the destiny of those whose independence is of concern to us.

Security policy for Asia must therefore be formed in global terms. Yet its requirements are uniquely complex. In Europe two alliance systems face each other directly across a clear line drawn down the center of the continent. The principal danger is external attack by organized military forces. The strengths and weaknesses of both sides are relatively calculable.

In Asia the balance is more multiple and fluid. The focal point is not solely between East and West—it includes the contention between the two major Communist powers, and the threats are highly diverse.

In some areas, such as Korea, the principal danger lies in armed attack across an established frontier. In others, such as Southeast Asia, the more immediate threats involve insurgency. Governments confront the difficult challenge of nation-building. Most are burdened by complex social problems arising from religious, racial, and cultural differences. Virtually all must contend with armed dissidents who are frequently ready to accept outside assistance.

As President Ford stated in Honolulu last December, the linchpin of our Asian security effort must be a strong and balanced U.S. military posture in the Pacific. Only if we are perceived to be clearly capable of supporting friends can we discourage aggression against them. Only by showing that we understand the necessities of the regional balance of power can we encourage free countries to see to their self-defense.

To the extent that the nations of Asia achieve a margin of security, the political forces that stand for democracy and human liberty are encouraged. By the same token, unilateral withdrawals from Asia diminish our security as well as our influence even over the domestic evolution of friendly countries.

It goes without saying that an American commitment is vital only if it is perceived to be as much in the interest of our allies as of ourselves. No nation should conduct its policy under the illusion that it is doing the United States a favor by permitting us to contribute to its defense. Those who seek to adjust their defense relationships with us will find us prepared to accommodate their desires in a spirit of reciprocity.

At the same time let there be no doubt about this Administration's firmness with regard to our treaty commitments. Allies needing our support will find us constant; adversaries testing our resolution will find us steadfast.

It is not possible to enumerate all our security interests in Asia in one speech. Let me therefore discuss three areas of special importance or complexity: Japan, Korea, and Southeast Asia.

Japan and Korea

No relationship is more important to the United States than our alliance with Japan. Mutual security remains fundamental to our collaboration; but in a new era we have extended our partnership to a broad range of common interests: easing tensions in Asia, solving regional and global problems, and combining our vast economic strength to spur stable and noninflationary world economic growth.

In the early 1970's, Japan and the United States passed through an inevitable period of adjustment from dependence and American predominance to equality and mutual responsibility. There were frictions over textiles and monetary policies and over the timing of our essentially parallel China policies. But these difficulties have been overcome; they proved to be the growing pains of a more mature and equal relationship.

Today our relations with Japan are better than they have ever been. There are no significant bilateral disputes. We have developed a clearer common perception of our security requirements, which will be further enhanced by the recently formed Joint Committee on Defense Cooperation. We have injected greater balance and reciprocity into our economic relations. We have learned to identify and deal with potential difficulties before they become politically explosive. We have consulted with greater frequency and frankness and in greater depth than in any previous period. Both nations are displaying sensitivity to the intangibles of our relationship and have built a wide base of public support for closer cooperation.

Our relationship with Japan plays a central role in furthering stability and progress in Asia and the world. Our security relationship is crucial for the global balance of power. Japan is our largest overseas trading partner. Each of us seeks to improve relations with Moscow and Peking, to ease tensions in Korea, to encourage a stable political evolution in Southeast Asia. Each of us cooperates in the development of effective international efforts to promote stable economic growth, strengthen bonds among the industrial democracies, and shape more positive ties between the industrial and developing countries.

Japan and the United States share a common dedication to the principles of democracy. And so close consultation on key regional and global issues is at the heart of our respective policies. The United States will make every effort to strengthen these bonds.

Americans fought and died to preserve South Korea's independence. Our experience and our sacrifice define our stake in the preservation of this hard-won stability; treaty obligations of mutual defense define our legal obligations. Our support and assistance will be available where it has been promised.

In fulfilling our commitments we will look to South Korea to assume the primary responsibility for its own defense, especially in manpower. And we will continue to remind the South Korean Government that responsiveness to the popular will and social justice are essential if subversion and external challenge are to be resisted. But we shall not forget that our alliance with South Korea is designed to meet an external threat which affects our own security and that of Japan as well.

Southeast Asia

Difficult as the situation still remains in Korea, it is the friendly nations of Southeast Asia that, in the wake of Indochina, are facing the greatest adjustment to new conditions.

Nations which once looked almost exclusively to us for their security have been forced by events into greater self-reliance and broader cooperation with one another. The members of the Association of Southeast Asian Nations (ASEAN)—the Philippines, Indonesia, Thailand, Malaysia, and Singapore—are determined to preserve their independence by hastening the pace of regional consolidation. All face serious problems that are endemic to the process of development; all seek to sustain and expand their relations with us; all hope that we will retain an active interest in their destiny.

President Ford, in his speech in Honolulu last December and in his visits to the Philippines and Indonesia, affirmed our continuing interest in the well-being and safety of Southeast Asia. We shall encourage the efforts of the ASEAN countries to bolster their independence; we welcome Southeast Asian regional cooperation.

Clearly our effort cannot substitute for, but only supplement, regional efforts. But we are prepared to continue to provide military assistance, though with greater emphasis on cash and credit sales. We will, as well, maintain our military presence in the western Pacific, especially our mobile naval and air power. We are in the process of negotiating a new base agreement with the Philippines. We will promote new patterns of economic cooperation. And we will cooperate with ASEAN countries, consistent with their own initiatives and concepts.

Easing Tensions To Strengthen Peace

Second, let me turn to the problem of easing tensions.

In the thermonuclear age, we have no more important obligation than to push back the shadow of nuclear confrontation. If crises occur, they must not result from any lapse of vision on our part. Accommodation without strength or principle leads to appeasement; but in the thermonuclear age, reliance on power—not coupled with a spirit of conciliation—can spell catastrophe for all of mankind.

Thus the United States, in concert with its allies, seeks to reach beyond security toward better relations—based on strict reciprocity and principle—with former or potential adversaries.

The People's Republic of China

No nation is more important to this process than the People's Republic of China. Together we have turned a dramatic new page, following a generation of mutual suspicion and hostility.

There have long been deep sentimental attachments between the American and Chinese peoples which have provided an important bond between our two nations even in the most difficult times. But it was mutual necessity that impelled us both to launch a fresh beginning in 1969. Our shared concern that the world remain free from domination by military force or blackmail—"hegemony," as we have described it in our various communiques—provided the strategic foundation for a new relationship. This mutual interest continues and is the basis for durable and growing ties.

Both sides derive benefits from constructive relations—improved prospects for maintaining a global equilibrium, reduced dangers of conflict in Asia, mutually beneficial trade and cultural exchanges, and expanded possibilities for cooperative or parallel action on specific global issues.

We have made significant progress in improving relations with China over the past several years. We have established liaison offices in each other's capitals. We have increased trade and promoted exchanges. Frequent and wide-ranging talks with Chinese leaders—including visits by two American Presidents and many congressional delegations—have deepened our mutual understanding. On some international issues there is substantial compatibility in our perspective, and where our interests diverge, we are diminishing the risks of miscalculation.

It is important to recognize that China's perception of the United States as a strong and resolute force in international events is an important factor in shaping our relations. We will keep Chinese views in mind in framing our approach to important international questions. But equally, if so subtle and complex a relationship is to prosper, the People's Republic of China must take our concerns and problems into account as well. We must deal with each other on the basis of equality and mutual benefit—and a continuing recognition that our evolving relationship is important for global stability and progress.

The new relationship between the United States and the People's Republic of China is now an enduring and important feature of the international scene. We are determined to work to improve it further. While difficult issues remain, we intend to continue to move toward the normalization of our relationship in keeping with the principles of the Shanghai communique.

The Korean Peninsula

On the Korean Peninsula, too, we are prepared to make serious efforts to ease tensions.

In recent years North Korea and its friends have mounted a major diplomatic campaign—especially in the so-called nonaligned forums and the United Nations—to alter the institutional arrangements of the armistice agreement which ended hostilities in Korea 23 years ago and helps to keep the peace today.

They insist upon unconditional dissolution of the U.N. Command, which, together with North Korea and China, is a signatory to the armistice agreement. They have gone so far as to claim that if the command is dissolved, the armistice agreement itself would cease to exist.

At the same time, North Korea demands the unilateral withdrawal of American forces from Korea. They propose that the issues of peace and security on the peninsula be discussed in bilateral talks with the United States alone, excluding the Republic of Korea, which represents two-thirds of the Korean population.

North Korea's proposals are designed not to promote peace but to isolate our ally, to precipitate unilateral American withdrawal, and to dissolve the existing legal arrangements into amorphous general negotiations.

The United States will never accept such proposals. No nation that truly believes in peace should support them; no country interested in genuine nonalignment should lend itself to so one-sided an approach.

We do not maintain that present arrangements in the Korean Peninsula must remain forever frozen. On the contrary, the United States favors new negotiations to promote security and to ease tensions there. We are prepared to discuss a new legal basis for the existing armistice. We are also ready to replace the armistice with more permanent arrangements.

But this Administration cannot, and will not, negotiate behind the back of our South Korean ally over issues which affect its very existence. Nor will the United States agree to terminate the U.N. Command without new arrangements which preserve the integrity of the armistice agreement—the only existing legal arrangement which commits the parties concerned to keep the peace—or which establish a new permanent legal basis. And the United States will not undermine stability and hopes for negotiation by withdrawing its forces unilaterally.

The U.S. position with respect to Korea is clear:

—First, we urge a resumption of serious discussions between North and South Korea.

—Second, if North Korea's allies are prepared to improve their relations with South Korea, then and only then, will we be prepared to take similar steps toward North Korea.

—Third, we continue to support proposals that the United Nations open its doors to full membership for South and North Korea without prejudice to their eventual reunification.

—Finally, we are prepared to negotiate a new basis for the armistice or to replace it with more permanent arrangements in any form acceptable to all the parties.

In this spirit, we proposed last September a conference including North and South Korea, the United States, and the People's Republic of China—the parties most immediately concerned—to discuss ways of preserving the armistice agreement and of reducing tensions in Korea. We noted that in such a meeting we would be ready to explore possibilities for a larger conference to negotiate more fundamental and durable arrangements.

Today, President Ford has asked me to call again for such a conference.

Specifically, the U.S. Government is prepared to meet with South Korea, North Korea, and the People's Republic of China during the coming session of the U.N. General Assembly. We propose New York, but we are ready to consider some other mutually agreeable place. We are willing to begin immediate discussions on issues of procedure and site. Such a conference could provide a new legal structure for the armistice if the parties agree. It could replace it with more permanent arrangements. It could ease tensions throughout Asia.

We urge other parties to respond affirmatively. Any nation genuinely interested in peace on the peninsula should be prepared to sit down and talk with the other parties on ways to improve the existing situation.

Indochina

Southeast Asia, as much as Northeast Asia, requires our careful attention. Indochina, an arena of war for generations, has yet to find a positive and peaceful role. Viet-Nam has been unified by force, producing a new and strong power in the region, and Communist regimes have taken over in Laos and Cambodia. The relations of the Indochinese states with one another are unsettled and unclear, as are Hanoi's longer term ambitions. Our policy is designed to bolster the independence of our friends, encourage the restraint of former foes, and help chart a more constructive pattern of relations within the region.

We have said on many occasions that for us the Indochina war is over. We are prepared to look to the future; we are willing to discuss outstanding issues; we stand ready to reciprocate gestures of good will. We have conveyed our willingness to open discussions with the Vietnamese authorities, with both sides free to raise any issues they wish.

For us the Americans missing in action remain the principal concern. Let there be no mistake: There can be no progress toward improved relations with Hanoi without a wholly satisfactory accounting for these men. Nor will we yield to cynical efforts to use the anguish of American families to extort economic aid.

If the Vietnamese meet our concerns for the missing in action and exhibit restraint toward their neighbors, they will find us ready to reciprocate and to join in the search for ways to turn a new page in our relations.

New Patterns of Cooperation

Third, the problem of international cooperation.

Beyond security, beyond the imperative of easing tensions, lies a new dimension of international relations: to help shape a global structure that responds to the aspirations of peoples and assures our children a world of prosperity, justice, and hope. We must meet this challenge because:

—There cannot be enduring tranquillity in a world scarred by injustice, resentment, and deprivation.
—There cannot be assured prosperity in a world of economic warfare and failed development.
—There cannot be an enduring international order in a world in which millions are estranged from decisions and practices which determine their national well-being.

As the world's strongest economy, the United States has accepted responsibility for leadership in this agenda of interdependence. In many international forums over several years, we have put forth comprehensive initiatives to produce concrete progress on the most compelling issues of our interdependent world: food, energy, commodities, trade, technology, the environment, and the uses of mankind's last frontiers—the oceans and outer space.

Nowhere are the possibilities and benefits of economic cooperation greater than in Asia. The record of developing countries in Asia is extraordinary. Most grew at annual rates of 6-7 percent a year for the entire decade prior to the 1973 oil embargo; Asian economies have flourished even in the face of global recession.

The secret of their economic performance is no mystery. Rich in natural resources, fertile land, and industrious people, East Asia—with few exceptions—is not burdened with massive overpopulation. Most countries in the area possess talented entrepreneurs and skilled administrators; most governments have rejected the confining straitjacket of statist economic practices; virtually all provide a hospitable climate for foreign investment.

If growth and vitality are a common feature, the developing nations of Asia otherwise reflect a considerable diversity. Some, despite abundant resources, remain among the world's poorest in terms of per capita income. Others are rapidly approaching the ranks of the advanced nations. Some export principally raw materials and foodstuffs, while others have joined Japan as industrial workshops for the world.

Although the impulse for regional integration is apparent, the Asian-Pacific market economy is open and accessible to the world. The United States, Japan, and others supply capital, markets, management skills, and technology. We in turn obtain from the developing countries of Asia reliable supplies of important raw materials, fair treatment of our investments, and expanding markets for our trade.

Economic development does not automatically insure tranquillity between states or within them. But it can enhance the ability of governments to obtain public support, strengthen the legitimacy of institutions, and consolidate national independence. These factors are of particular importance for Asian nations beset—as they often are—by the problems of nation-building and domestic dissidence.

Cooperative relations between the industrialized nations and the developing nations of Asia are both inescapable and vital.

The United States and the developing nations of Asia share important interests:

—We should both value an international economic system which insures steady, noninflationary growth and expands the opportunities of our citizens.

—We must both recognize that if economic development is to strengthen stability, it must enhance national self-reliance. The developing nations of Asia need concessional foreign assistance far less than support for their efforts to participate in the international economy on a more equal footing.

—We must deal with each other on the basis of parity and dignity, seeking responsible progress on issues, to liberalize trade, to expand investment opportunities, and to transfer technology.

—We must cooperate to improve the effectiveness of established institutions such as the Asian Development Bank. We must be ready to create new instruments, for example, the proposed International Resources Bank, to address the new range of issues in the field of commodities.

The nations bordering on the Pacific have an opportunity to usher in an era of cooperation which will enhance the prosperity of their peoples and give an impetus to the well-being of mankind.

America's Strength and Spirit

Three times in the past 35 years many thousands of American lives have been lost in wars on the Asian Continent. For us, World War II began and ended there. A blatant Communist attempt to conquer Korea was defeated there. And the tragedy of Viet-Nam, with its 50,000 dead and the wave of bitterness it created here at home, was played out there.

It must not happen again. It will not happen again if America's policy, profiting from the past, takes charge of its future, making aggression too costly to attempt and peace too tempting to reject.

Our greatest challenge abroad is to continue to act on the knowledge that neither peace nor prosperity—for ourselves or anyone else on our small planet—is possible without the wisdom and the continuing active involvement of the United States. Our size, our economy, our strength, and our principles leave us no alternative but to be concerned with events in the world around us.

Our greatest foreign policy need at home is steadiness, cohesion, and a realization that in shaping foreign policy we are engaged in an enterprise beyond party and not bounded by our electoral cycles. Today, Americans—of whatever party or political conviction—can have confidence that their country, as always, has the substance and the strength to do its duty:

—We have the military and economic power, together with our allies, to maintain the balance of stability upon which global peace must rest.

—We have the wisdom to see that an enduring peace requires dedicated and realistic measures to reduce tension.

—We have the vision to fashion new relationships among all nations in an interdependent world, to work toward a true and lasting world community.

The bond between America's spirit and America's achievement, between her courage and her responsibility, was expressed by a great poet here in Seattle.

As Theodore Roethke said:

I feel my fate in what I cannot fear.
I learn by going where I have to go.

That is the American way. We are a people accustomed to, and capable of, forging our own destiny. We are ready, as Americans always have been ready, to face the future without fear. We shall go where we have to go. We shall do what we have to do.

(25) The ANZUS Connection: Communiqué of the 25th Meeting of the ANZUS Council, Canberra, August 3-4, 1976.[2]

The ANZUS Council held its twenty-fifth meeting in Canberra on 3 and 4 August 1976. Attending were the Honourable B.E. Talboys, Deputy Prime Minister and Minister for Foreign Affairs of New Zealand; the Honourable Charles W. Robinson, Deputy Secretary of State of the United States; and the Honourable An-

[2]Department of State Press Release 365, Aug. 5; text from *Bulletin*, 75: 289-91.

drew Peacock, Minister for Foreign Affairs, and the Honourable D. J. Killen, Minister for Defence, of Australia.

The Council members exchanged views on a wide range of issues. They noted that consultation and cooperation had characterized the work of the Council during the quarter century of change since the ANZUS Treaty was concluded; and expressed their confidence that the close relationship among the three countries, based as it is on a shared community of interests, would endure and be further developed.

The Council members expressed support for the fabric of negotiations which had been developed between the United States and the Soviet Union and noted that the attempt to stabilize the balance between the most powerful nations is an important precondition of an enduring structure of peace.

The Council reviewed the situation in Korea and North East Asia and emphasized its interest in the maintenance of peace and stability in the area. In particular, the Council noted the close relations between each of the ANZUS partners and Japan and welcomed the signature of the basic Treaty of Friendship and Cooperation between Australia and Japan concluded on 16 June 1976.

The Council noted the potentially important contribution of the People's Republic of China in the affairs of the Asian/Pacific region and, generally, in world affairs.

The Council reviewed recent developments in the South Pacific and noted the general increase in external awareness of the region. The Council reaffirmed the importance which it attached to the security of the region and in this connection emphasized the contribution to be made by steady and sustained economic progress. The Council noted the intention of Australia and New Zealand to give greater priority to the South Pacific in their development assistance programs. It also welcomed the growing sense of regionalism among the countries of the South Pacific, as exemplified by the South Pacific Forum and the South Pacific Commission. It underlined the need for these and other institutions for regional cooperation active in the South Pacific to respond effectively and promptly in key development areas. The Council welcomed the Joint Declaration on the Law of the Sea issued by the South Pacific Forum at its recent meeting in Nauru, in which the member governments recognized the value of a coordinated approach.

The Council noted the importance of peaceful and cooperative relations among all the states of South East Asia. It welcomed the progress of the individual South East Asian nations in developing their countries and in strengthening their self-reliance. It also welcomed the continued progress of the Association of South East

Asian Nations (ASEAN) in developing broad-based regional cooperation. It expressed support for efforts among all countries of the region.

The Council noted with concern the increased Soviet military presence and capacity in the Indian Ocean. In this connection, it welcomed the actions taken by the Government of the United States to establish a modest facility at Diego Garcia to support United States forces in the region. The Council believed that a broad balance of military capability, coupled with a general forbearance from provocative actions, was an essential prerequisite for stability and for the restraint that was needed in the Indian Ocean.

The Council reviewed the efforts being made towards achieving satisfactory measures of arms limitation, which it considered were essential to the establishment of a peaceful and stable world order. In particular, the Council reaffirmed the dangers posed by the proliferation of nuclear explosives and weapons capabilities and the need to move against these dangers. It endorsed the various measures being taken to strengthen the nuclear non-proliferation regime including strengthened safeguards of and controls on the export of nuclear equipment, materials and technology. Concern was voiced that there remained important exceptions in all regions of the world to the general trend towards universal acceptance of the Nuclear Non-Proliferation Treaty and the hope was expressed that countries not yet party to it would accede.

The Council further supported the continuing negotiations between the United States and Soviet Union over strategic arms limitation as important to the maintenance of a stable world balance and hoped that these would lead to further curbs of the increase of strategic nuclear weapon levels. It also welcomed the signature of the agreement between the United States and the Soviet Union governing the conduct of and limiting the yield of peaceful nuclear explosions to supplement the Threshold Test Ban Treaty of 1974. The Ministers reaffirmed the hope that it would be possible at an early date to transform the present agreements limiting nuclear testing into a comprehensive test ban treaty.

The Council members expressed satisfaction at the degree of cooperation which existed between their respective armed forces. In this connection the members welcomed the decision by the Australian and New Zealand Governments to permit the resumption of visits to their ports by United States nuclear-powered warships. It was agreed that this was a natural part of the cooperation under the ANZUS Treaty. The Council also welcomed the Australian Government's decisions to accelerate the construction of a naval facility at Cockburn Sound in Western Australia.

In conclusion, the ANZUS partners confirmed the great importance that each attached to the alliance and stressed their desire to strengthen further their cooperation to meet changing circumstances. They emphasized that the Asian/Pacific region should continue to develop in peace and prosperity and agreed to maintain close consultation on matters of common concern.

(26) *"Southeast Asia: U.S. Interests and Policies": Statement by Arthur W. Hummel, Jr., Assistant Secretary of State for East Asian and Pacific Affairs, before the Special Subcommittee on Investigations of the Committee on International Relations, House of Representatives, September 28, 1976.*[3]

It is a pleasure to be with you today to discuss the situation in Southeast Asia and U.S. policy toward the area.

I think it would be most useful first to look at the broad trends that seem to be at work in Southeast Asia, then to move on to consider our interests and policies in the region, and after that to mention regional cooperation, before talking briefly about individual countries in the area, including those of Indochina.

First, I would like to review the broad trends evident in the foreign and domestic policies of the non-Communist states of Southeast Asia since the fall of Saigon.

These nations were greatly concerned that events in Indochina might cause the United States to withdraw from the region and that Hanoi might move strongly to undermine its neighbors. These initial fears have largely subsided as we have reassured these nations of our continued interest and commitment to the area. Our determination to continue to play a role in the area was symbolized by visits of President Ford to Indonesia and the Philippines last December and Vice President Rockefeller to Malaysia, Singapore, Australia, and New Zealand this spring.

At the same time, the nations of the area have modified their policies, often in directions already underway before 1975, to adapt themselves to the changed international environment.

As you know, these states had been moving toward improving relations with the People's Republic of China for some time, particularly since the visit of President Nixon to China in 1972. Malaysia established relations with China in 1974, and Thailand and the Philippines followed suit in 1975 after Saigon's fall. Singapore and Indonesia have not yet done so, but Prime Minister Lee of Singapore was well received on a recent trip to the People's Republic of China. These countries now all have diplomatic

[3]Text from *Bulletin*, 75: 469-75.

relations with the Soviet Union and also with the Socialist Republic of Vietnam.

At the same time as they balanced their close ties with the West by new openings to Communist countries, these nations have also modestly increased the attention they pay to their own security, recognizing that they must take the primary responsibility for their own defense, especially internal security.

Indochina developments have also encouraged these nations to emphasize their own self-reliance and independence in other ways. One aspect of this more self-reliant mood has been some increase in emphasis on ties with the Third World and the nonaligned movement and, more specifically, support for the New International Economic Order, the detailed program of Third World demands on the industrialized countries.

On the economic side, these countries are now emerging from the world recession in reasonably good shape. In some cases their recovery has lagged somewhat behind that of the industrialized countries, because improvement in their export picture necessarily depends on the prior improvement of the economies of the industrialized nations, including Japan.

Since the fall of Saigon we have not seen a major increase in the level of Communist insurgent activity in Southeast Asia. At present none of the insurgencies represents a threat to the existence of the central government of the country in which it operates, and these nations have a reasonably good chance of coping successfully with the various rebel movements even though it will be very difficult to suppress them entirely.

In concluding this discussion of the broader aspects of Southeast Asia at present, I would note there seems to be a rough equilibrium among the interests of the major powers at the present time. There have been continuing good ties with the United States, and in some ways our relationships are becoming broader and deeper. The People's Republic of China and the U.S.S.R. are competing for influence in the area but are doing so through such traditional means as diplomatic relations, trade, and aid, rather than through any significantly increased support to insurgent movements or Communist parties. Japan is an important economic influence and, like the United States, it would like to see stability in the area preserved. Thus at present no major power is aggressively seeking a predominant role in the region.

Policies Derived From U.S. Interests

Now, let me turn to U.S. interests in the region.

—First, we support the sovereignty and independence of the

countries in the region and would like to see the maintenance of an equilibrium which will preserve their independence.

—Second, American strength is basic to any stable balance of power in the Pacific and contributes to peace and progress. Our use of bases in the Philippines is important to us as an element of stability not only in Southeast Asia but in East Asia as a whole, as well as being related to the global strategic picture. Similarly we have an interest in maintaining free use of the sea and air lanes through this area connecting the western Pacific with the Indian Ocean.

—Third, we desire friendly political relationships with the non-Communist nations which will facilitate the resolution of bilateral problems and gain their support in multilateral forums.

—Fourth, we have mutually beneficial economic relationships with the non-Communist nations in this area. Indonesia supplies a growing percentage of our oil requirements and is even more important to our ally Japan. The area is also an important source of tin, copper, rubber, and other materials. It is also an important market and a region offering significant investment opportunities.

—Fifth, we have an interest in reducing tensions and working for a stable peace.

Our policies in the region derive quite naturally from the interests which I have just stated. As President Ford stated last December 7 in his review of our Asian policy: ". . . American strength is basic to any stable balance of power in the Pacific. . . . without security, there can be neither peace nor progress."

Part of our military presence in the Asia-Pacific region is the Philippine bases. We also undertake various diplomatic efforts to preserve our naval and aerial mobility by maintaining access to the various straits in the region. One aspect of this effort is carried out in the law of the sea negotiations designed to preserve our mobility on a worldwide basis.

We maintain a friendly political dialogue with the nations in this area. By discussing our policies with these countries on a regular basis, we help maintain the existing friendly relationships and also improve the prospects of gaining their support on broader international questions, especially in the United Nations.

In the economic area we seek to keep open the channels of trade and investment. In recent years there have been some efforts by these nations to increase the benefits they derive from foreign investment, which in some cases have had the effect of reducing their attractiveness to investors. This trend was compounded by the economic recession. Despite this, the leaders of these nations generally realize the vital role that private foreign investment can play in their economic development plans, and they understand that to attract foreign investment they have to permit foreign investors a fair return. It can also be said that American companies now understand more than before that their relations with these countries must involve mutual benefit.

These countries are also of interest to us in the global negotiations on economic issues which are usually referred to as the North-South dialogue. While they are firm supporters of changes in international economic relationships which they believe are necessary to increase the rate of development in their countries, these are moderate nations which have indicated their willingness to cooperate with the United States as we show them we are on a constructive path. Thus our economic relations with these nations also have an important multilateral element.

Our policies include continuing modest economic and military assistance to those nations that need it. In the economic sphere, obviously Singapore, with a per capita income well over $2,000, does not need our assistance; and we are phasing out economic aid to Thailand, which has a basically healthy and growing economy. On the other hand we are continuing aid to Indonesia, which has great natural resources but also great problems of population pressures and organization for development as well as a very low per capita gross national product. With regard to security assistance it should be noted that arms acquisitions in the area are modest and there is no arms race taking place. A significant proportion of our economic assistance is supplied through multilateral institutions, notably the Asian Development Bank, which utilizes its resources effectively and deserves more vigorous U.S. support.

Regional Cooperation

In 1967, Indonesia, Malaysia, Singapore, Thailand, and the Philippines formed a group for regional cooperation called the Association of Southeast Asian Nations (ASEAN).

The gradual development of this organization was given a new stimulus by Indochina developments, and the member countries held their first summit meeting last February in Bali, which gave further impetus to ASEAN's general cohesiveness and area of cooperation.[4] At this meeting the leaders signed a number of interlocking documents including a Declaration of Concord, a Treaty of Amity and Cooperation, and an agreement on the establishment of an ASEAN Secretariat. It also was agreed that the organization should move ahead with joint industrial projects, preferential trade

[4]Meeting of Feb. 23-24; details in *Keesing's:* 27676.

arrangements, and organization of a permanent secretariat with an Indonesian as the first ASEAN Secretary General. This organization has a consultative arrangement in the economic field with the European Economic Community and similar arrangements with several other countries.

We welcome the efforts of the Southeast Asian nations to strengthen their own independence by increasing their efforts at regional cooperation. We would be prepared to enter into economic consultation with the ASEAN nations but are leaving the initiative to them.

One of the question marks in Southeast Asia during the past year or more has been how relations would develop between the new Communist states of Indochina and the ASEAN grouping. In July and August the Vietnamese Vice Minister of Foreign Affairs made official visits to all ASEAN capitals except Bangkok, and the Thai Foreign Minister[5] went to Hanoi and Vientiane in August. During these visits the Vietnamese emphasized their desire for peaceful and friendly relations and seemed to accept the assurances of host government officials that ASEAN is a truly neutral group. Diplomatic relations were established with the Philippines July 12 and with Thailand August 6, completing the establishment of such relations between the Socialist Republic of Vietnam and all ASEAN members.

However, at the recent nonaligned meeting in Colombo, Vietnam and Laos opposed a Malaysian position advocating a zone of peace, freedom, and neutrality in Southeast Asia, which has been a standard ASEAN concept since 1971. Vietnam and Laos proposed language welcoming the Communist victories and demanding an end to U.S. alliances and bases. Furthermore, they sharply attacked ASEAN and ASEAN members for allegedly supporting U.S. "aggression" in the Indochina conflict. This incident suggests that the future of relations between Indochina and the ASEAN nations remains to be defined and that Hanoi can be expected to continue its efforts to reduce or eliminate the U.S. presence in Southeast Asia and to influence the foreign and domestic politics of its neighbors.

Indochinese Nations

Vietnam maintains ties with both the Soviet Union and the People's Republic of China, but their relations appear to be closer with Moscow than with Peking. The Vietnamese are very influential in Laos, and the two countries work together closely. Cambodia, on the other hand, has gone its own way. The Cambodian population has become strictly regimented, as the new

[5]Nguyen Duy Trinh and Upadit Pachariyangkun respectively.

Communist leaders have carried out their ruthless revolution. The Soviet Union is active in Hanoi and Vientiane but has not been allowed to open an Embassy in Phnom Penh, where there are only a handful of embassies and the principal foreign ties are with the People's Republic of China. Cambodia recently established nominal ties with a number of Western countries and with Japan.

During the first year after the fall of Saigon, Hanoi was largely occupied with moving toward the reunification of the country. This was formally accomplished in July of this year, although many problems of establishing firm political control over the South, of administration, and of economic unification and development remain to be overcome. In contrast to Cambodia, the new Socialist Republic of Vietnam has been conducting an active foreign policy and is seeking to enter a large number of international organizations, often claiming the seat previously held by the Republic of Vietnam.

We look to the future and not to the past in our relations with Vietnam. We are prepared to meet to discuss all issues and have indicated this willingness to the Vietnamese. So far no discussions have taken place. For us the most serious single obstacle in proceeding toward normalization of relations is the refusal of Hanoi to give us a full accounting for those missing in action (MIA's). Hanoi for its part continues to demand economic assistance under the Paris agreement. We believe that the Paris agreement was so massively violated by Hanoi that we have no obligation to provide assistance, and in any case Congress has prohibited such assistance by law.

On September 13 we indicated our intention to veto Vietnam's application for membership in the United Nations on the grounds that their actions so far on the MIA issue do not reflect willingness to fulfill the humanitarian obligations of the U.N. Charter. Security Council consideration of the Vietnamese application has been deferred.

We have maintained an Embassy in Laos, which has been headed by a Chargé for the past year. There is little substance to our relationship at the present time.

Non-Communist Southeast Asian Nations

I would now like to say a few words about each of the six non-Communist nations of Southeast Asia.

Burma

Burma attempts to maintain a policy of strict neutrality in its external relations, and the Burmese Government has chosen economic policies which offer little scope for American trade or investment. Thus our relationships with Burma are not so diverse as those with other Southeast Asian countries. The Burmese Government has an active antinarcotics effort, which is also, of course, a matter the United States is very concerned with, and we have provided the Burmese Government with some equipment for this purpose, including helicopters.

Thailand

The nation most affected by Indochina developments was Thailand, which has common borders with Laos and Cambodia. The fall of Saigon brought immediate concern based on the potential of a revolutionary and well-armed Hanoi and fear of a complete U.S. withdrawal from the region. One reaction was to proceed rapidly to establish diplomatic relations with the People's Republic of China, which was perceived as a counterweight to Hanoi, with the latter's close association with the Soviet Union.

Thailand also sought to initiate talks with the new Communist governments in order to establish friendly relations and discuss common problems. At present Thailand has diplomatic relations with all three Indochina states, although Embassies have not yet been established in Hanoi and Phnom Penh. Negotiations between Thailand and its neighbors have made some progress on such issues as trade, refugees, and the avoidance of border incidents. At the same time, Vietnam apparently has not increased its support for Thai insurgents, although the type of Hanoi support rendered in the past continues. Communist insurgencies continue to exist in the North and Northeast, and Moslem separatists are troublesome along the southern border.

We were already drawing down our troop presence in Thailand in the spring of 1975, and further reductions were contemplated for the future. We were prepared to retain some residual facilities; but it was not possible to come to agreement on status-of-forces issues, and our last troops departed July 20 of this year except for a small group involved with military assistance.

In 1973 Thailand's military government was overthrown. The most recent elections were held last April, bringing to power Prime Minister Seni Pramoj, who presides over a coalition of four parties in the National Assembly. We wish this democratic experiment well and hope it will succeed.

Thailand has a rather healthy economy which has permitted us to begin phasing out economic aid. We are still assisting the Thai with a modest military assistance program which is focusing increasingly on credit sales and less on grant aid.

Malaysia

This relatively prosperous and well-run nation, with a per capita gross national product of about $700, has a strategic location on the Malacca Strait and is a source of rubber and tin. Its moderate government shares our goal of a peaceful and stable Southeast Asia.

The new Prime Minister[6] is making a strong effort to continue strengthening the Malaysian economy and to deal equitably with the divisions between the Malay majority and the large Chinese minority. He must also deal with a longstanding Communist insurgency which, although not of a magnitude seriously to threaten the nation's security, has increased its activities noticeably since the fall of Saigon.

Singapore

Singapore is unique in the area for its small size (225 square miles) and its large per capita income ($2,200). Prime Minister Lee Kuan Yew is publicly skeptical of Hanoi and supportive of a continued American military presence in the region in order to balance other major powers.

We, of course, desire friendly relations with this strategically situated and energetic country. We are also interested in Singapore's position as the leading Southeast Asian commercial center, in its large oil-refining industry, and in encouraging our already large ($900 million) investment stake in this country.

Indonesia

Indonesia's 135 million people give it half the population of the region, and it stretches over an archipelago 3,000 miles long that dominates the sea routes between the western Pacific and the Indian Ocean. In spite of its great natural resources, especially oil, Indonesia remains among the poorest countries of the region in terms of per capita income. The government which took over in 1966 following an abortive Communist-supported coup in late 1965, although predominantly military, has consciously kept military spending to a minimum so as to devote the maximum of resources to economic development.

The changed situation in Southeast Asia following the fall of Saigon has indicated to the Indonesian leadership the need to

---

[6]Datuk Hussein bin Onn was sworn in Jan. 15, 1976 following the death of Tun Abdul Razak bin Hussein on the previous day.

upgrade modestly the efficiency and mobility of Indonesian forces to insure the defense of this farflung island nation. We are helping through a small program of grant aid and military sales credits.

Indonesia supplies about 8 percent of U.S. oil imports, and a larger percentage of Japan's. Indonesia has been a stable supplier; it did not participate in the 1973 Arab embargo. Increasing supplies of oil and liquefied natural gas are expected to be available in the future. We already have about $2 billion in private investment in the country, mostly in the energy field.

There is no question that Indonesia, its resources, and its friendly, moderate government are of political, strategic, and economic importance to us. Although Indonesia is careful to maintain its nonaligned position, our relations have been close. President Suharto visited Washington in July 1975, President Ford visited Jakarta last December, and consultations between Secretary Kissinger and Foreign Minister Malik, took place in Washington last June.[7]

Philippines

We have close historical ties with this nation, consecrated by our joint struggle in World War II. However, we are careful not to take the Philippines for granted, and we deal with that country as a fully independent nation which has the duty of safeguarding its own interests.

After the Communist takeover in Indochina, President Marcos called for a "reassessment" of the American military presence in his country. When President Ford visited the Philippines last December, he and President Marcos agreed that the military bases used by the United States in the Philippines remain important in maintaining an effective U.S. presence in the western Pacific in support of the mutual objectives of the defense of both countries, security of the Pacific region, and world peace. The two Presidents also agreed that negotiations to revise existing arrangements would be conducted "in the clear recognition of Philippine sovereignty." These negotiations began in April and are still continuing. We are confident that they will eventually prove successful, but complex issues remain to be resolved.

Our economic interests are significant—over $2 billion in investments and a flourishing trade relationship. Last year we began discussion with the Philippine Government of a new agreement regarding economic and commercial relations, which would replace the expired Laurel-Langley Agreement.

The Philippine Government's desire to make clear its in-

[7]Text of U.S.-Indonesian press statement, June 29, in *Bulletin*, 75: 145.

dependence, and also to further its economic interests, has led it to take an active part in the Group of 77, which coordinates economic policy among the less developed countries on certain issues. The Philippines has also balanced its close Western ties by establishing relations with the People's Republic of China in June 1975 and with the Soviet Union in June 1976. But I am confident we can continue to have close and friendly relations based on mutual respect and mutual interest.

U.S. Support for Southeast Asian Aspirations

In conclusion, I think it is important that we approach the problems of Southeast Asia with the understanding that the future of this area will depend primarily on the internal strength and efforts of the countries themselves. They themselves recognize this and indeed have made great strides over the years in improving their economies and modernizing their societies.

They have also gained experience and confidence in their own abilities. The international context of Sino-Soviet tension and U.S. détente policies with both of the major Communist powers has contributed to the general equilibrium which appears to have been established in the area.

We intend to maintain a strong military presence in the western Pacific. Our presence there is an important element for stability in Southeast Asia as well as for the strategic balance in the western Pacific region as a whole.

Under present conditions the challenges the countries of Southeast Asia face are primarily economic, political, and social in nature, with serious external threats a less likely contingency. In these circumstances we should do what we can to support the aspirations of the peoples of Southeast Asia, based on our common interest in the preservation of their sovereignty and independence.

(27) Incident at Panmunjom, Korea, August 18, 1976: Statement by Assistant Secretary Hummel before the Subcommittees on International Political and Military Affairs and on International Organizations of the Committee on International Relations, House of Representatives, September 1, 1976.[8]

I appreciate the opportunity to appear before these subcommittees and to testify on the August 18 incident at Panmunjom and its aftermath.

[8] Text from *Bulletin*, 75: 386-92.

As members of the subcommittees are fully aware, the Korean Peninsula has been in an armed truce since 1953, with the political problems that caused the Korean hostilities still unresolved and two heavily armed forces facing each other across a four-kilometer-wide demilitarized zone. Over the past 23 years of the armistice the consistent goal of the United States has been to prevent the outbreak of new hostilities and contribute to stability in an area where the interests of four great powers—ourselves, Japan, the U.S.S.R., and the People's Republic of China—all intersect. The security of Korea remains vital to peace in Northeast Asia and is closely linked to the security of Japan, a major ally.

Throughout the long period since the end of the Korean war, North Korea has not given up its goal of reunifying the peninsula on its own terms and views the use of force as one measure of achieving this goal. The North has remained intransigent on all the political issues which divide North and South and has posed a constant military threat. The demilitarized zone has thus been an area of major tension since the armistice agreement, with frequent military clashes which, over the years, have taken 49 American and over 1,000 Korean lives.

The United States, which was of course a major participant in the Korean hostilities, is firmly committed to the security of Korea through its important interests in the peninsula and the Mutual Defense Treaty of 1954 with the Republic of Korea. We continue to maintain forces in the Republic of Korea under this treaty to preserve the peace by deterring renewed aggression from the North.

You will recall that after the fall of Viet-Nam there was a period of time during which there was the possibility that the North Koreans might miscalculate our commitment to peace and stability on the Korean Peninsula and our commitment under the Mutual Defense Treaty of 1954 to the security of the Republic of Korea. This commitment was strongly restated by the President, Secretary Kissinger, and other high-level U.S. Government officials. We believe that this commitment, together with the state of readiness of the United States and the Republic of Korea forces, continues to deter any renewed major aggression by North Korea. We believe that neither the People's Republic of China nor the U.S.S.R. wishes to see North Korea make any move that would destabilize the situation on the Korean Peninsula.

At present there is on the peninsula a rough military balance between the forces of South Korea and the United States on the one hand and those of the North on the other. It has been a major goal of the North Koreans to destroy this balance by securing the withdrawal of U.S. forces from the Republic of Korea. North Korea has repeatedly called for such a withdrawal, trying to win international support for this goal by depicting the U.S. presence as a source of tension in the area.

Intensified Campaign Against the U.S.

Immediately prior to the August 18 incident, P'yongyang embarked upon a major intensification of this longstanding campaign. On August 5 they issued a strongly worded government statement attacking the United States and the Republic of Korea. The statement was accompanied by a supporting memorandum purporting to document the statement's allegations that the United States was about to make war on North Korea.

The statement said the United States had completed war preparations and was entering into a "phase of directly triggering war" from a "phase of directly preparing for war." It demanded that the United States withdraw all its military equipment from the Republic of Korea, abandon what it called a "two Koreas" policy, disband the U.N. Command, withdraw all foreign troops under the U.N. flag, and replace the armistice agreement with a peace agreement.

From earlier North Korean statements we know that the phrase "foreign troops under the U.N. flag" also means all U.S. forces in Korea under bilateral U.S.-Republic of Korea arrangements. The statement claimed that the reunification of Korea could then be achieved by the Korean people through a national congress. There was no recognition of the Government of the Republic of Korea. The statement also appealed to other nations to condemn alleged U.S. attempts to trigger a war in Korea.

This statement was also the culmination of anti-U.S. efforts among the nonaligned nations which were about to hold their nonaligned summit meeting in Colombo. At the nonaligned meeting, which took place in mid-August, we believe the North Koreans hoped for endorsement of very harsh anti-U.S. and anti-Republic of Korea language which they could subsequently utilize in lobbying for a resolution submitted by their supporters at the U.N. General Assembly.

As you may recall, the U.N. General Assembly last year approved two contradictory resolutions on Korea—one submitted by supporters of North Korea and one submitted by ourselves and other supporters of the Republic of Korea. We believe that at this year's U.N. General Assembly the North Koreans hope to score a diplomatic victory which would contribute to isolation of the Republic of Korea and its supporters by securing approval of its own propagandistic resolution and the defeat of the friendly resolution. I shall return to the U.N. General Assembly situation later.

The Joint Security Area

The August 18 incident came in the context of this heightened propaganda campaign. Before I describe this incident, let me make some comments on the Joint Security Area. This is a small, roughly circular area of the demilitarized zone some 800 yards in diameter in which the Military Armistice Commission meetings are held. It is a neutral area, maintained and patrolled by both sides. Each side is permitted to have 35 armed guards in the area at any given time. Larger groups of unarmed work personnel are permitted. Specific maintenance and groundskeeping tasks, such as the pruning of trees, have been carried out by each side without prior consultation with the other.

The North Koreans have frequently caused incidents in the Joint Security Area, harassing U.N. Command personnel, engaging in verbal threats and on occasion in physical assaults. In 1975 a U.N. Command officer was knocked to the ground and severely injured with a kick to the throat.

The August 18 Incident

With respect to the tree involved in the August 18 incident, it was found that the foliage on this tree was obstructing the line of sight between two U.N. Command guardposts. One of these guardposts was near the North Korean side of the military demarcation line near the Bridge of No Return. It was felt that if this guardpost were not fully visible from the other, the chances for its being subject to harassment or attack by North Korean personnel were increased. It was decided, therefore, to remove the obstruction.

On August 5 a work party went to the tree, which is located on the U.N. Command side of the military demarcation line, for the purpose of felling it. North Korean guards told them to leave the tree alone, although they did not lodge a formal protest over the matter. Subsequently, it was determined that guardpost visibility could be improved by trimming the tree rather than cutting it down.

On Wednesday, August 18, 1976, at approximately 10:30 local time, a U.N. Command work crew of five Korean laborers accompanied by three U.N. Command officers (two U.S. and one Republic of Korea) and a seven-man security force arrived in the Joint Security Area at Panmunjom. Their purpose was routine and nonthreatening; namely, to prune the tree.

Shortly after the party began its work, two North Korean Army officers and about nine enlisted men arrived in a truck. They inquired about the work in progress. After being told that the tree was to be trimmed, not cut down, one North Korean Army officer stated that this was "good." Work continued for 10-15 minutes during which some North Korean Army personnel tried to direct the U.N. Command workers on how to prune the tree. At about 10:50, some 20 minutes after work began, one North Korean Army officer told the U.N. Command officer to halt work. After a short discussion, the North Korean Army officer threatened the U.N. Command personnel. The U.N. Command officer told his men to keep working. The North Korean Army officer then ordered the Korean laborers to stop working. The U.N. Command officer indicated that work would continue, at which point the North Korean Army officer sent a guard across the bridge, apparently to summon reinforcements. Several minutes thereafter the number of North Korean Army guards on the scene had increased to approximately 30.

At this point, one North Korean Army officer put his watch, which he had wrapped in a handkerchief, into his pocket. Another rolled up his sleeves. One officer yelled "kill" and then struck Captain [Arthur G.] Bonifas, knocking him to the ground. Five other North Korean Army guards jumped on Bonifas and continued to beat him. Other North Korean Army guards attacked the other U.N. Command guards, beating them with ax handles and clubs. U.N. Command witnesses reported that North Korean Army guards picked up the axes used by the tree pruners. Captain Bonifas was beaten with the blunt heads of the axes while he was on the ground. All U.N. Command personnel received repeated beatings even though they tried to break contact and leave the area.

Casualties from this incident—which lasted less than five minutes—were two U.S. Army officers killed, four U.S. Army enlisted personnel wounded, and four enlisted Korean augmentees to the U.S. Army wounded.

We believe that the August 18 incident may have been an attempt by North Korea to underscore the theme of its propaganda campaign: that tensions were high in Korea as a result of the U.S. presence. The number of North Korean personnel involved in the incident, the ferocity of their attack, and their readiness to spill blood in the Joint Security Area, an area in which there had been no deaths during the 23 years of the armistice, all indicate that this was meant to be a major provocation. As a result, we believe that the North Koreans may have been seeking an incident which could be used extensively in their propaganda efforts to depict us as seeking war on the peninsula.

We also believe the incident was intended to test whether in the midst of a national election campaign we would firmly maintain our security commitment to the Republic of Korea. It threatened our goal of maintaining peace and stability on the peninsula.

U.S. Response and North Korean Reaction

We believe our response was sobering to the North Koreans. Our reactions were measured and calculated. Our military moves—the deployment of the F-4's from Okinawa, and the F-111's from Idaho to Korea, the dispatching of the Midway task force to the area, the raising of our defense alert status to DefCon 3, and daily B-52 flights from Guam to Korea—were swift and coordinated. They demonstrated to P'yongyang that we were willing and able to move decisively to counter any threat in this area.

In the context of this military response, the tree-cutting operation itself [August 21] made it clear to P'yongyang that we would not tolerate interference with our rights in the Joint Security Area under the armistice agreement and that we were determined to protect U.N. Command personnel in the area in order to maintain the viability of the armistice agreement.

Let me make a few further points with regard to the tree cutting. We are aware of critical comments to the effect that we took massive and expensive military moves simply to cut down a tree. This is not the case. The military augmentations were precautionary deployments designed to make it clear to P'yongyang that we were determined to meet any larger military threat which they might pose. The tree-cutting operation, as I have indicated, was meant to uphold the rights of the U.N. Command in the Joint Security Area and to help insure the future safety of the U.N. Command personnel.

P'yongyang was clearly taken aback by both our military response and the tree-cutting operation. It put its own forces on a so-called "war footing" and took certain defensive measures, but gave no indication that it was contemplating any military reaction to our moves. In the Joint Security Area, North Korean guards watched the tree-cutting operation without attempting to interfere.

A few hours later, North Korean President Kim Il-song took the unprecedented step of conveying a message through the Military Armistice Commission to the Commander in Chief of the U.N. Command, General [Richard] Stilwell, expressing regret that the August 18 incident had occurred and urging that further incidents in the area be avoided. Kim's conciliatory message has been widely viewed as an implicit acceptance of responsibility for the incident, particularly when contrasted with P'yongyang's usual rhetoric.

At subsequent Military Armistice Commission meetings, the North Koreans have been uncharacteristically subdued and businesslike and have reiterated Kim Il-song's expression of regret. They have also suggested a proposal for new security arrangements at Panmunjom to avoid incidents in the Joint Security Area.

The U.N. Command is now considering the proposal—which it put forth itself in 1970 and which the North has now picked up. One important element of this plan will be the removal of four guardposts which the North Koreans now have on the U.N. Command side of the military demarcation line. The U.N. Command has no guardposts on the North Korean side of the line.

We think the North Koreans have been chastened by the incident. It is not certain that the lesson will stick; however, it is evident that P'yongyang now has a clearer picture of our readiness to maintain the security of the Korean Peninsula and to uphold the armistice agreement. We believe the North Koreans may also fear that our response to any future incidents of the kind that occurred on August 18 could well be costly to them.

World Reaction

World reaction to the August 18 incident and its aftermath has of course varied according to the predisposition of the countries involved, but there has been widespread support for our position on the incident and for our subsequent moves.

Most significantly, both the Soviet and Chinese media were very restrained in their handling of the issue. They gave it only limited attention and confined themselves to quotes from the North Korean press, avoiding any editorial comment of their own. This clearly indicated a lack of enthusiasm for the North Korean provocation and a reluctance to be sharply critical of our response.

It is not clear to what extent the August 18 incident affected the language adopted on Korea at the nonaligned conference, which was in its final sessions at the time the incident occurred. The North Koreans were successful in ramming through the hard-line language they wanted, largely because the drafting committee was composed of P'yongyang's supporters. However, many countries recognized the one-sided nature of this language, and for the first time on any question in the nonaligned meetings, specific reservations to the language of the political declaration and resolution on Korea were entered. We do not yet have a full list of countries which did so, since reservations are still being submitted, but the total may reach 20 to 25. It well may be that the brutal murders in the Joint Security Area were seen as evidence of North Korean belligerence and not aggressiveness on the part of the United States.

Forthcoming U.N. General Assembly

It is also unclear at this point how the incident and its aftermath will affect the U.N. General Assembly's vote on the two resolutions which have been submitted on the Korean question.

We had made it clear this year that we, the Republic of Korea, and many other countries hoped to avoid another sterile Korean debate although we were prepared to meet the challenge if one was mounted by North Korea and its supporters.

North Korean supporters, however, submitted a harsh and inflexible resolution even before the nonaligned had finished their debate on a Korean position, thus demonstrating that North Korea was more interested in maintaining its inflexible position than in obtaining a true nonaligned consensus on Korea.

This resolution, which draws heavily on the August 5 government statement, calls for the withdrawal of all foreign forces under the U.N. flag. North Korea made clear last year that this also means the withdrawal of all U.S. forces in Korea under the bilateral arrangements with the Republic of Korea. There are now only about 300 personnel in Korea under the U.N. flag, of whom about 250 are Americans. It "demands" the withdrawal of "new" types of military equipment from the Republic of Korea and an end to alleged acts aggravating tensions and increasing the danger of war.

The resolution also calls for the unconditional dissolution of the U.N. Command. North Korea has said that if the Command is dissolved, the armistice agreement, the only legal document binding the parties to keep the peace, would cease to exist.

It also calls for the replacement of the armistice agreement with a peace agreement. The latter means an agreement with the United States and is an attempt to negotiate future security arrangements on the peninsula without the participation of the Government of the Republic of Korea, which represents two-thirds of the peninsula's population.

The resolution further "hopes" for reunification through a "great national congress." The Government of the Republic of Korea is not mentioned; this provision is an attempt to obfuscate North Korea's refusal to accept the necessity of South-North discussions and its failure to respond to repeated offers by the Republic of Korea to resume without preconditions the South-North discussions which both sides agreed to in 1972 and which were broken off by North Korea in 1973.

Through this resolution the North is attempting to isolate our ally the Republic of Korea, precipitate American troop withdrawal, and dissolve existing legal arrangements without substituting suitable arrangements to maintain peace and stability. We will not accept such proposals. We will not negotiate on future security arrangements on the Korean Peninsula without the participation of the Republic of Korea.

To meet this challenge, the United States and 18 other countries introduced on August 20 a noncontentious resolution on Korea which calls for the resumption of the South-North dialogue to achieve by negotiation the resolution of the outstanding problems between them. It calls on both sides to exercise restraint so as to create an atmosphere conducive to peace and dialogue. It also urges that South and North Korea and the other parties directly concerned, ourselves and the People's Republic of China, enter into early negotiations permitting the dissolution of the U.N. Command by adapting the armistice agreement or replacing it with more permanent arrangements to maintain the peace.

This provision refers to a major U.N. General Assembly initiative which we and the Republic of Korea undertook last year. On September 22, 1975, Secretary Kissinger proposed that we and the Republic of Korea meet with the other parties directly concerned, the People's Republic of China and North Korea, to discuss ways of preserving the armistice agreement and of reducing tensions in Korea. We said that in such a meeting we would be ready to explore possibilities for a larger conference to negotiate more fundamental arrangements to keep the peace.

This invitation was not accepted then and was dismissed by North Korea in its statement August 5, 1976, after the Secretary restated the proposal in a speech July 22, 1976.

U.S. Policy on Korea

Our position on Korea is clear:

—We urge the resumption of serious South-North discussions, which both sides agreed to in 1972 and which North Korea has broken off.

—If North Korea's allies are prepared to improve their relations with South Korea, we are prepared to take reciprocal steps toward North Korea.

—We continue to support proposals that the United Nations give full membership to both South and North Korea, without prejudice to eventual reunification.

—We are prepared to negotiate a new basis for the armistice or replace it with more permanent arrangements in any form acceptable to all the parties concerned.

As a result of North Korea's intransigence, we thus again face a tough and time-consuming confrontation in the U.N. General Assembly on Korea which is likely to be both contentious and unproductive. The effect of the August 18 incident on what will follow in the U.N. General Assembly confrontation, as I have said, is difficult to judge. We believe few countries take seriously the charge that the United States is about to make war on North Korea.

The pattern of North Korean propaganda, together with the brutality of the North Korean assault, the measured response from our side, and the subsequent backing down on P'yongyang's part may serve to convince some nonaligned countries that continued support of the North's inflexible position is not productive and may well increase tensions. We also believe many nonaligned countries recognize that there cannot be progress on the Korean question until South and North resume direct discussions and that the North's refusal to talk with the Government of the Republic of Korea is an unrealistic and self-defeating posture. The reservations on the Korea language at the nonaligned meeting that I mentioned earlier are a sign of this view.

We believe that our firm and judicious response to the August 18 incident has shown the North that we are prepared to resist aggression.

We do not view the August 18 incident as having a major effect on decisions regarding U.S. force levels in Korea. As then-Assistant Secretary Habib said before the Subcommittee on Foreign Assistance and Economic Policy of the Senate Foreign Relations Committee April 8:

> . . . the specific level of our forces in Korea is not immutable. It is a function of the North Korean threat, the ability of the Republic of Korea forces to meet that threat, and the prevailing international situation.

Mr. Habib went on to say that we intended to honor commitments and maintain our presence in the area and in this context we had no present plans for significant force reduction in Korea. Our response to the incident of August 18 has demonstrated that we will meet our commitments.

We would hope that the firmness we demonstrated in the aftermath of this incident will eventually cause the North to reassess its inflexible position of seeking to reunify the peninsula on its own terms. Meanwhile we and the Republic of Korea are prepared to seek the easing of tensions and more permanent security arrangements on the peninsula through negotiation rather than confrontation.

(28) "The Foundation of U.S.-Japan Ties: Common Interests and Shared Values": Address by Assistant Secretary Hummel before the Japan-America Society, Washington, October 19, 1976.[9]

⁹Text from *Bulletin,* 75: 582-6.

I am pleased to be your guest this evening. The Japan-America Society has long been a consistent and sensible advocate in this town of the importance of Japan to the United States and the need to maintain in good repair our ties with that country. There have been periods in the last decade when the priority of our relations with Japan has been temporarily obscured—by our concerns elsewhere in Asia or the world or, conversely, by a tendency to impute to the relationship a degree of automaticity, to assume that because Japan and the United States share so many common interests our relations are bound to proceed smoothly.

None of us wants the U.S.-Japan relationship to dominate the headlines, since headlines ordinarily highlight problems rather than accomplishments. Nor do we necessarily believe that the central preoccupation of policymakers in either government should be the bilateral relationship. In fact, for so complex an organism it does run remarkably smoothly. On the other hand, because it is so large, so successful, and so complex the U.S.-Japan relationship should be both a source of great satisfaction and a focus of our continuing intense attention. The Japan-America Society and other similar groups around the country help us in insuring that our Japan connection receives the recognition and the attention it deserves.

One problem which those of us who deal with Japan and speak about Japan constantly face is that the American people, and most particularly groups such as this one, are increasingly knowledgeable and sophisticated observers of U.S.-Japan relations. The broad outlines of our respective policies are known and understood, and in attempting to review them it is difficult to avoid what seem to be cliches. Quite correctly, people tend to challenge cliches. Even people in government.

I would say that our ties with Japan, and our policies toward it, are examined as constantly and as critically as is any other relationship this country maintains. We think we are on the right track. We do not believe that, simply because our approach toward Japan has achieved a certain maturity, sharp new departures are called for. We do not expect our present policies, or those of Japan, to prove immutable in every respect. Policies must reflect circumstances, and circumstances change. But we do think that the essential foundation of the U.S.-Japan relationship, constructed of common interests and shared values, will endure.

In other words, many of those cliches about Japan and the United States are true. At the risk of repeating a few of them I want to sketch briefly how we currently see our relations with Japan, as we near the end of what has been a very eventful year.

I think a useful way to approach a discussion of U.S.-Japan ties is to examine them in three broad categories, separate but interrelated—the economic, security, and political dimensions of our relationship.

Bilateral and Multilateral Economic Spheres

First, the economic. Despite the major challenges both our economies have faced in the last two years in restoring noninflationary growth, our bilateral economic ties have been remarkably trouble-free, in pleasant contrast to the situation of the early 1970's. The bilateral problems of those years—a massive trade imbalance; difficult textile negotiations; the need for Japan to eliminate import restrictions, liberalize foreign investment regulations, and revalue the yen—were largely resolved by 1974 to the satisfaction of both sides.

This was achieved through a process of continuing consultations at all levels and reflected both governments' awareness of the reality and the necessities of interdependence. And as that process went forward, I believe people on both sides of the Pacific came to understand better the importance of sustaining sound economic ties and to recognize that bilateral problems, however difficult they may appear, can indeed be resolved.

Today our bilateral economic ties are healthy and growing again after the 1974-75 recession. There are problems on specific trade issues, ranging from citrus fruits to specialty steel, and negotiations are now underway in two areas where we have significant differences—civil aviation and fisheries. In addition, as always, there is a need to keep an eye on the overall health of our trading relationship. Huge surpluses on one side tend to exacerbate protectionist sentiments on the other. In an economic relationship of this magnitude and complexity, there inevitably will be problems. But recent experience has demonstrated convincingly that those problems need not become contentious issues between our two countries. Where there is a will, there is a way.

As our techniques for resolving bilateral economic problems have become more refined and effective, both governments have been able to focus increasingly on the broader multilateral aspects of the U.S.-Japan economic relationship—e.g., questions of trade expansion, monetary reform, energy, food, and law of the sea—which have a pervasive influence on the prosperity of both countries and the world as a whole. The United States and Japan share a common approach to most of these global issues, and our two governments have cooperated effectively in seeking solutions to them.

For example, we have worked with Japan in the new International Energy Agency to strengthen cooperation among oil-consuming countries and coordinate our positions vis-a-vis the producers on price and supply questions. Our respective approaches toward the myriad North-South economic issues are similar, and we consult closely with Japan in this area. Japan is an increasingly weighty factor in world monetary affairs and has given important support to our initiatives in the IMF for reform of the international monetary system. Prime Minister Miki participated in the economic summits at Rambouillet and San Juan, which sought to improve the overall coordination of the economic policies of the major industrial nations. We consult closely with Japan on law of the sea issues, where major interests of both nations are at stake, i.e., with respect to a deep seabeds regime, continental shelf jurisdiction and the concept of an economic zone, and fisheries regulation. We are actively engaged with Japan in the multilateral trade negotiations (MTN); and in fact many formerly bilateral economic questions—e.g., liberalization of import quotas, standardization of antidumping codes, et cetera—are now treated in the MTN context.

There are of course important differences in the economic circumstances of Japan and the United States, the most obvious being Japan's virtually total dependence on outside sources of supply for its energy and raw materials needs; and these differences compel differing approaches toward certain specific multilateral economic issues. Nevertheless, U.S. and Japanese interests in the multilateral economic sphere are fundamentally alike: we wish to sustain conditions which are conducive to a stable world economic environment, in which the economic needs of our societies—and those of other industrialized and developing nations alike—can be fulfilled. Close cooperation between our two governments is essential if those interests are to be preserved and an equitable world economic order sustained. I have no doubt that such cooperation will continue to be forthcoming from both sides.

Cooperation on Security Issues

Secondly, let me touch upon the security dimension of our relationship. The U.S. alliance with Japan is a keystone of our security policy toward East Asia, an essential factor in the maintenance of the peace and stability of the region, and a crucial element in our worldwide security strategy. For Japan the alliance is a major pillar of the nation's foreign policy, providing a strategic foundation from which it can pursue with confidence its relations with potential adversaries. Both our governments are determined to preserve and strengthen cooperation on defense issues, based on a common recognition of the benefits to both nations of this constructive alliance.

Within the framework of the alliance, Japan's own security role remains limited, focusing on the defense of its home islands. We think this is appropriate and wise. The United States is not urging Japan to undertake a larger role. However, I believe both our governments would agree that while a major quantitative expansion of Japan's security responsibilities is inappropriate, there is room for qualitative improvement—particularly in the areas of antisubmarine warfare and airborne early-warning systems—and the Japanese Government is addressing this issue. There can also be, within established limits, more effective cooperation and coordination between U.S. and Japanese defense elements. One new instrumentality for that purpose has already been created—the Subcommittee for Defense Cooperation—and other approaches are being discussed.

During the past year and more, we have noticed in Japan a new tendency toward a more realistic, and less emotional, consideration of defense issues. Out of this has emerged a broader public awareness and understanding of the security environment in Northeast Asia and Japan's place in it. The essentiality of a Japanese defense role, albeit limited, and of Japan's security relationship with the United States, has become more broadly accepted. We think this is a healthy development: we also believe it is one that must proceed at its own speed. So long as this country continues to demonstrate steadiness in its approach to the security issues of East Asia, and sensitivity toward the particular political and historical characteristics of Japan and its people which shape Japan's approach toward those issues, the U.S.-Japan security relationship will remain strong, as it must.

Political Dimension of the Relationship

Finally, I would like to say a few words about a more intangible aspect of the interrelationship between Japan and the United States, but one which profoundly influences all the others. As one of the world's largest and most dynamic democratic societies, Japan shares with the United States a fundamental goal: that of preserving and strengthening democratic institutions and values in a world increasingly hostile to them. Japan is a strong and lively democracy. Its parliamentary system is firmly established, it has a free and highly irreverent press, and its people and government are second to none in their respect for human rights. These institutions and these values, and the importance both countries place on maintaining them, in themselves constitute a strong bond between us in a world in which authoritarianism of left or right is all too prevalent in other countries.

I think I should mention in this context a problem with which both our governments contended earlier this year and which remains a difficult issue in Japan—the Lockheed affair—because to be seen in proper perspective it must be viewed in relation to the institutions and values which were brought to bear in resolving it.

Both Japan and the United States, their people and their governments, deplore corruption, whether private or public, and recognize the corrosive effects of bribery upon society. In both countries, public opinion, the media, and governments demanded a thorough investigation of the allegations which were raised. The United States proposed, and the Japanese Government agreed, that cooperative efforts to investigate the scandal and punish the guilty should insofar as possible be removed from the political arena and placed in a legal framework. To that end, an agreement was reached between the U.S. Department of Justice and the Japanese Justice Ministry for the exchange of all relevant information, in a manner which would at the same time protect the rights of individuals to the due process of law.

The agreement—which became a model for agreements with other nations touched by this scandal—has worked well. The Japanese Government has expressed its appreciation for the assistance our investigators have provided, and our two governments are pledged to work together in an international effort to devise a code of conduct which will prevent repetitions of this brand of corporate misconduct.

Despite its potential for doing so, the Lockheed affair has not significantly damaged U.S.-Japan relations. By treating the affair as a legal issue and placing it solely within the purview of law enforcement agencies, the bilateral political relationship was successfully insulated.

In a broader sense, the common political values which anchor our relations with Japan also mean that our approaches to major international issues—whether political, economic, or security—stem from a similar world view and tend therefore to be complementary. For example:

—Japan, like the United States, seeks improved relations with both the Soviet Union and China on a basis of equality and reciprocal benefit, while avoiding any involvement in Sino-Soviet differences.

—In Southeast Asia, Japan, like the United States, supports the desires of the non-Communist nations of the region to maintain their independence and identity and to develop their economies, and its economic and political policies toward the area are designed toward this end.

—Toward the Third World, Japan's policies are positive and constructive as, I hasten to add, are ours. It recognizes the legitimate aspirations of the developing countries and is seriously seeking ways to meet them.

—In the United Nations, Japan eschews flamboyant and meaningless rhetoric, while working quietly behind the scenes in support of rational and equitable solutions to the political, economic, and security issues constantly before the world community.

—In the area of science and technology, including questions of nuclear power, Japan has a well-developed sense of the benefits as well as the potential hazards of new applications and brings a reasoned and measured approach to technological issues.

In short, as this audience well knows, Japan's is an increasingly active and influential voice in world affairs. As Japan's role grows, so too does the importance of our bilateral relationship and its potential for constructive action. While perhaps a truism, it is nonetheless correct to say that our two nations can accomplish far more working together than could be achieved through the sum of our separate efforts.

In a speech last year to the National Press Club [at Washington], Prime Minister Miki spoke of the broad mutuality of interests between Japan and the United States and termed Japanese-American amity "a powerful and positive force in the world." The U.S. Government fully shares that view. U.S. ties with Japan are indeed of vital importance to this country and to the peace and progress of mankind. I can report to you that they are in good shape. Our two countries can take pride in what we have achieved together, and we can face with confidence the challenges before us.

8. THE ECONOMIC DIMENSION

(29) Meeting of the Interim Committee of the Board of Governors of the International Monetary Fund (IMF), Kingston, Jamaica, January 7-8, 1976: Press communiqué.[1]

1. The Interim Committee of the Board of Governors of the International Monetary Fund held its fifth meeting in Kingston, Jamaica on January 7-8, 1976 under the chairmanship of Mr. Willy de Clercq, Minister of Finance of Belgium, who was selected by the Committee to succeed Mr. John Turner of Canada as Chairman. Mr. H. Johannes Witteveen, Managing Director of the Fund, participated in the meeting. The following observers attended during the Committee's discussions: Mr. Henri Konan Bédié, Chairman, Bank-Fund Development Committee, Mr. G. D. Arsenis representing the Secretary-General, UNCTAD, Mr. Wilhelm Haferkamp, Vice-President, EC Commission, Mr. Mahjoob A. Hassanain, Chief, Economics Department, OPEC, Mr. René Larre, General Manager, BIS, Mr. Emile van Lennep, Secretary-General, OECD, Mr. F. Leutwiler, President, National Bank of Switzerland, Mr. Olivier Long, Director General, GATT, and Mr. Robert S. McNamara, President, IBRD.

2. The Committee endorsed the recommendations contained in the report of the Executive Directors on the Sixth General Review of Quotas and the proposed resolution on increases in the quotas of individual members to be submitted to the Board of Governors for its approval. In this connection, the Committee reaffirmed its view that the Fund's holdings of each currency should be usable in the Fund's operations and transactions in accordance with its policies. Appropriate provisions for this purpose will be included in the draft amendments of the Fund's Articles. To give effect to the Committee's view in the period before the amendments become effective, it was agreed that, within six months after the date of the

[1] Text from *Bulletin*, 74: 197-9.

adoption of this resolution, each member shall make arrangements satisfactory to the Fund for the use of the member's currency in the operations and transactions of the Fund in accordance with its policies, provided that the Executive Directors may extend the period within which such arrangements shall be made.

3. The Committee considered the question of the implementation of the agreement reached at its fourth meeting regarding the disposition of a part of the Fund's holdings of gold. It was agreed that action should be taken to start without delay the simultaneous implementation of the arrangements referred to in paragraph 6 of the press communiqué issued by the Committee on August 31, 1975.[2] The sales of gold by the Fund should be made in public auctions according to an appropriate timetable over a four-year period. It is understood that the Bank for International Settlements would be able to bid in these auctions.

4. In its discussion of the world economic situation and outlook, the Committee noted that recovery from the severe international recession of 1974–75 was now under way in much of the industrial world. Nevertheless, current rates of both unemployment and inflation were still unacceptably high. The Committee called on the industrial countries, especially those in relatively strong balance of payments positions, to conduct their policies so as to ensure a satisfactory and sustained rate of economic expansion in the period ahead while continuing to combat inflation.

A special source of concern to the Committee was the deterioration in the external position of the primary producing countries, especially the developing ones. The general picture for the developing countries in 1975 was again one of large balance of payments deficits on current account, financed through heavy external borrowing and through the use of reserves already eroded by the inflation in recent years. With large current account deficits still in prospect this year, the Committee felt that the ability of many developing countries to maintain an adequate flow of imports in 1976, and to follow appropriate adjustment policies, would also depend on the availability of adequate credit from the Fund.

5. The Committee welcomed the recent decision of the Executive Directors liberalizing the Compensatory Financing Facility. Under the new decision the Fund will be prepared to authorize drawings up to 75 per cent of a member's quota, as against 50 per cent under the 1966 decision. Maximum drawings in any one year are raised from 25 per cent to 50 per cent of quota. Moreover, the decision enables the Fund to render assistance under the facility at an earlier stage of the development of a shortfall.

6. The Committee noted the report of the Executive Directors on

[2] Text in *Bulletin*, 73: 450-72; brief summary in *AFR, 1975:* 448.

their review of the Fund's policies on the use of its resources, and also on the Trust Fund for the benefit of the low income members. After consideration of the issues involved, the Committee reached the following conclusions:

(a) It was agreed that the necessary steps should be taken to establish the Trust Fund without delay. Its resources would be derived from the profits of the sales of the Fund's gold, which should be augmented by voluntary national contributions. It was agreed that the amount of gold available for sale in accordance with the agreement reached by the Committee at its fourth meeting should be disposed of over a four-year period. The resources of the Trust Fund should be used to provide balance of payments assistance on concessionary terms to members with low per capita incomes. Initially, eligible members would be those with per capita incomes in 1973 not in excess of SDR 300.

(b) It was further agreed, that, until the effective date of the amendment of the Articles, the size of each credit tranche should be increased by 45 per cent, which would mean that total access under the credit tranches would be increased from 100 per cent to 145 per cent of quota, with the possibility of further assistance in exceptional circumstances. The present kinds of conditionality for the tranches would remain unchanged. The Fund will in due course consider again the question of access to the Fund's resources if it becomes evident that the needs of members make it advisable to re-examine this question.

7. The Committee noted the report of the Executive Directors on amendment, welcomed the progress made toward the solution of the outstanding issues, and commended them for the voluminous and successful work that they had done in order to achieve a major revision of the Articles. In particular, it welcomed the agreement that has been reached on provisions concerning the important problem of exchange rates. In this respect, it has endorsed a new Article IV of the Articles of Agreement which establishes a system of exchange arrangements. The new system recognizes an objective of stability and relates it to achievement of greater underlying stability in economic and financial factors. The Committee considered the remaining issues on which its guidance has been requested by the Executive Directors and agreed as follows:

(a) The amended Articles of Agreement should include a provision by which the members of the Fund would undertake to collaborate with the Fund and with other members in order to ensure that their policies with respect to reserve assets would be consistent with the objectives of promoting better international surveillance of international liquidity and making the special drawing right the principal reserve asset in the international monetary system.

(b) The amended Articles would contain an enabling provision under which the Fund would be able to sell any part of the gold left after the distribution of 50 million ounces in accordance with the arrangements referred to in paragraph 3 above, and use the profits (1) to augment the general resources of the Fund for immediate use in its ordinary operations and transactions, or (2) to make balance of payments assistance available on special terms to developing members in difficult circumstances. On the occasion of such sales the Fund would have the power to distribute to developing members a portion of the profits on the basis of their quotas or to make a similar distribution by the direct sale of gold to them at the present official price. Any decision on such a distribution should be taken by an 85 per cent majority of the total voting power. These powers of the Fund would be in addition to the power that the Fund would have under another enabling provision to restitute to all members, on the basis of present quotas and at the present official price, any part of the gold left after the disposition of the 50 million ounces referred to above.

(c) Decisions of the Fund on the use of the profits from the sale of its gold in the regular operations and transactions of the Fund should be taken by a 70 per cent majority of the total voting power and on decisions on use of the profits in other operations and transactions by an 85 per cent majority of the total voting power.

(d) The Executive Directors are urged to review, during the final stage of their work on the draft amendments, the majorities for operational decisions that do not reflect com- promises of a political character with a view to considering the reduction, if possible, of the number and size of the special majorities that would be required under the amended Articles for such operational decisions. Such a review should be com- pleted within the coming weeks and should not delay the completion of the comprehensive draft amendment.

(e) The majority required for the adoption of decisions on the method of valuation of the SDR under the amended Articles should be 70 per cent of the total voting power, with the ex- ception of decisions involving a change in the principle of valuation or a fundamental change in the application of the principle in effect, which should be taken by an 85 per cent majority of the total voting power.

(f) The Executive Directors should continue their consideration of the subject of a substitution account without delaying completion of the comprehensive draft amendment.

(g) With respect to the obligation of participants in the Special Drawing Account to reconstitute their holdings of special drawing rights, it was agreed that the amended Articles should authorize the Fund to review the rules for reconstitution at any time and to adopt, modify, or abrogate these rules by a 70 per cent majority of the total voting power.

8. The Committee requested the Executive Directors to complete their work on amendment in the light of the guidance given by the Committee, and expects that the Executive Directors will be able to submit a comprehensive draft amendment for the approval of the Board of Governors, together with a report, within the coming weeks.

(30) "Expanding Cooperation for Global Economic Development": Address by Secretary of State Kissinger before the Fourth Ministerial Meeting of the United Nations Conference on Trade and Development (UNCTAD IV), Nairobi, Kenya, May 6, 1976.[3]

We are assembled here to carry forward one of the most important enterprises in history: the endeavor of independent nations to advance global economic development and so to better the quality of human life on earth. Our goal is nothing less than to shape an enduring structure of international collaboration that offers peace and prosperity, equal opportunity and dignity to all peoples.

Man has always yearned for peace and a just international order. In our time these twin goals have become a realistic possibility. Their attainment will require us to meet challenges whose scale eludes the grasp of individual nations, whose complexity mocks the slogans and solutions of the past, and whose pace outstrips the measured processes of traditional diplomacy.

There is before us all the imperative of world stability—the task of resolving conflicts, reducing tensions, and resisting the encroachment of new imperialisms, new oppressions, and new dangers. For this undertaking the United States, together with other nations, has assumed a heavy responsibility.

Beyond it lie our positive aspirations. The American people are a humane people. We know that stability is not enough; peace must

[3]Department of State Press Release 224; text from *Bulletin*, 74: 657-72.

extend mankind's reach for a better life. In the Declaration of Independence of the United States, the seminal document of our national existence, we have written that "all men are created equal" and entitled to "Life, Liberty, and the pursuit of Happiness." This pursuit has brought me to Nairobi—to advance on behalf of President Ford and the U.S. Government the great cause we all hold in common.

In the long sweep of history, the future of peace and progress may be most decisively determined by our response to the necessities imposed by our economic interdependence. This is the challenge which we have assembled here to address: the urgent need for cooperative solutions to the new global problems of the world economy. These issues dominate the agenda of the evolving relationship between North and South, the industrial and the developing countries.

They are issues of economics—of an effective system of trade, monetary relations, and development assistance, and of insuring that the prosperity of some nations does not come at the expense of others. They are issues of politics—of how nations deal with each other and of how we can construct an international order that promotes peace. They are issues of morality—the recognition that economic might does not make right. And they are issues of justice—the awareness that the well-being of our peoples depends upon an international system fair and open to all.

The modern age and our common morality insistently demand respect for human dignity and the fulfillment of the human personality. But a world in which poverty and misery continue to afflict countless millions would mock these imperatives. The daily preoccupation of men and women would be the harsh necessities of survival; the energies of nations would be consumed in hatred and rivalry. We must build instead a world of cooperation and widening human opportunity reflecting the fundamental interdependence of our destinies.

Today, the accelerating forces of modernization—technological, economic, social, and political—link the peoples of the world as never before. They can intensify conflict, or they can provide us with unprecedented possibilities to advance our common aims. All nations are part of a global economic system. If that system is to flourish it must rest on the firm foundation of security, fairness, and opportunity to all who wish to participate—rich and poor, North and South, consumer and producer. It must embrace the interests of all if it is to be supported by all. President Ford has sent me here, committed to bring about a constructive and cooperative relationship between the developed and the developing countries over the remainder of this century.

This ministerial meeting of UNCTAD is the first of its kind to be held in Africa. This is altogether fitting, for Africa's importance in world affairs is growing. And African countries have an especially high stake in a successful conference leading to concrete progress. No continent has been more vulnerable to worldwide economic instabilities. No continent suffers so cruelly when crops fail for lack of rain. No continent endures a heavier burden when commodity prices fluctuate violently. And no continent has more to gain from the organized cooperation of all nations to promote economic and social progress and to insure a greater role for the developing nations in the world's economic deliberations.

This is a continent of proud traditions and new nations, of rising aspirations and of determination in the face of monumental challenge. Here it can—indeed, it must—be demonstrated that men of all races and colors can live and prosper together in peace with equal rights and mutual respect.

During the past two weeks I have been privileged to be a guest in Africa and to enjoy the extraordinary hospitality of its people and leaders. I have greatly benefited from my discussions with African statesmen, and I have learned much about the concerns and hopes of the peoples of Africa. The nations of this continent can be confident that the United States is prepared to cooperate with them in their great struggles for justice, economic progress, and freedom from external intervention.

Today we are all especially indebted to the Republic of Kenya and its world-renowned leader, President Kenyatta, for making this beautiful city available as the site of this conference. The U.S. delegation has come to Nairobi to achieve, with representatives of other nations, a major step forward in international cooperation.

We begin this conference at a moment of opportunity. The world economy is recovering from a deep recession, my own country perhaps most rapidly. Increasing American demand for products of other countries will make a major contribution to recovery around the world. Many obstacles to sustained economic growth remain; but there are convincing signs that we have surmounted the worst part of the economic crisis and that before us, if we act with wisdom and energy, is the opportunity for a new and prolonged period of prosperity.

This, therefore, may be a decisive moment which offers us a brief, but special, opportunity to reinvigorate and improve the world's international economic system. Now is the time to free the world from disruptive cycles of boom and bust and to enhance the opportunities of the developing countries.

The United States, better than almost any other nation, could survive a period of economic warfare. We can resist confrontation and rhetorical attacks if other nations choose that path. And we can ignore unrealistic proposals and peremptory demands. But the historic opportunity which is at hand would slip away. It is up to us, as the spokesmen of nations meeting in this world forum, to reach beyond the doubts and temptations of the moment toward the permanent international interests of us all. In so doing, we can take courage from the knowledge that the means exist to achieve a brighter future. It lies within our power to shape a world where all men can live in dignity and aspire to progress.

Let us therefore hold before us as the goal of this conference, and of the dialogue between developed and developing nations, the motto of the Republic of Kenya: *"Harambee*—work together for the good of all."

Let us begin by building on the positive accomplishments of the seventh special session of the U.N. General Assembly last September. At that meeting the industrial and developing nations, in an encouraging demonstration of consensus, put aside ideological confrontation, declared their common purpose of moving forward cooperatively, and adopted an agreed agenda for action.

On behalf of President Ford, I call upon this conference to accelerate the efforts and continue the cooperative spirit which began then. I will introduce new proposals on all the priority concerns of this conference, to reflect what we have heard of your ideas and your aspirations in the Manila Declaration and in other forums, including the Conference on International Economic Cooperation in Paris.

These proposals represent the contributions of all relevant agencies of the U.S. Government, under the direction of the President. I have worked especially closely with my colleague Treasury Secretary Simon in shaping the program we are presenting.

The strong bipartisan support which our approach enjoys results from weeks of close consultations between the executive and both Houses of our Congress. It is demonstrated by the presence here of two distinguished Senators representing our two political parties.[4] Other Senators and members of the House of Representatives will follow as your work proceeds.

The United States pledges its dedication and willingness to cooperate over the decades ahead. We do so with an open mind. We want to hear your ideas and proposals. We are here to exchange views and to forge a fresh consensus.

The State of Our Efforts

Let me first review what our nations together achieved since last September.

[4] Jacob K. Javits (Republican) and Abraham A. Ribicoff (Democrat).

We agreed at the seventh special session to take measures to help insure basic economic security against cycles that devastate export earnings and undermine development. In January, the International Monetary Fund (IMF) expanded its compensatory financing facility, as we had proposed, to make available several billion dollars to stabilize export earnings.

In September, we pledged to accelerate economic growth by improving developing countries' access to capital and new technology. To these ends, the United States, other industrial countries, and several oil-producing countries have begun to marshal increased capital, technological, and human resources to promote development. Negotiations have been completed to increase World Bank capital by $8 billion; we will contribute our fair share to a $6 billion increase in the resources of the Inter-American Development Bank; we will contribute to an expansion of the African Development Fund; we are actively participating in discussions on replenishment of the Asian Development Fund and Bank.

At the special session, the world community dedicated itself to improving trade and investment in key commodities. International solutions have already been achieved on several key commodity issues, including the successful negotiation of coffee and tin agreements. Progress is also being made in expanding the world's supply of its most vital commodity—food.

And finally, at the special session, the world community made a commitment to meet the special needs of the poorest countries, which have suffered the most from recent economic dislocations. We have made significant progress by providing financial and technical assistance to increase food production and by introducing new measures to help relieve crushing balance-of-payments problems of the poorest nations.

These achievements are only the beginning of the process. We are, this year, in the midst of what may well be the most extensive series of international negotiations on trade, finance, commodities, and development in history—involving more nations, addressing more issues, and affecting more people than ever before. This conference has a major role to play. In particular we can advance our work in four key areas:

First, we must make renewed efforts on commodity issues, including the problems of resource investment and trade. Commodities—energy, food, and other primary products—are the building blocks of growth and prosperity. For many countries, development of resources is the key to industrialization, employment, decent incomes, and healthy diets. All nations need adequate supplies of primary products and fair compensation for their production. Solving the complex of these issues is a critical test of our ability to work together systematically to expand the world's wealth for the benefit of all.

Second, we must design a far-reaching long-term program to accelerate technology transfer. The quantity of capital investment by itself does not assure sustained development. There must be as well continuous improvements in productivity that only new technology and trained local manpower can bring. The subject deserves high priority, and comprehensive efforts will be required.

Third, we must deal with serious balance-of-payments and debt problems which face a number of developing countries. Rising import costs caused in large part by higher oil prices, and reduced export earnings due to recession in industrialized countries, have created unprecedented international payments problems. An improved world economy will automatically ease the problem for many countries. Nevertheless we must continue to seek means of assistance for the particular problems of certain developing countries.

Fourth, we must continue to respond to the special and urgent needs of the poorest countries. Helping these nations will not only demonstrate the capacity of the international economy to serve all countries equitably; it will also reflect our collective sense of responsibility.

Let me now suggest specific new approaches for dealing with each of these four problems.

A Comprehensive Approach to Commodities

Commodity exports are critical for development. The non-oil developing countries rely on primary products for nearly two-thirds of their export earnings. Yet production and export of these resources are vulnerable to the whims of weather, the swings of worldwide demand, and new technology. Cycles of scarcity and glut, of underinvestment and overcapacity, disrupt economic conditions in both the developing and the industrial world.

It has become clear in recent years that a piecemeal approach to these issues will not suffice. The UNCTAD Secretariat has made an important contribution to meeting these problems in its integrated commodities program. While the United States cannot accept all of its elements, there are many parts which we are prepared to consider.

At this conference, the United States proposes its own comprehensive approach to commodity issues. It reflects many of the objectives contained in the integrated program and our desire for constructive action on all aspects of the challenge. It contains the following elements:

—Insuring sufficient financing for resource development and for equitable sharing in the benefits by the host nation;
—Improving the conditions of trade and investment in individual commodities and moderating excessive price fluctuations;
—Stabilizing the overall export earnings of developing countries; and
—Improving access to markets for processed products of developing countries while assuring consumers reliability of supply.

Let me discuss each of these elements in turn.

Adequate Investment

Most of the world's raw material production in fact takes place in the industrial countries. But if development is to take hold, a special effort must be made to expand the production and exports of primary products of developing countries. Such a program must overcome the following problems.

First, we must deal realistically with the political and economic problems which are diverting investments from developing to developed countries. For, paradoxically, resource development is often discouraged by the very countries which are most in need of it. Nationalization and forced change in the terms of concessions in some developing countries have clouded the general climate for resource investment in the developing world. Social and political uncertainties have further complicated investment prospects. As a result, commercially viable projects have been postponed, canceled, or relocated; and capital, management, and technology have been diverted to production of higher cost raw materials in the industrialized world.

Second, in the next decade alone the total requirements for global investment in resources will be massive. Individual projects will require unprecedented sums of capital and complex financial arrangements. The time required between the beginning of a project and its completion is increasing. All these factors compound the political uncertainties and further inhibit rational investment.

Third, there is no one institution that can work comprehensively to facilitate resource development, particularly in energy and minerals, or to promote equitable sharing of its benefits.

If present trends continue, serious misallocations of capital, management, and technology are inevitable. The costs of raw material and agricultural production will escalate. Many potential producers will be unable to attract adequate capital. All countries will pay the price in accelerated inflation and retarded growth—with the poorest countries suffering the most.

To overcome these problems the United States proposes the establishment of an International Resources Bank (IRB). This new institution would promote more rational, systematic, and equitable development of resources in developing nations. It would facilitate technological development and management training in the developing countries. It would help insure supplies of raw materials to sustain the expansion of the global economy and would help moderate commodity price fluctuations.

The International Resources Bank would mobilize capital for sound resource development projects by assisting individual resource projects to secure direct financing and issuing bonds which could be secured by a specific commodity. Alternatively, these bonds could be retired through delivery of a specific commodity. "Commodity bonds" of this type could greatly improve conditions of supply and market access and help developing countries to stabilize export earnings.

To enhance confidence for both host governments and investors the International Resources Bank would begin operations with a capital fund of $1 billion. It would participate with foreign investors and the host government in project agreements specifying the conditions of the investment on a basis acceptable to all parties. Such an agreement could include a formula for production sharing and arrangements by investors to help develop the managerial, technological, and marketing capabilities of the host country. The Bank would support guarantees of both investor and host nation performance in accordance with conditions established in the project agreement.

To insure effective coordination with other public institutions, the International Resources Bank could be associated with the World Bank Group, in a form to be worked out by the participating countries. It could operate in close collaboration with—and render even more effective—other institutions such as the World Bank and its associate, the International Finance Corporation, and the Inter-American Development Bank as well as the U.N. revolving fund for mineral exploration.

The IRB proposal offers many advantages and new concepts:

—Its facilitating role as third party with the host country and the foreign investor will encourage conditions for project development consistent with internationally accepted standards of equity.

—The IRB mechanism provides multilateral guarantees of the performance of both the host nation and the foreign investor in accordance with the project agreement—thereby reducing the noncommercial risks. This cannot fail to promote greater flows of investment capital for resource projects on reasonable terms.

—The proposal contemplates production-sharing arrangements under which the foreign investor is assured of an established percentage of total production with disposition of the balance to be controlled by the host nation. This allows the host nation to share in production from the outset, providing it with the basis for further processing of the raw material should this prove to be economically feasible.

—Commodity bonds would be a fruitful new international instrument for forward purchases of commodities. They could contribute to earnings stabilization. They would also provide added assurance of market access for the host country and supply access for the consumer.

—Finally, through the IRB, modern technology would flow into developing nations. The two key elements required for development—management and technology—are provided by the foreign investor directly in a new form of capital investment. The trilateral agreement could include provision for the progressive acquisition of technology by the host country and thus contribute importantly to the process of technology transfer.

We consider the International Resources Bank to be an innovative and significant response to the basic needs of the developing nations and the international community. It will be a major advance in the sharing of benefits and responsibilities between industrialized and developing nations. It will help insure the essential flow of capital, management, and technology into resource development under conditions acceptable to host governments. And it will enhance the predictability that is essential to attract capital investment. We hope other countries will join us during the coming months to design and establish this global institution.

Improvement of the Conditions of Trade and Investment in Individual Commodities

We are all conscious of the problems the world economy has

faced recently in this area. Within only two years the tight supply and astronomical prices of many critical materials have been followed by a period of declining prices. Many economies have been severely shaken, and several countries have suffered balance-of-payments crises. Drastic price changes affect the developing countries most severely, playing havoc with foreign exchange earnings and development plans. And because raw material production projects require years to develop and involve high risks, volatile prices tend to lead to erratic patterns of investment.

There are a number of ways to improve commodity markets: long-term contractual arrangements, better exchange of market information, improved distribution, more efficient production methods, and better storage and transport facilities.

We agree with the UNCTAD Secretariat that buffer stocks deserve special attention. For those commodities where buffer stocks are feasible, sharp fluctuations in prices can be moderated by building stocks when markets are weak. And adequate supplies at reasonable prices can be assured through releasing stocks when markets are tight.

The United States believes that buffer stocks can be financed from a combination of sources: direct contribution by the participants, export taxes, commercial borrowing guaranteed by the countries participating in the buffer stock, or through the existing facilities of international institutions. Should existing sources prove inadequate, we would also be prepared to consider the IRB as a supplemental channel for financing a particular buffer stock. In these ways, we are convinced that adequate international financing for buffer stocks can be assured within the context of the specific commodity agreement under which the stock is established. Clearly, the United States would not want a buffer stock in which we had agreed to participate to fail for want of adequate financing.

The United States has pursued a constructive approach to other aspects of the commodities problem:

—We have joined with producers and consumers of key commodities to agree on measures to improve and stabilize markets.

—We have signed commodity agreements on coffee and tin, and we will participate in negotiations on sugar. We viewed cocoa as well suited to a buffer stock arrangement but were disappointed in the agreement negotiated a few months ago, which we believe is unlikely to improve the functioning of the cocoa market. If other parties are interested, we stand ready to renegotiate this agreement.

—The United States recently participated in the first meeting of producers and consumers of copper. We look forward to the establishment of a permanent producer-consumer group.

—Agricultural raw materials need serious attention as well. Those that face declining markets from growing competition from lower cost producers and synthetics can benefit from market promotion, research to improve productivity and marketability, or diversification into other products. We recommend that producer-consumer forums dealing with individual commodities focus on such possibilities. We urge that the World Bank and the regional development banks give high priority to funding projects for these purposes.

Today the United States proposes these additional measures:

—First, let us reach agreement on a definite timetable for the study of specific commodity problems of interest to developing countries. We are prepared to initiate concerted consideration in producer-consumer forums this year of measures to improve the stability, growth, and efficiency of markets for all key commodity exports of developing countries. Particular attention should be given to the formation of groups for bauxite and iron ore.

—Second, since many of the poorest countries are dependent on these products for export earnings, we urge the World Bank and regional institutions to sponsor projects to improve production efficiency and markets for jute, sisal, and other hard fibers or to facilitate diversification into other products in order to reduce excessive reliance on them.

—Finally, any program of resource development must emphasize the two most vital international resources: food and energy.

Forecasts of good harvests must not lull us into letting the progress begun at the World Food Conference slip away. At that conference, nations agreed to work toward a system of world grain reserves to improve food security, to increase support for agricultural research, to develop programs for nutritional improvement, and to increase agricultural development in low-income countries. We urge other countries to join us to make the concept of world food reserves a reality, to increase support for agriculture development in poorer nations, and to provide necessary food aid.

In energy we strongly support the efforts of oil producers and consumers from both the industrialized and the developing world to achieve cooperative solutions at the Conference on International Economic Cooperation. We urge that our proposal for an International Energy Institute—which would help developing countries take advantage of their domestic energy resources— receive priority attention in the months ahead.

Stabilizing Export Earnings of Developing Countries

At the seventh special session, the United States listed as its first priority the need to insure economic security for the developing world. We continue to believe that the world economic system must provide the developing nations greater security from the worst effects of fluctuating prices, recession, inflation, and other economic shocks which they are helpless to prevent or avoid.

We are gratified at the rapid implementation of our proposals to the special session for the far-reaching expansion of the International Monetary Fund. These innovations make available billions of dollars in new financing to offset steep declines in export earnings.

The most significant step forward has been the Fund's agreement to liberalize its compensatory financing facility. As of now, roughly $800 million from this improved facility has been provided. If this rate continues, more money will have been lent this year from the facility than the entire amount provided over the last 12 years.

Another major advance has been the establishment of an IMF trust fund to help meet the balance-of-payments needs of the poorest countries. While many developing countries have received substantial benefits from the compensatory financing facility, low-income countries whose export revenues depend on one or two commodities often need additional financial help to meet balance-of-payments problems. To assist the poorest countries, the United States has proposed that the trust fund provide concessional financing to poorer countries to offset declines in earnings from an agreed list of particularly significant commodities.

Moreover, the United States would be ready to join others in a review of the adequacy of the trust fund's resources, should they prove inadequate to stabilize earnings and provide general balance-of-payments financing for low-income developing nations. We especially urge those oil-producing nations with strong reserves to contribute to the trust fund's lending capacity.

Expanding Trade in Resources and Processed Goods

Trade has been an engine of growth for all countries; for many developing countries it is the most critical vehicle of development.

The United States has taken a number of initiatives to meet the special needs of developing countries. We have reduced global trade barriers, especially those affecting processed goods; provided preferential access to our market for many exports of developing countries; worked in the multilateral trade negotiations (MTN) in Geneva for reduction of barriers in tropical products; and recognized in our general trade policy the special trade needs of developing countries.

We now have these challenges:

—We must maintain the momentum in reducing world trade barriers.

—We must focus especially on reducing barriers against processed goods, which retard developing countries' efforts to industrialize.

—We need additional international arrangements to assure reliability of supply, for the steady flow of new materials is vital to every country.

To maintain momentum in reducing trade barriers, industrial countries of the OECD, despite the strains on their economies from higher energy costs and recession, have pledged themselves to avoid restrictive trade measures. The United States intends to join with other developed countries in a renewal of that pledge at the next OECD ministerial meeting in June.

In addition, at the multilateral trade negotiations now taking place in Geneva we will pay special attention to the interests of developing countries, particularly in such areas as processed exports, tropical products, and nontariff barriers.

The institution in January of a generalized system of preferences by the United States, combined with the preference systems of other industrial countries, has opened significant trading opportunities for developing nations. Our own preference system already covers more than 2,700 items from nearly 100 countries. The annual trade value of these items is roughly $2.5 billion. We are examining the possibility of including additional products.

The United States will give priority support to the U.N. Development Program (UNDP) financing of a joint GATT-UNCTAD program of technical assistance to developing countries. This will help those countries take full advantage of the preference schemes of industrialized countries by finding the most productive areas for new and increased exports and the best techniques of marketing their products.

In addition, intensive negotiation is now underway in the MTN on tariff treatment of tropical products, including processed goods and manufactures, that are of particular interest to developing countries. The United States intends to implement negotiated tariff reductions in this area as soon as possible once the tropical product package is agreed upon.

In keeping with the Tokyo Declaration,[5] the United States believes that the MTN negotiations on rules concerning nontariff barriers must give greater attention to the needs of developing countries. For example, the United States believes that a code to govern the use of countervailing duties against export subsidies should recognize the special conditions facing developing countries. We will urge that the special needs of developing nations be taken into account when new international rules pertaining to offsetting action are being developed.

With respect to new rules on safeguard measures against injury from imports, we will consider special treatment for less developed countries which are minor suppliers or possible new entrants into the U.S. market.

We recognize, too, that developing countries have interests in other reforms of the trading system which are not presently under negotiation. We will respond to these views with an open mind. We are confident that with good will on all sides, constructive agreement can be reached on specific reform issues within the time frame of the multilateral trade negotiations.

The reduction of tariffs against the exports of processed raw materials from developing countries is especially important. Lowering these barriers would provide fresh opportunities to expand and diversify exports, particularly in cases where tariffs now escalate with the degree of processing. To this end, the tariff-reduction proposal which the United States has made in the MTN will not only result in significant tariff cuts but also will reduce tariff escalation. We expect that developing countries will regard this as an incentive to positive cooperation in the current negotiations.

If more open market access is one pillar of an expanding international trading system, greater reliability of supply is another. Without reasonable assurance from producer countries that they will not arbitrarily interfere with exports, importers must turn to other sources. Consumers will then bear the cost of less efficient production; unreliable producers, the cost of lost markets and reduced foreign investment.

There is an urgent need to analyze methods to improve reliability of supply. We urge that work begin promptly in the GATT to determine whether an international code on export controls is feasible. Such a code should define more clearly the circumstances under which countries may legitimately apply export controls. It

[5] Text in *AFR, 1973:* 391-4.

would reduce the uncertainties for consumers and for exporters, and it would mitigate some of the political damage to relations between countries when restrictions are imposed on exports.

The United States will also continue to seek commitments of reliable supply in the context of specific arrangements negotiated for individual commodities.

This four-point program—a new International Resources Bank, a case-by-case effort to improve conditions of trade and investment in primary products, stabilization of export earnings, and improved market and supply conditions—recognizes that these issues are linked; yet it permits pragmatic and flexible treatment of specific problems. The approach I have described is a major effort by the United States to deal on a comprehensive basis with commodity issues. It is workable; it is achievable; it is a program which meets the needs of developing and developed nations alike. We urge favorable consideration and rapid collective action.

Technology for Development

Let me now turn to another area of major concern: the application of technology for development.

Technology is at the heart of the development process. It enables man to extend his horizons beyond the mere struggle for existence. Technology draws the fullest measure from the finite resources of our globe. It harnesses the intelligence of man and the forces of nature to meet human needs.

For two centuries technological progress has been fundamental to rapid industrial growth. A central challenge of our time is to extend the benefits of technology to all countries.

There are a number of impediments to a rapid and effective technology transfer from industrialized to developing countries.

First, in many cases technology from industrial countries may not fit the real needs of developing countries. By and large, the challenge is not to transfer a carbon copy of existing technology, but to develop new technology and technological institutions that are most relevant to the conditions of individual developing countries.

Second, developing countries often lack adequate information and expertise to identify the technology which best meets their needs.

Third, there is often a shortage of the trained manpower needed to select, adapt, and effectively manage technology.

Fourth, technology often cannot be separated from capital and management. Hence it is one element of the overall investment process. And to be successful, technology must be applied within a framework of government policies which facilitate and nourish the process of technology transfer.

The task therefore is not simply the turnover of formulas or blueprints. We must pursue a comprehensive approach which provides a broad range of programs and incentives to transfer both technology and the fundamental skills that will give it root and effectiveness. To promote this, the United States proposes a five-point approach:

First, to adapt technology to the needs of developing countries, the United States supports the establishment of a network of research and development institutions at the local, regional. and international level. We need to strengthen global research capacities for development and to expand intergovernmental cooperation. Therefore we propose the following:

—An International Industrialization Institute should be established to encourage research and development of industrial technology appropriate to developing countries. A founders conference involving all interested countries should be held no later than this fall.

—The Energy Commission of the Conference on International Economic Cooperation should establish an International Energy Institute to facilitate energy research and the application of energy-related technologies to the special needs of developing countries.

—We should extend existing networks for applied research in the fields of agriculture, health, and education. The creation of new institutions must be accompanied by measures to help the process of technology transfer. To improve cooperation between industrialized and developing countries, the United States proposes new programs in three fields of advanced science, to which we are prepared to make major contributions of knowledge and experience: in satellite technology, in water resources development, and in oceans technology.

—Satellite technology offers enormous promise as an instrument for development. Remote-sensing satellites can be applied to survey resources, forecast crops, and improve land use in developing countries. They can help to foresee and evaluate natural disasters. Modern communication technologies, including satellites, have large untapped potential to improve education, training, health services, food production, and other activities essential for development. Therefore, from July through October of this year the United States will make available to interested developing countries demonstrations of the various applications for development of the experimental ATS-6 communications satellite, the Landsat remote sensing satellite, and high resolution photography. We are prepared to cooperate with developing countries in establishing centers, training personnel, and where possible, adapting our civilian satellite programs to their needs.

—The United States will play a leading role in applying water resources technology to such objectives as improving the quality and productivity of agriculture and developing new industry. We will play an active role at the U.N. Water Conference to be held in March of next year, putting forward practical measures to share our knowledge and experience.

—The technology necessary to mine the deep seabed, to manage fisheries, and to exploit the vast potential of the oceans is rapidly being developed. The United States has made major advances in this field. We plan to invite scientists, managers, and technicians from different countries to participate in our scientific projects. And we strongly support provisions in the law of the sea treaty which will provide incentives for sharing of deep-seabed technology appropriate to developing-country needs.

—Finally, there is a pressing need to develop new ways to use technology to improve the basic condition of the poor. The United States is increasing the technical component of its development programs to provide basic nutrition, health, and education services.

The *second* element of our program is to improve the amount and quality of technological information available to developing countries and to improve their selection of technology relevant to their needs. We will support the efforts of the U.N. International Center for Exchange of Technological Information to provide comprehensive information on the capabilities and facilities of national and regional information services. For its part, the United States will inventory its national technological information resources and make available, both to developing countries and to the U.N. Center, consultants and other services to improve access to our national information facilities. These include the National Library of Medicine, the division of scientific information of the National Science Foundation, the National Agricultural Library, and the Smithsonian information service.

The United States also supports the proposed UNCTAD advisory service to strengthen the ability of developing nations to identify effectively, select, and negotiate for technology most appropriate to their requirements. We support the concept of regional advisory services under UNCTAD auspices, to provide expertise and resources to the technology requirements of particular regions and countries. These regional centers could act as conduits for the activities of other programs and institutions for the application of technology to developing countries.

Third, to nurture new generations of technologists and technology managers, the United States proposes a priority effort to train individuals who can develop, identify, and apply technology suited to the needs of developing countries. To this end:

—Training competent managers of future technology should be central objectives of the proposed International Industrialization Institute and the International Energy Institute.

—For its part, the United States will encourage universities, research institutes, and industrial training schools in the United States to create special institutes and curricula for technology training for the developing countries; we will provide for and assist their sister institutions in developing countries. We invite other developed countries to join us in this effort.

—Finally, the United States proposes that appropriate incentives and measures be devised to curb the emigration of highly trained manpower from developing countries; for the benefits which developing nations derive from trained technology managers are of no consequence if they leave their home countries.

In this connection, the U.S. Government will encourage the formation of a technology corps, which will parallel our executive service corps in organization and operation. This will be a private, nonprofit organization to which corporations and universities will contribute highly skilled personnel experienced in the management of scientific and technical operations. They will work with and help train local manpower in specific development projects.

The *fourth* element of our approach is to make the process of transferring existing technology more effective and equitable.

New technology in industrialized countries resides primarily in the private sector. Private enterprise is in the best position to provide packages of management, technology, and capital. To enhance that contribution, both industrialized and developing countries must create an environment conducive to technology transfer.

The United States recommends that voluntary guidelines be developed that set forth the conditions and standards of technology transfer which encourage, facilitate, and maximize the orderly transfer of technology.

The proposed International Resources Bank also contains features which can enhance the ability of developing countries to manage technology and thereby encourage its transfer. In the trilateral agreement with the host nation and the International Resources Bank, the foreign investor would generally undertake to provide both management and technology. The investment project could, by mutual agreement, include the obligation to progressively transfer some of the technology to the host nation over the period of the agreement—as well as accelerate the country's capacity to manage such technology.

The flow of technology in the channels of world commerce can be diverted by restrictive practices. Some practices may directly limit the transfer of technology; in addition, where technology is transferred, restrictive provisions on trade in high-technology products can limit its benefits for others. The United States proposes that international attention be focused on the full range of these practices, with a view to their reduction or elimination.

The *fifth* element of the U.S. program is to set goals for achievement before and during the U.N. Conference on Science and Technology for Development, now proposed for 1979. The United States strongly supports this conference and its objectives. Preparations for it provide a major opportunity for both developed and developing countries to review their responsibilities for the sharing and use of technology.

To speed our preparations, the United States will convene a national conference next year to bring together our best talent from universities, foundations, and private enterprise. They will be asked to consider the broad range of technological issues of concern to the developing world. They will be invited to help mobilize American resources to assist developing countries to meet their research requirements. And they will be encouraged to prepare detailed American proposals for the conferences and institutes I have described.

We recommend also that the OECD nations urgently study the possibilities of a greater contribution by all industrialized nations to overcoming the problems of technology transfer.

This five-point program represents the most comprehensive effort ever put forward by the United States to deal with the challenge of applying technology to development. We hope that the UNCTAD Conference will give these initiatives serious consideration. We invite your ideas and proposals. Working together, we can see to it that this age of technology will improve the quality of the lives of all of our peoples in a manner undreamed of by previous generations.

Balance-of-Payments and Debt Problems

Rising import costs caused in large part by higher oil prices, and reduced export earnings resulting from recession in the industrialized nations, have generated unprecedented international payments deficits. Although global economic recovery has begun, many countries will face persisting deficits this year.

A major institutional effort must be made if these countries are to avoid severe cutbacks in their imports and consequent reductions in their economic growth. There are three priority areas:

—We must insure that flows of funds for development projects are neither reduced nor diverted by short-term economic problems. In addition, long-term financing must be increased and its quality enhanced.

—We must enable private markets to continue to play a substantial role in providing development capital. For many countries, private capital flows are, and will continue to be, the principal form of development finance.

—We must see to it that the domestic economic policies of all our countries are sound. They should not place undue pressures on payments positions by unnecessary accumulations of debt. And we must give particular attention to those countries unable to avoid critical debt problems.

Resource Flows

We have been heartened by the immense effort made since the seventh special session to assure adequate balance-of-payments financing for less developed nations. Especially important has been the expansion of the International Monetary Fund's lending facilities. These efforts should help insure that sufficient balance-of-payments financing is available on an aggregate basis to developing countries.

But emergency lending cannot be a substitute for effective and high-quality foreign aid. Although most foreign assistance from the United States and other donors is provided on highly concessional terms, much can be done to improve the quality of resource flows. In many cases, the conditions of assistance restrict its financial and developmental impact; one example is the tying of aid to procurement in donor countries, which can reduce its value. The United States therefore will urge the OECD Development Assistance Committee to develop arrangements for the reciprocal untying of development assistance.

Private Capital

For many developing countries, particularly those in the midst of industrialization, private sources make up the bulk of development capital. Of the $35 billion balance-of-payments deficit of the non-oil-producing developing countries in 1975, nearly half was financed by private capital flows. Without this contribution, the

consequences of the mammoth deficit would have been un-
manageable. The IMF-IBRD Development Committee is studying
a wide range of measures to insure that international capital
markets continue their imaginative adaptation to the needs of
developing nations.

In addition, negotiations on the replenishment of the International Finance Corporation, which we proposed at the seventh
special session, have been completed. The IFC is actively engaged
in examining the U.S. proposal for an International Investment
Trust to mobilize portfolio capital for investment in local enterprises. The United States gives its full support to these efforts.

Debt Problems

Many countries have had to resort to short-term external
borrowing to finance deficits. Debt payment burdens are mounting; a number of countries are experiencing serious problems in
meeting their debt obligations.

Generalized rescheduling of debts is not the answer. It would
erode the creditworthiness of countries borrowing in private capital
markets. By tying financing to debt, it obscures the significant
differences among countries and prevents an appropriate focus on
those in most urgent need. And it would not be fair to those nations
which have taken strong policy measures to reduce their
obligations.

The debt problem must be addressed in relation to each country's
specific position and needs. The United States stands ready to help
countries suffering acute debt service problems with measures
appropriate to each case. The procedures must be agreeable to
creditor and debtor alike. The device of a creditor club is a flexible
instrument for negotiations.

To improve the basis for consideration of balance-of-payments
problems of particular developing countries, the United States
proposes that the Finance Commission of the Conference on International Economic Cooperation or another mutually acceptable
forum examine the economic and acute financing problems of
developing countries.

The Poorest Countries

The needs of many nations in the developing world are great, but
the special requirements of the poorest countries are massive. This
conference has a collective moral responsibility to respond to this
challenge. We must devote major efforts to improve programs for
the poorest countries and to devise new ones where necessary, for
without adequate assistance the poorest will be condemned to

continuing poverty and helplessness. We must increase resource flows, improve their terms, and enhance their quality. And aid must be given on softer terms, because the poorest countries are by definition unable to service debt except on a highly concessional basis.

Resource flows to the poorest countries must be freed from restrictions on procurement sources and the financing of local costs which distort the design of projects, waste resources, and cause excessive reliance on imported equipment.

The IMF trust fund now being established will importantly ease the immediate balance-of-payments problems of the poorest countries.

For the longer term, a substantial replenishment of the International Development Association is imperative. The United States will, as always, meet its commitments to this vitally important source of assistance. And we look forward to generous OPEC support for this important institution.

Thus the United States has already taken a number of steps to assist the most needy countries. We will do more:

—To meet the urgent needs of the Sahel region, we are actively participating in the deliberations of the *Club des Amis du Sahel*. In addition, we have proposed that an urgent study be undertaken on ways not merely to ease the drought but to end the water shortage by mobilizing the great African rivers—not to perpetuate relief but to initiate basic reform.

—The U.S. Congress has already authorized a contribution of up to $200 million for the International Fund for Agricultural Development;[6] we look forward to the June plenipotentiary conference which has been called to sign the agreement; and we urge others to contribute generously so that the $1 billion target can be met.

—We have secured authority under our Foreign Assistance Act to finance all costs of aid projects in least developed countries when necessary to insure their success.

—Seventy percent of our bilateral development assistance is now programed for countries with per capita GNP of $300 or less.

—For countries whose per capita GNP is less than $500, we strongly support proposals to increase their share to over 80 percent of all UNDP grants. One-third of this should go to the least developed countries in this category.

—We pledge a major expansion of our efforts to develop integrated systems for basic community health services. These

[6] Public Law 94-161, Dec. 20, 1975.

will combine medical treatment and family planning and nutritional information, while making full use of locally trained paramedical personnel.

In the law of the sea negotiations now underway in New York, the United States has made a detailed proposal that revenues from deep-seabed mining and resources exploitation be shared with the international community especially for the benefit of the poorest countries.

This is a substantial effort. It must be complemented, however, by improvement in the terms of bilateral assistance to the poorest countries. To this end, the United States proposes that all donor countries agree to provide all development assistance to the relatively least developed countries on the UNCTAD list on a grant basis.

The United States will seek authorization from the Congress to provide all development assistance to the poorest countries on this basis. We already have congressional authorization to convert repayment of a portion of our loans under Public Law 480 to grants under certain circumstances. Taken together, these two steps will significantly increase the grant element in our bilateral assistance programs.

Human suffering and human deprivation are not questions of ideology or bloc politics. They touch the elemental needs of mankind and the basic imperatives of universal moral values. We must not fail to do our duty.

Dimensions of Task of Development

Economic development is a task of many dimensions. Whatever may be our differing perspectives, the United States believes that a number of conclusions stand out clearly:

—Development is a mutually reinforcing endeavor. There is nothing permanent about the distinction between the developed and developing worlds. Developed countries thrive and advance most surely when the international economy grows vigorously and steadily. As the United States sees other nations develop and industrialize, we feel renewed confidence in the world economic system and in our own economic future. Sustained growth and development require that we work together cooperatively.

—Development involves mutual responsibility. International cooperation cannot be one-sided. The strength of the industrial countries must be regarded as a trust for the progress of all; the developing countries only hurt themselves if they weaken that strength through contrived scarcities, cartels, embargoes, or arbitrary seizures of property. At the same time, the developed countries have an obligation to do their utmost to spur development. Our efforts here must take into consideration the concerns and the contributions of all countries, developed and developing, producer and consumer, East and West, North and South.

—Development is a process of change and innovation. It must respond not only to rapidly changing technology but also to the evolution of political attitudes. The old relationships of donor and recipient are increasingly paternalistic and anachronistic to the recipient; they may also come to seem a one-sided burden to those who have long been donors. We must fashion a new sense of cooperation that is based on the self-respect and sovereign equality of all nations. Each nation must find its own path to development which allows it to retain its self-respect and identity, its culture, and its ideological preference. But development itself is not a function of ideology; it must unite practical solutions and a philosophy of international cooperation. It cannot grow from doctrines of confrontation and the exploitation of despair.

—Development is a human enterprise. It is the talents and efforts of individuals which make development a reality, and it is they who are its ultimate beneficiaries. Our first aim is the minimum essentials of life—food, clothing, shelter—and the relief of human suffering and monotony and debilitating illness and ignorance and demeaning servitude to others. Then development must look beyond survival to provide opportunities for education, greater personal freedom, and individual dignity and self-respect. Finally, development must deal with the quality of life: the dignity of the individual, personal freedom, and equality of opportunity regardless of race, religion, sex, or political belief.

The magnitude of the task before us will require unprecedented international collaboration. No nation alone can surmount—and only together can all nations master—what is inescapably a global challenge of historic proportions.

But we are not confronted by overwhelming odds or by intractable obstacles. We have it in our power to achieve in our generation a rate of economic advance that has no parallel in human experience.

In each age, men and women have striven for greater prosperity and justice and dignity. Yet always in the past there have been setbacks; history has recorded a surfeit of misery and despair. Our age is the first where we can choose to be different. And therefore we must.

If we succeed, this decade could be remembered as a turning point in the economic and political evolution of man. The new institutions and mechanisms we create could be perceived as building blocks of international cooperation that strengthened the world's sense of community. The implications for world peace, as well as for economic cooperation, are vast.

The United States proceeds from the conviction that both morality and practical interest point in the same direction, toward a dedicated enterprise of cooperation. If we are met in a cooperative and realistic spirit, we are prepared to offer our national capacities in support of a historic extension of the global economy and global development.

So let us get down to business. Let us make this task a priority of all our foreign policies. Let us set our sights high, but let us not make our desire for the ideal block achievement of the attainable. Let us reach agreement on practical steps that improve the lot of our fellow man. We owe our people performance, not slogans; results, not rhetoric.

The United States extends its hand to those who will travel with us on this road to a more humane and bountiful future. We must travel it together, and we must take another step at this conference.

(31) . The Organization for Economic Cooperation and Development (OECD): Meeting of the Council at Ministerial Level, Paris, June 21-22, 1976.

(a) Statement to the Council by Secretary of State Kissinger, June 21, 1976.[7]

The purposeful cooperation of our nations has been at the heart of the world's progress for three decades. Today, we are challenged to deepen and advance that common effort. The cooperation of the industrial democracies is decisive for world peace, prosperity, and the cause of justice and human dignity.

No group of nations is better equipped to master these challenges. Ours are the societies that launched the two great events that gave birth to the modern age—the political revolutions of the 18th and 19th centuries that shaped today's community of nation-states and the Industrial Revolution that produced the contemporary world economy. We share a heritage of pioneering effort in all the modern forms of commercial, social, and governmental organization. And we have been able to perceive and

[7]Department of State Press Release 311; text from *Bulletin*, 75: 73-83.

respond to new challenges, especially in giving effect to our recognition of the imperatives of interdependence.

Our democratic systems have disproved the doctrine that only repression and authoritarianism could advance human well-being. On the contrary, the industrial democracies assembled here have demonstrated conclusively that it is in freedom that men achieve the economic advances of which ages have dreamed. There is some irony in the fact that after years of disparaging our economic system, both the Socialist countries and the developing countries have turned to us to help them advance more rapidly. Today it is the industrial democracies which primarily have the resources, the managerial genius, the advanced technology, and the dedication which are needed for sustained economic development under *any* political system.

The advanced industrial nations have conducted themselves of late with vigor, determination, and a sense of shared purpose. Most of the OECD countries are now entering a period of economic expansion. We have worked together in the process of recovery, averting protectionist tendencies in trade and the selfish pursuit of oil and raw materials at each other's expense. Largely due to this, we are recovering quickly and with excellent prospects for continued progress.

We have acted together because we recognize that the world economy has become global. National interests cannot prosper or endure in isolation. And the nations assembled here are the engines of the world economy. Our performance is the pivot around which international trade and finance revolve. Our technology and investment are the catalysts of development and economic progress in developing nations.

Today the world economy faces new and demanding challenges. Our past cooperation must be given fresh impetus in our twofold task: to improve our performance in areas where we have already begun to work together and to create mechanisms of cooperation to deal with new issues and opportunities.

This organization is well suited to this task. Its history and durability are a demonstration of the unity and cooperation of the industrial democracies. It has provided a unique forum and necessary focus for dealing with the critical link between national aspirations and global opportunity. This is no accident; it reflects our fundamental moral and political fraternity. Our traditions of freedom give moral meaning and political purpose to our technical achievements.

This is why I wish to stress the importance of furthering our unity and progress through the OECD. The objective is not to forge a bloc for our own advantage or for purposes of confrontation. It is to shape a new international environment based on the consciousness that in an age of interdependence national interests can best be served by advancing the aspirations of all mankind through cooperative efforts.

Let me discuss three areas of challenge and opportunity:

—Strengthening the cohesion and prosperity of the industrialized democracies;
—The new issues we face in economic relations with the Communist world; and
—The ongoing international effort to promote economic development and a constructive long-term relationship between the industrial and developing worlds.

Relationship of the Industrial Democracies

Our first and fundamental concern must be economic cooperation and progress among the industrialized democracies of North America, Western Europe, and Asia. Tomorrow, finance and economic ministers will discuss these economic questions in detail. Today I want to sketch in broad terms four essential areas of our cooperation which have the greatest significance for world order and the future of the international system:

—Noninflationary economic growth;
—Strengthening our open international trade and monetary system;
—The encouragement of transnational investment; and
—Greater cooperation in energy.

I shall discuss each of these in turn.

First, as our nations move to recovery and expansion, we must insure steady, noninflationary economic *growth.* Only in this manner can we resolve conflicting claims on resources, reinforce the political vitality of our institutions, enhance our freedom of action in world affairs, and enlarge the economic horizons of all societies.

We must overcome cycles of boom and stagnation, which in the past have impaired productivity, constricted investment, and choked off our full economic potential. We can achieve sustained growth by containing inflation. The investment needed to create jobs for our growing labor forces will dry up in an environment of rapidly and constantly rising prices. Inflation erodes the progress made in raising the standard of living of our peoples; it strains the social fabric of our democratic societies.

The responsibility for noninflationary growth rests with national governments. But close consultation and collaboration are essential to insure that national policies are complementary and reinforcing; to contribute to exchange rate stability among us; to give special attention to members that are in difficulty; and to collaborate on policies of trade, energy, and relations with the developing countries. The summit meeting at Rambouillet last November made a major contribution to general recovery and promotion of these goals. The summit next week in Puerto Rico will assess the progress we have made and use it as a point of departure for future advances.

This meeting provides an opportunity for the nations assembled here to reaffirm our joint commitment to an open economic system, to national responsibility, and to international cooperation. With sound and concerted policies among us and with efforts to coordinate our strategies for expansion, the potential for the world's sustained economic growth can be realized.

At last year's OECD ministerial meeting, at U.S. recommendation, a Group of Distinguished Economists was set up, chaired by Professor McCracken.[8] It was assigned the task of examining the medium- and long-term and structural problems of sustained economic growth. It is exploring the problems of inflation, investment, structural imbalances, and adequate supplies of raw materials. We look forward to its conclusions and recommendations.

Strengthening our trade and monetary system also requires enhanced collaboration. In recent years, high unemployment and economic uncertainty have revived protectionist pressures in many countries; inflation and drastic differences in the performance of member nations have produced major payments imbalances, exchange rate pressures, and financial strains.

The Rambouillet summit and the IMF meeting in Jamaica last January were milestones in adapting the international monetary system to a new era. We have agreed to new IMF rules to avoid the shocks and disequilibrium which plagued the Bretton Woods system and to insure a smoother functioning of our trade and investment.

Today and tomorrow the OECD nations are continuing close and detailed consultations. We will examine both current problems and the long-term future, both the existing institutions and institutional reform. A recent example of our capacity for innovation was the agreement on the OECD Financial Support Fund, designed to help us deal cooperatively with serious economic dislocations aggravated by the oil price rises. The United States is seeking swift

[8] Paul W. McCracken, former Chairman of the Council of Economic Advisers.

ratification of this agreement so that the Fund may come into being soon.

In *trade*, two years ago the OECD nations jointly undertook an extraordinary political commitment to preserve an open economic system despite a period of general economic difficulty. On May 30, 1974, we pledged to avoid new restrictions on trade. We rejected policies which would tend to shift one nation's difficulties onto others. That declaration strengthened our successful efforts to resist protectionist pressures and thus benefit countries with particularly acute balance-of-payments problems. The declaration was renewed last year. We should now renew it for an additional year.

Our economic recovery provides significant opportunities for further progress:

—First, the political commitment represented by our trade pledge should be the basis for wider cooperation among us. The United States proposes that this organization recommend further areas for common action, not only on current trade problems and negotiations but on the long-term operation of our open trading system.

—Second, all nations assembled here should make a political commitment to accelerate the multilateral trade negotiations in Geneva. We are at the point where we must move forward at a more rapid pace if the negotiations are to reach a successful conclusion in 1977. To this end, the United States strongly recommends that we reach agreement this fall in Geneva on a tariff-cutting formula.

—Third, it is our shared obligation to improve the conditions of trade for developing countries. The postwar trading system was built on a consensus among industrial countries in which the developing countries did not participate and which they now challenge in several important respects. We need to reexamine the trading system, prepared to change or strengthen it where necessary. In the multilateral trade negotiations we will be negotiating new provisions in such areas as nontariff barriers, supply access, the settlement of disputes, and trade restrictions that are justified for balance-of-payments purposes. This organization and its members can play a crucial role in building a new global consensus on these issues.

Transnational investment is the third area calling for close collaboration among the industrial nations.

Investment is the lifeblood of our economies and vital to worldwide development. It has been a principal source of the economic growth and security and prosperity which the nations represented here enjoy. It has been the single largest source of development capital for Third World nations and a powerful force marshaling management and technology for their benefit. It has developed resources; it has increased income; it has provided jobs. Since the midsixties, foreign direct investment has been growing faster than international trade and global GNP.

The increasing importance of transnational investment to the global economy has been accompanied by no little concern over the activities of private investors, particularly the multinational corporations. Questions have been raised as to how the international firms can serve the national interests of their hosts as well as their own. A few notorious cases of illicit payments have stirred apprehension and cast a cloud over the overwhelming majority of international firms whose behavior has been beyond reproach.

Governments, too, have impeded the flow of capital through inconsistent policies or discriminatory treatment of international firms. And most industrial countries have been under pressure at home to take increasingly nationalist positions toward international investment.

If this trend is not halted, we shall face a gradual deterioration in the international investment climate, with serious consequences for economic development and the global economy.

It is highly significant, therefore, that this organization undertook two related tasks: to negotiate voluntary guidelines for multinational firms and to clarify governmental responsibilities to preserve and promote a liberal investment climate. We are able to announce today the acceptance by OECD member governments of a declaration on investment. This declaration extends the cooperation which has characterized our trade and monetary relations into the area of investment. It includes:

—Recommended guidelines for the activities of multinational corporations;

—An agreed statement of the basic responsibilities of our governments with respect to transnational investment;

—Provision for strengthened cooperation on the questions of incentives and disincentives to foreign direct investment; and

—Provision for increased consultations between our governments on all these matters.

The United States strongly endorses this declaration and urges its widest possible adoption and observance.

A framework for investment is now emerging. We must encourage its development. Therefore, in addition to our full support for the OECD declaration, the United States urges the following policies for our nations:

—First, we should support the work of the U.N. Commission on Transnational Corporations and the related U.N. Information and Research Center within its Secretariat, which will develop a comprehensive information system on issues relating to transnational corporations. This will contribute to a fuller understanding of investment issues among all nations.

—Second, we should review the proposal of the International Resources Bank which the United States put forward at UNCTAD at Nairobi last month. While the Bank will focus on energy and raw materials, its principal features—as a multilateral guarantor against noncommercial risk and as a facilitator of production sharing and technology transfer—have important implications for development generally.

—Third, we should take strong collective measures to eliminate corrupt payments. Bribery and extortion are a burden on international trade and investment. We reiterate our proposal that negotiation of a binding international agreement on corrupt practices begin at next month's session of the U.N. Economic and Social Council.

—Fourth, we should cooperate to restrain anticompetitive practices of firms which undermine the benefits of our open economic system. The United States proposes a dual effort: to reduce international procedural obstacles to the enforcement of laws against international restrictive business practices and to pursue bilateral and multilateral agreements for international antitrust cooperation similar to that about to be concluded between the United States and the Federal Republic of Germany.

—Fifth, we should strengthen the work of specialized OECD committees which deal with investment problems such as harmonizing statistical systems, cataloguing restrictive business practices, improving the exchange of tax information, dealing with tax haven problems, as well as their work now underway on the general topics of technology transfer and short-term capital movements.

The fourth crucial sphere of cooperation among the industrial nations is *energy*. The cooperation of energy-consuming nations has become an imperative, for the last few years have demonstrated the economic and political costs of loss of control over this critical component of industrial growth.

For the next several years, our nations' heavy dependence on imported oil will contribute to our political and economic vulnerability. The outlook for reducing our dependence in the next decade is not encouraging. Forecasts based on existing energy programs in the industrial countries indicate that our imports of

OPEC oil will increase from 27 million barrels a day in 1975 to as much as 37 million barrels per day by 1985. At the same time, it has become clear that oil reserves, while still large, are finite. Thus we must reduce our immediate dependence on imported oil side by side with beginning a long-term transition to alternative energy systems through the most rapid possible development of new and alternative sources of energy.

The industrial countries have begun to respond to the energy challenge. The difficult process of reorienting energy priorities and establishing new energy policies has been started. When the energy crisis became apparent, we moved rapidly to set up the new International Energy Agency (IEA), within the framework of the OECD. Through its impetus, a comprehensive structure of technical cooperation and policy coordination among industrial countries has grown up. At the same time, a dialogue with the OPEC countries has been started in the Conference on International Economic Cooperation (CIEC). And the importance of helping the poorer developing countries—especially those with limited energy resources—to survive the energy crisis has been recognized.

Despite these accomplishments, our efforts have fallen far short of our needs. They will neither adequately reduce our immediate energy vulnerability nor achieve a satisfactory global balance of energy supply and demand over the longer term. The United States therefore proposes that OECD members take the following cooperative steps:

—First, that we establish on an urgent basis joint energy production projects to pool technical know-how and financing in areas such as coal extraction and utilization, uranium enrichment, and synthetic fuels. Such actions would accord with the commitments we undertook in the IEA Long-Term Program. They will contribute to the early availability of commercially attractive additional energy sources.

—Second, that we establish collective and individual goals for substantially reduced dependence on imported oil by 1985. This will require agreed targets for additional energy production, particularly in the coal and nuclear energy sectors; these represent our best hope for substantially reducing our energy dependence in the next decade.

—Third, that we agree to intensify our national efforts to reduce the growth in demand for energy.

The United States urges that the Governing Board of the IEA launch these efforts on a priority basis. Member governments should endorse these goals for reduced dependence and also make the essential political commitments to specific and concrete actions to achieve them. We should aim for a ministerial meeting in six to nine months to accomplish these objectives. The ministerial meeting should also look beyond the next decade to the post-oil era and seek ways to build on cooperative research and development efforts in such areas as solar power and nuclear fusion. OECD countries not members of the IEA should be given an opportunity to participate fully in this process.

This agenda—of action for growth, trade and monetary affairs, investment, and energy—suggests an expanding role and responsibility for the OECD. Working together, the nations of the OECD face an unprecedented opportunity to advance their common welfare and prosperity. And from this foundation of cooperation we can more effectively deal with the issues which involve us with nations outside the OECD region.

Let me now turn to these relations with the rest of the world.

East-West Economic Relations

Our relations with the nations of the East turn primarily upon political and security issues. In the past, trade and economic relations with the Soviet Union and Eastern Europe have not been among our central concerns. But a new dimension of economic interaction between East and West has begun to take shape. It is time to act cooperatively so that this new economic factor becomes an increasingly positive element in the world economy.

The Soviet Union has the second largest economy in the world. Together with all COMECON countries, it accounts for about 20 percent of world output. But despite the size of its economy, the Soviet Union is not a major factor in the world economic system. Its trade is relatively small; it has made little contribution to economic development.

In recent years, however, the Soviet Union and the countries of Eastern Europe have moved toward greater economic contact with the West. The basic reason is plain. These countries have come to realize that they cannot provide for growing consumer demand or meet the technological imperatives of the more sophisticated economy they seek solely from their own economic resources. Further, many of the countries of Eastern Europe wish to diversify trading patterns that were established in the aftermath of World War II.

As a result, in the last four years, trade between the COMECON countries and the OECD countries has increased nearly fourfold. Most East European countries now depend on and prefer Western machinery, technology, and material imports for the dynamic element of their economic growth. And in matters of finance, the sudden increase in the external debt of the Soviet Union and the countries of Eastern Europe has been striking. Their net debt to private Western banks doubled in 1975 to $15 billion, and their total hard currency debt has reached nearly twice that amount.

The most familiar example of the impact of Communist countries on the international economy has been Soviet shortfalls in the production of grain, which has become the single most volatile element in the world food picture. In addition the Socialist countries can become an important element in the global energy balance. And in an era where adequate supplies of many other industrial raw materials can no longer be taken for granted, the extensive mineral reserves of the East can expand resource availability worldwide. It is therefore clear that in our multilateral efforts to build a strengthened international economic system, we will have to take account of the potential needs and contributions of the centrally planned economies.

For us, the industrial democracies in the OECD, the growing economic interaction between East and West and the Eastern influence on the global economy are realities that if arranged wisely can be positive developments, stabilizing relationships and broadening contacts. At the same time, managing relations between free economies and state trading systems has inevitable complications. Dealing with a centrally planned economy under strict political direction can never be treated simply as a commercial enterprise alone.

Certain principles stand out:

—All our nations have been engaged in this process.

—State trading countries must not be permitted to use their centrally directed systems for unfair advantage, nor should they be permitted to play off the industrial democracies against each other through selective political pressure.

—Growing East-West trade also presents hopeful prospects, both economic and political, if approached with understanding, skill, and foresight.

—In short, it is up to the industrial democracies to consult closely and to manage this process cooperatively.

Therefore the United States proposes that the OECD nations adopt a systematic work program for developing objectives and approaches for our economic relations with the Communist countries. To this end, some progress has already been made; for example, in aligning national export credit policies among the industrial countries. If we are to face this issue in an intelligent and harmonious fashion, many additional areas should be examined. Specifically, our nations should seek answers to the following questions:

—How can we insure effective reciprocity in trade between market and nonmarket countries?

—How do we deal with the problem of dumping and other unfair trade practices by countries in which prices need not bear a relation to costs or market forces?

—What are the implications of the growing external debt of the Communist countries?

—How can the industrial democracies deal with possible efforts to misuse economic relations for political purposes inimical to their interests?

—What should be the relationship between the nations of the East and the multilateral bodies dealing with economic affairs?

—How do we take account of the diversity of interests and needs that has already appeared among Eastern countries?

—And finally, is it possible to bring the Soviet Union and the Eastern European countries into the process of responsibly assisting development in the Third World?

The United States will elaborate its views on these issues at the next meeting of the Executive Committee in Special Session. The results of our examinations of these questions could be embodied in a report to the next ministerial meeting of this organization.

Growing East-West trade presents problems together with great opportunities. It is up to the countries assembled here to understand the process and its complexities and to manage it cooperatively. In that case, it can contribute to the vitality of our economies and to the stability of the international order.

The Relationship Between North and South

One of the most urgent and compelling challenges that summon our cooperation is the relationship between the industrial and the developing nations. The new era of international cooperation we seek must include economic relations that offer mutual prosperity and widening opportunity for all the peoples of the world.

Every nation has a stake in global stability and world peace. But the ultimate good must be to look beyond the maintenance of peace to a world which offers its children a hope of a better future.

The United States has made its commitment. We have demonstrated our determination at the seventh special session of the U.N. General Assembly, at the Conference on International Economic Cooperation in Paris, at Kingston in January, and at the UNCTAD Conference in Nairobi last month.

Our efforts begin from the conviction that an effective international system must be founded upon a consensus among all nations and peoples. The world community which is our ultimate aspiration can only be realized if all nations and peoples can pursue their goals with a sense of participation and an awareness that their concerns are heeded. If we are to live in a stable world, the preponderant number of nations must be persuaded that their legitimate concerns are taken seriously.

The poor nations cry out for development. Their objectives are clear: economic progress, a role in international decisions that affect them, and an equitable share of global economic benefits. The objectives of the industrialized nations are equally clear: widening prosperity for all peoples produced by an open world system of trade and investment with expanding markets for North and South. We want to see stable and equitable development of the world's resources of food, energy, and raw materials as the fundamental basis for a prosperous world economy.

Thus, the objectives of the industrial democracies and those of the developing nations should be complementary. The process of building a world community must therefore be shared by nations of both North and South and must address the issue of economic development in the context of growing global prosperity.

But this is not inevitable. Effective cooperation presupposes that both sides face certain realities without illusion.

The most critical of these realities is that development is a long-term process. Sustained economic development cannot possibly result from any one conference or any one set of proposals. It will depend primarily upon the internal effort, the domestic policy, and the national will of the developing countries themselves. In most cases the effort will extend over decades. Often this will require painful short-term sacrifices for longer term gains. Development cannot be created by rhetoric or by parliamentary victories in international forums.

Development further requires the sustained and collective effort of the industrial countries. The role of the industrial democracies is critical, for we possess the largest markets and most of the world's capital and technology. Thus real development presupposes a serious, unemotional, constructive North-South dialogue.

In such a dialogue it is futile for one party to seek to impose solutions to the problems of development on another. An atmosphere of extortion or pressure, unworkable proposals, or excessive reliance on parliamentary maneuvers will ultimately undermine public support in the only countries capable of contributing effectively to development.

We of the industrial democracies have a special responsibility. What we do—or fail to do—is critical to the future of the countries of the Third World. If we substitute competition among ourselves for a dispassionate analysis of the issues, the development process will falter. Our resources will be inefficiently scattered or misallocated; projects will too often prove fruitless for lack of careful analysis or want of wider support. We do no one a favor when we substitute rhetorical concessions for intelligent and realistic proposals that link the interests and concerns of both sides in a prospering global economy. Those who curry short-term favor may mortgage the long-term future.

It is imperative that the North-South dialogue advance in a way which benefits both sides. In the long run, progress, stability, and peace depend upon it.

The United States has done its utmost to be forthcoming in the dialogue. We have strained our domestic processes to develop pragmatic proposals to meet real problems in our relations with the developing world. As our economies improve and as we, together with the developing world, identify new areas for cooperation, we can look forward to widening global cooperation which can serve the interests of all.

The spirit of cooperation necessary between North and South requires first a commitment to cooperation among the industrial nations. This is not a call for confrontation with the Third World. It is an indispensable step we must take if we are not to fragment our efforts and fail in our objectives.

The United States believes that this organization should focus on three areas where our cooperation is most necessary and would be most effective:

—We must improve our ability to concert our development efforts in international forums, for it is in these meetings that ideas are launched, compromises are made, and political directions are set.

—We must enhance our collaboration in our bilateral and multilateral aid programs; for our resources are limited, and closer alignment of programs is essential for their effectiveness.

—We must develop a longer term strategy for development which integrates the diverse strands of North-South policy, including foreign aid, technology transfer, financial policy, and trade. For development is a comprehensive and never-ending process with implications for every area of the international economic system.

Let me discuss each area in turn.

First, we must improve the coordination of our positions at major international conferences. Recent unfavorable experiences at UNCTAD in Nairobi and at other international forums should make clear the importance of this step. We in this organization have supporting mechanisms for coordination of positions on energy, commodities, finance, and development, but their effectiveness has been frequently less than adequate. For the remainder of this year we will be relying on these bodies to continue to support our work in the Conference on International Economic Cooperation. It is therefore imperative that we review now our recent experience with the objective of strengthening the coordinating role of each OECD support mechanism as well as the relationship among them.

The United States recommends that the Secretary General undertake an immediate examination of the issues and present recommendations to the Executive Committee in Special Session on ways in which we may more closely align our positions.

We suggest as well that this organization take a more active role in developing views on key North-South issues than it has in the past. We believe this could most fruitfully be done by identifying in advance of international meetings specific issues of major concern to industrialized countries and arranging for consultations to develop mutually supporting positions. It makes no sense to work out our differences under the pressure of deadlines and of other participants at international conferences.

The next several months will be a test of our ability to work together in a variety of international settings. The agenda of conferences is full. We will be considering on a case-by-case basis measures to improve the functioning of individual commodity markets, including the reduction of excessive price fluctuations and methods of buffer stock financing. We will also be translating the analysis of the first six months of the year into concrete results in CIEC. In this forum, the United States looks forward to visible and concrete achievements in energy, raw materials, investment, trade, and measures to address the problems of the poorest countries. We will want:

—To explore possibilities for further consultations on energy, including ways to assist developing nations that have no energy resources;

—To facilitate progress on commodity discussions, including ways to improve the functioning of individual commodity markets; and

—To begin work on the International Resources Bank proposal, which we see as relating to the work of all the CIEC commissions, particularly those dealing with energy and raw materials.

Second, we must increase the effectiveness of our bilateral and multilateral aid efforts in addressing specific problems in the developing world. The OECD Development Assistance Committee has done important work to improve and coordinate development assistance policies. There are, as well, over 20 consultative groups working with regard to specific developing nations. We should review our coordination in all these areas. We may consider streamlining some of those mechanisms and eliminating duplication.

We must seek to enhance the coordination of assistance policies and programs which have a regional or even continental focus. The *Club des Amis du Sahel* is a recent successful effort to concert our resources to combat the problems of that African subregion. We should explore whether there are other regions, in Africa or elsewhere, where similar approaches are needed. The recent initiative by the President of France for focusing joint attention on specific problems on the African Continent is an example of the kind of effort we must make together in the future.

Third, we must devote a major portion of our efforts to longer range planning for global development. The problem of growth will not go away. No one policy will be decisive; no one conference will devise permanent solutions. We must begin to focus honestly and carefully on the development challenge through the distant future.

A high priority in this effort must be to consider together the various development issues we have been addressing separately. Development policies can be either mutually reinforcing or they can undermine one another. We must find a way to look at development as a comprehensive and integrated whole, harmonizing our long-range planning efforts in trade, aid, investment, and technology. These individual policies need to be placed into a larger coherent plan so that the industrial nations' development efforts can more efficiently respond to the most pressing issues in the developing world.

To achieve a more effective integrated development strategy, the United States proposes that OECD countries decide now to review the entire range of North-South issues which we will be addressing over the remainder of this decade and beyond. Over the next year we should develop a consistent and comprehensive set of objectives and strategies.

At the same time, we should now move to strengthen the institutional arrangements within this organization for handling North-South issues. There should be a central focal point in the OECD for consideration of all such activities. This will give a greater political impetus to our efforts. And it should also stimulate greater consideration for the needs and interests of developing nations in the ongoing work of specialized OECD committees.

The kind of coordination which I have suggested will require attention at the highest levels of our governments. It will, of course, also require compromises on policies and priorities which each of us has developed in the past. But it is our best, perhaps our sole, chance to accelerate the pace of constructive progress in our relations with the Third World while not undermining our relations with each other.

The Imperative of Cooperative Action

The nations assembled in this room proceed from two main premises: the interdependence among the OECD nations and our common desire to help shape a new era of global economic cooperation among *all* nations.

The central task before the industrialized democracies of the OECD is to give new focus and purpose to our own cooperative economic action. Economics is only part of that enterprise. The choices before us and the decisions we take will, above all, reflect our perception of ourselves as peoples and as nations. The tasks are long term, and they demand that we extend our line of sight beyond immediate technical issues or political controversies to more distant horizons.

Ours is a time when the centers of global power and influence are many and diverse. And ours, therefore, is a choice between cooperation or chaos. Today more than ever, the industrial democracies require leadership determined not to adapt to reality, but to shape it. Circumstances have provided us with a clear understanding of our interdependence, and our efforts to translate this reality into common progress are well begun. We have every reason for confidence in our capacities.

Our cooperative endeavor, which has accomplished so much in the past, can be even more dynamic as we turn to the new and long-term challenges of interdependence. What we elect to do together is bound to have vast meaning to a world that seeks progress and justice and needs from all of us in this room a fresh demonstration of what strong and free nations working together can accomplish.

(b) Communique on Independence, Development Cooperation, and Strategy for Sustained Economic Expansion, June 22, 1976.[9]

[9] OECD Press Release A(76)21, June 22; text from *International Legal Materials*, 15: 961-6 (July 1976).

COMMUNIQUE

1. The Council of the Organisation for Economic Co-operation and Development met at Ministerial level on 21st and 22nd June, in Paris under the Chairmanship of Mr. Panayis PAPALIGOURAS, Minister of Co-ordination and Planning of the Republic of Greece. Ministers took a number of decisions in the field of international investment and multinational enterprises and trade. They discussed world interdependence, development co-operation and the dialogue with developing countries. They exchanged views on the current economic situation and agreed on the main elements of a strategy for sustained economic expansion, to be carried out through their respective policies.

I. INTERDEPENDENCE AND CO-OPERATION AMONG OECD MEMBER COUNTRIES

2. OECD Member Governments, basing themselves on a market-oriented open economic system within which social progress, enhanced development co-operation and freedom of the individual can be ensured, are agreed that growing economic interdependence among nations is a source of strength and efficiency contributing to the maintenance of a peaceful and stable world, and leading to improvement in the conditions of life of all people. In this situation Member Governments bear a great responsibility to promote non-inflationary economic growth, employment and social progress not only among their countries but for the world at large.

3. Member Governments agreed that the high degree of interdependence among their countries, their recognition, in a spirit of solidarity, of each other's problems and their dedication to the same basic principles demand close consultation and co-operation among themselves in formulating and implementing their economic policies. Where appropriate, this co-operation may extend to the adoption of rules or guidelines for their behaviour as had been the case in specific areas such as trade, environment, energy and international investment and multinational enterprises.

Energy

4. Ministers noted the progress which has already been achieved in the Organisation in the field of energy co-operation. They received a report from the Chairman of the Governing Board of the International Energy Agency on the Agency's accomplishments over the past year.

5. Important policies have already been adopted to promote

rational use of energy resources. In addition, Ministers recognised, in view of the long lead times involved, that there was a need for early effective action to meet the long-term requirement of reducing dependence on depletable energy resources and thus meet the long-term needs of all nations for energy supplies; and that in the short-term, means will have to be found to provide for rational use and adequate supply of available energy sources, primarily oil. They therefore affirmed their resolve to pursue policies designed to meet these objectives, as well as to carry on a useful dialogue with oil-producing and other developing countries, seeking to establish a co-operative approach to these problems.

International Investment and Multinational Enterprises

6. Ministers are agreed that co-operation among Member countries can improve the foreign investment climate, encourage the positive contribution which multinational enterprises can make to economic and social progress, and minimise and resolve difficulties which may arise from their various operations. They therefore agreed to intensify their co-operation and consultation on international investment and multinational enterprises. On behalf of their Governments,[10] they adopted a Declaration related to guidelines for multinational enterprises, national treatment, international investment incentives and disincentives and consultations and review of these matters. The Council took three Decisions establishing the necessary procedures for intergovernmental consultations in these areas (see PRESS/A(76)20).[11] Continuing endeavours within the OECD may lead to further international arrangements and agreements in this field.

Trade

7. Member Governments[12] decided to renew, for a further year, their Declaration on Trade of 1974 aimed at avoiding restrictions on trade and other current account transactions which could lead to chain reactions and endanger the process of economic recovery. Bearing in mind that the Declaration was designed as a temporary measure to meet the exceptional economic problems of the time, and having in mind the prospect of continued improvement in the economic situation and hence the expected return to normal conditions, Ministers instructed the Organisation to review the

[10]The Government of Turkey did not participate in the Declaration. [Footnote in original.]

[11]Texts of the three decisions are printed in *Bulletin*, 75: 87-8.

[12]The Government of Portugal is not, at this stage, in a position to renew the Declaration. [Footnote in original.]

situation and to examine any appropriate proposals well in advance of the expiry of the Declaration in 1977. Ministers furthermore agreed to reinforce the Organisation's activities in the field of export credits.

8. Noting the important contribution international trade has made to world economic growth, Ministers recognised the need not only to resist protectionist pressures in all areas but to continue efforts towards further liberalising trade and strengthening the international trade system. In this regard they expressed their strong support for a successful outcome of the Multilateral Trade Negotiations.

II. WORLD INTERDEPENDENCE, DEVELOPMENT CO-OPERATION AND THE DIALOGUE

9. OECD Member Governments believe that intensified economic interchange will bring substantial gains in economic progress and prosperity to all nations including the developing countries. They recognise that growing interdependence means that countries are increasingly affected by the actions and events in other countries. They are therefore determined to contribute through appropriate policies and institutions to greater world economic security in such areas as balance-of-payments, commodities, energy and food.

10. Ministers noted that the strong recovery now under way in many industrialised countries will improve the economic and balance-of-payments situation of developing countries. At the same time Ministers stressed that progress towards more balanced and equitable economic relations between developed and developing countries is an essential element of an improved world economy. They recognised that policy measures are called for to ensure enhanced opportunities for developing countries in trade, investment and technology, noting that such measures are designed to support developing countries' own efforts. Ministers also emphasized that increased concessional development assistance is required in particular for those most in need. Member governments agreed to intensify their efforts, within the OECD, to strengthen policies to these ends.

11. Ministers reaffirmed that co-operation among industrialised countries within the OECD in pursuit of improved relations with the developing countries is essential to achieve a coherent approach to the evolving economic relations between the industrialised and developing countries and to lead to agreements on practical measures. They noted that the recently concluded meeting of the United Nations Conference on Trade and Development, following

the constructive outcome of the Seventh Special Session of the United Nations General Assembly in September 1975, had achieved progress on a number of issues which are being pursued. Ministers also noted that at the Conference on International Economic Co-operation the dialogue has now been well launched and the ground prepared for the achievement of concrete results in the second half of the year. They underlined the value they attach to the successful outcome of the Conference.

12. Ministers reaffirmed the determination of their governments, expressed in the Declaration on Relations with Developing Countries adopted by the Council in 1975, to pursue the dialogue with the developing countries in all appropriate fora in order to arrive quickly at concrete results which would make possible intensified co-operation with them and better meet their development needs. Ministers agreed that their governments are prepared to respond positively to the challenges of the continuing dialogue and evolving relationship between the industrialised and developing countries and stressed the necessity of close collaboration and strengthened co-ordination among industrialised nations in pursuing this objective.

III. STRATEGY FOR SUSTAINED ECONOMIC EXPANSION

13. Recognising that the continuation of present levels of unemployment and inflation would be unacceptable, Ministers agreed on the main elements of a strategy for sustained economic expansion, to be carried out through their respective policies. The basic premise on which this strategy rests is that the steady economic growth needed to restore full employment and satisfy rising economic and social aspirations will not prove sustainable unless all Member countries make further progress towards eradicating inflation. Due weight must also be given to features of the present situation which seem to point to the need for caution in the pursuit of expansionary policies. First, because of the fairly close synchronisation of the recovery in many countries, there is a risk that the strength of the expansionary forces at work may be underestimated. Second, because of the virulence of recent inflationary experience, there is a danger that inflationary expectations could revive quite strongly if the pace of the recovery is too fast. Third, because of inadequate investment in past years in some countries and in certain basic industries, there is a risk of supply bottlenecks at a comparatively early stage of the recovery.

14. Bearing these considerations in mind, Ministers agreed on a strategy whereby governments will direct their policies to attaining price stability and full employment through the achievement of an

economic expansion which is moderate but sustained. This implies that the restoration of full employment and normal levels of capacity utilisation in the OECD area will be progressive and take a number of years. Ministers are convinced that by adopting a strategy along these lines OECD countries will be making an essential contribution to the economic stability and well-being of the world at large.

15. The growth rates implied by this strategy will differ between countries. Because of the depth of the recent recession, a period of somewhat above-average growth will be possible and necessary to restore full employment, although care will be needed to avoid rekindling inflationary forces and to slow down demand in line with longer-term growth potential as the present slack is taken up. Allowing for this recovery element, Ministers consider that if the right policies are followed and inflation rates are further reduced, there is scope for the growth rate for the GNP of the OECD as a whole to average 5 per cent or somewhat more over the five years 1976-80, with world trade expanding by 8 per cent or somewhat more.

16. National economic policies in support of this general strategy of a moderate but sustained expansion should be guided by the following principles:

(a) Governments should make firm use of fiscal and monetary policy to achieve the general stability in their economies that non-inflationary growth requires. This means that action taken to dampen short-term fluctuations in demand must be formulated in the light of the need for greater steadiness and predictability of policies over the medium run.

(b) In many countries, continuing efforts to develop a better social consensus as to the aims of the economic policy will be needed, which may involve various forms of prices and incomes policy. Such policies can complement, but cannot replace, sound demand management policies which are essential in any event.

(c) Action should be taken appropriate to the circumstances to deal with unsatisfactory aspects of the employment situation in accordance with the 1976 Recommendation of the Council of the OECD on a General Employment and Manpower Policy as elaborated by the Manpower and Social Affairs Committee meeting at Ministerial level on 4th-5th March, 1976. This action may include selective policies to cope with sectors and areas which have particularly acute employment problems.

(d) In most countries, policies should be directed more towards promoting investment rather than consumption. In many cases, this will require an appropriate recovery of profits from the depressed levels of recent years. It may also require action to stimulate investment, to encourage savings over the medium run and to restrain the rise of public expenditure.

17. Ministers agree that national policies in pursuit of this strategy should be based on a clear recognition of countries' international responsibilities. They noted that some larger Member countries and quite a number of smaller Member countries are running unsustainably large current account deficits. So long as the OECD area continues to run a large current deficit with the OPEC countries, Member countries in a strong external position should, while pursuing their anti-inflationary policies, not resist market forces tending to push their current account into deficit. The priority task in countries in a weak external position must be effective policies to bring down the rate of inflation. Because of the interaction between domestic policies, inflation rates and exchange rates, the continuation of much stronger inflation in some countries than in others could have adverse effects on growth and international monetary stability. Ministers recognised the importance of inter-governmental consultation and co-operation to support national stabilization policies. Note was taken of the progress made towards ratifying the Agreement establishing the OECD Financial Support Fund, and there was agreement on the need to complete the process rapidly.

18. Ministers discussed the employment problems of European Member countries where emigration has been an important factor in the past. They agreed that more emphasis should be given to the creation of indigenous employment opportunities, and that this could be facilitated by the creation of conditions conducive to increased capital flows to, and imports from, these countries. Major changes in migration flows between some European Member countries call for intensified co-operation between host countries and countries of origin, so that the burden of adjustment can be equitably shared.

19. Ministers examined the current economic situation and concluded that the recovery now evident in almost all Member countries is on a course consistent with achieving sustainable expansion. They welcomed the fact that in many countries unemployment has stopped rising or begun to decline and that the outlook for labour costs offers hope of a further reduction in inflation. But care will be needed to ensure that the recovery is kept under control and to avoid the undue fiscal ease and excessive rates of monetary expansion which characterised the similar phase of the

last upswing; to this end, close international consultation and collaboration will be essential.

20. Ministers instructed the Organisation to examine regularly the extent to which the policies being followed are consistent with the agreed medium-term strategy. They stressed, in particular, the importance of analysis and consultations within the Organisation directed towards the early detection of changes in the pace of expansion in the OECD area, the avoidance of undue fiscal ease or excessive rates of monetary expansion and the identification of potential bottlenecks. They also requested the Secretary-General to ensure that careful attention is given to the problem of the recent divergence in the economic performance of Member countries by the appropriate bodies of the Organisation.

(32) The "Economic Summit," Dorado Beach, Puerto Rico, June 27-28, 1976: Joint Declaration of the participating Heads of State and Government, June 28, 1976.[13]

The heads of state and government of Canada, France, the Federal Republic of Germany, Italy, Japan, the United Kingdom of Great Britain and Northern Ireland and the United States of America[14] met at Dorado Beach, Puerto Rico, on the 27th and 28th of June, 1976, and agreed to the following declaration:

The interdependence of our destinies makes it necessary for us to approach common economic problems with a sense of common purpose and to work toward mutually consistent economic strategies through better cooperation.

We consider it essential to take into account the interests of other nations. And this is most particularly true with respect to the developing countries of the world.

It was for these purposes that we held a broad and productive exchange of views on a wide range of issues. This meeting provided a welcome opportunity to improve our mutual understanding and to intensify our cooperation in a number of areas. Those among us whose countries are members of the European Economic Community intend to make their efforts within its framework.

At Rambouillet, economic recovery was established as a primary goal and it was agreed that the desired stability depends upon the underlying economic and financial conditions in each of our countries.

[13]Text from *Presidential Documents*, 12: 1091-4.
[14]Respectively Prime Minister Pierre Elliott Trudeau, President Valéry Giscard d'Estaing, Chancellor Helmut Schmidt, Prime Minister Aldo Moro, Prime Minister Takeo Miki, Prime Minister James Callaghan, and President Gerald R. Ford.

Significant progress has been achieved since Rambouillet. During the recession there was widespread concern regarding the longer-run vitality of our economies. These concerns have proved to be unwarranted. Renewed confidence in the future has replaced doubts about the economic and financial outlook. Economic recovery is well under way and in many of our countries there has been substantial progress in combatting inflation and reducing unemployment. This has improved the situation in those countries where economic recovery is still relatively weak.

Our determination in recent months to avoid excessive stimulation of our economies and new impediments to trade and capital movements has contributed to the soundness and breadth of this recovery. As a result, restoration of balanced growth is within our grasp. We do not intend to lose this opportunity.

Our objective now is to manage effectively a transition to expansion which will be sustainable, which will reduce the high level of unemployment which persists in many countries and will not jeopardize our common aim of avoiding a new wave of inflation. That will call for an increase in productive investment and for partnership among all groups within our societies. This will involve acceptance, in accordance with our individual needs and circumstances, of a restoration of better balance in public finance, as well as of disciplined measures in the fiscal area and in the field of monetary policy and in some cases supplementary policies, including incomes policy. The formulation of such policies, in the context of growing interdependence, is not possible without taking into account the course of economic activity in other countries. With the right combination of policies we believe that we can achieve our objectives of orderly and sustained expansion, reducing unemployment and renewed progress toward our common goal of eliminating the problem of inflation. Sustained economic expansion and the resultant increase in individual well-being cannot be achieved in the context of high rates of inflation.

At the meeting last November, we resolved differences on structural reform of the international monetary system and agreed to promote a stable system of exchange rates which emphasized the prerequisite of developing stable underlying economic financial conditions.

With those objectives in mind, we reached specific understandings, which made a substantial contribution to the IMF meeting in Jamaica. Early legislative ratification of these agreements by all concerned is desirable. We agreed to improve cooperation in order to further our ability to counter disorderly market conditions and increase our understanding of economic problems and the corrective policies that are needed. We will continue to build on this structure of consultations.

Since November, the relationship between the dollar and most of the main currencies has been remarkably stable. However, some currencies have suffered substantial fluctuations.

The needed stability in underlying economic and financial conditions clearly has not yet been restored. Our commitment to deliberate, orderly and sustained expansion, and to the indispensable companion goal of defeating inflation provides the basis for increased stability.

Our objective of monetary stability must not be undermined by the strains of financing international payments imbalances. We thus recognize the importance of each nation managing its economy and its international monetary affairs so as to correct or avoid persistent or structural international payments imbalances. Accordingly, each of us affirms his intention to work toward a more stable and durable payments structure through the application of appropriate internal and external policies.

Imbalances in world payments may continue in the period ahead. We recognize that problems may arise for a few developed countries which have special needs, which have not yet restored domestic economic stability, and which face major payments deficits. We agree to continue to cooperate with others in the appropriate bodies on further analysis of these problems with a view to their resolution. If assistance in financing transitory balance of payments deficits is necessary to avoid general disruptions in economic growth, then it can best be provided by multilateral means coupled with a firm program for restoring underlying equilibrium.

In the trade area, despite the recent recession, we have been generally successful in maintaining an open trading system. At the OECD we reaffirmed our pledge to avoid the imposition of new trade barriers.

Countries yielding to the temptation to resort to commercial protectionism would leave themselves open to a subsequent deterioration in their competitive standing; the vigor of their economies would be affected while at the same time chain reactions would be set in motion and the volume of world trade would shrink, hurting all countries. Wherever departures from the policy set forth in the recently renewed OECD trade pledge occur, elimination of the restrictions involved is essential and urgent. Also, it is important to avoid deliberate exchange rate policies which would create severe distortions in trade and lead to a resurgence of protectionism.

We have all set ourselves the objective of completing the Multilateral Trade Negotiations by the end of 1977. We hereby reaffirm that objective and commit ourselves to make every effort through the appropriate bodies to achieve it in accordance with the Tokyo Declaration.

Beyond the conclusion of the trade negotiations we recognize the desirability of intensifying and strengthening relationships among the major trading areas with a view to the long-term goal of a maximum expansion of trade.

We discussed East/West economic relations. We welcomed in this context the steady growth of East/West trade, and expressed the hope that economic relations between East and West would develop their full potential on a sound financial and reciprocal commercial basis. We agreed that this process warrants our careful examination, as well as efforts on our part to ensure that these economic ties enhance overall East/West relationships.

We welcome the adoption, by the participating countries, of converging guidelines with regard to export credits. We hope that these guidelines will be adopted as soon as possible by as many countries as possible.

In the pursuit of our goal of sustained expansion, the flow of capital facilitates the efficient allocation of resources and thereby enhances our economic well-being. We, therefore, agree on the importance of a liberal climate for international investment flows. In this regard, we view as a constructive development the declaration which was announced last week when the OECD Council met at the Ministerial level.

In the field of energy, we intend to make efforts to develop, conserve and use rationally the various energy resources and to assist the energy development objectives of developing countries.

We support the aspirations of the developing nations to improve the lives of their peoples. The role of the industrialized democracies is crucial to the success of their efforts. Cooperation between the two groups must be based on mutual respect, take into consideration the interests of all parties and reject unproductive confrontation in favor of sustained and concerted efforts to find constructive solutions to the problems of development.

The industrialized democracies can be most successful in helping the developing countries meet their aspirations by agreeing on, and cooperating to implement, sound solutions to their problems which enhance the efficient operation of the international economy. Close collaboration and better coordination are necessary among the industrialized democracies. Our efforts must be mutually supportive, not competitive. Our efforts for international economic cooperation must be considered as complementary to the policies of the developing countries themselves to achieve sustainable growth and rising standards of living.

At Rambouillet, the importance of a cooperative relationship between the developed and developing nations was affirmed; particular attention was directed to following up the results of the Seventh Special Session of the UN General Assembly, and especially to addressing the balance of payments problems of some developing countries. Since then, substantial progress has been made. We welcome the constructive spirit which prevails in the work carried out in the framework of the Conference on International Economic Cooperation, and also by the positive results achieved in some areas at UNCTAD IV in Nairobi. New measures taken in the IMF have made a substantial contribution to stabilizing the export earnings of the developing countries and to helping them finance their deficits.

We attach the greatest importance to the dialogue between developed and developing nations in the expectation that it will achieve concrete results in areas of mutual interest. And we reaffirm our countries' determination to participate in this process in the competent bodies, with a political will to succeed, looking toward negotiations, in appropriate cases. Our common goal is to find practical solutions which contribute to an equitable and productive relationship among all peoples.

9. CALMER WEATHER AT THE UNITED NATIONS

(33) *"The Role of the United States in the United Nations":*
Statement by Samuel W. Lewis, Assistant Secretary of State
for International Organization Affairs, to the Committee on
Foreign Relations, United States Senate, March 18, 1976. [1]

I greatly appreciate your invitation to appear before this committee on behalf of the Administration to discuss U.S. policy toward the United Nations.

We are passing through a time of turbulence in that organization, and these hearings can help all of us, public and Administration alike, to steer a firmer course.

Consultation between the executive branch and the Congress on U.N. matters is growing, and we welcome that trend. Within the last half year there has been a particularly close and productive cooperation between members of Congress and the executive branch in connection with U.S. participation in the seventh special session of the General Assembly, held last September, on the subject of world economic cooperation. Several from this committee and other interested members of Congress met with Secretary Kissinger on several occasions during the months of preparation, commented on our ideas, and put forward many creative suggestions of their own. Many were reflected in the proposals we put forward in New York. A large number of Senators and Congressmen then joined our delegation at the session itself, participating actively in the negotiations.

The seventh special session endorsed a comprehensive agenda for action by consensus, a resolution which the United States was happy to support. We are convinced that the collaboration between the congressional and executive branches had a major bearing on the success of our efforts to shape the outcome. This example

[1] Department of State Press Release 134; text from *Bulletin*, 74: 443-55.

should surely provide the model for our efforts in future major U.N. endeavors.

But we are equally aware of more worrisome trends. The regular session of the General Assembly last fall was marked by high contention. The United States and some of its friends, particularly Israel, seemed to take it on the chin. Among other actions, a resolution was adopted which Americans fundamentally reject, which they rightly believe to be a wholly unjustified distortion of basic truths—the resolution equating Zionism and racism. And other hostile resolutions were adopted in an atmosphere of confrontation—raising serious questions in the minds of many Americans about the United Nations itself and about the utility of U.S. participation in its work.

Indeed, throughout recent decades there have been large-scale changes in the political environment at the United Nations, especially in the General Assembly. Originally, the organization consisted of about 50 countries, most of which practiced a fairly polite brand of diplomacy—along 19th-century lines. Now, however, membership has expanded to nearly 150 with the addition of about 100 new nations. These countries share a deep dissatisfaction over the cards they were dealt when they became independent. They want to narrow the great gulf of economic inequality. They want a weightier political role in the international state system. They are impatient, and many are eager to dramatize their causes even if this involves a disregard for traditional niceties of diplomacy. Americans understandably are affronted when our country is attacked, or repeatedly outvoted, by small new nations whose independence we championed.

At the same time, many Americans understand that global cooperation is more than ever essential to meet inescapable global problems. We are all increasingly aware that the interdependence of nations in both the economic and security spheres can have a direct effect on the lives of our citizens.

The oil embargo that followed the last major Middle East conflict produced serious hardship in many countries, including our own. Many saw vividly for the first time the inescapable facts of economic interdependence—that political decisions by other governments can damage America's prosperity, can impact on whether millions of Americans have jobs or suffer the economic and social hardships of unemployment, on whether our businesses and our economy grow and flourish, on whether or not our budget can readily sustain vital social, educational, and health programs.

In addition to these pragmatic concerns, there is another factor which makes your current review particularly important. Our government was the chief architect of the U.N. system. We acted in the shadow of a global disaster whose incalculable cost had convinced men and women in every land that a new basis for global cooperation had to be established. Through all the disappointments and setbacks of the past 30 years, we have remained among the chief supporters of constructive and innovative work within the U.N. system. This is because, as President Ford has said:[2]

The United States retains the idealism that made us the driving force behind the creation of the United Nations over three decades ago as a worldwide system to promote peace and progress.

Any assessment of the role of the United States in the United Nations must therefore take into account not merely the issues of the moment but our fundamental interests and the basic ideals of the American people.

Moreover, it is essential that we view our role in the United Nations as an integral part of our overall foreign policy, not as a separate segment. The United States seeks on many fronts to build an international system congenial to the pursuit of our national foreign policy goals. Our participation in the United Nations represents only one part—although certainly an important part—of that larger effort.

If this central point is accepted, it means that we can approach the United Nations in a practical way. We should ask ourselves:

—Not whether the United Nations can solve all of the world's evils, but whether it can contribute significantly to the achievement of American purposes.

—Not whether the United States can win every dispute in the United Nations, but whether through firm, imaginative, and patient participation we can help the United Nations to play its role in building a world order in which all countries, rich and poor, new and old, feel a genuine stake.

To help find answers to these fundamental questions, I would like today to review how we see U.S. interests in the U.N. system as a whole; second, how the General Assembly fits into this picture; third, where we stand now in our effort to encourage more responsible participation in the United Nations by other states; fourth, what future course it would be in our interest to follow; and lastly, what paths we should avoid if we are to protect our basic interests.

[2] Remarks at swearing-in ceremony for Ambassador Scranton; *Presidential Documents*, 12: 431.

The Nature of the U.N. System

The United Nations is often seen as a simple, single entity. As a consequence, simplistic judgments too often affirm that the United Nations is either good or bad, getting worse or better, in the U.S. interest or contrary to it.

The U.N. system, however, is composed of a vast array of institutions embracing an extremely wide spectrum of activities. It includes bodies of nearly universal membership and relatively small subgroups. It includes specialized agencies handling the regulation of daily international intercourse in technical fields like shipping, aviation, communications, finance. It includes bodies working on highly political security issues and others wrestling with the complexities of international economic policy. It includes organs which funnel development and humanitarian aid to many countries. Within many of these institutions there are different types of subbodies—conferences, executive boards, expert groups. Clearly, regarding this range of activities, no single, simple judgment of success or failure can be made.

I believe, however, it may assist in our review to consider U.N. activities in two broad spheres: First, those relating directly to the maintenance of international peace and security and, second, those relating to economic and social cooperation.

In the *security area*, the United Nations, and the Security Council in particular, has made vital contributions to maintaining world peace. Let me illustrate by recalling recent peacekeeping efforts in the Middle East.

During the fourth Arab-Israeli war in 1973, our efforts to achieve a cease-fire and avoid dangerous escalation of the conflict encountered enormous difficulties. In the negotiations it became clear that disengagement between the opposing forces would depend upon the availability of an independent, impartial organization that could provide peacekeeping forces and observe compliance with the disengagement plan. This was an element regarded as indispensable by all sides. The United Nations provided that indispensable element.

This experience, incidentally, underscores a key point in any overall assessment regarding the value of the United Nations. It would be completely misleading to attempt to tally up apparent successes and failures within the U.N. system and then draw a conclusion based on a comparison of the totals as if all of these events were of roughly equal importance. In fact, they are not.

The U.N. operations in the Middle East were an essential ingredient in terminating the fourth Arab-Israeli war. We all know that the conflict, had it continued, would not only have deepened the misery within the area, but it would have gravely jeopardized world peace. No one can be certain that another world war including the United States would not ultimately have ensued. The United Nations performed a role of incalculable importance to the United States.

The United Nations continues to play such a role. The mandates of the U.N. forces both in Sinai and on the Golan Heights have been extended. These forces remain integral elements in preserving options for negotiations toward a just and lasting peace.

As Secretary of State Kissinger recently said:[3]

If this organization had no other accomplishment than its effective peacekeeping role in this troubled area, it would have well justified itself.

In other areas of political tension, the Security Council has also played an important role. It has served increasingly as one of the mechanisms through which a growing crisis may be defused or negotiated or at least kept from erupting. On a number of occasions, it has permitted a government being pressed toward a military reaction or intransigence to allay such pressures by taking the issue to the Council. This was true, for example, of a number of the sessions devoted to Cyprus, to the Spanish Sahara, to Djibouti, and to Iceland as well. In Cyprus, a peacekeeping force has been deployed at the direction of the Council since 1964.[4] The Force, in addition to patrolling the lines of confrontation, has contributed to the satisfaction of humanitarian needs.

The Security Council continues to be occupied with important business, including the problems of southern Africa and the thorny Middle East dispute. Although inevitably there will be conflicting viewpoints, we find that the Council has been conducting its proceedings in a serious and responsible atmosphere, employing relatively new informal procedures which reduce somewhat the temptation for delegates to play to world propaganda galleries.

The Security Council will continue to be available in the event of unforeseen crises—ready to meet at all times and at a moment's notice. Its constant availability provides an appropriate check against efforts by other bodies to issue recommendations bearing on security matters. Since the charter has assigned the Council primary responsibility in the area of peace and security, recommendations of other bodies remain only that. It is only the Council—in which the United States retains its veto—which can take binding decisions.

[3]From address to the 30th Regular Session of the U.N. General Assembly, Sept. 22, 1975, in *AFR, 1975:* 468.
[4]Resolution 186 (1964), Mar. 4, 1964; text in *Documents, 1964:* 103-5.

Let me turn now to the U.N.'s activities affecting *international economic and social cooperation*. This is a vast realm involving both the conduct of day-to-day work in regulating the world's continuing business and also the development of goals and concrete programs regarding global problems of economic interdependence, as at the seventh special session.

I would like first to sketch several examples of continuing day-to-day business within the U.N. system which are of intrinsic importance to our citizens:

The International Civil Aviation Organization, for example, helps to set and maintain high standards for international air transportation. Needless to say, for our citizens, who probably use international air transportation more than the citizens of any other country in the world, international cooperation in improving safety and efficiency is of vital, direct importance. And the standards developed by the ICAO will assist many countries to take measures that can lessen the occurrence of aircraft hijacking.

For many years the World Health Organization has worked patiently and with determination to rid the world of the highly contagious and age-old disease smallpox. These endeavors have been outstandingly successful. The WHO also maintains a worldwide alert system to warn governments of the outbreak of serious contagious diseases anywhere in the world, and this activity is clearly of great value to our own health officials and to Americans—millions of them—who travel abroad.

The Food and Agriculture Organization maintains programs which directly lessen the threat of introduction into the United States of foreign plant and animal diseases and pests. This organization has established a program in which over 100 countries participate to maintain internationally accepted food standards. The United States, as a major food exporter and importer, directly benefits, not only because international trade is facilitated, but also because the health and safety of Americans is better protected. Moreover, new research programs sponsored by the FAO are expected to improve the varieties of our food crops.

Several bodies within the U.N. system are encouraging programs to control production of opium and other dangerous drugs and to curtail international drug trafficking. These efforts largely respond to priorities we have urged, and they are of undoubted benefit in the overall U.S. effort to counter drug abuse among our citizens.

The International Monetary Fund, another organization within the U.N. system, plays an indispensable role in promoting international monetary cooperation, facilitating international trade and finance, and promoting world economic stability. These are areas in which our own country has huge interests which would be difficult to exaggerate.

A little known body within the U.N. system is the U.N. Disaster Relief Office. It helps to coordinate assistance from many parts of the world when a country has been overwhelmed by natural disaster.

The International Atomic Energy Agency plays an indispensable role in the effort to prevent the spread of nuclear weapons. The Agency is responsible for establishing safeguards standards and carrying out international inspections to insure that nuclear materials are not being transferred from peaceful uses to weapons uses.

The World Meteorological Organization maintains a World Weather Watch—a global network of meteorological stations collecting and exchanging weather information on a continuous basis. This program has made possible improved forecasts for U.S. passenger jets crossing the Atlantic and the Pacific. It has also enabled more accurate forecasts of hurricanes originating in the Caribbean which affect the eastern half of the United States. Large-scale research programs coordinated by this U.N. body will improve our understanding of climate changes which are fundamental to agricultural and economic planning.

The Intergovernmental Maritime Consultative Organization is developing standards which nations are generally following to prevent pollution of the seas. This organization's work in the field of safety at sea has long been recognized as of the highest value to all countries whose ships and peoples travel the oceans.

This list of examples could be extended almost indefinitely. I have mentioned only a few to illustrate the range of work being done within the U.N. system today which affects directly the interests and concerns of our citizens.

I have already referred to last September's seventh special session of the General Assembly on world economic cooperation. At that session our government presented a comprehensive set of proposals which resulted in the adoption of a wide-ranging practical program for improving economic cooperation between the developing countries and the industrial world.

The important point to bear in mind about the special session is that it provided an opportunity for us to see whether it was possible to fashion approaches to current economic problems which would be *in the mutual interest of all countries.* I cannot stress this point too strongly. What the U.S. Government was proposing at the special session was a nonideological approach to problems of economic interdependence, based on concrete steps of benefit to poor countries and rich countries alike. We found an overwhelming majority of governments in the Third and Fourth Worlds ready to try this path with us.

Since September, we have been vigorously following up on our special session proposals. At meetings of the International Monetary Fund in Jamaica two months ago, the United States took the lead in achieving adoption of measures to stabilize the earnings of developing countries and to help meet the severe balance-of-payments problems which many of them are experiencing We have gotten well underway in the North-South dialogue at the Conference on International Economic Cooperation taking place in Paris. At the multilateral trade negotiations in Geneva, we are vigorously promoting our special session proposals. And in anticipation of the fourth UNCTAD, the U.N. Conference on Trade and Development in May of this year, the Department of State is working intensively on further practical proposals to implement more of the broad negotiating agenda adopted at the special session.

Let me conclude this part of my statement with this observation: As we build on the program begun at the seventh special session, we will not merely be assisting the less fortunate; we will be helping to create healthier conditions throughout the world which provide more opportunities for American business. The long-term results will create more jobs for American workers and also lessen the danger of raw material scarcities which can fuel a worldwide inflation that would erode the real income of consumers in the United States and throughout the developed world.

It is easy for most Americans to agree that bodies like the World Health Organization or the Security Council are indispensable and continue to merit full American support. But many question the usefulness of the General Assembly or other parts of the U.N. system whose utility is less obvious; they are prone to call on our government to cease participating or to reduce our financial support.

This issue has recently arisen with respect to the General Assembly because of parliamentary abuses which have taken place there and because that body has recently taken a number of irresponsible actions—such as passage of the resolution equating Zionism and racism. The question is a valid one. But in order to answer it, we must first take a careful look at the overall activity of the General Assembly to see how it fits with other activities of the United Nations and how American interests are affected by its work.

The Role of the General Assembly

The General Assembly is the central body of the United Nations.

It considers and disposes of certain subjects which are dealt with nowhere else in the U.N. system, but it also provides guidance and coordination for many activities handled by specialized and technical bodies. Moreover, many of the activities of the United Nations which we strongly support are financed through decisions taken by the General Assembly.

The best way for me to explain the Assembly's role might be to provide a series of illustrations showing the interconnection between the General Assembly and other activities:

Support for Middle East peacekeeping operations. Peacekeeping operations in the Middle East and elsewhere have been financed in accordance with decisions of the General Assembly. While the members of the Security Council take policy decisions which set the basic lines of action, *all* U.N. members have a responsibility to contribute to the costs. All members jointly determine the amount and apportionment of the assessed expenses and in fact have done so through the General Assembly. Needless to say, the essential peacekeeping operations in the Middle East could not be carried out unless there were successful cooperation in determining how to pay for the troops, supplies, and other burdens inherent in these large operations. We are pleased that a pattern of cooperation in providing financial support for Middle East peacekeeping has continued within the General Assembly.

Consideration of security issues. It is often thought that security issues are dealt with seriously only within the Security Council. This is not so. Many of the most important security issues of significance to the United States have been considered by both the Security Council and the General Assembly, and there is unavoidable interaction between the two bodies. This has, for example, been the case with the Middle East, with Korea, and with Cyprus. In the latter case, the General Assembly has adopted resolutions which the United States considered moderate and constructive and which have had a direct influence in stimulating talks between the Greek and Turkish communities. It is encouraging that talks have recently resumed under the auspices of the Secretary General, who is pursuing his mission with skill and dedication. I should also mention in passing that the Security Council and the General Assembly are further interconnected because it is the General Assembly which elects the nonpermanent members of the Security Council.

Promotion of economic and social cooperation. Within the United Nations, the General Assembly has not merely a partial role, but a predominant one. I have already cited the seventh special session of the Assembly on world economic cooperation. A meeting of that sort could only have taken place in the General

Assembly. It will be the General Assembly and some of its subsidiary bodies, the Second Committee and the Economic and Social Council, which will monitor implementation of many of the concrete measures for economic cooperation which the United States has proposed.

U.N. involvement in international drug control. As the result of a U.S. initiative, the General Assembly adopted in 1970 a resolution authorizing establishment of the U.N. Fund for Drug Abuse Control.[5] The technical and executing personnel for many of the projects financed by the Fund come from the Division of Narcotic Drugs, part of the U.N. Secretariat, which is supported by the budget of the United Nations as voted by the General Assembly. The Fund's most important project has been its assistance to Turkey in setting up strict controls over its poppy production. It was not so long ago that it was feared that heroin from Turkish opium might once again appear on the streets of American cities. In 1975 the Fund-supported Turkish program prevented this from happening. Today the Fund is helping the Turkish Government to make this success permanent.

The General Assembly is also responsible for supporting unprecedented diplomatic efforts to achieve international agreement at a series of U.N. conferences on the law of the sea. I think it is broadly recognized that the United States must persevere, no matter how hard the task, in working out with other countries fair, sound, and effective rules to govern this enormous sector of our planet. World peace and security are at stake, as is the future rational and peaceful exploitation of the resources of the oceans and the seabeds. The third major session of the conference is now underway in New York, and we are hopeful that a comprehensive oceans treaty may soon be in sight.

The U.N. Fund for Population Activities is another activity directly connected with the General Assembly. Many members of the Congress and public have been deeply concerned with the difficult dilemma of trying to make meaningful gains through development assistance when population growth outstrips economic growth. The U.N. Fund for Population Activities is supporting important projects that help countries to slow down explosive population growth rates. The Fund's connection with the General Assembly is very direct. Several years ago the General Assembly debated and adopted a world plan of action on this subject[6]—a major step forward for the nations of the world. This General Assembly action provides a fundamental framework and

[5] Resolution 2719 (XXV), Dec. 15, 1970.
[6] Resolution 2211 (XXI), Dec. 17, 1966.

impetus for all population control activities, including particularly those of the U.N. Fund.

The U.N. Environment Program is a creature of the General Assembly, having been established by a resolution of the Assembly in 1972, and the budget of the United Nations contributes to its work. Since the U.N.'s Stockholm Conference on the Human Environment, the United States has attached great importance to the mounting of a major U.N. program to begin the work necessary to reverse worldwide deterioration of the human environment. A concerted worldwide program can only be realized within the U.N. system, and the Assembly has taken the essential steps to launch and support this effort.

The General Assembly has also recently played a constructive role in planning worldwide cooperative efforts to cope with international food problems. The Assembly decided, as a result of a U.S. initiative, to convene a World Food Conference.[7] Held in November 1974, the conference was generally successful. Among many other actions, the conference led to the formation of the World Food Council, which reports to the General Assembly. World food problems clearly are of central importance to the United States, both for humanitarian reasons and because they have direct impact on our own economic well-being.

The U.N. Disaster Relief Office, to which I earlier referred, is another activity guided and supported by the General Assembly. We believe that the worldwide coordination efforts of this organization can save the American Government, and thus the American taxpayer, significant sums by helping to avoid overlapping or duplicative disaster relief efforts. The United States has always responded generously when other countries are struck by natural disaster, as recently occurred in Guatemala. I am sure that we will continue to do so. The functioning of the U.N.'s disaster relief coordination effort is of real practical value to the United States.

Finally, the General Assembly also serves as the only truly global forum for promoting disarmament agreements which are in our interests and the broad interests of all other nations. Certain negotiations, like the Strategic Arms Limitation Talks, must of course be carried out by the nations most directly involved, the United States and the U.S.S.R. But there are other vital disarmament areas, like the current effort to control forms of warfare based upon manipulation of man's environment, which should merit wide international support and participation. The General Assembly has recently discussed a draft agreement proposed by the

[7]Cf. *AFR, 1974:* 427-42.

United States. The Assembly's activities are a necessary part of the process of achieving broad international support for a sound treaty.

There is another aspect of the General Assembly which I have not so far discussed. That is its role as a universal forum to debate basic viewpoints, to develop consensus when this is possible, and to register honest disagreement.

We must expect to encounter serious differences in point of view among the nearly 150 countries that comprise the United Nations. These differences do not derive primarily from hostility to the United States, though hostility is sometimes a factor. More often they reflect the diversity of interests among countries widely differing in geography, state of development, and historical background. Amid such diversity, the United States will not always have its way, and indeed it should not expect to. What is important is that countries pursue their differences in a spirit of mutual respect and that they still attempt, to the greatest extent possible, to agree on concrete measures from which there can be common gain.

Obviously, these precepts have not always been followed and there have been recent instances when countries have gone beyond the bounds of vigorous, constructive debate and have attempted to establish by "parliamentary victories" doctrines which a substantial part of the world cannot accept.

But even where there is sharp conflict, it is important that all of us keep in mind this fundamental aspect of the United Nations: It is not some abstract entity called the United Nations which is responsible for disagreements or irresponsible and confrontational acts; it is individual countries acting through their representatives which make decisions about what should be proposed, supported, or opposed at the United Nations. In this sense the United Nations is but a mirror of the attitudes of governments throughout the world.

Certainly any parliamentary body can distort the reflection of the real views of those represented. For example, there is no doubt that in many representational bodies, including the United Nations, the extent of support for or opposition to a particular proposal is often affected by old-fashioned "log-rolling" or by whether a particular representative desires to build personal support for an elected office in the body. In general, however, the opinions and concerns of governments are mirrored in the actions of their U.N. representatives.

Let us keep one point firmly in mind: The United States does not fear vigorous debate. When widespread disagreement about an important issue exists, it is in our interest that it be exposed and debated. The reality of differing viewpoints, differing objectives, will not go away simply because countries may find it expedient in one forum or another to hold back in expressing their opinions. Open discussion of differing viewpoints is an essential first step toward making progress in understanding the full dimensions of a problem, the interests at stake, and in identifying and enlarging on those areas where there may be common ground.

This does not mean that we welcome or enjoy hostile or exaggerated attacks. When debate is carried on in an irresponsible fashion, positions can harden and the prospects for accommodation diminish. We will therefore work in every way to encourage serious, responsible debate, while forcefully rebutting unwarranted attacks on our good name. But the United States is a strong enough country, and our overall record of past constructive achievements is impressive enough, that we need not shrink timidly from the fray—even when the going gets pretty tough.

Where We Stand

I have already discussed where we stand with respect to some of the main substantive subjects within the U.N. system. As I have indicated, we believe the United Nations has done, and is continuing to do, responsible work in many areas relating to maintaining international peace and security. We also believe that the United Nations is doing essential work on many economic and social issues. What I would like to focus on now is where we stand in our reinforced diplomatic efforts to encourage a greater degree of responsibility and genuine cooperation among all countries in the United Nations.

The United States has for some time been distressed by what has seemed a growing trend toward confrontation within the U.N. system. We witnessed an acute example of this confrontation nearly two years ago at the sixth special session of the General Assembly. Many less developed and nonaligned countries seemed much more interested at that session in preserving an artificial bloc unity through which they could score "victories" over the industrial world than in coming to grips with the real economic issues at stake. We were distressed not solely because of the negative political ramifications of this attitude but also because the practice of ramming through "precooked," confrontational resolutions would destroy all possibility of practical cooperation.

Our concern led us to begin a sustained effort to encourage a turning away from confrontation toward cooperation. The Secretary of State made a series of major statements during 1975 in which he spelled out with utmost clarity that countries cannot have it both ways: they cannot expect to challenge and confront us in some arenas and then automatically expect our full cooperation in others. And we did much more. We attempted to demonstrate, not only in conjunction with the Secretary's statements, but in numerous diplomatic representations, that through the practice of cooperation and conciliation, through the beginning of genuine dialogue, there were concrete gains to be realized by all.

Since confrontation seemed to have reached a peak at the sixth special session, we decided to focus special effort on our preparations for the seventh special session in September of last year. We viewed that session as a test case, to see whether countries would negotiate rather than confront in the General Assembly when we ourselves made major efforts to present concrete action proposals.

We believe this effort was a success, and I am pleased to say that this is not solely a view of the Administration but also one that has been expressed by the congressional group which participated in the special session. The congressional advisers reported that the session "marks a significant turning point in U.S. relations with the developing countries and sets the stage for a new era of economic partnership between rich and poor nations." They also said that the session "eases a decade of confrontation over how to narrow the widening gap in the distribution and control of global resources." And they referred to "the success of the Seventh Special Session, in creating a positive dialog and an atmosphere of negotiation on North/South issues."

Shortly after these encouraging developments were taking place, however, the General Assembly was also the scene of some actions based on confrontation and political antagonism. One such action stood out at the last General Assembly—the resolution equating Zionism and racism.[8] It was a distressing and deplorable resolution which we know to be wholly unjustified. Nonetheless, it is our duty, no matter how strongly we feel about that resolution, to assess it objectively:

The *first* thing which needs to be said is that the resolution is not binding on us, or on any other member of the United Nations. Like most General Assembly resolutions, it is merely a recommendation. As Secretary Kissinger has said: "The United States will ignore this vote, pay no attention to it. . . ."[9]

Second, we must recognize that, throughout this deplorable episode, some countries displayed objectivity and good sense. In other words, a substantial number of countries, including many from the Third World, refused to be bulldozed by the extremist leadership. This means that the extremists had no iron grip on all votes of the nonaligned. True, in the end the numerical vote

[8] Resolution 3379 (XXX), Nov. 10, 1975; text in *AFR, 1975:* 507-8.
[9] Remarks of Nov. 12, 1974, Pittsburgh, in *Bulletin*, 73: 766.

went against us, but in the long run, it may be of more significance that bloc solidarity was fractured.

Third, we must ask ourselves: What are the practical consequences of the Zionism resolution? Is it likely to lead to the exclusion of Israel from the General Assembly? It should be recalled that some U.N. members did try last year to begin an effort to exclude Israel. Fortunately the effort was thwarted, largely because many African and nonaligned countries did not support it. Some of the countries which were against expulsion did, however, support the resolution equating Zionism and racism. They have said that they did so because they believed it represented a way to register a strong protest regarding the Palestinian problem. We will, in any event, continue as we have in the past to resist with the utmost seriousness any unconstitutional exclusion of a member of the United Nations from General Assembly activities. Such an abuse of the charter would pose the gravest threat to the viability of the organization as a whole and call fundamentally into question continuing U.S. support and participation.

Fourth, will there be other consequences of the Zionism resolution affecting the work of the United Nations? Yes, there will be. Of most immediate significance, the Zionism resolution applies to other recently adopted resolutions relating to the Decade for Action To Combat Racism and Racial Discrimination, which was launched in 1973.[10] We therefore decided not to participate in this activity. Recently we took concrete steps to implement this policy. We instructed our representative at UNESCO to inform the Director General that we would not participate in a meeting of experts to draft a UNESCO declaration on racism. The meeting was postponed.

U.S. Policy in the Future

I would like now to discuss, in light of this review, what we in the Administration believe should be the American approach to participation in the United Nations. I shall do so first in terms of the direct positive steps we think should be pursued in order to advance American interests, and then I would like to outline some of the policies which we believe it would be contrary or harmful to American interests to adopt.

First, the steps we intend to pursue:

—The Administration intends to continue to support in an effective, vigorous, and tough-minded way all of those programs in

[10]Designated by Resolution 3057 (XXVIII), Nov. 2, 1973.

the United Nations which offer benefits to the American people. As I think I have demonstrated, there are programs and activities of benefit throughout the entire system: in the Security Council, in specialized agencies, in many technical and ad hoc committees, and in the General Assembly itself.

—We will continue selectively to refuse to participate in U.N. activities which we believe are fundamentally unsound or grossly irresponsible. An immediate consequence of this approach is our decision, caused by the resolution equating Zionism and racism, not to participate in the Decade To Combat Racism. We hope that our firm stand will give many countries serious second thoughts about the wisdom of letting a situation develop in which over the longer term they lose more than they gain.

On the diplomatic front, we have intensified our efforts to impress on other governments that standards of cooperation and restraint largely prevalent in the conduct of bilateral relations should also prevail in multilateral relations. We are doing everything possible to counter the belief that attacks on the motivation and the basic good faith of the United States can be safely and inexpensively delivered in international forums. While we welcome honest and vigorous debate over issues, countries should not believe, without any concern for the consequences, that they can attack the vital interests of the United States in behalf of some abstract concept of group solidarity, particularly when their own national interests are not involved. When we see a consistent pattern of hostility toward the United States, unjustified by any reasonable and honest differences of policy, we will consider whether there are appropriate direct bilateral responses that we should carry out. It will of course continue to be our duty in any such cases to keep in mind the practical balance of American national interests.

—In meetings of international organizations, and particularly in the General Assembly, we will continue to speak out firmly and forcefully in behalf of American interests. There may be differences of judgment from time to time on precisely how this may best be done, but basically an approach of vigor and candor on our part strengthens our participation in the United Nations. Others will know that we care more about the work of the United Nations and about their opinions when we take the time and the trouble to engage ourselves in vigorous give-and-take. Moreover, it seems clear that such an approach will be strongly supported by the American people and will be important for maintaining the public's confidence in our work.

—To strengthen our capacity to interrelate effectively our multilateral and bilateral diplomacy, the Department of State has taken important new organizational steps. We have established within the Bureau of International Organization Affairs a new Office of Multilateral Affairs, under the supervision of a Deputy Assistant Secretary of State. The basic responsibility of this office is to work even more intensively than in the past with our regional bureaus and our embassies in order to achieve maximum possible support from other countries in pursuing issues of greatest concern to the United States. The overall thrust of this effort will be to increase our effectiveness in persuading others on the merits of the issues. There is a tremendous job to be done here. We need to approach governments early. We need to build up serious and frank dialogues with many countries which continue throughout the year. We need to frame our arguments in ways which are most meaningful to countries with dissimilar backgrounds. In short, we need to use all opportunities, both in our bilateral and multilateral contacts, to *persuade*—to build a climate of greater understanding.

—In addition to these specific immediate actions, we are taking broader long-range actions to build up the capability of the personnel of the Department of State and the Foreign Service to perform more effectively in advancing American interests in international organizations. We are building up work on multilateral affairs as a specialty. To be sure that the best officers are attracted to assignments in multilateral diplomacy, we are establishing new training programs and designating positions in our embassies to concentrate on multilateral affairs problems on a year-round basis. The success of all of our efforts in multilateral affairs ultimately will depend to a large measure on the talents, skills, and training of our personnel.

Let me discuss now certain courses of action which we do *not* think are in the American interest:

First, withdrawal from the United Nations as a whole. The President has made clear that the United States continues to support the United Nations. We believe that the organization as a whole serves many important American interests. This option would hurt, not help, the United States.

Second, cessation of our active participation in the General Assembly. We do not believe this is either a desirable or a practical course of action. There are many Assembly activities which are beneficial to us and many which are intertwined with vital activities in other forums like the Security Council. For us to cease our active participation in the Assembly's work would deprive us of an influential voice on such issues as: the funding and administration of peacekeeping operations; the planning and shaping of important international conferences, like the World Food Conference and the

Law of the Sea Conference; the development of new international institutions like the International Fund for Agricultural Development; the formulation and approval of the U.N. budget, which supports such activities as international drug control and worldwide efforts to improve the environment.

Third, reduction in the U.S. contribution to the U.N.'s budget. This also would be a self-defeating course. We have a treaty obligation to pay our assessed contribution to a U.N. budget properly adopted by its members. The Administration does not intend to disregard the treaty obligations of the United States, and we are certain the Congress would agree. But even if this fundamental consideration were not present, it would still serve no practical purpose to reduce unilaterally our contribution. There is no realistic way to prevent activities which we do not like as a result of such a reduction. The Soviet Union tried this course when it refused to pay its assessments for U.N. bonds required to relieve financial strains arising out of U.N. peacekeeping operations. The net result was not to stop the peacekeeping operations, but to place additional burdens on the funding of all activities covered by the U.N. budget. We should not ourselves consider reductions which would only have the impact of making it harder to support the many activities which we feel are beneficial. I would note in passing that under the present assessment rates the United States is treated specially—and favorably. If the formula used for calculating the dues of others—for example, the United Kingdom, France, the Soviet Union—were applied strictly to the United States, we would pay more than the 25 percent we do now. A great many countries now contribute a larger share of their gross national product to the United Nations than does the United States.

Fourth, cutting off U.S. bilateral assistance to all countries which supported the Zionism resolution or other resolutions which were egregiously irresponsible or hostile. We believe that this type of shotgun approach would harm American interests. It would be playing into the hands of extremist adversaries for us to lash out equally at all who voted for the Zionism resolution, without recognizing important differences in underlying situations and even some possible differences in motives. In short, our bilateral programs serve a great many American interests and are carried out for a wide and complex variety of reasons. We should not subordinate all of these American interests to a single vote, no matter how offensive, on a recommendatory resolution which we and many other members intend to disregard.

Fifth, reduction of U.S. support for multilateral development assistance, especially through the U.N. Development Program. This also would be contrary to American interests. By cutting back on our own contributions, we would be lessening significantly the money available for many close friends who benefit from UNDP programs. In addition, we would be lessening the assistance available to many of the poorest countries, like the drought-stricken nations in Africa. This dimension—that some aid is of an essentially humanitarian character—also argues against proposals to cut back on our bilateral economic assistance. But there is an even more fundamental point involving the calculation of U.S. interests. We do not support UNDP as a favor to other nations. We do so because we believe it is in our interest. We believe that the development efforts fostered by the UNDP and other multilateral programs will over time contribute to creating a healthier, expanding world economy—one in which there will be more opportunities for American business, for growing and profitable trade, all of which can have the consequence of greater American prosperity.

Conclusion

Mr. Chairman,[11] this hearing provides a valuable occasion for the Congress and the Administration to consider together issues of fundamental importance to the American people. The breadth of our interests involved comprehends our physical security, our economic well-being, and even our ability to pursue the kind of way of life which we cherish.

It is clear that it would be wrong, even tragic, to take only a short-range view of individual activities within the U.N. system. As the Secretary of State commented last year in Pittsburgh, "we also will keep in mind that we have long-term obligations and that we will not be driven by the emotions of the day."[12] All of us, I submit, must make every conceivable effort to keep our sights fixed on our larger long-range goals.

We will not, Mr. Chairman, ever experience in any continuing body, domestic or international, a steady and straight graph of successes or failures. There will be ups and downs. We have recently experienced a serious low point. But we have also experienced some points that are very high indeed. Foremost among these is the outstanding American success at the seventh special session on international economic cooperation. We do not exclude that other high points, other successes, are possible. In fact, we believe that they are. But we can achieve them not by withdrawing but by participating—by staying and fighting for what we know to be right.

We will not ignore our difficulties. We will not pretend that we have not had setbacks—because indeed we have. But equally, we in

[11]John Sparkman, Democrat of Alabama.
[12]News conference statement, Pittsburgh, Nov. 12, 1975, in *Bulletin*, 73: 772.

the Administration, and we hope and trust that this is true of Americans generally, will not give up in a fight where there are important and fundamental gains to be made for our country.

And we must maintain historical perspective. Since the United Nations was founded some 30 years ago at San Francisco, the world has witnessed fundamental changes which no one could have predicted.

Ambassador Adlai Stevenson, on the occasion of the U.N.'s 20th anniversary, shortly before his death, described the situation this way:[13]

> In the bright glow of 1945 too many looked to the United Nations for the full and final answer to world peace. And in retrospect that day may seem to have opened with the hint of a false dawn.
>
> Certainly we have learned the hard way how elusive is peace, how durable is man's destructive drive, how various are the forms of his aggressions.
>
> We have learned, too, how distant is the dream of those better standards of life in larger freedom, how qualified our capacity to practice tolerance, how conditional our claims to the dignity and worth of the human person, how reserved our respect for the obligations of law.

He then described the changes taking place in the world:

> Already science and technology are integrating our world into an open workshop where each new invention defines a new task, and reveals a shared interest, and invites yet another common venture.
>
> In our sprawling workshop of the world community, nations are joined in cooperative endeavor: improving soils, purifying water, harnessing rivers, eradicating disease, feeding children, diffusing knowledge, spreading technology, surveying resources, lending capital, probing the seas, forecasting the weather, setting standards, developing law, and working away at a near infinitude of down-to-earth tasks—tasks for which science has given us the knowledge and technology has given us the tools, and common sense has given us the wit to perceive that common interest impels us to common enterprise.
>
> Common enterprise is the pulse of world community, the heartbeat of a working peace . . . .

[13]Ambassador Adlai E. Stevenson died in London July 14, 1966. Text of Stevenson address, June 25, 1965, in *Bulletin*, 53: 101-5 (July 19, 1965).

Mr. Chairman, I can find no words that better express my own view of the United Nations than those spoken by this great American on that occasion:

. . . we support the United Nations; and we shall work in the future, as we have worked in the past, to add strength, and influence, and permanence to all that the organization stands for in this, our tempestuous, tormented, talented world of diversity in which all men are brothers and all brothers are somehow, wondrously, different—save in their need for peace.

(34) Third United Nations Conference on the Law of the Sea: Statement by Secretary of State Kissinger on the conclusion of the Fifth Session, held in New York August 2-September 17, 1976.[14]

The law of the sea negotiations have just ended their current session in New York on September 17. The work they have undertaken is among the most important, complex, and difficult of any negotiations in this century. The delegations are attempting to establish a legal regime for nearly three-quarters of the surface of the globe. With some 150 nations participating, each seeking to protect its interests, it is not surprising that progress has been slow, given the diversity of views represented. However, significant progress has been made since the first substantive session in 1974.

The present revised single negotiating text represents a consensus on a large number of issues before the conference. This text has been maintained in this session as the basis for negotiations. A broad consensus already exists in certain key areas, including a 12-mile territorial sea, establishing coastal state resource and other rights in a 200-mile economic zone, protecting navigational rights, and marine pollution. However, the United States believes the present text remains imperfect and requires further changes in a certain number of key areas, such as:

—A regime for mining deep seabed minerals.
—The nature of the economic zone.
—The provisions for marine scientific research in the economic zone.
—The articles dealing with the exploitation of resources in the continental margin beyond 200 miles.

[14]Department of State Press Release 446, Sept. 17; text from *Bulletin*, 75: 451-3.

—The rights of landlocked and geographically disadvantaged states in the economic zone.

During meetings between myself and certain other delegations September 1–2, the United States put forward important new ideas on a number of key topics still at issue. With respect to deep seabed mining we proposed a package approach which would include assured access in all its aspects to deep seabed mining sites by all nations and their citizens along with a financing arrangement to enable the proposed Enterprise (the independent operating arm of the International Seabed Authority) to get into business. As part of that package we further proposed that there could be a review, in 25 years perhaps, to determine if the provisions of the treaty regarding the system of seabed exploitation were working adequately. This was a significant move which generated considerable interest which we believe can be transformed at the next session into specific treaty language.

A number of delegations, representing all concerned groups, have expressed to us their belief that our package proposal represented a constructive contribution to the negotiations. This reaction is encouraging, and we intend in this same spirit to follow up this initiative both during the period between sessions and at the next session. On the other hand, some delegations chose tactics of confrontation. Such tactics cannot work and will inevitably lead to deadlock and unilateral action.

With respect to the issues in Committee II of the conference dealing with navigation and the nature of the economic zone, the United States continues to believe that a satisfactory solution is within reach. While specific language on the nature of the proposed economic zone has not yet been agreed, several promising ideas have been considered. We believe that a solution can be found which will provide for both the legitimate interests of the coastal states in protecting their resource and other interests and the high seas freedoms of the international community in the economic zone. These provisions are important in maintaining global security and supporting our allies in this dangerous age.

In Committee III the United States is seeking protection of the marine environment and preservation of the right to conduct marine scientific research. The present text already contains important provisions on ocean pollution which we seek to strengthen. With respect to marine scientific research in the economic zone, we have proposed a compromise which will give the coastal states the right to control marine scientific research directly related to resource exploitation but which will insure the right to conduct other forms of marine scientific research which benefit all mankind.

In order for an overall package settlement to be viable, the treaty must contain provisions for comprehensive, obligatory, and binding third-party dispute settlement. This session has made considerable progress toward that goal.

We believe that equitable resolution of these and other key issues in these negotiations can be found. Unless this is the case various governments may conclude agreement is not possible, resulting in unilateral action which can lead to conflict over the uses of ocean space.

The United States has a major interest as a global power in preventing such conflict and thus will continue to seek overall solutions acceptable to all groups of countries. In so doing, however, we will continue vigorously to safeguard essential American interests. We will work cooperatively with other nations, but we expect a reciprocal attitude of good will and reasonableness. There are limits beyond which the United States will not go, and we are close to such limits now.

We must now move toward businesslike negotiations and toward a recognition that the alternative to a treaty would serve no national or international community interest. I continue to believe that a law of the sea convention can be achieved. The United States will seek to build on the progress made to date and will continue its intensive efforts to achieve a treaty. A successful outcome will bring major benefits to this nation and help shape a more peaceful and prosperous international community.

(35) 31st Regular Session of the United Nations General Assembly (Part One), New York, September 21-December 22, 1976.

(a) "Toward a New Understanding of Community": Address by Secretary of State Kissinger to the Assembly, September 30, 1976.[15]

Let me first congratulate this body for electing Ambassador Amerasinghe of Sri Lanka to preside over this 31st session of the General Assembly. He is a diplomat of great international stature who, among his many distinctions, has provided indispensable leadership to the crucial negotiations on the law of the sea.

I would also like to pay tribute to the Secretary General for his tireless efforts on behalf of the world community. He successfully embodies the charter's principles of fairness, impartiality, and dedication to the causes of global peace and human dignity.

The United Nations was born of the conviction that peace is both

[15]Department of State Press Release 485; text from *Bulletin*, 75: 497-510.

indivisible and more than mere stability, that for peace to be lasting it must fulfill mankind's aspirations for justice, freedom, economic well-being, the rule of law, and the promotion of human rights. But the history of this organization has been in considerable measure the gradual awareness that humanity would not inevitably share a single approach to these goals.

The United Nations has survived—and helped to manage—30 years of vast change in the international system. It has come through the bitterness of the cold war. It has played a vital role in the dismantling of the colonial empires. It has helped moderate conflicts and is manning truce lines in critical parts of the world. It has carried out unprecedented efforts in such areas as public health, development assistance, and technical cooperation.

But the most important challenge of this organization lies still ahead: to vindicate mankind's positive and nobler goals and help nations achieve a new understanding of community.

With modern communications, human endeavor has become a single experience for peoples in every part of the planet. We share the wonders of science and technology, the trials of industrialization and social change, and a constant awareness of the fate and dreams of our fellow men.

The world has shrunk, but the nations of the world have not come closer together. Paradoxically, nationalism has been on the rise at the precise time when the most serious issues we all face can only be resolved through a recognition of our interdependence. The moral and political cohesion of our world may be eroding just when a sense of community has become indispensable.

Fragmentation has affected even this body. Nations have taken decisions on a bloc or regional basis by rigid ideologies, before even listening to the debate in these halls; on many issues positions have been predetermined by prior conferences containing more than half the membership of the United Nations. The tendency is widespread to come here for battle rather than negotiation. If these trends continue, the hope for world community will dissipate and the moral influence of this organization will progressively diminish.

This would be a tragedy. Members of this organization are today engaged in a multiplicity of endeavors to find just solutions for complex and explosive problems. There is a fragile tranquillity, but beneath the surface it is challenged by fundamental forces of change—technological, economic, social. More than ever this is a time for statecraft and restraint, for persistence but also daring in the pursuit of peace and justice. The dogmas of perpetual strife produce only bloodshed and bitterness; they unleash the forces of destruction and repression and plant the seeds of future conflict. Appeals to hatred—whether on the basis of race or class or color or nationality or ideology—will, in the end, rebound against those who launch them and will not advance the cause of freedom and justice in the world.

Let us never forget that the United Nations benefits the smaller and weaker nations most of all. It is they that would suffer most from its failure. For without the rule of law, disputes would be settled as they have been all too frequently and painfully in history—by test of strength. It is not the weak that will prevail in the world of chaos.

The United States believes that this 31st General Assembly must free itself of the ideological and confrontational tactics that marked some of its predecessors and dedicate itself to a program of common action.

The United States comes to the General Assembly prepared to work on programs of common action. We will offer concrete proposals. We will listen to the ideas of others. We will resist pressure and seek cooperation.

The Problem of Peace

Let me now discuss the three principal challenges we face: the problem of peace, the challenge of economic well-being, and the agenda of global interdependence.

The age of the United Nations has also been an age of frequent conflict. We have been spared a third world war but cannot assume that this condition will prevail forever, or without exertion. An era of thermonuclear weapons and persistent national rivalries requires our utmost effort to keep at bay the scourge of war. Our generation must build out of the multitude of nations a structure of relations that frees the energies of nations and peoples for the positive endeavors of mankind, without the fear or threat of war.

Central to American foreign policy are our sister democracies— the industrial nations of North America, Western Europe, the southern Pacific and Japan, and our traditional friends in the Western Hemisphere. We are bound to these nations by the ties of history, civilization, culture, shared principles, and a generation of common endeavors.

Our alliances, founded on the bedrock of mutual security, now reach beyond the common defense to a range of new issues: the social challenges shared by advanced technological societies, common approaches to easing tensions with our adversaries, and shaping positive relations with the developing world. The common efforts of the industrial democracies are not directed at exclusive ends but as a bridge to a broader, more secure and cooperative international system and to increasing freedom and prosperity for all nations.

The United States is proud of its historical friendships in the

Western Hemisphere. In the modern era they must be—and are—based on equality and mutual benefit. We have a unique advantage: the great dialogue between the developed and the developing nations can find its most creative solution in the hemisphere where modern democracy was born and where cooperation between developed and developing, large and small, is a longstanding tradition.

Throughout history, ideology and power have tempted nations to seek unilateral advantage. But the inescapable lesson of the nuclear age is that the politics of tests of strength has become incompatible with the survival of humanity. Traditional power politics becomes irrational when war can destroy civilized life and neither side can gain a decisive strategic advantage.

Accordingly, the great nuclear powers have particular responsibilities for restraint and vision. They are in a position to know the full extent of the catastrophe which could overwhelm mankind. They must take care not to fuel disputes if they conduct their rivalries by traditional methods. If they turn local conflicts into aspects of a global competition, sooner or later their competition will get out of control.

The United States believes that the future of mankind requires coexistence with the Soviet Union. Tired slogans cannot obscure the necessity for a more constructive relationship. We will insist that restraint be reciprocal not just in bilateral relations but around the globe. There can be no selective détente. We will maintain our defenses and our vigilance. But we know that tough rhetoric is not strength, that we owe future generations more hopeful prospects than a delicate equilibrium of awesome forces.

Peace requires a balance of strategic power. This the United States will maintain. But the United States is convinced that the goal of strategic balance is achievable more safely by agreement than through an arms race. The negotiations on the limitation of armaments are therefore at the heart of U.S.-Soviet relations.

Unprecedented agreements limiting and controlling nuclear weapons have been reached. A historic effort is being made to place a ceiling on the strategic arsenals of both sides in accordance with the Vladivostok accord. And once this is achieved we are ready to seek immediately to lower the levels of strategic arms.

The United States welcomes the recent progress that has been made in further curtailing nuclear weapons testing and in establishing a regime for peaceful nuclear explosions for the first time. The two treaties now signed and awaiting ratification should be the basis for further progress in this field.

Together with several of our European allies, we are continuing efforts to achieve a balanced reduction in the military forces facing each other in Central Europe. In some respects this is the most complex negotiation on arms limitation yet undertaken. It is our hope that through patient effort reciprocal reductions will soon be achieved that enhance the security of all countries involved.

The United States remains committed to the work of the Geneva Disarmament Committee. We welcome the progress there on banning environmental modification for destructive purposes. We will seriously examine all ideas, of whatever origin, to reduce the burdens of armaments. We will advance our own initiatives not for purposes of propaganda or unilateral advantage but to promote peace and security for all.

But coexistence and negotiations on the control of arms do not take place in a vacuum. We have been disturbed by the continuing accumulation of armaments and by recent instances of military intervention to tip the scales in local conflicts on distant continents. We have noted crude attempts to distort the purposes of diplomacy and to impede hopeful progress toward peaceful solutions to complex issues. These efforts only foster tensions; they cannot be reconciled with the policy of improving relations.

And they will inevitably be resisted. For coexistence to be something better than an uneasy armistice, both sides must recognize that ideology and power politics today confront the realities of the nuclear age and that a striving for unilateral advantage will not be accepted.

In recent years the new relationship between the United States and the People's Republic of China has held great significance for global security.

We came together out of necessity and a mutual belief that the world should remain free of military blackmail and the will to hegemony. We have set out a new path: in wide-ranging consultations, bilateral exchanges, the opening of offices in our respective capitals, and an accelerating movement toward normalization. And we have derived reciprocal benefits: a clear understanding of the aspirations of our peoples, better prospects for international equilibrium, reduced tensions in Asia, and increased opportunities for parallel actions on global issues.

These elements form the basis for a growing and lasting relationship founded on objective common interests. The United States is committed to strengthen the bonds between us and to proceed toward the normalization of our relations in strict conformity with the principles of the Shanghai communique. As this process moves forward, each side must display restraint and respect for the interests and convictions of the other. We will keep Chinese interests in mind on all international issues and will do our utmost to take account of them. But if the relationship is to prosper, there must be similar sensitivity to our views and concerns. On this basis, the progressive development of our relations with the world's most populous nation will be a key element of the foreign policy of the United States.

The world today is witness to continuing regional crises. Any one of them could blossom into larger conflict. Each one commands our most diligent efforts of conciliation and cooperation. The United States has played, and is prepared to continue to play, an active role in the search for peace in many areas: southern Africa, the Middle East, Korea, and Cyprus.

Southern Africa

Racial injustice and the grudging retreat of colonial power have conspired to make southern Africa an acid test of the world's hope for peace and justice under the charter. A host of voices have been heard in this chamber warning that if we failed quickly to find solutions to the crises of Namibia and Rhodesia, that part of the globe could become a vicious battleground with consequences for every part of the world.

I have just been to Africa, at President Ford's request, to see what we could do to help the peoples of that continent achieve their aspirations for freedom and justice.

An opportunity to pull back from the brink now exists. I believe that Africa has before it the prize for which it has struggled for so long: the opportunity for Africans to shape a future of peace, justice, racial harmony, and progress.

The United Nations since its inception has been concerned with the issue of Namibia. For 30 years that territory has been a test of this institution's ability to make its decisions effective.

In recent months the United States has vigorously sought to help the parties concerned speed up the process toward Namibian independence. The United States favors the following elements: the independence of Namibia within[16] a fixed, short time limit, the calling of a constitutional conference at a neutral location under U.N. aegis, and the participation in that conference of all authentic national forces including, specifically, SWAPO.

Progress has been made in achieving all of these goals. We will exert our efforts to remove the remaining obstacles and bring into being a conference which can then fashion, with good will and wisdom, a design for the new state of Namibia and its relationship with its neighbors. We pledge our continued solicitude for the independence of Namibia so that it may, in the end, be a proud

[16]Text corrected from *Bulletin*, 75: 596.

achievement of this organization and a symbol of international cooperation.

Less than a week ago the Rhodesian authorities announced that they are prepared to meet with the nationalist leaders of Zimbabwe to form an interim government to bring about majority rule within two years. This is in itself a historic break from the past. The African Presidents, in calling for immediate negotiations, have shown that they are prepared to seize this opportunity for a settlement. And the Government of the United Kingdom, in expressing its willingness to assemble a conference, has shown its high sense of responsibility and concern for the rapid and just independence of Rhodesia.

Inevitably after a decade of strife, suspicions run deep. Many obstacles remain. Magnanimity is never easy, and less so after a generation of bitterness and racial conflict. But let us not lose sight of what has been achieved: a commitment to majority rule within two years, a commitment to form immediately a transitional government with an African majority in the Cabinet and an African prime minister, a readiness to follow this with a constitutional conference to define the legal framework of an independent Zimbabwe.

The United States, together with other countries, has made major efforts, and we will continue to do what we can to support the hopeful process that is now possible. But it is those in Africa who must shape the future. The people of Rhodesia, and the neighboring states, now face a supreme challenge. Their ability to work together, their capacity to unify, will be tested in the months ahead as never before.

There may be some countries who see a chance for advantage in fueling the flames of war and racial hatred. But they are not motivated by concern for the peoples of Africa or for peace. And if they succeed they could doom opportunities that might never return.

In South Africa itself, the pace of change accelerates. The system of apartheid, by whatever name, is a denial of our common humanity and a challenge to the conscience of mankind. Change is inevitable. The leaders of South Africa have shown wisdom in facilitating a peaceful solution in Rhodesia. The world community takes note of it and urges the same wisdom—while there is still time—to bring racial justice to South Africa.

As for the United States, we have become convinced that our values and our interests are best served by an Africa seeking its own destiny free of outside intervention. Therefore we will back no faction, whether in Rhodesia or elsewhere. We will not seek to impose solutions anywhere. The leadership and the future of an independent Zimbabwe, as for the rest of Africa, are for Africans to decide. The United States will abide by their decision. We call on all other non-African states to do likewise.

The United States wants no special position or sphere of influence. We respect African unity. The rivalry and interference of non-African powers would make a mockery of Africa's hard-won struggle for independence from foreign domination. It will inevitably be resisted. And it is a direct challenge to the most fundamental principles upon which the United Nations is founded.

Every nation that has signed the charter is pledged to allow the nations of Africa, whose peoples have suffered so much, to fulfill at long last their dreams of independence, peace, unity, and human dignity in their own way and by their own decisions.

Middle East

The United Nations, since its birth, has been involved in the chronic conflict in the Middle East. Each successive war has brought greater perils: an increased danger of great-power confrontation and more severe global economic dislocations.

At the request of the parties, the United States has been actively engaged in the search for peace in the Middle East. Since the 1973 war, statesmanship on all sides has produced unprecedented steps toward a resolution of this bitter conflict. There have been three agreements that lessen the danger of war, and mutual commitments have been made to pursue the negotiating process with urgency until a final peace is achieved. As a result we are closer to the goal of peace than at any time in a generation.

The role of the United Nations has been crucial. The Geneva Conference met in 1973 under its aegis, and the implementation of subsequent agreements has been negotiated in its working groups. Security Council resolutions form the only agreed framework for negotiations. The U.N. Emergency Force, Disengagement Observer Force, and Truce Supervision Organization are even now helping maintain peace on the truce lines. I want to compliment the Secretary General and his colleagues in New York, Geneva, and on the ground in the Middle East for their vigorous support of the peace process at critical moments.

The United States remains committed to help the parties reach a settlement. The step-by-step negotiations of the past three years have now brought us to a point where comprehensive solutions seem possible. The decision before us now is how the next phase of negotiations should be launched.

The United States is prepared to participate in an early resumption of the work of the Geneva Conference. We think a preparatory conference might be useful for a discussion of the structure of future negotiations, but we are open to other suggestions. Whatever steps are taken must be carefully prepared so that once the process begins the nations concerned will advance steadily toward agreement.

The groundwork that has been laid represents a historic opportunity. The United States will do all it can to assure that by the time this Assembly meets next year it will be possible to report significant further progress toward a just and lasting peace in the Middle East.

Since the General Assembly last met, overwhelming tragedy has befallen the people of Lebanon. The United States strongly supports the sovereignty, unity, and territorial integrity of that troubled country. We oppose partition. We hope that Lebanese affairs will soon be returned to the hands of the people of Lebanon. All members of the United Nations, and all the conflicting parties in Lebanon, have an obligation to support the efforts of the new President of Lebanon to restore peace and to turn energies to rebuilding the nation. And the agencies of the U.N. system can play an important role in the reconstruction effort.

Korea

The confrontation between North and South Korea remains a threat to international peace and stability. The vital interests of world powers intersect in Korea; conflict there inevitably threatens wider war.

We and many other U.N. members welcome the fact that a contentious and sterile debate on Korea will be avoided this fall. Let this opportunity be used, then, to address the central problem of how the Korean people can determine their future and achieve their ultimate goal of peaceful reunification without a renewal of armed conflict.

Our own views on the problem of Korea are well known. We have called for a resumption of a serious dialogue between North and South Korea. We have urged wider negotiations to promote security and reduce tensions. We are prepared to have the U.N. Command dissolved so long as the armistice agreement—which is the only existing legal arrangement committing the parties to keep the peace—is either preserved or replaced by more durable arrangements. We are willing to improve relations with North Korea provided that its allies are ready to take similar steps toward the Republic of Korea. We are ready to talk with North Korea about the peninsula's future, but we will not do so without the participation of the Republic of Korea.

Last fall the United States proposed a conference including all the parties most directly concerned—North and South Korea, the United States, and the People's Republic of China—to discuss ways of adapting the armistice agreement to new conditions and replacing it with more permanent arrangements. On July 22 I stated our readiness to meet immediately with these parties to consider the appropriate venue for such a conference. I reaffirm that readiness here today.

If such a conference proves impracticable right now, the United States would support a phased approach. Preliminary talks between North and South Korea, including discussions on the venue and scope of the conference, could start immediately. In this phase the United States and the People's Republic of China could participate as observers or in an advisory role. If such discussions yielded concrete results, the United States and China could join the talks formally. This, in turn, could set the stage for a wider conference in which other countries could associate themselves with arrangements that guarantee a durable peace on the peninsula.

We hope that North Korea and other concerned parties will respond affirmatively to this proposed procedure or offer a constructive alternative suggestion.

Cyprus

The world community is deeply concerned over the continuing stalemate on the Cyprus problem. Domestic pressures, nationalistic objectives, and international rivalries have combined to block the parties from taking even the most elementary steps toward a solution. On those few occasions when representatives of the two Cypriot communities have come together, they have fallen into inconclusive procedural disputes. The passage of time has served only to complicate domestic difficulties and to diminish the possibilities for constructive conciliation. The danger of conflict between Greece and Turkey has spread to other issues, as we have recently seen in the Aegean.

All concerned need to focus on committing themselves to achieve the overriding objectives: assuring the well-being of the suffering Cypriot people and peace in the eastern Mediterranean.

A settlement must come from the Cypriot communities themselves. It is they who must decide how their island's economy, society, and government shall be reconstructed. It is they who must decide the ultimate relationship of the two communities and the territorial extent of each area.

The United States is ready to assist in restoring momentum to the negotiating process. We believe that agreeing to a set of principles might help the parties to resume negotiations. We would suggest some concepts along the following lines:

—A settlement should preserve the independence, sovereignty, and territorial integrity of Cyprus;

—The present dividing lines on Cyprus must be adjusted to reduce the area currently controlled by the Turkish side;

—The territorial arrangement should take into account the economic requirements and humanitarian concerns of the two Cypriot communities, including the plight of those who remain refugees;

—A constitutional arrangement should provide conditions under which the two Cypriot communities can live in freedom and have a large voice in their own affairs; and

—Security arrangements should be agreed that permit the withdrawal of foreign military forces other than those present under international agreement.

I have discussed this approach with the Secretary General and with several Western European leaders. In the days ahead the United States will consult along these lines with all interested parties. In the meantime we urge the Secretary General to continue his dedicated efforts.

Economic Development and Progress

The economic division of our planet between the Northern and Southern Hemispheres, between the industrial and developing nations, is a dominant issue of our time. Our mutual dependence for our prosperity is a reality, not a slogan. It should summon our best efforts to make common progress. We must commit ourselves to bring mankind's dreams of a better life to closer reality in our lifetime.

There are many reasons why cooperation has not made greater strides:

—The industrial democracies have sometimes been more willing to pay lipservice to the challenge of development than to match rhetoric with real resources.

—The oil-producing nations command great wealth, and some have been generous in their contribution to international development. But the overall performance in putting that wealth to positive uses has been inadequate to the challenge.

—The countries with nonmarket economies are quite prepared to undertake verbal assaults, but their performance is in inverse ratio to their rhetoric. Their real contribution to development assistance has been minimal. Last year, for example, the nonmarket economies provided only about 4 percent of the public aid flowing to the developing nations.

—The developing nations are understandably frustrated and impatient with poverty, illiteracy, and disease. But too often they have made demands for change that are as confrontational as they are unrealistic. They sometimes speak of new economic orders as if growth were a quick fix requiring only that the world's wealth be properly redistributed through tests of strength instead of a process of self-help over generations. Ultimately such tactics lose more than they gain, for they undermine the popular support in the industrial democracies which is imperative to provide the resources and market access—available nowhere else—to sustain development.

The objectives of the developing nations are clear: a rapid rise in the incomes of their people, a greater role in the international decisions which affect them, and fair access to the world's economic opportunities.

The objectives of the industrial nations are equally plain: an efficient and open system of world trade and investment; expanding opportunities and production for both North and South; the reliable and equitable development of the world's resources of food, energy, and raw materials; a world economy in which prosperity is as close to universal as our imagination and our energies allow.

These goals are complementary; indeed they must be, for neither side can achieve its aims at the expense of the other. They can be realized only through cooperation.

We took a major step forward together a year ago, at the seventh special session of this Assembly. And we have since followed through on many fronts:

—We have taken steps to protect the economic security of developing nations against cyclical financial disaster. The newly expanded compensatory finance facility of the International Monetary Fund (IMF) has disbursed over $2 billion to developing nations this year alone.

—An IMF trust fund financed by gold sales has been established for the benefit of the low-income countries.

—Replenishments for the World Bank, the Inter-American Development Bank, and the Asian Development Bank will provide additional resources for development.

—Worldwide food aid has expanded. We have committed ourselves to expand the world supply of food. With a U.S.

contribution of $200 million, we have brought the International Fund for Agricultural Development close to operation.

—The major industrial nations have moved to expand trade opportunities for the developing world. We have joined in a solemn pledge to complete by next year the liberalization of world trade through the Tokyo round of multilateral trade negotiations. For its part, the United States has established a system of generalized preferences which has significantly stimulated exports from developing nations to the United States.

The United States continued this process by putting forward a number of new proposals at the fourth ministerial United Nations Conference on Trade and Development in May 1976. We proposed a comprehensive plan to improve the capacity of the developing countries to select, adapt, improve, and manage technology for development. We committed ourselves to improvements in the quality of aid, proposing that a greater proportion of aid to poor countries be on a grant basis and untied to purchases from donor nations. We agreed to a serious effort to improve markets of 18 basic commodities.

These measures undertaken since we met here just a year ago assist—not with rhetoric and promises, but in practical and concrete ways—the peoples of the world who are struggling to throw off the chains of poverty.

Much remains to be done.

First, the application of science and technology is at the very heart of the development process. The United States, conscious of its pioneering role in technology, has put forward three basic principles, which we will support with funds and talent:

—To train individuals who can identify, select, and manage the future technology of the developing world;

—To build both national and international institutions to create indigenous technology, as well as adapt foreign designs and inventions; and

—To spur the private sector to make its maximum contribution to the development and transfer of technological progress.

To achieve these goals, we are today extending an invitation to the World Conference on Science and Technology for Development, now scheduled for 1979, to meet in this country. In preparation for that meeting, we have asked members of the industrial, academic, and professional scientific communities throughout the United States to meet in Washington in November. They will review the important initiatives this country can take to expand the technological base for development, and they will strive to develop new approaches.

Second, the ministerial meeting of the Conference on International Economic Cooperation in Paris should be given new impetus. We are making several new proposals:

—We will seek to help nations facing severe debt burdens. For acute cases we will propose guidelines for debt renegotiation. For countries facing longer term problems, we will propose systematic examination of remedial measures, including increased aid.

—We will advance new ideas for expanded cooperation in energy including a regular process of information exchange among energy producers and users, and an expanded transfer of energy-related technology to energy-poor developing nations.

Third, the industrial democracies have been far too willing to wait for the demands of the developing countries rather than to advance their own proposals. Now, however, the OECD countries, at the suggestion of the United States, have agreed to examine long-range development planning and to develop a more coherent and comprehensive approach to global growth and economic justice.

Fourth, natural disaster each year takes thousands of lives and costs billions of dollars. It strikes most those who can afford it the least, the poorest peoples of the world. Its toll is magnified by a large array of global issues: overpopulation, food scarcity, damage to the ecology, and economic underdevelopment. The United Nations has a unique capacity to address these global concerns and thus improve man's odds against nature. We urge this body to take the lead in strengthening international cooperation to prevent and alleviate natural calamity.

Our dream is that all the children of the world can live with hope and widening opportunity. No nation can accomplish this alone; no group of nations can achieve it through confrontation. But together there is a chance for major progress—and in our generation.

Interdependence and Community

It is an irony of our time that an age of ideological and nationalistic rivalry has spawned as well a host of challenges that no nation can possibly solve by itself:

—The proliferation of nuclear weapons capabilities adds a new dimension of danger to political conflicts, regionally and globally.

—As technology opens up the oceans, conflicting national claims and interests threaten chaos.

—Man's inventiveness has developed the horrible new tool of terror that claims innocent victims on every continent.

—Human and civil rights are widely abused and have now become an accepted concern of the world community.

Let me set forth the U.S. position on these topics.

Nuclear Nonproliferation

The growing danger of the proliferation of nuclear weapons raises stark questions about man's ability to insure his very existence.

We have lived through three perilous decades in which the catastrophe of nuclear war has been avoided despite a strategic rivalry between a relatively few nations.

But now a wholly new situation impends. Many nations have the potential to build nuclear weapons. If this potential were to materialize, threats to use nuclear weapons, fed by mutually reinforcing misconceptions, could become a recurrent feature of local conflicts in every quarter of the globe. And there will be growing dangers of accidents, blackmail, theft, and nuclear terrorism. Unless current trends are altered rapidly, the likelihood of nuclear devastation could grow steadily in the years to come.

We must look first to the roots of the problem:

—Since the 1973 energy crisis and drastic rise in oil prices, both developed and developing nations have seen in nuclear energy a means both of lowering the cost of electricity and of reducing reliance upon imported petroleum.

—In an age of growing nationalism some see the acquisition and expansion of nuclear power as symbols of enhanced national prestige. And it is also clear that some nations, in attaining this peaceful technology, may wish to provide for themselves a future option to acquire nuclear weapons.

A nation that acquires the potential for a nuclear weapons capability must accept the consequences of its action. It is bound to trigger offsetting actions by its neighbors and stimulate broader proliferation, thereby accelerating a process that ultimately will undermine its own security. And it is disingenuous to label as "peaceful" nuclear devices which palpably are capable of massive military destruction. The spread of nuclear reactor and fuel cycle capabilities, especially in the absence of evident economic need and combined with ambiguous political and military motives, threatens to proliferate nuclear weapons with all their dangers.

Time is of the essence. In no area of international concern does the future of this planet depend more directly upon what this generation elects to do—or fails to do. We must move on three broad fronts:

—First, international safeguards must be strengthened and strictly enforced. The supply and use of nuclear materials associated with civilian nuclear energy programs must be carefully safeguarded so that they will not be diverted. Nuclear suppliers must impose the utmost restraint upon themselves and not permit the temptations of commercial advantage to override the risks of proliferation. The physical security of nuclear materials—whether in use, storage, or transfer—must be increased. The International Atomic Energy Agency must receive the full support of all nations in making its safeguards effective, reliable, and universally applicable. Any violator of the IAEA safeguards must face immediate and drastic penalties.

—Second, adherence to safeguards, while of prime importance, is no guarantee against future proliferation. We must continue our efforts to forge international restraints against the acquisition or transfer of reprocessing facilities which produce separated plutonium and of enrichment facilities which produce highly enriched uranium—both of which are usable for the construction of nuclear weapons.

—Third, we must recognize that one of the principal incentives for seeking sensitive reprocessing and enrichment technology is the fear that essential nonsensitive materials, notably reactor-grade uranium fuel, will not be made available on a reliable basis. Nations that show their sense of international responsibility by accepting effective restraints have a right to expect reliable and economical supply of peaceful nuclear reactors and associated nonsensitive fuel. The United States, as a principal supplier of these items, is prepared to be responsive in this regard.

In the near future President Ford will announce a comprehensive American program for international action on nonproliferation that reconciles global aspirations for assured nuclear supply with global requirements for nuclear control.

We continue to approach the proliferation problem in full recognition of the responsibility that we and other nuclear powers have—both in limiting our weapons arsenals and in insuring that the benefits of peaceful nuclear energy can be made available to all states within a shared framework of effective international safeguards. In this way the atom can be seen once again as a boon and not a menace to mankind.

Law of the Sea Negotiations

Another issue of vast global consequence is the law of the sea. The negotiations which have just recessed in New York represent one of the most important, complex, and ambitious diplomatic undertakings in history.

Consider what is at stake:

—Mankind is attempting to devise an international regime for nearly three quarters of the earth's surface.

—Some 150 nations are participating, reflecting all the globe's diverse national perspectives, ideologies, and practical concerns.

—A broad sweep of vital issues is involved: economic development, military security, freedom of navigation, crucial and dwindling living resources, the ocean's fragile ecology, marine scientific research, and vast potential mineral wealth.

—The world community is aspiring to shape major new international legal principles: the extension of the long-established territorial sea, the creation of a completely new concept of an economic zone extending 200 miles, and the designation of the deep seabeds as the "common heritage of mankind."

We have traveled an extraordinary distance in these negotiations in recent years—thanks in no small part to the skill and dedication of the distinguished President of this Assembly. Agreement exists on key concepts: a 12-mile territorial sea, free passage over and through straits, a 200-mile economic zone, and important pollution controls. In many fields we have replaced ideological debates with serious efforts to find concrete solutions. And there is growing consensus that the outstanding problems must be solved at the next session.

Bult there is hardly room for complacency. Important issues remain which, if not settled, could cause us to forfeit all our hard-won progress. The conference has yet to agree on the balance between coastal state and international rights in the economic zone, on the freedom of marine scientific research, on arrangements for dispute settlement, and most crucially, on the regime for exploitation of the deep seabeds.

The United States has made major proposals to resolve the deep seabed issue. We have agreed that the seabeds are the common heritage of all mankind. We have proposed a dual system for the exploitation of seabed minerals by which half of the mining sites would be reserved for the International Authority and half could be developed by individual nations and their nationals on the basis of their technical capacity. We have offered to find financing and to transfer the technology needed to make international mining a practical reality. And in light of the many uncertainties that lie ahead, we have proposed that there be a review—for example, in 25 years—to determine whether the provisions on seabed mining are working equitably.

In response some nations have escalated both their demands and the stridency with which they advocate them.

I must say candidly that there are limits beyond which no American Administration can, or will, go. If attempts are made to compel concessions which exceed those limits, unilateralism will become inevitable. Countries which have no technological capacity for mining the seabeds in the foreseeable future should not seek to impose a doctrine of total internationalization on nations which alone have this capacity and which have voluntarily offered to share it. The United States has an interest in the progressive development of international law, stable order, and global cooperation. We are prepared to make sacrifices for this—but they cannot go beyond equitable bounds.

Let us therefore put aside delaying tactics and pressures and take the path of cooperation. If we have the vision to conclude a treaty considered fair and just by mankind, our labors will have profound meaning not only for the regime of the oceans but for all efforts to build a peaceful, cooperative, and prosperous international community. The United States will spend the interval between sessions of the conference reviewing its positions and will approach other nations well in advance of the next session at the political level to establish the best possible conditions for its success.

International Terrorism

A generation that dreams of world peace and economic progress is plagued by a new, brutal, cowardly, and indiscriminate form of violence: international terrorism. Small groups have rejected the norms of civilized behavior and wantonly taken the lives of defenseless men, women, and children—innocent victims with no power to affect the course of events. In the year since I last addressed this body, there have been 11 hijackings, 19 kidnapings, 42 armed attacks, and 112 bombings perpetrated by international terrorists. Over 70 people have lost their lives, and over 200 have been injured.

It is time this organization said to the world that the vicious

murder and abuse of innocents cannot be absolved or excused by
the invocation of lofty motives. Criminal acts against humanity,
whatever the professed objective, cannot be excused by any
civilized nation.

The threat of terrorism should be dealt with through the
cooperative efforts of all countries. More stringent steps must be
taken now to deny skyjackers and terrorists a safe haven.

Additional measures are required to protect passengers in both
transit and terminal areas, as well as in flight.

The United States will work within the International Civil
Aviation Organization to expand its present technical assistance to
include the security of air carriers and terminal facilities. We urge
the universal implementation of aviation security standards
adopted by the ICAO. We are prepared to assist the efforts of other
governments to implement those standards.

The United States will support new initiatives which will insure
the safety of the innocent. The proposal of the distinguished
Foreign Minister of the Federal Republic of Germany[17] against the
taking of hostages deserves the most serious and sympathetic
consideration of this Assembly.

The United States will do everything within its power to work
cooperatively in the United Nations and in other international
bodies to put an end to the scourge of terrorism. But we have an
obligation to protect the lives of our citizens as they travel at home
or abroad, and we intend to meet that obligation. Therefore, if
multilateral efforts are blocked by those determined to pursue their
ends without regard for suffering or death, then the United States
will act through its own legislative processes and in conjunction
with others willing to join us.

Terrorism is an international problem. It is inconceivable that an
organization of the world's nations would fail to take effective
action against it.

Human Rights

The final measure of all we do together, of course, is man
himself. Our common efforts to define, preserve, and enhance
respect for the rights of man thus represent an ultimate test of
international cooperation.

We Americans, in the year of our Bicentennial, are conscious—
and proud—of our own traditions. Our founders wrote 200 years
ago of the equality and inalienable rights of all men. Since then the
ideals of liberty and democracy have become the universal and
indestructible goals of mankind.

[17] Hans-Dietrich Genscher.

But the plain truth—of tragic proportions—is that human rights are in jeopardy over most of the globe. Arbitrary arrest, denial of fundamental procedural rights, slave labor, stifling of freedom of religion, racial injustice, political repression, the use of torture, and restraints on communications and expression—these abuses are too prevalent.

The performance of the U.N. system in protecting human rights has fallen far short of what was envisaged when this organization was founded. The principles of the Universal Declaration of Human Rights are clear enough. But their invocation and application, in general debates of this body and in the forums of the Human Rights Commission, have been marred by hypocrisy, double standards, and discrimination. Flagrant and consistent deprivation of human rights is no less heinous in one country or one social system than in another. Nor is it more acceptable when practiced upon members of the same race than when inflicted by one race upon another.

The international community has a unique role to play. The application of the standards of the Universal Declaration of Human Rights should be entrusted to fair and capable international bodies. But at the same time let us insure that these bodies do not become platforms from which nations which are the worst transgressors pass hypocritical judgment on the alleged shortcomings.

Let us together pursue practical approaches:

—To build on the foundations already laid at previous Assemblies and at the Human Rights Commission to lessen the abominable practice of officially sanctioned torture;

—To promote acceptance of procedures for protecting the rights of people subject to detention, such as access to courts, counsel, and families and prompt release or fair and public trial;

—To improve the working procedures of international bodies concerned with human rights so that they may function fairly and effectively; and

—To strengthen the capability of the United Nations to meet the tragic problems of the ever-growing number of refugees whose human rights have been stripped away by conflict in almost every continent.

The United States pledges its firm support to these efforts.

Mr. President, Mr. Secretary General, distinguished delegates: The challenge to statesmanship in this generation is to advance from the management of crises to the building of a more stable and just international order—an order resting not on power but on

restraint of power, not on the strength of arms but on the strength
of the human spirit.

Global forces of change now shape our future. Order will come
in one of two ways: through its imposition by the strong and the
ruthless or by the wise and farsighted use of international institutions through which we enlarge the sphere of common interests
and enhance the sense of community.

It is easy and tempting to press relentlessly for national advantage. It is infinitely more difficult to act in recognition of the
rights of others. Throughout history, the greatness of men and
nations has been measured by their actions in times of acute peril.
Today there is no single crisis to conquer. There is instead a persisting challenge of staggering complexity—the need to create a
universal community based on cooperation, peace, and justice.

If we falter, future generations will pay for our failure. If we
succeed, it will have been worthy of the hopes of mankind. I am
confident that we can succeed.

And it is here, in the assembly of nations, that we should begin.

(b) Assessment of the Session: Statement by Ambassador Scranton to the Assembly, December 22, 1976.[18]

A year ago the problems of disarmament, the Middle East, and
southern Africa were acute. Negotiations, however, were stagnant.
The deteriorating situation in Lebanon kept Arabs and Israelis
from seeking ways to move toward solutions. As prospects for
peaceful solution in southern Africa dwindled, a downward spiral
toward violence gained momentum. Superpower commitment to
strategic arms discussions and disarmament talk in general was
questionable.

This world situation affected the United Nations. The lack of
progress or even a prospect for progress was aggravated by one of
the sharpest and most dangerous confrontations in General
Assembly history: the dispute over the equation of Zionism with
racism. There, another divisive factor was added to an already
intensely complex Middle East debate. This wounding rhetoric and
other acts nearly as excessive embittered many people toward the
United Nations, certainly in the United States.

Today, hope exists for settlement in the Middle East. This results
partly, though only partly, from a winding down of the tragic
struggle in Lebanon. Equally important, the energies of all parties
are today engaged productively in pursuing ways for the parties to

[18]USUN Press Release 200, Dec. 22; text from *Bulletin*, 76: 68-70.

come together. For the first time all sides have manifested a renewed determination to achieve peace. For the first time all parties desire a negotiating process.

As to southern Africa, determination is strong to bring about majority rule for multiracial nations living in peace. Meaningful talks concerning Rhodesia are in process. Talks on Namibia are within reach—talks allowing peaceful change, change by negotiations, the only course that will avoid the horror of mass violence.

This positive tone extends to the difficult issues of arms control and disarmament, including nuclear proliferation—issues that will be with us after many others are solved. Today, none doubt the necessity of resolution or that superpowers must take the first steps.

These developments are no cause for euphoria, but they do offer a basis for hope. In contrast with the last General Assembly, this session has had a lessening of confrontation. Some significant changes in the world situation combined with a more mature tone here to alter the atmosphere for the better. A small but perceptible change of mood took place. The U.N.'s cup, last year half empty, this year became half full.

I repeat: There is no reason for euphoria, but it just may be that we have turned a corner. It just may be that this new tone will permit us to do more together. Having approached the brink and drawn back, perhaps we will now turn to our common tasks with resolve to make substantive progress rather than political points.

At the very least, our growing recognition of the value of small steps taken together is indeed an accomplishment.

And now, Mr. President and fellow delegates, once again I ask your indulgence for some personal comments, a habit of mine to which you have become accustomed but to which you will not be subjected much longer. Having been the American Representative for nine months, I have become an instant expert on all aspects of the United Nations. More seriously, I am deeply indebted to each of you and many others for this educational process, and when I leave in another month, it will be with more understanding of the United Nations than when I arrived.

Let me begin with a few basic thoughts. Although the United Nations has many purposes, three are most frequently and clearly enunciated in the charter: maintaining international peace and security, assisting in economic development, and promoting human rights.

As to the first, we are making progress. Let me cite one example: Eight years ago on a trip to the Middle East, I was informed by the leaders of all six countries I visited that they believed there was no further role for the United Nations in the Middle East dispute.

Today, none deny the essential role of the U.N. presence between Syria and Israel and between Egypt and Israel. Through these temporary peacekeeping forces the United Nations is giving the world time to find a way to bring peace in the Middle East. And there is virtually unanimous opinion that the route to peace definitely and prominently involves the United Nations.

In this geo-economic era, increasing interdependence and an acceleration of the desire by people everywhere for a better way of life bring economic problems and opportunities to the United Nations to a greater degree than ever before. The nations of the world now recognize that new mechanisms must be initiated and developed in the U.N. system for world resources and world trade to meet the special needs of many while benefiting us all.

In both these areas—peacekeeping and economic development— I am encouraged, as I think we all are, not only by the demands on the United Nations but by its response, even though it is limited. Time will tell, and a short time at that, whether we take further opportunities now before us.

But while much is encouraging with regard to two of the main purposes of the United Nations, little can be said about the third. With the exception of successful action on the initiative of the Federal Republic of Germany in regard to hostages, for which I congratulate the General Assembly, little has happened during this session to improve protection of human rights where human rights most need protection. The strong and unswerving views of the U.S. Government on this subject were recently made plain to the Third Committee.

This brings me to the United States. Over and over again I am told here that the United States must lead—that it must lead with regard to a settlement in the Middle East; that it must lead with regard to majority rule in southern Africa; that, with the Soviet Union, it must lead in disarmament initiatives; that it must lead and be forthcoming in regard to interdependence in the economic field; that the United States must lead the West in the East-West dialogue and it must lead the North in the North-South dialogue.

I believe that, working with many of your countries, the United States has important roles to play in the effort to find "proximate solutions to the insoluble problems" of mankind. How will each of our nations meet the test? Will all of us measure up to our responsibilities?

I can speak only as one American But at this moment my feelings are clear and my hopes high.

Like all nations and all governments and all peoples, we have made mistakes. That came home dramatically to Americans in the last decade.

We have been looking at ourselves—just as you have been

looking at us—with confusion, with anger in some cases, and with some effort at dispassionate analysis.

Every one of you sees the United States firsthand. You are here. You read about us in our newspapers every day. You hear about us on radio and you see us on television. Our assets and liabilities are wide open to you.

When I look at the United States as our Bicentennial year comes to a close, I have a simple emotion: I rejoice. I find an America which is quieter, calmer, more modest, but sounder and more secure. Also, we are becoming better listeners. Though we no longer expect the rest of the world to copy our economic system, we believe that of all the economic systems in the world, it is the most productive, the most creative, and the most beneficial to the people.

We also know that we are joined irrevocably with the rest of the world, that neither we nor anyone else can "go it alone."

But out of 30 years of postwar turbulence has come a more important security than simply an economic one, and this Bicentennial year epitomizes it. There is a deeper dedication to the basic precepts of this country as declared in the Bill of Rights of our Constitution. I believe the people of the United States are more firmly convinced today than ever before in our history that our individual freedoms, our open society, are the most precious part of our lives. They are our inspiration and our only real security.

What does all this mean for the United Nations? I think it means that the United States will take leadership. It means that we will try with our hearts and our minds to work for a lasting peace in the Middle East, to bring majority rule to southern Africa, to build the mechanisms necessitated by economic interdependence, and to progress in arms control and disarmament.

It also means that you will hear a great deal from us about freedom and human rights—for we believe in them. We believe there is a natural desire in people everywhere to live not only in peace but also in freedom; that governments are installed foremost to secure those rights; and that no human being has peace or freedom where his or her human rights are denied.

I believe you will find us easier to live with and a better leader. I believe Americans respect you, and you willl have good reason to respect us.

One final thought: The United Nations is not a parliament. It cannot enforce its will by enacting laws. It cannot define reality or establish truth by majority vote. The United Nations is a gathering of sovereign states, born out of consensus and destined to survive only by consensus. Consensus comes down simply to this: commitment from each of us to strive for a safer and better life for human beings everywhere, now and for generations to come.

10. FOREIGN POLICY AND PRESIDENTIAL POLITICS

(36) Campaign Platform of the Democratic Party, adopted July 14, 1976 by the Democratic National Convention in New York.[1]

(Excerpts)

VI. International Relations

The next Democratic administration must and will initiate a new American foreign policy.

Eight years of Nixon-Ford diplomacy have left our nation isolated abroad and divided at home. Policies have been developed and applied secretly and arbitrarily by the executive department from the time of secret bombing in Cambodia to recent covert assistance in Angola. They have been policies that relied on ad hoc, unilateral maneuvering, and a balance-of-power diplomacy suited better to the last century than to this one. They have disdained traditional American principles which once earned the respect of other peoples while inspiring our own. Instead of efforts to foster freedom and justice in the world, the Republican administration has built a sorry record of disregard for human rights, manipulative interference in the internal affairs of other nations, and, frequently, a greater concern for our relations with totalitarian adversaries than with our democratic allies. And its efforts to preserve, rather than reform, the international status quo betray a self-fulfilling pessimism that contradicts a traditional American belief in the possibility of human progress.

Defense policy and spending for military forces must be consistent with meeting the real security needs of the American people.

[1]Text from *The National Democratic Platform 1976* (Washington: Democratic Platform Committee, 1976): 12-17.

We recognize that the security of our nation depends first and foremost on the internal strength of American society—economic, social and political. We also recognize that serious international threats to our security, such as shortages of food and raw materials, are not solely military in nature and cannot be met by military force or the threat of force. The Republican Administration has, through mismanagement and misguided policies, undermined the security of our nation by neglecting human needs at home while, for the first time in our nation's history, increasing military spending after a war. Billions of dollars have been diverted into wasteful, extravagant and, in some instances, destabilizing military programs. Our country can—and under a Democratic administration it will—work vigorously for the adoption of policies of full employment and economic growth which will enable us to meet both the justified domestic needs of our citizens and our needs for an adequate national defense.

A Democratic administration will work to create a foreign policy that does justice to the strength and decency of the American people through adherence to these fundamental principles and priorities:

We will act on the premise that candor in policy-making with all its liabilities, is preferable to deceit. The Congress will be involved in the major international decisions of our government, and our foreign policies will be openly and consistently presented to the American people. For even if diplomatic tactics and national security information must sometimes remain secret, there can be no excuse for formulating and executing basic policy without public understanding and support.

Our policy must be based on our nation's commitment to the ideal of individual freedom and justice. Experience has taught us not to rely solely on military strength or economic power, as necessary as they are, in pursuit of our international objectives. We must rely too on the moral strength of our democratic values—the greatest inspiration to our friends and the attribute most feared by our enemies. We will ensure that human needs are not sacrificed to military spending, while maintaining the military forces we require for our security.

We will strengthen our ties to the other great democracies, working together to resolve common economic and social problems as well as to keep our defenses strong.

We will restore the Democratic tradition of friendship and support to Third World nations.

We must also seek areas of cooperation with our traditional adversaries. There is no other option, for human survival itself is at stake. But pursuit of detente will require maintenance of a strong American military deterrent, hard bargaining for our own interest, recognition of continuing competition, and a refusal to oversell the immediate benefits of such a policy to the American public.

We will reaffirm the fundamental American commitment to human rights across the globe. America must work for a release of all political prisoners—men and women who are in jail simply because they have opposed peacefully the policies of their governments or have aided others who have—in all countries. America must take a firm stand to support and implement existing U.S. law to bring about liberalization of emigration policy in countries which limit or prohibit free emigration. America must be resolute in its support of the right of workers to organize and of trade unions to act freely and independently, and in its support of freedom of the press. America must continue to stand as a bulwark in support of human liberty in all countries. A return to the politics of principle requires a reaffirmation of human freedom throughout the world.

The Challenge of Interdependence

The International Economy

Eight years of mismanagement of the American economy have contributed to global recession and inflation. The most important contribution a Democratic administration will make to the returning health of the world economy will be to restore the health of our own economy, with all that means to international economic stability and progress.

* * *

Energy

The United States must be a leader in promoting cooperation among the industrialized countries in developing alternative energy sources and reducing energy consumption, thus reducing our dependence on imports from the Middle East and restraining high energy prices. Under a Democratic Administration, the United States also will support international efforts to develop the vast energy potential of the developing countries.

We will also actively seek to limit the dangers inherent in the international development of atomic energy and in the proliferation of nuclear weapons. Steps to be given high priority will include: revitalization of the Nonproliferation Treaty, expansion of the International Atomic Energy Agency and other international safeguards and monitoring of national facilities, cooperation against potential terrorism involving nuclear weapons, agreement by suppliers not to transfer enrichment or reprocessing facilities, international assurance of supply of nuclear fuel only to countries cooperating with strict nonproliferation measures, subsidization of multinational nuclear facilities, and gradual conversion to international control of non-weapons fissionable material.

The Developing World

We have a historic opportunity in the next decade to improve the extent and quality of cooperation between the rich and poor countries. The potential benefits to our nation of a policy of constructive cooperation with the developing world would be considerable: uninterrupted access at reasonable cost to raw materials and to basic commodities; lower rates of global inflation; improved world markets for our goods; and a more benign atmosphere for international negotiation in general. Above all, the prospects for the maintenance of peace will be vastly higher in a world in which fewer and fewer people suffer the pangs of hunger and the yoke of economic oppression.

* * *

A primary object of American aid, both military and economic, is first of all to enhance the condition of freedom in the world. The United States should not provide aid to any government— anywhere in the world—which uses secret police, detention without charges, and torture to enforce its powers. Exceptions to this policy should be rare, and the aid provided should be limited to that which is absolutely necessary. The United States should be open and unashamed in its exercise of diplomatic efforts to encourage the observance of human rights in countries which receive American aid.

* * *

Defense Policy

The size and structure of our military forces must be carefully related to the demands of our foreign policies in this new era. These should be based on a careful assessment of what will be needed in the long-run to deter our potential adversaries; to fight successfully, if necessary, conventional wars in areas in which our national security is threatened; and to reassure our allies and friends—notably in Western Europe, Japan and the Near East. To this end, our strategic nuclear forces must provide a strong and credible deterrent to nuclear attack and nuclear blackmail. Our conventional forces must be strong enough to deter aggression in areas whose security is vital to our own. In a manner consistent with these objectives, we should seek those disarmament and arms control agreements which will contribute to mutual reductions in both nuclear and conventional arms.

* * *

By its undue emphasis on the overall size of the defense budget as the primary measure of both our national resolve and the proficiency of our armed forces, the administration has forgotten that we are seeking not to outspend, but to be able to deter and, if necessary, outfight our potential adversaries. While we must spend whatever is legitimately needed for defense, cutbacks on duplication and waste are both feasible and essential. Barring any major change in the international situation, with the proper management, with the proper kind of investment of defense dollars, and with the proper choice of military programs, we believe we can reduce present defense spending by about $5-billion to $7-billion. We must be tough-minded about the development of new weapons systems which add only marginal military value. The size of our defense budget should not be dictated by bureaucratic imperatives or the needs of defense contractors but by our assessment of international realities. In order to provide for a comprehensive review of the B-1 test and evaluation program, no decision regarding B-1 production should be made prior to February 1977.

* * *

U.S.-U.S.S.R. Relations

The United States and the Soviet Union are the only powers who, by rivalry or miscalculation, could bring general nuclear war upon our civilization. A principal goal must be the continued reduction of tension with the U.S.S.R. This can, however, only be accomplished by fidelity to our principles and interests and through businesslike negotiations about specific issues, not by the bad bargains, dramatic posturing, and the stress on general declarations that have characterized the Nixon-Ford administration's detente policy.

* * *

Our task is to establish U.S.-U.S.S.R. relations on a stable basis, avoiding excesses of both hope and fear. Patience, a clear sense of our own priorities, and a willingness to negotiate specific firm agreements in areas of mutual interest can return balance to relations between the United States and the Soviet Union.

* * *

Our stance on the issue of human rights and political liberties in the Soviet Union is important to American self-respect and our moral standing in the world. We should continually remind the Soviet Union, by word and conduct, of its commitments in Helsinki to the free flow of people and ideas and of how offensive we and other free people find its violations of the Universal Declaration of Human Rights. As part of our programs of official, technical, trade, cultural and other exchanges with the U.S.S.R., we should press its leaders to open their society to a genuine interchange of people and ideas.

* * *

America in the World Community

Many of the critical foreign policy issues we face require global approaches, but an effective international role for the United States also demands effective working with the special interests of specific foreign nations and regions. The touchstone of our policy must be our own interests, which in turn means that we should not seek or expect to control events everywhere. Indeed, intelligent pursuit of our objectives demands a realization that even where our interests are great and our involvement essential, we do not act alone, but in a world setting where others have interests and objectives as well.

* * *

Europe

* * *

The military security of Europe is fundamental to our own. To that end, NATO remains a vital commitment. We should retain in Europe a U.S. contribution to NATO forces so that they are sufficient to deter or defeat attack without premature resort to nuclear weapons. This does not exclude moderate reductions in manpower levels made possible by more efficiency, and it affirmatively requires a thorough reform and overhaul of NATO forces, plans and deployments. We encourage our European allies to increase their share of the contributions to NATO defense, both in terms of troops and hardware. By mutual agreement or through modernization, the thousands of tactical nuclear weapons in Europe should be reduced, saving money and manpower and increasing our own and international security.

* * *

Middle East

We shall continue to seek a just and lasting peace in the Middle East. The cornerstone of our policy is a firm commitment to the independence and security of the State of Israel. This special relationship does not prejudice improved relations with other nations in the region. Real peace in the Middle East will permit Israel and her Arab neighbors to turn their energies to internal development, and will eliminate the threat of world conflict spreading from tensions there.

* * *

Asia

We remain a Pacific power with important stakes and objectives in the region, but the Vietnam War has taught us the folly of becoming militarily involved where our vital interests were not at stake.

Friendship and cooperation with Japan are the cornerstone of our Asian interests and policy.

* * *

We reaffirm our commitment to the security of the Republic of Korea, both in itself and as a key to the security of Japan. However, on a prudent and carefully planned basis, we can redeploy, and gradually phase out, the U.S. ground forces, and can withdraw the nuclear weapons now stationed in Korea without endangering that support, as long as our tactical air and naval forces in the region remain strong. Our continued resolve in the area should not be misunderstood. However, we deplore the denial of human rights in the Republic of Korea, just as we deplore the brutal and aggressive acts of the regime in North Korea.

* * *

The Americas

* * *

In the last eight years, our relations with Latin America have deteriorated amid high-level indifference, increased military domination of Latin American governments, and revelations of extensive American interference in the internal politics of Chile and other nations. The principles of the Good Neighbor Policy and the Alliance for Progress, under which we are committed to working with the nations of the Americas as equals, remain valid today but seem to have been forgotten by the present administration.

* * *

We pledge support for a new Panama Canal treaty, which insures the interests of the United States in that waterway, recognizes the principles already agreed upon, takes into account the interests of the Canal work force, and which will have wide hemispheric support.

* * *

Africa

Eight years of indifference, accompanied by increasing cooperation with racist regimes, have left our influence and prestige in Africa at an historical low. We must adopt policies that recognize the intrinsic importance of Africa and its development to the United States, and the inevitability of majority rule on that continent.

* * *

(37) Campaign Platform of the Republican Party, adopted August 18, 1976 by the Republican National Convention in Kansas City.

    (a) Sections on Foreign Policy, National Defense and International Economic Policy.[2]

(Excerpt)

[2]Text from *New York Times*, Aug. 16, 1976.

Foreign Policy, National Defense and International Economic Policy

National Defense

A superior national defense is the fundamental condition for a secure America and for peace and freedom for the world. Military strength is the path to peace. A sound foreign policy must be rooted in a superior defense capability, and both must be perceived as a deterrent to aggression and supportive of our national interests.

The American people expect that their leaders will assure a national defense posture second to none. They know that planning for our national security must be a joint effort by the President and Congress. It cannot be the subject of partisan dispute. It should not be held hostage to domestic adventurism.

A minimum guarantee to preserve freedom and insure against blackmail and threats, and in the face of growing Soviet military power, requires a period of sustained growth in our defense effort. In constant dollars, the present defense budget will not more than match the defense budget of 1964, the year before a Democratic Administration involved America so deeply in the Vietnam war. In 1975 Soviet defense programs exceeded ours in investment by 85 percent, exceeded ours in operating costs by 25 percent, and exceeded ours in research and development by 66 percent. The issue is whether our forces will be adequate to future challenges. We say they must be.

Our national defense will include the continuation of the major modernization program for our strategic missile and bomber forces, the development of a new and intercontinental ballistic missile, a new missile-launching submarine force and a modern bomber—the B-1—capable of penetrating the most sophisticated air defenses of the 1980's. These elements will comprise a deterrent of the first order.

Our Navy, the guarantor of freedom of the seas, must have a major ship-building program, with an adequate balance between nuclear and non-nuclear ships. The composition of the fleet must be based on a realistic assessment of the threat we face, and must assure that no adversary will gain naval superiority.

An important modernization program for our tactical air forces is under way. We will require new fighters and interceptor aircraft for the Air Force, Navy and Marines. As a necessary component of our long-range strategy, we will produce and deploy the B-1 bomber in a timely manner, allowing us to retain air superiority.

Our investments in military research and development are of great importance to our future defense capabilities. We must not lose the vital momentum.

As a vital component of our overall national security posture, the United States must have the best intelligence system in the world. The effectiveness of the intelligence community must be restored, consonant with the reforms instituted by President Ford. We favor the creation of an independent oversight function by Congress and we will withstand partisan efforts to turn any part of our intelligence system into a political football. We will take every precaution to prevent the breakdown of security controls on sensitive intelligence information, endangering the lives of U.S. officials abroad, or affecting the ability of the President to act expeditiously whenever legitimate foreign policy and defense needs require it.

NATO and Europe

The economic strength of Western Europe has increased to the point where our NATO partners can now assume a larger share of the common defense; in response to our urging, our allies are demonstrating a greater willingness to do so. This is not the time to recommend a unilateral reduction of American military forces in Europe. We will, however, pursue the balanced reduction of forces in both Western and Eastern Europe, based on agreements which do not jeopardize the security of the alliance.

Some of our NATO allies have experienced rapid and dynamic changes. We are encouraged by developments in the Iberian peninsula, where both Portugal and Spain now face more promising futures. Early consideration should be given to Spain's accession to the North Atlantic Treaty Organization.

Asia and the Pacific

When Republicans assumed executive office in 1969, we were confronted with a war in Vietnam involving more than 500,000 U.S. troops, and to which we had committed billions of dollars and our national honor and prestige. It was in the spirit of bipartisan support for Presidential foreign policy initiatives, inaugurated in the postwar era by Senator Arthur Vandenberg, that most Republicans supported the United States commitment to assist South Vietnam resist Communist-sponsored aggression. The human cost to us was great; more than 55,000 Americans died in that conflict, and more than 300,000 were wounded.

A policy of patient, persistent and principled negotiations extricated the United States from that ill-fated war with the expectation that peace would prevail. The refusal of the Democrat-controlled Congress to give support to Presidential requests for military aid to the beleaguered nations of South Vietnam, Cambodia and Laos, coupled with sustained military assaults by the

Communists in gross violation of the Paris peace accords, brought about the collapse of those nations and the subjugation of their people to totalitarian rule.

We recognize that there is a wide divergence of opinion concerning Vietnam, but we pledge that American troops will never again be committed for the purpose of our own defense, or the defense of those to whom we are committed by treaty or other solemn agreement, without the clear purpose of achieving our stated diplomatic and military objectives.

United States-Chinese Relations

A development of significance for the future of Asia and for the world came to fruition in 1972 as our communications were restored with the People's Republic of China. This event has allowed us to initiate dialogue with the leaders of a quarter of the earth's population and trade channels with the People's Republic have been opened, leading to benefits for each side.

Our friendly relations with one great power should not be construed as a challenge to any other nation, large or small. The United States Government, while engaged in a normalization of relations with the People's Republic of China, will continue to support the freedom and independence of our friend and ally, the Republic of China, and its 16 million people. The United States will fulfill and keep its commitments, such as the mutual defense treaty with the Republic of China.

The Americas

The present Panama Canal treaty provides that the United States has jurisdictional rights in the Canal Zone as "if it were the sovereign." The United States intends that the Panama Canal be preserved as an international waterway for the ships of all nations. This secure access is enhanced by a relationship which commands the respect of Americans and Panamanians and benefits the people of both countries. In any talks with Panama, however, the United States negotiators should in no way cede, dilute, forfeit, negotiate or transfer any rights, power, authority, jurisdiction, territory or property that are necessary for the protection and security of the United States and the entire Western Hemisphere.

The Middle East

Our commitment to Israel is fundamental and enduring. We have honored and will continue to honor that commitment in every way—politically, economically and by providing the military aid that Israel requires to remain strong enough to deter any potential aggression. Forty percent of all United States aid that Israel has received since its creation in 1948 has come in the last two fiscal years, as a result of Republican initiatives. Our policy must remain one of decisive support for the security and integrity of Israel.

An equally important component of our commitment to Israel lies in continuing our efforts to secure a just and durable peace for all nations in that complex region. Our efforts have succeeded, for the first time since the creation of the state of Israel, in moving toward a negotiated peace settlement which would serve the interests and the security of all nations in the Middle East. Peace in the Middle East now requires face-to-face, direct negotiations between the states involved with the recognition of safe, secure and defensible borders for Israel.

Africa

We support all forces which promote negotiated settlements and racial peace. We shall continue to deplore all violence and terrorism and to urge all concerned that the rights of tribal, ethnic and racial minorities be guaranteed through workable safeguards. Our policy is to strengthen the forces of moderation, recognizing that solutions to African problems will not come quickly. The peoples of Africa can coexist in security, work together in freedom and harmony, and strive together to secure their prosperity. We hope that the Organization of African Unity will be able to achieve mature and stable relationships within Africa and abroad.

United States-Soviet Relations

Our trade in nonstrategic areas creates jobs here at home, substantially improves our balance-of-payments position, and can contribute to an improved political climate in the world. The overseas sale of our agricultural products benefits American farmers and consumers. To guard against any sudden shift in domestic prices as the consequence of unannounced purchases, we have instituted strict reporting procedures and other treaty safeguards. We shall not permit concessional sales of agricultural products to the Soviet Union, nor shall we permit the Soviet Union or others to determine our agricultural policies by irregular and unpredictable purchases.

Our relations with the Soviet Union will be guided by solid principles. We will maintain our strategic and conventional forces; we will oppose the deployment of Soviet power for unilateral advantages or political and territorial expansion; we will never tolerate a shift against us in the strategic balance, and we will remain firm in the face of pressure, while at the same time expressing our willingness to work on the basis of strict reciprocity toward new agreements which will help achieve peace and stability.

International Cooperation

The United States should promptly withdraw from the International Labor Organization if that body fails to stop its increasing politicization.

We favor an extension of the territorial sea from three to 12 miles, and we favor in principle the creation of a 200-mile economic zone in which coastal states would have exclusive rights to explore and develop natural resources.

We strongly condemn illegal corporate payments made at home and abroad. To eliminate illegal payments to foreign officials by American corporations, we support passage of President Ford's proposed legislation and the O.E.C.D. declaration on investment setting forth reasonable guidelines for business conduct.

International Economic Policy

The Republican Administration will cooperate fully in strengthening the international trade and monetary system which provides the foundation for our prosperity and that of all nations. We shall bargain hard to remove barriers to an open economic system, and we shall oppose new restrictions to trade. We shall continue to represent vigorously our nation's economic interests in the trade negotiations taking place in Geneva, guard against protectionism, and insist that the principles of fair trade be scrupulously observed. When industries and jobs are adversely affected by foreign competition, adjustment assistance under the Trade Act of 1974 is made available. This act must be under continuous review to ascertain that it reflects changing circumstances.

Conclusion

The American people can be proud of our nation's achievements in foreign policy over the past eight years.

We are at peace.

We are strong.

We re-emphasize the importance of our ties with the nations of the Americas.

Our relations with allies in the Atlantic community and with Japan have never been closer.

Significant progress has been made toward a just and durable settlement in the Middle East.

We have sought negotiation rather than confrontation with our adversaries, while maintaining our strategic deterrent.

The world economic recovery, led by the United States, is producing sustainable growth.

In this year of our nation's Bicentennial, the American people have confidence in themselves and are optimistic about the future.

We, the Republican Party, proudly submit our record and our platform to you.

(b) Amendment on Morality in Foreign Policy, accepted by the Convention August 18, 1976.[3]

The goal of Republican foreign policy is the achievement of liberty under law and a just and lasting peace in the world. The principles by which we act to achieve peace and to protect the interests of the United States must merit the restored confidence of our people.

We recognize and commend that great beacon of human courage and morality, Aleksandr Solzhenitsyn, for his compelling message that we must face the world with no illusions about the nature of tyranny. Ours will be a foreign policy that keeps this ever in mind.

Ours will be a foreign policy which recognizes that in international negotiations we must make no undue concessions; that in pursuing détente we must not grant unilateral favors with only the hope of getting future favors in return.

Agreements that are negotiated, such as the one signed in Helsinki, must not take from those who do not have freedom the hope of one day gaining it.

Finally, we are firmly committed to a foreign policy in which secret agreements, hidden from our people, will have no part.

Honestly, openly, and with a firm conviction, we shall go forward as a united people to forge a lasting peace in the world based upon our deep belief in the rights of man, the rule of law and guidance by the hand of God.

(38) Debate on Foreign Policy: Verbatim record of the televised debate between President Ford and Governor Jimmy Carter, Democratic candidate for the Presidency, San Francisco, October 6, 1976.[4]

---

[3] Text from *New York Times*, Aug. 18, 1976.
[4] Text from *Presidential Documents*, 12: 1445-59.

THE MODERATOR. Good evening. I am Pauline Frederick of NPR [National Public Radio], moderator of the second of the historic debates of the 1976 campaign between Gerald R. Ford of Michigan, Republican candidate for President, and Jimmy Carter of Georgia, Democratic candidate for President.

Thank you, President Ford, and thank you, Governor Carter, for being with us tonight.

This debate takes place before an audience in the Palace of Fine Arts Theatre in San Francisco. An estimated 100 million Americans are watching on television as well. San Francisco was the site of the signing of the United Nations Charter, 31 years ago. Thus, it is an appropriate place to hold this debate, the subject of which is foreign and defense issues.

The questioners tonight are Max Frankel, associate editor of the New York Times, Henry L. Trewhitt, diplomatic correspondent of the Baltimore Sun, and Richard Valeriani, diplomatic correspondent of NBC News.

The ground rules tonight are basically the same as they were for the first debate 2 weeks ago. The questions will be alternated between candidates. By the toss of a coin, Governor Carter will take the first question.

Each question sequence will be as follows: The question will be asked and the candidate will have up to 3 minutes to answer. His opponent will have up to 2 minutes to respond. And prior to the response, the questioner may ask a follow-up question to clarify the candidate's answer, when necessary, with up to 2 minutes to reply. Each candidate will have 3 minutes for a closing statement at the end.

President Ford and Governor Carter do not have notes or prepared remarks with them this evening, but they may take notes during the debate and refer to them.

Mr. Frankel, you have the first question for Governor Carter.

MR. FRANKEL. Governor, since the Democrats last ran our foreign policy, including many of the men who are advising you, the country has been relieved of the Vietnam agony and the military draft; we've started arms control negotiations with the Russians; we've opened relations with China; we've arranged the disengagement in the Middle East; we've regained influence with the Arabs without deserting Israel. Now, maybe, we've even begun a process of peaceful change in Africa.

Now you've objected in this campaign to the style with which much of this was done, and you've mentioned some other things that you think ought to have been done. But do you really have a quarrel with this Republican record? Would you not have done any of those things?

MR. CARTER. Well, I think this Republican administration has been almost all style and spectacular, and not substance. We've got a chance tonight to talk about, first of all, leadership, the character of our country, and a vision of the future. In every one of these instances, the Ford administration has failed. And I hope tonight that I and Mr. Ford will have a chance to discuss the reason for those failures.

Our country is not strong any more; we're not respected any more. We can only be strong overseas if we're strong at home, and when I become President, we'll not only be strong in those areas but also in defense—a defense capability second to none.

We've lost, in our foreign policy, the character of the American people. We've ignored or excluded the American people and the Congress from participation in the shaping of our foreign policy. It's been one of secrecy and exclusion.

In addition to that, we've had a chance to become now, contrary to our longstanding beliefs and principles, the arms merchant of the whole world. We've tried to buy success from our enemies and, at the same time, we've excluded from the process the normal friendship of our allies.

In addition to that, we've become fearful to compete with the Soviet Union on an equal basis. We talk about détente. The Soviet Union knows what they want in détente, and they've been getting it. We have not known what we've wanted, and we've been outtraded in almost every instance.

The other point I want to make is about our defense. We've got to be a nation blessed with the defense capability that's efficient, tough, capable, well-organized, narrowly focused fighting capability. The ability to fight if necessary is the best way to avoid the chance for, or the requirement to fight.

And the last point I want to make is this: Mr. Ford, Mr. Kissinger have continued on with the policies and failures of Richard Nixon. Even the Republican platform has criticized the lack of leadership in Mr. Ford, and they've criticized the foreign policy of this administration. This is one instance where I agree with the Republican platform.

I might say this in closing, and that is, that as far as foreign policy goes, Mr. Kissinger has been the President of this country. Mr. Ford has shown an absence of leadership and an absence of a grasp of what this country is and what it ought to be. That's got to be changed, and that is one of the major issues in this campaign of 1976.

THE MODERATOR. President Ford, would you like to respond?

THE PRESIDENT. Governor Carter again is talking in broad generalities. Let me take just one question that he raises—the military strength and capability of the United States. Governor Carter, in November of 1975, indicated that he wanted to cut the defense budget by $15 billion. A few months later, he said he wanted to cut the defense budget by $8 billion or $9 billion. And more recently, he talks about cutting the defense budget by $5 billion to $7 billion. There is no way you can be strong militarily and have those kinds of reductions in our military appropriations.

Now let me just tell you a little story. About late October of 1975, I asked the then Secretary of Defense, Mr. Schlesinger, to tell me what had to be done if we were going to reduce the defense budget by $3- to $5-billion. A few days later, Mr. Schlesinger came back and said if we cut the defense budget by $3- to $5-billion, we will have to cut military personnel by 250,000, civilian personnel by 100,000, jobs in America by 100,000. We would have to stretch out our aircraft procurement. We would have to reduce our naval construction program. We would have to reduce the research and development for the Army, the Navy, the Air Force, and Marines by 8 percent. We would have to close 20 military bases in the United States immediately. That's the kind of a defense program that Mr. Carter wants.

Let me tell you this, straight from the shoulder: You don't negotiate with Mr. Brezhnev from weakness. And the kind of a defense program that Mr. Carter wants will mean a weaker defense and a poorer negotiating position.

THE MODERATOR. Mr. Trewhitt, a question for President Ford.

MR. TREWHITT. Mr. President, my question really is the other side of the coin from Mr. Frankel's. For a generation, the United States has had a foreign policy based on containment of communism; yet, we have lost the first war in Vietnam; we lost a shoving match in Angola. Communists threaten to come to power by peaceful means in Italy, and relations generally have cooled with the Soviet Union in the last few months. So let me ask you, first, what do you do about such cases as Italy and, secondly, does this general drift mean that we're moving back toward something like an old cold war relationship with the Soviet Union?

THE PRESIDENT. I don't believe we should move to a cold war relationship. I think it's in the best interest of the United States and the world as a whole that the United States negotiate rather than go back to the cold war relationship with the Soviet Union.

I don't look at the picture as bleakly as you have indicated in your question, Mr. Trewhitt. I believe that the United States has had many successes in recent years and recent months as far as the Communist movement is concerned. We have been successful in

Portugal where, a year ago, it looked like there was a very great possibility that the Communists would take over in Portugal. It didn't happen. We have a democracy in Portugal today.

A few months ago—or I should say maybe 2 years ago—the Soviet Union looked like they had continued strength in the Middle East. Today, according to Prime Minister Rabin, the Soviet Union is weaker in the Middle East than they have been in many, many years. The facts are the Soviet Union relationship with Egypt is at a low level; the Soviet Union relationship with Syria is at a very low point. The United States today, according to Prime Minister Rabin of Israel, is at a peak in its influence and power in the Middle East.

But let's turn for a minute to the southern African operations that are now going on. The United States of America took the initiative in southern Africa. We wanted to end the bloodshed in southern Africa. We wanted to have the right of self-determination in southern Africa. We wanted to have majority rule with the full protection of the rights of the minority. We wanted to preserve human dignity in southern Africa. We have taken the initiative, and in southern Africa today, the United States is trusted by the black frontline nations and black Africa. The United States is trusted by the other elements in southern Africa.

The United States foreign policy under this administration has been one of progress and success. And I believe that instead of talking about Soviet progress, we can talk about American successes.

And may I make an observation—part of the question you asked, Mr. Trewhitt: I don't believe that it's in the best interests of the United States and the NATO nations to have a Communist government in NATO. Mr. Carter has indicated he would look with sympathy to a Communist government in NATO. I think that would destroy the integrity and the strength of NATO, and I am totally opposed to it.

MR. CARTER. Well, Mr. Ford, unfortunately, has just made a statement that's not true. I have never advocated a Communist government for Italy. That would, obviously, be a ridiculous thing for anyone to do who wanted to be President of this country. I think that this is an instance for deliberate distortion, and this has occurred also in the question about defense. As a matter of fact, I've never advocated any cut of $15 billion in our defense budget. As a matter of fact, Mr. Ford has made a political football out of the defense budget.

About a year ago, he cut the Pentagon budget $6.8 billion. After he fired James Schlesinger, the political heat got so great that he added back about $3 billion. When Ronald Reagan won the Texas primary election, Mr. Ford added back another $1½ billion.

Immediately before the Kansas City convention, he added back another $1.8 billion in the defense budget. And his own Office of Management and Budget testified that he had a $3-billion cut insurance added to the defense budget under the pressure from the Pentagon. Obviously, this is another indication of trying to use the defense budget for political purposes, which he's trying to do tonight.

Now, we went into south Africa late, after Great Britain, Rhodesia, the black nations had been trying to solve this problem for many, many years. We didn't go in until right before the election, similar to what was taking place in 1972, when Mr. Kissinger announced peace is at hand just before the election at that time.

And we have weakened our position in NATO, because the other countries in Europe supported the democratic forces in Portugal long before we did. We stuck to the Portugal dictatorships much longer than other democracies did in this world.

THE MODERATOR. Mr. Valeriani, a question for Governor Carter.

MR. VALERIANI. Governor Carter, much of what the United States does abroad is done in the name of the national interest. What is your concept of the national interest? What should the role of the United States in the world be? And in that connection, considering your limited experience in foreign affairs and the fact that you take some pride in being a Washington outsider, don't you think it would be appropriate for you to tell the American voters, before the election, the people that you would like to have in key positions such as Secretary of State, Secretary of Defense, national security affairs adviser at the White House?

MR. CARTER. Well, I'm not going to name my Cabinet before I get elected; I've got a little ways to go before I start doing that. But I have an adequate background, I believe. I am a graduate of the U.S. Naval Academy, the first military graduate since Eisenhower. I've served as Governor of Georgia and have traveled extensively in foreign countries—in South America, Central America, Europe, the Middle East, and in Japan.

I've traveled the last 21 months among the people of this country. I've talked to them, and I've listened. And I've seen at firsthand, in a very vivid way, the deep hurt that's come to this country in the aftermath of Vietnam and Cambodia and Chile and Pakistan and Angola and Watergate, CIA revelations.

What we were formerly so proud of—the strength of our country, its moral integrity, the representation in foreign affairs of what our people are, what our Constitution stands for—has been gone. And in the secrecy that has surrounded our foreign policy in the last few years, the American people and the Congress have been excluded.

I believe I know what this country ought to be. I've been one who's loved my Nation, as many Americans do. And I believe that there is no limit placed on what we can be in the future if we can harness the tremendous resources—militarily, economically—and the stature of our people, the meaning of our Constitution in the future.

Every time we've made a serious mistake in foreign affairs, it's been because the American people have been excluded from the process. If we can just tap the intelligence and ability, the sound commonsense and the good judgment of the American people, we can once again have a foreign policy to make us proud instead of ashamed.

And I'm not going to exclude the American people from that process in the future, as Mr. Ford and Kissinger have done. This is what it takes to have a sound foreign policy: strong at home, strong defense, permanent commitments, not betray the principles of our country, and involve the American people and the Congress in the shaping of our foreign policy.

Every time Mr. Ford speaks from a position of secrecy—in negotiations and secret treaties that have been pursued and achieved, in supporting dictatorships, in ignoring human rights— we are weak and the rest of the world knows it.

So these are the ways that we can restore the strength of our country. And they don't require long experience in foreign policy— nobody has that except a President who served a long time or a Secretary of State. But my background, my experience, my knowledge of the people of this country, my commitment to our principles that don't change—those are the best bases to correct the horrible mistakes of this administration and restore our own country to a position of leadership in the world.

MR. VALERIANI. How, specifically, Governor, are you going to bring the American people into the decisionmaking process in foreign policy? What does that mean?

MR. CARTER. First of all, I would quit conducting the decisionmaking process in secret, as has been a characteristic of Mr. Kissinger and Mr. Ford. In many instances we've made agreements, like in Vietnam, that have been revealed later on to our embarrassment.

Recently, Ian Smith, the President of Rhodesia, announced that he had unequivocal commitments from Mr. Kissinger that he could not reveal. The American people don't know what those commitments are. We've seen in the past a destruction of elected governments, like in Chile, and the strong support of military dictatorship there. These kinds of things have hurt us very much.

I would restore the concept of the fireside chat, which was an integral part of the administration of Franklin Roosevelt. And I would also restore the involvement of the Congress. When Harry Truman was President, he was not afraid to have a strong Secretary of Defense—Dean Acheson, George Marshall were strong Secretaries of State, excuse me, State. But he also made sure that there was a bipartisan support. The Members of Congress, Arthur Vandenberg, Walter George, were part of the process. And before our Nation made a secret agreement, and before we made a bluffing statement, we were sure that we had the backing not only of the President and the Secretary of State, but also of the Congress and the people.

This is a responsibility of the President, and I think it's very damaging to our country for Mr. Ford to have turned over this responsibility to the Secretary of State.

THE MODERATOR. President Ford, do you have a response?

THE PRESIDENT. Governor Carter again contradicts himself. He complains about secrecy, and yet he is quoted as saying that in the attempt to find a solution in the Middle East, that he would hold unpublicized meetings with the Soviet Union—I presume for the purpose of imposing a settlement on Israel and the Arab nations.

But let me talk just a minute about what we've done to avoid secrecy in the Ford administration. After the United States took the initiative in working with Israel and with Egypt and achieving the Sinai II agreement—and I am proud to say that not a single Egyptian or Israeli soldier has lost his life since the signing of the Sinai agreement—but at the time that I submitted the Sinai agreement to the Congress of the United States, I submitted every single document that was applicable to the Sinai II agreement. It was the most complete documentation by any President of any agreement signed by a President on behalf of the United States.

Now, as far as meeting with the Congress is concerned, during the 24 months that I've been the President of the United States, I have averaged better than one meeting a month with responsible groups or committees of the Congress, both House and Senate.

The Secretary of State has appeared, in the several years that he's been the Secretary, before 80 different committee hearings in the House and in the Senate. The Secretary of State has made better than 50 speeches all over the United States explaining American foreign policy. I have made, myself, at least 10 speeches in various parts of the country, where I have discussed with the American people defense and foreign policy.

THE MODERATOR. Mr. Frankel, a question for President Ford.

MR. FRANKEL. Mr. President, I'd like to explore a little more deeply our relationship with the Russians. They used to brag, back in Khrushchev's day, that because of their greater patience and because of our greed for business deals, that they would sooner or later get the better of us. Is it possible that, despite some setbacks in the Middle East, they've proved their point? Our allies in France and Italy are now flirting with communism; we've recognized a permanent Communist regime in East Germany; we virtually signed, in Helsinki, an agreement that the Russians have dominance in Eastern Europe; we bailed out Soviet agriculture with our huge grain sales—we've given them large loans, access to our best technology and, if the Senate hadn't interfered with the Jackson Amendment, maybe you would have given them even larger loans. Is that what you call a two-way street of traffic in Europe?

THE PRESIDENT. I believe that we have negotiated with the Soviet Union since I've been President from a position of strength. And let me cite several examples.

Shortly after I became President, in December of 1974, I met with General Secretary Brezhnev in Vladivostok. And we agreed to a mutual cap on the ballistic missile launchers at a ceiling of 2,400, which means that the Soviet Union, if that becomes a permanent agreement, will have to make a reduction in their launchers that they now have or plan to have.

I negotiated at Vladivostok with Mr. Brezhnev a limitation on the MIRVing of their ballistic missiles at a figure of 1,320, which is the first time that any President has achieved a cap either on launchers or on MIRVs.

It seems to me that we can go from there to the grain sales. The grain sales have been a benefit to American agriculture. We have achieved a 5¾-year sale of a minimum of 6 million metric tons, which means that they have already bought about 4 million metric tons this year and are bound to buy another 2 million metric tons, to take the grain and corn and wheat that the American farmers have produced in order to have full production. And these grain sales to the Soviet Union have helped us tremendously in meeting the cost of the additional oil and the oil that we have bought from overseas.

If we turn to Helsinki—I am glad you raised it, Mr. Frankel—in the case of Helsinki, 35 nations signed an agreement, including the

Secretary of State for the Vatican. I can't under any circumstances believe that His Holiness the Pope would agree, by signing that agreement, that the 35 nations have turned over to the Warsaw Pact nations the domination of Eastern Europe. It just isn't true. And if Mr. Carter alleges that His Holiness, by signing that, has done it, he is totally inaccurate.

Now, what has been accomplished by the Helsinki agreement? Number one, we have an agreement where they notify us and we notify them of any military maneuvers that are to be undertaken. They have done it in both cases where they've done so. There is no Soviet domination of Eastern Europe, and there never will be under a Ford administration.

MR. FRANKEL. I'm sorry, could I just follow—did I understand you to say, sir, that the Russians are not using Eastern Europe as their own sphere of influence and occupying most of the countries there and making sure with their troops that it's a Communist zone, whereas on our side of the line the Italians and the French are still flirting with the possibility of communism?

THE PRESIDENT. I don't believe, Mr. Frankel, that the Yugoslavians consider themselves dominated by the Soviet Union. I don't believe that the Romanians consider themselves dominated by the Soviet Union. I don't believe that the Poles consider themselves dominated by the Soviet Union.

Each of those countries is independent, autonomous; it has its own territorial integrity. And the United States does not concede that those countries are under the domination of the Soviet Union. As a matter of fact, I visited Poland, Yugoslavia, and Romania, to make certain that the people of those countries understood that the President of the United States and the people of the United States are dedicated to their independence, their autonomy, and their freedom.

THE MODERATOR. Governor Carter, have you a response?

MR. CARTER. Well, in the first place, I am not criticizing His Holiness the Pope. I was talking about Mr. Ford.

The fact is that secrecy has surrounded the decisions made by the Ford administration. In the case of the Helsinki agreement, it may have been a good agreement at the beginning, but we have failed to enforce the so-called Basket 3 part, which insures the right of people to migrate, to join their families, to be free to speak out.

The Soviet Union is still jamming Radio Free Europe. Radio Free Europe is being jammed. We've also seen a very serious problem with the so-called Sonnenfeldt document which, apparently, Mr. Ford has just endorsed, which said that there is an organic linkage between the Eastern European countries and the Soviet Union. And I would like to see Mr. Ford convince the Polish-Americans and the Czech-Americans and the Hungarian-Americans in this country that those countries don't live under the domination and supervision of the Soviet Union behind the Iron Curtain.

We also have seen Mr. Ford exclude himself from access to the public. He hasn't had a tough, cross-examination-type press conference in over 30 days. One press conference he had without sound.

He's also shown a weakness in yielding to pressure. The Soviet Union, for instance, put pressure on Mr. Ford, and he refused to see a symbol of human freedom recognized around the world—Alexander Solzhenitsyn.

The Arabs have put pressure on Mr. Ford—and he's yielded and he has permitted a boycott by the Arab countries of American businesses who trade with Israel, who have American Jews owning or taking part in the management of American companies. His own Secretary of Commerce had to be subpoenaed by the Congress to reveal the names of businesses who were subject to this boycott. They didn't volunteer the information; he had to be subpoenaed.

And the last thing I'd like to say is this: This grain deal with the Soviet Union in '72[5] was terrible, and Mr. Ford made up for it with three embargoes—one against our own ally in Japan. That's not the way to run our foreign policy, including international trade.

THE MODERATOR. Mr. Trewhitt, a question for Governor Carter.

MR. TREWHITT. Governor, I'd like to pick up on that point, actually, and on your appeal for a greater measure of American idealism in foreign affairs. Foreign affairs come home to the American public pretty much in such issues as oil embargoes and grain sales, that sort of thing. Would you be willing to risk an oil embargo in order to promote human rights in Iran, Saudi Arabia—withhold arms from Saudi Arabia for the same purpose? As a matter of fact, I think you have perhaps answered this final part, but would you withhold grain from the Soviet Union in order to promote civil rights in the Soviet Union?

MR. CARTER. I would never single out food as a trade embargo item. If I ever decided to impose an embargo because of a crisis in

[5]Cf. *AFR, 1972:* 114-19.

international relationships, it would include all shipments of all equipment. For instance, if the Arab countries ever again declare an embargo against our Nation on oil, I would consider that not a military but an economic declaration of war. And I would respond instantly and in kind. I would not ship that Arab country anything—no weapons, no spare parts for weapons, no oil-drilling rigs, no oil pipe, no nothing. I wouldn't single out just food.

Another thing I'd like to say is this: In our international trade, as I said in my opening statement, we have become the arms merchant of the world. When this Republican administration came into office, we were shipping about $1-billion worth of arms overseas; now, $10- to $12-billion worth of arms overseas to countries that quite often use these weapons to fight each other.

The shift in emphasis has been very disturbing to me, speaking about the Middle East. Under the last Democratic administration, 60 percent of all weapons that went into the Middle East were for Israel. Nowadays—75 percent were for Israel before—now, 60 percent go to the Arab countries, and this does not include Iran. If you include Iran, our present shipment of weapons to the Middle East—only 20 percent goes to Israel. This is a deviation from idealism; it's a deviation from a commitment to our major ally in the Middle East, which is Israel; it's a yielding to economic pressure on the part of the Arabs on the oil issue; and it's also a tremendous indication that under the Ford administration, we have not addressed the energy policy adequately.

We still have no comprehensive energy policy in this country, and it's an overall sign of weakness. When we are weak at home economically—high unemployment, high inflation, a confused Government, a wasteful Defense Establishment—this encourages the kind of pressure that's been put on us successfully. It would have been inconceivable 10, 15 years ago for us to be brought to our knees with an Arab oil embargo. But it was done 3 years ago, and they're still putting pressure on us from the Arab countries to our discredit around the world.

These are the weaknesses that I see, and I believe it's not just a matter of idealism. It's a matter of being tough. It's a matter of being strong. It's a matter of being consistent. Our priorities ought to be, first of all, to meet our own military needs; secondly, to meet the needs of our allies and friends, and only then should we ship military equipment to foreign countries. As a matter of fact, Iran is going to get 80 F-14's before we even meet our own Air Force orders for F-14's, and the shipment of Spruance Class Destroyers to Iran are much more highly sophisticated than the Spruance Class Destroyers that are presently being delivered to our own Navy. This is ridiculous, and it ought to be changed.

MR. TREWHITT. Governor, let me pursue that, if I may. If I understand you correctly, you would, in fact, to use my examples, withhold arms from Iran and Saudi Arabia even if the risk was an oil embargo and if they should be securing those arms from somewhere else. And then, if the embargo came, then you would respond in kind. Do I have it correctly?

MR. CARTER. If—Iran is not an Arab country, as you know, it's a Moslem country. But if Saudi Arabia should declare an oil embargo against us, then I would consider that an economic declaration of war. And I would make sure that the Saudis understood this ahead of time, so there would be no doubt in their mind. I think under those circumstances, they would refrain from pushing us to our knees as they did in 1973 with the previous oil embargo.

THE MODERATOR. President Ford.

THE PRESIDENT. Governor Carter apparently doesn't realize that since I've been President, we have sold to the Israelis over $4 billion in military hardware. We have made available to the Israelis over 45 percent of the total economic and military aid since the establishment of Israel 27 years ago. So the Ford administration has done a good job in helping our good ally, Israel, and we're dedicated to the survival and security of Israel.

I believe that Governor Carter doesn't realize the need and necessity for arms sales to Iran. He indicates he would not make those.

Iran is bordered very extensively by the Soviet Union. Iran has Iraq as one of its neighbors. The Soviet Union and the Communist-dominated Government of Iraq are neighbors of Iran, and Iran is an ally of the United States. It's my strong feeling that we ought to sell arms to Iran for its own national security and as an ally, a strong ally, of the United States.

The history of our relationship with Iran goes back to the days of President Truman, when he decided that it was vitally necessary for our own security, as well as that of Iran, that we should help that country. And Iran has been a good ally. In 1973, when there was an oil embargo, Iran did not participate; Iran continued to sell oil to the United States. I believe that it's in our interest and in the interest of Israel and Iran and Saudi Arabia, for the United States to sell arms to those countries. It's for their security as well as ours.

THE MODERATOR. Mr. Valeriani, a question for President Ford.

MR. VALERIANI. Mr. President, the policy of your administration is to normalize relations with mainland China. That means establishing, at some point, full diplomatic relations and, obviously, doing something about the mutual defense treaty with Taiwan. If you are elected, will you move to establish full diplomatic relations with Peking and will you abrogate the mutual defense treaty with Taiwan and, as a corollary, would you provide mainland China with military equipment if the Chinese were to ask for it?

THE PRESIDENT. Our relationship with the People's Republic of China is based upon the Shanghai Communiqué of 1972. That communiqué calls for the normalization of relations between the United States and the People's Republic. It doesn't set a time schedule; it doesn't make a determination as to how that relationship should be achieved in relationship to our current diplomatic recognition and obligations to the Taiwanese Government.

The Shanghai Communique does say that the differences between the People's Republic on the one hand and Taiwan on the other shall be settled by peaceful means. The net result is this administration—and during my time as the President for the next 4 years—we will continue to move for normalization of relations in the traditional sense. And we will insist that the disputes between Taiwan and the People's Republic be settled peacefully, as was agreed in the Shanghai Communiqué of 1972.

The Ford administration will not let down, will not eliminate or forget our obligation to the people of Taiwan. We feel that there must be a continued obligation to the people, the some 19 or 20 million people in Taiwan, and as we move during the next 4 years, those will be the policies of this administration.

MR. VALERIANI. Sir, the military equipment for the mainland Chinese?

THE PRESIDENT. There is no policy of this Government to give to the People's Republic, or to sell to the People's Republic of China, military equipment. I do not believe that we, the United States, should sell, give, or otherwise transfer military hardware to the People's Republic of China or any other Communist nations such as the Soviet Union, and the like.

THE MODERATOR. Governor Carter.

MR. CARTER. I'd like to go back just one moment to the previous question, where Mr. Ford, I think, confused the issue by trying to say that we're shipping Israel 40 percent of our aid. As a matter of fact, during this current year, we are shipping Iran—or have contracted to ship to Iran—about $7½-billion worth of arms and also to Saudi Arabia about $7½-billion worth of arms.

Also, in 1975, we almost brought Israel to their knees after the Yom Kippur war by the so-called reassessment of our relationship to Israel. We, in effect, tried to make Israel the scapegoat for the problems in the Middle East. And this weakened our relationship with Israel a great deal and put a cloud on the total commitment that our people feel toward the Israelis. There ought to be a clear, unequivocal commitment without change to Israel.

In the Far East, I think we need to continue to be strong, and I would certainly pursue the normalization of relationships with the People's Republic of China. We opened up a great opportunity in 1972—which has pretty well been frittered away under Mr. Ford— that ought to be a constant inclination toward friendship. But I would never let that friendship with the People's Republic of China stand in the way of the preservation of the independence and freedom of the people on Taiwan.

THE MODERATOR. Mr. Frankel, a question for Governor Carter.

MR. FRANKEL. Governor, we always seem, in our elections, and maybe in between, too, to argue about who can be tougher in the world. Give or take a few billion dollars, give or take one weapons systems, our leading politicians, and I think you two gentlemen, seem to settle roughly on the same strategy in the world at roughly the same Pentagon budget cost.

How bad do things have to get in our own economy, or how much backwardness and hunger would it take in the world to persuade you that our national security and our survival required very drastic cutbacks in arms spending and dramatic new efforts in other directions?

MR. CARTER. Well, always in the past we have had an ability to have a strong defense and also to have a strong domestic economy and also to be strong in our reputation and influence within the community of nations. These characteristics of our country have been endangered under Mr. Ford. We are no longer respected. In a showdown vote in the United Nations or in any other international council, we are lucky to get 20 percent of the other nations to vote with us. Our allies feel that we've neglected them. The so-called Nixon shocks against Japan have weakened our relationships there. Under this administration, we have also had an inclination to keep separate the European countries, thinking that if they are separate, then we can dominate them and proceed with our secret Lone Ranger type diplomatic efforts.

I would also like to point out that we in this country have let our economy go down the drain—the worst inflation since the Great Depression, the highest unemployment of any developed nation of the world. We have a higher unemployment rate in this country than Great Britain, than West Germany; our unemployment rate is twice as high as it is in Italy; it's three or four times as high as it is in Japan. And that terrible circumstance in this country is exported overseas. We comprise about 30 percent of the world's economic trade power influence. And when we are weak at home, weaker than all our allies, that weakness weakens the whole free world. So, strong economy is very important.

Another thing that we need to do is to reestablish the good relationships that we ought to have between the United States and our natural allies and friends—they have felt neglected. And using that base of strength, and using the idealism, the honesty, the predictability, the commitment, the integrity of our own country—that's where our strength lies. And that would permit us to deal with the developing nations in a position of strength.

Under this administration, we've had a continuation of a so-called "balance of power politics" where everything is looked on as a struggle between us on the one side and the Soviet Union on the other. Our allies, the smaller countries, get trampled in the rush.

What we need is to try to seek individualized, bilateral relationships with countries regardless of their size and to establish world order politics, which means we want to preserve peace through strength. We also want to revert back to the stature and the respect that our country had in previous administrations.

Now, I can't say when this can come, but I can guarantee it will not come if Gerald Ford is reelected and this present policy is continued. It will come if I am elected.

MR. FRANKEL. If I hear you right sir, you are saying guns and butter both, but President Johnson also had trouble keeping up both Vietnam and his domestic programs. I was really asking, when do the needs of the cities and our own needs and those of other backward and even more needy countries and societies around the world take precedence over some of our military spending? Ever?

MR. CARTER. Let me say very quickly that under President Johnson, in spite of the massive investment in the Vietnam war, he turned over a balanced budget to Mr. Nixon. The unemployment rate was less than 4 percent. The inflation rate under Kennedy and Johnson was about 2 percent—one-third what it is under this administration. So we did have at that time, with good management, the ability to do both.

I don't think anybody can say that Johnson and Kennedy

neglected the poor and the destitute people in this country or around the world. But I can say this: The number one responsibility of any President, above all else, is to guarantee the security of our Nation, an ability to be free of the threat of attack or blackmail, and to carry out our obligations to our allies and friends, and to carry out a legitimate foreign policy. They must go hand-in-hand. But the security of this Nation has got to come first.

THE MODERATOR. President Ford.

THE PRESIDENT. Let me say very categorically, you cannot maintain the security and the strength of the United States with the kind of defense budget cuts that Governor Carter has indicated. In 1975, he wanted to cut the budget $15 billion. He is now down to a figure of $5 billion to $7 billion. Reductions of that kind will not permit the United States to be strong enough to deter aggression and maintain the peace.

Governor Carter apparently does not know the facts. As soon as I became President, I initiated meetings with the NATO heads of state and met with them in Brussels to discuss how we could improve the defense relationship in Western Europe. In November of 1975, I met with the leaders of the five industrial nations in France for the purpose of seeing what we could do, acting together, to meet the problems of the coming recession.

In Puerto Rico this year, I met with six of the leading industrial nations' heads of state to meet the problem of inflation so we would be able to solve it before it got out of hand.

I have met with the heads of government, bilaterally as well as multilaterally. Our relations with Japan have never been better. I was the first United States President to visit Japan. And we had the Emperor of Japan here this past year. And the net result is Japan and the United States are working more closely together now than at any time in the history of our relationship. You can go around the world—and let me take Israel, for example. Just recently, President Rabin said that our relations were never better.

THE MODERATOR. Mr. Trewhitt, a question for President Ford.

MR. TREWHITT. Mr. President, you referred earlier to your meeting with Mr. Brezhnev at Vladivostok in 1974. You agreed on that occasion to try to achieve another strategic arms limitation, SALT, agreement, within the year. Nothing happened in 1975 or not very much publicly, at least, and those talks are still dragging, and things got quieter as the current season approached. Is there a bit of politics involved there, perhaps on both sides or perhaps more important, are interim weapons developments, and I am thinking such things as the cruise missile and the Soviet SS-20 intermediate range rocket, making SALT irrelevant, bypassing the SALT negotiations?

THE PRESIDENT. First, we have to understand that SALT I expires October 3, 1977. Mr. Brezhnev and I met in Vladivostok in December of 1974 for the purpose of trying to take the initial steps so we could have a SALT II agreement that would go to 1985. As I indicated earlier, we did agree on a 2,400 limitation on launchers of ballistic missiles. That would mean a cutback in the Soviet program. It would not interfere with our own program. At the same time we put a limitation of 1,320 on MIRV's.

Our technicians have been working since that time in Geneva trying to put into technical language an agreement that can be verified by both parties. In the meantime, there has developed the problem of the Soviet Backfire, their high performance aircraft, which they say is not a long-range aircraft and which some of our people say is an intercontinental aircraft.

In the interim, there has been the development on our part primarily, the cruise missiles—cruise missiles that could be launched from land-based mobile installations; cruise missiles that could be launched from high performance aircraft like the B–52's or the B–1's, which I hope we proceed with; cruise missiles which could be launched from either surface or submarine naval vessels. Those gray area weapons systems are creating some problems in the agreement for a SALT II negotiation.

But I can say that I am dedicated to proceeding. And I met just last week with the Foreign Minister of the Soviet Union, and he indicated to me that the Soviet Union was interested in narrowing the differences and making a realistic and a sound compromise.

I hope and trust in the best interests of both countries and in the best interests of all peoples throughout this globe that the Soviet Union and the United States can make a mutually beneficial agreement because, if we do not and SALT I expires on October 3, 1977, you will unleash again an all-out nuclear arms race with the potential of a nuclear holocaust of unbelievable dimensions. So, it is the obligation of the President to do just that, and I intend to do so.

MR. TREWHITT. Mr. President, let me follow that up. I'll submit that the cruise missile adds a whole new dimension to the arms competition, and then cite a statement by your office to the arms control association a few days ago in which you said that the cruise missile might eventually be included in a comprehensive arms limitation agreement but that in the meantime it was an essential part of the American strategic arsenal. Now may I assume from that that you are tending to exclude the cruise missile from the next SALT agreement or is it still negotiable in that context?

THE PRESIDENT. I believe that the cruise missiles which we are now developing in research and development across the spectrum, from air, from the sea, or from the land can be included within a SALT II agreement. They are a new weapons system that has a great potential, both conventional and nuclear armed. At the same time, we have to make certain that the Soviet Union's Backfire, which they claim is not an intercontinental aircraft and which some of our people contend is, must also be included if we are to get the kind of an agreement which is in the best interests of both countries.

And I really believe that it's far better for us and for the Soviet Union and, more importantly, for the people around the world that these two super powers find an answer for a SALT II agreement before October 3, 1977. I think good will on both parts, hard bargaining by both parties, and a reasonable compromise will be in the best interests of all parties.

THE MODERATOR. Governor Carter.

MR. CARTER. Well, Mr. Ford acts like he is running for President for the first time. He has been in office 2 years and there has been absolutely no progress made toward a new SALT agreement. He has learned the date of the expiration of SALT I, apparently.

We have seen in this world a development of a tremendous threat to us. As a nuclear engineer myself, I know the limitations and capabilities of atomic power. I also know that as far as the human beings on this Earth are concerned, that the nonproliferation of atomic weapons is number one. Only in the last few days with the election approaching has Mr. Ford taken any interest in a nonproliferation movement.

I advocated last May, in a speech at the United Nations, that we move immediately as a nation to declare a complete moratorium on the testing of all nuclear devices, both weapons and peaceful devices, that we not ship any more atomic fuel to a country that refuses to comply with strict controls over the waste which can be reprocessed into explosives. I've also advocated that we stop the sale by Germany and France of reprocessing plants to Pakistan and Brazil. Mr. Ford hasn't moved on this. We also need to provide an adequate supply of enriched uranium. Mr. Ford again, under pressure from the atomic energy lobby, has insisted that this reprocessing or rather reenrichment be done by private industry and not by the existing government plants.

This kind of confusion and absence of leadership has let us drift now for 2 years with the constantly increasing threat of atomic weapons throughout the world. We now have five nations that have atomic bombs that we know about. If we continue under Mr. Ford's policy, by 1985 or '90, we will have 20 nations that have the capability of exploding atomic weapons. This has got to be stopped. That is one of the major challenges and major undertakings that I will assume as the next President.

THE MODERATOR. Mr. Valeriani, a question for Governor Carter.

MR. VALERIANI. Governor Carter, earlier tonight you said America is not strong anymore, America is not respected anymore, and I feel I must ask you, do you really believe that the United States is not the strongest country in the world; do you really believe that the United States is not the most respected country in the world, or is that just campaign rhetoric?

MR. CARTER. No, it's not just campaign rhetoric. I think that militarily we are as strong as any nation on Earth. I think we've got to stay that way and continue to increase our capabilities to meet any potential threat. But as far as strength derived from commitment to principles; as far as strength derived from the unity within our country; as far as strength derived from the people, the Congress, the Secretary of State, the President, sharing in the evolution and carrying out of a foreign policy; as far as strength derived from the respect of our own allies and friends, their assurance that we will be staunch in our commitment, that we will not deviate, and we will give them adequate attention; as far as strength derived from doing what is right, caring for the poor, providing food, becoming the breadbasket of the world instead of the arms merchant of the world—in those respects we are not strong. Also, we will never be strong again overseas unless we are strong at home. And with our economy in such terrible disarray, and getting worse by the month—we have got 500,000 more Americans unemployed today than we had 3 months ago; we have got 2½ million more Americans out of work now than we had when Mr. Ford took office—this kind of deterioration in our economic strength is bound to weaken us around the world.

And we not only have problems at home, but we export those problems overseas. So, as far as the respect of our own people toward our own Government, as far as participation in the shaping of concepts and commitments, as far as a trust of our country among the nations of the world, as far as dependence of our country in meeting the needs and obligations that we've expressed to our allies, as far as the respect of our country, even among our potential adversaries, we are weak. Potentially, we are strong. Under this administration, that strength has not been realized.

THE MODERATOR. President Ford.

THE PRESIDENT. Governor Carter brags about the unemployment during Democratic administrations and condemns the unemployment at the present time. I must remind him that we are at peace and during the period that he brags about unemployment being low, the United States was at war.

Now let me correct one other comment that Governor Carter has made. I have recommended to the Congress that we develop the uranium enrichment plant at Portsmouth, Ohio, which is a publicly owned U.S. Government facility, and have indicated that the private program which would follow on in Alabama is one that may or may not be constructed, but I am committed to the one at Portsmouth, Ohio.

The Governor also talks about morality in foreign policy. The foreign policy of the United States meets the highest standards of morality. What is more moral than peace, and the United States is at peace today. What is more moral in foreign policy than for the administration to take the lead in the World Food Conference in Rome in 1974, when the United States committed 6 million metric tons of food, over 60 percent of the food committed for the disadvantaged and underdeveloped nations of the world?

The Ford administration wants to eradicate hunger and disease in our underdeveloped countries throughout the world. What is more moral than for the United States under the Ford administration to take the lead in southern Africa, in the Middle East? Those are initiatives in foreign policy which are of the highest moral standards. And that is indicative of the foreign policy of this country.

THE MODERATOR. Mr. Frankel, a question for President Ford.

MR. FRANKEL. Mr. President, can we stick with morality? For a lot of people it seems to cover a bunch of sins.

Mr. Nixon and Mr. Kissinger used to tell us that instead of morality we had to worry in the world about living with and letting live all kinds of governments that we really didn't like—North and South Korean dictators, Chilean fascists, Chinese Communists, Iranian emperors, and so on. They said the only way to get by in a wicked world was to treat others on the basis of how they treated us and not how they treated their own people.

But more recently, we seem to have taken a different tack. We seem to have decided that it is part of our business to tell the Rhodesians, for instance, that the way they are treating their own black people is wrong and they've got to change their government. And we put pressure on them. We were rather liberal in our advice to the Italians as to how to vote.

Is this a new Ford foreign policy in the making? Can we expect that you are now going to turn to South Africa and force them to change their government, to intervene in similar ways to end the bloodshed, as you called it, say in Chile or Chilean prisons, and to throw our weight around for the values that we hold dear in the world?

THE PRESIDENT. I believe that our foreign policy must express the highest standards of morality, and the initiatives that we took in southern Africa are the best examples of what this administration is doing and will continue to do in the next 4 years.

If the United States had not moved when we did in southern Africa, there is no doubt there would have been an acceleration of bloodshed in that tragic part of the world. If we had not taken our initiative, it's very, very possible that the government of Rhodesia would have been overrun and that the Soviet Union and the Cubans would have dominated southern Africa.

So, the United States, seeking to preserve the principle of self-determination, to eliminate the possibility of bloodshed, to protect the rights of the minority as we insisted upon the rights of the majority, I believe followed the good conscience of the American people in foreign policy, and I believe that we have used our skill. Secretary of State Kissinger has done a superb job in working with the black African nations, the so-called frontline nations. He has done a superb job in getting the Prime Minister of South Africa, Mr. Vorster, to agree that the time had come for a solution to the problem of Rhodesia.

Secretary Kissinger, in his meeting with Prime Minister Smith of Rhodesia, was able to convince him that it was in the best interests of whites, as well as blacks, in Rhodesia to find an answer for a transitional government and then a majority government.

This is a perfect example of the kind of leadership that the United States, under this administration, has taken. And I can assure you that this administration will follow that high moral principle in our future efforts in foreign policy, including our efforts in the Middle East, where it is vitally important because the Middle East is the crossroads of the world. There have been more disputes, and it's an area where there is more volatility than any other place in the world. But because Arab nations and the Israelis trust the United States, we were able to take the lead in the Sinai II agreement.

And I can assure you that the United States will have the leadership role in moving toward a comprehensive settlement of the Middle Eastern problems—I hope and trust as soon as possible—and we will do it with the highest moral principles.

MR. FRANKEL. Mr. President, just clarify one point, there are lots of majorities in the world that feel they are being pushed around by minority governments. And are you saying they can now expect to look to us for not just good cheer but throwing our weight on their side in South Africa, or on Taiwan, or in Chile, to help change their governments as in Rhodesia?

THE PRESIDENT. I would hope that as we move to one area of the world from another—and the United States must not spread itself too thinly; that was one of the problems that helped to create the circumstances in Vietnam—but as we as a nation find that we are asked by the various parties, either one nation against another or individuals within a nation, that the United States will take the leadership and try to resolve the differences.

Let me take South Korea as an example. I have personally told President Park that the United States does not condone the kind of repressive measures that he has taken in that country. But, I think in all fairness and equity, we have to recognize the problem that South Korea has. On the north they have North Korea with 500,000 well-trained, well-equipped troops. They are supported by the People's Republic of China. They are supported by the Soviet Union. South Korea faces a very delicate situation.

Now, the United States in this case, this administration, has recommended a year ago—and we have reiterated it again this year—that the United States, South Korea, North Korea, and the People's Republic of China sit down at a conference table to resolve the problems of the Korean peninsula. This is a leadership role that the United States, under this administration, is carrying out. And if we do it—and I think the opportunities and the possibilities are getting better—we will have solved many of the internal domestic problems that exist in South Korea at the present time.

THE MODERATOR. Governor Carter?

MR. CARTER. I noticed that Mr. Ford didn't comment on the prisons in Chile. This is a typical example, maybe of many others, where this administration overthrew an elected government and helped to establish a military dictatorship. This has not been an ancient history story. Last year, under Mr. Ford, of all the Food for Peace that went to South America, 85 percent went to the military dictatorship in Chile.

Another point I want to make is this: He says we have to move from one area of the world to another. That is one of the problems with this administration's so-called shuttle diplomacy. While the Secretary of State is in one country, there are almost 150 others that are wondering what we are going to do next, what will be the next secret agreement. We don't have a comprehensive, understandable foreign policy that deals with world problems or even regional problems.

Another thing that concerned me was what Mr. Ford said about unemployment, that insinuating that under Johnson and Kennedy that unemployment could only be held down when this country is at war. Karl Marx said that the free enterprise system in a democracy can only continue to exist when they are at war or preparing for war. Karl Marx was the grandfather of communism. I don't agree with that statement. I hope Mr. Ford doesn't, either.

He has put pressure on the Congress, and I don't believe Mr. Ford would even deny this, to hold up on nonproliferation legislation until the Congress agreed for an $8 billion program for private industry to start producing enriched uranium.

And the last thing I want to make is this: He talks about peace, and I am thankful for peace. We were peaceful when Mr. Ford went into office, but he and Mr. Kissinger and others tried to start a new Vietnam in Angola. And it was only the outcry of the American people and the Congress when this secret deal was discovered that prevented our renewed involvement in that conflagration which was taking place there.

THE MODERATOR. Gentlemen, I am sorry to say we do not have time enough for two complete sequences of questions. We now have only 12 minutes left. Therefore, I would like to ask for shorter questions and shorter answers. And we also will drop the follow-up question. Each candidate may still respond, of course, to the other's answer.

Mr. Trewhitt, a question for Governor Carter.

MR. TREWHITT. Governor Carter, before this event the most communication I received concerned Panama. Would you, as President, be prepared to sign a treaty which at a fixed date yielded administrative and economic control of the Canal Zone and shared defense which, as I understand it, is the position the United States took in 1974?

MR. CARTER. Well, here again, the Panamanian question is one that has been confused by Mr. Ford. He had directed his diplomatic representative to yield to the Panamanians full sovereignty over the Panama Canal Zone at the end of a certain period of time. When Mr. Reagan raised this question in Florida, Mr. Ford not only disavowed his instructions but he also even dropped, parenthetically, the use of the word "détente."

I would never give up complete control or practical control of the Panama Canal Zone, but I would continue to negotiate with the Panamanians. When the original treaty was signed back in the early 1900's, when Theodore Roosevelt was President, Panama retained sovereignty over the Panama Canal Zone. We retained control as though we had sovereignty.

Now, I would be willing to go ahead with negotiations. I believe that we could share more fully responsibilities for the Panama Canal Zone with Panama. I would be willing to continue to raise the payment for shipment of goods through the Panama Canal Zone. I might even be willing to reduce to some degree our military emplacements in the Panama Canal Zone, but I would not relinquish practical control of the Panama Canal Zone any time in the foreseeable future.

THE MODERATOR. President Ford.

THE PRESIDENT. The United States must and will maintain complete access to the Panama Canal. The United States must maintain a defense capability of the Panama Canal, and the United States will maintain our national security interests in the Panama Canal.

The negotiations for the Panama Canal started under President Johnson and have continued up to the present time. I believe those negotiations should continue. But there are certain guidelines that must be followed, and I've just defined them.

Let me take just a minute to comment on something that Governor Carter said on nonproliferation. In May of 1975, I called for a conference of nuclear suppliers. That conference has met six times. In May of this year, Governor Carter took the first initiative, approximately 12 months after I had taken my initiative a year ago.

THE MODERATOR. Mr. Valeriani, a question for President Ford.

MR. VALERIANI. Mr. President, the Government (General) Accounting Office has just put out a report suggesting that you shot from the hip in the *Mayaguez* rescue mission and that you ignored diplomatic messages saying that a peaceful solution was in prospect. Why didn't you do more diplomatically at the time? And a related question: Did the White House try to prevent the release of that report?

THE PRESIDENT. The White House did not prevent the release of that report. On July 12, of this year, we gave full permission for the release of that report. I was very disappointed in the fact that the GAO released that report because I think it interjected political, partisan politics at the present time.

But let me comment on the report. Somebody who sits in Washington, D.C., 18 months after the *Mayaguez* incident can be a very good grandstand quarterback. And let me make another observation: This morning I got a call from the skipper of the *Mayaguez*. He was furious, because he told me that it was the action of me, President Ford, that saved the lives of the crew of the *Mayaguez*. And I can assure you that if we had not taken the strong and forceful action that we did, we would have been criticized very, very severely for sitting back and not moving.

Captain Miller is thankful, the crew is thankful. We did the right thing. It seems to me that those who sit in Washington 18 months after the incident are not the best judges of the decisionmaking process that had to be made by the National Security Council and by myself at the time the incident was developing in the Pacific.

Let me assure you that we made every possible overture to the People's Republic of China and, through them, to the Cambodian Government; we made diplomatic protest to the Cambodian Government through the United Nations. Every possible diplomatic means was utilized. But at the same time, I had a responsibility, and so did the National Security Council, to meet the problem at hand, and we handled it responsibly. And I think Captain Miller's testimony to that effect is the best evidence.

THE MODERATOR. Governor Carter.

MR. CARTER. Well, I am reluctant to comment on the recent report. I haven't read it. I think the American people have only one requirement—that the facts about *Mayaguez* be given to them accurately and completely.

Mr. Ford has been there for 18 months. He had the facts that were released today immediately after the *Mayaguez* incident. I understand that the report today is accurate. Mr. Ford has said, I believe, that it was accurate and that the White House made no attempt to block the issuing of that report. I don't know if that is exactly accurate or not.

I understand that both the Department of State and the Defense Department have approved the accuracy of today's report, or yesterday's report, and also the National Security Agency. I don't know what was right or what was wrong or what was done. The only thing I believe is that whatever the knowledge was that Mr. Ford had should have been given to the American people 18 months ago, immediately after the *Mayaguez* incident occurred.

This is what the American people want. When something happens that endangers our security, or when something happens that threatens our stature in the world, or when American people are endangered by the actions of a foreign country, just 40 sailors on the *Mayaguez*, we obviously have to move aggressively and quickly to rescue them. But then, after the immediate action is taken, I believe the President has an obligation to tell the American people the truth and not wait 18 months later for the report to be issued.

THE MODERATOR. Gentlemen, at this time we have time for only two very short questions. Mr. Frankel, a question for Governor Carter.

MR. FRANKEL. Governor Carter, if the price of gaining influence among the Arabs is closing our eyes a little bit to their boycott against Israel, how would you handle that?

MR. CARTER. I believe that the boycott of American businesses by the Arab countries because those businesses trade with Israel or because they have American Jews who are owners or directors in the company, is an absolute disgrace. This is the first time that I remember in the history of our country when we've let a foreign country circumvent or change our Bill of Rights. I will do everything I can as President to stop the boycott of American businesses by the Arab countries.

It's not a matter of diplomacy or trade with me, it's a matter of morality. And I don't believe that the Arab countries will pursue it when we have a strong President, who will protect the integrity of our country, the commitment of our Constitution and Bill of Rights, and protect people in this country who happen to be Jews—it may later be Catholics, it may later be Baptists—who are threatened by some foreign country. But we ought to stand staunch. And I think it is a disgrace that so far Mr. Ford's administration has blocked the passage of legislation that would have revealed by law every instance of the boycott, and it would have prevented the boycott from continuing.

THE MODERATOR. President Ford?

THE PRESIDENT. Again, Governor Carter is inaccurate. The Arab boycott action was first taken in 1952, and in November of 1975, I was the first President to order the executive branch to take action—affirmative action through the Department of Commerce and other Cabinet Departments—to make certain that no American businessman or business organization should discriminate against Jews because of an Arab boycott.

And I might add that my administration—and I am very proud of it—is the first administration that has taken an antitrust action against companies in this country that have allegedly cooperated with the Arab boycott. Just on Monday of this week, I signed a tax bill that included an amendment that would prevent companies in the United States from taking a tax deduction if they have in any way whatsoever, cooperated with the Arab boycott.

And last week, when we were trying to get the Export Administration Act through the Congress—necessary legislation—my administration went to Capitol Hill and tried to convince the House and the Senate that we should have an amendment on that legislation which would take strong and effective action against those who participate or cooperate with the Arab boycott.

One other point: Because the Congress failed to act I am going to announce tomorrow that the Department of Commerce will disclose those companies that have participated in the Arab boycott. This is something that we can do. The Congress failed to do it, and we intend to do it.[6]

THE MODERATOR. Mr. Trewhitt, a very brief question for President Ford.

MR. TREWHITT. Mr. President, if you get the accounting of missing in action you want from North Vietnam—or from Vietnam, I am sorry, now—would you then be prepared to reopen negotiations for restoration of relations with that country?

THE PRESIDENT. Let me restate our policy. As long as Vietnam, North Vietnam, does not give us a full and complete accounting of our missing in action, I will never go along with the admission of Vietnam to the United Nations. If they do give us a bona fide, complete accounting of the 800 MIA's, then I believe that the United States should begin negotiations for the admission of

[6]President Ford on October 7 instructed the Department of Commerce to make future reports concerning compliance with the boycott available for public inspection. *Presidential Documents*, 12: 1460-61.

Vietnam to the United Nations, but not until they have given us the full accounting of our MIA's.

THE MODERATOR. Governor Carter?

MR. CARTER. One of the most embarrassing failures of the Ford administration, and one that touches specifically on human rights, is his refusal to appoint a Presidential commission to go to Vietnam, to go to Laos, to go to Cambodia, and try to trade for the release of information about those who are missing in action in those wars. This is what the families of MIA's want. So far, Mr. Ford has not done it. We have had several fragmentary efforts by Members of the Congress and by private citizens.

Several months ago the Vietnam Government said we are ready to sit down and negotiate for release of information on MIA's. So far, Mr. Ford has not responded.

I also would never normalize relationships with Vietnam, nor permit them to join the United Nations until they have taken this action. But that is not enough. We need to have an active and aggressive action on the part of the President, the leader of this country, to seek out every possible way to get that information which has kept the MIA families in despair and doubt, and Mr. Ford has just not done it.

THE MODERATOR. Thank you, Governor Carter.
That completes the questioning for this evening. Each candidate now has up to 3 minutes for a closing statement. It was determined by the toss of a coin that Governor Carter would take the first question, and he now goes first with his closing remarks.
Governor Carter.

MR. CARTER. The purpose of this debate and the outcome of the election will determine three basic things—leadership, upholding the principles of our country, and proper priorities and commitments for the future.

This election will also determine what kind of world we leave our children. Will it be a nightmare world, threatened with the proliferation of atomic bombs, not just in five major countries, but dozens of smaller countries that have been permitted to develop atomic weapons because of a failure of our top leadership to stop proliferation? Will we have a world of hunger and hatred, and will we be living in an armed camp, stripped of our friendships and allies, hiding behind a tight defense that has been drawn in around us because we are fearful of the outside world? Will we have a government of secrecy that excludes the American people from participation in making basic decisions and therefore covers up mistakes and makes it possible for our Government, our Government, to depart from the principles of our Constitution and Bill of Rights? Or will we have a world of peace with the threat of atomic weapons eliminated, with full trade, with our people at work, inflation controlled, openness in Government, our people proud once again, Congress, citizens, President, Secretary of State, working in harmony and unity toward a common future, a world where people have enough to eat, and a world where we care about those who don't? Can we become a breadbasket of the world, instead of the arms merchant of the world? I believe we can and we ought to.

Now we have been hurt in recent years in this country, in the aftermath of Vietnam, Cambodia, Chile, Pakistan, Angola, Watergate, CIA. We have been hurt. Our people feel that we have lost something precious. That's not necessary. I want to see our Nation return to a posture and an image and a standard to make us proud once again. I remember the world of NATO and the world of point four and the world of the Marshall Plan and a world of the Peace Corps. Why can't we have that once again?

We ought to be a beacon for nations who search for peace, and who search for freedom, who search for individual liberty, who search for basic human rights. We haven't been lately. We can be once again.

We will never have that world leadership until we are strong at home, and we can have that strength if we return to the basic principles. It ought not to be a strength of bombast and threats. It ought to be a quiet strength based on the integrity of our people, the vision of the Constitution, and an innate strong will and purpose that God has given us in the greatest nation on Earth, the United States.

THE MODERATOR. President Ford.

THE PRESIDENT. As we have seen tonight, foreign policy and defense policy are difficult and complex issues. We can debate methods. We can debate one decision or another, but there are two things which cannot be debated—experience and results.

In the last 2 years, I have made policy decisions involving long-range difficulties and policies and made day-to-day judgments, not only as President of the United States but as the leader of the free world.

What is the result of that leadership? America is strong, America is free, America is respected. Not a single young American today is fighting or dying on any foreign battlefield. America is at peace, with freedom.

Thank you, and good night.

THE MODERATOR. Thank you, President Ford. Thank you, Governor Carter. I also want to thank our questioners and the audience here this evening.

The third and final debate between President Ford and Governor Carter will take place on October the 22d at 9:30 p.m., eastern daylight time, on the campus of the College of William and Mary in Williamsburg, Virginia. The subject matter will cover all issues.

These debates are sponsored by the League of Women Voters Education Fund to help voters become better informed on the issues and to generate greater voter turnout in the November election.

Now, from the Palace of Fine Arts Theatre in San Francisco, good night.

APPENDIX:
SELECTED HISTORICAL DOCUMENTS
1945-1975

(A checklist of historical documents referred to in this volume)

1945

The IMF Articles of Agreement: Articles of Agreement of the International Monetary Fund, opened for signature at Washington Dec. 27, 1945 and entered into force on the same day (TIAS 1501; 60 Stat. 1401).

1947

The Rio Treaty: Inter-American Treaty of Reciprocal Assistance, opened for signature at Rio de Janeiro Sept. 24, 1947 and entered into force Dec. 3, 1948 (TIAS 1838; 62 Stat. 1681); text in *Documents, 1947:* 534-40.

1948

The OAS Charter: Charter of the Organization of American States, signed at Bogotá Apr. 30, 1948 and entered into force Dec. 13, 1951 (TIAS 2361; 2 UST 2394); text in *Documents, 1948:* 484-502.

The Genocide Convention: Convention on the Prevention and Punishment of the Crime of Genocide, done at Paris Dec. 9, 1948 and entered into force Jan. 12, 1951 (not in force for the U.S.); text in *Documents, 1948:* 435-8.

The Universal Declaration of Human Rights: U.N. General Assembly Resolution 217 A (III), adopted in Paris Dec. 10, 1948; text in *Documents, 1948:* 430-35.

1949

The North Atlantic Treaty, signed at Washington Apr. 4, 1949 and entered into force Aug. 24, 1949 (TIAS 1964; 63 Stat. 2241); text in *Documents, 1949:* 612-15.

1951

The ANZUS Treaty: Tripartite Security Treaty between the Governments of Australia, New Zealand, and the United States, signed at San Francisco Sept. 1, 1951 and entered into force Apr. 29, 1952 (TIAS 2493; 3 UST 3420); text in *Documents, 1951:* 263-5.

1953

The Korean Armistice: Agreement Concerning a Military Armistice in Korea, signed at Panmunjom and entered into force July 27, 1953 (TIAS 2782; 4 UST 234); partial text in *Documents, 1953:* 289-97.

The U.S.-Korean Treaty: Mutual Defense Treaty between the U.S. and the Republic of Korea, signed at Washington Oct. 1, 1953 and entered into force Nov. 17, 1954 (TIAS 3097; 5 UST 2368); text in *Documents, 1953:* 312-13.

1954

Public Law 480: Agricultural Trade Development and Assistance Act of 1954, approved July 10, 1954 (Public Law 480, 83rd Cong.).

The Manila Pact: South-East Asia Collective Defense Treaty, signed in Manila Sept. 8, 1954 and entered into force Feb. 19, 1955 (TIAS 3170; 6 UST 81); text in *Documents, 1954:* 319-23.

1959

The Antarctic Treaty, signed at Washington Dec. 1, 1959 and entered into force June 23, 1961 (TIAS 4790; 12 UST 794); text in *Documents, 1959:* 528-35.

1960

The U.S.-Japan Security Treaty: Treaty of Mutual Cooperation and Security between the U.S. and Japan, signed at Washington Jan. 19, 1960 and entered into force June 23, 1960 (TIAS 4509; 11 UST 1632); text in *Documents, 1960:* 425-31.

1963

The "Hot Line" Agreement: U.S.-Soviet Memorandum of Understanding Regarding the Establishment of a Direct Communications Link, signed at Geneva and entered into force June 20, 1963 (TIAS 5362; 14 UST 1825); text in *Documents, 1963:* 115-16.

The Nuclear Test Ban Treaty: Treaty Banning Nuclear Weapon Tests in the Atmosphere, in Outer Space and Under Water, signed in Moscow Aug. 5, 1963 and entered into force Oct. 10, 1963 (TIAS 5433; 14 UST 1313); text in *Documents, 1963:* 130-32.

The Tokyo Convention: Convention on Offenses and Certain Other Acts Committed on Board Aircraft, done at Tokyo Sept. 14, 1963 and entered into force Dec. 4, 1969 (TIAS 6768; 20 UST 2941).

1966

International Covenant on Economic, Social and Cultural Rights, adopted by U.N. General Assembly Resolution 2202 A (XXI) of Dec. 16, 1966 and entered into force Jan. 3, 1976; signed by the U.S. Oct. 5, 1977.

International Covenant on Civil and Political Rights, adopted by U.N. General Assembly Resolution 2202 A (XXI) of Dec. 16, 1966 and entered into force Mar. 23, 1976; signed by U.S. Oct. 5, 1977.

1967

The Outer Space Treaty: Treaty on Principles Governing the Activities of States in the Exploration and Use of Outer Space, Including the Moon and Other Celestial Bodies, signed Jan. 27, 1967 and entered into force Oct. 10, 1967 (TIAS 6347; 18 UST 2410); text in *Documents, 1966:* 391-8.

Protocol of Amendment to the Charter of the Organization of American States, signed at Buenos Aires Feb. 27, 1967 and entered into force Feb. 27, 1970 (TIAS 6847; 21 UST 607); summary in *Documents, 1968-9:* 399-401.

U.N. Security Council Resolution 242 (1967), enunciating principles for peace in the Middle East, adopted Nov. 22, 1967; text in *Documents, 1967:* 169-70.

1968

The Astronaut Rescue Agreement: Agreement on the Rescue of Astronauts, the Return of Astronauts, and the Return of Objects Launched into Space, signed Apr. 22, 1968 and entered into force Dec. 3, 1968 (TIAS 6599; 19 UST 7570); text in *Documents, 1967:* 392-6.

The Nuclear Nonproliferation Treaty: Treaty on the Non-Proliferation of Nuclear Weapons, signed in London, Moscow and Washington July 1, 1968 and entered into force Mar. 5, 1970 (TIAS 6839; 21 UST 483); text in *Documents, 1968-9:* 62-8.

1970

Declaration on Friendly Relations: Declaration on Principles of International Law concerning Friendly Relations and Co-operation Among States, adopted as U.N. General Assembly Resolution 2625 (XXV), Oct. 24, 1970.

The Hague Convention: Convention for the Suppression of Unlawful Seizure of Aircraft, done at The Hague Dec. 16, 1970 and entered into force Oct. 14, 1971 (TIAS 7192; 22 UST 1641); text in *Documents, 1970:* 350-55.

1971

The Anti-Terrorist Convention: Convention to Prevent and Punish the Acts of Terrorism Taking the Form of Crimes Against Persons and Related Extortion That Are of International Significance, done at Washington Feb. 2, 1971 and entered into force Oct. 20, 1976 (TIAS 8413); text in *AFR, 1971:* 437-41.

The Seabed Arms Limitation Treaty: Treaty on the Prohibition of the Emplacement of Nuclear Weapons and Other Weapons of Mass Destruction on the Seabed and the Ocean Floor and in the Subsoil Thereof, opened for signature Feb. 11, 1971 and entered into force May 18, 1972 (TIAS 7337; 23 UST 701); text in *Documents, 1970:* 69-73.

The Berlin Agreement: Quadripartite Agreement on Berlin Between the United States of America and Other Governments, signed at Berlin September 3, 1971 and entered into force June 3, 1972 (TIAS 7551; 24 UST 283); text in *AFR, 1971:* 166-70.

The Montreal Convention: Convention for the Suppression of Unlawful Acts Against the Safety of Civil Aviation, done at Montreal Sept. 23, 1971 and entered into force Jan. 26, 1973 (TIAS 7570; 24 UST 565); text in *AFR, 1971:* 548-55.

Agreement on Measures to Reduce the Risk of Outbreak of Nuclear War Between the United States of America and the Union of Soviet Socialist Republics, signed in Washington and entered into force Sept. 30, 1971 (TIAS 7186; 22 UST 1590); text in *AFR, 1971:* 110-12

The Second "Hot Line" Agreement: Agreement Between the United States of America and the Union of Soviet Socialist Republics on Measures to Improve the U.S.A.-U.S.S.R. Direct Communications Link, signed in Washington and entered into force Sept. 30, 1971 (TIAS 7187; 22 UST 1598); text in *AFR, 1971:* 113-14.

1972

The Shanghai Communiqué: Joint Statement issued at Shanghai on the conclusion of President Nixon's visit to the People's Republic of China, February 27, 1972; text in *AFR, 1972:* 307-11.

The Space Liability Convention: Convention on International Liability for Damage Caused by Space Objects, done at London, Moscow, and Washington Mar. 29, 1972, and entered into force Sept. 1, 1972 (TIAS 7762; 24 UST 2389); text in *AFR, 1971:* 555-65.

The Biological Warfare Convention: Convention on the Prohibition of the Development, Production and Stockpiling of Bacteriological (Biological) and Toxin Weapons and on Their Destruction, opened for signature in London, Moscow, and Washington on April 10, 1972 and entered into force Mar. 26, 1975 (TIAS 8062; 26 UST 583); text in *AFR, 1971:* 90-95.

The ABM Treaty: Treaty Between the United States of America and the Union of Soviet Socialist Republics on the Limitation of Anti-Ballistic Missile Systems, signed in Moscow May 26, 1972 and entered into force Oct. 3, 1972 (TIAS 7503; 23 UST 3425); text in *AFR, 1972:* 90-95.

The Interim Agreement: Interim Agreement Between the United States of America and the Union of Soviet Socialist Republics on Certain Measures with Respect to the Limitation of Strategic Offensive Arms, signed in Moscow May 26, 1972 and entered into force Oct. 3, 1972 (TIAS 7504; 23 UST 3462); text in *AFR, 1972:* 97-101.

Declaration on the Human Environment, adopted by the U.N. Conference on the Human Environment at Stockholm June 16, 1972; text in *AFR, 1972:* 470-75.

1973

U.N. Security Council Resolution 338 (1973), calling for peace negotiations on the Middle East, adopted Oct. 22, 1973; text in *AFR, 1973:* 459.

The War Powers Act: Public Law 93-148, passed by the Senate October 10 and by the House of Representatives Oct. 12, 1973 and repassed over the President's veto on Nov. 7, 1973; text in *AFR, 1973:* 484-90.

The Diplomatic Protection Convention: Convention on the Prevention and Punishment of Crimes Against Internationally Protected Persons, Including Diplomatic Agents, done at New York Dec. 14, 1973 and entered into force Feb. 20, 1977 (TIAS 8532); text in *AFR, 1973:* 586-94.

1974

Declaration on the Establishment of a New International Economic Order, adopted as U.N. General Assembly Resolution 3201 (S-VI), May 1, 1974; text in *AFR, 1974:* 103-7.

The ABM Protocol: Protocol to the Treaty on the Limitation of Anti-Ballistic Missile Systems, signed in Moscow July 3, 1974 and entered into force May 24, 1976 (TIAS 8276; 27 UST 1645); text in *AFR, 1974:* 226-8.

The Threshold Test Ban (TTB) Treaty: Treaty on the Limitation of Underground Nuclear Weapons Tests, signed in Moscow July 3, 1974 but not in force as of Jan. 1978; text in *AFR, 1974:* 229-33.

The IEA Agreement: Agreement on an International Energy Program, done at Paris Nov. 18, 1974 and entered into force Jan. 19, 1976 (TIAS 8278; 27 UST 1685); text in *AFR, 1974:* 466-90.

The Vladivostok Statement: Joint statement on the limitation of strategic offensive arms, released in Vladivostok Nov. 24, 1974; text in *AFR, 1974:* 508-9.

Charter of Economic Rights and Duties of States, adopted as U.N. General Assembly Resolution 3281 (XXIX), Dec. 12, 1974; text in *AFR, 1974:* 528-41.

1975

The Space Registration Convention: Convention on the Registration of Objects Launched into Outer Space, opened for signature at New York Jan. 14, 1975 and entered into force Sept. 15, 1976 (TIAS 8480).

Fifth International Tin Agreement, done at Geneva June 21, 1975 and entered into force June 14, 1977 (TIAS 8607).

The Helsinki Final Act: Final Act of the Conference on Security and Cooperation in Europe, signed in Helsinki Aug. 1, 1975; text in *AFR, 1975:* 292-360.

The Anti-Zionist Resolution: U.N. General Assembly Resolution 3379 (XXX), adopted Nov. 10, 1975; text in *AFR, 1975:* 507-8.

International Coffee Agreement, 1976, done at London Dec. 3, 1975 and entered into force Aug. 1, 1977 (TIAS 8683).

INDEX

A

ABM Protocol (signed Moscow July 3, 1974), 20-21

ABM Treaty (signed Moscow May 26, 1972), 20

ACDA, *see* Arms Control and Disarmament Agency

Afars and Issas, Territory of, 59

Africa, 2, 3, 12, 45, 48-61, 64, 68, 94; Kissinger statement (May 13), 294-304; Kissinger remarks (New York, Oct. 8), 310-15

African Development Fund, 53, 111; Kissinger reference (Nairobi, May 6), 398

Agency for International Development (AID), 11

AID, *see* Agency for International Development

Albania, 27

Allende Gossens, Salvador, 63, 65, 69

Amerasinghe, H.S., 101, 102, 103

American Declaration on the Rights and Duties of Man (signed at Bogotá May 2, 1948), Kissinger reference (Santiago, June 8), 333

Amin Dada, Idi, 54-5

Andreotti, Giuseppe, 35

Angola, 3, 6, 17-18, 48-50, 58, 61, 68-9; in U.N., 59, 94, 103, 109; Schaufele statement, 275-83; Kissinger reference (San Francisco, Feb. 3), 177-80

ANZUS Pact, 74; 25th Council meeting (Canberra, Aug. 3-4): communiqué, 362-5

Arab-Israeli conflict, 38-9, 41-2, 45-7, 112; Geneva Conference on the Middle East, 38, 41, 47; Atherton address (Omaha, June 30), 259-67; Lebanon, civil conflict in, 254-9; Kissinger remarks (New York, Sept. 29), 267-9; Scranton statement to U.N. General Assembly (Dec. 9); Entebbe rescue, 54-6; Scranton statement to U.N. Security Council (July 12), 304-10; Lewis reference (Mar. 18), 448-9, 453; Scranton reference (Dec. 22), 487-8

Arab League, 44

Arafat, Yasir, 40, 41

541

B

F

J

K

L

M

N

T

U

V

W